Attacks on the Press
in 1997

Cover Photo: Argentine photojournalists raise their cameras on January 28 to protest the murder of fellow photographer José Luis Cabezas. Cabezas' charred, handcuffed body was found in the burned-out hull of his rental car on January 25 near Pinamar, a resort where he had been on assignment. (Reuters/Eduardo Farre/Archive Photos)

330 Seventh Avenue, 12th Floor
New York, New York 10001
Phone: (212) 465-1004 • Fax: (212) 465-9568
E-Mail: info@cpj.org • website: http://www.cpj.org

Begun in 1981, the Committee to Protect Journalists responds to attacks on the press everywhere in the world. CPJ investigates more than 2,000 cases every year and takes action on behalf of journalists and their news organizations without regard to political ideology. Join CPJ and help promote press freedom by defending the people who report the news. To maintain its independence, CPJ accepts no government funding. We depend entirely on your support.

Agence France-Presse, The Associated Press, IDT, LEXIS•NEXIS, and Reuters provided electronic news and Internet services that were used to conduct research for this report.

The Committee to Protect Journalists is most grateful to the following foundations, whose long-term commitments to the cause of global press freedom constitute the core operating support for our organization's programs:

The Ford Foundation
The Freedom Forum
John S. and James L. Knight Foundation
Robert R. McCormick Tribune Foundation

Editor: Alice Chasan
Associate Editor: Jesse T. Stone

Attacks on the Press in 1997: A Worldwide Survey by the Committee to Protect Journalists
ISSN: 1078-3334
ISBN: 0-944823-17-3

Preface

by Gene Roberts

It is difficult to read this volume without feeling despair that so many journalists could have died, languished in jail, or have been brutalized in a single year. But before you let the despair burrow too deeply, remember that journalists can put a stop to many, arguably most, of the murders and assassinations and atrocities.

How? By doing our jobs. By regarding the murder and assassination and brutalization of journalists as major news stories and covering them thoroughly and prominently. By launching investigations into the murders of reporters and editors, and publishing the findings. And by completing the work of reporters who were killed while uncovering a story.

When journalists are murdered or brutalized, it is almost always by some government, some organization, some criminal cartel, some individual wanting to prevent the flow of embarrassing or incriminating information to the public. If the assassins learned that when they killed journalists the inevitable result was that they got more coverage, rather than less, the killings would subside.

In the United States in 1976, Don Bolles, an investigative reporter in the midst of an investigation for *The Arizona Republic*, was fatally injured by a car bomb in downtown Phoenix. Thirty-eight journalists from 28 newspapers and television stations formed a team to complete Bolles' investigation. The result was a series that ran in newspapers such as the *Boston Globe*, the *Miami Herald*, and *Newsday* on Long Island. The Associated Press moved stories developed from the series to the vast majority of U.S. newspapers. The coverage was broad enough and deep enough to make any would-be assassin think twice about violence against journalists anywhere in the United States.

The killing of journalists has halted the flow of any semblance of honest journalism in Pakistan and in most of Algeria. And terrorism threatens the flow of information in many parts of Asia, Africa, and Latin America. It is urgently essential for journalists whose colleagues are killed to cover the deaths and to pick

---

Gene Roberts is CPJ's chairman. He also chairs the International Press Institute. Currently, he is professor of journalism at the University of Maryland. From 1994 until September 1997, he was managing editor of *The New York Times*. Between 1965 and 1972, Roberts worked for the *Times* as chief Southern and civil rights correspondent, chief war correspondent in South Vietnam, and national editor. From 1972-90, he was executive editor of the *Philadelphia Inquirer*. During his tenure there, the *Inquirer's* staff won 17 Pulitzer Prizes. Roberts himself is the recipient of numerous awards, including The National Press Club's Fourth Estate Award, presented to him in 1993 for lifetime achievement in journalism. He received a B.A. degree in journalism from the University of North Carolina in 1954.

up the story—even if the dead journalist is a competitor. Not to react is to risk extinction of tell-it-as-it-is journalism in many nations of the world and its most populous continents—Africa, Asia, the Americas, Europe.

Is it discriminatory and unfair to cover the murder of a journalist more thoroughly than the murder of the average person?

No. The state of the press in any nation is a litmus test of how free the nation's people are. If press freedom is missing—whether by government suppression or by the intimidation of terrorists and assassins—so, inevitably, will be freedom of speech, and true economic opportunity, and, often, freedom of religion. And the murder of a journalist is important news because it is an attack on freedom of expression and the flow of information to the public. When freedom of the press and of speech are absent, people cannot settle issues through open discussion. Then, war and uprisings or lives of fear almost certainly will be the result.

Freedom of expression, which very much depends upon press freedom, is not a guarantee of world peace. But it is a vital first step. Our planet is becoming more complex and more problem-ridden with each passing year. But the problems cannot be solved in the next century, or ever, if the people of all nations cannot be involved in the discussion. Thus, when there is an absence of press freedom in any nation, it should become the concern of all nations. And if journalists and peace-seekers do not support, cover, and constantly struggle for the cause of press freedom across national boundaries, then who will?

Table of Contents

Introduction

by William A. Orme, Jr.

For journalists, 1997 was a year of unusual scrutiny—most of it by journalists themselves.

Photographers were pilloried for their purported role in Princess Diana's fatal car crash. Editors were criticized for their indefensibly (take your pick) disrespectful or hagiographic coverage of Diana's death and life. In a paroxysm of self-analysis, journalists then assiduously covered the criticism of the journalists.

In editorial meetings and academic conferences, meanwhile, American newspaper editors and media scholars earnestly debated the merits of "public" or "civic" journalism, without ever quite clarifying what this means when translated into front-page agate.

In early 1998, the all-absorbing preoccupation of the press was President Clinton's sex life and—even more—its own reporting on same. Media critics observed that the public seemed at once hostile to the relentless focus on alleged Oval Office dalliances and riveted by the salacious content of the unfolding scandal. News commentators soberly questioned their reliance on anonymous leaks, lamented the overshadowing of Pope John Paul II's Cuba visit and preparations for war with Iraq, and examined anew the ethics and logistics of public reporting on private lives.

Are these the great journalistic issues of the day?

Such concerns seem somewhat remote when viewed from the confines of a Lagos prison, where *Sunday Magazine* editor Christine Anyanwu is serving a 15-year term for publishing stories challenging the official version of an alleged coup plot, or from a Tijuana hospital, where editor-publisher Jesús Blancornelas recuperated from a machine-gunning by the drug traffickers his newsweekly *Zeta* so zealously covers.

In Kashmir, local journalists who face violent retribution from all sides in the armed conflict must decide every day if a story is worth the risk of an abduction or a terror bombing. Editors in West Africa and Eastern Europe aim thumb-in-your-eye satire at their presidents, deliberately testing the boundaries of discourse

William A. Orme, Jr. *is the executive director of the Committee to Protect Journalists. Before joining CPJ in 1993, he covered Latin America for 15 years as a magazine editor and correspondent for* The Washington Post, The Economist, *and other publications. He is the author of* Understanding NAFTA: Mexico, Free Trade and the New North America *(University of Texas Press, 1996), and the editor of* A Culture of Collusion: An Inside Look at the Mexican Press *(University of Miami North-South Center Press, 1997).*

in societies where offending a head of state is an act of treason; many end up in court, bankrupted by huge fines and legal bills.

The professional dilemma for a journalist in Algiers is whether even to try to venture outside the capital to report on vicious massacres, knowing that you risk summary execution by insurgents while you are reporting, and prosecution by the military if you get back safely and publish your reporting. In Chechnya, where NTV reporter Yelena Masyuk spent 101 days as the hostage of a rebel splinter group, the questions for Russian journalists are basic: Do they succumb to the intimidation of terrorists and the hostility of their military, and walk away from a raging civil war within the borders of their own country? And if they persist despite these pressures, who will defend them?

Hong Kong newspaper publishers must gauge Beijing's tolerance for real journalism—fearing that despite all official assurances to the contrary, overstepping certain undefined lines could jeopardize not only their own publications, but freedom of expression for the entire former colony. In countries as different as Indonesia and Cuba and Turkey, reporters seek out alternative foreign outlets for stories they fear would otherwise be suppressed—often working without pay, or bylines, simply to get information out into the world.

The truly critical challenges for journalism today can be found in the scores of countries that are only now slipping free of the authoritarian shackles of the past—countries where reporters can now operate, but where the concept of an independent press is not yet enshrined in law or comprehended by political leaders. In some of these countries, making the problems much more acute, a brief flowering of press freedom in the recent past is being washed away by a new wave of repression and intolerance.

Just by doing their jobs, journalists in these societies are challenging authority and demonstrating to society at large the value—and the risks—of independent newsgathering and commentary. They are fighting openly for their rights, and sometimes for their lives.

They are also grappling daily with fundamental philosophical dilemmas: How does a newly aggressive, critical press expose the inevitable kickback scams, cronyism, and political abuses in fledgling democracies without undermining popular support for the entire fragile democratic experiment—especially since most citizens heard nothing of such seamy things when the authoritarians ruled? Is it possible for a young and sometimes irresponsible popular press to police its ethics without inviting official reprisals against colleagues whose ethics are found wanting?

Can a country torn asunder by intra-ethnic violence survive open democratic discourse without restricting "hate speech"—and can it survive as a democracy if the government dictates what can and cannot be said? In a society without a legacy of constitutional and common-law press freedom guarantees, will well-intentioned free-media statutes be used to regulate rather than protect the press? Is it responsible for editors to assign investigative reporters to stories on drug cartels and arms traffickers when the enemies of these criminal gangs are executed with apparent impunity—and, conversely, is it responsible to succumb to intimidation and leave such stories untold?

Should mainstream journalists in places where the press is under siege unite in defense of marginal muckrakers or firebrands who face jail or censorship—and suffer the consequences of perceived association with extremist or even repugnant viewpoints?

Even when the answers appear self-evident, the cost of doing the right thing can be extraordinarily high.

In contrast to their jaded brethren in London or Washington, these editors and writers and broadcasters are quite consciously engaged in nation-building. They see themselves—correctly, though not necessarily happily—as actors, not just scribes. Some unhesitatingly cross a line their first-world colleagues perceive as dividing journalism from activism. Americans, especially, should look back at their own history before passing judgment: Dissident journalists in Zagreb or Hanoi may have less in common with the editor of *The Washington Post* than with John Peter Zenger or Tom Paine. It is not just that the news media are an integral part of the political process: In some places, they *are* the political process. In Central Europe or sub-Saharan Africa, where emerging antigovernment forces are fractious or inexperienced, or in South America, where old political parties have been fatally weakened by corruption and compromise, the independent press becomes almost by default the de facto opposition. And those in power respond to that threat accordingly.

These are the people on the profession's front lines, uncovering news that matters, in their own countries and beyond, at great risk to their news organizations and themselves.

It is not as if the rest of us don't have a stake in this. Almost invariably, it is local journalists who alert the international media to what is really going on in Russia, or Mexico, or Nigeria, or Israel, or even China. And in this age of instantaneous satellite feeds and Internet news services, local journalists increasingly provide the text and video we see from the latest global flash points.

The chief concerns confronting many of these journalists are whether it is possible to go with a story and stay in business, or stay out of jail, or simply stay alive. At least 26 journalists were murdered in 14 countries in 1997 because they were working journalists. At the end of the year at least 129 journalists were held in prison in 24 countries because of alleged offenses directly related to their journalistic work. Scores more were threatened with legal reprisals or violent retribution.

These people are the focus of CPJ's work. We have learned that international pressure, from journalists on behalf of their fellow journalists, can be highly effective. "I look at CPJ as a kind of giant crane that suddenly appeared overhead and plucked me out of jail," Ocak Isik Yurtçu told me last year, shortly after a CPJ mission had persuaded the new Turkish government to release the imprisoned newspaper editor and six colleagues. (See special report on Turkey, p. 82). But at least 29 journalists remain in prison in Turkey, plus 17 in Nigeria, 16 in Ethiopia, 15 in China, and 8 in Burma.

In 1997, CPJ put extra emphasis on illuminating and, ideally, reversing disturbing trends in places we view as leading indicators for press freedom worldwide: China, Mexico, Jordan, Turkey, and the Caucasus region. Our findings are contained in the special reports excerpted here. Some of CPJ's work, such as in Azerbaijan and Hong Kong, was largely fact-finding: documenting the details of the life of the daily press under difficult new circumstances. In other cases, such as Turkey and Mexico, our emphasis was on working with local journalists to reform repressive laws, get journalists out of jail, or to keep journalists from being sent to jail.

But the bedrock of CPJ's work are the many specific cases of threats and abuse we document and respond to on a daily basis. They make up the bulk of this book, which we present not as an encyclopedia of press freedom violations, but as a record of CPJ's work through the year. Without this detailed, painstakingly documented case information, and our track record of rapid and effective response to such incidents, CPJ's more analytical work would be an essentially academic exercise.

The hundreds of cases reported in this book represent just a fraction of the year's attacks on journalists and press freedom violations, but we attempt to include the most significant incidents in the more than a hundred countries we regularly cover. In aggregate, these incidents provide a compelling picture of the challenges facing journalists in places where journalism is constantly under siege. They also give a sense of the magnitude of the problem: The cases that CPJ can actively and effectively address are in themselves a small fraction of the minority of cases that we are able to confirm and put on the public record in the course of the year.

The often grim statistics punctuating this book—journalists jailed, newsrooms ransacked, reporters murdered—should not be misinterpreted as a kind of inversely proportional press freedom index. For journalists to get into trouble, there must first be journalists: In truly totalitarian societies there are no independent editors or reporters to attack or prosecute. In Russia today, journalists work under constant fear of legal reprisals, political coercion, and violent attack—at least 13 reporters, editors, and broadcasters have been murdered because of their work in the 1990s. A decade ago, CPJ had little to report about the former Soviet

Union, save for the occasional harassment of a foreign correspondent and the repression of *samizdat* dissidents. Yet it would be absurd to conclude that were was less press freedom in Russia in 1997 than in 1987. In scores of other shakily emerging democracies, CPJ now has a full logbook of press freedom violations, whereas a decade ago we would have simply noted for the record the continuing restrictions on press freedom and moved on.

Most of the approximately one hundred countries CPJ routinely covers are neither the best nor the very worst examples of journalistic freedoms. We also focus our advocacy work on behalf of local journalists in countries where international opinion is likely to have an influence. That leads to what some governments perceive as a double standard on our part. We pay much closer attention to South Korea, now one of Asia's most democratic societies, than we do to North Korea, one of the most repressive regimes on earth. For the past year, CPJ's highest research and advocacy priority has been the imprisonment of journalists in Turkey, and even some of our colleagues in Istanbul ask why we aren't spending equivalent energy on neighboring Iraq, for example, where an independent journalist would risk not jail, but execution.

We are also often chastised for ignoring the real press freedom problems in our own country. Because CPJ was founded with the express intent of not replicating the work of well-funded and effective domestic journalism organizations, we do not cover the United States—or, for that matter, the other industrial democracies, where journalists also tend to be well organized in defense of their own interests. The exceptions we make are rare. We are vigorous in demanding investigations when journalists in the United States are murdered, an occurrence not as uncommon as is often supposed. We make our views known on U.S. actions or policies which we believe endanger journalists abroad, whether they are nationals or visiting correspondents (an example is the CIA's insistence on having the option to recruit journalists as spies and use journalism credentials as cover for its own agents in the field).

Both are fair criticisms. We concentrate our limited resources on countries where journalists tell us that they want and need international support, and that skews both our newsgathering process and our reporting priorities.

We are also sometimes accused of defending people—the imprisoned, even the dead—who are in the view of some not really journalists. This is a critique we respectfully reject.

Of the 26 cases of murdered journalists confirmed by CPJ in 1997, all but six were the victims of deliberate political assassination, and all were clearly targeted because of their work. This pattern has held true for more than a decade: Homicide is the leading cause of job-related death among journalists worldwide.

Accidental deaths while on assignment, including combat casualties, are the relatively rare exceptions to this rule.

Again, it is not the number of deaths that we should emphasize. Thousands of innocent civilians lose their lives every year in civil conflicts, and journalism is by no objective statistical measure among the world's most dangerous professions. What matters is the *intent* of those murders, and their result. These are calculated and all too frequently effective acts of censorship. The ultimate target is not a journalist as an individual, but society at large.

Governments are rarely directly responsible for these crimes, but governments—especially in self-described democracies—are responsible for aggressively investigating and prosecuting those responsible for these crimes. Yet this rarely happens, and almost never without sustained domestic and international pressure. That is why it is always a priority for CPJ to document these cases carefully, to publicize them as widely as possible, and to hold government accountable. Still, the pattern in 1997, as always, has been one of impunity: Only 5 of the 26 cases have led to arrests, and even in those instances those believed to have ordered the killings have not been charged or even questioned. There were many other cases of journalists murdered last year where there is reason to suspect a causal relationship between the crime and the victim's work, but where governments have failed to conduct even the most basic investigations.

Some of the horrors of recent years abated in 1997, reducing the numbers of journalists killed in the line of duty. For the second straight year there were no journalists killed in any part of the former Yugoslavia, a dramatic change wholly attributable to the Dayton peace process. Algeria, which had seen 60 journalists murdered since 1993—more than any other country—was spared the tragedy of additions to this toll in 1997. Tajikistan, which had by mid-decade become one of the most dangerous places for journalists on the globe, with at least 29 documented assassinations, was also absent from 1997's list. The apparent contract murders of investigative reporters in Moscow and the kidnapping and executions of correspondents in Chechnya had combined to make Russia a nation with an alarmingly high death toll in recent years. In 1997, however, there were no instances where the evidence made clear that a reporter or broadcaster or editor had been murdered as a result of his or her professional work.

Still, the continued inability of the Yeltsin government to find and prosecute those responsible for earlier murders put a palpable chill on Russian investigative journalism in 1997. And the fact that no Algerian journalists were killed last year should not be misinterpreted as a sign of improvement in press freedom there. Algerian journalists continue to function under a virtual state of siege, suffering threats of violence from militant Islamists and threats of legal reprisals from the military government. There are fewer victims in large part because so many Algerian journalists have gone underground, fled into exile, or left the profession entirely, while those who remain on the job live and work under the most extreme security precautions. In the former Yugoslavia, where at least 47 journalists were killed in the past decade, there have been no casualties among journalists since the 1995 signing of the Dayton peace accords. The Dayton accords put at least a temporary stop to the killings. But the press in Bosnia and Croatia and Serbia is still far from independent, or free from the fear of violent reprisals.

In every reported case of a press freedom abuse, CPJ must first determine the people involved were journalists and the attack or prosecution was related in some direct way to their profession. This is necessarily a somewhat subjective process. Who is a journalist? For the purposes of our work, we define the profession as broadly as possible. Journalists who are sentenced to prison or targeted for assassination include renowned newspaper editors and struggling provincial stringers, political polemicists and by-the-book news service reporters, star television correspondents and shoestring community radio activists. In totalitarian societies, where by definition there is no independent journalism, dissident pamphleteers or pirate radio operators will be defended by CPJ if punished for what they have written or broadcast. Journalists jailed for campaigning for freedom of expression also get our support: If journalists don't stand up for other journalists who are fighting for press freedom, who will?

We will also defend as journalists those who would not define themselves primarily as journalists: That is because governments sometimes define people into our profession for us by prosecuting them for what they have published in newspapers or said on the radio. If a political leader who pens occasional opinion columns is assassinated, we would presume that the murderer was motivated by politics, not by a specific newspaper piece. Such a case would be a tragedy, but not an entry in CPJ's ledger. But if a politician were prosecuted and imprisoned on the basis of what he had written as a columnist, we would defend the politician as a journalist—because journalism would be the nature of that alleged offense.

It is a painful paradox that as press freedom increases around the world, so does the number of casualties in the press corps. But the multiplying incidents of violence and legal harassment against journalists should not obscure the real news: There is more press freedom and more independent journalists are taking advantage of that freedom than ever before in history.

That doesn't mean that press freedom progress is now a straight, unbroken line, or that it is obtained without a struggle. In part, the story of 1997 was one of worrisome backsliding in many countries where this decade had begun with unprecedented freedoms.

The 1990s have witnessed an unprecedented explosion of independent news media around the world. In scores of countries, regimes marked by authoritarianism or outright despotism were forced to cede power to new, more pluralistic governments which at least in principle ascribed to the notion that freedom of expression is a fundamental right. State propaganda networks were dismantled or transformed into genuine news agencies, while upstart private newspapers and broadcast outlets vied for audiences hungry for real, uncensored news and commentary.

The triggering event was the collapse of Soviet communism, the single most dramatic advance of the century for press freedom. Almost overnight, journalists in the former Warsaw Pact republics began aggressively asserting their independence, and courting an audience that was no longer a captive of state media. In Central Asia, a region that had in its history never experienced an independent press, tiny newspapers and fledgling radio outlets appeared within months of the Soviet Union's dissolution. The short-lived democracy movement in China, propelled by reverberations from Gorbachev's Moscow, revealed a generation of eager, idealistic young reporters and commentators. One of the instructive surprises of this transformation was that so many reporters and editors for Soviet-era state media—whom many Western journalists had viewed not as colleagues but as apparatchik cogs in a Communist propaganda machine—were both eager and able to act as authentic journalists, once given the political chance. This is an important, encouraging lesson for those of us dealing today with reporters for state news services in China, or Vietnam. We should give them the benefit of the doubt.

Not only the Communist world—or the ex-Communist world—was caught up in this revolution. In Africa and Latin America, military dictators and civilian autocrats who had survived by exploiting Cold War rivalries were abandoned by foreign patrons, and then by their own people. In contrast to the Soviet bloc, where independent media emerged in the aftermath of the system's collapse, the local news media in these countries were in the vanguard of change from the start. From Central America to Southern Africa, fledgling news organizations of the 1990s have their roots in democratic rebellions and popular insurgencies of the 1980s. This thawing effect seemed contagious: In the Middle East, the news media in Algeria and Jordan and Yemen became much more openly critical at the beginning of the decade, while in East Asia the best newspapers of Manila and Taipei and Seoul aggressively asserted their independence. Not all of this new-found media independence was handled responsibly: unverified rumors were often peddled as news, and hatemongers in Central Europe and Central Africa took to the airwaves to incite genocide. Much more the pattern, though, was an almost startlingly fast and lasting consolidation of a vibrant, independent, and increasingly professional news media, from Bangkok to Warsaw to Buenos Aires.

Now, however, the distressing pattern in many places is a return to repression. The Algerian military has clamped down on coverage of Islamists and counterinsurgency campaigns. In most of Central Asia the once-nascent independent press has been smothered out of existence by violence and censorship. In the Caucasus, Azeri censors and Georgian hit men keep independent reporters under control. Peruvian journalists again live in fear of military harassment. Hanoi has abruptly turned away from the path of liberalization. In Liberia and Sierra Leone, the once-independent press functions under something akin to martial law. And in nearby Lagos, once home to perhaps the most vigorous press on the continent, journalists are ruthlessly driven underground or into exile. These are the exceptions to the rule, but they are necessarily the places where CPJ must focus its efforts in the coming months and years.

This annual report can be read as a catalogue of horrors, and the physical dangers and political pressures facing journalists around the world are unquestionably acute and increasing. But beneath this press-abuse case log is a substratum of good news: Journalists around the world are defying this intimidation and creating loyal new audiences for fearless, independent newsgathering, and neither they nor their readers will easily tolerate a return to the days of state propaganda and censorship.

This book is a chronicle of resistance. It is a reminder that the highest standards of our profession are being upheld at great personal cost by journalists like Nigeria's Christine Anyanwu, Mexico's Jesús Blancornelas, and Turkey's Ocak Isik Yurtçu. This latest annual edition of *Attacks on the Press* is dedicated not just to the 129 journalists who were imprisoned at year's end and to the 26 journalists who lost their lives in the line of duty in 1997, but to the hundreds of bold, enterprising reporters and editors and broadcasters who insist on doing their jobs under conditions that would make most of us abandon the profession for dentistry or carpentry. They are paying a price, but they are also making history. By paying attention, by offering moral support, by reporting to the world about them and their stories, we can help them to continue to do their jobs.

26 Journalists Murdered in 1997

Verifying and responding to cases of murdered journalists is at the heart of CPJ's mission, and it often cuts to the heart, too.

In 1997, CPJ confirmed 26 deaths in 14 countries of journalists killed while on assignment or as a direct result of their professional work. Seven journalists were murdered in **India**, four in **Colombia**, three in **Mexico**, and two in **Cambodia**.

Assassinations also claimed the lives of journalists in another 10 countries— **Argentina, Brazil, Guatemala, Indonesia, Iran, Pakistan, the Philippines, Rwanda, Sierra Leone**, and **Ukraine**.

In 1997, as in years past, assassination was the leading cause of job-related death for journalists around the world. In 1996, CPJ also documented 26 murders, plus one accidental job-related death.

Because the motive behind these attacks is censorship, CPJ urges governments to investigate and prosecute these murders not as common homicides, but as crimes against society. Yet with few exceptions, those believed responsible for the murders have not been apprehended, or even officially identified.

In another 10 cases of journalists reported murdered in 1997, CPJ suspects but could not document a direct link between the killing and the victim's professional work. We have listed such troubling but inconclusive cases as "unconfirmed," and are urging the governments of the countries in which the deaths occurred to undertake thorough investigations.

The seven documented killings in India in 1997 reflect increasing political violence there and heightened risks for local reporters and photographers. Five journalists, members of a television production crew, died while on assignment in Hyderabad in a terrorist car bombing. Two Kashmiri Muslim journalists were murdered in apparent reprisal for their work as government broadcast journalists, bringing to eight the number of journalists assassinated in Kashmir since the onset of armed conflict in 1990 between separatist militants and Indian government forces.

In Colombia, the four 1997 deaths bring to 43 the number of journalists murdered there in the past decade, by far the largest number in the Americas. The three brutal murders of Mexican journalists last year show a disturbing trend toward Colombian-style violence against journalists on the northern border and other drug-trafficking centers.

The two deaths of journalists in Cambodia were casualties of the tragic reversal of what had been a trend toward genuine democratization in the Southeast Asian nation. None of the 26 murders documented in 1997 was more poignant than the case of 23-year-old Michael Senior, a Cambodian who was orphaned as an infant in the Pol Pot terror years and adopted by a Canadian family. Two years ago, yearning to learn about his birthplace, he returned to Cambodia, where he taught English and began to work in the profession he most aspired to, journalism. On July 7 Michael Senior was shot dead by soldiers—before the eyes of his wife and brother-in-law—because his outrage moved him to photograph their looting in the aftermath of the coup two days earlier that brought Hun Sen to full power. "He had put the camera down and was apologizing," his anguished mother told CPJ from her home in Port Moody, British Columbia, "but they shot him anyway."

Whenever CPJ receives word that a journalist has been killed, the region's program coordinator investigates whether the journalist's murder was indeed a manifestation of the most vicious form of censorship. Painstaking, time-consuming research is required to verify the facts of each case and to determine, first, if the victim is indeed a journalist, and, second, that the journalist was killed *because* he or she was a journalist.

A journalist by CPJ criteria is someone who covers news or writes commentary or works as an editor, publisher, or director of a news organization. Photojournalists, members of radio, television, and cable news teams, and editorial staff of online news publications are journalists to CPJ. When a death is attributable to the journalist's professional work, it is categorized as "confirmed." This includes not just assassination victims, but journalists killed covering armed conflicts, whether they were caught in crossfire or targeted by combatants. When a journalist is killed in an accident, on an assignment that placed him or her in harm's way, that is also considered a death in the line of duty.

This listing almost certainly omits other cases of journalists who were also killed in 1997 because of their profession. The following are cases CPJ has been able to document. It is often extraordinarily difficult to demonstrate that a murder was committed in retribution for someone's professional work. In most of the countries where these murders are committed, the majority of homicides of all kind remain unsolved. CPJ welcomes information on these cases and calls on governments to conduct vigorous investigations into all such deaths and to prosecute those responsible for the killings.

JOURNALISTS KILLED IN 1997

Twenty-six Journalists Murdered in 1997

Research by CPJ and Reporters Sans Frontières (RSF) indicates that the following individuals were murdered in 1997 because of their work as journalists. They either died in the line of duty on assignment, or were deliberately targeted for assassination because of their reporting or their affiliation with a news organization.

Listed by name, affiliation, date of death, and place of attack.

Argentina: 1

José Luis Cabezas, *Noticias,* **January 25, Pinamar**

Cabezas was a photographer for the news magazine *Noticias.* His handcuffed, charred corpse was discovered on January 25 inside a burned rental car outside of Pinamar, a beach resort where Cabezas was working on a story. He was one of the first photojournalists to take a picture of Alfredo Yabrán, a well-known and reclusive tycoon described by a prominent politician as head of the Argentine mafia. His murder evoked memories of brutal killings in Argentina's "dirty war" of the 1980s—outraging journalists, who took to the streets in protest and pressured the government for a thorough investigation. The Justice Minister was forced to resign after it became known that he had received phone calls from Yabrán. Numerous arrests have been made in connection with the murder, among them current and former police officers and Yabrán's security chief. Journalists covering the investigation have been threatened.

Brazil: 1

Edgar Lopes de Faria, FM Capital, October 29, Campo Grande

Lopes de Faria was host of the programs "O Escaramuça" ("The Fighter") on the local radio station FM Capital and "Boca do Povo" ("The Mouth of the People") on television station TV Record. He was murdered on October 29 in Campo Grande, capital of the state of Mato Grosso do Sul, while on his way to the radio station. Police believe his murder was carried out by trained assassins, who fired with accuracy and left no trail. Lopes de Faria had reported on the hired killers who investigators say are responsible for recent murders in Mato Grosso do Sul.

Cambodia: 2

Chet Duong Daravuth, *Neak Prayuth,* **March 30, Phnom Penh**

Chet had worked as a reporter for the newspaper *Neak Prayuth* (The Fighter) and had recently obtained permission to publish a new paper. He was killed March 30 in a grenade attack outside the National Assembly while covering a Khmer National Party rally at which opposition leader Samuel Rainsy was speaking. Other journalists were injured and at least 26 people were killed. The motive for the attack is believed to be political.

Michael Senior, July 7, Phnom Penh

Senior, 23, a Canadian citizen, was born in Cambodia, where he was orphaned as an infant during the Pol Pot terror years. He was adopted in 1975 by a family in Canada, where he was raised. Two years ago he returned to Cambodia and fournd work in Phnom Penh as an English teacher and television newscaster. He also worked at the *Cambodia Daily* in Phnom Penh. Senior was assassinated while photographing looting by soldiers in a public market on July 7 in the aftermath of the coup begun two days earlier by Second Prime Minister Hun Sen. He was accosted by the soldiers—Hun Sen loyalists— who shot him first in the knee. As he lay in the street pleading for mercy, he was shot again, executed before the eyes of his Cambodian wife and brother-in-law. Phnom Penh editors say that Senior's pictures, had they been recovered, would have been used in their coverage of the coup.

Colombia: 4

Gerardo Bedoya Borrero, *El País*, March 20, Cali

Bedoya was the opinion editor of the Cali daily newspaper *El País* and a harsh critic of drug trafficking. He was assassinated as he was getting into his car on the night of March 20 by a gunman who shot him repeatedly and fled the scene on a motorcycle. Colleagues said in a public statement that they believed the perpetrators of the crime were drug traffickers. Bedoya had three weeks earlier written a column defending the controversial U.S. decision to decertify Colombia as a recipient of U.S. economic aid because of its government's alleged ties to the cocaine cartels. "Even though they call me pro-Yankee, I prefer the pressure of the U.S. government to the pressure of the narcos," he wrote.

Freddy Elles Ahumada, March 18, Cartagena

Elles was a free-lance photojournalist who drove a taxi to supplement his income. He was abducted by three unidentified individuals in Cartagena on March 17 and found assassinated in his taxi on March 18. He had been shot several times and his body showed signs of torture. Local journalists believe that Elles may have been assassinated in reprisal for his photographs of police violence published in the Bogotá daily *El Espectador*. Only the spare tire of his taxi was missing, making robbery an unlikely motive for the crime.

Francisco Castro Menco, Fundación Cultural, November 8, Majagual

Castro was president of the Fundación Cultural, a community foundation that broadcasts daily by radio in the violence-ridden town of Majagual in the department of Sucre. Castro was at home when he was fatally shot by unidentified killers. While Castro tried to make the Fundación Cultural a neutral forum for community news, it represented an independent voice in a region where both armed guerrillas and paramilitary forces are active.

Fundación provided air time for all three mayoral candidates in the October municipal elections without endorsing any. Castro, a community leader and a candidate for the departmental assembly in October, hosted a daily program on community topics and often called for an end to the violence. Local journalists believe he was murdered because of his appeals for peace, but are unsure if the guerrillas or the paramilitary are responsible.

Jairo Elías Márquez Gallego, *El Marqués*, November 20, Armenia

Márquez was director of the magazine *El Marqués*, known for its critical reporting on corruption. He was killed in a drive-by shooting by two gunmen on a motorcycle as he was entering his car on a downtown street in the town of Armenia in western Colombia. Márquez had received numerous death threats in the past two years because of his crusade against corruption in the region. Márquez was the fourth journalist murdered in Colombia in 1997. The deaths of two other Colombian journalists are still under investigation.

Guatemala: 1

Jorge Luis Marroquín Sagastume, *Sol Chortí*, June 5, Jocotán

Marroquín was founding director of the local monthly *Sol Chortí*, which has reported extensively about corruption in the mayor's office. He was also a member of the ruling Partida de Avanzada Nacional (National Vanguard Party) in the department of Chiquimula. He was fatally shot in the town of Jocotán June 5 by two assassins, according to eyewitnesses. Brothers Neftalí and José Gabriel López León, who are being tried for the murder, said that Jocotán mayor José Manuel Ohajaca hired José Gabriel to kill Marroquín. Guatemalan law protects mayors from prosecution for common crimes, but the Human Rights Office of the Archbishop in Guatemala City has petitioned the court to lift the immunity for Ohajaca. The request was rejected by the Sixth Court of Appeals in Jalapa and is pending before the Supreme Court.

India: 7

Altaf Ahmed Faktoo, Doordarshan TV, January 1, Srinagar

Faktoo was an anchor for the state-owned Doordarshan television station in Srinagar, Kashmir. He was assassinated on January 1, reportedly by militant separatists, who fired two shots at the journalist with a gun equipped with a silencer. He had received repeated threats from militant separatists because of his work and had been kidnapped and detained by a militant group in 1994. Faktoo had aired pro-government news reports that were critical of the separatist movement. Shortly before his death he started working for a news program about Kashmir that is broadcast by satellite throughout India, but not in Kashmir. He was the seventh journalist assassinated in Kashmir since the militant movement began in 1989 and the third who was specifically targeted because of his work with the state-owned broadcast media.

Saidan Shafi, Doordarshan TV, March 16, Srinagar

Shafi was a reporter for Doordarshan TV, the official Indian television network, for "Kashmir File," a weekly news program, and "Eyewitness," a five-minute nightly news capsule. He was fatally shot March 16 in an ambush by two gunmen in Srinagar, Kashmir. His personal security guard also was killed in the attack. "Kashmir File" was critical of militant Kashmiri separatists in the state, and he told colleagues he had received threats from separatists for what they said was his "biased" reporting. Shafi was the eighth journalist to be assassinated in Kashmir since the militant separatist movement began in 1989 and the fourth targeted because of his work with the state-owned broadcast media. Both Shafi and Altaf Ahmed Faktoo, killed January 1, were Kashmiri Muslim journalists.

Jagadish Babu, G. Raja Sekhar, S. Gangadhar Raju, P. Srinivas Rao, and S. Krishna, E-TV, November 19, Hyderabad

Five members of a production crew of E-TV (Eenadu Television), a private channel, were covering the making of a film November 19 when they were killed in a car bomb explosion. As they were leaving the Rama Naidu Studios, their vehicle caught the brunt of the massive blast, which police said was caused by a remote-control car bomb parked by the studio entrance. The television crew's driver, P. Chandra Sekhar Reddy, was also killed. At least 17 others died and more than 30 were injured. The attack is believed to have been motivated by political rivalry targeted at the film's producer, Paritala Ravi, a former guerrilla leader pardoned in return for his surrender. Ravi who is a state legislator and member of the governing Telugu Desam party.

JOURNALISTS KILLED IN 1997

Indonesia: 1

Muhammad Sayuti Bochari, *Pos Makasar* , June 11, Luwu, Sulawesi

Sayuti was a reporter with the Ujungpandang-based weekly *Pos Makasar*. He died June 11 of head and neck injuries after he was found unconscious June 9 on a village street in Luwu, 400 kilometers north of Ujungpandang, the provincial capital in the south of Sulawesi. His motorbike, found beside his body, was not damaged, according to news reports. Family members and friends said his bruises and injuries showed that he had been beaten. Sayuti recently had written articles on local officials who had allegedly embezzled government funds earmarked for poverty relief. He had also reported on the front page of *Pos Makasar* June 1 on timber theft involving a village chief. The editor of *Pos Makasar* told the *Jakarta Post* that Sayuti's death was related to his reporting on local corruption. Local police said Sayuti died in a traffic accident. The state-sponsored Association of Indonesian Journalists (PWI) is investigating Sayuti's death.

Iran: 1

Ebrahim Zalzadeh, *Mayar*, February 22, Tehran

Zalzadeh was publisher of the monthly magazine *Mayar*. The magazine, which frequently criticized government censorship practices against the media, was forced to close by the authorities in 1995. Zalzadeh's body was identified in a Tehran morgue on March 29, 35 days after he disappeared. According to witnesses, there were three or four stab wounds visible on his chest. A coroner's report said that his body had been discovered on or about February 24 by a road in the outskirts of Tehran. Zalzadeh was one of several Iranian writers and publishers who had volunteered to share the punishment of magazine editor Abbas Maroufi, who was sentenced in January 1996 to six months in prison and 35 lashes for criticizing the government.

Mexico: 3

Jesús Abel Bueno León, *7 días*, May 22, Chilpancingo

Bueno León was a director at the regional weekly *7 días* (7 Days). His bullet-ridden body was found next to his burned car on a road close to the city of Chilpancingo, the state capital of Guerrero, 120 miles south of Mexico City. Members of the National Union of Journalists (SNRP) said they had asked the governor to protect Bueno León after the journalist had received death threats. He left a letter to be made public in the event of his death, listing names of those who may have wanted him dead. Topping the list was José Rubén Robles

Catalán, former secretary of state for Guerrero, who was suing Bueno León and other journalists for defamation for reporting on criminal allegations against him which were the subject of government investigations. After Bueno León's murder, 50 local journalists marched to the central plaza in Chilpancingo, where they called on the governor to investigate the circumstances of the crime.

Benjamín Flores González, *La Prensa*, July 15, San Luis Río Colorado

Flores González was editor and owner of the daily *La Prensa* in San Luis Río Colorado, Sonora State, in northern Mexico. He was gunned down July 15 as he was arriving at the newspaper's offices. Flores González was known for his aggressive coverage of the drug trade, including a story published in May reporting that a half-ton of cocaine confiscated by federal authorities had disappeared from the Federal Judicial Police Headquarters in San Luis Río Colorado. His newspaper had recently reported on the special treatment being given an imprisoned drug lord. On July 18, police arrested a gunman allegedly hired by the drug lord's brother and charged him with the crime.

Víctor Hernández Martínez, *Como*, July 26, Mexico City

Hernández was a police reporter for the magazine *Como*. He was hit on the head with a blunt instrument July 25, and died July 26 of the traumatic head injury. Hernández was attacked upon leaving the office of the Federal Judicial Police, where he had gone in connection with a story he was working on. Colleagues at *Como* suspect that he may have been killed by federal agents working for the judiciary or by individuals connected to the police. Hernández often covered stories on the police and drug trafficking and had received threats and was the target of an attempted car bombing.

Pakistan: 1

Z.A. Shahid, *Khabrain*, January 18, Lahore

Shahid was a photographer with the Urdu-language daily *Khabrain*. He was killed in a bomb blast at a court house. The bombing targeted leaders of the Sipah Sahaba Pakistan, an anti-Shiite party, who were being brought from jail to a hearing. At least 19 people were killed and more than 80 injured. Five of the injured were journalists.

Philippines: 1

Danny Hernandez, *People's Journal Tonight*, June 3, Manila

Hernandez was the news editor of a popular tabloid daily, *People's Journal Tonight*, for which he wrote a column called "Sunday Punch." He specialized in exposing drug syndicates and police corruption. He was fatally shot in a taxi after leaving the *Journal* office just before dawn. It was later learned the taxi had been stolen hours earlier and was apparently waiting for him, police said. Colleagues said Hernandez had told them he had been receiving death threats from members of drug rings.

Rwanda: 1

Appolos Hakizimana,
***Umuravumba*, April 27, Kigali**

Hakizimana was editor in chief of the independent bimonthly *Umuravumba* and former editor of the weekly *Intego*. He was accosted on his way home, gagged, shot, and killed by two assailants. He had been the target of an attempted kidnapping three weeks earlier. In July 1996 he was arrested and charged with being a Hutu accomplice to a mass killing. He was released August 19.

Sierra Leone: 1

Ishmael Jalloh, June 3,
Allentown

Jalloh was a free-lance reporter for the independent newspapers *Punch*, *Storm*, and *Vision*. He was killed while covering the June 3 battle at Allentown of the combined battalion of the Revolutionary United Front (RUF) and Sierra Leone Armed Forces Revolutionary Council (AFRC) with Nigerian soldiers of the West African peace monitoring force, ECOMOG.

Ukraine: 1

Borys Derevyanko, *Vechernyaya*
***Odessa*, August 11, Odessa**

Derevyanko, editor in chief of *Vechernyaya Odessa*, a popular and influential thrice-weekly newspaper, was fatally shot at point-blank range on his way to work on the morning of August 11 near the Press House, where the newspaper's offices are located. Colleagues believe the killing of Derevyanko, who was editor of *Vechernyaya Odessa* for 24 years, was related to the newspaper's opposition to the policies of Odessa's mayor. The chief regional prosecutor declared the murder a contract killing and launched an official investigation. Local authorities announced in September that they had arrested a suspect, described as a professional assassin, who confessed to killing Derevyanko, but they gave no details about his confession.

Ten Journalists Killed: Motive Unconfirmed

When the motive for a journalist's murder is unclear, but there is reason to suspect that it was related to the journalist's profession, CPJ classifies that death as "unconfirmed." CPJ continues its research to identify the reasons for the crime and its efforts to persuade authorities to investigate the killings and apprehend and punish the culprits.

Brazil

Natan Pereira Gatinho, Ouro Verde, January 11, Paragominas

Gatinho was a correspondent for the television station Ouro Verde, also known as TV Mundial. Until November 1996 he also hosted a program for Radio Cidade, in which he read letters from farmers and workers complaining about their dire conditions. He was fatally shot January 11. He had been receiving death threats because of his radio program. He also was a militant activist of the Worker's Party and a candidate in the 1996 municipal elections. A truck driver with whom Gatinho had had a fight two days before his death was arrested for the murder, but he has denied the charges. Brazilian press groups suspect that Gatinho was murdered by local landowners because of his work as a journalist, but some journalists believe he was killed because of a personal feud with the truck driver. Gatinho had accused him of running over and killing a woman who was a colleague at Ouro Verde.

Colombia

Alejandro Jaramillo, October 24, Pasto

Jaramillo last worked in journalism as deputy director of the newspaper *El Sur* in Pasto, from June through August. Before taking that job he had lived in exile in Ecuador, where he fled in 1989 after receiving death threats. Several years earlier, in an incident that may have been related to his work as a police reporter, he was shot and injured while working for *El País* in Cali. He was reported missing on October 24, and his dismembered body was found the following week. Because of the gruesome nature of his murder, involvement by organized crime is suspected.

Cambodia

Ou Sareoun, *Samleng Reas Khmer*, October 14, Phnom Penh

Ou was a reporter for *Samleng Reas Khmer* (Voice of the Cambodian People), according to his father, who owns and edits the newspaper. The newspaper was investigating extortion in the central market of Phnom Penh. On the morning of October 14, as he was distributing newspapers to vendors in the market, Ou was dragged into the street by security guards, who had been the target of the newspaper's investigation, and shot dead. The official report of Ou's death said he was drunk and had been killed in a dispute over a card game, but the Khmer Journalists Association maintains that he was killed because of the newspaper's reporting. Police arrested the guard who shot Ou, but he was later released, and no charges were filed against him.

El Salvador

Lorena Saravia, Radio RCS, August 25, San Salvador

Saravia was a prominent newscaster in El Salvador and a news anchor at radio station RCS. She was abducted from her car August 25, murdered with a shot to the head, and found dead in a vacant lot the following morning. Her car was found a week later in Santa Ana, 50 kilometers from San Salvador. Nothing was stolen. The investigation has not produced any leads, and it is not clear why Saravia was killed. Prior to working at Radio RCS, Saravia was a television news presenter. Radio RCS airs political talk shows hosted by ex-military officers and ex-guerrillas.

Guatemala

Luis Ronaldo De León Godoy, *Prensa Libre*, November 14, Guatemala City

De León was head of the weekend supplement section of the leading daily *Prensa Libre*. He was stabbed as he was leaving his house in central Guatemala City by an assailant who had been waiting in a nearby car for several hours, eyewitnesses reported. He died as a result of his injuries after three hours of surgery. Neither money nor personal documents were taken in the attack, local journalists reported, making robbery an unlikely motive.

Hernández Pérez, Radio Campesina, July 16, Tiquisate

Pérez was a news reader at Radio Campesina in Tiquisate, Escuintla. He was ambushed by a group of heavily armed men as he was leaving the station on the morning of July 16 and killed instantly by gunfire. Another employee of the station, Haroldo Escobar Noriega, a messenger, was also killed. The motive for the murders is not known.

Indonesia

Naimullah, *Sinar Pagi*, July 25, Pantai Penibungan

Naimullah was a reporter with the Jakarta-based morning daily newspaper *Sinar Pagi*. His mutilated body was found in the back seat of his car on July 25 in the remote area of Pantai Penibungan, about 90 kilometers north of Pontianak, the provincial capital of West Kalimantan. He had recently reported on timber theft and had been conducting an investigation of illegal logging in Kalimantan. Police in the area said he was killed in a traffic accident. The editor of *Sinar Pagi* was widely quoted as saying that Naimullah was no longer working for the paper at the time of his death. Some officials of the Jakarta-based Alliance of Independent Journalists believe he was targeted by logging interests as a result of his earlier reporting.

Peru

Tito Pilco Mori, Radio Frecuencia Popular, September 3, Rioja

Pilco was owner and director of Radio Frecuencia Popular in Rioja and host of the program "El Pueblo Quiere Saber" ("The People Want to Know"), which frequently criticized public prosecutors, judges, and police officials. He was assaulted August 27 on the outskirts of Rioja as he was returning home from a visit with a cousin. He was found, severely injured and unable to speak, at 5 a.m. on August 28, some distance from his motorcycle. He died September 3 in a Lima hospital. Two witnesses reported seeing assailants in a white car without license plates intercept Pilco on his motorcycle and beat him. But the official report said his death resulted from head wounds received when he crashed his motorcycle because he was drunk. The investigation was initially headed by José Monteverde, a provincial prosecutor whose integrity had been questioned by Pilco on his radio show, according to the local press. After a Lima newspaper published an account of Pilco's death, the case was reopened.

Russia

Valery Krivosheyev, *Komsomolskaya Pravda*, September 6, Lipetsk

Krivosheyev was a special correspondent for the national daily *Komsomolskaya Pravda* in Lipetsk in Central Russia. He was found dead from skull trauma, near a coffee shop where the reporter frequently met his sources. Colleagues at the newspaper and at the Glasnost Defense Foundation claim that Krivosheyev's killing was related to his work as an investigative journalist covering local and national public figures. Later reports indicated that he was killed in a brawl during a wedding reception at the café. The day before his death he told friends at *De-Fakto*, the newspaper where he had formerly worked, that he had scheduled a meeting with a source on a story he called "a bombshell of national proportions."

Ukraine

Petro Shevchenko, *Kievskiye Vedomosti*, Ukrainian, March 13, Kiev

Shevchenko was a correspondent for the Kiev daily *Kievskiye Vedomosti*. He was found hanged in an abandoned building. Kiev police labeled Shevchenko's death a suicide, but his colleagues at the newspaper believe he was murdered because he had co-authored a series of articles published in the weeks before his death about disputes between the mayor of Luhansk and the local branch of the Ukrainian Security Service (SBU), successor to the KGB. At year's end, CPJ was unable to confirm whether Shevchenko's death was a suicide or murder.

CPJ Confirms 474 Journalists Killed* in Past 10 Years

From 1988 through 1997, the most dangerous countries for journalists were: Algeria, Colombia, Russia, Tajikistan, Croatia, India, Bosnia and Herzogovina, Philippines, Turkey, Peru, and Rwanda.

120 in the AMERICAS
Colombia: 43
Peru: 18
Mexico:12
Brazil: 10
El Salvador: 10
United States: 7
Guatemala: 4
Haiti: 4
Argentina: 2
Honduras: 2
Venezuela: 2
Canada: 1
Chile: 1
Dominican Republic: 1
Ecuador: 1
Panama: 1
Paraguay: 1

128 in EUROPE & THE REPUBLICS OF THE FORMER SOVIET UNION
Russia: 29**
Tajikistan: 29
Croatia: 26
Bosnia and Herzegovina: 21
Soviet Union: 8**
Georgia: 3
Ukraine: 3
Azerbaijan: 2
Romania: 2
Slovenia: 2
Belgium: 1
Ireland: 1
Lithuania: 1

95 in the MIDDLE EAST & NORTH AFRICA
Algeria: 60
Turkey: 20
Lebanon: 6
Iraq: 5
Egypt:2
Cyprus: 1
Iran: 1

78 in ASIA
India: 24
Philippines: 20
Pakistan: 9
Cambodia: 6
Afghanistan: 5
Sri Lanka: 5
Indonesia: 4
Bangladesh: 1
China: 1
Papua New Guinea: 1
Thailand: 1
Vietnam: 1

53 in AFRICA
Rwanda: 16
Somalia: 9
Angola: 6
Chad: 4
South Africa: 4
Burundi: 3
Ethiopia: 3
Liberia: 2
Zaire: 2
Sierra Leone: 1
Sudan: 1
Uganda: 1
Zambia: 1

All figures above reflect the number of journalists killed in the line of duty.

**Between 1988 and 1991, eight journalists were killed in what was then the Soviet Union: three in Azerbaijan, three in Russia, and two in Latvia.*

129 Journalists in Jail: As of December 31, 1997

As the world prepared to commemorate the 50th anniversary of the Universal Declaration of Human Rights, at least 129 journalists were being held in prison for exercising the right guaranteed to them in Article 19 to "seek, receive and impart information and ideas through any media, and regardless of frontiers." The Committee to Protect Journalists is calling for their immediate release.

A t the end of every year, CPJ attempts to document every case of everyone held in prison anywhere in the world on charges related to journalistic work. This includes newsgathering, writing, editing, publishing, broadcasting, and photojournalism. It applies to opinion, analysis and commentary, as well as to factual reportage. We undoubtedly miss some cases. Information about these journalists and their convictions is often extremely difficult to obtain and verify. There are many reported instances of journalists' jailings we do not include because we cannot verify the information or because we cannot demonstrate a direct relationship between the imprisonment and the journalist's work.

What follows is a listing of journalists whose imprisonment was—according to all available information—related directly to some facet of journalism: **129 cases in 24 countries as of December 31, 1997, including 29 in Turkey, 17 in Nigeria, 16 in Ethiopia, and 15 in China.** The cases are presented chronologically and by country, from Algeria to Zambia.

One year earlier, CPJ had reported a record 185 confirmed cases of journalists in prison in 24 countries. The significant reduction in 1997 to 129 journalists in prison is due largely to a dramatic drop in **Turkey**, from 78* confirmed cases at the close of 1996 to 29 at the end of 1997. This is attributable to a convergence of international pressure and a mid-year change of government in Ankara. At least 37 of the journalists who CPJ reported in prison on December 31, 1996, were released from Turkish prisons in 1997, including six editors who were freed by a limited amnesty measure passed by parliament in August following a CPJ mission to Turkey in July. Among those released was Ocak Isik Yurtçu, a recipient *in absentia* of a 1996 International Press Freedom award from CPJ and the focus of a sustained CPJ campaign for his release. Yurtçu, who was imprisoned in 1994 and had faced another 10 years in prison, traveled to New York after his

* See footnote on p. 24

release to speak at the ceremony honoring recipients of the 1997 International Press Freedom Awards. The release of 37 Turkish journalists was perhaps the single most positive press-freedom development in the world last year.

Still, with 29 confirmed cases of journalists in prison as of December 31, 1997, Turkey once again heads CPJ's list, with more journalists in jail than any other country. This compares to 78* journalists in prison at the close of 1996, 51 in 1995, and 74 in 1994. It is CPJ's hope and expectation that these numbers will continue to decline. The statutes under which these journalists were convicted remain on the books, however. The Yilmaz government has pledged to CPJ and others that it will undertake sweeping reform of the Anti-Terror Law and articles of the Turkish Penal Code that have been used to prosecute working journalists. (More information on CPJ's research on imprisoned Turkish journalists is presented on page 49; for further background, see the Special Report on CPJ's Turkish press freedom campaign on page 82.)

The most disturbing development of 1997 was the increasing persecution of journalists in **Nigeria**, where at least 17 reporters and editors were in jail at the end of the year—up from eight in 1996. The Abacha government refuses in most cases to permit visitors to these prisoners, who are said to be confined under extremely primitive conditions and subjected to physical abuse by security officials. Among the prisoners is *Sunday Magazine* editor Christine Anyanwu, a 1997 recipient of CPJ's International Press Freedom Award. More than 400 leading American journalists and news media executives have petitioned the Abacha government for her immediate release. It is CPJ's commitment to intensify our campaign on behalf of Christine Anyanwu in 1998. (For more information on Nigeria and Christine Anyanwu, see pp. 139 and 169.)

In **Ethiopia**, 16 journalists were jailed at year-end, all of them newly imprisoned during 1997. This compares to 18 in 1996 and 31 in 1995. For more than five years now, the Meles regime has made a habit of punishing outspoken journalists with sentences ranging typically from six to 18 months for allegedly "false" reporting or inciting "anxieties" and ethnic strife. Journalists are also routinely detained for weeks or months at a time without charges.

---

* In *Attacks on the Press in 1996* we reported that there were 78 confirmed cases of Turkish journalists in prison at the end of that year. We now believe that the correct number as of December 31, 1996, was 74. In the current 1997 report, we have omitted four cases included in the 1996 list because newly obtained information showed that those prosecutions were not connected to the journalists' work. We reclassified another nine of the original 78 cases as "unconfirmed" due to new information raising questions about the relationship between the charges and the journalists' profession (another four imprisoned journalists on the 1996 list are listed as "unconfirmed" in 1997 because CPJ could not verify reports that they had been released). We have also since learned of four other journalists who were imprisoned as of December 31, 1996; two remained in jail a year later, and two had been released. For more information on Turkey, see pages 49 and 82.

In **China**, at least 15 journalists remain in jail, for publishing alleged "state secrets" or writing and distributing political leaflets critical of Communist Party rule. In one of the more recent prosecutions, Gao Yu, a correspondent for a Hong Kong monthly, was sentenced to prison for reporting government financial data. She was the recipient of UNESCO's 1997 Guillermo Cano World Press Freedom Prize. There were no new prosecutions of Chinese journalists in 1997.

The military government of **Burma** continues to hold eight opposition journalists in jail, while Kuwait keeps in custody seven foreign-born reporters— most of them Jordanians and Palestinians—convicted of treasonous "collaboration" with Iraqi occupying forces in 1991. **Vietnam** has five indepen- dent journalists in prison, including Doan Viet Hoat, the recipient of CPJ's 1993 International Press Freedom Award and the 1997 Golden Pen of Freedom prize from the World Association of Newspapers.

Peru was the Western Hemisphere's leading jailer of journalists, with four imprisoned reporters at the end of 1997. In prosecutions based exclusively on their published articles, the four were convicted by secret tribunals of alleged membership in the Tupac Amaru and Sendero Luminoso guerrilla bands. **Algeria**, **Cuba**, **Indonesia**, **Pakistan**, **Russia**, **Sudan**, and **Tunisia** each held two journalists in prison. Journalists were also in jail at year's end in **Azerbaijan**, **Cameroon**, **Eritrea**, **Iran**, **Iraq**, **Malaysia**, **South Korea**, and **Zambia**.

These are not simple statistics. Every name on this list represents someone whom we as fellow journalists believe to have been unjustly imprisoned because of his or her work. We have learned that with sufficient international attention and pressure, many could and would be freed.

Not everyone on this list was a career journalist prior to his or her arrest. We include political analysts, human rights activists, and others who have been prose- cuted because of opinion columns or news features they have written. All working journalists in these countries are directly threatened by such prosecutions, and we believe that we have an obligation to defend such imprisoned writers as colleagues. Journalism is not the exclusive domain of a professional fraternity. Anyone who is prosecuted for writing or broadcasting political commentary or factual reportage should be defended as a colleague by journalists around the world.

In totalitarian societies where independent journalism is not permitted, CPJ often defends prosecuted writers who would be defined by their governments as political dissidents, rather than journalists. This category would embrace the *samizdat* publishers of the former Soviet Union, the wall-poster essayists of the pre-Tiananmen period in China, and the underground pamphleteers of today's Burma. CPJ also classifies as an imprisoned journalist anyone with a news media

IMPRISONED JOURNALISTS

background in an authoritarian in or totalitarian state who, like several recent cases in Cuba, is prosecuted for campaigning on behalf of the cause of free expression. We believe that working in the defense of press freedom is as legitimate an activity for a journalist as reporting or editing.

We also object in principle to any imprisonment of a journalist on the basis of a conviction for criminal libel. Legitimate cases of defamation should be matters for civil courts to resolve.

In addition to the 129 confirmed cases reported here, we have listed a further 30 "unconfirmed" cases of imprisoned journalists in eight countries (see page 75). In some of these cases, we could not confirm reports that a jailed journalist had been released from prison before the end of 1997. In others it remains uncertain whether the prosecution was directly connected to the journalist's work. In all these cases CPJ is seeking additional information from local sources and clarification from the governments in question.

This year-end accounting offers an instructive global snapshot of patterns of repression of journalists around the world. Though it omits the many cases of journalists who have been jailed and released in the course of the year, these incidents are often noted in the country sections of this 1997 report. Such cases are simply too numerous for CPJ to document comprehensively, however. The annual year-end listing permits accurate year-to-year as well as country-to-country comparisons, and focuses attention on long-term prisoners whose cases might otherwise be forgotten.

The common denominators of the year-end case list are summary convictions and harsh sentences equating some form of journalistic activity with treason. There is little ambiguity in these cases. Governments explicitly or implicitly acknowledge that the charges were prompted by critical reporting or commentary, and that the intent of prosecution was censorship. Formal charges do not always refer to journalistic work, however. In some countries—Turkey is the main offender—journalists are often accused of unlawful collaboration with armed insurgents, but the motivation for the prosecution and the evidence for the charge appears to stem wholly or largely from the publication of reportage or opinions deemed to be supportive of those rebel movements. In other places—Ethiopia, Nigeria—journalists critical of the government are often jailed with no formal charges at all.

With few exceptions, the journalists held in prison at the end of December 1997 will still be in jail when this report is published at the end of March 1998. Most of them have been on CPJ's lists before. We again call on the leaders of the 24 countries holding these 129 journalists in jail to expedite their immediate release. We urge all journalists to join us in appealing for the freedom of our imprisoned colleagues.

Imprisoned Journalists (129)

The following is a list of journalists imprisoned around the world. Cases appear chronologically, and are grouped according to the countries in which the journalists are held.

Algeria (2)

Please send appeals to:
His Excellency Liamine Zeroual
President of the High Council of State
The Presidential Palace
El Mouradia
Algiers, Algeria
Fax: 213 2 60 96 18

Djamel Fahassi, Alger Chaîne III
Detained: May 7, 1995

State security officials detained Fahassi, a reporter for the government-run French-language radio station Alger Chaîne III, and formerly a contributor to *Al-Forqane*, a weekly organ of the Islamic Salvation Front (FIS) that was banned in March 1992. Officials have refused to acknowledge his arrest.

Aziz Bouabdallah, *Al-Alam al-Siyassi*
Detained: April, 12, 1997

Bouabdallah, a journalist who covered Islamist groups in Algeria for the Arabic-language daily *Al-Alam al-Siyassi*, was abducted by three armed men from his home in Algiers. The men identified themselves as Algerian security agents and forced Bouabdallah into a waiting car. CPJ later received information that Algerian authorities were holding Bouabdallah in an Algiers detention center. He was reported to have been tortured repeatedly. Authorities have denied any knowledge of his detention.

Azerbaijan (1)

Please send appeals to:
His Excellency Heydar Aliyev
President of Azerbaijan
Baku, Azerbaijan
FAX: 994-12- 92-26-63

Savalan Mamedov, *Istintag*
Imprisoned December 22, 1997

On December 22, Salavan Mamedov, editor of the Baku weekly *Istintag*, was arrested and imprisoned. He was charged with libel (article 121 of the Azerbaijani penal code) against the former Prosecutor of the Lenkoran district, Nazim Tagiev. In a number of articles Mamedov claimed that Tagiev had cooperated with Alikram Gumbatov, who was convicted of treason and attempting to stage an uprising. According to *Yeni Nesil*, Mamedov was released from police custody on January 23, 1998. Court hearings have not yet been scheduled. Mamedov could serve a sentence of up to five years if he is found guilty.

Burma (8)

Please send appeals to:
His Excellency General Than Shwe
Prime Minister and Minister of Defense
Chairman of the State Peace and Development Council
Ministry of Defense
Signal Pagoda Road
Yangon (Rangoon), Myanmar (Burma)
Tel: 87862

U Win Tin
Imprisoned: July 4, 1989

U Win Tin, former editor of two daily newspapers and vice-chair of Burma's Writers Association, was arrested and sentenced to three years' hard labor—a sentence that was subsequently extended. U Win Tin was active in establishing independent publications during the 1988 student democracy movement, and he also worked closely with imprisoned National League for Democracy leader Daw Aung San Suu Kyi.

Authorities extended U Win Tin's sentence by five more years on March 28, 1996, after they convicted him of smuggling letters describing conditions at Insein prison to Professor Yozo Yokota, the U.N. Special Rapporteur for human rights in Burma.

In an October alert, Human Rights Watch cited reports that U Win Tin was seriously ill and perhaps close to death in Rangoon General Hospital. He was apparently transferred to the hospital in early October from Myingyan jail, known to be one of the worst in Burma.

U Maung Maung Lay Ngwe
Imprisoned: September 1990

U Maung Maung Lay Ngwe was arrested and charged with writing and distributing publications that "make people lose respect for the government." The publications were titled, collectively, *Pe-Tin-Tan.*

In 1997, CPJ was unable to obtain new information on his status.

U Myo Myint Nyein, U Sein Hlaing, *What's Happening*
Imprisoned: September 1990

U Myo Myint Nyein and U Sein Hlaing were arrested for contributing to the preparation, planning, and publication of the satirical news magazine *What's Happening*, which the Burmese government claims is anti-government propaganda. They were sentenced to seven years in prison. On March 28, 1996, they were among 21 prisoners tried inside Insein Prison and given an additional seven years sentence under the Emergency Provisions Act for smuggling letters describing prison conditions to Professor Yozo Yokota, the U.N. Special Rapporteur for human rights in Burma. In 1997, CPJ was unable to obtain new information on their case.

Daw San San Nwe
U Sein Hla Oo
Imprisoned: August 5, 1994

Dissident writer Daw San San Nwe and journalist U Sein Hla Oo were arrested on charges of spreading information damaging to the state and contacting anti-government groups. San San Nwe and Sein Hla Oo were sentenced on October 6, 1994 to 10 years and seven years in prison, respectively. Three other dissidents, including a former UNICEF worker, were sentenced to between 7 and 15 years in prison on similar charges. Officials said the five had "fabricated and sent anti-government reports to some diplomats in foreign embassies, foreign radio stations, and visiting foreign journalists." San San Nwe allegedly met two French reporters visiting Burma in April 1993 and appeared in a video they produced to spread propaganda about the government. According to reports citing Burmese officials, authorities seized confidential Energy Ministry data, as well as documents and compact discs containing anti-government materials from one of the dissidents. Both U Sein Hla Oo and Daw San San Nwe were previously imprisoned for their involvement in the National League for Democracy, Burma's main pro-democracy party. As of December 1994, all five were being held at the Insein Prison in Rangoon. In 1997, CPJ was unable to obtain new information on their case.

Ma Myat Mo Mo Tun
Imprisoned: 1994

The daughter of imprisoned dissident Daw San San Nwe, Ma Myat Mo Mo Tun, was arrested in 1994 and sentenced to seven years in prison for spreading information injurious to the state. She is alleged to have recorded "defamatory letters and documents," made contact with "illegal" groups and sent anti-government articles to a journal published by an expatriate group. In 1997, CPJ was unable to obtain new information on her case.

Ye Htut
Imprisoned: September 27, 1995

Ye Htut was arrested on charges of sending fabricated news abroad to Burmese dissidents and opposition media. Among the organizations to which Ye Htut allegedly confessed sending reports was the Thailand-based Burma Information Group (BIG), which publishes the human rights newsletter *The Irrawaddy*. Burma's official media claimed that BIG had presented a false picture of the country to foreign governments and human rights organizations. He was sentenced to seven years in prison. In 1997, CPJ was unable to obtain new information on his status.

Cameroon (1)

Please send appeals to:
His Excellency Paul Biya
President of the Republic of Cameroon
Presidential Palace
Yaoundé, Cameroon
Fax: 237-221-699

Evariste Menouga, *Hebdo*
Imprisoned: March 20, 1997

Menouga, editor in chief of the independent newspaper *Hebdo*, was convicted of "inciting rebellion within the army" and "spreading false news," and remanded to the central prison in Keondengui. Menouga was arrested in Yaounde after a warrant was issued against him on March 13 by Defense Minister Philippe Menye. The arrest was in connection with an article titled "Rebellion in the Army" published in the March 12 issue of *Hebdo.* Menouga was scheduled for a court hearing on April 17.

China (15)

Please send appeals to:
President Jiang Zemin
Guowuyuan
9 Xihuangcheng Genbeijie
Beijing, People's Republic of China

Ji Kunxing, Shang Jingzhong, Shi Qing, Yu Anmin, *Pioneers*
Tried: September 1989

Ji, Shang, Shi, and Yu were tried in Kunming on charges of "fomenting a counter-revolutionary plot." They had published an underground magazine called *Pioneers,* circulated anti-government leaflets, and put up anti-government posters. Though they were tried in 1989, their sentences have never been publicized. According to reports from 1994, Ji was sentenced in 1991 and the others were still being detained. In 1997, CPJ was unable to obtain new information on this case.

Chen Yanbin, *Tielu*
Imprisoned: Late 1990

Chen, a former University student, was arrested in late 1990 and sentenced to 15 years in prison and four years without political rights after his release. Together with Zhang Yafei, he had produced an unofficial magazine called *Tielu* (Iron Currents) about the 1989 Tiananmen Square massacre. Several hundred mimeographed copies of the magazine were distributed. The government termed the publication "reactionary" and charged Chen with dissemination of counter-revolutionary propaganda and incitement.

Zhang Yafei, *Tielu*
Imprisoned: September 1990

Zhang, a former student at Beifang Communications University, was arrested and charged with dissemination of counterrevolutionary propaganda and incitement. In March 1991, he was sentenced to 11 years in prison and two years without political rights after his release. Zhang edited an unofficial magazine called *Tielu* (Iron Currents) about the 1989 crackdown at Tiananmen Square.

Wu Shishen, Xinhua News Agency
Imprisoned: October or November 1992

Arrested in the fall of 1992, Wu, a Xinhua News Agency reporter, received a life sentence in August 1993 for allegedly providing a Hong Kong journalist with a "state-classified" advance copy of President Jiang Zemin's 14th Party Congress address.

Gao Yu, free-lancer
Imprisoned: October 2, 1993

Gao was detained two days before she was to depart for the United States to start a one-year research fellowship at Columbia University's Graduate School of Journalism. On November 10, 1994, she was tried without counsel and sentenced to six years in prison for "leaking state secrets" about China's structural reforms in articles for the pro-Beijing Hong Kong magazine *Mirror Monthly*. Gao had previously been jailed for 14 months following the June 1989 Tiananmen Square demonstrations and released in August 1990 after showing symptoms of a heart condition. In January 1997, Chinese authorities rejected an appeal for bail on medical grounds. On May 3, 1997, Gao Yu was awarded the World Press Freedom Prize by the United Nations Educational, Scientific, and Cultural Organization (UNESCO). The Chinese government attacked UNESCO and condemned its director general, Federico Mayor, for supporting the presentation of the award to Gao Yu.

Ma Tao, *China Health Education News*
Sentenced: August 1993

Ma, editor of *China Health Education News*, received a six-year prison term for allegedly helping Xinhua News Agency reporter Wu Shishen provide a Hong Kong journalist with President Jiang Zemin's "state-classified" 14th Party Congress address. According to the Associated Press, Ma is believed to be Wu's wife.

Wang Dan
Imprisoned: May 21, 1995

Wang, a former student leader, pro-democracy activist, and frequent contributor to overseas publications, was detained at an undisclosed location. On October 30, 1996, he was sentenced to 11 years in prison for conspiring to subvert the government. Wang's offenses consisted of publishing articles in the overseas press that were deemed objectionable by Beijing and receiving donations from overseas human rights groups. Foreign reporters were barred from the courtroom during his trial, and the domestic press was prohibited from reporting on the trial. Following the denial of his appeal on November 10, Wang was sent to a prison in remote Jinnzhou, in Liaoning province, 500 kilometers northeast of Beijing. Wang had previously been jailed for three-and-a-half years after he lead pro-democracy protests in Tiananmen Square in 1989.

Bai Weiji, Zhao Lei
Arrested: April 1993
Sentenced: May 1993

Bai, who once worked for the Chinese Foreign Ministry, monitoring foreign news and writing news summaries, was sentenced in May 1993 to ten years in prison for passing information and leaking national secrets to Lena Sun, a correspondent for the *Washington Post*. His appeal was rejected in July 1993. His wife, Zhao Lei, and two friends were also

IMPRISONED JOURNALISTS

31

arrested for involvement in this case. Bai organized a march of Foreign Ministry colleagues in June 1989 and reportedly lost his job as a result. Zhao was working as a translator for Lena Sun when she was tried in secret and sentenced to six years in prison for "illegally providing national secrets to a foreigner," said to be Lena Sun.

Khang Yuchun
Sentenced: December 1994

Khang was tried with 16 others on charges of being members of counter-revolutionary organizations, most notably the Chinese Progressive Alliance, the Liberal Democratic Party of China and the Free Labor Union of China. Among the accusations against him was that he commissioned people to write articles and set up *Freedom Forum*, the magazine of the Chinese Progressive Alliance. He was sentenced in December 1994, to 12 years in prison for "organizing and leading a counter-revolutionary group" and an additional seven year imprisonment for "counter-revolutionary propaganda."

Liu Jingsheng, *Tansuo*
Tried: 1994

Liu, a former writer and co-editor for the pro-democracy journal *Tansuo*, was sentenced to 15 years in prison for "counterrevolutionary" activities after being tried secretly in July 1994. Liu was arrested in May 1992 and charged with being a member of labor and pro-democracy groups, including the Liberal Democratic Party of China, Free Labor Union of China, and the Chinese Progressive Alliance. Court documents stated Liu was involved in organizing and leading anti-government and pro-democracy activities. Prosecutors also accused him and other dissidents who were tried on similar charges of writing and printing political leaflets that were distributed in June 1992, during the third anniversary of the Tiananmen Square demonstrations.

Wang Ming
Arrested: November 1996

Wang was sentenced to three years re-education through labor for writing "Declarations on Citizens' Freedom of Speech," an open letter which called on the government to release dissidents Wei Jingsheng and Wang Dan. He is being held in Xishanping Reeducation Brigade in Sichuan Province

Cuba (2)

Please send appeals to:
His Excellency Fidel Castro Ruz
President of Cuba
c/o Permanent Mission of Cuba to the United Nations
315 Lexington Avenue
New York, NY 10016
United States
Fax: (212)779-1697

Lorenzo Páez Nuñez, *Buro de Prensa Independiente de Cuba* **Imprisoned: July 10, 1997**

Páez was sentenced to 18 months in prison for defaming the national police. He was detained because of his report about a police officer who allegedly killed a young man during harvest celebrations in Pinar del Río. Páez was convicted after a one-day trial during which he was not permitted legal assistance. On December 19, CPJ sent a letter to the Cuban authorities, asking for information on Páez's legal status. No reply was received. On January 20, CPJ sent a letter asking that Páez be released.

Bernardo Arévalo Padrón, *Línea Sur 3* **Imprisoned: November 18, 1997**

On October 31, Arévalo was sentenced to six years in prison by the Provincial Chamber of the Court of Aguada de Pasajeros, a town in the province of Cienfuegos. He was convicted on the charge of "lack of respect" for Fidel Castro and Carlos Lage, a member of the Cuban State Council. The conviction stems from a story Arévalo published on the leaders' privileges. He reported that a helicopter transported meat from a farm in Aguada de Pasajeros to Havana, while the Aguada de Pasajeros inhabitants do not have enough to eat. Arévalo was detained and jailed on November 18. He is serving his sentence in Ariza prison in Cienfuegos, where Arévalo shares a filthy cell with common criminals. On November 28, the Aguada de Pasajeros Court rejected Arévalo's petition to review the conviction. On December 19, CPJ wrote a letter to Cuban authorities inquiring about the legal status of Arévalo. No reply was received. On January 20, CPJ sent a letter calling for Arévalo's release.

Eritrea (1)

Please send appeals to:
His Excellency Issaias Afewerki
President of Eritrea
Asmara, Eritrea
Fax: 291-1-125123

Ruth Simon, **Agence France-Presse** **Imprisoned: April 25**

Simon, an Eritrean national who works as a correspondent for the Agence France-Presse news agency, was arrested and charged with endangering state secuirty. In a story she filed the day before, she had quoted President Issaias Afewerki as saying Eritrean troops were fighting alongside rebels in neighboring Sudan.

At press time, Simon remained in detention. Her colleagues have been denied visitation. She is allowed visits from her family members only. In a letter to Afewerki, CPJ called for Simon's immediate and unconditional release. According to the Eritrean foreign ministry, Simon has been charged under a press law which states that "any journalist who disinforms the public or any institution is liable to the damage he/she may cause as a result."

IMPRISONED JOURNALISTS

Ethiopia (16)

Please send appeals to:
His Excellency Prime Minister Meles Zenawi
Office of the Prime Minister
Addis Ababa, Ethiopia
Fax: 251-1-552-030 (c/o Ministry of Foreign Affairs)

Abay Hailu, *Wolafen*
Detained: February 1997

Abay was sentenced to one year in prison on November 25. He had been in detention since February. At press time, CPJ learned that Abay had died in custody on February 13, 1998.

Sisay Negussie, *Agere*
Imprisoned: March 1997

Sisay appeared before court on April 7, and was detained at Kerchele prison for failing to present a bail guarantor of approximately US$600. At press time, CPJ had no further information about this case.

Samson Seyoum, *Tequami* **and**
Agere
Imprisoned: April 18, 1997

Samson, former editor in chief of *Agere* and *Tequami*, was sentenced to an undisclosed prison term, on charges of "inciting war and spreading Islamic Fundamentalism," for articles he had published in *Agere*. Detained before the sentencing and unable to produce the bail of approximately US$730, Samson had just completed an 18-month prison sentence which he had begun in December 1995 after his conviction on charges of libel for an article in *Tequami*.

Tolera Tessema, *Mede Welabu*
Imprisoned: April 23, 1997

Tolera, deputy editor in chief of *Mede Welabu*, was sentenced to a year in prison. At press time, CPJ had no further information on this case.

Nega Tariku, *Quiyit*
Imprisoned: September 3, 1997

Nega, a reporter with *Quiyit* magazine, was arrested, detained, and charged with publishing pornography. His whereabouts are unknown.

Sisay Agena, *Ethiop*
Imprisoned: September 8, 1997

Sisay, publisher of *Ethiop*, was arrested on September 8 on as yet unknown charges, and detained. He was released on bail on September 10, but on September 16 had been taken back into custody and moved from the Region 14 Criminal Investigation Office to the Central Criminal Investigation Office Prison.

Tamrat Serbessa, *Wenchif*
Admassu Tesfaye, *Wenchif*
Imprisoned: October 14, 1997

Tamrat, editor in chief of *Wenchif*, and Admassu, the paper's deputy editor, were detained at the Central Criminal Investigation Office Prison. The two journalists are each charged on five counts, one of which is libel against President Negasso Gidada. This charge stemmed from a report in *Wenchif* that claimed the president was drunk at a gathering of Oromos.

Tesfaye Deressa, *Urjii*
Solomon Nemera, *Urjii*
Imprisoned: October 16, 1997

Tesfaye, editor in chief of the *Urjii* newspaper, and Solomon, the paper's deputy editor, were abducted from a tea room near *Urjii* 's offices. The journalists were first detained at the

Central Criminal Investigation Office Prison and were later taken to a district police prison. The two were held on charges related to a report in *Urjii* about the recent killing of alleged Oromo Liberation Front (OLF) members in the Mekanissa area. The article contradicted the government media's version of the same story.

Tesfaye and Solomon appeared three times before a district court but were given new appointments each time because of requests by police for more time to continue their investigation. After the journalists' court appearance on December 12, police said they had concluded their investigation but were awaiting the prosecutor's decision as to bail. However, no decision had been made when Tesfaye and Solomon appeared again in court on December 19. They were scheduled for another court appearance on January 9.

Garoma Bekele, *Urjii*
Imprisoned: October 27, 1997

Garoma, publisher of the newspaper *Urjii*, was detained on suspicion of being a member of the outlawed Oromo Liberation Front (OLF). Garoma is being held at the Central Investigation Office Prison along with others who have been detained for their alleged connection to a series of OLF bomb attacks in Addis Ababa, Dire Dawa, and Harar. On October 31, Garoma appeared in court and made an appeal for release on bail, but was denied by the prosecutor. He was given a new court appointment for January 13.

Fekadu Mahtemwork
Imprisoned: October 28, 1997

Fekadu, a distributor of private newspapers, was detained at the Central Criminal Investigation Bureau prison. He was given a court appointment for a week later but has not yet appeared. The charges against him are not known.

Garedew Demisse, *Wenchif*
Imprisoned: October 31, 1997

Garedew appeared in court on charges of false information regarding a number of stories in *Wenchif*. The journalist was served a trial date of two weeks later. He was detained on October 28 at the Central Criminal Investigation Office Prison.

Iskinder Nega, *Wenchif*
Imprisoned: December 6, 1997

Iskinder, owner and publisher of *Wenchif*, was detained at the Central Criminal Investigation Office Prison, and charged with reporting false information. He was later moved to Wereda 9 Police Station.

Waqshum Bassa, *Urjii*
Alemu Tolessa, *Urjii*
Imprisoned: December 23, 1997

Waqshum and Alemu were called in for questioning and detained at the Central Criminal Investigation Office. After properly registering at the Press Licensing Office of the Ministry of Information and Culture, the two had taken over publishing the *Urjii* newspaper. The paper's previous editors, Solomon Nemera and Tesfaye Deressa, were arrested on October 16 and are still in detention. Alemu and Waqshum were ordered to appear in court on January 9, 1998. The status of their trial is unknown.

Indonesia (2)

Please send appeals to:
His Excellency Suharto
Office of the President
Istana Merdeka
Jakarta, Indonesia
Fax: 62-21-345-2685

Andi Syahputra
Sentenced: April 1997

Syahputra, who manages the printing house that produces the *Suara Independen* magazine, was sentenced to 30 months in prison on charges of defaming President Suharto. The magazine published an article titled "Suharto in the Process of Becoming a Naked King" in October 1996. Chief Judge Marsel Buchari of the South Jakarta District Court ruled that the article had "clearly" shown intent to defame Suharto.

Syahputra was sentenced several months after being arrested in a raid of the printing house on October 28, 1996, when police confiscated 5,000 copies of the issue containing the article. They also arrested Nasrul, a press operator.

After the two were taken into custody at a South Jakarta police station, security forces searched Syahputra's home. Syahputra and Nasrul were charged with defaming the president.

Syahputra is a member of Indonesia's only independent journalists union, the Alliance of Independent Journalists (AJI).

These actions were part of the government's suppression of *Suara Independen*, published by the Melbourne-based Society of Indonesian Alternative Media, and its predecessor, *Independen*, published by AJI.

Adnan Beuransyah, *Serambi*
Indonesia
Imprisoned: August 16, 1990

Beuransyah, a journalist with the newspaper *Serambi Indonesia*, was arrested. He was tried and convicted in March 1991 in Banda Aceh on charges of subversion and sentenced to eight years in prison.

Iran (2)

Please send appeals to:
His Excellency Mohammed Khatemi
President of the Islamic Republic of Iran
The Presidency, Palestine Avenue
Azerbaijan Intersection
Tehran, Islamic Republic of Iran
Telex: 214231 MITI IR or 213113 PRIM IR
Fax: 98 21 674790 (via Foreign Affairs; ask for fax to be forwarded)

Faraj Sarkoohi, *Adineh*
Imprisoned: January 27, 1997

Sarkoohi, editor in chief of the monthly literary magazine *Adineh*, was arrested by Iranian authorities and in September

1997, sentenced to one year in prison for "slandering the Islamic Republic," a charge which stemmed from a letter he smuggled out of Iran in January describing his detention and torture at the hands of Iranian authorities in 1996. Previously, in 1994, Sarkoohi had been one of 134 writers and intellectuals who petitioned the Iranian government to end censorship and launch official efforts to foster greater freedom of expression.

Morteza Firouzi, *Iran News*
Imprisoned: November 9, 1997

The official Iranian daily *Joumhouri Islami* reported that Firouzi, editor in chief of the English-language daily *Iran News*, was arrested on charges of espionage. Prior to *Joumhouri Islami's* announcement, Firouzi had been rumored "disappeared" for several months, since about the time of the presidential election in May. Authorities have provided no further details about his case, but CPJ has received reports that Firouzi's arrest was related to articles published in *Iran News* calling for the release of foreign nationals from Iranian prisons, and for warmer relations with the United States. The charge of espionage is frequently brought against individuals viewed as threats to the regime. The charge has also been used by political factions within the government to attack their opponents' allies.

Iraq (1)

Please send appeals to:
President Saddam Hussein
c/o Iraqi Mission to the United Nations
14 East 79th Street
New York, NY 10021 United States

Aziz al-Syed Jasim, Al-Ghad,
Al-Thawra
Imprisoned: April 18, 1991

Jasim, editor of Al-Ghad magazine and former editor of the official daily *Al-Thawra*, was taken into custody at a secret police station in Baghdad and has not been heard from since. Reports suggest that his refusal to write a book about Iraqi President Saddam Hussein precipitated his arrest. Government officials deny that he is in prison.

Kuwait (7)

Please send appeals to:
His Highness Shaikh Sa'ad al-'Abdallah al-Sabah,
Crown Prince and Prime Minister
Al-Diwan al-Amiri
Al-Safat
Kuwait City, Kuwait
Telegrams to: His Highness Shaikh Sa'ad al-'Abdallah al-Sabah,
Kuwait City, Kuwait Fax: 965-243-0121

Ibtisam Berto Sulaiman al-Dakhil
Usamah Suhail Abdallah Hussein
Abd al-Rahman Muhammad Asad al-Husseini
Ahmad Abd Mustafa
Sentenced: June 1991

The four journalists were given life sentences for working for the Iraqi occupation newspaper *Al-Nida*. They were taken into custody after Kuwait's liberation and charged with collaboration. The trials, which began on May 19, 1991, in martial-law courts, failed to comply with international standards of justice. The defendants were reportedly tortured during their interrogations. Their defense—that they were coerced to work for the Iraqi newspaper—was not rebutted by prosecutors. On June 16, 1991, the journalists were sentenced to death. Ten days later all martial-law death sentences were commuted to life terms, following international protests.

Nawwaf Izzedin al-Khatib
Sentenced: June 20, 1992

Al-Khatib, a Palestinian journalist, was convicted of having worked for the Iraqi occupation newspaper *Al-Nida* and sentenced by the State Security Court to 10 years in prison. The court also fined him KD2000 and ordered that he be expelled from the country upon termination of his sentences.

Mufid Mustafa Abd al-Rahim
Ghazi Alam al-Dine
Sentenced: July 28, 1992

The State Security Court convicted Abd al-Rahim and Alam al-Dine of working for the Iraqi occupation newspaper *Al-Nida*. Abd al-Rahim, a Palestinian, and Alam al-Dine, a Jordanian citizen and former editor at the Kuwait News Agency (KUNA), were sentenced to 10 years in prison. Alam al-Dine had only worked a total of 12 hours for *Al-Nida*. The court also fined each of the two men KD2000 and ordered that they be expelled from the country upon termination of their sentences. Abd al Rahim, who is in his sixties, suffers from paralysis in one of his hands—the result of torture at the hands of Kuwaiti authorities. Alam al-Dine, who is reported to be in his late fifties, is said to suffer from a serious heart condition.

Malaysia (1)

Please send appeals to:
His Excellency Dato' Seri Dr. Mahathir Mohamad
Prime Minister and Minister of Home Affairs
Jabatan Perdana Menteri
Jalan Dato' Onn
Kuala Lumpur 50502
Malaysia
Fax: 60-3-298-4172; 60-3-255-6264

Nasiruddin Ali, Karya One
Imprisoned: May 6, 1996

Nasiruddin, a director of the publishing firm Karya One, which published four magazines linked to the banned Islamic movement al-Arqam—*Tatih*, *O.K!*, *Ayu*, and *Dunia Baru*—was arrested and imprisoned at the Kemunting Detention Center near Ipoh, 25 miles north of Kuala Lumpur. The magazines were suspended on June 4, 1996. Authorities detained Ali for the 60-day period allowed under section 73(1) of the Internal Security Act (ISA), then on July 7 invoked section 8 of the ISA, which allows up to two years' imprisonment without trial. The charges against Nasiruddin have never been made public. However, the pro-government daily *New Straits Times* reported in May 1996 that Nasiruddin had been arrested along with three other Al-Arqam members for attempting to revive the activities of the sect, which the government banned in 1994 for allegedly deviating from true Islamic teachings.

Nigeria (17)

Please send appeals to:
General Sani Abacha
Chairman of the Provisional Ruling Council
and Commander in Chief of the Armed Forces
State House
Abuja
Federal Capital Territory, Nigeria
Fax: 234-95-232-138

Kunle Ajibade, *TheNews*
Imprisoned: May 5, 1995

Police arrested Ajibade, editor in chief of the daily *TheNews*, and demanded to know the source of the articles "No One Guilty: The Commission of Inquiry Presents an Empty File Regarding Suspects in the Coup d'Etat." They held him because he refused to divulge the whereabouts of his colleague Dapo Olorunyomi, who went underground. In July 1995, a special military tribunal held a secret trial for Ajibade and George Mbah of *Tell* Magazine (see below), charging them as accessories to treasonable felony and sentencing them to prison terms of undisclosed length. On October 1, 1995, Nigeria's Independence Day, the Provisional Ruling Council amended the sentence to 15 years in prison. Ajibade is in Makurdi Prison, Benue State.

Christine Anyanwu,
The Sunday Magazine
Imprisoned: May 31, 1995

Anyanwu, publisher and editor in chief of *The Sunday Magazine*, was arrested for her reports on an alleged coup plot in March. In July 1995, a special military tribunal secretly tried Anyanwu, along with Ben Charles Obi, editor of *Weekend Classique*. [See below] Both got life sentences. On October 1, 1995, Nigeria's Independence Day, the Provisional Ruling Council commuted their sentences to 15 years in prison. Anyanwu and Obi have since been transferred to a prison in Bama, northeastern Nigeria, notorious for its poor conditions. On four occasions, CPJ protested the arrests in letters to the Abacha government and called for the journalists' immediate and unconditional release. In October,

IMPRISONED JOURNALISTS

Anyanwu was named a 1997 International Press Freedom awardee by CPJ. At the end of 1997, she was being held at Kadu Prison in Kaduna State.

George Mbah, *Tell*
Imprisoned: May 5, 1995

Soldiers arrested Mbah, assistant editor of *Tell*, for contributing to a report about a military officer who died during interrogation about his involvement in an alleged coup plot. In July 1995, a special military tribunal tried Mbah and Kunle Ajibade of *TheNews*, charging them with being accessories to treasonable felony. They were sentenced to life in prison. On October 1, 1995, Nigeria's Independence Day, the Provisional Ruling Council commuted their sentences to 15 years in prison. Mbah and Ajibade have since been transferred to a prison in Bama, northeastern Nigeria, notorious for its poor conditions. There are reports that Mbah, who suffers from epilepsy, is consistently denied his medication. On four occasions, CPJ protested the arrests in letters to the Abacha government and called for the journalists' immediate and unconditional release. CPJ also demanded that Mbah receive prompt and proper medical care. At the end of 1997, Mbah was being held at Biu Prison in Borno State.

Charles Ben Obi, *Weekend Classique*
Imprisoned: May 1, 1995

Obi, editor of the weekly newsmagazine *Weekend Classique*, was arrested for his reports on an alleged attempted coup in March 1995. In July 1995, a special military tribunal tried Obi and Christine Anyanwu of *The Sunday Magazine*. (See above) Both received life sentences. On October 1, 1995, Nigeria's Independence Day, the Provisional Ruling Council commuted their sentences to 15 years in prison. Obi was transferred to a prison in northeastern Nigeria notorious for its poor conditions. On four occasions, CPJ has protested his arrest in letters to the Abacha government and called for his immediate and unconditional release. At the end of 1997, Obi was being held at Agodi Prison in Ibadan (Oyo State).

Jude Sinnee, newspaper vendor
Imprisoned: March 1, 1996

Armed agents of the Rivers State Internal Security Task Force arrested Sinnee, a newspaper vendor in Bori, an Ogoni settlement in Rivers State, at his newsstand. The agents also seized 500 copies of various publications and the vendor's accumulated sales of the day. They then transported Sinnee to the Internal Security Task Force's office at Kpor, near Bori, where he is being held incommunicado. Sinnee, who is disabled, went on a hunger strike to protest his detention.

Okina Deesor, Radio Rivers
Imprisoned: July 31, 1996

Deesor, a producer with Radio Rivers in the state of Rivers, was arrested and detained at the Government House Cell prison, reportedly without food or water. On August 3, 1996, he was transferred to the Mobile Police Headquarters in Port Harcourt. According to Maj. Obi Umabi, who ordered the arrest, Deesor's detention was in connection with the July 18, 1996, Radio Rivers broadcast of the national anthem of the Ogoni people. In a letter to Gen. Sani Abacha, CPJ denounced Deesor's continued detention and asked for his immediate and unconditional release. At the end of 1997, Deesor was still detained by the Rivers State Internal Task Force in Kpor.

Moshood Fayemiwo, *Razor*
Imprisoned: February 1, 1997

Fayemiwo, publisher of the now-defunct weekly *Razor*, was arrested and detained at the Directorate of Military Intelligence (DMI) in Lagos. Fayemiwo, who had been temporarily living in exile in Cotonou, Benin, was kidnapped by Nigerian security agents and returned to Lagos. Fayemiwo was reportedly tortured and his already poor health was deteriorating when he was imprisoned.

Mohammed Adamu, *African*
Concord
Imprisoned: July 27, 1997

Adamu, the Abuja correspondent of *African Concord* magazine, was arrested by three security agents at his Abuja residence. The agents did not give a reason for the arrest, but informed Adamu that he was being "invited for a chat." Friends believed Adamu's arrest was in connection with the July 14 *African Concord* cover story titled "Ali Mustapha: Ruthless Man Behind Abacha."

In a letter to Gen. Sani Abacha, CPJ called for Adamu's immediate and unconditional release.

Soji Omotunde, *African Concord*
Imprisoned: October 25, 1997

Omotunde, editor of the *African Concord*, was abducted by two security agents as he was driving along a street in Ikeja, in mainland Lagos. The agents tied, gagged, and bundled him into their car. He was driven to an unknown location. At the end of the year, Omotunde was still being detained, reportedly in the town of Abuja.

Adetokunbo Fakeye, *PM News*
Imprisoned: November 4

Fakeye, the defense correspondent of *PM News*, disappeared while on assignment at Army Defense Headquarters in Lagos. Staffers at *PM News* said that Fakeye was detained at the Defense Headquarters. No reason was given for the journalist's detention.

Jenkins Alumona, *TheNEWS*
Imprisoned: November 8

Three plainclothes operatives of the State Security Service (SSS) arrested Alumona, editor of *TheNEWS* magazine, on the premises of the Nigerian Television Authority (NTA), located on Victoria Island, Lagos.

A female member of the security team approached Alumona

and escorted him out of the NTA offices. Her colleagues then placed him in one of two waiting vehicles and drove him to the State Security Services detention camp in Abuja.

Alumona was released on December 31.

Onome Osifo-Whiskey, *Tell*
Imprisoned: November 10, 1997

Osifo-Whiskey, managing editor of *Tell* magazine, was arrested by officials of the Directorate of Military Intelligence as he was on his way home from church with his family. His whereabouts and the reason for his arrest are unknown.

Akin Adesokan, *Post Express*
Imprisoned: November 12, 1997

Adesokan, a reporter with the *Post Express* newspaper, was arrested by State Security Service (SSS) officers on November 12, at the Nigeria-Benin border. He was returning to Lagos from Austria, where, as an author and member of the Association of Nigerian Authors, he had attended a four-month writer-in-residence program. The security officers apparently objected to photographs of dissidents such as Ken Saro-Wiwa that Adesokan had in his possession. Adesokan was held at the State Security Service (SSS) Detention Camp, in Ikoyi, Lagos.

Adesokan was released on December 31.

Rafiu Salau,
TheNews/Tempo/PM News Group
Imprisoned: November 14, 1997

Salau, administration manager of TheNews/TEMPO/PM News group, was arrested and detained at the Directorate of Military Intelligence (DMI) in Apapa, Lagos, on November 18. Salau had gone to the offices of the DMI to check on his colleague Adetokunbo Fakeye. Fakeye, defense reporter for *PM News*, who had been imprisoned since October 25, was later released without charge. Salau remains in detention at DMI.

Babafemi Ojudu,
TheNews/Tempo/PM News Group
Imprisoned: November 17, 1997

Operatives of the State Security Service arrested Ojudu, managing editor of TheNews/TEMPO/PM News group, upon his return to Lagos from Nairobi, Kenya, where he had taken part in a seminar organized by the Freedom Forum. He is being held at the Ikoyi prison. Although authorities have given no reason for his imprisonment, it follows a pattern of harassment of the publishing group, which has resulted in the arrests of several other journalists affiliated with the group.

In a letter to Gen. Sani Abacha, CPJ protested the November arrests of Ojudu and other journalists affiliated with the publishing group, and called for an end to the systematic censorship of the group's publications.

Ben Adaji, *TheNews*
Imprisoned: December 4, 1997

Adaji, Taraba State correspondent for *TheNews* magazine, was arrested by state security officers in Jalingo. He is being held at an undisclosed location.

Security officers had launched a full-scale manhunt for Adaji. He was wanted in connection with a story titled "War in Taraba," which he wrote in the October 27 edition of the *TheNews*. The story detailed the build-up and outbreak of a factional conflict in the Takum district of Taraba State and the roles of some military officers in this conflict.

Niran Malaolu, *The Diet*
Imprisoned: December 28, 1997

Niran Malaolu, editor of the daily newspaper *The Diet*, was arrested December 28 by Directorate of Military Intelligence (DMI) officers at the newspaper's editorial offices. He was transported to Military Intelligence Headquarters in Apapa, Lagos, where he is being held incommunicado.

Pakistan (2)

Please send appeals to:
His Excellency Muhammad Nawaz Sharif
Prime Minister of Pakistan
Office of the Prime Minister
Islamabad, Pakistan
Fax: 92-51-920-1835

Irfanul Haq, Iftikhar Adil
Lashkar
Sentenced: December 26, 1997

The Baluchistan High Court in Quetta sentenced sub-editor Irfanul Haq and printer/publisher Iftikhar Adil of the Lahore-based Urdu-language evening newspaper *Lashkar* to six months in prison for inaccurate reporting. Despite their written apologies, the two journalists were convicted after publishing a report on the alleged theft of court records. The journalists were also fined Rs. 5000 (US$109). On January 12, 1998, Iftikhar Adil was released from prison after the Baluchistan High Court accepted his appeal and said that the days he spent in jail were adequate for his punishment. Haq was released a few days later.

Peru (4)

Please send appeals to:
His Excellency Alberto Fujimori
President of the Republic of Peru
Palacio de Gobierno
Lima 1, Peru
Fax: 51-14-266-770

Javier Tuanama Valera, *Hechos*
Imprisoned: October 16, 1990

Tuanama, editor in chief of the magazine *Hechos*, was sentenced to 10 years in prison by a "faceless" judge from the Superior Court of Lambayeque. He was first detained on October 16, 1990, and charged with having links to the guerrilla group Revolutionary Movement Tupac Amaru (MRTA). He was found not guilty of the charges in two trials held in 1994. He was subsequently released but arrested again soon after. Under the Repentance Law, which allows terrorists to turn themselves in and inform on former comrades, a former member of the MRTA confessed that Tuanama had recruited him into the MRTA. CPJ protested his November 7, 1994, conviction in a trial that fell far below international standards of due process. In June 1995, one of his sisters complained that Tuanama's medical condition seriously worsened as he had no access to specialized medical care his arthritis required. In April 1996, he was transferred to the Huacariz prison in Cajamarca. Tuanama appealed the sentence. The Oversight Commission (Comisión de Indultos) is currently reviewing the case. The Oversight Commission was created by the government of Alberto Fujimori to examine cases of those convicted under Peru's anti-terrorism laws. CPJ inquired about Tuanama's legal status in a December 22, 1997, letter, to which the Peruvian authorities did not reply.

Hermes Rivera Guerrero, Radio Oriental
Imprisoned: May 8, 1992

Rivera, a reporter for Radio Oriental, in the province of Jaén in the Andean department of Cajamarca, was sentenced to 20 years in prison on May 13, 1994, for alleged terrorist activity. In his defense, Rivera said policeman Idelfonso Ugarte Valdivia arrested him arbitrarily on May 8, 1992, and brought the false charges against him. Rivera's wife, Dilsia Miranda, also accused the policeman of demanding $500 for the release of her husband and making uninvited sexual advances. When she refused to cooperate, Miranda said, Ugarte apparently falsified evidence to show Rivera's participation in terrorist attacks in the area. On January 26, 1995, Rivera, who was being held at the Picsi prison in the city of Chiclayo, sewed his mouth closed with thread and began a hunger strike in protest of the ratification of his sentence. He ended his hunger strike three weeks later. On March 7, his defense lawyer presented an appeal for review of his case before the Supreme Court of Peru. On September 5, 1995, the Supreme Court revoked the 20-year prison sentence and ordered a retrial.

CPJ sent a letter of inquiry on December 22, but Peruvian authorities did not provide any information on Rivera's legal status.

Augusto Ernesto Llosa Giraldo,
***El Casmeno*, Radio Casma**
Imprisoned: February 14, 1995

Llosa, editor in chief of the newspaper *El Casmeno* and a reporter with Radio Casma, was arrested in the northern city of Casma and charged with involvement in a 1986 terrorist incident in Cuzco, where he was staying in a hotel at the time. Police raided his home and confiscated several documents, including National Association of Journalists (ANP) posters urging the release of several detained journalists, and an issue of ANP's newsletter. A secret tribunal of the Fifth Criminal Chamber of the Superior Court of Cuzco convicted him of involvement in the terrorist incident, and on August 10, 1996, he was sentenced to six years in prison. Three weeks after the verdict, he was unexpectedly transferred to the maximum security Yanamayo prison. He is the only journalist among the inmates, most of whom are serving life sentences. Llosa requested the nullification of the sentence before the Surpeme Court of Peru, which was accepted.

On June 30, a new verdict was reached, and Llosa was sentenced to five years. Llosa again requested the sentence be nullified. CPJ did not receive a reply to the letter it sent on December 22, inquiring about Llosa's legal status.

Pedro Carranza Ugaz, Radio Oriental
Imprisoned: November 29, 1993

Carranza, a correspondent with Radio Oriental de Jaén in Cajamarca, was detained on November 29, 1993, and sentenced on November 7, 1994, to 20 years in prison on the charges of being a member of the terrorist group Revolutionary Movement Tupac Amaru (MRTA). He is currently being held in the Picsi prison in Chiclayo. Carranza lived in Moyabamba.

In 1997, the Oversight Commission (Comisión de Indultos) is currently reviewing the case. The Oversight Commission was created by the government of Alberto Fujimori to examine cases of those convicted under Peru's anti-terrorism laws.

Russia (2)

Please send appeals to:
President Boris Yeltsin
The Russian Federation
Moscow, Russia
Fax: 011-7-095-224-0366
And also to:
President Aslan Maskhadov
The Chechen Republic
Grozny, Chechen Republic
Fax: 011-90-212-257-6817

Krzysztof Galinski, *Mac Pariadka* and *Zycie*
Marek Kurzyniec, *Marscho* and *Zycie*
Imprisoned: December 17, 1997

Galinski and Kurzyniec were kidnapped in Chechnya along with three other Polish citizens by unknown assailants while trying to deliver a shipment of food aid. All five undertook the mission on behalf of the National Federation of Anarchists in Poland, of which they are members.

Galinski is an editor with the Gdansk-based *Mac Pariadka*, the country's largest national anarchist monthly magazine. Kurzyniec edits his own small political bulletin *Marscho*, also in Gdansk.

Although their primary mission was the food aid delivery, both carried press credentials from *Zycie*, a national daily newspaper in Gdansk. They had agreed to a request from the editor to write free-lance articles about the situation in Chechnya upon their return.

The National Federation of Anarchists reported that all five hostages were safe as of mid-January. Rumors that the hostage-takers demanded ransom from *Zycie* and the anarchists' group could not be confirmed.

The kidnapping is the latest in a long series of abductions of foreign journalists and aid workers in Chechnya, usually for ransom.

South Korea (1)

Please send appeals to:
President Kim Dae Jung
The Blue House
#1 Sejong-no, Chongno-gu
Seoul
Republic of Korea
Fax: 822-770-0253

Richard Choi, Radio Korea
Imprisoned: December 19, 1997

Choi, a veteran reporter and the vice president of Radio Korea, a Korean-language radio station in Los Angeles, was arrested at the Koreana Hotel in Seoul and charged with criminal slander and defamation on the basis of a story he broadcast from Seoul to Los Angeles. The brief report, which aired on December 15 in Los Angeles on Radio Korea (KBLA AM-1580), concerned the current economic difficulties of the Korea Times/Hankook Ilbo publishing company and its rumored merger with the Hyundai Corporation. The report was not broadcast in South Korea.

According to Jang Hee Lee, the owner of Radio Korea, the report angered the owners of the *Korea Times*, which brought the defamation suit against Choi that led to his arrest. At the year's end, Choi was being detained in the Seoul Jail. On January 7, 1998, the South Korean government released Choi on his own recognizance. Choi must still stand trial on charges of criminal slander. He is being prosecuted under a section of the Korean criminal code which allows private companies to file a criminal complaint against persons accused of defaming their reputation. He faces up to five years in jail if convicted.

Sudan (2)

Osama Ghandi, Sudanese Television
Hassan Saleh, Sudanese Television
Imprisoned: February 1996

Television cameraman Osama Ghandi and technician Hassan Saleh of the state-owned Sudanese Television were arrested and accused of being involved in an alleged coup attempt. They were among 10 civilians who went on trial in late August 1996 in an in-camera military court trial, in which most of the defendants were military officers. Ghandi told the court on September 18 that military intelligence agents had coerced his confession by torturing him. CPJ received reports in 1997 that the military court had reached a verdict, although it was not clear whether the two journalists were convicted or if they remained in prison.

Syria (5)

Faisal Allush
Imprisoned: 1985

Allush, a journalist and political writer who has been in jail since 1985, was sentenced in June 1993 to 15 years' imprisonment for membership in the banned Party for Communist Action. He is reportedly being held in Sednaya Prison.

Anwar Bader, Syrian Radio and Television
Imprisoned: December 1986

Bader, a reporter for Syrian Radio and Television who has been in jail since his arrest by the Military Interrogation Branch in December 1986, was convicted in March 1994 of being a member in the Party for Communist Action. He was sentenced to 12 years in prison.

Samir al-Hassan, *Fatah al-Intifada*
Imprisoned: April 1986

Al-Hassan, Palestinian editor of *Fatah al-Intifada*, who has been in jail since his arrest in April 1986, was convicted in June 1994 of being a member of the Party for Communist Action. He was sentenced to 15 years in prison.

Salama George Kila
Imprisoned: March 1992

Kila, a Palestinian writer and journalist, was arrested in March 1992 by Political Security in Damascus. His trial began in the summer of 1993. According to the London-based International PEN, Kila had "reportedly written an article on censorship in Syria for a Jordanian daily paper." The court ruled that he was guilty of a misdemeanor rather than a felony. Since the maximum sentence for a misdemeanor is three years, his release was expected in March 1995. But he remains in prison.

Nizar Nayouf, free-lancer
Imprisoned: January 1992

Nayouf, a free-lance journalist who has contributed to *Al-Huriyya* and *Al-Thaqafa al-Ma'arifa*, was arrested in January 1992 in Damascus with several human rights activists from the Committees for the Defense of Democratic Freedoms and Human Rights in Syria. In March 1992, he was sentenced by the State Security Court to 10 years in prison for "disseminating false information and receiving money from abroad." He was severely tortured during his interrogation. He remains in solitary confinement in Mezze military prison.

Tunisia (2)

Please send appeals to:
M. Zine El Abidine Ben Ali
President of the Republic of Tunisia
Presidential Palace
Tunis, Tunisia
Fax: 216 1 744 721

Hamadi Jebali, *Al-Fajr*
Imprisoned: January 1991

Jebali, editor of *Al-Fajr*, the weekly newspaper of the banned Islamist Al-Nahda party, was sentenced to 16 years in prison by the military court in Bouchoucha on August 28, 1992. He was tried along with 279 others accused of belonging to Al-Nahda. Jebali was convicted of "aggression with the intention of changing the nature of the state" and "membership in an illegal organization." During his testimony, Jebali denied the charges against him and displayed evidence that he had been tortured while in custody. Jebali has been in jail since January 1991, when he was sentenced to one year in prison after *Al-Fajr* published an article calling for the abolition of military courts in Tunisia. International human rights groups monitoring the mass trial concluded that it fell far below international standards of justice.

Abdellah Zouari, *Al-Fajr*
Imprisoned: February 1991

Zouari, a contributor to *Al-Fajr*, the weekly newspaper of the banned Islamist Al-Nahda party, was sentenced to 11 years in prison by the military court in Bouchoucha on August 28, 1992. He was tried along with 279 others accused of belonging to Al-Nahda. He has been in jail since February 1991, when he was charged with "association with an unrecognized organization." International human rights groups monitoring the trial concluded that it fell far short of international standards of justice.

❧❧❧❧❧❧❧

THE CASE OF TURKEY: VERIFYING REPORTS OF IMPRISONED JOURNALISTS

There were at least 29 Turkish journalists in prison on journalism-related charges at the end of 1997—more than in any other country. Turkey has topped the list of countries which imprison journalists every year since 1994.

There were also at least 37 Turkish journalists released from jail in the course of 1997—the largest number of releases CPJ has ever recorded in one year in one country. International pressure and the growing assertiveness of Turkish journalists combined with the installation at mid-year of a more reform-minded government put a brake on new prosecutions of reporters and editors. There was one new case of a journalist convicted and imprisoned in 1997, as compared to 55 in 1994, 30 in 1995, and 27 in 1996. Yet the laws under which these journalists were prosecuted remain on the books, despite promises of sweeping reform.

Both because of their sheer numbers and the complexity of their cases, the journalists imprisoned in Turkey have been a special focus of CPJ's research efforts over the past year. Establishing a causal link between the prosecution and the professional activities of an imprisoned journalist often requires a subjective assessment of the political context and evidentiary basis of the conviction.

CPJ's analyses of these cases are based primarily on information gathered first-hand from court documents and interviews with imprisoned journalists' colleagues and attorneys. CPJ's research also incorporates information from the Turkish government itself. In January 1997, we submitted our research on imprisoned journalists in Turkey to the Turkish authorities for comment. In July 1997, the Justice Ministry responded with detailed remarks on 21 of the 78 cases we had documented. In September 1997, CPJ submitted further documentation about these cases to members of the Turkish cabinet for their review. CPJ also shared and compared documentation with the Paris-based Reporters sans Frontières and the Press Council of Turkey, which provided invaluable assistance in locating and analyzing court records. The Press Council also played a critical role in 1997 in interceding with CPJ on behalf of Turkey's imprisoned journalists, including 1996 International Press Freedom Award recipient Ocak Isik Yurtçu, who was freed in August.

As a result of this collaborative research effort CPJ removed four cases from its listing of imprisoned Turkish journalists, based on court documents showing that the four journalists had been convicted on charges unrelated to their profession. Newly obtained information also raised questions about the linkage between the profession and the conviction in another four cases of imprisoned journalists previously reported by CPJ; these cases are now listed as "unconfirmed," pending further inquiry. Also on the basis of new information, CPJ confirmed four previously unreported cases of journalists who were in prison as of December 31, 1996; two were later released, and two remained in prison.

CPJ has concluded that on December 31, 1997:

• At least 29 journalists were in prison in Turkey because of their work, compared to 74* confirmed cases one year earlier; they included one journalist who was sentenced in 1997, plus two journalists whose earlier imprisonments were not confirmed by CPJ until 1997.

• All but two of the imprisoned journalists were prosecuted under Articles 168 or 169 of the Penal Code for allegedly aiding or joining a banned "terrorist" or "separatist" organization.

• Thirty-seven journalists who had been imprisoned as of December 1996 were released in the course of 1997; all but two were on the list of 78 published by CPJ a year ago in *Attacks on the Press in 1996*. The 37 released journalists include six newspaper editors released as a result of a limited amnesty for jailed editors passed by parliament in August 1997 following CPJ's July mission to Turkey. One imprisoned journalist was freed prior to an appeal hearing. Another 12 who had been held in pre-trial detention were released on bail, pending the outcome of their trials; five others were acquitted. Four journalists were released after serving out their terms; another nine were released for reasons CPJ has been unable to document.

• We categorize 13 journalists as "unconfirmed" cases of imprisonment. In four cases we have been unable to confirm reports of their release; in another nine, as noted above, newly obtained information raises doubt about whether the journalists' work was the main reason for their prosecution.

This list is not exhaustive. We believe that there may be other journalists who are now in prison for exercising their internationally guaranteed right to freedom of expression.

* See footnote on p. 24

And we are aware of cases which we continue to investigate because we have not confirmed the initial report or are attempting to gather information about their prosecutions and alleged offenses that has hitherto been unavailable.

Background

Since 1994, Turkey has consistently imprisoned more working journalists than any other nation. Most of the journalists jailed in Turkey have been prosecuted for news coverage or opinion articles related to the conflict with Kurdish insurgents in Southeastern Turkey or for their affiliation with far-left publications that are viewed as sympathetic to armed guerrilla groups inside Turkey.

In January, CPJ submitted detailed information on 78 imprisoned journalists to Turkish authorities for their review and comment. The Turkish Embassy in Washington, which had challenged the accuracy of CPJ's information publicly and in subsequent private meetings with CPJ representatives, agreed to forward the list to the Justice Ministry. We received no response until July, shortly before CPJ sent its delegation to Turkey, when the embassy sent CPJ a memo conveying comments from the Turkish Justice Ministry on 21 of CPJ's 78 cases. It is significant that in only four of the 78 cases of jailed journalists we documented did Turkish authorities challenge any of the factual information. In three of four, we were not able to verify the Justice Ministry's statements about the charges against the defendants. In the fourth case, we verified the Justice Ministry's statement about the charge against the defendant and, based on court records, we determined that the case was not related to the defendant's work as a journalist.

In 14 cases about which CPJ received official comment, Turkish authorities either reiterated information that CPJ had previously reported—for example, stating that a journalist was convicted for membership in a specific outlawed organization—or provided details about the criminal prosecutions that did not contradict CPJ's original reports.

CPJ Methodology and Classifications

The preponderance of the information below comes from CPJ investigations in Turkey between July and December 1997. The information was gathered in Istanbul and Ankara, through dozens of interviews with reporters and editors, as well as with lawyers who had represented newspapers, magazines, and individual journalists indicted under the provisions of Turkey's Penal Code and Anti-Terror Law for a variety of criminal offenses.

IMPRISONED JOURNALISTS

51

We have relied heavily on documents, such as indictments, transcripts of court proceedings, and court decisions, in ascertaining the facts about the state's prosecution of imprisoned journalists, evaluating Turkish authorities' assertions about the nature of the offenses, and determining whether the journalists in prison are in fact there for their journalistic work. Since many of the journalists whose imprisonment we have documented have been formally charged with violent offenses, court documents containing detailed accounts of the prosecution's rationale and evidentiary process and the defense's response are essential to our analysis of the cogency of the state's accusations. These documents rarely provide conclusive evidence about whether a journalist was imprisoned because of his or her journalistic work. Rather, they typically offer a window into a defendant's trial, noting the state's accusations against the defendant, evidence it presented in court to support its claim, and, often, the defense's argument. And they often reveal the vicious circularity that characterizes many prosecutions of journalists in Turkey, when the state claims that the journalist's affiliation with a legal publication or possession of copies of a legally circulating newspaper constitutes proof of illegal activity.

Because the documents are not always available and what is available is sometimes incomplete, we have cross-checked the available information on the imprisoned journalists using a variety of sources, including the independent research of other international and local press freedom organizations and human rights groups, and interviews with the imprisoned journalists' colleagues and lawyers.

Confirmed cases of journalism-related prosecutions include working journalists and others who have been prosecuted as a result of journalistic activities. When a journalist has been formally charged with a criminal offense such as membership in a proscribed organization or specific acts of terrorism, we have used the following criteria in making our determination that the underlying motive for the prosecution is the journalist's work: 1) Court documents indicate that the state has based its accusations, wholly or in part, on a journalist's affiliation with or work for a particular publication; 2) There has been a pattern of government harassment of the journalist and/or his or her publication; 3) An imprisoned journalist appears to have been denied due process or contends that confessions or other self-incriminating statements were given under torture; credible accounts of the torture of defendants, coercion of witnesses, and falsification of documents in Turkish criminal justice proceedings are too numerous to disregard such claims.

All but two of the cases in the "confirmed" category involve journalists charged and convicted under Articles 168 or 169 of Turkey's Penal Code, under which it is a crime to belong or provide assistance to armed insurgent groups or proscribed political organizations. Membership and assistance are both loosely defined. The Turkish government has used the broad provisions of these articles against journalists and publications affiliated with or sympathetic to Kurdish separatists or banned leftist political groups. Many of the cases in this category demonstrate a pattern of harassment of particular publications which we believe makes credible the contentions of journalists convicted under Articles 168 and 169 that they were prosecuted because of their work as journalists. We have grouped those cases by the publication with which the journalist is or was affiliated and have provided a brief explanation about the publication's content and political history.

e/ɔe/ɔe/ɔe/ɔe/ɔe/ɔ

Turkey (29)

Please send appeals to:
His Excellency Mesut Yilmaz
Prime Minister
Basbakanlik
06573 Ankara, Turkey

Sinan Yavuz,
Yoksul Halkin Gücü
Imprisoned: August 9, 1993

CPJ believes that Yavuz, editor of the left-wing weekly *Yoksul Halkin Gücü*, was arrested during a police raid on an Istanbul fabric shop. Police reportedly had been told that the shop served as a front and arms-trafficking station for Devrimci Sol (Dev Sol), an outlawed leftist organization responsible for numerous armed terrorist operations in Turkey. The charges under which Yavuz was prosecuted show that he was alleged to be a member of Dev Sol, apparently on the basis of his affiliation with *Yoksul Halkin Gücü*, which the state asserts is the group's publishing arm. The evidence against Yavuz consisted of unspecified "documents" relating to Dev Sol and two copies of the magazine *Kurtulus* (a legal, far-left publication), which had allegedly been discovered during a search of the shop. Yavuz was alleged to have resisted arrest after attempting to flee the raid. He had been detained on previous occasions but released for lack of evidence.

Yavuz confessed to nothing in police custody, but the prosecution said that other members of Dev Sol who were detained in the same roundup stated that Yavuz was a member of the group. According to court documents, Yavuz waved a Dev Sol banner in the courtroom. He was convicted, sentenced on December 29, 1994, to 12 years and six months in jail, and sent to Canakkale Prison.

໑ຩຩຩ

Atilim

Journalists in Turkey and informed observers of Turkish politics regarded the now-defunct weekly socialist newspaper *Atilim* (Leap Forward) and its successor publications as sympathetic to the outlawed Marxist-Leninist Communist Party (MLKP), an extreme-left urban guerrilla group which the government holds responsible for acts of domestic terrorism, including bombings and robberies. *Atilim*'s predecessor was the monthly *Emegin Bayragi* (Labor's Flag) and the magazine *Iscinin Yolu*. *Atilim* began publication in October 1994; in 1996, it changed its name to *Ozgur Atilim* (Free Leap Forward). In September 1997, *Ozgur Atilim* changed its name to *Ozgurluk ve Sosyalizm Yolunda Atilim* (Leap Forward for Freedom and Socialism), under which it continues to publish as a weekly newspaper based in Istanbul. *Ozgurluk ve Sosyalizm Yolunda Atilim* and its predecessors have all been legally registered publications.

The Turkish government has repeatedly harassed *Atilim*, confiscating editions of the newspaper and detaining and allegedly torturing its reporters. On March 29, 1996, Istanbul's State Security Court ordered *Atilim* closed for one month and sentenced Ismail Akkin, the weekly's editor, to six months in prison for allegedly disseminating "separatist propaganda." The order also suspended publication of *Ozgür Genclik*, a magazine for young people, published by *Atilim*'s parent company.

The government has prosecuted *Atilim*'s journalists on numerous occasions:

Bülent Öner, *Atilim*
Imprisoned: June 15, 1995

CPJ believes Öner is imprisoned for his work as a reporter for *Atilim*. He was taken into custody during a police raid on the newspaper's Mersin bureau on June 15, and formally charged with membership in the outlawed Marxist-Leninist Communist Party (MLKP) on June 24.

Investigators reportedly found numerous unspecified "documents" linking Öner to the MLKP. Two witnesses testified for the state, which asserted that *Atilim* was the publication of the MLKP and further accused Öner of writing and distributing unspecified declarations of the group. According to court documents, the prosecutor had stated that banners depicting a "disappeared" political activist were found in Öner's office. Öner was convicted and sentenced to 12 years and six months in jail; he was sent to Erzurum Prison.

Mesut Bozkurt, *Atilim*
Imprisoned: June 15, 1995

Bozkurt, bureau chief of *Atilim*'s Iskenderun office, was convicted of membership in the outlawed Marxist-Leninist Communist Party (MLKP), evidently on the basis of his work for the paper. He was arrested during a police raid on *Atilim*'s offices in June 15, 1995.

Court documents reveal that copies of *Atilim*—described

by the prosecution as "bulletins" of the MLKP—comprised the principal evidence in his trial. The prosecution also said that Bozkurt had rented a house in Mersin on behalf of the MLKP, and that police searching the premises found unspecified "illegal documents." It is not clear whether these confiscated documents were introduced as material evidence.

Bozkurt was sentenced to 12 years and six months in prison on January 26, 1996, along with *Atilim* colleagues Fatma Harman, Bulent Öner, and Hasan Abali.

**Fatma Harman, *Atilim*
Imprisoned: June 15, 1995**

Harman, a reporter for *Atilim*, was taken into custody during a police raid on the newspaper's Mersin bureau in June 15, 1995. CPJ believes that her arrest was the result of a crackdown on the publication and that she has been imprisoned for work as a journalist.

Harman was formally arrested on June 24, 1995, and sentenced on January 26, 1996, to 12 years and six months in prison under Article 168 of the Penal Code. *Atilim's* lawyer reports that she was convicted of membership in the outlawed Marxist-Leninist Communist Party (MLKP) on the argument that *Atilim* was the publication of that group. The prosecution reportedly offered copies of *Atilim* found in Harman's possession as evidence of her affiliation, and said that several unspecified banners were found in the *Atilim* office. Further, the prosecution said that Harman and Bulent Öner, another *Atilim* reporter, lived together in a house belonging to the MLKP. Harman is in Adana Prison.

**Ibrahim Çiçek, *Atilim*
Imprisoned: March 15, 1996**

The use of articles from *Atilim* as material evidence against Çiçek leads CPJ to believe that he was prosecuted for his work as a journalist. According to court documents, Çiçek, former editor in chief of the leftist weekly *Atilim*, testified that he was detained on March 15, 1996, on his way to his father's home, and his wife was detained the following day at their home. Çiçek was charged with membership in an illegal organization, but his lawyer reports that the only evidence against Çiçek was his affiliation with *Atilim*, which the state asserted was the mouthpiece of the Marxist-Leninist Communist Party (MLKP).

According to the Ministry of Justice, Çiçek "was taken into custody in relation to the armed attack carried out by the MLKP illegal leftist organization against government office buildings in the Sultanbeyli district of Istanbul as well as the offices of the MHP political party in the same district around 1 a.m. on March 14, 1996. The incident prompted the decision of the Istanbul State Security Court to detain Mr. Çiçek with his collaborators on March 29, 1996. Currently, he is in Bayrimpasa Prison in Istanbul."

Court documents show that Çiçek was charged with being a leader of the MLKP (Article 168/1 of the Penal Code)—specifically, of ordering an armed assault on the offices of an ultra-right-wing party in Istanbul—and of running *Atilim*. The prosecutor produced as evidence a story that appeared in *Atilim*'s March 23, 1996, issue, about the assault on the ultra-right-wing party in Istanbul. Two peopke gave statements to authorities which implicated Çicek. According to the defense statement, Çiçek said that he was tortured by police, but made no confession. He was sentenced to a minimum of 15 years in prison.

Nabi Kimran, *Iscinin Yolu*
Imprisoned: September 9, 1996

CPJ believes that Kimran's prosecution and imprisonment resulted from his work as editor of the leftist weekly *Iscinin Yolu*, which was subject to repeated government harassment during his tenure.

Kimran is currently being held in Sakarya Prison for alleged membership in an outlawed organization under Article 168 of the Penal Code. His lawyer told CPJ that Kimran had also faced charges under Articles 7 (engaging in propaganda for an outlawed organization) and 8 (disseminating separatist propaganda) of the Anti-Terror Law. Staffers from the socialist weekly *Atilim* said these charges arose from news articles that appeared in *Iscinin Yolu* during his tenure. The Penal Code violation case was prosecuted but the Anti-Terror Law cases were eventually suspended following the government's August 14, 1997, amnesty for jailed editors.

According to court documents, Kimran was apprehended by police on a bus on September 9, in a police operation in advance of the anniversary of the Marxist-Leninist Communist Party (MLKP). The prosecution claimed that Kimran was a leader of the organization. The charge was based on a statement of an alleged MLP sympathizer, made while in police custody, that Kimran had given instructions to bomb a city bus. Kimran was also caught with a counterfeit I.D., which he admitted having because of his fear of being detained in the course of his journalistic work. The prosecution stated that police searching Kimran's apartment found documents in his handwriting that demonstrated his affiliation with the MLKP.

かめかめ

Alinteri

Alinteri (Sweat of the Laborer), a now-defunct Istanbul-based socialist weekly, began publication on October 31, 1993. Since 1995, it has published under the name *Emekci' nin Alinteri*. Both are/were legal publications. Journalists in Turkey and informed observers of Turkish politics regarded *Alinteri* as sympathetic to the outlawed Turkish Revolutionary Communist Union (TIKB), a small urban guerrilla group. The government has confiscated editions of the newspaper and prosecuted its journalists on numerous occasions:

Erdal Dogan, *Alinteri*
Imprisoned: July 10, 1995

Dogan, an Ankara reporter for *Alinteri*, was detained by police on July 10, 1995, and later tried and convicted of membership in the Turkish Revolutionary Communist Union (TIKB) on the basis of his attendance at opposition events in his capacity as a journalist.

Court papers indicate that the prosecution argued that *Alinteri* was the publication of the TIKB. The case against Dogan was based on the following evidence: 1) A photograph of Dogan, taken at a 1992 May Day parade, allegedly showing him standing underneath a United Revolutionary Trade Union banner; 2) A photograph of Dogan taken on the anniversary of a TIKB militant's death; 3) A photograph alleged to show Dogan attending an illegal demonstration in Ankara; 4) Statements of an alleged member of the TIKB, who said Dogan belonged to the organization. The defense claimed that the incriminating statement was extracted under torture. Dogan's lawyer told CPJ that the photograph from the militant's memorial was blurry, and Dogan testified in court that he had attended the May Day parade as a journalist. He was sentenced to 12 years and six months in prison under Article 168/2 of the Penal Code. and has been confined to Bursa Prison.

Serpil Günes, *Alinteri*
Imprisoned: September 7, 1996

Günes, an editor and owner of *Alinteri*, was arrested in Izmir when police raided a vacation apartment where she and several of her *Alinteri* colleagues were staying. She has been in jail since her arrest.

The prosecution stated that police found a counterfeit identification card in Günes' possession, and seized unspecified illegal publications and handwritten documents which purportedly linked her and her colleagues to the Turkish Revolutionary Communist Union (TIKB). Günes was accused of membership in an outlawed organization based on the these allegations, as well as on witness testimony. Günes denied all the accusations.

Former *Alinteri* staffers said Günes was charged and convicted of violating Article 7 of the Anti-Terror Law (propagandizing on behalf of an outlawed organization) and Article 312 of the Penal Code (inciting racial hatred) for articles published in the newspaper during her tenure. She was also charged with membership in the TIKB.

Günes' lawyer told CPJ that there had been about 20 cases against her as editor and owner of *Alinteri*, all of which were suspended following the August 14, 1997, amnesty for editors. Her lawyer said Günes has been fined nearly one billion TL in her capacity as owner of *Alinteri*. CPJ sees in these previous convictions a pattern of state harassment against *Alinteri* for publishing news and dissenting opinion.

As a result of the raid, Günes was also charged in a separate indictment with "membership in an outlawed organization" under Article 168 of the Penal Code. Günes' lawyer characterized her conviction in this case as a "political decision" and said that she received the maximum 15-year sentence because the state considers *Alinteri* the mouthpiece of the TIKB. Günes is in Usak Prison.

Erhan Il, *Devrimci Emek*
Imprisoned: February 16, 1996

Il is a reporter for the magazine *Devrimci Emek*, and was editor in chief from 1993 to 1994. Court documents state that Il was arrested and charged under Article 168/2 of the Penal Code with belonging to the Turkish Communist Leninist Labor Party's (TKEP-L) youth organization. The prosecution also alleged that he rented a house in December 1994 for the TKEP-L, stored weapons for the organization, and possessed a counterfeit I.D.

Il's colleagues at *Devrimci Emek* told CPJ that he was prosecuted on the basis of articles published in the magazine during his tenure as editor. In response to an inquiry from CPJ, the Ministry of Justice stated that Il was convicted "according to amended Article 8/1 of the Anti-Terror Law [disseminating separatist propaganda], and not according to Article 168 of the Penal Code[.]" He is in Byrampasa Prison.

e⁄oe⁄oe⁄o

Kurtulus and *Mücadele*

Kurtulus, a weekly socialist magazine based in Istanbul, is the latest incarnation in a series of publications that since 1986 has included *Çözüm*, *Yeni Çözüm*, and *Mücadele*. Although its circulation is relatively small, *Kurtulus* is available at major kiosks and bookstores in Ankara and Istanbul.

Journalists in Turkey and informed observers of Turkish politics regard *Kurtulus* (Liberation) as the publication sympathetic to the outlawed armed group Revolutionary People's Liberation Party-Front (DHKP-C), formerly known as Dev Sol. Over the years, these militant Marxist organizations have claimed responsibility for the killings of generals, police officers, government officials, and foreigners. The group also took responsibility for the 1996 assassination of a member of one of Turkey's most powerful business families.

Examples of state harassment of *Kurtulus* and its predecessors include:

Hüseyin Solak, *Mücadele*
Imprisoned: October 27, 1993

Solak, the Gaziantep bureau chief of *Mücadele*, was arrested, charged with membership in the outlawed Dev Sol, and convicted on the strength of statements from people who said they had seen him distributing the magazine.

Transcripts of Solak's trial indicate the prosecution witness also testified that Solak had hung unspecified banners in public, and had served as a lookout while members of Dev Sol threw a Molotov cocktail at a bank in Gaziantep. The prosecution also cited "illegal" documents found after searches of Solak's home and office. Solak confessed to the charges while in police custody, but recanted in court.

Solak was sentenced on November 24, 1994, to 12 years and six months in prison under Article 168/2 of the Penal Code. He is in Cankiri Prison.

Serdar Gelir, *Mücadele*
Imprisoned: April 16, 1994

Gelir, Ankara bureau chief for *Mücadele*, was detained on April 16, 1994, and arrested 10 days later for being a member of an illegal organization. CPJ believes he has been imprisoned for attending an opposition rally as a reporter and his association with *Mücadele*.

During the trial, the prosecution introduced into evidence a handwritten note—written on a copy of *Kurtulus* magazine—found in Gelir's possession, which discussed local elections in Turkey. Excerpts from the document said that "the state has held elections in Kurdistan by force, with the force of 150,000 soldiers. The state has shown that it can hold elections in this region by blood. By disqualifying the representatives of the Kurdish people, by massacring the Kurdish people, that [sic] the state can get the results it wants from the elections…"

The prosecution also claimed that Gelir had handwritten a four-page document that discussed revolution, colonialism, and armed struggle. Prosecutors further alleged that Gelir had attended an illegal demonstration and distributed copies of the magazine. This was cited as proof of his membership in Dev Yol, an outlawed organization affiliated with Dev Sol. They said that Gelir had confessed to the accusations in police custody but later recanted.

In his defense, Gelir insisted that he was covering the demonstration for *Mücadele*, and his lawyer added that Gelir had filed a story on the event. Gelir said that he had been detained on April 6 and held for 16 days but was released due to lack of evidence. On April 25, he was arrested again and then charged. Gelir cited the Turkish government's hostility toward the press, which he said that such groups as RSF and the Press Council have documented.

The Ministry of Justice told CPJ that Gelir was tried under Article 168/2 of the Penal Code and Article 5 of the Anti-Terror Law 3713 and sentenced to 15 years imprisonment by the Ankara State Security Court for being a member of an armed, illegal leftist organization (Revolutionary Left/Dev Sol). Court records, however, indicate that he was sentenced to 12 years and six months in Ankara Closed Prison.

Aysel Bölücek, *Mücadele*
Imprisoned: October 11, 1994

Bölücek, a correspondent in Ankara for *Mücadele*, was arrested at her home and charged under Article 168/2 of the Penal Code, based on information the police had obtained and on a handwritten document allegedly linking her to Dev Sol. She has been in prison since her arrest.

Court documents show the state also used as evidence the October 8, 1994, issue of *Mücadele*, arguing that the weekly was the publication of Dev Sol. The prosecutor claimed that the October 8 issue insulted the security forces and state officials, and praised Dev Sol guerrillas who had been killed in clashes with security forces.

The defense argued that it was illegal for the defendant to be tried twice for the same crime. (Earlier in 1994, Bölücek had been acquitted of a charge of membership in Dev Sol for which the primary evidence had been the same handwritten document.) The defense accepted the claim that Bölücek had written the document, but said that she was forced under torture to write it while in police custody. The defense also said that a legal publication could not be used as evidence, and that the individuals who made incriminating statements about Bölücek to the police had done so under torture and subsequently recanted. Bölücek was sentenced to 12 years and six months on December 23, 1994. She is being held in Canakkale Prison.

Burhan Gardas, *Mücadele*
Imprisoned: March 23, 1995

Gardas, the Ankara bureau chief for *Mücadele*, has been the target of several prosecutions since 1994 relating to his work as a journalist.

Court records state that Gardas was detained on January 12, 1994, at his office. During a search of the premises, the police reportedly found four copies of "news bulletins" of the outlawed Dev Sol. The prosecution also said that police found banners with left-wing slogans and photographs of Dev Sol militants who had been killed in clashes with security forces. The prosecution said that when Gardas was taken into custody he shouted anti-state slogans. The prosecution said that Gardas was using *Mücadele's* office for Dev Sol activities.

He was charged with violating Article 168/2 of the Penal Code.

Gardas denied all charges. His attorney argued that the confiscated illegal publications were part of the magazine's archive, and that Gardas had been tortured while in detention. His lawyer presented a medical report to document the torture. Gardas was released on May 14, 1994, pending the outcome of his trial. While awaiting the verdict, he was arrested again on March 23, 1995, on new charges of violating Article 168/2 of the Penal Code, this time in connection with his activity as Ankara Bureau Chief of *Kurtulus* (the successor publication to *Mücadele*).

The police raided his office in connection with the later charges and seized three copies of *Kurtulus* "news bulletins" and six articles from *Kurtulus* regarding the announcement of some illegal rallies. His second trial was held at the Number 2 State Security Court of Ankara. Court documents reveal that the prosecution's evidence against Gardas consisted of his refusal to talk during a police interrogation—allegedly a Dev Sol policy—and his possession of publications which the prosecution contended were the mouthpieces of outlawed organizations, including *Mücadele* and *Kurtulus*. The state also introduced the statements of Ali Han, who worked at *Kurtulus*' Ankara bureau and stated that Gardas was a Dev Sol member. Gardas denied the claim, and his defense argued that his silence during police interrogation was a constitutional right and proved nothing.

On July 4, 1995, the Number 1 State Security Court of Ankara sentenced Gardas to 15 years in prison on the *Mücadele* charges. In 1996, he was sentenced to an additional 15 years on the second set of charges. He has thus been convicted twice of membership in Dev Sol, in each case based on his work as a journalist. Gardas is reportedly serving these sentences successively at Aydin Prison.

Özlem Türk, *Mücadele*
Imprisoned: January 17, 1995

Türk, a reporter for *Mücadele* in Samsun, was arrested at a relative's home and charged with being a member of the outlawed Revolutionary People's Liberation Party-Front, an offshoot of Dev Sol. She has been in prison since her arrest.

Court documents state that the prosecution cited as evidence the fact that Türk collected money for *Mücadele*, as well as a handwritten autobiography allegedly found in the home of a member of the Revolutionary People's Liberation Party-Front. Two people stated that she was a member of the group.

Türk maintained that the money she had collected came from sales of copies of *Mücadele*. The same court documents reveal that Türk said she was forced to confess to the charges under torture. The only material evidence presented in the case were copies of legal publications—*Mücadele, Tavir,* and *Devrimci Genclik*—found at her home, and copies of her alleged autobiography. Police provided expert testimony to authenticate the incriminating document.

According to court documents, Türk was sentenced to 15 years in prison. She is in Canakkale Prison.

Necla Can, *Kurtulus*
Imprisoned: April 9, 1995

CPJ believes Can, a reporter for the leftist weekly *Kurtulus,* was imprisoned for attending an insurgent's funeral in her capacity as a journalist.

Trial documents obtained in December 1997 state that Can was apprehended by police at her home on April 9, 1995, after two people made incriminating statements about her to authorities. They alleged that Can was a member of the Revolutionary People's Liberation Party-Front (DHKP-C) but later recanted. Can was tried along with 19 other alleged members of the DHKP-C.

Can's lawyer told CPJ that the basis for the charge against her had been her attendance at the funeral of a member of the DHKP-C. In defending Can, her lawyer had said that she had been there as a journalist. The lawyer also said that Can had testified in court to being beaten while in custody.

Can was tried along with 19 other alleged members of the DHKP-C. Can was convicted on December 21, 1997, and sentenced to 12 years and six months in prison under Article 168/2 of the Penal Code. She is in Istanbul's Umraniye Prison.

Özgür Güdenoglu, *Mücadele*
Imprisoned: May 24, 1995

Güdenoglu, *Mücadele*'s Konya bureau chief, was arrested, charged, and convicted under Article 168 of the Penal Code. He was sentenced to 12 years, 6 months in prison for alleged membership in Dev Sol. CPJ believes his prosecution is related to the state's well-documented harassment of *Mücadele*. He is in Konya Prison.

Kamber Inan, *Kurtulus*
Imprisoned: July 11, 1995

CPJ believes Inan has been jailed as part of a campaign of harassment against *Kurtulus,* for which he was a reporter. Inan was arrested in his home in Istanbul and charged under Article 168/2 of the Penal Code for membership in the Revolutionary People's Liberation Party-Front (DHKP-C). Court documents obtained from Inan's lawyer in December 1997 said that he had refused to answer questions during his detention and upon conviction was sentenced to 15 years in prison. He is in Bayrampasa Prison.

Ufuk Dogubay, *Kurtulus*
Imprisoned: July 27, 1995

CPJ believes that the prosecution of Dogubay, a former editor of *Kurtulus*, was motivated by his work as a journalist and is part of a pattern of harassment against the magazine.

Court documents state that Dogubay was arrested and imprisoned on July 27, 1995, and accused of writing a document that indicated that *Kurtulus* was the publication of the Revolutionary People's Liberation Party-Front (DHKP-C). He denied the charge, but an expert witness for the prosecution concluded that he had written the document. The prosecution cited statements from two people allegedly incriminating Dogubay, and claimed that Dogubay shouted leftist slogans during his arrest. He was convicted and sentenced to 12 years and six months in prison under Article 168/2 of the Penal Code. The court documents refer to him as a journalist and an engineer. He is in Sagmalcilar Prison.

Sadik Çelik, *Kurtulus*
Imprisoned: December 23, 1995

Although Çelik was detained and formally charged with membership in the outlawed Revolutionary People's Liberation Party-Front (DHKP-C), the state's case rested almost exclusively on his activities as a reporter and Zonguldak bureau chief for *Kurtulus*.

Court documents state that Çelik was detained on December 23, 1995. The prosecution asserted that *Kurtulus* was the publication of the DHKP-C, and that Çelik's position with the magazine proved he was a member of the group. Çelik was accused of conducting "seminars" for the DHKP-C in the magazine's office, propagandizing for the organization, transporting copies of the magazine from Istanbul to Zonguldak by bus, and organizing the paper's distribution in Zonguldak. The prosecution said that Çelik's name appeared in a document written by a leader of the DHKP-C (it is not clear whether the document was introduced as material evidence). Moreover, the prosecution said Çelik's refusal to testify in police custody proved his guilt.

The defense argued that the prosecution could not substantiate any of its claims. Çelik acknowledged distributing the magazine in his capacity as *Kurtulus'* bureau chief. He said that he held meetings in the office to discuss matters pertaining to the magazine. The defense presented the statements of two *Kurtulus* reporters, corroborating Çelik's statements.

Çelik was sentenced on October 17, 1996, to 12 years and six months in prison. Court documents indicate he was sent to Ankara Closed Prison.

He was reportedly released in February 1998.

IMPRISONED JOURNALISTS

Asaf Sah, *Kurtulus*
Imprisoned: January 4, 1996

CPJ believes that Sah, an Antakya reporter for *Kurtulus*, was imprisoned as part of the state's campaign of harassment against the magazine. Sah was convicted under Article 169 of the Penal Code for aiding an outlawed organization. He was sentenced on April 16, 1996, to three years and nine months in jail and is currently in Nevsehir Prison.

Yazgül Güder Öztürk, *Kurtulus*
Imprisoned: March 31, 1996

CPJ believes Öztürk has been prosecuted as part of the state's harassment of *Kurtulus*, for which she was a reporter. Court documents obtained in December 1997 state that Öztürk was detained and imprisoned on March 31, 1996, charged with violating Article 168/2 of the Penal Code for membership in the Revolutionary People's Liberation Salvation Party-Front (DHKP-C). The prosecution accused her of gathering information for DHKP-C in Gaziantep, near the Syrian border, and Konya, in central Turkey. She was also accused of attending unspecified illegal demonstrations in Istanbul and the funeral in Adana of two members of the DHKP-C who were killed during a robbery in Ankara.

According to Öztürk's lawyer, the prosecution additionally claimed that she had coordinated the propaganda activities of the DHKP-C.

In her defense, Öztürk cited her work as a journalist and denied all charges. She was convicted of membership in the DHKP-C and is in Bayrampasa Prison.

Ayten Öztürk, *Kurtulus*
Imprisoned: October 13, 1997

Court documents suggest strongly that Öztürk has been imprisoned because she published and edited *Kurtulus*. In September 1997, Öztürk was already facing charges, under Article 7 of the Anti-Terror Law, of spreading propaganda in the press on behalf of an outlawed organization. Those charges were voided on September 4 by an Istanbul State Security Court in accordance with the government's August 14 amnesty for editors. On September 19, however, a warrant was issued for her arrest for a violation of Article 168/1 of the Penal Code—a statute not covered by the amnesty.

Özturk surrendered to the court on October 13, and thereupon was charged with leading the outlawed Revolutionary People's Liberation Party-Front (DHKP-C). The main evidence cited at her trial was her publication and distribution of an unspecified "special edition" of *Kurtulus*. The prosecution also said she had met with two alleged members of the DHKP-C. She was convicted on December 24 and sentenced to 12 years and six months. She is currently in Ankara Closed Prison.

❧❧❧❧

Utku Deniz Sirkeci, *Tavir*
Imprisoned: August 6, 1994

CPJ believes that Sirkeci, the Ankara bureau chief of the leftist cultural magazine *Tavir*, was imprisoned for attending the funeral of a Dev Sol activist in his capacity as a journalist. He was convicted of membership in Dev Sol and sentenced to 12 years and six months in prison.

Court records show the state accused Sirkeci of throwing a Molotov cocktail at a bank in Ankara, but the documents do not stipulate what evidence was introduced to support this charge. It is not clear that a Molotov cocktail was ever thrown. Prosecutors also cited Sirkeci's attendance at the funeral of a political activist to support the charge that he was a Dev Sol member. Sirkeci maintained he attended the funeral in his capacity as a journalist. During the trial, he provided detailed testimony of his torture at the hands of police, who he alleged coerced him to confess. He is in Ankara Closed Prison.

Baris Yildirim, *Tavir*
Imprisoned: March 21, 1995

CPJ believes that Yildirim, a columnist for the leftist cultural magazine *Tavir*, was imprisoned for his work as a journalist. He was arrested, charged, and subsequently tried and convicted under Article 168 of the Penal Code for membership in Dev Sol, but interviews with his colleagues in 1996 indicated that his conviction was based largely on the fact that he worked for the magazine.

The prosecution stated that Yildirim was arrested in Izmir and tried in the State Security Court for membership in Dev Sol. Informants told the court that Yildirim was a spokesman for the organization, taking part in throwing Molotov cocktails, and hanging banners around Izmir on orders from the organization. The prosecution alleged that he had participated in the occupation of the center-right True Path Party's Izmir offices.

Yildirim was convicted on December 17, 1996, and sentenced to 12 years and six months. He is being held in Buca Prison in Izmir.

Bülent Sümbül, *Özgür Halk*
Imprisoned: April 24, 1995

Sümbül, a reporter in the Diyarbakir bureau of the pro-Kurdish monthly magazine *Özgür Halk*, was arrested during a police raid on his Diyarbakir office. CPJ believes that the state's case stemmed from Sümbül's work as a journalist.

Sümbül's lawyer told CPJ his client had been accused of violating Article 169 of the Penal Code, aiding the outlawed Kurdistan Workers' Party (PKK). To establish Sümbül's guilt, the prosecution relied on photographs of alleged PKK members which they claimed Sümbül delivered to an imprisoned colleague in Diyarbakir Prison. Sümbül's lawyer

IMPRISONED JOURNALISTS

responded: "When you take something to the prison, every-thing is searched. There is no way that he [Sümbül] could have given her the photos of some PKK members. The guards would have found them...inside the stationery. So, he [Sümbül] denies that he had given [the imprisoned colleague] the photos."

The prosecution's statement said that Sumbul was also accused of "being the leader of an organizational cell, taking an active role in an illegal organization, [and] acting as liaison for militants in rural and urban areas." According to this lawyer, the prosecution also produced a written confession, which police coerced him to sign.

Sümbül denied the charges. He was convicted and sentenced to three years and nine months. He is in Bismil Prison.

**Mehmet Çakar, *Partizan Sesi*
Imprisoned: February 13, 1995**

Çakar, Izmir bureau chief of the leftist monthly *Partizan Sesi*, was arrested and charged with being a member the outlawed Marxist-Leninist Communist Party.

According to Çakar's lawyer, the prosecution had based its case on the fact that Çakar had distributed copies of the magazine. The prosecution also said that Çakar had met with two members of an unspecified outlawed organization—a charge that Çakar denied, according to his attorney. Court documents obtained in December 1997 verified the lawyer's statements.

Çakar's lawyer told CPJ that his client had been convicted of membership in the Marxist-Leninist Communist Party and sentenced to 12 years and six months in Bursa Prison.

e/ɔe/ɔe/ɔ

Özgür Gündem

The pro-Kurdish daily *Özgür Gündem* published from 1992 to 1994 before being forced to close under sustained government pressure. Successor papers have included *Yeni Ulke, Özgür Ulke, Yeni Politika, Özgür Yasam*, and *Demokrasi*. Each was forced to close because of state legal action. The paper currently publishes under the name *Ulkede Gündem*. Journalists in Turkey and informed observers of Turkish politics regard the paper as sympathetic to the outlawed Kurdistan Workers' Party (PKK).

Throughout its existence, *Özgür Gündem* experienced systematic government harassment in response to its coverage of the state's ongoing conflict with Kurdish insurgents in southeastern Turkey. In 1993, CPJ documented 246 cases pending against the newspaper. Authorities suspended or confiscated numerous issues of the newspaper and prosecuted its journalists under various pro-visions of the Anti-Terror Law and Penal Code for articles published in the paper. At least four of its responsible editors have served or are currently serving prison terms.

Ismail Besikçi
Imprisoned: November 13, 1993

Besikçi, a prominent scholar and author of numerous books and articles on the Kurds in Turkey, was arrested and charged with violating the Anti-Terror Law for an article he wrote in the now-defunct daily *Yeni Ülke*. He was tried and sentenced to one year in prison. Since this initial conviction, however, Besikçi has been found guilty in other cases for articles he published on the Kurdish question in *Özgür Gündem*, and for books he has written on the subject. By the end of 1997, he had been sentenced to more than 100 years in prison. He remains in Bursa Prison, with additional charges pending against him.

Hasan Özgün, *Özgür Gündem*
Imprisoned: December 9, 1993

CPJ believes that Özgün's imprisonment is a result of his work as a journalist and is of a piece with the state's well-documented harassment of *Özgür Gündem*. Özgün, Diyarbakir correspondent for *Özgür Gündem*, was taken into custody during a police raid on the paper's Diyarbakir bureau and charged under Article 168 of the Penal Code with being a member of the outlawed Kurdistan Workers' Party (PKK). He was sentenced to 12 years and five months in prison.

Transcripts of Özgün's trial show that the prosecution based its case on what it described as *Özgür Gündem's* pro-PKK slant. The prosecution also used as evidence copies of banned PKK publications (*Serkhabun* and *Berxehun*) found in Özgün's possession, as well as photographs and biographical sketches of PKK members found in the newspaper's archive. The state further cited Özgün's possession of an unauthorized handgun as evidence of his membership in the PKK.

In his defense, Özgün maintained that the PKK publications were used as sources of information and that the photos of PKK members found in the archive were related to interviews the newspaper had conducted. Özgün admitted to purchasing the gun on the black market, but denied all other charges.

The Ministry of Justice replied to CPJ's request for information saying that "In fact, Mr. Özgün had extensive ties to the PKK terrorist organization. Accordingly, he was convicted of the following charges: being an active member of the PKK terrorist organization; being a courier for the PKK's mountain team; inciting the public to participate in propaganda activities organized by the PKK; informing the PKK of rich locals who could be targeted for extortion and ransom schemes organized by the organization; supplying food and medicine for the members of the PKK terrorist organization; carrying a gun without a license; providing arms for PKK mountain teams; distributing separatist propaganda material on behalf of the PKK terrorist organization."

RSF and International PEN have voiced strong objections to Özgün's prosecution. RSF reported that on the day after Özgün's arrest, more than 150 journalists and employees of *Özgür Gündem* were arrested throughout the country. RSF noted that the accusation against Özgün was based on the discovery in the *Özgür Gündem* office of petitions signed by detained PKK members. Responding to an RSF letter, the Turkish Embassy in France stated that "Mr. Hasan Özgün, not having the title of journalist, was accused of belonging to the terrorist organization PKK, for having organized activities on behalf of this organization, for publicity and praise of said organization in the paper, for having given the organization the names of wealthy people for levying a compulsory tax for financing PKK, for possession of an illegal weapon, for having smuggled arms to terrorists posted in the mountainous areas of southeastern Anatolia, for having kept in his house and distributed numerous pamphlets and other pro-PKK publicity materials."

According to RSF, Özgün told the court that petitions belonging to detained PKK members had been entrusted to him by people close to the prisoners so that he could write an article about their case. Özgün denied ever having been a PKK member and complained that both he and *Özgür Gündem* were being persecuted.

International PEN, in its mid-year 1997 report, concluded that Özgün did not receive a fair trial, noting that he had additionally been accused of arranging medical treatment for PKK guerrillas and having communicated with PKK guerrillas in prison. PEN's report said that "part of the evidence [was] said to relate to [an] interview with [a] PKK leader published in *Özgür Gündem*. Defense says the [same] interview was run in other Turkish newspapers without charges being brought."

Özgün is currently in Aydin Prison.

Kemal Sahin, *Özgür Gündem*
Imprisoned: November 1995

Sahin, the former editor in chief of *Ozgür Gündem*, was arrested and charged with membership the outlawed Kurdistan Workers' Party (PKK). CPJ believes that his prosecution and imprisonment are part of a campaign of harassment against *Özgur Gündem*.

Sahin had initially been convicted of violating Articles 6, 7, and 8 of the Anti-Terror Law and Article 312 of the Penal Code for articles published in the newspaper during his tenure as editor. Court documents from his trial on the Article 8 charges (disseminating separatist propaganda) show that among the numerous, mostly unspecified articles cited by the prosecution was one that appeared in *Özgür Gündem* on October 10, 1994, titled "Escape from the Army."

Sahin was sentenced to seven years and eight months in prison and fined more than 319 million TL (US$1,595) for the Article 8 conviction. It is unclear whether he was ever imprisoned on these charges, which were subsequently suspended by the government's August 14 limited amnesty for editors. Additional charges were brought against him under Article 168 of the Penal Code, however, for which he was arrested, charged, and eventually imprisoned.

Sahin's lawyer told CPJ that the new charges against him were based on the testimony of Sahin's brother, who accused him of being a member of the PKK. It is unclear whether Sahin's brother had been coerced into giving this testimony. Sahin is being held in Umraniye Prison in Istanbul.

Vietnam (5)

Please send appeals to:
His Excellency Le Kha Phieu
General Secretary of the Central Committee
Communist Party of Vietnam
1 Hoang Van Thu
Hanoi, Socialist Republic of Vietnam

Doan Viet Hoat,
Dien Dan Tu Do
Imprisoned: November 17, 1990

Public security police arrested Hoat, editor and publisher of the pro-democracy newsletter *Dien Dan Tu Do* (Freedom Forum). The Ho Chi Minh City People's Court sentenced him in late March 1993 to 20 years of hard labor for his involvement with the newsletter. He is currently serving out his sentence, commuted to 15 years on appeal, in Thanh Cam Prison. Located in northern Vietnam, near the Laotian border, Thanh Cam is normally reserved for serious criminal offenders. Hoat suffers from kidney stones, a condition that developed during his previous 12-year incarceration by the Hanoi regime. In November 1997, the World Association of Newspapers awarded its Golden Pen of Freedom for press freedom to Doan Viet Hoat for his "extraordinary courage" in the fight for press freedom in Vietnam.

Nguyen Van Thuan (Chau Son), *Dien Dan Tu Do*
Imprisoned: Late 1990

Thuan, whose pen name is Chau Son, was arrested in the fall of 1990 and in March 1993 was sentenced to 12 years in prison for his involvement with the pro-democracy newsletter *Dien Dan Tu Do* (Freedom Forum). His sentence was reduced on appeal to eight years. Thuan suffered a stroke on February 25, 1994, that left him partially paralyzed. He is reportedly being held in a re-education camp where he is not forced to carry out labor, although the lack of medical facilities raises concerns for his health.

Le Duc Vuong, *Dien Dan Tu Do*
Imprisoned: Late 1990

Vuong was arrested in the fall of 1990 and sentenced in late March 1993 to seven years in prison for his involvement with the pro-democracy newsletter *Dien Dan Tu Do* (Freedom Forum). CPJ believes Vuong is incarcerated at Xuan Phuoc labor camp.

Nguyen Dan Que
Sentenced: November 1991

Que was convicted of compiling and distributing subversive literature and sentenced to 20 years in prison. Before he was imprisoned, he had distributed political handbills and sent documents abroad. Que, who suffers from hypertension and a bleeding gastric ulcer, is imprisoned at the Xuyen Moc labor camp in Dong Nai Province.

Nguyen Hoang Linh,
Doang Nghiep
Arrested: October 8, 1997

Hoang Linh, editor of the state-run business newspaper *Doang Nghiep*, was arrested on charges of revealing state secrets. The charges were linked to articles he wrote that explored questionable practices of Vietnam's General Customs Department in the purchase of coastal patrol boats. Local journalists said the arrest was interpreted as a warning to reporters to stay away from stories about government corruption. The arrest followed restrictions imposed earlier in the year concerning financial and banking information. The government also barred Vietnamese journalists from giving information to their foreign counterparts without first obtaining state permission.

Zambia (1)

Please send appeals to:
His Excellency Frederick Chiluba
President of the Republic of Zambia
State House
Independent Avenue
Lusaka, Zambia
Fax: 260-1-221-939

Fredrick Mwanza
Imprisoned: November 14, 1997

Mwanza, a writer and journalist, was detained under the Preservation of Public Security Act of 1960, accused of involvement with a failed coup attempt on October 28. He appeared in court on November 26, but was not charged. Mwanza then applied for a writ of habeas corpus, challenging the government to show cause why he could not be released. At a hearing on December 2, the government responded by serving Mwanza with a presidential detention order, which allows the police to hold the journalist indefinitely under the state of emergency currently in force.

Mwanza has denied all allegations that he was present at a meeting finalizing the coup plot against President Frederick Chiluba's government. The journalist has been questioned in prison about several articles critical of government policies. His lawyer, Patrick Mvunga, has stated that Mwanza was tortured during interrogation and has been denied access to his family.

Unconfirmed Cases of Imprisoned Journalists (30)

CPJ could not confirm that the journalists below remained in prison as of December 31, 1997, or that their imprisonment was directly related to their work. We are continuing to investigate these cases, and welcome any information.

China (5)

The following five journalists were arrested in 1989 and received a sentence of four years in prison. There is therefore reason to believe that they have been released, although CPJ has not obtained information of their release.

Fan Jianping, Jin Naiyi, *Beijing Ribao*
Imprisoned: 1989

Fan, an editor at *Beijing Ribao* (Beijing Daily), and Jin, a journalist for the same newspaper, were arrested sometime after the June 4, 1989, Tiananmen Square crackdown.

Li Jian, *Wenyi Bao*
Imprisoned: July 1989

Li, a journalist with *Wenyi Bao* (Literature and Arts News), was arrested sometime after the June 4, 1989, Tiananmen Square crackdown.

Yang Hong, *Zhongguo Qingnian Bao*
Imprisoned: June 13, 1989

Yang, a reporter for *Zhongguo Qingnian Bao* (China Youth News), was arrested in Kunming and charged with circulating "rumormongering leaflets" and protesting against corruption.

Yu Zhongmin, *Fazhi Yuekan*
Imprisoned: 1989

Yu, a journalist with *Fazhi Yuekan* (Law Monthly) in Shanghai, was arrested sometime after the June 4, 1989, Tiananmen Square crackdown. He was later described in an article in *Wenhui Daily* as an "agitator" of the Shanghai student demonstrations.

Shang Ziwen, Sun Liyong
Arrested: 1991

Shang, a cadre at Thorough Transport Corporation and a major member of the group producing the underground magazine *Zhong Sheng* (The Sound of the Bell), was sentenced to six years in prison. Sun, the founder of *Zhong Sheng*, was sentenced to seven years imprisonment. Both were convicted of "counter-revolution" for publishing *Zhong Sheng*. Shang's prison term was expected to end in 1997. Sun is expected to be released in 1998, although CPJ was not able to obtain evidence that either had been released.

Democratic Republic of Congo (formerly Zaire) (4)

Mukalayi Mulongo, *OZRT-Shaba*
Kabemba wa Yulu, *OZRT-Shaba*
Imprisoned: May 19, 1995

Lubumbashi security service officers arrested Mulongo, the program director of the state-owned radio station OZRT and wa Yulu, a journalist with the station. Mulongo was arrested for granting the president of the Shaba province branch of the

Union of Independent Republicans Party (UFERI) the right to respond to statements made by the national UFERI president. CPJ has been unable to confirm his status since Mobutu's regime was ousted on May 17, 1997, by Laurent Kabila.

Jean Muadianvita, free-lancer
Imprisoned: January 23, 1997

Muadianvita, a free-lance journalist for the independent newspapers *La Tempete des Tropiques*, *Umoja*, and *L'Example*, was arrested at his home in Mont Ngafula, a county of Kinshasa, by soldiers of the Military Action and Intelligence Service (SARM) on the orders of General Bolozei Ngbudu. Muadianvita was transported to SARM headquarters at Kitambo in Kinshasa, where he is being held incommunicado.

On the same day, SARM soldiers returned with Muadianvita to his home to search for documents. After the search, he was transported back to SARM headquarters, which was controlled by a Major Boyombo.

Muadianvita's arrest was in connection with a series of articles published in November 1996 about President Mobutu's U.S.-based political lobbyists. The articles reported that the lobbyists were paid to maintain a foreign network that was acting to keep then-President Mobutu in power. Muadianvita published a list of these lobbyists, detailing how much Mobutu had paid each for their services.

Muadianvita's attorney was denied access to his client after he was taken into custody, and SARM has refused to send the journalist to court because he will not reveal his sources for the articles.

On January 30, CPJ wrote a letter to then-Prime Minister Kengo wa Dondo, protesting the incommunicado arrest of Muadianvita.

CPJ has been unable to confirm the journalist's whereabouts since Mobutu was ousted by Laurent Kabila on May 17.

Nepa Bagili Mutita, *La Voix de L'Islam*
Imprisoned: February 11, 1997

Mutita was arrested on February 11 on charges of spreading false rumors about the civil war and faced up to three years in jail. The journalist, who was also president of the Mouvement National Congolais-Lumumba, had published in his monthly *La Voix de l'Islam* a list of people wanted by then-rebel leader Laurent Kabila. The list included the names of the president and the prime minister. CPJ has been unable to confirm his whereabouts since Kabila came to power on May 17.

Ethiopia (3)

Melese, *Kayete*
Imprisoned: September 3, 1997

CPJ has been unable to determine whether Melese is still in prison.

Andualem Mohammed, *Tame Feker*
Imprisoned: September 3, 1997

CPJ has been unable to determine whether Mohammed is still in prison.

Getachew Teffera, *Agere*
Imprisoned: September 3, 1997

CPJ has been unable to determine whether Teffera is still in prison.

Guinea (2)

Ousmane Camara, *L'Oeil*
Imprisoned: August 1, 1997

L'Oeil publications director Camara, and editor in chief Louis Celestin, were arrested and detained, charged with "spreading false information and defamation" after Justice Minister Maurice Zogbelemou Togba lodged a complaint. The June 25 and July 2 editions of *l'Oeil* contained criticism of Togba. On August 4, the journalists appeared in court for preliminary questioning. Although the court granted them an official release on August 6, Camara and Celestin remained in jail. Celestin was later released and began to work again, but was expelled from Guinea to the Ivory Coast on December 22 after writing an article on an opposition press conference. Camara's whereabouts are unknown.

Foday Fofana, *L'Independant*
Imprisoned: October 13, 1997

Fofana, a reporter with the weekly paper *L'Independant*, was arrested at the Alpha Yaya military camp in Conakry. Fofana had gone there to interview the camp's associate commander in connection with reports that the commander was behind several assaults on a civilian. When Fofana stated the reason for his visit, he was charged with "gathering information on behalf of a foreign power." Police transported Fofana to police headquarters, where he was held for a month, before moving him to the central detention facility. Other charges brought against Fofana include "attempting to threaten the security of the State," "falsehood and use of deception," and "attempting to usurp in name and deed."

Nigeria (1)

Babatunji Wusu, *TheNews*
Imprisoned: September 17, 1997

Security operatives who presented themselves as Federal Intelligence and Investigation Bureau officers arrested Wusu, an administrator with *TheNews*, at the magazine's editorial office in Lagos. The men were unable to find the editors they were seeking, so they arrested Wusu instead and took him to their Ikoyi office. The action appears to have been in connection with an article published in the September 15 issue of *TheNews* titled, "Panic Over Abacha's Illness." CPJ has been unable to confirm Wusu's whereabouts.

Sierra Leone (1)

Suliman Janger, *New Tablet*
Imprisoned: July 28, 1997

Janger, production manager of the *New Tablet* newspaper, was arrested while he was distributing the newspaper's second edition. The soldiers who detained him also seized about 900 copies. Five unidentified newspaper vendors were also arrested along with Janger.

Turkey (13)

(+ = Charges and convictions suspended under the government's August 14, 1997, limited amnesty for editors.)

Bektas Cansever,
Devrimci Çözüm
Imprisoned: December 26, 1993

CPJ believes that Cansever may have been prosecuted and imprisoned as a result of his affiliation with *Devrimci Çözüm*. He was taken into custody in Istanbul and subsequently charged under Article 168/2 of the Penal Code with membership in the outlawed organization Dev Sol.

The Ministry of Justice informed CPJ that "Mr. Bektas Cansever, whose alias was Yusuf Yilmaz, was taken into custody on December 26, 1993. During a physical body search, police found an unauthorized pistol on Mr. Cansever. Like the CPJ states, it was also found that Mr. Cansever was also a member of Dev Sol, an outlawed leftist organization categorized as such in the annual U.S. State Department's Patterns of Global Terrorism report."

Prosecution documents show that Cansever was accused of hanging banners in public, throwing Molotov cocktails in Izmir in 1991, and other Molotov cocktail incidents. The prosecution claimed that Dev Sol had sent Cansever to Istanbul in 1992 in order to elude capture, and that he then began working for *Devrimici Çözüm*. The state alleged that at the time of his arrest, police found in his possession a gun, two counterfeit I.D.s, and a handwritten document outlining Dev Sol's organizational structure. Three people were said to have made statements incriminating him—but there was no record of their statements in the court documents.

According to court documents, Cansever admitted throwing a Molotov cocktail in Istanbul.

Cansever was convicted on April 10, 1997, and sentenced to more than 24 years in jail. He is in Gebze Prison.

Kemal Topalak,
Devrimci Çözüm
Imprisoned: December 26, 1993

CPJ believes that Topalak may have been prosecuted for his work as a reporter for *Devrimci Çözüm*.

Court documents indicate that Topolak was detained in a coffee shop and was found to be carrying a counterfeit I.D., which prosecutors said had been acquired in Switzerland through Dev Sol. He was charged under Article 168 of the

Penal Code with membership in the outlawed Dev Sol organization.

Police searched Topolak's house, where they found copies of *Devrimci Çözüm* and sketches of a hammer and sickle as well as documents allegedly handwritten by Topolak, which the prosecution said linked him and his wife to Dev Sol, for which he allegedly served as a courier. Police said they had statements incriminating Topalak as a Dev Sol member. Topalak admitted to the charges while in police custody but denied them in court. The prosecution alleged that Topolak had visited Damascus "for bomb and gun training," and that he had two guns in his possession upon arrest.

In his defense, Topolak admitted to having false identification, which he said he procured in Switzerland after losing his real one, but denied receiving the I.D. from Dev Sol. His lawyer said the state's case relied upon testimony coerced from Topolak under torture during an interrogation at police headquarters. He believes that his client was prosecuted because he is a journalist.

The Ministry of Justice responded to CPJ's request for information by stating that Topolak had been taken into custody with Bektas Cansever on December 26, 1993: "It was discovered that Mr. Topolak was a member of the illegal leftist organization Dev Sol. Hence, like CPJ reports, he was charged under Article 168/2 of the Penal Code with being a member of an outlawed organization and sentenced to prison. He is in Gebze Prison." Topolak is serving a sentence of 12 years and six months.

Ibrahim Özen, *Devrimci Çözüm*
Imprisoned: December 28,
1993

CPJ believes that Özen may have been prosecuted and imprisoned because of a crackdown on *Devrimci Çözüm*, which he owned. He was taken into custody during a police raid on his home in Istanbul and charged with violating Articles 5 and 7/2 of the Anti-Terror Law (aid and propaganda for a terrorist organization) and Article 312/2 of the Penal Code (inciting racial hatred). He is serving a 12-year sentence in Gebze Prison in Istanbul.

The defense argued that *Devrimci Çözüm* was a legal publication, and that the authorities would have rejected Özen's application to publish the magazine had he been affiliated with any outlawed organization. Özen's lawyer said his client had committed no crime.

The Ministry of Justice responded to CPJ's request for information saying: "As a result of exhaustive investigations, certain members of [Dev Sol] and some terrorists acting on its behalf were apprehended. From their testimony, it was discovered that Mr. Ibrahim Özen was a member of the organization and acted on its behalf. In the search of his hideout [sic], an unauthorized arm was found. Like CPJ reports, Mr. Özen, like Bektas Cansever and Kemal Topalak, who were members of the same organization, was arrested by the State Security Court for being a member of an outlawed organization. Ibrahim Özen was convicted under Penal Code Article 168/2 and is currently serving time at Gebze Prison."

Court documents from Özen's trial state that he was detained during a police raid on his home—the "hideout" referred to above. He was convicted of membership in Dev Sol and Dev Genc, another outlawed organization, in violation of Article 168 of the Penal Code. Based on witness testimony, the prosecution said that Özen traveled to the Bekaa Valley in Lebanon and sent other members there as well. He is also accused of providing written instructions to other alleged Dev Sol members and using the magazine's office on behalf of the organizations. According to the court documents, he confessed to the charges against him in police custody but later recanted. His lawyers argued in court that he was tortured. They asserted that the prosecution had no concrete evidence to support its claims.

Hanim Harman, *Mücadele*
Imprisoned: January 19, 1994

Harman, a reporter in Malatya for *Mücadele*, was detained and accused of membership in the banned organization Dev Sol. CPJ believes that Harman may have been prosecuted for her work as a journalist and as part of a state campaign of harassment against *Mücadele*. She was sentenced on May 2, 1995, to 12 years and six months in jail.

Court documents obtained in December 1997 said that the prosecution accused Harman of communicating with members of Dev Sol, providing them with information about the police, and reporting to her superiors. The state said Harman had interrogated a Dev Sol defector.

In her defense, Harman cited her work as a correspondent for *Mücadele* in Malatya and denied all the charges against her. She is in Sakarya Prison.

Nuray Gezici,
Yoksul Halkin Gücü
Imprisoned: April 16, 1994

Gezici, a reporter for *Yoksul Halkin Gücü*, was arrested and is currently serving a 15-year prison term in Ankara Closed Prison. Transcripts of her trial show she was charged with membership in the Revolutionary People's Liberation Party-Front.

Gezici was detained in Ankara while exiting a taxi with two other people. Police claimed she was on her way to the meeting house of an illegal organization. Police said Gezici was carrying copies of *Kurtulus* and unspecified "left wing books."

The state asserted that Gezici's presence at a ceremony commemorating Turkish revolutionaries who had been killed by security forces in the 1960s and 1970s was evidence of membership in the outlawed group. Gezici said that she had attended the ceremony in her capacity as a journalist. She was also accused of having thrown two Molotov cocktails at an Ankara bank on March 29, 1993, and of having hung two Dev Sol flags in public on April 16, 1993. The prosecution claimed that Gezici had previously confessed to throwing Molotov cocktails, but Gezici testified that her confession had been extracted under torture by police and subsequently denied participating in the attack.

Mustafa Çoskun, *Partizan Sesi*
Imprisoned: May 25, 1994
Released: October 25, 1994 [?]

CPJ first reported this case in March 1996, stating that Çoskun, Elazig bureau chief of the leftist monthly *Partizan Sesi*, was arrested and charged with being a member of an outlawed organization and was being held in Elazig Prison. Çoskun was said to have been convicted under Article 168 of the Penal Code for membership in an outlawed organization and was sentenced to prison.

Çoskun's lawyer told CPJ that his client had been convicted of membership in the Marxist-Leninist Communist Party and was in Bursa Prison. According to the lawyer, Çoskun was accused of distributing copies of *Partizan Sesi*, which the prosecution deemed as evidence of his membership in the organization.

CPJ read court documents stating that Çoskun had been detained on May 25, 1994, and accused of membership in the outlawed Marxist-Leninist Communist Party under Article 168/2 of the Penal Code and formally arrested on June 3, 1994. The documents indicated that the State Security Court dropped the charge on June 16, 1994, and instead charged him under Article 7/2 of the Anti-Terror Law (propagandizing on behalf of an outlawed organization). Çoskun was said to have been convicted of the Article 7/2 charge on an unspecified date, sentenced to 10 months in prison, and fined 333 million TL. He was released prior to the expiration of his term on October 25, 1994, according to the documents.

In the fall of 1997, Çoskun's lawyer told CPJ that his client was in prison. CPJ is attempting to determine if he was in fact released on October 25, 1994, or if he was released and subsequently arrested and imprisoned on an additional charge or charges.

Ali Sinan Çaglar, *Mücadele*
Imprisoned: August 6, 1994

Çaglar, *Mücadele*'s Ankara correspondent, was arrested at the funeral of a political activist and charged with membership in an illegal organization. He has been in prison since his arrest. On January 23, 1995, he was sentenced to 12 years and six months in prison for alleged membership in the outlawed Dev Sol organization. CPJ believes Çaglar's work as a journalist may have led to his prosecution.

The state based its case on Çaglar's testimony and the statements of two people who said that Çaglar was a member of Dev Sol. The prosecution said that Çaglar had admitted to hanging posters with leftist slogans around the city, and stated that Çaglar had burned a U.S. flag at Ankara University and shouted leftist slogans during the funeral at which he was arrested. He was also accused of resisting arrest on that occasion.

In his defense, Çaglar recanted the testimony he gave while in police custody. He denied all charges, saying that he had attended the funeral in his capacity as a journalist. Upon conviction he was sent to Konya Prison. He is now in Ankara Closed Prison.

Bülent Ecevit Özdemir,
Kurtulus
Imprisoned: December 7, 1995
Released: October 1997 [?]

Özdemir, a reporter for *Kurtulus*, was charged with membership in an illegal organization under Article 168 of the Penal Code. He was last known to be held in Konya Prison.

CPJ has been unable to obtain any court documents in the case. In December 1997, the editor of *Kurtulus* told CPJ that Özdemir had been released from prison in October 1997 pending the outcome of his trial. CPJ has been unable to verify this report or determine his status.

Semiha Topal, *Kurtulus*
Imprisoned: December 12,
1995

Topal, a reporter for the Antakya bureau of *Kurtulus*, was arrested, charged, and convicted under Article 168/2 of the Penal Code. She was sentenced to 12 years and six months in Malatya Prison.

Court documents obtained by CPJ state that Topal was detained on December 12, 1995, in an apartment along with two other suspects, for membership in the outlawed Revolutionary People's Liberation Party-Front (DHKP-C). She was accused of taking part in throwing a Molotov cocktail into a car showroom. Topal denied the allegation and denied being at the scene of the crime. The prosecution presented four witnesses who said she was there, a photo negative that they claimed showed her standing behind the showroom's broken windows, and footprints from the crime scene which they said were Topal's. She was also accused of hanging leftist banners around the city.

IMPRISONED JOURNALISTS: UNCONFIRMED

CPJ is still investigating this case out of concern that Topal's prosecution is part of a pattern of state harassment of *Kurtulus*.

Tekin Aygün, *Kurtulus*
Imprisoned: 1996 [?]
Released: ?

Aygün, a reporter for the leftist weekly *Kurtulus*, was reportedly arrested and jailed in Umraniye Prison. *Kurtulus* staffers told CPJ that Aygün had been convicted of membership in an outlawed organization under Article 168 of the Penal Code and sentenced to 12 years and six months in prison. CPJ has obtained court documents stating that prosecutors had dropped all charges against Aygün on November 30, 1995. But CPJ has been unable to determine if Aygün was facing trial on other charges, or his whereabouts.

Özgür Öktem, *Devrimci Emek*
Imprisoned: February 19, 1996

CPJ believes that Öktem may have been imprisoned because of his work as a reporter for the leftist magazine *Devrimci Emek*, which we believe to have been the target of a state harassment campaign.

Öktem was arrested for alleged membership in the Turkish Communist Labor Party-Leninist and tried under Articles 146/1, 168/2, and 169 of the Penal Code. Prosecution documents state that Öktem was accused of participating in throwing Molotov cocktails, burning a city bus, hanging leftist banners in Istanbul, and organizing illegal demonstrations. He is said to be held in Bayrampasa Prison.

Aysel Sarica, *Demokratik Universite Bulteni*
Imprisoned: September 7, 1996

CPJ believes that Sarica's imprisonment may be related to her work as editor of the youth magazine *Demokratik Universite Bulteni* (published by *Alinteri*). She was detained in Izmir on September 7, 1996, along with Serpil Günes, *Alinteri*'s editor, when police raided a vacation apartment where she and several of their *Alinteri* colleagues were staying. Her colleagues said Sarica faced charges under Articles 6, 7, and 8 of the Anti-Terror Law and Article 312 and 155 of the Penal Code in connection with numerous stories that appeared in the magazine. Sarica's lawyer told CPJ that she had been charged in nine separate cases stemming from articles published in *Demokratik Universite Bulteni*, but that the government's August 14 amnesty for editors had suspended those prosecutions.

Sarica was also charged, and ultimately jailed, for membership in an outlawed organization, the Turkish Revolutionary Communist Union (TIKB), a violation of Article 168 of the Penal Code.

According to court documents, the prosecution stated that Sarica had given police a counterfeit identification card on

September 7. Upon determining her true identity, the police learned that she was wanted for allegedly attacking a police officer during a May Day demonstration in Istanbul in 1996.

At the time of the raid, a photograph alleged to show Sarica beating the officer had been published across the country and a warrant had already been issued for her arrest. The prosecution offered the photograph as evidence.

CPJ is concerned that the circumstances of her arrest—albeit on outstanding charges ostensibly unconnected to her work—contribute to and follow from a pattern of harassment of *Alinteri*. No explanation has been given for the police raid on the meeting at which Sarica was detained. Furthermore, CPJ has not been able to verify that the allegedly incriminating photograph is in fact a photograph of Sarica. CPJ continues to investigate the extent to which Sarica's *Alinteri* affiliation was a factor in her prosecution.

**Özden Özbay, *Özgür Ülke*
Imprisoned: November 1996
Released: 1997 [?]**

Özbay, a former editor of the now-defunct pro-Kurdish daily *Özgür Ülke*, was arrested and charged with violating Article 312 of the Penal Code and Articles 6, 7, and 8 of the Anti-Terror Law.

Former staffers of *Özgür Ülke* told CPJ that Özbay had been released, although they provided no information on the date or circumstances.

CPJ has been unable to verify Özbay's status or whereabouts.

Zambia (1)

**Gerard Gatare, Rwandan
National Television
Imprisoned: October 10, 1995**

Gatare, a former editor at Rwandan National Television, was arrested and later imprisoned in Kabwata Central Prison in Lusaka. Early in 1995, Gatare, fearing for his life, had fled to Zambia from a refugee camp outside Rwanda. No charges have been brought against him. His arrest came after a Rwandan government minister visited Zambia, reportedly bringing a list of "wanted" Rwandan intellectuals with him. He had been awarded the 1994-95 Fulbright Hubert Humphrey Fellowship for International Journalists.

CPJ's 1997 Turkey Campaign: Background and Chronology

by William A. Orme, Jr.

Turkey has been a preoccupation of the Committee to Protect Journalists for many years. CPJ sent several high-level missions to the country earlier in the 1990s and devoted substantial staff resources to documenting and responding to press freedom violations there—more, in fact, than for any other single country.

In June 1997, CPJ's board of directors decided to make Turkey CPJ's greatest immediate priority. The number of journalists in jail was again setting world records—CPJ had documented an extraordinary 78 cases of imprisonment at the beginning of the year, many of them long-term sentences for reporting and opinion pieces about Kurdish separatism. In the spring of 1997 two more journalists had been jailed, two were detained and tortured, and eight other reporters and editors from leading dailies had been summoned to court. Police who had been arrested for beating a journalist to death in 1996 were openly refusing to appear for trial. An independent television station was attacked by unidentified gunmen feared to have connections to the powerful foreign minister, True Path Party boss and former prime minister Tansu Çiller, whose allegedly corrupt business dealings were being subjected to aggressive media scrutiny. The year-old coalition regime led by Prime Minister Necmettin Erbakan of the pro-Islamist Welfare Party, after reneging on campaign promises to remove strictures on freedom of expression, was now courting alliances with Nigeria's Abacha, Libya's Qadhafi, and other foreign leaders notorious for their ruthless suppression of independent media.

Alarmed at these trends, Turkish journalists were seeking more visible public support from CPJ and other Western press groups—

William A. Orme, Jr. *is the executive director of the Committee to Protect Journalists. Before joining CPJ in 1993, he covered Latin America for 15 years as a magazine editor and correspondent for* The Washington Post, The Economist, *and other publications. He is the author of* Understanding NAFTA: Mexico, Free Trade and the New North America *(University of Texas Press, 1996), and the editor of* A Culture of Collusion: An Inside Look at the Mexican Press *(University of Miami North-South Center Press, 1997).*

and urging us to come.

In July, using resources from a new CPJ Emergency Response Fund (underwritten by a grant from the Knight Foundation), CPJ sent a high-profile delegation to Turkey for meetings with the president, prime minister, other senior cabinet officers, influential minority party leaders, and local journalists.

Led by vice chairman Terry Anderson, the CPJ delegation included board members Peter Arnett of CNN and Josh Friedman of *Newsday*, Executive Director Bill Orme, and Middle East program coordinator Joel Campagna. Arnett's celebrated coverage of the Gulf War gave him great credibility in Turkey as a CPJ representative. Friedman's knowledge of the country—he had traveled throughout Turkey for a 1990 CPJ report on press freedom abuses there—further strengthened the CPJ team. As our spokesman, Anderson was especially effective. His seven years as a hostage in Lebanon had been covered closely by the Turkish press. Anderson's personal experience with terrorism—and his insistence that terrorism should never be a pretext for censorship—effectively refuted the assertion by Turkish officials that Western free speech advocates simply do not comprehend the security threat presented by armed extremists.

Our goal was to get imprisoned journalists out of jail and halt further prosecutions of editors, reporters, and opinion writers. CPJ's efforts so far have been instrumental in securing the release of seven imprisoned newspaper editors, all of whom were facing another two to 10 years in jail. The new Turkish government has pledged further to amend or eliminate the many provisions of its criminal code which are used to prosecute journalists for their work. It also largely ceased new prosecutions of journalists. Still, as of October 15, at least 45 journalists were in jail, far more than in any other country. And as the Turkish parliament reconvened in October, it remained uncertain whether the minority coalition government of Prime Minister Mesut Yilmaz has the political ability or will to implement the sweeping press freedom reforms it has promised.

In order to raise awareness in the United States and to underscore for Turkish authorities the depth of concern among U.S. journalists, CPJ first undertook an intensive publicity campaign in the American news media about the Turkish issue, generating editorials in more than a dozen leading American newspapers. This aspect of the campaign later proved invaluable in meetings with officials in Ankara: The press clips showed that this issue—the jailing of journalists, the suppression of free speech—was defining Turkey in the eyes of the media in the United States, the country's major supplier of economic and military aid and chief supporter of Turkish membership in the European Union.

CPJ was warned by many experts in Turkish affairs that the government would prove impervious to pressure from foreign press freedom advocates. European journalists' groups and international human rights organizations had tried and failed to exact concessions from Erbakan and from Çiller before him. There were doubts about whether a CPJ delegation would even be received by Turkish leaders. However, both the prime minister and foreign minister indicated through aides that they would agree to discussions in Ankara with CPJ, as did President Suleyman Demirel, the ostensibly powerless but enormously influential head of state. At that point, though, it was becoming clear that the Erbakan-Çiller government could not survive much longer. Opposition parties were intensifying demands for a criminal investigation of Çiller and—more important—the staunchly secular and coup-prone military was in open rebellion against Erbakan's pro-Islamist policies.

An abrupt change in governments in mid-1997 presented a unique opportunity to put press freedom on Turkey's domestic political agenda and urge immediate and longer-term legal reforms. Erbakan, succumbing to pressure from the army, resigned on June 18. Mesut Yilmaz, leader of the center-right Motherland Party, was tapped by President Demirel to form a new government. In naming Yilmaz—a moderate but somewhat colorless figure who has earlier served two brief stints as prime minister—Demirel was deliberately returning power to Turkey's secular mainstream and sending the Welfare-True Path coalition into political exile.

The army high command was presumably pleased, but the new Yilmaz government still faced a vote of confidence with less than a parliamentary majority. It needed to demonstrate to skeptics at home and abroad that it was not a docile creature of Demirel and the military, yet did represent a sharp, pro-Western break with the Islamist-oriented Erbakan regime. Through intermediaries, CPJ and the Turkish Press Council suggested to Yilmaz aides that free-ing journalists from jail would be an especially effective and appropriate signal, and requested formal meetings with the new prime minister and senior cabinet officials in Ankara in July.

The word came back that our request would be granted—if the new minority government survived a vote of confidence. CPJ decided to proceed with the mission.

Imprisonment and Censorship

A self-described democracy, Turkey has for decades enforced laws which effectively criminalize independent reporting about military actions and policies and prohibit the written expression of a wide number of views which the government deems seditious. Journalists and political commentators writing in left-wing or Kurdish-oriented periodicals have been the principal targets, but scores of mainstream reporters and editors—as well as many lead-ing poets, novelists, and playwrights—have been prosecuted and imprisoned as a result of these laws. The statutes are broadly and vaguely worded, and enforcement is highly selective and arbitrary. Prosecuting magistrates have great discretionary power and, seem-ingly, significant political autonomy. State security courts maintain a parallel system of enforcement.

In the cosmopolitan circles of Ankara journalists and Istanbul's literary elite, these prosecutions are seen as an anachronistic, unpredictable, and sometimes literally Kafkaesque fact of Turkish intellectual life. It is a world in which a straightforward news dis-patch from the southeastern border zone can provoke an unexpected criminal prosecution and swift conviction a full year later, where a column about Kurdish cooking or folklore can be seized as an example of terrorist propaganda, where a composer can be sent to jail for reading aloud in court passages from *The Trial*.

The journalists jailed at the beginning of 1997 were exception-al in number, but typical in their political profile and the nature of their alleged infractions. Most of the 78 had been convicted of alleged membership in proscribed organizations, a charge fre-quently made against journalists whose writings or whose publications are deemed sympathetic to the Kurdistan Workers' Party (PKK) and other separatist or leftist insurgents. Others were imprisoned for "aiding" one of these illegal organizations with writings classified as "separatist" or "terrorist propaganda." Still others were jailed without ever having been formally charged. Whatever the purported reason, the Committee to Protect Journalists considers such prosecutions indefensible. They are clear violations of the right "to seek and impart information and ideas through any media and regardless of frontiers," as guaranteed by the Universal Declaration of Human Rights, to which Turkey is a signatory.

Violent repression has also been a problem. Over the past decade, at least 20 Turkish journalists were murdered as a direct result of their work. Reporters foraying into areas of military engagement in the Southeast were harassed, threatened, and subjected to arbitrary detention, all in a generally successful effort to suppress field reporting about the counterinsurgency campaign against the guerrilla forces of the PKK. In 1990, a CPJ fact-finding mission to Turkey led by Josh Friedman produced an extensive report, titled "Forced Restraint," documenting and analyzing the problems faced by local journalists.

Those problems became even more acute: By the end of 1993, at least 19 Turkish journalists were serving time in prison as a direct result of their published reporting or political opinions. Only China held more journalists in jail.

In 1994, the criminal prosecution of journalists accelerated. As civil warfare escalated in the heavily Kurdish southeast, the rightist True Path government of Prime Minister Çiller responded with aggressive enforcement of articles of the Penal Code and the Anti-Terror Law which effectively labeled any independent reporting or sympathetic political commentary about the Kurdish insurgency as "separatist propaganda" or even "terrorism." By the end of the year CPJ had documented a stunning 74 cases of journalists in jail, more than in the next four worst-offending countries combined. In part due to the resulting international outcry, especially among Europeans who cited this crackdown as an argument for denying Turkey entry into the European Union, some of these journalists were released before serving their full sentences. Still, at the close of 1995, Turkey held 51 journalists in prison—again, far more than any other country.

In diplomatic travels outside Turkey, the U.S.-educated Çiller presented herself as a pro-Western reformer who was by her account holding Islamic fundamentalist forces at bay while keeping military hard-liners in check—though she was lamentably unable to withstand military pressure for "thought crimes" prosecutions. Inside the country, however, she was widely reviled as repressive and corrupt and considered directly responsible for the campaign of repression against a press which had begun to subject her government and her family business dealings to unusually close scrutiny. In 1995, Walter Cronkite and Kati Marton separately undertook CPJ missions to Turkey, during which they met with Çiller. Cronkite spoke to Çiller about the case of Reuters correspondent Aliza Marcus, who was facing criminal charges for her reporting about counterinsurgency campaigns in southeastern Turkey—reporting classified as inciting "racial hatred." The charges against Marcus were dropped soon after. Marton raised concerns about the jailings of journalists with Çiller and other Turkish officials.

In June 1996, in a turnabout which stunned Turkey's traditional political leadership and infuriated the resolutely secular armed forces, the Welfare Party ticket led by Erbakan emerged as the leading vote-getter—and Çiller deserted her former allies and formed a majority coalition as Erbakan's junior partner. The prosecutions of journalists continued to rise under the Erbakan-Çiller regime, reaching 78 documented cases by the end of the year.

CPJ's Turkey Campaign Strategy: 1996-1997
CPJ's strategy in 1996 was to first focus worldwide attention on one emblematic case—the sentencing to a 15-year term of a widely respected newspaper editor, Ocak Isik Yurtçu—and then press the government to free him along with others who have been imprisoned for similar offenses.

In 1994, Yurtçu had been sentenced to 15 years and 10 months in prison as editor of the pro-Kurdish daily *Özgür Gündem*, which was previously forced to close. He was convicted by a state security court under provisions of the Anti-Terror Law and Penal Code for news articles that appeared in the newspaper during his brief stint as editor. Although he was urged by colleagues to leave the country before the trial and then again before his sentencing, Yurtçu rejected exile and chose to remain in his country to fight against the injustice.

On November 26, 1996, the Committee to Protect Journalists

gave Yurtçu its International Press Freedom Award. It was presented to him in absentia by Terry Anderson, who spoke movingly of the personal toll inflicted by imprisonment. The awards ceremony at New York's Waldorf-Astoria Hotel marked the beginning of an intensive CPJ campaign to free Yurtçu and to bring to light the predicament of all independent Turkish journalists. More than 300 editors, columnists, broadcasters, reporters, and news executives signed petitions calling for Yurtçu's released. Other international journalism organizations soon followed suit, honoring Yurtçu with more awards and further raising the profile of the case of the imprisoned editor within Turkey and abroad.

After the November ceremony, CPJ addressed numerous appeals to Turkish government officials, urging Yurtçu's release. In January 1997, Kati Marton, Bill Orme, and Joel Campagna met in Washington with Ambassador Nuzhet Kandemir to present him with the signed petitions on Yurtçu's behalf and to express CPJ's concern about the escalation of prosecutions against journalists. The Turkish diplomat acknowledged that many leading Turkish journalists and some government officials agreed with CPJ that Yurtçu should never have been prosecuted, but questioned the accuracy of CPJ's information about other imprisoned journalists. The CPJ representatives presented Ambassador Kandemir with a then-unpublished, detailed list of 78 cases of journalists who according to CPJ's information were in jail as of January 1 for alleged crimes related directly to their work. Ambassador Kandemir agreed to CPJ's request to present the list to the Justice Ministry for its internal review and to report back its findings to CPJ.

To sustain attention on Turkey, CPJ made the country a principal focus of the March 1997 release of its annual report, *Attacks on the Press in 1996*. With Turkey leading the list of countries that imprison journalists for the third straight year, the deteriorating press freedom situation there was spotlighted in the extensive U.S. and international press coverage of the report. On May 3, World Press Freedom Day, CPJ named Prime Minister Erbakan to its annual list of Top Ten Enemies of the Press, generating further international press attention and prompting widespread commentary in the Turkish media.

In June, CPJ's board of directors, led by incoming chairman Gene Roberts, decided to send an emergency mission to Turkey.

Politically, the timing was problematic: We had no firm assurances about which government would end up in power after Erbakan and whether its leaders would agree to see us. But the political turbulence also worked in CPJ's favor. Prime Minister Erbakan's resignation on June 18 and President Suleyman Demirel's subsequent offer to Mesut Yilmaz to form a new coalition provided a unique opportunity for CPJ to persuade an incoming government to put press freedom at the top of its agenda—and to let Yurtçu and others out of jail.

CPJ Mission Chronology: July 13-16, 1997
On July 13, the day after the Yilmaz government was confirmed in office by a vote of confidence, the CPJ-led delegation began a series of talks with the president, the prime minister, and other officials of the new administration. Deputy Prime Minister Bulent Ecevit, Justice Minister Oltan Sungurlu, and Foreign Minister Ismail Cem, along with the leaders of the major political parties supporting the Yilmaz coalition, agreed to meet with the international delegation on the first working day of the new government.

The foreign delegation included three executive directors—of CPJ, the Vienna-based International Press Institute (IPI), and Reporters Sans Frontières of France. Spokesman Terry Anderson opened each of our meetings with a statement urging the government to expedite the release of as many as possible of the 78 imprisoned journalists, including Ocak Isik Yurtçu; to undertake sweeping long-term legal reforms; and to put a stop to police violence against the working press.

Oktay Eksi, a prominent Istanbul columnist and chairman of the Turkish Press Council, an independent centrist journalism organization, acted as the host for the visiting delegation, voicing support in the meetings for the intervention of foreign journalists and playing a key role in negotiating for appointments. Other participants included Sebnem Senyener, New York bureau chief of the Turkish dailies *Sabah* and *Yeni Yuzyil*, who served as a consultant to CPJ; Johann P. Fritz, Peter Goff, and Christian Ultsch of IPI; Robert Menard, Nadire Mater, and Ragip Duran of Reporters Sans Frontières; and Emer Ersoz of the Turkish Union of Newspaper Owners.

Day 1
July 13, 1997
President Suleyman Demirel: An Amnesty Offer

The delegation held an open meeting with President Demirel at the president's ornate Ankara offices in the presence of scores of print and broadcast journalists. Demirel, a veteran politician and former prime minister, is perhaps Turkey's best-known statesman. Foreign human rights advocates with whom he had met often in the past said that while he expressed sympathy for their goals, he had never committed himself to a meaningful reform of the country's freedom of expression restrictions.

After Yurtçu was honored with CPJ's 1996 International Press Freedom Award last November, Demirel privately informed a visiting group from the Turkish Press Council that he would be willing to grant Yurtçu a presidential pardon, but could do so only on medical or other non-political grounds. Yurtçu, despite his ill health, refused the offer, insisting that any pardon should include implicit recognition that the original prosecution and conviction were unjust and should be extended as well to other less-celebrated imprisoned journalists.

Despite the largely symbolic status of the Turkish presidency, Demirel had in the weeks before the meeting displayed his continuing political strength. In choosing Yilmaz instead of then-foreign minister Tansu Çiller, who had asked to lead a new government, the president had in effect ousted the Welfare-True Path coalition and reinforced his credentials as a committed defender of Ataturk's secularist legacy. In the meeting with CPJ, Demirel was both cordial and blunt, decrying restrictions on press freedom generically but defending what he called Turkey's right to take harsh measures against "separatists" and "terrorists." Demirel said he recognized that Turkey's record on press freedom was cause for "sorrow" and said he was committed to "protecting journalists and journalism... and freedom of thought." Yet he suggested that the prosecutions of journalists were still a legitimate prerogative of the courts: "We are trying to preserve justice and the proper functioning of the judiciary."

Terry Anderson, speaking for the group, asked Demirel to take a leadership role in support of a comprehensive legal reform of Turkey's harsh Anti-Terror Law and Penal Code and amnesty legislation for Yurtçu and other jailed journalists. Delegation members raised concern over the numerous incidents of police violence against journalists and asked Demirel to state publicly that the policemen indicted for the January 1996 murder of *Evrensel* journalist Metin Goktepe should be forced to appear at the trial. Demirel replied only that those responsible for the killing "should be punished."

CPJ executive director Bill Orme gave Demirel the hundreds of signed appeals from leading U.S. journalists and news media executives urging Yurtçu's release gathered at its November 1996 International Press Freedom Awards ceremony. Demirel reiterated publicly his former private offer to grant a presidential pardon to Yurtçu on humanitarian grounds, and said he intended to ask the prime minister for the required legal documents.

Justice Minister Oltan Sungurlu: The Hard Line
In his first official meeting as the Minister of Justice, Oltan Sungurlu made it clear that even members of the new government were willing to defend the imprisonment of journalists. A career justice ministry functionary charged with enforcing laws against journalists, Sungurlu could not argue—as could some of his colleagues in the new cabinet—that this was a problem he had simply inherited from previous governments. Sungurlu's meeting with the CPJ delegation was covered by many members of the Turkish press.

Terry Anderson urged Sungurlu to undertake a comprehensive legal reform that would lead to the release of journalists now in prison and prevent further such prosecutions. He suggested that Sungurlu direct prosecutors under the Ministry's control to use their discretionary authority to decline to prosecute and to expedite the release of journalists on appeal. He also asked for Sungurlu's support of a partial amnesty proposal which was submitted to members of parliament and political party heads in June by the independent Journalists Association of Turkey. The proposal effectively called for a suspension of prison terms of Ocak Isik Yurtçu and other jailed "responsible editors," a term of art for editors who are registered with the government as the person legally responsible for material published in their newspapers. Anderson said that as a democracy, Turkey should eschew the repressive practices toward the press that put it in the company of countries such as China, Burma, and Ethiopia.

Sungurlu, a hard-line conservative from Mesut Yilmaz's Motherland Party, previously served as Justice Minister under the eight-year government of Turgut Ozal, and is known for his legal defense of many of the restrictive changes to Turkey's constitution following the 1980 military coup. The minister was cautious, and often defensive, in responding to the group's demands for reform. Conceding that he had not had the opportunity to discuss the press issues with the cabinet, Sungurlu strongly defended Turkey's use of the Anti-Terror Law, insisting that "journalists in jail are actually in jail for terrorism." He noted that Turkish law forbids insulting the president, parliament, or military forces of Turkey, as well as "terrorist propaganda."

And he expressed doubts about the desirability and likelihood of a broad amnesty of imprisoned journalists, citing significant political obstacles such as the need to repeal Article 14 of the Turkish constitution.

The article, applied in conjunction with Article 87, was inserted into the constitution by the 1980-83 military government; it prohibits amnesty for individuals convicted of offenses that "violate[s] the indivisible integrity of the state,. . . [or] jeopardize[s] the existence of the Turkish State and Republic." Most journalists in prison have been convicted for such offenses under the Anti-Terror Law and Penal Code and would hence be ineligible for amnesty without a constitutional amendment, which requires a three-fifths majority.

When asked why the 11 police officers indicted in the January 1996 murder of journalist Metin Goktepe had failed to appear in court, Sungurlu claimed to be unaware of their failure to appear but termed it "unacceptable." He said that "as in other countries, police should be brought to justice for crimes they commit."

Foreign Minister Ismail Cem: A Former Journalist As Diplomat

In what was the foreign minister's first official session at his residence, Ismail Cem met with the delegation for two hours over lunch. Cem, a career journalist who has worked for several newspapers including *Politika* and *Gunes*, intends to remain a columnist for the daily *Sabah* in spite of his new cabinet post. The minister lamented Turkey's poor record on press freedom and its dubious distinction as the world leader in imprisoning journalists. In a cordial luncheon discussion, Cem said international attention is helpful for those in Turkey who are trying to effect reforms. He acknowledged that Turkey's record on freedom of expression issues is obstructing its quest for European Union membership. He said he was surprised and impressed by the many editorials in U.S. newspapers about the issue, and said he would distribute the editorials to cabinet colleagues. "One journalist imprisoned is too much," Cem said. Yet, like other Turkish diplomats, he expressed doubts about the validity of many of the cases of imprisoned journalists documented by CPJ and other press groups.

Cem was not optimistic about repealing Article 14 of the constitution, given the government's minority status and the extreme sensitivity of any initiative that could be interpreted as a gesture toward Kurdish separatists. He contended that pressure from political constituents was as much of a factor as the military. Terrorism remains a serious problem, he said, and with the ever-mounting toll of draftees lost in combat, many ordinary Turks would be hostile to the proposal.

Still, he said, the government is committed to reform. "If you come back in six months, you will see a lot of changes," said Cem. He said that when parliament reconvened in October the government would initiate efforts for broader legal reform to enhance protection for journalists and to release those remaining in prison. He pledged public support for a partial amnesty for jailed editors, including Yurtçu.

Turkish Democratic Party Leader Husamettin Cindoruk: A Kingmaker

Cindoruk, a veteran politician, heads the tiny, centrist Turkish Democratic Party (TDP). His support is crucial to the Yilmaz coalition government. Cindoruk received the delegation at the TDP headquarters in Ankara for a one hour meeting witnessed by a group of Ankara newspaper reporters. Before throwing his support to Yilmaz's new government, Cindoruk had said his party's chief concern was a commitment to freedom of thought and expression. During the meeting, he reiterated his view that the suppression of press freedom "is the most important problem in Turkey."

Cindoruk said his parliamentary delegation supported passage of the partial amnesty bill for jailed "responsible" editors, as did at least two other parties in the Yilmaz coalition. In response to Terry Anderson, he said confidently that Yurtçu could expect to have his freedom soon: "This is his democratic right, and it will be given back to him as soon as the parliament has time to deliberate."

Day 2
July 14, 1997
Republican Peoples Party Leader Deniz Baykal: Ataturk's Heir
Baykal's Republican Peoples Party (RPP), the party of Mustafa Kemal Ataturk, is not part of the Yilmaz coalition, but gave it crucial support in the vote of confidence. The party vowed support for the limited amnesty initiative, while acknowledging the need for more sweeping changes. "First, I think that we must undertake legal reforms," Baykal told the CPJ group. "But unfortunately, this is not enough to solve all of the problems, because threats against press freedom come from extra-legal forces. I think we must change so many things, including the attitude of the government toward the press."

He added: "We also need a quick solution to find a formula to immediately release those in jail for expression of opinion...As a member of parliament and leader of the RPP, I want to say that the RPP is ready to support any kind of initiative that favors freedom of the press and freedom of thought."

Deputy Prime Minister Bulent Ecevit: A Friend In Court
Considered by many the real political heavyweight of the new government, Ecevit spoke passionately and without prompting of the importance of new guarantees for press freedom. "As a journalist, I suffered imprisonment in the past, and I consider freedom of expression as a vital component of democracy," said Ecevit, a former journalist who served as prime minister in the 1970s. "I am personally disturbed by the number of journalists in jail in Turkey and the physical aggressions against them."

Ecevit said he had met with the prime minister earlier that day to discuss press freedom issues and a plan for government action. He said that the first order of business would be to ensure that the "responsible editors" amnesty bill would be presented for debate before parliament adjourned for its summer recess in August. "Our first step will be to achieve the release of journalists in prison and then to achieve a wider scope of press freedom through legislation," he said. He also stated that reform should not be limited to journalists, but should also include writers and intellectuals. Ecevit noted the example of Ismail Besikci, the well-known academic and writer on Kurdish affairs who has been sentenced to more than 100 years in prison for his writings. The deputy prime minister called his court convictions and imprisonment unacceptable and unfitting of a democracy.

He said he was confident that the jailed "responsible editors" would be released. Ecevit said he supported a broader amnesty for imprisoned journalists, but underscored the political difficulties in passing such a law, given the constitutional impediments.

Prime Minister Mesut Yilmaz

No political novice, Yilmaz served two short stints as prime minister during the last six years and also held cabinet posts in the Ozal government. As leader of the conservative Motherland Party, he led the vocal opposition in parliament against the Erbakan-Çiller coalition. He had been seen by many local political analysts as a cautious and somewhat calculating figure, and Turkish commentators were surprised by his willingness to criticize past prosecutions of journalists and commit his new government to major press freedom reforms.

The jailing of journalists and other restrictions on press freedom "were explained away in the past by the fight against terrorism," Yilmaz said in the meeting with the CPJ delegation. "That was unacceptable then, and it is unacceptable now."

Admitting that Turkey's dubious "record for imprisoned journalists is not a record to be proud of," Yilmaz promised to pursue change on two tracks. The first was support for a limited amnesty for jailed editors who were legally responsible for—and subsequently convicted for—the content of their publications. "For me, it is an issue of responsibility with no crime," Yilmaz said. He acknowledged, though, that the amnesty would help only "a limited number" of imprisoned journalists. He informed the group that his government had already begun work on the proposed law and that it would be presented to parliament within a week.

Second, Yilmaz promised to pursue comprehensive legal reform of the Anti-Terror Law and Penal Code in order to repeal articles that have been used to prosecute journalists for their writing. He also pledged to press for legislative initiatives to amnesty those remaining in prison. Echoing the caveat voiced by other Turkish officials, Yilmaz warned that such a reform is contingent on parliament's repeal of Article 14 of the constitution, a move that would require a three-fifths majority—no easy task for a minority government.

Yilmaz said he would order Interior Minister Murat Basesgioglu to take steps to end police harassment—including violence against working journalists. "I will talk to Murat Basesgioglu," he said, "and give instructions to him to treat journalists like gentlemen of the press, not like terrorists."

"My government is one that will take press issues more seriously than any other, because the deputy prime minister and the foreign minister are both journalists," Yilmaz noted during the one-hour private meeting.

Asked whether he was willing to see his government stand or fall on press reform issues, the prime minister responded, "That is my commitment."

Yilmaz was asked to reiterate the pledges he had made privately to the CPJ delegation to the Turkish press corps, which he did, with even greater emphasis. Immediately following the meeting, he told local reporters that his government would back the amnesty bill for "responsible editors" and begin work on a comprehensive press reform package.

The Prime Minister kept his word. On August 14, the bill was passed by parliament, resulting in the release of six editors, among them Isik Yurtçu. The law effectively suspended the sentences of "responsible" editors for a period of three years, after which time the convictions are dropped. If one of those released by the amnesty commits the same "offense" before the three years are up, he/she will be entitled to serve out the old sentence in addition to any new convictions confirmed by the courts. Observers noted that the prime minister's criticism of the suppression of independent journalism was the most pointed such statement ever articulated by a Turkish prime minister.

Day 3
July 15, 1997
Journalists' Round Table Discussion
Following two days of meetings in Ankara, the delegation traveled
to Istanbul, where we held a two-hour open forum with local jour-
nalists, sponsored by the Turkish Press Council and *Sabah*, one of
Turkey's leading newspapers. The symposium was attended by more
than a hundred Turkish reporters and Istanbul based foreign correspondents. The panelists were Terry Anderson, Peter Arnett, Josh
Friedman, and Bill Orme of CPJ; Johann Fritz of the International
Press Institute; Robert Menard of Reporters Sans Frontières, and
Oktay Eksi of the Turkish Press Council. The discussion focused on
subjects ranging from government censorship of Kurdish issues and
media access to combat zones in southeastern Turkey to the role of
international organizations in the fight for free expression.

The Turkish journalists repeatedly expressed frustration at
their inability to cover the country's biggest story: the PKK-led
separatist rebellion and the army's counterinsurgency campaign.
Arnett compared Turkish censorship to his own experiences with
the U.S. military during the Gulf War, "the most censored war in
modern history." The Turkish army's attempts to suppress and
control news are "unfortunately" typical of most military establish-
ments, he noted.

The local journalists described incidents of harassment, prosecutions, and the forced closure of their newspapers in retaliation for their
coverage of the Kurdish conflict. One journalist who had worked in
the southeast said that after her first day in the office of a pro-Kurdish
newspaper she was summoned by authorities, who formally charged
her with PKK "membership," a serious criminal offense.

The fear of prosecution keeps most journalists from reporting
in or about the southeast, said one veteran editor. "I only censor
news articles on the Kurdish issue," he said. "Otherwise, my colleagues will be put in prison."

Day 4
July 16, 1997
Yurtçu Receives His Press Freedom Award:
CPJ's Visit to Saray Prison
The four-day mission culminated in a dramatic visit to Saray

Prison in the remote town of Tekirdag in northwestern Turkey, where Isik Yurtçu was serving his prison sentence. Approximately 100 journalists accompanied the CPJ delegation, traveling by bus from Istanbul for the two-hour journey. Accompanying them was Yasar Kemal, Turkey's most famous novelist and an outspoken press freedom advocate. (Prosecuted on "separatist propaganda" charges, Kemal had another bond with Yurtçu: In his youth, he had worked in a small newspaper bureau together with Yurtçu's late father.)

The foreign press delegation met for more than an hour with Yurtçu inside the prison, where Terry Anderson presented him with his 1996 International Press Freedom Award. The emotional ceremony was covered live by national television outside the prison and by a pool camera from within the jail.

"We would like to present this award to you for your fight for press freedom in Turkey and to honor you for your courage and integrity," Anderson told Yurtçu upon presenting him the award. "I know that your actions have been taken not just for yourself but for all Turkish journalists and for all Turkish citizens."

"I would like to share this honor with all journalists fighting for press freedom and freedom of expression in Turkey and throughout the world," Yurtçu said. "I hope that not only journalists but everyone imprisoned for their thoughts can win their freedom."

Yurtçu waved his award plaque through the barred prison window, sparking applause from the Turkish press contingent gathered outside. "I have been a journalist for 40 years," Peter Arnett told Turkish reporters covering the story, "and I count today as one of the most important and joyful days of my journalistic career, to see a colleague on the verge of being released from custody."

Exactly one month later, Ocak Isik Yurtçu was freed.

Enemies of the Press:
The 10 Worst Offenders of 1997

On May 3, in conjunction with World Press Freedom Day, CPJ announced its annual list of the top 10 enemies of the press worldwide. Those who made the list this year, as in the past, earned the dubious distinction by exhibiting particular zeal for the ruthless suppression of journalists. For the second consecutive year, the leader of Algeria's Armed Islamic Group took first place on a roster that includes a number of repeat offenders and a troubling cast of newcomers.

Antar Zouabri, Algeria
Zouabri, head of the militant Armed Islamic Group (GIA), ensured that Algeria remained the most dangerous place in the world for journalists. Under his leadership and that of his predecessor, Abu Abdul Rahman Amin, who was killed in 1996, the GIA has waged an unprecedented campaign of assassination that has claimed the lives of 59 journalists since the brutal civil conflict began in 1992. "Those who fight with the pen shall die by the sword," warns the GIA, creating fear in a press corps trying to continue its work under impossible conditions.

President Jiang Zemin, China
Jiang has waged a continuing battle against all independent reporting, threatening to close down one-third of all publications as part of a crackdown on press that fail to toe the Communist Party line—a harsh reminder that the media's only role is to be the party's mouthpiece. Jiang made it clear that press freedom in Hong Kong would be greatly constrained after China took over on July 1.

President Fidel Castro, Cuba
Castro has continued his relentless harassment of independent journalists, using tactics such as organized demonstrations outside journalists' homes. Castro's security police routinely detain journalists and steal their effects and money, while threats of reprisals

instill fear in their families, neighbors, and colleagues. Under Castro's rule, Cuba is the only country in the Western Hemisphere that tolerates no free or independent domestic journalism.

Gen. Sani Abacha, Nigeria

Abacha has escalated his vicious tactics to decimate the country's once-thriving independent press and has driven scores of journalists into exile. He ended 1996 with a rash of detentions of journalists for their critical coverage of the government and the establishment of a press court solely for the prosecution of journalists. The assassination in broad daylight of the wife of *Concord* publisher and Nigerian president-elect Moshood Abiola and the attempted assassination of *Guardian* publisher Alex Ibru illustrated the lengths to which Abacha will go to silence the media. The continued imprisonment of *The Sunday Magazine* founder and editor Christine Anyanwu in the face of an international appeal for her release demonstrates his contempt for press freedom.

Prime Minister Necmettin Erbakan, Turkey

Erbakan maintained Turkey's pattern of repression of independent journalists. The press remained under threat from the sweeping provisions of the Anti-Terror Law and the Penal Code, which permit the arrest and prosecution of journalists for critical reporting on the government's ongoing conflict with Kurdish insurgents. Broadening his assault, Erbakan increasingly subjected journalists to arbitrary detention and trial for expression of unfavorable political opinions. Under Erbakan's regime, 78 journalists were in jail at the beginning of 1997—more than in any other country.

President Alexander Lukashenko, Belarus

Lukashenko has bullied the press with Soviet-era tactics, tightening his stranglehold by shutting down independent media and publicly denouncing journalists. He expelled Russia's best-known independent television bureau chief for "distorted coverage." In March, before signing an integration agreement with Russia, he instituted prior censorship of television broadcasts and blocked the dissemination of information "deemed harmful to the interests of Belarus."

Prime Minister Meles Zenawi, Ethiopia

Meles has waged a deliberate campaign to restrict press freedom, inflicting harassment, censorship, arrest, and months-long detention on journalists, as the total of 104 documented imprisonments in Ethiopia in the last four years attests. At the end of January 1997, for the fourth consecutive year, more journalists were in prison in Ethiopia than in any other African country.

President Suharto, Indonesia

Suharto continued to stifle any independent press, banning and censoring both foreign and local publications at will, and permitting the severe beatings of journalists covering demonstrations against his suppression of political opposition. He ignored international appeals for the release of imprisoned leader of the independent journalists union, Ahmed Taufik, and his colleague Eko Maryadi—instead further isolating them by frequent moves to increasingly remote prisons.

Senior Gen. Than Shwe, Burma

Chairman of the State Law and Order Restoration Council (SLORC), Than Shwe kept the media under tight control with a barrage of laws restricting the flow of information. Writing or saying anything to "disrupt and deteriorate the stability of the state" brings a 20-year prison sentence; owning or using a fax machine or modem, 15 years. Jamming of BBC and Voice of America Burmese-language broadcasts effectively denied Burmese citizens access to any independent, reliable information on developments in their country.

President Sali Berisha, Albania

Berisha, until recently the West's favorite East European anti-communist, adopted his predecessors' tactics by muzzling the press during a state of emergency he declared in March to quash mass public protests over failed pyramid investment schemes. Berisha's dreaded secret police raided and then torched the newsroom of the main opposition daily, *Koha Jone*. Journalists, beaten and intimidated, were forced to flee the country or seek refuge in foreign embassies in Tirana. Continued attacks on journalists and seizure of critical publications belied his claim to have lifted censorship.

The 1997 International Press Freedom Awards

The International Press Freedom Awards are given annually by CPJ to journalists around the world who have courageously provided independent news coverage and viewpoints under difficult and often dangerous conditions. To defend press freedom, award winners have risked arrest, imprisonment, violence against themselves and their families, and even death.

The following six journalists received awards on October 23 in New York City at the Seventh Annual International Press Freedom Awards ceremony:

Publisher and editor in chief of the now-defunct national news weekly *The Sunday Magazine*, **Christine Anyanwu** was arrested on May 31, 1995, because of articles she had published reporting that there was no evidence of an alleged plot to overthrow Nigeria's military regime headed by Gen. Sani Abacha. The regime had used the allegation to round up political opponents who challenged Abacha's annulment of the June 12, 1993, presidential elections. *The Sunday Magazine* also had published a list of people who had been wrongfully arrested at that time. Charged as an "accessory to a treasonable felony," Anyanwu was tried before a secret military tribunal and sentenced to life in prison. Three other journalists—George Mbah, assistant editor of *Tell* magazine; Ben Charles Obi, editor of *Weekend Classique*; and Kunle Ajibade, editor in chief of *TheNEWS*—were also tried, convicted, and sentenced with Anyanwu on the same charges. After an international protest and campaign for their release was initiated by CPJ, the sentence was commuted to 15 years.

Anyanwu, a former state commissioner of information and a well-known energy correspondent and diplomatic/foreign correspondent on Nigerian television, founded *The Sunday Magazine* in 1990. She received a master's degree in mass communications from Florida State University in 1979, and is the mother of two children. She is in deteriorating health after more than two years in prison, much of that in dank solitary confinement and without needed medication. Reports indicate that Anyanwu is in danger of losing her sight if she does not receive specialized treatment available only in eye clinics abroad. (For more on CPJ's campaign to free Christine Anyanwu, see p. 169.)

U.S. correspondent and contributing editor **Ying Chan** and Taiwan bureau chief **Shieh Chung-liang** of the Hong Kong magazine *Yazhou Zhoukan* (Asia Week) were the first journalists to point the way toward the role of Taiwan money in the unfolding investigation into Asian influence on U.S. elections. With Chan investigating the U.S. angle and Shieh reporting in Taiwan, the two wrote an article published on October 25, 1996, reporting that Liu Tai-ying, the powerful business manager of the ruling Kuomintang (KMT) party, had offered $15 million to the Clinton re-election campaign in a meeting with a former White House aide. Their story exposed a nerve in Taiwanese ruling circles, landing them in court. Liu denied that he had made the offer. He sued the reporters and the magazine for criminal libel in a case that for many observers called into question Taiwan's commitment to democracy and became a test case for press freedom in Asia. At stake was a possible two-year jail term and civil damages of $15 million.

Chan, who was then a reporter for the *Daily News* in New York, was born in Hong Kong and came to the United States in 1972 to do graduate work at the University of Michigan at Ann Arbor. Though an American citizen, she was determined to go to Taiwan to stand with her colleague and answer the charges—and risk going to jail. Using skills acquired as a Nieman Fellow at Harvard in 1995, she created a Web site on the case and worked tirelessly to inform an international audience about the libel action.

Veteran journalist Shieh, who holds a master's degree from the University of Minnesota, did the difficult reporting on the KMT in his own country. He broke the story with full awareness of the risk he was taking. The publisher and editor of *Yazhou Zhoukan*, to their credit, supported their reporters and refused to settle the suit out of court. On April 22, a Taiwanese district court ruled in favor of Ying Chan and Shieh Chung-liang, accepting arguments made in an amicus brief filed on behalf of the defendants by CPJ and 10 major U.S. media companies. The acquittal has been widely hailed as a major victory for freedom of the press in Asia.

While Liu Tai-ying has appealed the decision, Chan and Shieh have proven themselves worthy defenders of the finest traditions of press freedom. Their courage sets an example in a region noted for both widespread self-censorship and government intervention in the functioning of the press.

Born Teiti Roch D'Assomption in 1956 in the Ivory Coast, **Freedom Neruda** was inspired as a youth by the writings of the Chilean poet Pablo Neruda and chose his name to symbolize his ideals. He became a teacher after graduation from the University of Abidjan. In 1988 he began his journalism career as a copy editor with the daily newspaper *Ivoir Soir*. Two years later he was an investigative reporter, first with *Ivoir Soir*, then with *La Chronique du Soir*, and next with *La Voie*, where he is currently chief editor.

As a journalist, he has lived up to his adopted name. Freedom Neruda has demonstrated unflinching commitment to the cause of press freedom despite President Henri Konan Bédié's persistent efforts to silence the independent *La Voie*'s critical coverage of the government's policies and the actions of its officials. And *La Voie*, with a daily circulation of 25,000, has become the country's best-selling independent newspaper.

Freedom Neruda's ordeal began on December 18, 1995, when *La Voie* ran his satirical article headlined "He Brought Bad Luck to ASEC," which suggested that the presence of President Bédié at the African Champions Cup final against South Africa may have jinxed the Ivoirien soccer team, which lost the match. The article poked fun at Bédié's election campaign poster, which had proclaimed that Bédié was good luck for the country.

On January 2, 1996, Neruda was arrested on charges of seditious libel. Two of his colleagues, publisher Abou Drahamane Sangaré and reporter Emmanuel Koré, had been arrested 12 days earlier. Each of the three journalists was sentenced to two years in prison for "offenses against the head of state," and *La Voie* was fined and banned for three months. An appeals court later confirmed the sentences. President Bédié in a televised statement promised to pardon the *La Voie* journalists if they agreed to withdraw their appeal to the Supreme Court, but the journalists immediately rejected that course of action as being tantamount to acknowledging they had committed seditious libel. The three were quietly released from prison on January 1 of this year.

Neruda and his colleagues of the Nouvelle Horizons Publishing Group have been subjected to routine arrests, physical assaults, charges of "insulting the dignity of the head of state," and levying of excessive fines. In October 1995, a firebomb destroyed their editorial offices. Freedom Neruda's experiences exemplify those of many of Africa's dedicated independent journalists. He is a victim of one of the region's most pernicious abuses: the use of seditious libel charges to silence the press in democratic states as well as those under single-party rule or military dictatorship.

Under the leadership of editor in chief **Viktor Ivancic**, *Feral Tribune*, a weekly newspaper based in the Croatian city of Split, has enraged President Franjo Tudjman for its independent news coverage, biting lampoons, and satirical political cartoons. In 1996, Ivancic and reporter Marinko Cucic were indicted on charges of seditious libel for an article titled "Bones in the Mixer," which criticized Tudjman's plans to inter soldiers of Croatia's World War II fascist regime alongside their Serb, Jewish, Roma, and Croat victims, buried at the site of a former concentration camp. The criminal charges were brought under new amendments to the penal code that made libeling the president a crime punishable by six months to three years in prison.

CPJ board member James C. Goodale, a noted First Amendment attorney, traveled to Zagreb to present an amicus brief in support of the defendants. In June 1996, the two journalists were acquitted in a victory praised by international and local press freedom advocates. The Croatian government then appealed the acquittal.

At a December 22 hearing, the defense attorneys argued that Tudjman's burial plan had historical parallels in a plan initiated by Francisco Franco, the late Spanish fascist dictator. The judge responded by declaring that he would need to petition the Spanish Justice Ministry for its assessment of the comparison, and adjourned the trial until the court received a response from the Spanish government.

The feisty and irreverent *Feral Tribune* faces a daunting array of other lawsuits. For example, Tudjman's daughter, Nevenka Kosutic, has filed two libel suits against the paper for exposing her commercial activities. Ivancic has been slapped with spurious taxes and fines, and the newspaper has been castigated in official speeches as being the product of "anarchists and heretics" under "foreign influence." *Feral Tribune* news vendors have been attacked, and pro-government thugs burned bundles of the newspaper in the town square.

Ivancic and *Feral Tribune* staff received numerous death threats in response to the newspaper's publication on September 1 of an interview with a former Croatian policeman who confessed to murdering scores of ethnic Serbs during Croatia's war of independence. The confession and the subsequent international attention it received spotlighted the four-year-old *Feral Tribune*, one of the boldest papers in Eastern Europe, and its role as one of a handful of national newspapers outside state control that dare to report on developments generally ignored by the official press.

NTV correspondent **Yelena Masyuk** captured the world's attention when she was kidnapped by Chechen rebels May 10 and held, along with her two crew members, for 100 days in inhumane conditions—most of the time in damp mountain caves. She had covered the Chechen war in 1994 for NTV and had endeavored "to show the Chechen side of the story, to give them a chance to tell their point of view, to show how terrible the war was for civilians and even Russian soldiers," she told CPJ in an interview. Masyuk and NTV provided the world with in-depth coverage of the fighting in the breakaway republic—coverage that earned her Russia's top television awards. It also earned her interrogation and threats from Russia's intelligence services. And two weeks before she was taken captive, a right-wing Russian newspaper, *Zavtra*, carried a Russian colonel's threat to physically harm her for her critical coverage of Chechnya. Although pulled from the Chechen assignment for a time because of this and other threats, Masyuk reluctantly agreed to venture into the secessionist region again in May on the eve of a peace treaty.

Masyuk, cameraman Ilya Mordyukov, and sound engineer Dmitri Ulchev were released on August 18, the 101st day of their captivity—the day of a meeting in

Moscow between Russian president Yeltsin and Chechen president Aslan Maskhadov. Although the identity of her captors and the reason for her release are unclear, one thing is certain: Masyuk is driven by a journalist's need to report the story. "I want the exclusive story, the story that no one else is able to get," she told CPJ. And less than a month after her release, she was off again on assignment to Kamchatka, to report on the high cost but low standard of living in that remote region.

At 31, Masyuk is already a seasoned journalist renowned for her bold and objective reporting. A special correspondent for Russian independent television since 1994, she has, in addition to covering events in Russia's "flash points"—the ethnic conflict zones—reported from Afghanistan, Tajikistan, Pakistan, and Iran. A journalism graduate of Moscow State University, she was a media fellow in 1995 at Duke University's DeWitt Wallace Center for Communications and Journalism. While in the United States in May 1996, she testified before Congress about dangers to journalists in the Chechen war zone. In a region characterized by partisan journalism where few women rise to prominence in the profession, Masyuk is an extraordinary exception.

Ted Koppel was honored with CPJ's **Burton Benjamin Memorial Award** for his lifelong dedication to press freedom. During his 34 years at ABC News, Koppel has upheld the highest principles of professionalism and independence and has been a standard-bearer for press freedom worldwide. His landmark broadcasts from Israel and South Africa are prominent examples of the critical role that frank, independent hard-hitting journalism can play in societies where such practice has been rare or suppressed. His signature program, "Nightline," is one of the few serious broadcast news forums providing daily in-depth coverage of events and issues in countries around the world where the press is under attack or constraint, from Bosnia, to Russia, to the Middle East, to China.

Koppel has refused to underestimate the public's capacity for analytical news coverage. In defiance of conventional wisdom, he has brought hard reporting, tough interviewing, and serious debate to television and shown that press freedom is essential to an informed and educated public.

CPJ also presented a special tribute to **Fred Friendly**. In a distinguished career spanning 60 years, Friendly has been an inspiring and courageous leader. A principal exponent of the importance of a free press in a democracy, he challenged the fledgling television industry to realize its potential to inform and enlighten public opinion. His landmark "See It Now" documentaries with Edward R. Murrow broke new ground with bold programming that unmasked McCarthyism, revealed the shameful plight of migrant farm workers, and set a standard for investigative reporting that endures to this day.

As president of CBS News in the 1960s, he put principle into practice when he resigned in protest over the network's decision to air more profitable sitcom reruns instead of continuing live broadcasts of the U.S. Senate hearings on the Vietnam War. The experience led to his resolve to promote the concept of non-commercial television, and he became the driving force behind the creation of the Corporation for Public Broadcasting.

As a journalism educator at Columbia University later in his career, he took his powerful dictum—"to make the agony of decision-making so intense that you can escape only by thinking"—from the classroom to the American public and beyond in the Columbia University Media and Society Seminars television series. Those programs examined the complexity, role, and responsibility of the news media and have profoundly broadened the public's understanding of its obligations in a democratic society, and of the importance to the nation of a free press.

✂✂✂✂✂✂

Following are Ted Koppel's remarks upon receiving the Burton Benjamin Memorial Award for distinguished achievement in the cause of press freedom. The award honors the late CBS News senior producer and former CPJ chairman, who died in 1988.

I have heard wonderful things about Bud Benjamin throughout my professional life. I never worked for him; but nothing would please me more than to think that my selection for this award, which bears his name, would also have his approval. To members of the Committee, who have honored me this evening, and to the rest of you, who've contributed your financial support and your presence here: To all of you, in other words, I can think of no better way to express my appreciation than by keeping my remarks brief. Which I will do.

What I have to say doesn't require a great deal of elaboration. It looms inescapably before us. It is as clear as them and us. They function, when they can, at the risk of their freedom and often their lives. Many of my friends and colleagues here this evening have worked in dangerous places and have certainly taken risks; but the danger has rarely if ever come from our own government. The risks we took tended to be overseas. We could always come home.

And yet, in some respects, journalism in America today may be in greater peril than in some of the more obviously dangerous places that are so clearly inhospitable to our profession. We celebrate tonight the men and women whose dedication to the collection and distribution of facts threatens their very existence. When they antagonize those with money, political power, and guns, they risk their lives. *We*, on the other hand, tremble at nothing quite so much as the thought of boring our audiences. Antagonizing the rich and powerful is our bread and butter. Far from involving any great risk to our safety, it is one of the more reliable paths to professional advancement. The preferred weapons of the rich and powerful here in America are the pollster and the public relations consultant. But they are no threat to the safety of journalists. Our enemies are far more insidious than that. They are declining advertising revenues, the rising cost of newsprint, lower ratings, diversification, and the vertical integration of communications empires.

They are the breezier, chattier styles insinuating themselves onto the front pages of our more distinguished newspapers. They are the fading lines between television news and entertainment. There is, after all, a haunting paradox in the notion that, even as we honor journalists abroad for "risking personal and political peril in upholding the highest standards of their profession," their own stories and the stories they cover are increasingly unlikely to lead any of our broadcasts or appear on any of our front pages. We celebrate their courage even as we exhibit increasingly little of our own. It is not death, or torture, or imprisonment that threatens us as American journalists, it is the trivialization of our industry. We are free to write and report whatever we believe is important. But if what is important does not appeal to the reading or viewing appetites of our consumers, we'll give them something that does. No one is holding a gun to our heads. No one lies awake at night, dreading a knock on the door. We believe it to be sufficient excuse that "we are giving the public what it wants."

We have the responsibility to do more: To focus on foreign events and to explain to the American public how and why those events have an impact on us; to resist and reject the comfortable illusion that Americans don't care about what's happening overseas. They don't care only because they've been lulled into believing that what happens overseas will have no real impact on their own lives. We need to help our readers and viewers find their way through the blankets of fog laid down by spin doctors and press secretaries, media advisers and public affairs officers. We react too much and anticipate too little. We struggle to be first with the obvious. The more important events of the last couple of years have not been the O.J. Simpson trial and the death of Princess Diana.

We have more tools at our disposal and we are more skillful at applying them than any previous generation of journalists. But we're afraid of the competition; afraid of earning less money; afraid of losing our audience. They face death and torture and imprisonment, and we are afraid.

That cannot continue to be the case. Those of you assembled here tonight are the very best of our profession. You cannot allow that to continue to be the case. Because it is only when each of us accepts the challenge to reinvigorate what we do with a genuine sense of mission that we can sustain the hope that American journalism will remain a shining example to the rest of the world.

International Press Freedom Award Winners 1991-1996

1991
Pius Njawe, *Le Messager*, Cameroon
Wang Juntao and Chen Ziming,
Economics Weekly, China
Bill Foley and Cary Vaughan, United States
Tatyana Mitkova, TSN,
former Soviet Union
Byron Barrera, *La Epoca*, Guatemala

1992
David Kaplan, ABC News, United States
Muhammad *Al-Saqr, Al-Qabas*, Kuwait
Sony Esteus, Radio Tropic FM, Haiti
Gwendolyn Lister, *The Namibian*, Namibia
Thepchai Yong, *The Nation*, Thailand

1993
Omar Belhouchet, *El Watan*, Algeria
Doan Viet Hoat, *Freedom Forum*, Vietnam
Nosa Igiebor, *Tell* magazine, Nigeria
Veran Matic, Radio B92, Yugoslavia
Ricardo Uceda, *Si*, Peru

1994
Iqbal Athas, *The Sunday Leader*, Sri Lanka
Aziz Nesin, Turkey
Yndamiro Restano, Cuba
Daisy Li Yuet-Wah, Hong Kong
  Journalists Association, Hong Kong
In memory of staff journalists, *Navidi*
  Vakhsh, Tajikistan

1995
Yevgeny Kiselyov, NTV, Russia
José Rubén Zamora Marroquín,
  Siglo Veintiuno, Guatemala
Fred M'membe, *The Post*, Zambia
Ahmad Taufik, Alliance of Independent
  Journalists (AJI), Indonesia
Veronica Guerin, *Sunday Independent*, Ireland

1996
Yusuf Jameel, *Asian Age*, India
J. Jesús Blancornelas, *Zeta*, Mexico
Daoud Kuttab, Internews Middle East,
  Palestinian National Authority
Oscak Isik Yurtçu, *Özgür Gündem*, Turkey

Burton Benjamin Memorial Award

1991
Walter Cronkite
CBS News

1992
Katharine Graham
The Washington Post Company

1993
R.E. Turner
Turner Broadcasting System Inc.

1994
George Soros
The Soros Foundations

1995
Benjamin C. Bradlee
The Washington Post

1996
Arthur Ochs Sulzberger
The New York Times

How CPJ Investigates and Classifies Attacks on the Press

CPJ's research staff investigated and verified the cases of press freedom violations described in this volume. Each account was corroborated by more than one source for factual accuracy, confirmation that the victims were journalists or news organizations, and verification that intimidation was the probable motive. CPJ defines journalists as people who cover news or write commentary on a regular basis. For additional information on individual cases, contact CPJ at (212) 465-1004. CPJ classifies the cases in this report according to the following definitions:

Attacked
In the case of journalists, wounded or assaulted. In the case of news facilities, damaged, raided, or searched; non-journalist employees attacked because of news coverage or commentary.

Censored
Officially suppressed or banned; editions confiscated; news outlet closed.

Expelled
Forced to leave a country because of news coverage or commentary.

Harassed
Access denied or limited; materials confiscated or damaged; entry or exit denied; family members attacked or threatened; dismissed or demoted (when it is clearly the result of political or outside pressure); freedom of movement impeded.

Imprisoned
Arrested or held against one's will; held for no less than 48 hours.

Killed
Murdered, or missing and presumed dead, with evidence that the motive was retribution for news coverage or commentary. Includes accidental deaths of journalists in the line of duty.

Legal Action
Credentials denied or suspended; fined; sentenced to prison; visas denied or canceled; passage of a restrictive law; libel suit intended to inhibit coverage.

Missing
No group or government agency takes responsibility for the journalist's disappearance; in some instances, feared dead.

Threatened
Menaced with physical harm or some other type of retribution.

AFRICA

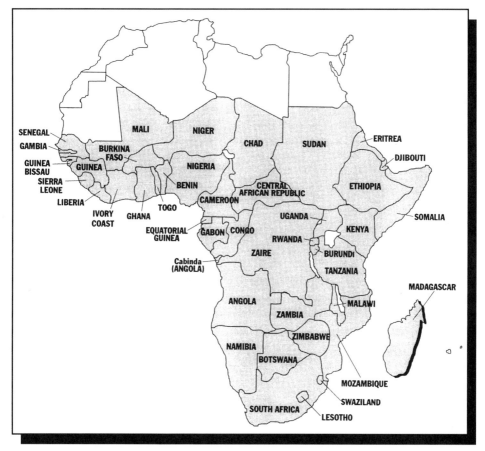

OVERVIEW OF
AFRICA
by Karen Petersen

Political upheaval, civil wars, and fragile democracies presented extraordinary challenges to Africa's independent press. The murder of veteran journalist Appolos Hakazimana was a chilling reminder of the fact that Rwanda continues to be one of the most dangerous countries in the region for journalists to work. Despite threats to their safety, journalists like Ishmael Jalloh, who was killed while covering a battle in post-coup Sierra Leone, continue to risk their lives in order to practice their profession.

In the Democratic Republic of Congo, Laurent Kabila rapidly began consolidating power after driving former dictator Mobutu Sese Seko into exile. Kabila's intolerance for journalists' calls for transparency and accountability and his tendency to target both state and private media for reprisals have bitterly disappointed journalists hoping for a freer climate in which they could practice their profession.

Nigeria has taken the regional lead for imprisoned journalists—17 at the end of the year. The alarming jump beyond last year's eight reflects the escalating brutality of the Abacha regime. Among the prisoners is *Sunday Magazine* editor Christine Anyanwu, a 1997 recipient of CPJ's International Press Freedom Award. (For more information on Nigeria and CPJ's campaign to release Christine Anyanwu, see pp. 139 and 169.) Ethiopia holds 16 journalists in jail, all of them newly imprisoned during 1997. From 1994 through 1996, Ethiopia had the greatest number of journalists in prison of any country in the region. As CPJ documented in its 1996 report on Ethiopia, "Clampdown in Addis," the Meles regime routinely punishes outspoken journalists with sentences ranging from six to 18 months for "false" reporting or inciting "anxieties"

Kakuna Kerina *has been program coordinator for Africa since September 1995. An award-winning documentary filmmaker, she has worked in and traveled throughout Africa for 35 years.*
Karen Petersen *served as a consultant to CPJ's Africa program from September 1997 through January 1998. She is a New York-based journalist and photojournalist with more than a decade's experience overseas covering foreign affairs for a variety of international publications.*
Selam Demeke, *research assistant for Africa, and* **Cornelius Howland,** *who served as a research assistant for Africa in December 1997 and January 1998, contributed significantly to this report.*
CPJ is grateful for the cooperation of a number of press freedom and human rights groups, professional journalists associations, and news organizations across the region, including the International Journalism Center (Lagos), the Media Institute of South Africa, and the West African Journalists Association.

and ethnic strife. Journalists are also detained for weeks or months at a time without charges.

In the midst of environments where the media are relentlessly targeted by governments that reject their calls for accountability and erect formidable obstacles to a free press, the region is home to a remarkable number of vibrant media outlets. Journalists working with Zambia's *Post*, Benin's *Echo du Jour*, *The Nation* in Kenya, *The Independent* in Ghana, and Nigeria's *TELL* and *TheNEWS* deserve praise for their courage and professionalism as they face a daily struggle for survival.

The barrage of criminal libel suits throughout sub-Saharan Africa, used ruthlessly by governments seeking to break the back of the media, places tremendous financial burdens on the independent press. A single libel conviction can force a newspaper to stop publishing or go financially bankrupt. In the Ivory Coast, the government of Henri Konan Bédié has stepped up its prosecutions of journalists sympathetic to the opposition. Although a CPJ campaign led to the release on January 1 of Freedom Neruda, editor of the independent opposition newspaper *La Voie*, along with reporter Emmanuel Koré, and publisher Abou Drahamane, after they had served a year of a two-year sentence for insulting the president, seditious libel suits continue unabated in their country. In October, Neruda received CPJ's 1997 International Press Freedom Award. (For more on Freedom Neruda, see page 103.)

Publications willing to run stories critical of public officials often suffer a loss of revenue when governments pull their advertising. Concerned about offending the state, many private businesses follow suit.

In a region where newspapers and magazines reach only a fraction of the population, the influence of international radio networks such as the British Broadcasting Corporation, Radio France Internationale, the Voice of America, and others who broadcast in numerous African and European languages, is significant. In addition to often being the sole source of international news, foreign radio networks provide local news that does not make it onto state-run broadcasts. In many African countries, the relative affordability of FM radio equipment makes it possible for nongovernmental organizations and private entrepreneurs to invest in broadcasting, but many governments refuse to relinquish control of the airwaves.

Although electronic mail and the Internet have revolutionized information-gathering and dissemination in many African countries, the availability of this technology is limited by high access fees, government regulatory practices, and the scarcity and unreliability of telephone lines. In recent years, a number of large-scale telecommunications infrastructure-building projects have been announced, representing a growing trend toward private foreign investment in the continent's underdeveloped telecommunications industry.

Newspapers in Ghana, Ivory Coast, Kenya, South Africa, Tanzania, Zambia, and Zimbabwe post editions on the Internet, thereby disseminating critical information worldwide and providing a direct link to African communities abroad.

Although the new technologies have significantly benefited African journalists by reversing the historical flow of information, the region's media professionals remain vulnerable because they work in environments with repressive press laws, weak judiciaries, and government officials who target them with impunity.

Angola

In April, after two decades of civil war, former Union for the Total Independence of Angola (UNITA) rebels entered into a power-sharing agreement with the majority Popular Movement for the Liberation of Angola (MPLA) government led by Eduardo Dos Santos. UNITA, under the leadership of Jonas Savimbi, failed to surrender territory or disarm its soldiers as stipulated under the peace treaty, however, and has subsequently faced sanctions imposed by the United Nations Security Council.

Although the constitution provides for freedom of expression and of the press, the government does not respect these rights. Continuing a trend that began during the war, most journalists still work and live in poverty and fear, and self-censorship is common. In addition to the 1995 murder of Ricardo de Mello, editor of the independent newsletter *Imparcial Fax*, last year's murder of Antonio Casemero, a journalist with the state-run Angolan Popular Television remains unsolved.

There were no investments in the private media from the business community, and the media were hampered by the collapse of much of the country's infrastructure. National distribution of newspapers and other publications was virtually impossible. Stepping into the information vacuum, the state attempted to manipulate public opinion by monopolizing the airwaves. Although there are three private weekly and biweekly newspapers, the government runs and tightly controls the only daily newspaper, the only television station, and the major radio station.

In April, the privately owned FM station Radio 2000 in Lubango was banned by the government from broadcasting the Voice of America's Portugal-to-Africa program, "Angola: Linha Directa, Linha Aberta."

Radio 2000 was the only station inside Angola carrying this programming, and is believed by many Angolans to be the most informative and unbiased source of information. This action, taken after the implementation of the new unity government, directly contradicted the government's professed commitment to democracy and freedom of expression.

April 10
Radio 2000 CENSORED

The Lubango-based Radio 2000, a privately owned FM radio station, was banned from broadcasting a Voice of America program called "Angola: Linha Directa, Linha Aberta." The program had been broadcasting daily to Angola from Portugal since late 1996. The government also banned Radio 2000 from sending its own reports to be broadcast on VOA.

CPJ sent a letter to President Jose Eduardo dos Santos strongly protesting the banning of the program and the censorship of the station.

Benin

In February, Benin's parliament adopted a new media law that allows for private ownership of radio and television stations but imposes harsh criminal penalties for libel. Journalists' groups believe that the law spells an end to the relative era of press freedom that began in 1991 when Benin moved from a Marxist/Leninist government to a republic under multi-party, democratic rule. The law, first proposed in 1991, was reworked over the years into its present formulation. In the context of harsher legislation in effect since the colonial era, however, it is considered potentially tolerable.

In the present local context of flourishing independent publications—the fifth weekly to be published in Benin, *Le Point*

Au Quotidien, appeared on the newsstands in August—virtually no one foresees enforcement of the more extreme provisions of the law. Under the new law, insulting the president, foreign heads of state and foreign ministers is punishable by five years in prison or a fine of up to 10 million CFA francs (US$17,700). Those accused of libel or defamation have seven days in which to substantiate their allegations; in the past most cases of defamation were settled through negotiations resulting in retractions or in the right to reply. But many journalists point with satisfaction to the law's authorization of private radio and television broadcasting, also noting that the new statute replaced a 1960 law that was extremely repressive although not fully enforced.

Botswana

Botswana's positive democratic image was tarnished on May 28, when the government released the Mass Media Communications Draft Bill. The legislation mandated the establishment of a separate broadcasting board, a state newspaper registration system, accreditation procedures, and a legislated press council to be appointed and managed by the Ministry of Information. Protests against the draft bill by international and local media and human rights groups successfully pressured the government to hold a meeting with media representatives on July 3, after which the government agreed to table the bill. A task force comprised of government officials and private press journalists was appointed on July 10 to draft a new mass media communications bill.

While Botswana has a free and vigorous print media, repressive laws regarding sedition, treason, defamation, and presidential powers of deportation remain threats to

freedom of expression and political activity. In addition, journalists and individuals have been charged for contravention of clauses of legislation such as the Alarming Publications Act, which prohibits the publication of material that "may create panic or disturb public peace," the National Security Act, which prohibits reporting on classified or confidential information, and the Directorate on Corruption and Economic and Crime Act, which bars the publication of information relating to an ongoing criminal investigation. Two precedent-setting cases currently in Botswana courts invoke the Alarming Publications Act and a law barring defamation or ridicule of the president.

Discussions to end the current government control of the airwaves have been underway since a mass media communications bill was passed last year to allow for private ownership of the broadcast media.

June 4
The Gazette CENSORED

The Botswana Defense Force (BDF) stopped the sale of copies of the independent newspaper The Gazette on the grounds of the Sir Seretse Khama Army Barracks.

The action followed a front-page story published in the May 21 edition titled, "Is The BDF A Family Business?" The article reported that the BDF had reacted angrily to the newspaper's queries about Army Comm. Lt. Gen. Ian Khama's management style.

December 9
Caitlin Davies, *Okavango Observer* LEGAL ACTION
Cobrie Kgaodi, *Okavango Observer* LEGAL ACTION

Criminal Investigation Department (CID) officers ordered Davies, former editor of the now-defunct *Okavango Observer* newspaper, and Kgaodi, who was a reporter for the paper, to report to court to take a plea on charges of "alarming the public" with an article they published two years ago. The article in the September 29, 1995, edition of the *Okavango Observer* reported on violent street gang activity in the northern Botswana town of Maun. Davies said that she had never been formally charged or arrested at the time of publication, but that she had been interrogated along with several other employees of the paper in January 1996.

Kgaodi and Davies obeyed the summons and appeared in court on December 10. They did not make a plea, noting that they had only been given one day's notice for the summons. Their next court appearance was set for February 2, 1998. If convicted they face a sentence of two years' imprisonment, or an unspecified fine, or both.

Burkina Faso

Entering the year with a new national motto of "Unity, Progress and Justice," Burkina Faso's parliament voted overwhelmingly to repeal constitutional provisions which had previously limited President Blase Compaore to two seven-year terms. Viewed as a setback to a tide of democratic reform that had swept the region after the collapse of communism in 1990, the new amendment did not help the cash-strapped country in the eyes of foreign donors. Although the 1990 Information Code, drafted at the same time as the new constitution, provided for freedom of speech and the press, in actuality these freedoms still remain subject to the practice of self-censorship. The independent press includes four dailies, a dozen weeklies, and a monthly news magazine. There are six radio stations and one private television station.

But despite this thriving press, the country's image was tarnished when Moustapha Thiombiano, the president general of the

Horizon-FM radio station—the first independent station broadcasting in Burkina Faso since 1987—was attacked by four supporters of the ruling Congress for Democracy and Progress party. The attack followed the airing of critical commentary on one of the station's call-in programs.

On December 24, four commercial radio stations announced a seven-hour blackout of their stations to protest the government's recent ban on local stations re-transmitting broadcasts from international stations such as Voice of America, the BBC, Radio Vatican, and Radio France International.

February 17
Moustapha Thiombiano, Horizon-FM
ATTACKED

Thiombiano, president general of the independent radio station Horizon-FM, was physically attacked by four supporters of the Congress for Democracy and Progress (CDP), the ruling party, in front of the CDP's offices and at the U.S. Embassy. The attack followed the February 16 broadcast of a call-in program, "Sondage Democratique," during which listeners are invited to voice their opinions on democracy in Burkina Faso.

Because of Thiombiano's fear of government reprisals against news programs, Horizon-FM suspended broadcasting on February 17. It resumed on-air programming on February 19 with an all-music format. In a letter to President Blaise Compaore, CPJ condemned the attack against Thiombiano.

March 14
Horizon-FM CENSORED

The government's Conseil Superieur d'Information (CSI) served Horizon-FM with documents instructing the radio station to suspend the listener call-in programs "Sondage Democratique" and "Ca Ne Va Pas" until the CSI creates regulations governing radio broadcasting.

The ban is believed to be designed to quash the program's broadcasting of anonymous callers' critical comments on government policies.

According to CSI documents, "those who call in under the protection of anonymity are making serious attacks on the honor and dignity of others, and are threatening the public order. The programs mislead the public into thinking that there is freedom without any sense of responsibility."

December 22

Horizon FM Radio CENSORED
Radio Pulsar CENSORED
Radio Maria CENSORED
Energy Radio CENSORED

The Central Information Council (CSI), citing concern for "the sovereignty of Burkina Faso," ordered the four radio stations to stop relaying news broadcasts from the BBC, Voice of America, Radio France International (RFI), and Radio Vatican. The four stations complied immediately.

The CSI said of the re-broadcasts that "manipulation of frequency use poses problems for the editorial responsibility of the station concerned," and noted that foreign radio stations wishing to transmit in Burkina Faso would be required themselves to obtain formal permission from the CSI.

Burundi

Since the assassination of Burundi's first elected head of state in 1993 by a small group of extremist army troops, the population has been decimated by violence, mainly pitting the Tutsi-dominated army against Hutu rebels, with both Hutu and Tutsi civilians caught in the crossfire. In this climate, being part of the independent press is equated with betrayal, and taking an independent stance is extremely dangerous.

Consequently, reporters have begun to work in multi-ethnic teams since the Balkanization of much of the country had made reporting physically impossible for individual journalists from either side. Studio Ijambo set the model for others to follow, and its courageous radio broadcasts reporting on more than 40 massacres involving the national army or armed rebels form the sole coverage of pivotal events that would otherwise have gone undocumented.

Cameroon

President Paul Biya waged an unrelenting assault on the media during the run-up to the second round of multi-party national elections in October, which followed highly flawed spring legislative elections. Repeated violations of the right to freedom of expression undermined the rocky process of democratic transition.

The first half of the year brought continuing harassment of the print media, as the government banned and seized newspapers. Police frequently attacked or harassed vendors selling independent papers, and arrested people reading banned publications. Of 400 registered newspapers, only about 30 published at the start of 1997, and fewer than 10 on a regular schedule. Although constitutional amendments ratified in January 1996 provide for an independent judiciary, corruption and inefficiency in the courts remain serious problems, and the judiciary is subject to political influence. Many print journalists continue to be prosecuted and sentenced to jail for criticizing the government, and some are physically attacked.

While some legal restraints on press freedom—such as pre-publication censorship—have been eased since the country joined the British Commonwealth in

November 1995, the government has added some repressive press laws to the books. Criminal libel and insult laws are favorite weapons against the independent press, and frequent banning orders and prohibitive fines push newspapers toward acute financial difficulty and even insolvency.

The state maintains its firm grip on broadcasting. Radio, which reaches a far wider audience than the print media, is Cameroon's most important medium because of high illiteracy rates and the vicissitudes of newspaper distribution outside major urban centers. Taking advantage of a loophole in the Law on Mass Communications allowing for the establishment of independent broadcast media without as yet establishing regulations for licensing them, five community radio stations began broadcasting in remote areas of the country. Nevertheless, it is highly unlikely that the state monopoly on the broadcast media will be surrendered in the coming year.

January 22
Eyoum Ngangue, *Le Messager Popoli*
IMPRISONED

Ngangue, co-publisher of the satirical independent weekly *Le Messager Popoli*, was arrested at the police station in Douala. He had turned himself in after being summoned on January 21.

Ngangue's arrest is believed to be related to his mocking editorial and cartoons published in the December 1, 1995, edition of *Le Messager Popoli*. He was convicted on October 3, 1996, for "abusing and insulting" the president and members of the National Assembly and for "spreading false news." He was sentenced to a year in prison and fined 300,000 CFA (US$600). The topic of his editorial was proposed constitutional reforms in Cameroon.

After his arrest in January, Ngangue was held until the Supreme Court in Douala granted him bail and he was released on March 31.

February 26
Christian Mbipgo Ngah, *The Herald*
ATTACKED

Ngah, a reporter for the local English-language paper *The Herald*, was arrested, tortured, and beaten for several hours at the Santa Gendarmerie Brigade, and released after promising to stop writing articles critical of former prime minister Achidu Achu or the gendarmerie.

Ngah was hospitalized for injuries resulting from the torture.

March 10
Claude Eyoum Ndoumbe, *Cameroon Tribune*
CENSORED

Ndoumbe, who edits a column called "Society" in the state-owned daily *Cameroon Tribune*, was suspended by the newspaper's director.

Ndoumbe, in an open letter to President Paul Biya, had protested the incarceration of his brother, a journalist with the privately owned satirical weekly *Le Messager Popoli*.

On July 7, Ndoumbe was dismissed from his job after the government sent a letter to the *Cameroon Tribune* accusing Ndoumbe of publishing articles likely to damage the image of the president, as well as Cameroon and its institutions.

March 17
Evariste Menouga, *Hebdo* IMPRISONED

Menouga, editor in chief of the independent newspaper *Hebdo*, was arrested in Yaounde after Defense Minister Philippe Menyea issued a warrent on March 13. The arrest was in connection with an article titled "Rebellion in the Army" published in the March 12 issue.

On March 20, Menouga was convicted of "inciting rebellion within the army" and for "spreading false news," and remanded to the central prison in Keondengui.

At press time, Menouga was still in prison.

May 27
Joseph Nyada Mani, *Le Proces* IMPRISONED

Mani, director of publication for the privately owned newspaper *Le Proces*, was arrested in Yaounde and placed in detention in Nkodengui. He was convicted of defamation and sentenced to six months in prison and 500,000 CFA francs (US$1,000) in damages. Mani's conviction followed the publication, in February 1997, of an article about corrupt activities surrounding the entrance exams at the Teachers' Training Academy.

At press time, Mani was still in prison.

August 18
L'Expression CENSORED
Le Messager CENSORED
Mutations CENSORED
Dikalo CENSORED
La Plume du Jour CENSORED

Copies of five independent weeklies, *L'Expression*, *Le Messager*, *Mutations*, *Dikalo*, and *La Plume du Jour*, were seized by police following the publication of a transcript of a telephone conversation between the minister of state in charge of economy and finances, Edouard Akame Mfoumou, and the secretary general of the Office of the President, Ahamadou Ali. The conversation reportedly was about dissension within the government. The five publications were seized from kiosks and delivery trucks. Authorities gave no official reason for the confiscation.

October 12
Marie Noelle Nguichi, *Le Messager* HARASSED

Nguichi, a reporter with the biweekly paper *Le Messager*, was arrested on the day of the presidential elections by a police officer in a barrack in Yaounde where a voting booth had been set up.

The officer accused Nguichi of being a spy for *Le Messager*. Nguichi was released after being detained for six hours.

October 12
Alain Bengono, *Expression* ATTACKED

During the presidential elections, Bengono, a reporter with *Expression*, was assaulted in front of a voting booth in Yaounde after questioning the booth's supervisor regarding irregular practices he had observed.

October 20
Mutations CENSORED

Security forces confiscated copies of *Mutations* from kiosks and roadstands. The action followed the publication, in that day's edition of the magazine, of an article titled "A Former Putschiste Sows Panic in Etoudi." The article alleged that Captain Guerandi Mbara, one of the instigators of a failed coup in 1984, wanted to seize power again.

Although the June 24 ban against *Mutations* was lifted on July 4, censorship of the magazine has continued.

December 29
Pius Njawe, *Le Messager* IMPRISONED

Njawe, editor of the weekly *Le Messager*, was charged with disseminating unsourced news with the intention of affecting the head of state and undermining national security. Njawe, detained in Douala's central prison, was arrested on December 24 because of an article published in the paper's December 22 edition. The article, written by reporter Franck Esomba, reported that President Paul Biya had possibly suffered a heart attack while at the Cameroon Cup soccer finals. On January 13, 1998, Njawe was sentenced to two years in prison and fined 500,00 CFA francs (US$1000) for "spreading false rumors."

Central African Republic

Reverberations of last year's mutiny and continued political strife plagued the Central African Republic this year. The Inter-African Mission to Monitor the Implementation of the Bangui Agreements (MISAB), a United Nations-authorized African peacekeeping force, was stationed in the country's capital, Bangui, to restore peace and oversee the implementation of key provisions of an African-brokered accord to end the recurring cycle of political, military, and ethnic violence.

The private print media suffered little direct government interference compared to previous years. At least a dozen newspapers publish with varied regularity. The state dominates the broadcast media, and the only licensed private radio stations air music or religious programming.

The primary threat to press freedom is an inefficient and compromised judiciary which, despite constitutional obligations, does not adhere to the principles of due process. The fate of the newly created government appeared uncertain as nine opposition party ministers resigned in protest over the domination of President Patasse's Movement for the Liberation of the Central African People (MLPC) and allied parties. The ministers rejoined the national unity government in August following an agreement between President Patasse and 11 opposition parties. Parliamentary elections are set for August 1998, and presidential elections will be held in 1999.

Congo

The continued fighting between government troops loyal to President Pascal Lissouba and the private militia of the country's former dictator, Gen. Denis Sassou-Nguesso, resulted in the indefinite postponement of the presidential election originally scheduled for July. In October, Gen. Sassou-Nguesso seized Brazzaville, overthrowing President Lissouba, who fled the country. At the close of the year, Sassou-Nguesso announced he was working on a timetable for elections and a return to democracy.

The government monopoly over the broadcast media is not expected to change with the new regime. Although the 1991 constitution provided for freedom of expression and called for the establishment of an independent council to oversee the media and safeguard press freedoms, it has not yet been established.

Rural Radio, a community station in operation since 1976 and once acclaimed by Congolese villagers as their authentic voice, was the latest casualty in the struggle for power between Lissouba and Sassou-Nguesso. Crippled by lack of funds, trained staff, and recording material, the station was reduced to re-broadcasting old shows instead of producing new ones.

AFRICA

The Democratic Republic Of Congo (formerly Zaire)

Zaire ostensibly began a transition to multi-party rule seven years ago, when President Mobutu Sese Seko gave in to the pro-democracy pressures that were sweeping the continent, and announced the end of the one-party state. Since that time, however, there have been more than 10 different governments appointed by Mobutu, and no transition. But in September 1996, a rebellion began in the eastern part of the country and then spread, ultimately leading to the formation of a rebel coalition headed by Laurent Kabila and reportedly backed by neighboring Uganda and Rwanda. By mid-February, a panicky Zairian cabinet had banned all public demonstrations and introduced strict censorship guidelines to quash coverage of the rebellion by the state-owned and private press.

Angered by television footage showing Kabila speaking to cheering crowds in eastern Zaire, Information Minister Kin Kiey Mulumba on February 15 issued a decree banning private radio and television stations from airing political programs and news. Journalists were also banned from publishing information coming from sources other than the Ministry of Defense on the conflicts in eastern Zaire.

In April, angered by reports in the foreign press of the steadily mounting crisis, the Minister of Information announced restrictive measures requiring the reaccreditation of all journalists and the creation of an ethics committee. After eight months of fighting his way across the country, Kabila seized Kinshasa on May 17 and declared himself president of the Democratic Republic of Congo, as Mobutu fled the country for Morocco, only to die of prostate cancer there in August.

In the days following Kabila's victory, much of the staff of public radio and television station OZRT were fired or given off-air assignments, and on May 26, shortly after the new government was formed, the new information minister, Raphael Ghenda, announced a ban on advertising on private radio and television stations. On June 17, state radio reported that the government planned to nationalize the private television network Tele Kin Malebo and take up to 40-percent shares in all the private non-religious television and radio stations. The year ended with Ghenda's announcement that FM stations could no longer rebroadcast programs from foreign broadcasters, who had been a significant source of news for the population.

Dozens of daily newspapers exist in Kinshasa, but only a small percentage of the literate population read them, and few reach the interior. The government owns the national radio and television networks, but reception of both is limited largely to the capital. Regional radio and television stations are tightly controlled by the regional authorities, although private radio and television are developing.

January 14
Michel Luya, *Le Palmares* IMPRISONED

Luya, publisher and director of the opposition weekly *Le Palmares*, was arrested by agents of the National Intelligence and Protection Service. He appeared before the State Security tribunal on January 16 and was charged with "seriously threatening the security of the state."

Luya's incarceration follows the publication, in the January 13 edition of *Le Palmares*, of a series of articles by the Belgian and French media concerning the hospitalization of Zairean President Mobutu Sese Seko. In the same edition, editor Germain Kadima wrote an article titled "Mobutu Signs Deceptive Ordinances," about presidential ordinances involving the restructuring of the army, information which had already been published by the state media.

On January 21, the Interior Ministry issued an order refusing to free Luya after the State Security Court had requested Luya's release from Makala prison. Luya was released on January 24.

January 19
Emmanuel Katshunga, *La Tempete des Tropiques* IMPRISONED

Security Service agents arrested Katshunga, a reporter with the independent newspaper *La Tempete des Tropiques*, at the newspaper's editorial offices. The arrest was in connection with an article Katshunga had written about an army unit called the President's Special Division. The agents told Katshunga that he should not write about the army during the civil war. Katshunga was released on January 27.

January 23
Jean Muadianvita, *La Tempete des Tropiques*, *Umoja*, and *L'Example* IMPRISONED

Muadianvita, a free-lance journalist for the independent newspapers *La Tempete des Tropiques*, *Umoja*, and *L'Example*, was arrested at his home in Mont Ngafula, a county of Kinshasa, by soldiers of the Military Action and Intelligence Service (SARM) on the orders of General Bolozei Ngbudu. Muadianvita was transported to SARM headquarters at Kitambo in Kinshasa, where he was held incommunicado.

The arrest was in connection with a series of articles published in November 1996 about President Mobutu's U.S.-based political lobbyists. The articles reported that the lobbyists were paid to maintain a foreign network that did everything it could to keep Mobutu in power. Muadianvita published a list of these lobbyists and how much Mobutu paid each of them for their services.

Muadianvita's attorney was denied access to his client, and SARM refused to send the journalist to court because he would not reveal his sources.

In a letter to Prime Minister Kengo wa Dondo, CPJ protested the incommunicado arrest of Muadianvita. CPJ has been unable to determine his status since the change in government in Zaire in May.

February 11
Ghislaine Dupont, Radio France Internationale (RFI) HARASSED
Thomas Sotinel, *Le Monde* HARASSED

The acting governor of the town of Kinsangani told Dupont, special correspondent for Radio France Internationale (RFI), to leave the town. The official was acting on orders from the Ministry of the Interior. The ministry accused Dupont of carrying out a "disinformation campaign" on the air. Sotinel, the West Africa correspondent for the French daily *Le Monde*, was also expelled from Kisangani. The two journalists went to Kinshasa the following morning.

February 11
Nepa Bagili Mutita, *La Voix de l'Islam* IMPRISONED

Mutita was arrested on February 11 on charges of spreading false rumors about the civil war and faced up to three years in jail. The journalist, who was also president of the Mouvement National Congolais-Lumumba, had published in his monthly *La Voix de l'Islam* a list of people wanted by rebel leader Laurent Kabila. The list included the names of the president and the prime minister.

February 15
Private Radio and Television CENSORED

The Ministry of Information and Press banned private radio and television stations from "producing, broadcasting or relaying political programmes." The ministry's decree also prohibited private electronic media from broadcasting radio and television newscasts and press reviews. The government justified this action by citing a need to smother enemy propaganda during the civil war.

February 23
Jean-Philippe Ceppi, *Liberation*, BBC
EXPELLED

Zairian authorities expelled Jean-Phillipe Ceppi, a correspondent for the French daily *Liberation* and the French service of the British Broadcasting Corporation (BBC), after detaining him for questioning for 48 hours. Authorities objected to his report, published in the February 21 edition of *Liberation* and broadcast on the BBC, concerning the retreat of the Zairian army during the civil war.

March 3
Television-Kin Malebo CENSORED

The Ministry of Information and Press ordered a three-month suspension of the private television station Television-Kin Malebo (TKM). TKM had refused to comply with the Ministry's decree, which two weeks earlier banned all political programs on private television and radio.

Ngogo Luwow, owner of TKM and a member of the transitional parliament, said that he considered the suspension illegal and intended to ignore it, as he had the initial ban.

March 21
Karen Lajon, *Le Journal du Dimanche*
EXPELLED

Lajon, special correspondent in Lubumbashi

for the French weekly *Le Journal du Dimanche*, was arrested by police at the airport as she was leaving the city. Police interrogated her for an hour and confiscated her notes, then put her on a plane to the capital.

When she arrived in Kinshasa, Lajon was detained for four hours and prevented from telephoning her newspaper's editorial offices or the French Embassy. After an interrogation, police told her that she was being expelled from Zaire because she had been in Lubumbashi without official authorization.

Authorities told Lajon "never to set foot in Zaire again." She was deported to Brazzaville in neighboring Congo, then was forced by Congolese authorities to board a plane to Paris.

April 3
Marie-Laurie Colson, *Liberation* HARASSED
Jean-Jacque Lourane, Radio France Internationale (RFI) HARASSED
Ed O'Loughlin, *The Independent*, *Sunday Times*, Associated Press (AP) HARASSED

Colson, special correspondent of the French daily *Liberation*; Lourane, a reporter with Radio France Internationale; and O'Loughlin, a correspondent for the daily *The Independent*, the Associated Press, and a contributor to the South African weekly *Sunday Times*, were all detained by Zairean authorities at the Lubumbashi airport.

The authorities barred the journalists from entering the city, despite the fact they possessed all the necessary government accreditation and permits. After a night of detention under military surveillance, the journalists were forcibly returned to Kinshasa the following day.

April 21
All foreign journalists LEGAL ACTION

Minister of Information Kin Kiey Mulumba announced restrictive measures on foreign journalists covering Zaire. The measures, which Mulumba said were to ensure journalists' safety, included the re-accreditation of journalists and the creation of an "ethics committee" that would look for "misinformed and unbalanced" articles.

Beginning on April 23, journalists were required to register at the Zaire Press Union. The union would then forward its opinion of the applications to the Information Ministry, which would make the final decision on whether a journalist's accreditation was renewed. The ethics committee, comprised of Zairean journalists, judges, representatives of human rights organizations, and church leaders, was to meet weekly to judge material containing "erroneous information."

September 8
Polydor Moboyayi Mubanga, *Le Phare*
IMPRISONED

Mubanga, director of the opposition daily *Le Phare*, was arrested at his home by four armed and uniformed men. Authorities gave no official explanation for the arrest.

The arrest seemed to be in connection with *Le Phare*'s publication on September 5 of an article that reported on President Laurent Kabila's wish to create a new elite or "special division" presidential guard similar to that of former President Mobutu.

In a letter to Kabila on September 15, CPJ asked that the government make public the reasons for Mubanga's arrest and called for Mubanga's immediate and unconditional release if his arrest was because of his work as a journalist.

Mubanga appeared before an examining judge on September 17 and the charges against him were made public. He was charged with spreading false news and inciting ethnic hatred. He could face up to two years in prison if found guilty on the first charge.

Mubanga was released on November 19.

December 15
Pontien Tshisungu, RTNC IMPRISONED

Tshisungu, a broadcast journalist with the

Democratic Republic of Congo's national television station, RTNC, was arrested and detained at Goma Central Prison. His arrest came after the disclosure of information about an attempted attack on then-Minister of the Interior Mwenze Kongolo when the minister traveled to the Nord-Kivu region and to Rwanda. Tshisungu was a member of Kongolo's entourage during the trip. He had given a first-hand account of shots being fired at the minister's motorcade. Mwenze, now Minister of Justice, ordered the journalist's arrest. Tshisungu was released on December 19.

December 22
Elima ATTACKED

Soldiers from the Democratic Republic of Congo army who since October 20 had been occupying the offices of the privately owned newspaper *Elima*, ransacked the newspaper's offices and its printing facilities. The soldiers then left the premises, taking with them the building's doors and windows. No official explanation has been given for this action.

Eritrea

This year marked the ratification of a new constitution for Africa's youngest nation and the drafting of electoral laws in preparation for parliamentary elections. Eritrea, which came into being in 1991 after the Eritrean People's Liberation Front (EPLF) defeated the Ethiopian army, became a formal state in 1993 following a U.N. supervised referendum in which citizens voted for independence from Ethiopia. The new constitution contains provisions for press freedom, but many of the country's institutions are still evolving after its 30-year war with Ethiopia, and the current centralized provisional government of President Issaias Afewerki will be replaced after the parliamentary elections.

Although magazines and newspapers are beginning to appear, and are sold and read freely, the media are controlled by the government, and there is one television and one radio station. Private ownership of newspapers, but not broadcast media, is allowed but newspapers must first obtain a license from the Ministry of Information before publication, and all reporters must be registered. 1997 produced the first controversial press incident in Eritrea, that of the arrest without charges of Ruth Simon, an Agence France-Presse correspondent.

April 25
Ruth Simon, Agence France-Presse
IMPRISONED

Simon, an Eritrean national who works as a correspondent for the Agence France-Presse news agency, was arrested and charged with endangering state secuirty. In a story she filed the day before, she had quoted President Issaias Afewerki as saying Eritrean troops were fighting alongside rebels in neighboring Sudan.

At press time, Simon remained in detention. Her colleagues have been denied visitation. She is allowed visits from her family members only. In a letter to Afewerki, CPJ called for Simon's immediate and unconditional release. According to the Eritrean foreign ministry, Simon has been charged under a press law which states that "any journalist who disinforms the public or any institution is liable to the damage he/she may cause as a result."

Ethiopia

There were at least 16 journalists in jail at the end of the year. All of them were newly imprisoned during the course of 1997, sustaining Ethiopia's status as one of the world's worst offenders of press freedom.

Most of the mass media are owned, funded, and controlled by the state.

In January, the government of Prime Minister Meles Zenawi announced its first state-owned Internet service provider with a capacity of 5,000 clients whose rates favored large organizations, effectively shutting out most individual users and smaller nongovernmental organizations.

As the cost of printing continues to rise, Zenawi's government has attempted to bring a poorly funded but boisterous independent press in line by the use of arbitrary restrictions on the print media—detention, imprisonment, and the imposition of prohibitive fines and bail on journalists and editors is commonplace. Journalists and editors work under threat of arrest and prosecution by either a poorly trained police force or an inexperienced, partisan judiciary working in a backlogged court system. The authorities regularly use the Press Law of 1992 to detain journalists for lengthy periods and sometimes try them for allegedly publishing false information or incitement against the government.

January 7
Arega Wolde-Kirkos, *Tobia* IMPRISONED

Three police officers arrested Wolde-Kirkos, acting editor in chief of the independent *Tobia*, at the newspaper's editorial offices. He was detained at the Ma'ekelawi Central Criminal Investigation Office.

Wolde-Kirkos was released on February 28 on a bail of 5,000 birr (US$780).

February 7
Kefle Mulat, *Ethio Times* IMPRISONED, LEGAL ACTION

Kefle, editor in chief of *Ethio Times*, was arrested and detained at Kerchle Prison in connection with an article titled "The Case of the Attempt to Assassinate Mengistu Haile

Mariam in Harare," published in the December 3, 1995, issue of *Ethio Times*. Kefle appeared on February 9 in the Addis Ababa Region 40 court, where he was charged and convicted of "disseminating false information" and sentenced to six months in prison. As of press time, Kefle was free, but new charges had been filed against him and a court case is pending.

February 24
Atenafu Alemayhu, *Tomar* IMPRISONED, LEGAL ACTION

Atenafu, editor in chief of the privately owned Amharic-language weekly *Tomar*, was detained and charged in connection with a report published in late 1995. The article had reported on the relationship between a Muslim relief organization called Blessed Relief and Sudanese religious leaders Hassan Al Turabi and Mohammed Sirage.

Atenafu could not pay the 5,000 birr (US$780) bail granted by the Federal High Court and was being detained in the Addis Ababa Central Prison. As of press time, Atenafu was free but new charges had been filed against him and a court case was pending.

February 24
Kidist Belachew, *A'emrio* HARASSED

Kidist, former editor in chief of and shareholder in the independent Amharic-language weekly *A'emrio*, was detained and charged in connection with a story she had published in late 1995 disclosing a relationship between Blessed Relief, a Muslim relief organization, and the Sudanese religious leaders Hassan Al Turabi and Mohammed Sirage.

Kidist was released the same day on a bail of 5,000 birr (US$780).

February 24
Tesihalene Mengesha, *Mebruk* HARASSED

Mengesha, former editor in chief of the private-

ly owned Amharic-language weekly *Mebruk*, was detained in connection with articles published in late 1995 disclosing a relationship between Blessed Relief, a Muslim relief organisation, and the Sudanese religious leaders Hassan Al Turabi and Mohammed Sirage. Mengesha was released that day on 5,000 birr (US$780) bail.

May 6
Birru Tsegaye, *Tobia* HARASSED
Goshu Moges, AKPAC HARASSED

Tobia editor in chief Birru, and Goshu, the acting manager of *Tobia*'s publisher, AKPAC, were arrested without charge and detained. Their arrest was in connection with an article published on April 17 titled "When Will It Stop?" suggesting that Ethiopians should mobilize and peacefully demonstrate to inform the government of their basic demands. Birru and Goshu were released on bail of 10,000 birr (US$1,600) each.

September 8
Sisay Agena, *Ethiop* IMPRISONED

Sisay, publisher of *Ethiop*, was arrested near his office on September 8 on as yet unknown charges, and detained at the Region 14 location. He was released on bail on September 10, but on September 16 had been taken back into custody and moved from the Region 14 Criminal Investigation Office to the Central Criminal Investigation Office Prison.

October 14
Tamrat Serbessa, *Wenchif* IMPRISONED
Admassu Tesfaye, *Wenchif* IMPRISONED

Tamrat, editor in chief of *Wenchif*, and Admassu, the paper's deputy editor, were detained at the Central Criminal Investigation Office Prison. The two journalists are each charged on five counts, one of which is libel against President Negasso Gidada. This charge stemmed from a report in *Wenchif* that claimed the president was drunk at an Oromo gathering.

October 16
Tesfaye Deressa, *Urjii* IMPRISONED
Solomon Nemera, *Urjii* IMPRISONED

Tesfaye, editor in chief of the newspaper *Urjii*, and Solomon, the paper's deputy editor, were abducted from a tea room near *Urjii*'s offices. The journalists were first detained at the Central Criminal Investigation Office Prison and were later taken to a district police prison. The two were held on charges related to a report in *Urjii* about the recent killing of alleged Oromo Liberation Front (OLF) members in the Mekanissa area. The article contradicted the government media's version of the same story.

Tesfaye and Solomon appeared three times before a district court but the proceedings were repeatedly postponed because of requests by police for more time to continue their investigation. After the journalists' court appearance on December 12, police said they had concluded their investigation but were awaiting the prosecutor's decision as to bail. No decision had been made when Tesfaye and Solomon appeared again in court on December 19. They were scheduled for another court appearance on January 9.

October 27
Garoma Bekele, *Urjii* IMPRISONED

Garoma, publisher of the newspaper *Urjii*, was detained on suspicion of being a member of the outlawed Oromo Liberation Front (OLF). Garoma is being held at the Central Criminal Investigation Office Prison along with others who have been detained for their alleged connection to a series of OLF bomb attacks in Addis Ababa, Dire Dawa, and Harar. On October 31, Garoma appeared in court and made an appeal for release on bail, but was denied by the prosecutor. He was given a new court appointment for January 13.

October 31
Garedew Demisse, *Wenchif* IMPRISONED

Garedew appeared in court on charges of false information regarding a number of stories in *Wenchif*. He was detained on October 28 at the Central Criminal Investigation Office Prison.

December 6
Iskinder Nega, *Wenchif* IMPRISONED

Iskinder, owner and publisher of *Wenchif*, was detained at the Central Criminal Investigation Office Prison, and charged with reporting false information. He was later moved to Wereda 9 Police Station.

December 23
Waqshum Bacha, *Urjii* IMPRISONED
Alemu Tolessa, *Urjii* IMPRISONED

Waqshum and Alemu were called in for questioning and detained at the Central Criminal Investigation Office.

After the arrest of *Urjii*'s former editors, Waqshum and Alemu had taken over as publishers of the newspaper. The paper's previous editors, Solomon Nemera and Tesfaye Deressa, were arrested on October 16 and are still in detention. Alemu and Waqshum were ordered to appear in court on January 9, 1998. The status of their trial is unknown.

Gabon

The October elections consolidated the Democratic Party of Gabon's grip on power and virtually eliminated all opposition parties from participation in government. A new constitution revised the already existing National Communication Council, which in the past had both elected and appointed members. It will now be comprised solely of appointees.

Despite moves by the government toward press freedoms in recent years, such as a constitution that provides for freedom

of speech and the press, President Omar Albert-Bernard Bongo's administration has made no public commitment to encouraging and safeguarding an independent press. A press code, adopted in 1993, requires newspapers to register with the Minister of Communication and with the Minister of Commerce and allows for the suspension of a newspaper for up to three months for publishing material offensive to the government. There are currently seven independent newspapers and five private radio stations. The government controls the national electronic media, which reach all areas of the country.

May 20
La Radio Commercial ATTACKED

The Libreville-based independent radio station was vandalized by several unidentified armed men who stormed the station's broadcast studios. The transmitter was completely destroyed, forcing the station off the air.

The Gambia

The government of Col. Yahya Jammeh renewed its assault on the independent press by continuing its pattern of attacks, detentions, and forced repatriation of non-Gambian media workers. Under Jammeh, who first took power in a military coup in 1994 and was elected president in 1996 in an election that was widely regarded as flawed and unfair, the country has no domestic television service, and radio news is censored.

In 1997, the cost of licenses to operate private radio stations were increased from 12,000 dalasi to 25,000 dalasi (US$1,200-$2,500).

The passage of arbitrary laws, such as the 1996 Newspaper Decrees #70 and #71, which massively increased the fine for any

contravention of the Newspaper Act and the sum required as a bond for the registration of all existing newspapers by 100 percent, has aided in dismantling the democratic tradition of the Gambia, producing ever-increasing difficulties for journalists.

January 6
***Daily Observer* CENSORED**

Immigration officials entered the editorial offices of the *Daily Observer* and ordered all of the privately owned daily's Senegalese employees to stop working immediately. The employees were forced to exit the building. Night-shift employees were prevented from entering the premises. Because Senegalese workers comprise the bulk of trained printing press technicians and lithographers in The Gambia, *Daily Observer* management believes the government was using the dismissal of the Senegalese employees as a way to prevent the newspaper from publishing.

The *Daily Observer*'s acting editor assembled a small crew of trained Gambians to perform the duties of the Senegalese workers and successfully published the following day's edition. In a similar incident a month earlier, immigration officials ordered all the *Daily Observer*'s Liberian employees to cease working for the newspaper.

February 27
Goodwin Okon, *Daily Observer* HARASSED

Okon, assistant editor and senior reporter for The *Daily Observer*, was harassed for a week by National Intelligence Agency (NIA) officials.

The harassment began a day after Okon published an article about hit-and-run accidents-including an incident on February 19 in which Okon was hit by a car driven by NIA agents. Okon, who was knocked unconscious in the accident, was hospitalized for four days.

Four NIA agents went to Okon's home in the Bakau Newtown residential district on February 28 and searched it, confiscated Okon's passport, and ordered him to report to NIA headquarters the following day. Okon went to the NIA on March 1 and was detained for six hours without questioning, then released and ordered to return the following day. That harassment was repeated every day through March 4, when NIA agents returned Okon's passport and warned him not to publish negative reports about the government or he would face reprisals.

July 12
Yorro Jallow, BBC HARASSED

The Gambian police arrested Jallow, a stringer for the BBC, and shuttled him between various police stations in Banjul making it difficult for his relatives to ascertain where he was being held. The next day he was taken to the Banjul police station and charged with "causing fear and alarm," because of a July 10 item on the BBC concerning recent prison riots. He was released on bail and has been reporting to the police station daily since then. At press time, his trial has yet to be scheduled.

November 1
Muhamed E. Seade, *Daily Observer*
EXPELLED

Seade, editor in chief of the privately owned newspaper the *Daily Observer*, was expelled from The Gambia by the immigration department. No official reason has been given for the expulsion. Seade, who is originally from Ghana, had worked for the *Daily Observer* since 1995.

Ghana

Ghana's independent press, reborn after the country's return to constitutional rule in 1991, remains one of the most vociferous and energetic on the continent. In the past, newspapers folded often, only to be resurrected under different names. But in recent years,

the print press has stabilized. Twelve papers published regularly this year, but the government controlled the only two national dailies, the *Ghanaian Times* and the *Daily Graphic*.

Numerous outdated laws are frequently used to harass the press. Many journalists are prosecuted under Section 185 of the penal code, a hold-over from the colonial era which makes libel a criminal offense.

The government-controlled Ghana Broadcasting Corporation radio reaches most of the 10 million citizens who own radios. While previously the only television station in the country was government-owned, private broadcasters have now received station licenses and 15 private radio stations broadcast in urban areas.

November 3
Kweku Baako Jr., *The Guide* LEGAL ACTION
Ian Mortey, *The Guide* LEGAL ACTION

Baako, editor in chief of the newspaper *The Guide*, and Mortey, a reporter for the paper, were sued by Franklin Aheto, a member of parliament, for libel. The suit is in connection with the article titled "NDC MP 'Chops' 100 Million Cedis," published in the October 16-22 edition of their paper. Aheto asked the Accra High Court to restrain Baako, Mortey, their agents, and Western Publication Ltd., which owns *The Guide*, from further publishing the allegedly libelous statements.

Guinea

Following the tide of democratic reform that swept Africa in the early 1990s, voters in 1991 approved a new constitution. In 1993 elections, former dictator and military strongman Col. Lansana Conte became president. Although the constitution provides for some freedom of expression, defamation and slander are criminal offenses, and speech that personally insults the president is considered seditious. Consequently, the deterioration of working conditions in recent years for both local and foreign journalists in Guinea has been marked by expulsions, arrests, and harassment under the guise of violations of restrictive press laws.

August 1
Ousmane Camara, *L'Oeil* IMPRISONED
Louis Esperant Celestin, *L'Oeil* IMPRISONED

L'Oeil publications director Camara, and editor in chief Celestin, were arrested and detained. The journalists were charged with "spreading false information and defamation" after Justice Minister Maurice Zogbelemou Togba lodged a complaint. The June 25 and July 2 editions of *L'Oeil* contained criticism of Togba.

On August 4, the journalists appeared in court for preliminary questioning. Although the court granted them an official release on August 6, Camara and Celestin remained in jail.

December 22
Louis Esperant Celestin, *L'Oeil* EXPELLED

Celestin, editor in chief of the independent weekly *L'Oeil*, was expelled from Guinea to the Ivory Coast. He was charged with "inciting violence and riots" following the publication of an article concerning a press conference held by The Democratic Opposition Coalition (CODEM). The article reported comments by a CODEM spokesperson, who said that the opposition "would no longer leave room for the ruling Party for Unity and Progress (PUP)."

December 26
Le Lynx HARASSED
L'Independant HARASSED

Le Lynx and L'Independant, two independent news groups that publish a total of five newspapers, were shut down by authorities in what the

government called "a routine operation." Security Minister Koureissy Conde said that officials had seized production materials from the papers' offices for "investigative purposes related to public security." The materials were returned to their owners after three days.

This action followed the government's December 22 expulsion of journalist Louis Esperant Celestin. Celestin had been editor of *L'Oeil*, one of the titles published by the two news groups. He was ordered to leave Guinea after writing an article about a news conference called by an opposition party.

Ivory Coast

Despite a peaceful constitutional succession in December 1993 and multiparty elections in October 1995-February 1996, the government of President Henri Konan Bédié increased its prosecutions of journalists sympathetic to the opposition, often resulting in sentences of up to three years in jail. On January 1, after serving a year in jail on a two-year conviction for "offenses against the head of state," deputy editor Freedom Neruda, journalist Emmanuel Koré, and publisher Abou Drahamane, all of the independent opposition newspaper *La Voie*, were released. Neruda subsequently received CPJ's 1997 International Press Freedom Award.

Although independent newspapers, opposition leaders, and student groups still voice their disapproval of government or presidential actions, self-censorship among journalists is common, since the government refuses to tolerate what it considers to be insults or attacks on the honor of the country's highest officials. While independent radio stations have complete control over editorial content and foreign broadcasts are available, the state continues to exercise considerable influence over official media program content, news coverage, and

other matters of its two nationally broadcast radio and television stations, using these media to promote the policies of the President's own political party, the Parti Democratique Cote D'Ivoire.

Almost a dozen daily papers, including *Le Jour*, *La Voie*, *La Nouvelle Republique*, and *Fraternité Matin* went online this year, providing access to local news for Ivorians living abroad.

May 15
Daniel Opeli, *La Voie* ATTACKED

Opeli, a reporter with *La Voie* newspaper, was severely beaten by the Abidjan police after identifying himself as a journalist while covering a meeting of the student organization FESCI at the University of d'Abobo-Adjame.

Kenya

In September, in an attempt to defuse escalating unrest in the run-up to year-end parliamentary and presidential elections, Kenya's parliament adopted constitutional reforms which allowed the political opposition equal access to the state-run media and also provided for the repeal of detention-without-trial laws. On November 7, the reforms were signed into law by President Daniel arap Moi, who was later re-elected to a fifth and final term in December elections that were marked by delays and confusion, forcing the Electoral Commission to extend the general election into a second day.

Although press freedoms have expanded somewhat since the advent of political pluralism in 1991 and the growth of privately owned independent weeklies and magazines, Moi's government still displays rigid intolerance of any criticism by the independent press. Officials employ such techniques as harassment and threats of legal action to muzzle the media, and in 1997 journalists were ejected from meetings and assaulted by politicians.

The government uses outdated colonial-era laws, such as those on seditious libel, to intimidate and silence the press. In July, a court rendered the largest libel judgment in Kenya's history against the independent weekly newspaper *The People*. Citing a recent ruling in Britain, the court ordered the paper to pay a 10-million shilling award (US $185,000) to an aide to the president. The ruling was ultimately overturned, but only after it had sent a collective shudder through the media.

Since most of the dailies and all of the weeklies are in English, the official language, the few Kenyan-language newspapers suffer great difficulties with financing and distribution. The English-language Nation Group newspapers, considered to be pro-opposition by the government, in March launched a state-of-the-art printing facility, with a production capacity of 60,000 papers an hour. The group has five daily and weekly titles, but despite its status as East Africa's leading newspaper chain, the Nation Group's 1991 application for radio and television licenses has continued to languish.

Broadcast licensing was to have been overseen by a Media Task Force, appointed two years ago to review media laws, but the government bypassed this procedure last year when authorities began to issue permits on a selective basis. The handful of private broadcasting licenses awarded since 1996 have gone to applicants linked to the ruling Kenya Africa National Union party (KANU), or to stations without news programming schedules. The Kenyan Television Network (KTN), which has had protracted court battles over its ownership, was finally bought by the *East African Standard* for an undisclosed amount a few days before the election. Thirty staff members were later dismissed in spite of the even-handed coverage the station showed toward the election.

Radio is the primary medium for more than 30 million Kenyans, most of whom live in rural areas, but the government continues to retain an effective monopoly for the Kenya Broadcasting Corporation on nationwide radio and television.

January 13
Nation CENSORED
Kenya Times CENSORED
East African Standard CENSORED

Nairobi High Court Judge Moijo ole Keiwua barred reporters from the dailies *Nation*, *Kenya Times*, and *East African Standard* from covering court proceedings on the controversial sale of the Grand Regency Hotel by the Central Bank of Kenya.

January 19
Rebecca Nduku, *Nation* ATTACKED

Nduku, a photographer for the daily *Nation*, was hospitalized after being attacked by a senior police officer in the presence of more than 20 other armed officers. Nduku was on assignment covering interdenominational prayer in a Nairobi slum village. Police clubbed Alphonse Muthoka, a driver for the *Nation*, as he sat in the newspaper's vehicle attempting to call for help on the car radio.

February 3
Kalamka Ltd. LEGAL ACTION

Kulei, a Nairobi businessman and member of President Daniel arap Moi's cabinet, filed a defamation lawsuit against Kalamka Limited, publishers of the independent weekly newspaper *The People*. The lawsuit was sparked by an article in the January 23-24 edition of *The People* titled "Asian Link in Moi's Kitchen Cabinet." Kulei's attorney, Mohammed Ibrahim, gave the publishers seven days to carry a correction and a written apology.

February 7
The People LEGAL ACTION

State House deputy comptroller John Lolorio sued the independent weekly newspaper *The People* over an article that associated him with the so-called "Asian link" in President Daniel arap Moi's cabinet. Lolorio is seeking, among other reliefs, an injunction restraining Kalamka Ltd., publisher of *The People*, and its employees from reprinting the offending story or repeating any similar accusations. He is also seeking general damages for alleged defamation and reimbursement of legal expenses.

June 12
All media CENSORED

The government banned 30 publications for printing seditious or immoral material, Minister of State Jackson Kalwo told parliament. The publications included *Development Agenda*, *Sauti ya Urafiki*, *Return to Reason*, *Inooro*, *Beyond*, *Playboy*, and *Men Only*. Parliament Deputy George Nthenge asked the government to appoint a committee to review the banned publications, but the request was denied.

July 4
Jennifer Wachie, *East African Standard* ATTACKED

Police beat Wachie, a photographer, while she was covering Nairobi University students protesting against a proposed higher education law. She was treated for injuries sustained during the attack and released.

July 7
Kalamka Limited LEGAL ACTION
Gordon Ondiek, *The People* LEGAL ACTION

Kalamka Limited, publisher of the Nairobi weekly *The People*, and Ondiek, a reporter for *The People*, were charged with defamation in a case filed by the Trypanosomiasis Research

Institute and its two senior officers, Joseph Mathu Ndungu and Mbaruk Abdala Suleiman. The suit stems from an article published in the February 21-27 edition of *The People*, which reported that the institute's top officials colluded with staff and suppliers to embezzle money from the World Health Organization.

July 8
Osman Njuguna, All-Africa Press Service ATTACKED
Peter Karuri, *Nation* ATTACKED

Njuguna, a correspondent for All-Africa Press, was beaten inside a cathedral in Nairobi after police lobbed tear-gas canisters and broke up a prayer service during a pro-reform rally. Njuguna was treated for his injuries and released.

Police also beat Karuri, a free-lance photojournalist affiliated with the *Nation* Group of newspapers, and destroyed his camera.

July 9
Vitalis Musebe, Kenya Television Network (KTN) CENSORED
Isaiya Kabira, Kenya Television Network (KTN) CENSORED

KTN editors Musebe and Kabira were suspended indefinitely as a result of the station's July 7 coverage of riots which erupted in Nairobi and other major Kenyan cities after the government outlawed pro-reform rallies.

Musebe and Kabira's suspension is to be reduced to one month upon the recommendation of the KTN board of directors on July 17.

Musebe and Kabira were officially and unconditionally reinstated on October 1 after a suspension of nearly three months.

October 21
Finance CENSORED

Groups of people believed to be security officers prevented the sale of the October 21 issue of *Finance* magazine by purchasing virtually all available copies. Vendors reported that they were asked for all of the copies they had on hand, whereupon the buyers paid in cash and loaded the magazines into waiting vehicles. By 2:00 p.m. *Finance* was almost entirely unavailable, and some vendors reported that they were warned not to try to buy extra stock.

The magazine's cover story may have prompted this action: it concerned serious allegations made by Central Bank of Kenya lawyer Philip Murgor against President Daniel arap Moi's son, Gideon Moi.

Lesotho

Although Lesotho has had a turbulent political history since gaining independence from Britain in 1966, the media have been threatened and harassed by security forces only occasionally since the democratically elected government of Prime Minister Ntsu Mokhehle came to power in April 1993. Nevertheless, since 1995, the government has not actively promoted press freedom, and 1997 was a politically tense year with extreme government sensitivity to critical voices in the media. There are no strong independent media organizations in the country to protect journalists from intimidation.

With general elections slated for next year, journalists working for the state-run media were forbidden to cover opposition press conferences. Armed police abused and harassed reporters covering rallies and the parliamentary sessions, and on September 1-5, the media were banned from entering parliament to cover a feud between the ruling Basutoland Congress Party (BCP) and the new, breakaway Lesotho Congress for Democracy (LCD). Although the media were eventually allowed access to the upper house of parliament, the ban was not completely lifted until September 15—when Speaker Teboho Kolane succumbed to pres-

sure from CPJ and other international press freedom groups.

On a positive note, in June the Ministry of Information and Broadcasting accepted a draft media policy after consulting with the press. The draft policy, which will come before parliament in 1998, recommends the creation of an independent press council, a code of ethics, and protection of sources.

August 28
All journalists CENSORED

Journalists in Lesotho were banned from entering the Parliament to cover proceedings. Parlimentary Speaker Teboho Kolane invoked Standing Order No. 83, blacking out media coverage to prevent the public from following the worsening power struggle between the ruling Basutoland Congress Party and the breakaway Lesotho Congress for Democracy. In the first week of September, armed police dispersed journalists who had denounced the ban as unconstitutional and had organized a petition against it. On September 15, Speaker Kolane lifed the ban without explanation.

Liberia

After more than a dozen peace accords and close to 20 cease-fire agreements, Liberia's devastating seven-year civil war finally ended with a monitored election in July that brought faction leader Charles Taylor and his party, the National Patriotic Front of Liberia, into power. The election selected a new president and seated a broadly recognized government for the first time since the assassination of military dictator Samuel K. Doe in 1990 in a war initially launched by Taylor in 1989.

During the transitional government prior to elections, the Liberian police,

under commissioner Joe Tate, were responsible for many arbitrary arrests, detentions without charge, and brutality toward the media.

In the volatile atmosphere leading up to Liberia's mid-year presidential elections, powerful business leaders and government officials targeted by investigative reporting used the threat of lawsuits against the media as an effective tool of repression. Journalists found it increasingly difficult to gather information from sources, who would not come forward to produce defense evidence out of fear of the inevitable wrath of factional agents. Without tangible evidence or witnesses to exonerate them before a court of law, many organizations faced the prospect of financial ruin from expensive criminal libel suits. Although many of the threatened suits never materialized, they had their desired effect: self-censorship became common among Liberia's journalists.

In August, the legislature reaffirmed the 1986 constitution, which guarantees freedom of speech and of the press, as well as fundamental human rights. But journalists fear that the outcome of government discussions in January 1998 to revamp the 1972 media registration law will impose not only annual registration deadlines with the Ministry of Information for all newspapers but also hefty fees and mandatory inspection of media houses as part of the registration process.

January 7
Phillibert Browne, *National Chronicle* HARASSED
Sayon Kieh, *National Chronicle* HARASSED
Finley Karago, *National Chronicle* HARASSED

Agents of the National Security Agency (NSA) detained *National Chronicle* publisher Browne, news editor Kieh, and typesetter Karago in connection with a story in the January 2 edition of the newspaper. The story reported that a Lebanese businessman had evaded taxes and engaged in illegal business practices, and that he gave a "bribe" to Ruth Perry, chairperson of the Council of State. The businessman reportedly had been prevented from leaving the country and allegedly bribed Perry to drop the restrictions on his freedom of movement. Browne, Kieh, and Karago were released later the same day.

January 7
Liberian Broadcasting Service
CENSORED

The Liberian Broadcasting Service, a state-run radio station operated by opposition members, suspended the broadcast of human rights programming. The suspension stemmed from government disapproval of the critical coverage of the warring factions and of the Council of State's activities on the program "Justice and Peace Forum."

January 7
Momo Varfolay Kanneh, *Heritage*
THREATENED

National Patriotic Front of Liberia faction leader and councilman Charles Taylor threatened Kanneh, managing editor of the independent daily *Heritage*, with a lawsuit because of a front-page story in the January 7 edition. The article, titled "Inside Watanga, The Story of Torture, Horror, Death," reported on gross human rights abuses, including torture and killings, in an area called Watanga Base, near Taylor's residence.

September 24
Phillip Wesseh, *The Inquirer* HARASSED

Wesseh, managing editor of *The Inquirer* newspaper, was arrested at the paper's office by Joe Tate, the director of National Police. Tate produced no arrest warrant, but detained Wesseh

nonetheless and subjected him to hours of harsh interrogation before releasing him.

The arrest occured as a result of an article published in *The Inquirer* that raised serious concerns about police conduct in Liberia.

November 18
New Democrat HARASSED

The Liberian Information Ministry rejected the weekly *New Democrat's* request for annual press registration, effectively preventing the paper from printing a new issue until 1998. The *New Democrat* has been unable to publish since April 1996, when its offices and all of its equipment were destroyed by arson. The Information Ministry's explanation, that the *New Democrat's* registration request was denied because it was too late in the year, angered the paper's editors, who were willing to pay the annual permit fee despite the fact that they would have to pay again at the beginning of 1998, only a month away.

December 21
Alex Redd, Radio DC101 IMPRISONED

Redd, a reporter for Radio DC101, was arrested in Gbarnga by one of President Charles Taylor's security units as he returned home from slain Unity Party leader Sam Dokie's funeral. Originally charged with "criminal attempt to commit treason," which carries the death penalty or a long prison sentence, Redd was released on bail on December 29, when authorities reduced his charge to "false report to law enforcement officers."

Redd's detention, and the first charge against him, appear to have stemmed from interviews the journalist conducted with Dokie's family after the opposition leader's murder. Police chief Joe Tate explained the later purjury charge by claiming that Redd had lied about being abducted and tortured by security forces.

No date has been set for the trial.

December 21
Forkpa Nyenkan, *The News* HARASSED
Musue Haddad, *The News* HARASSED
Stanley Seakor, *The News* HARASSED

On December 22, Nyenkan, Haddad, and Seakor, respectively managing editor and reporters for the daily *The News*, were arrested and detained by police in Monrovia. The three were interrogated for several hours about an article *The News* published the same day, which reported the death of a suspect in police custody. Before releasing the journalists, the police director cautioned them against using his photograph in the paper and criticized the article's suggestion that the police department was culpable for the prisoner's death.

Mali

In a continent dominated by almost constant government harassment of the press, Mali continues to serve as a hopeful example for the future. With two notable exceptions this year—the arrest and beating of 15 journalists covering an opposition press conference in August, and the censorship of a private radio station—there has been no organized government harassment of the media. The free press, consisting of 30 print media houses, 35 weeklies, and four dailies, operates without fear of reprisal. Self-censorship is rare, and although the country's press law, with its extremely punitive presumption-of-guilt standard, is one of the most repressive in Africa, it is seldom applied. The legislature has discussed extensive revisions to the law, which was written in 1991, during wartime.

There are an estimated 75-200 stations in the Union of Free Radio and Television Broadcasters, and Mali's radio programming is considered the freest in Africa. The country has 52 radio stations (10 in the capital of Bamako alone), and even the most remote regions of the country receive broadcasts. There is one government television station, and on the 1997-98 agenda for the national assembly are plans to revise the statutes to allow for private-sector television ownership. The country gained access to the Internet in September through the state telecommunications company SOTELMA. Four private companies operate the new network, which will have a capacity of 80,000 lines by the end of 1998.

April 25
Kayira radio station CENSORED

Programming of the independent radio station Kayira was been jammed for several months during 1997, particularly its news broadcasting.

A complaint lodged by the station on April 25 to authorities at the Communications Board was not acted on.

CPJ wrote a letter to President H. E. Alpha Omar Konare on August 19 asking for a timely and thorough investigation into the matter.

August 11
Yero Diallo, *Le Tambour* ATTACKED, HARASSED
Basse Diarra, *L'Essor* ATTACKED, HARASSED
Said Penda, BBC ATTACKED, HARASSED
12 other journalists HARASSED

The 15 journalists, who attended a press conference of the opposition party Movement for Independence, Rebirth and African Integration, were arrested. They were taken to police headquarters and beaten for two hours before they were released.

Diallo, director of publication of the independent magazine *Le Tambour*; Diarra, a journalist with the government newspaper *L'Essor*; and Penda, a correspondent for the BBC, were all treated for serious injuries sustained during the attack.

AFRICA

Namibia

President Sam Nujoma and government officials have displayed increasing hostility toward
the media. Their intolerance, coupled with
their rhetorical attacks on the press, threaten
to irreparably damage the country's reputation
as one of Africa's most solid democracies.
Local and international media organizations,
including the Journalists Association of
Namibia, strongly protested government officials' sweeping public statements
characterizing the media as irresponsible for
publishing leaked state reports.

Pending legislation, such as the
Powers, Privileges and Immunities Act of
1996, threatens to restrict the media,
which to date have been free to practice
their profession. The act would grant parliamentary committees the right to
subpoena journalists and force them to
reveal their sources, and it would also bar
journalists from interviewing members of
parliament about pending legislation that
is the subject of debate.

State-owned television and radio stations
regularly air reports critical of the government, and private radio stations and
independent newspapers operate without
much government interference. The electronic media are primarily state-controlled.

Niger

Like many of its neighbors in sub-Saharan
Africa, Niger launched democratic reforms in
the 1990s after the collapse of communist rule
in the Soviet Union. But they proved to be
short-lived when a military coup in January
1996 led by Col. Ibrahim Ba'are Mainassara
ousted democratically elected president
Mahamane Ousmane. Although presidential
elections six months later were widely considered to be fraudulent, Mainassara remained as
head of state, despite opposition protests.
This year produced a wave of arbitrary arrests,
systematic intimidation, and unfair trials, in
addition to the June 27 passage of a harsh and
repressive press law.

The law established obligatory licensing
of journalists and made defamation and
insulting the president criminal offenses—
the latter with two-to-five-year sentences
and stiff fines of 200,000 to five million CFA
(US$340-$8,600). Only journalism school
graduates or those who have worked in the
profession for five years are eligible for
press cards, an accreditation which could
easily be rescinded under the new law for
any writing construed as a threat to the
government.

The control that Niger's media regulatory body, the Upper Communication
Council, exercises is so extensive that it
threatens pluralism of information.
Currently, there are few independent radio
stations, and the state still maintains tight
control over Africa's most powerful broadcasting tool. When the privately owned
Radio Anfani was ransacked and forced off
the air in March by uniformed men, state
media gave little attention to the event.

March 1
Radio Anfani ATTACKED

Five men, armed and wearing military uniforms,
entered the premises of Radio Anfani (FM 100)
and forced the station off the air. They held the
night security guard and janitor at gunpoint, and
ransacked and destroyed equipment worth an
estimated US$80,000. The security guard rec-
ognized the assailants as military personnel and
questioned them about their actions. They
responded merely that they were under orders.

In a letter to Gen. Ibrahim Ba'are Mainassara,
CPJ condemned the attack on Radio Anfani and
called for a thorough and timely investigation
of the incident.

March 15
Mahamane Radiou Dogo, Radio Anfani
IMPRISONED
Salifou Rabi, Radio Anfani IMPRISONED
Abdoulaye Moussa, Radio Anfani
IMPRISONED

Police arrested Dogo, associate director for
Radio Anfani; Rabi, technical director; and
Moussa, a radio technician. The arrests followed a complaint by the military against the
bimonthly newspaper Anfani, run by the management of Radio Anfani. Anfani had reported
that the military was responsible for the March
1 raid and destruction of the Radio Anfani studios by armed men.

Dogo, Rabi, and Moussa were released on
March 19. No charges were filed.

March 20
Gremah Boucar, Radio Anfani IMPRISONED

On March 20, Radio Anfani director Gremah
Boucar and night security guard Harouna
Issoufou were brought before a judge and
charged with "swindling." They were accused of
organizing the attack on Radio Anfani to attract
financial aid from sympathetic international agencies. They were brought to Niamey Civil Prison
and were released from detention the next day.

Also on March 20, another Radio Anfani
security guard, Adamou Douka, was taken into
custody, questioned, and released the same day.

April 10
Souleymane Adji, *Le Republicain, Citoyen,*
L'Alternative, La Democrate ATTACKED

Adji, a columnist for the *Le Republicain, Citoyen,*
L'Alternative, and *La Democrate*, was attacked
while riding his motorcyle at about 2 a.m. by four
men driving a car without license plates. One of
the attackers was dressed in a military uniform.

Adji was hospitalized for wounds sustained
in the attack.

October 3
Moussa Tchangari, *Alternative* IMPRISONED,
LEGAL ACTION

Tchangari, director of publication for the independent weekly *Alternative*, was convicted of
"publishing an administrative document intended for internal use" and sentenced to three
months in prison. He was also fined CFA
50,000 (about US$100).

Tchangari was arrested at his office in
Niamey in connection with an article titled "A
[CFA franc] 300 Million Deal of Indulgence"
published in the October 2 edition of the newspaper. The article reproduced correspondence
between Prime Minister Cisse Amadou and
Minister of Universities Sanoussi Djakon concerning the legality of the prime minister's
suggestion to award two businessmen a CFA300
million (US$500,000) deal involving equipment
at the University of Niamey.

Tchangari was tried on October 7 in an
emergency procedure usually applied in cases of
flagrant violations of the law for contravention
of an article in the July 25 press law, which prohibits the circulation or reproduction of all
administrative documents intended for internal
use. Tchangari is currently appealing his conviction and the constitutionality of the law used
against him.

Tchangari was released on appeal in
December.

Nigeria

**After a year marked by the most extreme
deterioration of conditions for the press in
Africa, Nigeria holds at least 17 journalists in
prison—more than any other country in the
region. The first multi-party elections since
the Babangida regime in the early 1980s
were held on March 15, and these local
government council contests were a crucial
indicator of the direction of Gen. Sani**

Abacha's military regime's promised transition to democracy in 1998. Not surprisingly—the election was riddled with irregularities—Abacha supporters swept the polls. Reflecting voter dissatisfaction with the nature of the process, turnout was extremely low in state assembly elections at the end of the year. Elections of state governors, also slated for late 1997, were postponed to coincide with presidential elections in late 1998.

Freedom of expression violations continue to be rampant in Nigeria, which was suspended from the Commonwealth in November 1995 for the execution of Ken Saro Wiwa and eight other environmental activists. Gen. Abacha has since jailed more than 300 activists, journalists, politicians, and labor leaders, and in March charged Nobel laureate Wole Soyinka with treason. Continuing a pattern of incessant government attacks on the press, thousands of copies of newspapers were seized in 1997, and news vendors, as well as journalists, were thrown in jail for publishing or selling news that offended the government. Leading editors continue to serve long prison terms on trumped-up charges or are detained without trial under executive decree. Many journalists have fled the country in fear of their lives, and others simply have "disappeared." This relentless government crackdown on the media has forced editors to operate in increasingly clandestine conditions as "guerrilla journalists," often going underground to work by laptop computer, and frequently changing the location of newsrooms and printers to evade capture.

In addition to cruder attacks on the media, the government has implemented new press laws severely restricting the media. A provision in the 1995 draft constitution—upon which the promised transition to civilian rule in 1998 will be based—proposed a National Mass Media Commission, which will regulate the existence of radio, television, newspapers, magazines, and publications generally, as well as restrict newspaper circulation to their provinces and interfere in the daily affairs of already existing media organizations.

The already economically embattled independent press was forced to assume another financial burden when the Newspaper Registration Decree #43, issued in 1993, finally went into effect. The decree requires a non-refundable annual application fee of N100,000 (US$1,250), a pre-registration deposit of N250,000 (US$3,100), and allows the government to arbitrarily assert control over which newspapers receive licenses.

Although Nigeria boasts hundreds of newspapers, magazines, radio, television, and cable satellite organizations, in the last eight years more than 44 newspapers and magazines were shut down by government decree, and in 1997 the National Broadcasting Commission (NBC) approved astronomical new television and radio license rates, increasing the previous cost of US$5,000 to as much as US$37,500. In August, Minister of Information and Culture Walter Ofonagoro announced that the government would not grant any additional television licenses, and would instead spend its energies monitoring already existing stations. In the same month, the minister announced that the government had acquired the technology to jam the transmission of opposition radio station Radio Kudirat International.

The Nigerian press is enduring the darkest period of its 140-year existence. But in spite of the unavailability of full Internet service and the government's continuing efforts to erect financial impediments to that service, the rapid growth of E-mail networks both within Nigeria and abroad has provided the country's embattled journalists with a revolutionary means of freely receiving and disseminating news.

Attacks on the Press in 1997

January 24
Dele Sobowale, *Vanguard* IMPRISONED

State Security Service agents arrested Sobowale, deputy assistant general manager and columnist for the *Vanguard* newspaper, at the newspaper's editorial offices. The agents gave no reason for his arrest and did not present a warrant. Authorities did not disclose Sobowale's whereabouts. On January 28, he was released without formal charges.

February
Moshood Fayemiwo, *Razor* IMPRISONED

Fayemiwo, publisher of the now-defunct weekly *Razor*, was arrested and detained at the Directorate of Military Intelligence in Lagos. Fayemiwo, who was temporarily living in exile in Cotonou, Benin, was kidnapped by Nigerian security agents and returned to Lagos. Fayemiwo's already poor health deteriorated as a result of torture during his detention.

March 1
Emman Amaize, *Vanguard* IMPRISONED

Amaize, the Benin City correspondent for the *Vanguard*, was arrested by security agents and detained at the State Intelligence and Investigation Bureau. The arrest was in connection with a story he wrote titled "Fresh Human Skull Found in a School." Amaize appeared in court March 18 and was released on bail.

March 18
Tokunboh Olorun Tola, *Today's News Today* (TNT) IMPRISONED
Bola Owolola, *Today's News Today* (TNT) ATTACKED
Owei Lakemfa, *Today's News Today* (TNT) THREATENED

Today's News Today (TNT) news editor Tola was arrested at the newspaper's editorial office by Lagos State Police on the orders of Lagos State Police Commissioner Abubakar Tsav. The

arrest was in connection with a TNT article that reported Tsav had been transferred from Lagos. Tsav alleged that his political enemies were using the reporters to smear him and have him transferred out of Lagos because of his aggressive anti-crime tactics, which had targeted police and some military officers. Tola was released on March 20 without charges.

TNT reporter Owolola was severely beaten by police, and editor Lakemfa immediately went into hiding because the police are searching for him in connection with the same story.

March 20
Ladi Olorunyomi, International Journalism Center (IJC) IMPRISONED

Olorunyomi, journalist and assistant director of IJC, was arrested at her home in Lagos. Olorunyomi has also worked for the *Concord* and the *Herald* newspapers.

Four agents from military intelligence and one army officer searched the residence but did not remove anything. They then brought Olorunyomi to Apapa, to a military intelligence holding facility where she was held incommunicado. Olorunyomi is the wife of Nigerian journalist Dapo Olorunyomi, who is in exile in the United States.

On May 6, Olorunyomi was released from the Military Intelligence Headquarters where she had been held incommunicado, without charge, since March 20. To fulfill the conditions of her release, Olorunyomi was required to report to the facility every Tuesday and Friday for an unspecified time.

June 4
Olatunji Dare, *The Guardian* HARASSED

Dare, former editorial board chairman of the independent newspaper *The Guardian*, was detained by security agents at the Lagos airport upon his arrival from the United States. Dare was released the same day but his passport was confiscated. Authorities did not give an explanation for the detention.

AFRICA

June 19
Stanley Yakubu, *Punch* IMPRISONED

Three security agents arrested Yakubu, a
Punch correspondent based in Adamawa State,
at the newspaper's editorial office. The arrest
was in connection with an article, published in
the June 12 edition, titled "Oyakhire's Wife
Threatens DG (Director General)."

Yakubu was detained for four days on
charges of "false and seditious publications."

June 18
Nwobodo Onyekwere, *Punch* IMPRISONED

Armed soldiers arrested Onyekwere, assistant news
editor for *Punch*. Onyekwere's arrest was in connection with an article in the June 15 issue about
the collapse of a building under construction.
Onyekwere was taken to an unknown location and
tortured. He was released on June 23.

June 30
Bayo Awogbemi, *Nigerian Tribune*
IMPRISONED

Awogbemi, assistant editor of the *Nigerian
Tribune* in Benin City was arrested by security
operatives and detained at the Criminal
Investigation Department headquarters. The
arrest was linked to a story on the front page
of the June 1997 *Sunday Tribune* which reported on a violent clash between two rival cults.

Awogbemi was later released.

July 1
Chief Oni Egbunine, *The Horn* ATTACKED

Egbunine, publisher of Owerri-based *The Horn*
newspaper, was arrested by eight soldiers and
brought to the Imo State Government House.
He was beaten with a horse whip into a coma.

The arrest was in connection with a June 26
article that reported concerns about possible corrupt practices by top state government officials.

July 1
Newspaper vendors ATTACKED,
HARASSED

On July 1, Godfrey Chukwu, a newspaper vendor in Lagos, died after being shot in the head
by agents of "Operation Sweep," a government
anti-crime unit which began patrolling the
streets of Lagos in July, targeting newspaper
vendors. The agents had fired without warning
into a crowd at a bus station.

On September 11, Segun Olatunji, a journalist with the privately owned newspaper *The
Daily Sketch*, was whisked away by "Operation
Sweep" agents, who extorted money from him
at gunpoint before releasing him.

July 13
PM News HARASSED

The chief judge of the Federal High Court,
Justice Babatunde Belgore, reportedly told
State Security Service officers to harass
reporters of the independent newspaper *PM
News*. The order followed a story, published
June 13, that reported an arson attempt on the
judge's home in Lagos.

July 27
Mohammed Adamu, *African Concord*
IMPRISONED

Adamu, the Abuja correspondent of *African
Concord* magazine, was arrested by three security agents at his Abuja residence. The agents
did not give a reason for the arrest, but
informed Adamu that he was being "invited for
a chat."

Friends believed Adamu's arrest was in connection with the July 14 *African Concord* cover
story titled "Ali Mustapha: Ruthless Man
Behind Abacha."

In a letter to Nigerian leader Gen. Sani
Abacha, CPJ called for Adamu's immediate and
unconditional release.

August 23
Nigeria Union of Journalists HARASSED

During the weekend of August 23 and 24, armed policemen occupied and sealed the club house of the Lagos State Council of the Nigeria Union of Journalists (NUJ). Journalists and others who attempted to enter the club, located in the Lagos suburb Somolu, were turned away.

While the police gave no official reason for the action, The NUJ Executive Committee said that the authorities most probably closed the club to prevent an anticipated opposition press conference on the continued imprisonment of Chief M.K.O Abiola, the winner of the annulled 1993 presidential election.

Lanre Arogundade, chairman of the NUJ, condemned the seizure of the club, noting his group's record of peaceful and responsible meetings, and pointing out the police action as just one more example of the repression of free speech in Nigeria.

September 16
TheNEWS ATTACKED, THREATENED, HARASSED

Several security operatives raided the Kano office of *TheNEWS* magazine, claiming they had instructions to arrest the paper's Kano correspondent, Babajide Kolade-Otitoju. They presented a warrant, dated September 15, asking Kolade-Otitoju to report to the police in Abuja on September 17. Unable to find him, they forced his friend, who was in the office, to sign for the arrest warrant and produce Otitoju within 24 hours.

The raid was believed to be connection with a story titled "Panic Over Abacha's Illness" published in the September 15 issue of *TheNEWS*. Security operatives had also arrested news agents, sub-agents and vendors, and confiscated copies of the magazine in Abuja, the federal capital.

September 17
Babatunji Wusu, *TheNEWS* IMPRISONED

Security operatives who presented themselves as Federal Intelligence and Investigation Bureau officers arrested Wusu, an administration officer with *TheNEWS*, at the magazine's editorial office in Lagos. The men were unable to find the editors whom they had intended to arrest, so they arrested Wusu instead and took him to their Ikoyi office.

The arrest seemed to be in connection with an article published in the September 15 issue of *TheNEWS* titled, "Panic Over Abacha's Illness."

September 17
Gareth Yomi Ateloye, *Fame* IMPRISONED

Ateloye, the librarian for the magazine *Fame*, was arrested and placed in an overcrowded cell in the Federal Bureau of Intelligence and Investigation (FIIB) in Iyoki, Lagos. Ateloye, who was suffering from poliomyelitis at the time he was detained, became increasingly ill in prison and was moved to the military hospital in Ikoyi on September 20. On September 22, when his condition improved slightly, he was released. Soon thereafter his family took him to the Zeco Specialist Hospital in Ketu, where he died on October 5. The exact cause of his death is still not known.

Security officers from the FIIB had come to the *Fame* offices looking for the magazine's editor, Niyi Akinsijuor, whom they sought in connection with an article from the magazine's July 29-August 4 issue. The men arrested Ateloye because Akinsijuor was not in the office at the time, and reportedly intended to hold him until Akinsijuor reported to police in Lagos.

September 22
News vendors IMPRISONED
TheNEWS CENSORED

Two news vendors were arrested in Abuja during a sweep by security agents of newspaper distribution centers in the city. All copies of *TheNEWS* magazine displayed for sale were also impounded. The two vendors were released later that day. The security operatives were on the streets again on September 23 and 24 to ensure that other copies of the magazine were not displayed for sale.

The arrest and censorship was believed to be in connection with the week's cover story of *TheNEWS*, reporting on Western pressures on Gen. Sani Abacha's government.

October 1
Tenkum Kokoh, *The Democrat* IMPRISONED
Folu Oyewusi, *The Daily Sketch* IMPRISONED

Kokoh of *The Democrat* and Oyewusi of *The Daily Sketch* were arrested and detained by police in Makurdi, capital of Benue State on October 1. The two journalists were conducting a seminar on the topic "Nigeria '98 and the Principles of Rotational Presidency," to mark the 37th anniversary of Nigeria's independence, when they were called in to meet with the police. A police spokesman in Benue State said the two journalists were being held on "security matters." They were released a few days later.

October 3
Bayo Onanuga, *TheNEWS* THREATENED, HARASSED

Two plainclothes policemen appeared at the offices of *TheNEWS* and ordered the company's guards to sign for the arrest warrant of Onanuga, the managing director of TheNEWS/TEMPO/PM News Group. The warrant, which was dated October 2, ordered Onanuga to appear before a chief superintendent of police in the Criminal Investigation Department of the Police Force Headquarters, Abuja, at 10:00 a.m. on October 6. Onanuga and all other editors of the magazine are in hiding.

On November 3, security officers from the Directorate of Military Intelligence (DMI) twice stormed the editorial offices of *TheNEWS* in Lagos demanding to know

Onanuga's whereabouts. Unable to find him, the officers left.

October 6
Eight staffers, Yobe State Television (YTV) ATTACKED

Eight staffers of Yobe State Television (YTV) in Damaturu, the capital of Yobe State, were severely beaten on the orders of the state military administrator, Wing Commander John Ben Kalio. The administrator was said to have been annoyed over YTV's airing of a 45-minute documentary on the achievements of his predecessor, Police Commander Dabo Aliyu.

The staffers were brought to Government House, where they were severely beaten and then thrown into a van, which transported them to the state headquarters of one of the security agencies before being taken to the hospital for treatment.

October 10
Henry Ugbolue, *TheNEWS* and *TEMPO* HARASSED

Ugbolue, the Kaduna State correspondent of *TheNEWS* and *TEMPO* magazines, was arrested in Kaduna by security operatives attached to the Kaduna Government House. Ugbolue was taken to the Government House, where he was severely beaten and tortured. He was released that evening on the condition that he report daily to the state security services office.

Ugbolue's arrest was in connection with a story titled "Goodbye Justice," which was published in the October 8 edition of *TEMPO*. The story reported on the firing of 30,000 government workers by Lt. Col. Hamed Ali, the military administrator of Kaduna State.

Ugbolue went into hiding after his release. Security agents searching for him have stormed *TheNEWS* offices on three occasions during the first week after his release.

October 17
Demola Abimboye, *TheNEWS* IMPRISONED
Gbenga Alaketu, *TEMPO* IMPRISONED

Abimboye and Alaketu, editors of *TheNEWS* and *TEMPO* magazines respectively, were arrested by four plainclothes policemen while having dinner in a restaurant in Ogba, a Lagos suburb.

The two journalists were taken to police headquarters in Alagbon Close, Ikoyi, Lagos, and then transported to the Police Force Criminal Investigation Department (CID) Headquarters, Garki District, Abuja. Officials did not issue a statement on the reason for their arrest.

Abimboye and Alaketu were released on the evening of October 19. The two journalists said that during their detention they were interrogated about several stories published in recent editions of their magazines.

October 18
Casmir Igbokwe, *TheNEWS* HARASSED, THREATENED
Wisdom Dike, *The Week* HARASSED, THREATENED
Joseph Ollor-Obari, *The Guardian* HARASSED, THREATENED
Tokunbo Awoshakin, *This Day* HARASSED, THREATENED
Doifie Ola, *Post Express* HARASSED, THREATENED

Igbokwe, Dike, Ollor-Obari, Awoshakin, and Ola were arrested at Ogbia Town, Bayelsa State, while covering a youth rally protesting activity by the Shell oil company and the Nigerian government in the Niger Delta.

Security men swooped on Ogbia to abort the rally, but the organizers had secretly shifted the venue to Itokopiri, a neighboring town. The journalists, unaware of the change, were trying to locate the new site when they were arrested. They were interrogated and released hours later with a strong warning that they must not publish any story on the incident.

October 25
Soji Omotunde, *African Concord* IMPRISONED, ATTACKED

Omotunde, editor of the *African Concord*, was abducted by security agents as he was driving along a street in Ikeja, in mainland Lagos. The two agents stopped him, then bound and gagged him and forced him into their car. He was driven to an unknown location.

At press time, Omotunde was still in detention, at an unknown location in Abuja. Omotunde's case is of particular concern because his failing health. At the time he was abducted he had not fully recovered from serious injuries he sustained in a car crash in January.

November 3
Ladi Olorunyomi, Independent Journalism Centre (IJC) HARASSED

Olorunyomi, journalist and assistant director of the IJC, was arrested at her home at 1:00 a.m. by armed military intelligence officers.

Olorunyomi was interrogated about the whereabouts of her husband Dapo Olorunyomi, a journalist currently living in the United States, and Bayo Onanuga, editor of *TheNEWS*. Her colleagues believe her arrest may be connected to her husband's attendance at the Commonwealth Heads of Government Meeting in Edinburgh in October.

Olorunyomi was released in the afternoon of November 3 on the condition that she reports every day to the Military Intelligence Headquarters. CPJ protested the harassment of Olorunyomi in a November 12 letter to Gen. Sani Abacha.

November 4
Adetokunbo Fakeye, *PM News* IMPRISONED

Fakeye, the defense correspondent of *PM News*, disappeared while on assignment at Army Defense Headquarters in Lagos. *PM News* was

AFRICA

certain that Fakeye was detained at the Defense Headquarters. No reason was given for the journalist's detention.

November 8
Jenkins Alumona, *TheNEWS* IMPRISONED

Three plainclothes operatives of the State Security Service (SSS) arrested Alumona, editor of *TheNEWS* magazine, on the premises of the Nigerian Television Authority (NTA), located on Victoria Island, Lagos.

A female member of the security team approached Alumona and escorted him out of the NTA offices. Her colleagues then placed him in one of two waiting vehicles and drove him to the State Security Services detention Camp in Abuja.

Alumona was released on December 31.

November 10
Nosa Igiebor, *Tell* HARASSED
TheNEWS CENSORED

Security forces invaded the home of Igiebor, the editor in chief of the privately owned magazine *Tell*. They claimed that they were searching for an article titled, "Abacha's Illness Worsens," which reported that the head of state was very ill and suffering from cirrhosis.

The same story, published in the September 7 edition of the magazine *TheNEWS*, led to the arrest of an administration officer, a correspondent, 10 news agents, and many vendors of the magazine. All copies of that edition of *TheNEWS* were impounded.

November 12
Akin Adesokan, *Post Express* IMPRISONED

Adesokan, a reporter with the *Post Express* newspaper, was arrested by State Security Service (SSS) officers on November 12, at the Nigeria-Benin border. He was returning to Lagos from Austria, where, as an author and member of the Association of Nigerian Authors, he had attended a four-month writer-in-residence program.

The security officers apparently objected to photographs of dissidents such as Ken Saro-Wiwa that Adesokan had in his possession. Adesokan was held at the SSS Detention Camp, in Ikoyi, Lagos.

Adesokan was released on December 31.

November 14
Nduka Obaigbena, *THIS DAY* IMPRISONED

Obaigbena, publisher and editor in chief of the newspaper *THIS DAY*, was arrested shortly after his arrival at the Nicon Noga Hilton Hotel in Abuja. He is being detained at an unknown location. While authorities have offered no explanation as to Obaigbena's arrest, sources at *THIS DAY* believe it resulted from the paper's November 9 cover story, which analyzed the strategic importance of four officials in Gen. Sani Abacha's administration.

Obaigbena was released on November 20.

November 17
Ben Adaji, *TheNEWS* THREATENED

Adaji, Taraba State correspondent for *TheNEWS* magazine, was arrested by state security officers in Jalingo. He is being held at an undisclosed location.

Security officers had launched a full-scale manhunt for Adaji. He was wanted in connection with a story titled "War in Taraba," which he wrote in the October 27 edition of the *TheNEWS*. The story detailed the build-up and outbreak of a factional conflict in the Takum district of Taraba State and the roles of some military officers in this conflict.

November 17
Babafemi Ojudu, TheNEWS/TEMPO/PM News Group IMPRISONED

Ojudu, managing editor of TheNEWS/ TEMPO/PM News Group, was arrested by operatives of the state security service on November 17. He is being detained at an undisclosed location and authorities have given no reason for his arrest.

Ojudu was arrested upon his return to Lagos from Nairobi, Kenya, where he had taken part in a seminar organized by the Freedom Forum.

His imprisonment appears to be linked to a recent government clampdown on TheNEWS publishing group, which has resulted in the arrests of several other journalists affiliated with the group.

In a letter to Gen. Sani Abacha, CPJ protested the November arrests of Ojudu and other journalists affiliated with TheNEWS/TEMPO/PM News Group, and called for an end to the systematic censorship of the group's publications.

November 18
Rafiu Salau, TheNEWS/TEMPO/PM News Group IMPRISONED

Salau, administration manager of TheNEWS/TEMPO/PM News Group, was arrested and detained at the Directorate of Military Intelligence (DMI) in Apapa, Lagos. Salau had gone to the offices of the DMI to check on his colleague Adetokunbo Fakeye, the defense reporter for *PM News*, who had been imprisoned since November 4. Fakeye was later released without charge. Salau remains in detention at DMI.

November 25
Owei Lakemfa HARASSED
Charles Oni HARASSED

Lakemfa and Oni were detained at the State Security Service (SSS) offices in Ibadan, Oyo State. They were accused of "holding a workshop without the knowledge of the Police Commissioner or SSS director," interrogated, and released after several hours. Lakemfa had been coordinating a four-day training program for labor reporters in Oyo Township, Oyo State. Oni was a participant in the program.

The journalists were picked up and taken to the local police station before being moved to the SSS offices. After the two were released, the organizers of the workshop changed venues, only to have the program stopped again by security men.

December 1
Mahmud Jega, *New Nigerian* HARASSED

Jega, acting editor of the *New Nigerian*, was arrested by police in Kaduna, Kaduna State, because of an article the paper had run a few days earlier. He was detained for five hours at the State Police Command Offices in Kaduna and then released. According to a statement Jega made after his release, the police took issue with a November 27 editorial advocating a judicial inquiry into a number of suspicious fires that had razed several markets in and around Kaduna. The police were angered further that the editorial recalled reports of as many as 12 deaths in the fires.

December 2
Sunday Orinya, *TheNEWS* ATTACKED

Soldiers savagely beat and tortured Orinya, Benue State correspondent for *TheNEWS* magazine, after arresting him at the Benue Hotel where he was on assignment. They transported him to the Government House in Makurdi, and, led by the Chief Security Officer, 15 soldiers stripped Orinya of his clothes, horsewhipped and beat him for over an hour, and forced him to walk on his knees across rocks. He collapsed repeatedly and was eventually left unconscious in a bathroom for two hours. Orinya was released when he awoke, and was treated for severe injuries at a private clinic in Makurdi.

The soldiers who assaulted Orinya said they had been ordered to do so by the state military administrator, who objected to a December 8 article by the journalist reporting a series of unexplained fires and the presence of prostitutes at official Government House activities.

December 28
Niran Malaolu, *The Diet* IMPRISONED

Malaolu, editor of the daily newspaper *The Diet*, was arrested by Directorate of Military Intelligence (DMI) officers at the newspaper's editorial offices. He was transported to Military Intelligence Headquarters in Apapa, Lagos, where he is being held incommunicado.

Three weeks earlier, Hakizimana had been the target of an attempted kidnapping at his home. He was rescued by neighbors who intervened as he was being forced at gunpoint into a waiting car.

Hakizimana had been critical of the Rwandan government's activities for years and recently had received several threats on his life.

Rwanda

The murder of *Umuravumba* editor in chief Appolos Hakizimana on April 27 was a chilling reminder to the few journalists who survived Rwanda's genocide that they remain targets for any perceived critical reporting of the government and its officials.

Although a half-dozen newspapers and a few magazines still publish, much of the country is struggling to stabilize and rebuild itself. In the western part of the country, an ongoing clandestine battle between the government and organized opposition forces has put the countryside off-limits for civilian travel and destabilized the northwestern region. This largely unreported civil war and a government intolerant of dissent or disclosure intrude on all aspects of civic communication and discussion. But the fledgling Rwanda News Agency, established in 1997 by Jean-Baptiste Kayigamba, intends to supply articles to international news outlets.

April 27
Appolos Hakizimana, *Umuravumba* KILLED

Hakizimana, editor in chief of the privately owned bi-monthly *Umuravumba* and former editor of the independent weekly *Intego*, was murdered while returning to his home in Kigali. He was attacked and gagged by two men, who shot him twice in the ear, killing him instantly, and then fled.

Senegal

The climate for the media in Senegal is one of the most tolerant in Africa. Yet the laws are written so that the burden of proof rests with the accused, placing the media in a difficult position. On February 2, the National Assembly adopted a press code which emphasizes ethics and responsibility and requires publishers to report their press runs.

The ruling in the 1996 defamation case against the independent daily newspaper *Sud Quotidien*, published by the Sud Communications Group, one of the leading private press groups in francophone Africa, was upheld on appeal in June, sounded a sour note for press freedom in the country.

Since the state released its hold on broadcasting a little more than three years ago, call-in radio talk shows have increased in popularity and added to the openness of Senegalese society. But the exorbitant broadcasting fees charged by the government have made it difficult for private stations to survive. In August, three stations—Sud FM, Nostalgie, and Dunya—were given a three-month suspension for nonpayment of fees ranging from CFA 20 million (US$32,000) to CFA 30 million (US$48,000). In a revolutionary move, in September, Sud FM—which owns eight radio stations—signed an agreement with Worldspace, a U.S. company founded in 1990 to provide direct satellite delivery of digital audio communications to emerging world markets.

June 13
Abdoulaye Ndiaga Sylla, Sud Communication, *Sud Quotidien* LEGAL ACTION
Abdou Latif Coulibaly, *Sud Quotidien* LEGAL ACTION
Demba Ndiaye, *Sud Quotidien* LEGAL ACTION
Omar Khoureysi, *Sud Quotidien* LEGAL ACTION

Sylla, vice-president of Sud Communication and director of the newspaper *Sud Quotidien*, and reporters Coulibaly, Ndiaye, and Khoureysi, were charged with distributing false information and defaming the president. The charges were in connection with articles printed in the June 2, 6, and 7 issues of *Sud Quotidien* about the awarding of the nation's highest honor, the "Chevalier de l'Ordre National du Lion," to Jean Claude Mimran and his brother Robert, sugar importers whom the newspaper has implicated in corruption scams.

Sylla, Coulibaly, Ndiaye, and Khoureysi appeared in court on June 18. The state prosecutor's request for their detention was refused.

August 8
Sud FM CENSORED
Nostalgie CENSORED
Dunya CENSORED

The Senegalese government leveled a three-month broadcasting suspension against private radio stations Sud FM, Nostalgie, and Dunya, for broadcast fee arrears. Sud FM owed the state CFA 20 million (US$32,000) and Nostalgie and Dunya each owed the state CFA 30 million (US$48,000). All three stations resumed broadcasting in late August after paying the fees.

Sierra Leone

The election of President Ahmed Tejan Kabbah in 1996 ended five years of civil war and army rule, and later that same year his signing of a cease-fire agreement with Revolutionary United Front (RUF) leader Foday Sankoh appeared to put the country on the path to democracy. The media's efforts to get rid of the former military dictatorship were expected to be rewarded by the new government's liberalized approach to press freedom—a "reward" that came in the form of counseling, reprimands, and police action. In March, an amendment to the current press law was introduced in parliament whose changes were so severe that, if passed, would effectively dissolve 30 of the country's 42 newspapers.

Despite the cease-fire, fighting in the countryside in the early part of the year left the peace accord on the verge of collapse. Citing national security concerns, the government began to harass a variety of media. Many of the newer radio stations and newspapers were established for short-term gain or political reasons and staffed by non-professionals. There were 12 newspapers in 1996; in 1997, there were more than 50. In an attempt to stem what was perceived as a disturbing trend, the Sierra Leone Association of Journalists, headed by Frank Kposowa, drew up a code of ethics which included minimum requirements for editors and journalists, and sent it to the government for ratification.

As political conditions and general security in Sierra Leone rapidly degenerated, journalists experienced an unprecedented increase in harassment and intimidation at the hands of military officers. The crisis further escalated when junior army officers took over the capital, Freetown, on May 25 and overthrew Kabbah's civilian government in a bloody coup, the third in five years for war-torn Sierra Leone. The coup leaders, headed by Maj. Johnny Paul Koroma of the Armed Forces Revolutionary Council (AFRC), scrapped the constitution and banned all political parties. Announcing his opposition to the recently passed Newspaper Act of 1997 and the Media Practitioner's Act of 1997, Koroma then proceeded to shut down the country's private radio stations. Fearing looting of their premises by armed robbers, military officers, or RUF soldiers, newspapers closed of their own accord. Journalists who wrote articles critical of the armed forces were routinely harassed, attacked, or detained by junior officers acting on their own.

The complete collapse of the legal system, coupled with most journalists' inability to pay the monthly 80,000 Leones (US$80) fee to hire a free-lance bodyguard for protection, led many journalists to practice self-censorship or go into hiding. Many others left to live in exile and poverty in neighboring countries. Newspaper vendors were mercilessly beaten in the streets, arrested, and detained, and their papers confiscated and burnt as the Koroma junta declared outright war on the pro-democracy press. Free-lance journalist Ishmael Jalloh, who was killed covering a battle between ECOMOG and an alliance of AFRC and RUF soldiers, was an early victim of the state of anarchy that has prevailed in the capital since the coup.

Only two pro-government and two independent newspapers, out of 50 prior to the coup, still publish, albeit irregularly. Radio stations FM96.2 and FM104 resumed broadcasting, with their content restricted to religious and music formats. On September 22, the government told the independent and state-run press that newspapers wishing to keep their publishing licenses would have to submit to annual registration requirements. Registration fees were set at 100,000 Leones (US$100) for the independents, and 50,000 Leones (US$50) for the state-controlled publications.

After initially stating that presidential elections would be delayed until 2001, at year-end Koroma agreed to reinstate deposed President Kabbah by April 1998, bowing to pressure, including the 16-nation Economic Community of West Africa's economic sanctions and blockade, and the British Commonwealth's decision to continue to suspend the country until democracy was restored.

As this book went to press, the media remained effectively shut down. Journalists who had been forced into exile in neighboring countries and abroad awaited President Kabbah's reinstatement and the anticipated accompanying return of security and stability to the country.

January 24
Pat Kawa, *Punch* HARASSED, LEGAL ACTION

Police arrested Kawa, *Punch* correspondent in Bo, the capital of the Southern district, at his home. Kawa was taken to police headquarters and charged with four counts of defamation. He was released the same day on bail equivalent to US$250.

The arrest was in connection with Kawa's article in the January 24 issue of *Punch* about alleged financial improprieties on the part of the provisional secretary of the South, Soluku Bockari, and the chair of the Bo City Council, Elais Toma. Aro John Bockari, Soluku Bockari's brother and Toma's attorney, asked police to arrest Kawa.

In a letter to President Ahmed Tejan Kabbah, CPJ called for Kawa's unconditional release. Kawa appeared in court on March 3, and the case against him was dismissed.

March 3
Mohammed Karim, *Footprints* IMPRISONED
Njai Kanthba, *Footprints* IMPRISONED

Footprints magazine editor Mohammed Karim

and staff writer Njai Kanthba were arrested on charges of drug possession. Police said Prof. Harry Turay of Njala University accused the journalists of drug possession when they met with Turay in his office to confirm a story. Turay denied accusing the journalists, who were released three days later. The journalists said they planned to sue police for wrongful arrest and detention.

It is believed that Karim and Kanthba were arrested in connection with an article in the February 28 issue of *Footprints*, which reported that the presidential affairs minister had used his position to avoid customs tax on 50 cars he imported into Sierra Leone amounting to 23 million leones (US$23,000). Customs officials and the minister denied that the cars were imported into the country.

March 6
Harry Evans, *Footprints* IMPRISONED

Police arrested *Footprints* publisher Harry Evans and asked him to produce evidence confirming that the presidential affairs minister had imported 50 cars into the country, as his publication had reported.

Evans, who was not charged, was held for nearly a week before police released him on March 12.

An article printed in the February 28 issue of *Footprints* reported that the Minister of Presidential Affairs imported the cars into the country and used his position to avoid paying custom taxes of 23 million leones (US $23,000). Customs officials and the minister denied the cars were imported.

March 19
Gibril Koroma, *Expo Times* IMPRISONED
Charles Davis, *Expo Times* IMPRISONED
Ibrahim Seaga Shaw, *Expo Times* IMPRISONED

Expo Times editors Koroma and Davis and publisher Shaw were arrested without charge at the paper's editorial office. The arrest was in con-

nection with an article published in the March 19 issue of *Expo Times* titled "Abacha's Gangsterism," referring to Nigerian leader Sani Abacha. The journalists were detained at the Criminal Investigation Department in Freetown.

In a letter to Sierra Leone's president Ahmed Tejan Kabbah, CPJ protested the arrests and called for the journalists' immediate and unconditional release.

After denying bail applications four times, the authorities released the three men on April 7.

April 20
James Murray, *Punch* LEGAL ACTION

Murray, a reporter for the independent newspaper *Punch*, was arrested on charges of drug possession. Murray had gone to the police station to confirm a story that police officers had released an accused drug dealer after accepting a bribe from him. Murray was released the next day after posting bond.

Murray's case was later dismissed.

June 3
Ishmael Jalloh, *Punch*, *Storm*, and *Vision* KILLED

Jalloh, a free-lance correspondent for a number of independent newspapers including *Punch*, *Storm*, and *Vision*, was killed. He had been covering a battle in Allentown between a combined battalion of the Revolutionary United Front and the Sierra Leone Armed Forces Revolutionary Council against Nigerian ECO-MOG soldiers.

Jalloh died of wounds sustained from a rocket-propelled grenade. Jalloh was identified the following day by another journalist.

June 4
Phillip Neville, *Standard Times* ATTACKED

Neville, managing editor of the *Standard Times*, was severely beaten by two armed men who broke into his home. They demanded to know if Neville was harboring a government minister from ousted President Ahmed Tejan Kabbah's cabinet.

July 8
Saloman Conteh, *The Democrat*
IMPRISONED
Jeff Bowlay Williams, *The Democrat*
IMPRISONED

Reporter Conteh and free-lance correspondent Williams were arrested by 20 soldiers, interrogated at military headquarters, then brought to prison without charge. They were released on July 19.

The Democrat stopped publication on the day of their arrest. The soldiers originally had gone to *The Democrat* offices to arrest editor Pius Foray, who was not there at the time.

July 8
Budu Hayes, *The Point* IMPRISONED

Hayes, managing editor of the independent newspaper *The Point*, was arrested at his home by soldiers and transported to Cockrill Military Headquarters, where he was detained until the following day. Soldiers who arrested Hayes alleged that he was harboring local militia men who were "fighting against the revolution."

July 8
Hilton Fyle, WBIG (FM 103) IMPRISONED

Fyle, owner of independent radio station WBIG (FM 103), was arrested and detained in connection with a story he filed reporting that Sierra Leone soldiers had recaptured Lungi Airport from the ECOMOG (Economic Community of West African States Monitoring group) soldiers. Fyle was released on July 10.

July 19
Martins I. Martins, *Business Vision*
IMPRISONED

Martins, a reporter, was arrested and detained at military headquarters. He was accused of faxing intelligence reports to ousted President Ahmed Tejan Kabbah. Martins, who was released on July 21, returned to his home and found it had been looted.

July 26
Dominick Lamine, *Unity Now* IMPRISONED
Sahr Mbayoh, *Unity Now* IMPRISONED
Frank Kposowa, *Unity Now* THREATENED

Unity Now deputy editor Lamine and news editor Mbayoh were arrested by AFRC soldiers at the independent newspaper's editorial offices. Soldiers confiscated the publication's computer system; military officials later said they took subversive materials that would compromise the July 29 peace talks between the AFRC and ministers from the Economic Community of West African States (ECOWAS).

The journalists were held incommunicado at military headquarters. Mbayoh was released on July 30 and Lamine was released on August 2. No charges were filed.

AFRC soldiers continued to search for *Unity Now*'s editor in chief and president of the Sierra Leone Association of Journalists, Frank Kposowa, who went into hiding to avoid arrest.

July 26
Suliman Momodu, *Concord Times* and the BBC
THREATENED

Momodu, a Kenema-based BBC stringer and *Concord Times* correspondent, went into hiding after learning he was being sought by AFRC soldiers.

July 28
Suliman Janger, *New Tablet* IMPRISONED
Gibril Foday Musa, *New Tablet*
THREATENED
New Tablet CENSORED

Janger, production manager of the *New Tablet* newspaper, was arrested while he was distributing the newspaper's second edition. The soldiers who detained him also seized about 900 copies. Five unidentified newspaper vendors were also arrested along with Janger. AFRC soldiers searched for Musa, the paper's editor in chief, who went into hiding to avoid arrest.

July 30
***Standard Times* CENSORED**
Phillip Neville, *Standard Times* THREATENED

AFRC soldiers seized about 1,500 copies of the *Standard Times* newspaper at the newspaper's editorial offices. The soldiers were searching for *Standard Times* managing editor Phillip Neville, who went underground to avoid arrest.

August 25
Ibrahim El-Tayyib Bah, *The Eastern Front* ATTACKED

Armed men broke into the home of Bah, editor of *The Eastern Front* and vice president of the Sierra Leone Association of Journalists (SLAJ). The house was ransacked. Bah later fled to Guinea to escape further persecution.

October 8
David Tambaryoh, *Punch* IMPRISONED

Three armed men of the Criminal Investigation Division (CID) arrested Tambaryoh, editor of the newspaper *Punch* at his home. Tambaryoh was charged with the aggravated assault of Ibrahim Seaga Shaw, editor of the *Expo Times* and subversion for allegedly communicating sensitive information to ousted president Tejan Kabbah, Ambassador to the United Nations James Jonah, and Ambassador John Ernest Leigh in Washington. Tambaryoh denied all charges.

Upon his release after 72 hours of detention, security guards stopped by the *Punch* offices looking for him and his deputy director. Tambaryoh is currently in hiding.

During Tambaryoh's detention, his wife, who is also in hiding, transported some of his

belongings to her elder sister's house. That night, armed men arrived at Tambaryoh's sister-in-law's house and demanded his property. She denied having it and the soldiers looted her house before leaving.

October 11
Umaru Fofana, *Vision*, BBC ATTACKED

Fofana, a free-lancer for the *Vision* newspaper and a stringer for the British Broadcasting Corporation (BBC), was shot in the leg and tortured by army officers who claimed he was suspected of reporting for former president Tejan Kabbah's clandestine radio station, FM 98.1. At the time he was attacked, Fofana was assessing damage done to Kabbah's house, which was set on fire October 8 by the AFRC/RUF junta. Fofana was treated at the Military Hospital in Freetown and released.

October 11
John Foray, *Democrat* IMPRISONED
Abdul Kposwa, free-lancer IMPRISONED

Foray, acting editor of the newspaper *Democrat*, and Kposwa, a free-lancer, were beaten and arrested by army officers who then escorted them to Pademba Road Prison, where they was detained without charge.

Eight days after his arrest, officers bound Foray together with Jonathan Leigh, a reporter with the *New Observer* who had been in detention at Pademba when Foray was brought there, and drove the two journalists to Allentown, a region to the east of Freetown, where the military was attacking ECOMOG (Economic Community of West African States Monitoring Group) troops stationed in the area. The officers apparently wanted Foray to closely witness the civil strife they and other journalists had been covering. Foray was subsequently taken to a military camp. Kposwa was transferred from Pademba to the same military camp on October 19.

Foray was released on October 25 without

charge. He is reported to be suffering from a spinal injury.

Kposwa was also later freed. He reported, however, that after his release soldiers had come to his house looking for him.

October 13
Jonathan Leigh, *New Observer* IMPRISONED

Leigh was picked up by military officers, who accused him of subversion, and was detained at the Pandemba Road Prison. Six days after his arrest, officers tied him up, together with John Foray, the editor of *The Democrat*, who was also being held at Pademba, and drove the two journalists to Allentown, a region to the east of Freetown. The officers wanted to provide Leigh with a close look the civil strife he and other journalists had been covering. Leigh was subsequently taken to a military camp, from which he was released on October 25 without charge.

October 16
Paul Kamara, *For Di People* IMPRISONED
For Di People ATTACKED, CENSORED

Paul Kamara of the newspaper *For Di People* was arrested and detained for two days. Kamara was accused of providing reports to the illegal underground radio station 98.1 FM. The same day, junta soldiers ransacked *For Di People*'s offices, confiscating phones, computers, and other equipment, as well as Kamara's car. The newspaper was forced to close because of the attack.

November 21
Ibrahim Karim Sei, *Standard Times*
IMPRISONED
Dorothy Awoonor-Gordon, *Concord Times*
IMPRISONED

Sei, editor of the *Standard Times*, and Awoonor-Gordon, acting editor of the *Concord Times*, were arrested and detained at the Criminal Investigation Department headquarters. Their arrest resulted from the publication of articles in their respective papers. A principal liaison officer of the ruling Armed Forces Revolutionary Council, known to reporters by the nickname "Zagalo," found the various articles inappropriate and ordered the journalists' arrest. Awoonor-Gordon, who was nursing an infant at the time of her arrest, and Sei were released after nine days.

Somalia

Despite Hussein Aideed's election as president of Somalia by a council of clan leaders after the death of his father, warlord Gen. Mohammed Farah Aideed, in August 1996, there is still no recognized central government. Two years after the withdrawal of U.N. troops, the country remains under the control of various clan leaders. State institutions and public services have barely begun reconstruction. And although there is now relative peace in many parts of the country, several regions are still subject to frequent flare-ups of factional fighting.

Press freedom has been virtually nonexistent in Somalia since independence was declared in 1960. Today, after more than six years of civil war and famine, there are about a dozen publications, and they survive with very little equipment. The weekly *Sanca*, for example, publishing with three typewriters, an old photocopier, scissors and some glue, is one of the better-equipped newspapers in the capital of Mogadishu.

Somali journalists are poorly paid and under constant pressure from the various armed factions. Often the victims of reprisals, journalists have been intimidated with death threats, arrests, and interrogations, and certain topics have been banned. Members of the press must observe safety

precautions, including abiding by a 5 p.m. curfew, driving with an escort of several cars, and regularly changing bodyguards. Nevertheless, they continue to try to practice their profession in an extremely dangerous environment.

January 5
Qaran ATTACKED

Heavily armed men stormed and looted the editorial office of the Mogadishu daily *Qaran*. The men removed a computer, office equipment, and furniture. The theft forced the newspaper to cease publication until January 12.

September 8
Hassan Siad, *Jamhuria* IMPRISONED
Mahmud Abdu Shide, *Jamhuria* IMPRISONED
Jamhuria CENSORED

Siad, editor in chief of the daily *Jamhuria*, was arrested by police, and the Hargeisa police commander ordered the closure of the newspaper, cordoning off its printing press on September 9. The owner of the newspaper building, Mahmud Abdu Shide, was also detained for allegedly printing fake tax-collecting receipts.

Both Siad and Shide were released on September 16, and the closure order on *Jamhuria* was lifted. The newspaper resumed publication September 17. No official explanation was given for the arrests or the closure order.

South Africa

Since President Nelson Mandela came to power in South Africa's first all-race elections in 1994, his government has surprised many of its critics by pursuing market-friendly policies. One of the casualties of this new free market and privatization was the giant South African Broadcasting Corporation (SABC), which lost about one-third of its administrative, management, broadcasting, and technical staff as a result of downsizing, resignations, and retirements. The elimination of more than a thousand jobs resulted in the large-scale restructuring of the corporation. In a related matter, with the departure of former president F.W. de Klerk from National Party (NP) politics in August, the embattled NP in November accused SABC-Television News of politically biased reporting in giving over 90 percent of its coverage to the African National Congress (ANC) and not acting in the spirit of promoting multi-party democracy.

But while the SABC has reduced itself to a state of near collapse with a succession of misguided policy decisions, the Independent Broadcasting Authority (IBA) has been steadily reshaping the face of South African broadcasting since its inception three years ago. By creating more than 100 community radio stations in a country with low literacy rates and a high radio listenership, and selling off six SABC stations and licensing seven new commercial ones, the IBA has opened the airwaves to previously neglected sectors of society. In March, after the SABC got tough with license defaulters and proceeded with legal action against hundreds of people, the IBA began hearings for a new private commercial television station which would provide even more variety and is expected to go on the air by the middle of 1998 to compete with the three stations owned by SABC.

In August, the IBA began controversial inquiries into the existing license of M-Net, the only private pay-television station. Within the next 18 months, Posts, Telecommunications and Broadcasting Minister Jay Naidoo plans to merge IBA with the South African Telecommunications Regulatory Authority (SATRA), raising fears for IBA's independence, because the minister is able to intervene directly in the affairs of SATRA.

In mid-year, SATRA heard arguments concerning a battle for the Internet between Telkom, the state-owned phone company which enjoys a monopoly over telecommunications in South Africa, and the private Internet Service Providers Association. In an interim decision handed down on June 11, SATRA ruled that Telkom could not claim exclusive rights to Internet service provision.

The year was characterized by strained relations between the media and various levels of government. In a controversial statement at the beginning of the year, President Mandela described the press as "still controlled by white conservative pro-prietors" who are "embittered ...and out of touch with black society," and who co-opt black journalists to do their "dirty work." Tensions also rose at provincial and local levels of government, resulting in lawsuits and threats of lawsuits. These actions and threats were particularly worrisome for the future of small independent and community media, which often do not have the financial resources to pay legal fees.

Overall, the legal position of the press has changed significantly in recent years. Virtually all statutes aimed at the press—which in the past imposed a wide range of restrictions and provided for harsh mea-sures of control by the government—have now been repealed or are under review. In February, after more than two years of drafting, the country's new constitution came into effect, and although it protects the right to freedom of expression and speech, it does not provide protection against certain forms of hate speech as some had hoped it would. In June, Minister of Safety and Security Sydney Mufamadi assured the press that authorities would not use the infamous Section 205 of the Criminal Procedures Act against journalists until it is reviewed—an announcement met with relief because the section has been used in the past to compel journalists to reveal their sources.

President Mandela in July set up an advi-sory panel to choose the senior members of two new administrative bodies, the Films and Publications Board and the Review Board, which have the power to classify—or even ban—films and publications.

On a more positive note, the Open Democracy Bill was approved by the cabinet in June and made public in October. It is intended to protect citizens against invasion of privacy, either by the government or the private sector, and to protect government whistleblowers, as well as to allow citizens access to government information, and to force private information banks to disclose personal information they have gathered.

The Truth and Reconciliation Commission (TRC) set May 30 as the dead-line for submissions on the role the media played in South Africa from 1960 to the 1994 election, especially those journalists whose stories of abuse under apartheid had not yet been heard. In June, the Freedom of Expression Institute submitted research on the role of the media during the apartheid years and found that the mainstream news-paper industry had fallen short of its role to properly inform the public, and at times had engaged in collusion and self-censorship. In a stunning mea culpa in October, more than 100 journalists from Afrikaans publications presented written apologies to the TRC for the role played by their medium in promot-ing human rights abuses during apartheid.

April 30
Mapule Sibanda, *City Press* IMPRISONED, LEGAL ACTION

Sibanda, a reporter for the *City Press*, was arrested at a police station in Johannesburg for possession of narcotics after submitting drugs to the police for forensic testing. Sibanda had contacted the police a week earlier to ask them to test the drugs to determine their authenticity and potency. Police said Sibanda had contacted them the week before and that they told her she would be violating the law.

Sibanda appeared in the Johannesburg Magistrates Court the day of her arrest and was released on bail of R2,000 (US$500).

The government dropped the charges against Sibanda on May 27.

July 2
Derek Fleming, free-lancer IMPRISONED

Police arrested Fleming and detained him for six days. They searched Fleming's home and confiscated a number of documents, his computer's hard-drive, computer diskettes, a video cassette, and news clippings.

The police action was believed to be related to Fleming's investigation of Craig Kotze, the communications adviser to Police Commissioner George Fivaz.

July 20
Sunday Independent LEGAL ACTION
Sunday Argus LEGAL ACTION
Sunday Tribune LEGAL ACTION
Newton Kanhema, free-lancer LEGAL ACTION

Denel, an arms manufacturer, filed charges against the *Sunday Independent*, the *Sunday Argus*, the *Sunday Tribune*, the newspaper's editors, and reporter Newton Kanhema under the 1968 Armaments Development and Production Act. They were charged with publishing details of the company's large armaments deal with an undisclosed Middle Eastern country.

November 6
Justin Arenstein, *Mail & Guardian* THREATENED

The African National Congress (ANC) in the Mpumalanga province said that it intended to press charges against Arenstein, a reporter for the *Mail & Guardian*, to force him to reveal his

sources for an article he had published the week before. Arenstein's article quoted members of the ANC's Provincial Executive Committee as saying that the committee had unanimously agreed to withdraw the nomination of Provincial Premier Matthews Phosa for the position of ANC deputy president. ANC spokesman Jackson Mthembu denied that any such agreement had been made and vowed to root out the "malicious informants" who leaked the story to Arenstein.

Sudan

The state has maintained a firm grip over the media since the June 1989 military coup that brought to power the Islamist-led regime of Lt. General Omar Hassan al-Bashir. The independent press, which flourished during the brief period of multi-party government (1986-89), was dealt a serious blow when the regime banned all privately owned publications on the day it assumed power. Although some privately owned publications eventually reappeared after submitting to government re-licensure, the prohibition on newspapers affiliated with opposition parties has continued, and many of the journalists formerly affiliated with those papers are now living in exile. The existing private press is subject to close state scrutiny of their reporting on sensitive political issues such as the country's ongoing civil conflict in southern Sudan, government corruption, and domestic unrest. Over the last eight years, the authorities have suspended or permanently closed outspoken newspapers, and meted out long-term detentions and torture to offending journalists. As a result, self-censorship is widespread.

Following a peace accord signed in April with seven rebel factions, al-Bashir said that he was prepared to tolerate a more liberal

press. In an apparent sign of goodwill, the independent daily *Al-Rai Al-Akher*, which was closed in 1996 following a series of run-ins with authorities, was permitted to resume publication on June 23. The government also announced that it would no longer arrest or detain journalists while they are being investigated for press law violations. Amidst these developments, however, al-Bashir stressed that the press is still obligated to work within the limits of the law—a warning that criticism of the state or commentary on taboo political issues will continue to place journalists in jeopardy.

January 13
Nureddin Madani, *Al-Khaleej* IMPRISONED

Sudanese authorities detained Madani, the Sudan correspondent for the United Arab Emirates-based daily *Al-Khaleej*, in Khartoum. Security agents questioned Madani about what they called the paper's unbalanced reporting on the political situation in Sudan. He was released two days later.

August 9
Kamel Hassan Bakhit, *Al-Majallis*
IMPRISONED
Abdel Majuid Mansour, *Al-Majallis*
IMPRISONED

Sudanese security authorities detained Bakhit, editor in chief of the daily *Al-Majallis*; and Mansour, chairman of the board of Dar al-Ahlah, the publishing house that owns *Al-Majallis*. Security forces held them incommunicado for two days before releasing them on August 11. There was no official explanation, but the incident appeared to be a retaliation for an article published the week before that reported on the theft of Interior Minister Brig. Bakri Hassan Salih's portable telephone.

CPJ wrote to President Omar al-Bashir on August 13, urging that Sudanese authorities conduct a thorough investigation and to prosecute responsible members of the security forces.

Swaziland

Swaziland is the only country in southern Africa without a constitution. King Mswati III rules by a decree passed in 1973 which effectively nullified the 1968 constitution and prohibited political activity and freedom of expression. Over the last two years, however, the country has been going through intense labor and political unrest. There have been calls for constitutional reform, but the king has remained unmoved and instead has resorted to intimidation tactics to quash dissent.

Government censorship and pressure continue to stifle the press. In February, the cabinet ordered a blanket ban on state-controlled radio and television broadcasters' coverage of a national labor strike. And in April, the Minister of Public Service and Information, Muntu Mswane, issued a stern warning to an increasingly frustrated press to stop reporting on antigovernment organizations, citing the 1973 decree barring the media from covering news events involving opposition parties. The harassment of journalists working for government-owned media intensified during an April 12 political rally organized by opposition parties to protest the 1973 decree and mark the 24th year of the state of emergency.

In October, as dismayed journalists looked on, the cabinet approved a media council bill which would give it even tighter control over the press. Journalists or publications found by a seven-member media council to have committed a serious breach of ethics could be ordered to publish the council's findings, issue a retraction, publish an apology, or be deregulated. Journalists who fail to comply could face a fine of up to 15,000 rand (US$3,200) or five years in jail and a fine of 100,000 rand (US$21,000). Media owners would risk hefty fines or up to seven years in jail if they publish a newspaper without first receiving accreditation from the media council. But in a stunning reversal at the end of the year, the government, which had seemed intent on steamrollering the bill through parliament without any outside consultation, gave in to intense media pressure and allowed the bill to be reviewed by a special committee.

February 1
All journalists THREATENED

Pamphlets with warnings to journalists were distributed in the towns of Mbabane and Manzini. They warned that any journalist who reported favorably on the strike planned for February 3, organized by the Swaziland Federation of Trade Unions, "would be dealt with appropriately."

No individual or organization has claimed responsibility for the pamphleting action.

February 1
State-controlled broadcast media CENSORED

The Swaziland cabinet prevented state-controlled radio and television stations from broadcasting information about a country-wide labor stoppage. The blanket ban prohibited coverage of the Swaziland Federation of Trade Unions' strike. It was promulgated under Section 12 of the 1997 Criminal Procedure and Evidence Act, which makes illegal all materials likely to "incite the public against the government."

May 21
Paul Loffler, *Times of Swaziland* THREATENED

Loffler, finance manager for the *Times of Swaziland*, was summoned to appear in royal court without legal representation. The action was in connection with a story, published May 12, reporting that King Mswati owed the

Mbabane City Council 30,000 Lilangani (US$6,400) in back taxes for a hotel he owns.

Senator Bhekimpi Dlamini, a member of the royal family, reportedly told the newspaper that he intended to sponsor a motion to close the paper because he was angry about the article.

Tanzania

After three decades of one-party rule, the introduction of pluralism into Tanzanian politics in the early 1990s resulted in the break up of the government's monopoly over the print and electronic media, producing an unprecedented proliferation of media outlets and the emergence of a lively free press. As state efforts to suppress the independent media have increased, however, the number of functioning newspapers has dwindled to 38 from more than a hundred earlier in the decade. There are myriad oppressive laws which authorities have used to clamp down on the media, harassing, detaining, and arresting journalists and banning publications. In the early part of 1997, the Association of Journalists and Media Workers began legal proceedings challenging the constitutionality of these laws in a bid to check the escalating harassment of the press.

Despite the existence of five television stations and eight new FM radio stations, the euphoria that greeted the liberalization of Tanzania's airwaves has turned to disappointment as broadcast stations offer pro-government programs with very little independent reporting or criticism. In addition, the broadcast range of television and FM radio is geographically confined to only 25 percent of the country. The government has been extremely selective in granting licenses, thereby limiting the expression of dissenting views.

After considerable opposition, the government deferred the enactment of legislation to regulate the standard of conduct and activities of the media. In October, journalists established the Media Council of Tanzania, which set up a voluntary code of ethics and intends to mediate disputes in a profession that has become, along with the rest of the country, increasingly vulnerable to corruption because of poor working conditions, low pay, and the lack of job security.

On the island of Zanzibar—which, although part of the United Republic of Tanzania since 1964, can pass legislation independent of the mainland—the Zanzibar Information Service announced the compulsory licensing of journalists at the beginning of the year. The information service said that journalists working without a license would be fined 500,000 TS (US$1,000) or sentenced to five years in jail. This is the first time that Zanzibar has enforced the licensing of journalists since the passage of the Newspapers Act in 1988.

February 28
Adam Mwaibabile, free-lancer IMPRISONED

Mwaibabile, a free-lance journalist working in the Ruvuma region, was sentenced to a year in prison for possession of a secret government document as defined in the 1976 National Security Act. The document in question was a letter from the Ruvuma regional commissioner's office to the town council director, instructing him not to issue a 1995-96 business license to Mwaibabile, who runs a small business to supplement his income.

Mwaibabile's colleagues believe he was imprisoned for his investigative reporting exposing corruption among Ruvuma officials.

In an April 1 letter to President Benjamin Mkapa, CPJ protested Mwaibabile's arrest and imprisonment and demanded his immediate and unconditional release.

On April 29, Tanzania's High Court acquitted Mwaibabile, who had been released on bail on March 21.

March
All journalists THREATENED

Zanzibar authorities threatened to arrest any journalist who had failed to become licensed under new licensing policies.

The Zanzibar Information Services (ZIS) said on December 13, 1996, that it would begin a licensing process for journalists in January 1997. The deadline for compliance was February 28. Annually renewed licensing became compulsory for both private and state-sponsored journalists, at a fee of Tshs 6,000 (US$12).

Failure to follow the licensure procedure carries a fine of Tshs 500,000 ($1,000) or a jail sentence of up to five years. ZIS Deputy Director Rafii Makame said the licensing program was created to enforce the 1988 Newspapers Act.

April 10
Tryphone Mwenji, *The Guardian*
IMPRISONED

Dar es Salaam police arrested and detained Mwenji, a photojournalist for the independent Tanzanian newspaper *The Guardian*. Mwenji had been photographing police arresting loiterers in Dar es Salaam's city center. Police destroyed Mwenji's camera during the arrest. Mwenji was later released without charge.

April 25
Betty Masanja, Dar es Salaam Television
IMPRISONED
Lilian Kalaghe, *Business Times* and *Majira*
IMPRISONED

Zanzibar police searched the hotel rooms of Tanzania-based journalists Masanja and Kalaghe. Police confiscated their documents and briefly detained them at Mwembemadema Central Police Station and interrogated them about Zanzibar politics.

Regional Police Commander Musa Msheba

said the arrests followed a tip that the two journalists were from Malawi and were smuggling gemstones and trafficking drugs.

Togo

Gnassingbe Eyadema, Africa's longest-serving head of state, who seized power in 1967 and was elected president in 1993, is preparing to run for re-election in August 1998. Although the democratization movement of 1990-1992 broke the state monopoly on the print media, Eyadema's government has gradually regained control over the press through the increasingly frequent use of repressive statutes.

In an attempt to muzzle the press, the government has refused to repeal the draconian, 7-year-old law #90-25, despite persistent appeals from the Togolese Union of Journalists. The law's provisions include criminal penalties for defamation, and specific provisions for defaming the head of state. Because Togolese law permits investigative detention for 48 hours, arrests on defamation charges have occured frequently since 1993, sometimes resulting in the closure of newspapers.

A half-dozen private radio and television stations now broadcast, but independent local coverage is limited. And the government-controlled nationwide broadcast media rarely give access to the opposition. A number of newspapers have folded because of the ever-increasing cost of printing materials.

February 4
Abass Dermane, *Le Regard* IMPRISONED

Dermane, director of publication for the weekly *Le Regard*, was arrested at the interior ministry and transported to the gendarmerie. The state prosecutor said Dermane was accused of "disturbing the public order" and "defaming the

head of state." Dermane's arrest followed the January 14 publication of an article titled "Horrors Under the Regime of [President Etienne Gnassingbe] Eyadema."

Dermane was released on February 8.

February 5
Augustin Assiobo, *Tingo-Tingo* IMPRISONED

Assiobo, publications director of the weekly *Tingo-Tingo*, was arrested at his home and detained because of a complaint lodged by the family of former External Affairs Minister Alasounouma Boumbera. Assiobo was accused of making death threats against Boumbera, apparently a trumped-up charge by authorities angered by a story about a government payoff to a French journalist and a series of articles alleging abuses by the gendarmerie.

On May 1, Assiobo's case was settled with a jail sentence of four months, with two months suspended, and a fine of 50,000 francs CFA (US$83). Because he had already spent three months in jail, he was freed.

February 19
Gabriel Agah, *Forum Hebdo* LEGAL ACTION
Forum Hebdo CENSORED

A court order, issued by the Togo attorney general's office, suspended publication of the independent weekly *Forum Hebdo* for six months. The court sentenced *Forum Hebdo* publisher Agah in absentia to a one-year prison term and a fine of 1 million CFA (US$1,900).

The newspaper had received no prior notification of the court actions. Records of the court proceedings stated only that two default judgments were handed down in the cases of "RPT vs. Gabriel Agah" and the "National Police vs. Agah." The RPT (Rassemblement du Peuple Togolais) is the ruling party of President Gnassingbe Eyadema.

December 5
Basile Agboh, *Crocodile* IMPRISONED
Afatchao Siliadin, *Nouveau Journal*
IMPRISONED

Agboh, a school teacher and editor of the news-paper *Crocodile*, was arrested on December 5, in the town of Vogan (about 40 kilometers north-east of Lome). The arrest stemmed from the publication of an article concerning President Eyadema's alleged aid to forces battling Laurent Kabila of the Democratic Republic of Congo. Agboh was released on December 8.

Siliadin, publisher of *Nouveau Journal*, another paper which ran the article, was also arrested on December 5. Armed police arrived at his house at 4:30 a.m. and took Siliadin's entire family into custody. His wife and two sons were soon released, but Siliadin remained in detention at the Police Judiciary headquarters. At 7:00 a.m. on December 8, Siliadin was freed.

Uganda

Since coming to power in 1986, President Yoweri Museveni has been credited with ushering in peace, economic reform, and a fledgling democracy. In the northern region of the country, however, a rebel group known as the Lord's Resistance Army has been fighting Museveni in a 10-year war that has left the area unstable and underde-veloped. On the western front, Museveni is now paying a heavy price for having aided Laurent Kabila in his military campaign to overthrow Zairean dictator Mobutu Sese Seko. A Ugandan group called the Alliance of Democratic Forces has teamed up with former Rwandan and Zairean soldiers to attack Ugandan towns near the border with the Democratic Republic of the Congo.

In the midst of this instability, the press has emerged as one of the strongest under-pinnings of civil society in Uganda, openly expressing divergent views in a country which prohibits political parties and orga-nized dissent. Although the 1995 constitution contains fairly liberal provisions governing freedom of expression and the press, the country has draconian statutes governing the media, some of which, such as the law on sedition, were modeled on colonial-era laws. When the state chooses to enforce these laws, journalists are arrest-ed, detained, charged, and released after paying colossal amounts in bail. Heavy fines in defamation suits—usually brought by politicians and government officials—have caused a number of newspapers to suspend publication or go bankrupt. Most newspa-pers resort to self-censorship.

In June, the Uganda Journalists Safety Committee (UJSC), a press freedom watch-dog organization, filed two petitions in the Constitutional Court challenging the consti-tutionality of two controversial press laws—the sedition and criminal libel sections of the penal code, which have historically been used to intimidate, arrest, and detain journalists; and the repressive Press and Journalists Law of 1995, which requires strict licensing procedures. In December, the court dismissed the UJSC's petition.

January 26
Muasazi Namiti, *Crusader, Secrets*
IMPRISONED

Namiti was arrested and charged with seditious libel. The arrest was in connection with two articles, one titled "1,000 Women-Lovers in Trouble," published in the January 23 issue of *The Crusader*, and the other, "Uganda No. 1 Womanizer, 1001 Women Down ... How Many More to Go?" published in the January 30 issue of *Secrets* magazine.

Namiti's source for these stories, Hassan Kato, was arrested January 22 on the same charge.

Both men appeared in court in Mengo on

February 2. Namiti was released that day on a bail of 100,000 Ugandan shillings (US$90). Kato was unable to secure the bail. The men are required to appear in court every month beginning February 17.

In a letter to President Yoweri Museveni, CPJ protested the use of seditious libel charges against the journalist and his source.

March 26
Nathan Etengu, *The New Vision* CENSORED
Adams Wamakesi, *The Monitor* CENSORED
Arthur Wamangu, Capital Radio CENSORED
Mazuni Douglas, *The Crusader* CENSORED
Jack Nambafu, *The Crusader* CENSORED
David Zamanga, free-lancer CENSORED

Mbale District Local Council 5 Chairman Namangala Mwambu ordered an armed guard to prevent six journalists from different publications from attending a meeting that Mwambu was chairing. It is believed the journalists were barred because they wanted to question Mwambu about allegations of mismanagement.

May 21
Peter Busiku, *Uganda Express* LEGAL ACTION

The trial of Busiku, editor of the Kampala weekly *Uganda Express* who was arrested in December 1996, began on May 21, before Magistrate Precious Nyabriano of Buganda Road Court, Kampala. At press time, the trial was still in progress.

Busiku was charged with publishing "false statements or reports which are likely to cause fear and alarm to the public." The newspaper had published an article titled "Uganda, Burundi, Rwanda Plan Assault on Tanzania" in the November 27-December 4, 1996 issue. Busiku was remanded to Luzira Prison and later released on US$500 bail. He was scheduled to appear in court on December 19, but the trial was postponed for unknown reasons.

October 24
Charles Onyango-Obbo, *The Monitor* LEGAL ACTION
Andrew Mwenda, *The Monitor* LEGAL ACTION

Onyango-Obbo and Mwenda of the independent Ugandan daily *The Monitor* were charged with publishing false information in connection with an article published in the paper's September 21 edition titled, "Kabila Paid Uganda in Gold, Says Report."

Onyango-Obbo and Mwenda were released that day on bail of Ushs 2 million (US$2,000) cash each and non-cash sureties in the amount of Ushs 5 million (US$5,000).

Zambia

After President Frederick Chiluba's November 1996 election to a second five-year term in controversial elections boycotted by opposition parties, the president and his party, the Movement for Multiparty Democracy (MMD), continued their persistent campaign against the independent press, specifically targeting individual editors and journalists in a blatant pattern of criminalization of their work. Using the country's harsh media laws, a number of MMD leaders, including President Chiluba and Vice President Godfrey Miyanda, are pursuing criminal defamation suits and other legal actions against the media. There are more court cases pending against journalists in Zambia than anywhere else in Africa, the state's intention being to financially incapacitate the independent press. While the overburdened judiciary has shown autonomy in the disposition of some of these cases, it has appeared influenced by the executive branch in others.

The government's most zealous critic is *The Post*, an independent newspaper

launched in 1991 several months before the MMD government came to power. Since then, it has been served with more than 100 writs. Editor in chief Fred M'membe—a 1995 winner of CPJ's International Press Freedom Award—and some of his senior editorial staff have been detained for weeks in dangerously overcrowded jails where scurvy, malaria, and tuberculosis are common. Several of the *The Post*'s staff face the prospect of up to 25 years in jail in ongoing court cases. M'membe alone could be sentenced to more than 100 years' imprisonment for more than 50 suits, the first of which went before the High Court in January.

Recognizing that a free press and an active civil society are the main threats to its hold on power, Chiluba's government in January tried to introduce regulatory legislation in the form of a media council bill, which called for compulsory registration of journalists and gave the council powers to reprimand, suspend, or withdraw their accreditation. Failure to comply could result in prison terms and fines. The legislation was unanimously rejected by five of the country's major media organizations. In February, the Zambian Independent Media Association (ZIMA) established the Independent Media Council, maintaining that an independent council rather than a legislated body was the best regulatory solution and would provide a mechanism for complaints. Bowing to intense pressure from journalists, in April the government withdrew the bill, and in July, ZIMA began a weekly radio show called "Facing the Media" to highlight the activities of ZIMA's new council and other press issues in the country.

On August 22, the Zambian High Court ruled in favor of the Press Association of Zambia (PAZA); this voluntary association of journalists had challenged the government's 1995 decision to replace it with a statutory body with mandatory membership

for all journalists. The government said it would appeal the ruling to the Supreme Court.

The state controls television as well as the mainstream newspapers, which constitute 90 percent of the print media. There are an estimated 700,000 television sets in the country and about half the population has access to them. Most newspapers are sold in the capital and in mining towns in the north and south. Few copies reach the rest of the country and no joint distribution organization exists. Privately owned newspapers, which have scant financial backing, have been particularly hard hit by the increasing cost of newsprint and falling circulation. In February, *The Post*, which receives only 35 percent of its income from advertising, was forced to double its cover price.

As part of an ongoing national disinvestment program—one of the most successful in Africa—a bill was introduced to parliament in early October to privatize the *Times of Zambia, Zambia Daily Mail,* and the Zambian National Broadcasting Corporation (ZNBC). But affairs of state ground to a halt on October 28, when coup plotters calling themselves the National Redemption Council briefly took control of ZNBC, only to be crushed by a government strike force three hours later. The following day, under a state of emergency declared by President Chiluba, police were granted sweeping powers to search homes and detain anyone indefinitely for interrogation. Since the failed coup, government pressures on the independent press, including surveillance and denial of printing facilities, have increased significantly.

January 1
Fred M'membe, *The Post* LEGAL ACTION

In late January, editor in chief M'membe appeared in the High Court to face the first of more than 50 charges pending against him and his paper, *The Post*. In this first case, the journalist was charged under the State Security Act with receiving and publishing classified information after *The Post* reported in February that the government was considering holding a referendum on the country's constitution. M'membe faced as much as 25 years', imprisonment if convicted.

M'membe and *The Post* were tried on myriad other charges as the year progressed, resulting from articles published in *The Post* as long ago as 1994. The charges included criminal defamation, criminally defaming President Chiluba, publishing false information with intent to cause fear and alarm to the public, receiving and publishing classified information, treason, sedition, and inciting the army to revolt.

M'membe, a 1995 winner of CPJ's International Press Freedom Award, has been a target of harassment and persecution for many years. In February 1996, M'membe, *The Post* managing editor Bright Mwape, and columnist Ruth Sichone were convicted of contempt of parliament and held for 23 days in a maximum-security prison. CPJ protested the charges and arrests in letters to President Chiluba and to Robinson Nabulyato, speaker of the National Assembly, and launched a letter-writing campaign to secure the journalists' release.

January 22
Kunda Mwila, *The Post* HARASSED

Mwila, a reporter with the independent daily *The Post*, was arrested and detained for four hours by a plainclothes police officer for "conduct likely to cause a breach of the peace." Mwila was arrested in apparent retaliation for exposing the police officer at a press conference where he had claimed he was a journalist from the privately owned newspaper *The Chronicle*.

February 6
Zambia National Broadcasting Corp. (ZNBC) THREATENED, HARASSED

Zambian Vice President Godfrey Miyanda accused the state-owned ZNBC television station of screening "dirty programs that run contrary to Christian values" and warned of impending government action.

February 11
Masautso Phiri, *The Post* IMPRISONED, LEGAL ACTION

The Supreme Court sentenced Phiri, special projects editor of the privately owned daily *The Post*, to a three-month prison term. Phiri had been charged with contempt of court in connection with an article titled "Praising God Loudly," published December 11, 1996. The story reported that the seven judges of the Supreme Court had been paid a total of 7 billion kwacha (US$5 million) to rule in the state's favor in a case brought by the opposition parties, which challenged the candidacy of President Frederick Chiluba in the November 1996 elections.

February 15
George Jambwa, *The Chronicle* HARASSED

Plainclothes police officers arrested Jambwa, a reporter for *The Chronicle*, and detained him for 10 hours at the Lusaka Central Police Station. The officers demanded to know the identity of his source for an article in the February 14-17 issue of *The Chronicle* that alleged that presidential aide Everisto Mutale was using a stolen vehicle. Jambwa was released the same day without charge.

February 16
Lweendo Hamusankwa, *The Chronicle* IMPRISONED, LEGAL ACTION

Police detained Hamusankwa, editor of the privately owned newspaper *The Chronicle*, in connection with two articles published in the February 11-13 and February 14-17 editions. One article reported that arms and ammunition had been stolen from the Mikango Barracks in Lusaka;

the second article reported that presidential aide Everisto Mutale was using a stolen vehicle.

Hamusankwa was charged with criminal libel and with "publishing false news with intent to cause fear and alarm to the public." Hamusankwa denied both charges before a Lusaka magistrate. He was released on February 18 on bail of 500,000 kwacha (US$383).

February 17
Boyd Phiri, *The Chronicle* IMPRISONED, LEGAL ACTION

Phiri, a reporter for the privately owned newspaper *The Chronicle*, was detained by police in connection with two articles published in the newspaper. The February 11-13 edition reported that arms and ammunition had been stolen from the Mikango Barracks in Lusaka, and the February 14-17 edition reported that presidential aide Everisto Mutale was using a stolen vehicle.

Phiri was taken into custody at Woodlands police station in Lusaka and charged with criminal libel and with "publishing false news with intent to cause fear and alarm to the public." He was released after a hearing on February 18 on bail of 500,000 kwacha (approximately US$383).

August 5
The Post CENSORED

Zambia's High Court granted Finance Minister Ronald Penza an injunction preventing the independent newspaper *The Post* from publishing articles that might impugn his character. *The Post* had published a number of articles between July 18 and August 5 that reported on Penza's alleged corruption and theft.

August 23
Matsautso Phiri, *The Post* IMPRISONED, ATTACKED

Phiri, editor of *The Post*, was assaulted and

detained by police after he took photographs of a riot squad's dispersal of people gathered at a rally. The protest was organized by Zambia's former president Kenneth Kaunda and his party, the United National Independence Party (UNIP). Police seized Phiri's camera and removed the film. Phiri was detained in a Kabwe police station along with scores of other detainees picked from the rally. Phiri was released on August 25 on bail. He was to appear in Kabwe Magistrate's Court on September 3 to challenge his arrest.

Kaunda's rally in the town of Kabwe was dispersed because he did not have a license for public assembly.

September 2
FM Radio Phoenix CENSORED

Zambian Information Minister David Mpamba banned the privately owned FM Radio Phoenix from relaying live BBC programs. He said relaying live broadcasts was contrary to the conditions of the station's broadcasting license, which was issued in February 1996.

The BBC broadcasts on Radio Phoenix included "Newsdesk," "Network Africa," and "BBC World News."

Managing director Erol Hickey said the BBC programs were introduced to broaden the range of news programs on Phoenix, which carries local news. The BBC programs were already available on shortwave directly from the BBC.

When applying for a broadcasting license, FM Radio Phoenix outlined its intent to broadcast BBC programs and was informed that the request would be considered at a later date.

A fire during the night of September 19 destroyed Radio Phoenix's offices. Equipment valued at US$350,000 was lost in the fire, which burned through eight floors of the 22-story Society House Building. Police have not established the cause of the blaze. It was the fifth serious fire in the capital in weeks.

September 8
Dickson Jere, *The Post* HARASSED
Reuben Phiri, *The Post* HARASSED
George Chilembo, *The Post* HARASSED
Amos Malupenga, *The Post* HARASSED

Zambia Air Force (ZAF) personnel at Lusaka City Airport seized a camera and harassed Jere, Phiri, Chilembo, and Malupenga. The journalists, along with other journalists from the state-owned media, were covering the departure to London of Chief Litunga of Barotseland. *The Post*'s journalists were singled out and accused of entering airport premises "illegally."

When journalists inquired about the camera on September 9, ZAF public relations officer Lt. Col. Chrispin Mukumano told them the matter was in the hands of the police and the journalists were likely to face criminal charges.

November 14
Frederick Mwanza IMPRISONED

Writer and journalist Mwanza was detained under the Preservation of Public Security Act of 1960 and accused of involvement with a failed coup attempt on October 28. He appeared in court on November 26, but was not charged. Mwanza then applied for a writ of habeas corpus, challenging the government to show cause why he could not be released. At a hearing on December 2, the government responded by serving Mwanza with a presidential detention order, which allows the police to hold the journalist indefinitely under the state of emergency currently in force.

Mwanza has denied all allegations that he was present at a meeting finalizing the coup plot against President Frederick Chiluba's government. The journalist has been questioned in prison about several articles critical of government policies. His lawyer, Patrick Mvunga, has stated that Mwanza was tortured during interrogation and has been denied access to his family.

November 19
Reggie Marobe, Phenyo Film and Television Production EXPELLED
Abraham du Preez, Phenyo Film and Television Production EXPELLED

Marobe and du Preez, filmmakers for the South African Phenyo Film and Television Production company, had their press accreditation revoked and were expelled from Zambia by the Zambia Information Services (ZIS) on the grounds that the two were "a threat to national security." The journalists were in Lusaka to film a documentary about the African National Congress's (ANC) work in Zambia before the end of apartheid, which Phenyo was producing for the South African Broadcasting Corporation.

Marobe and du Preez had been granted prior permission to film. When they arrived in Lusaka, however, they learned that their accreditation had been revoked. They were reportedly told by Press Secretary Laurah Harrison that their presence in the country was "undesirable" because of the state of emergency prevailing since a failed coup attempt on October 28.

Although on December 2, the Third Secretary in the South African High Commission, Peter Pretorius, confirmed the expulsion, Deputy Information Minister Ernest Mwansa claimed that the story was false, and that he knew nothing of the canceled accreditation.

December 19
Mukalya Nampito, *The Post* HARASSED
Sheikh Chifuwe, *The Post* HARASSED
Sandra Mubiana, *The Sun* HARASSED

Soldiers barred Nampito, a reporter, Chifuwe, a photojournalist, and Mubiana, a reporter, from attending an army graduation ceremony at which President Chiluba officiated. The journalists were prevented from entering the Zambia Defense Services Command and Staff College in Lusaka and were told that "only the government-run media (were) invited" to cover the event. *The Post* and *The Sun* are both privately owned, *The Sun* by Sikota Wina, chairman of the ruling Multiparty Movement for Democracy (MMD).

Zimbabwe

Despite an August 1995 Supreme Court ruling against the government's monopoly on telecommunications and cabinet promises to free the airwaves in 1997, radio and television remain government-owned and controlled. So far, however, the state has failed to control the booming sale of satellite dishes by wealthy individuals, and it is just a matter of time before a prospective independent private broadcasting company challenges the constitutionality of current broadcasting laws.

Zimbabwe's independent press is relatively open and critical of President Robert Mugabe's government, but there is still a high degree of self-censorship in both the government-controlled and independent print media, which must navigate a minefield of civil and criminal anti-defamation laws and extremely broad and repressive colonial-era laws restricting access to information.

Unlike a number of other southern African countries, Zimbabwe's constitution provides no explicit protection for freedom of the press, and the current legal climate for the media is one of official secrecy and inaccessibility. An amendment to the Broadcasting Act which would allow independent radio and television stations to operate is expected to gain parliamentary approval sometime in 1998. Three independent television stations are now in operation, but they must buy air time on the government-controlled channel in order to broadcast.

March 12
***Independent* THREATENED**

Businessman Roger Boka threated to shoot journalists from the *Independent* newspaper who questioned him about his bid for a hotel property. The journalists were investigating a report that Boka had bid 7 million Zimbabwe dollars (US$875,000) for a hotel in Mutare.

March 20
Thompson Publications ATTACKED, HARASSED

Businessman Roger Boka, along with four armed bodyguards, raided the Harare offices of Thompson Publications, assaulted a Thompson employee with a walking stick, and ranted at the staff to express Boka's displeasure with an article published in the February issue of *Tobacco Magazine*. The article reported on a 7 million Zimbabwe dollar (US$875,000) bid that Boka had made on a hotel property in Mutare.

Thompson Publications filed civil and criminal charges against Boka for his attack.

December 13
Gerry Jackson, Zimbabwe Broadcasting Corporation (ZBC) HARASSED

Jackson was summarily dismissed from her position as a presenter with the Zimbabwe Broadcasting Corporation (ZBC), four days after she broadcast news of workers protesting tax increases in Harare. The letter terminating Jackson's contract with the ZBC accused her of "insubordination and total disregard for authority."

During her broadcast on December 9, Jackson took calls from listeners reporting on rioting that had erupted during the protests, some of whom mentioned instances of police brutality.

CPJ's Campaign for the Release
of Christine Anyanwu

Imprisoned Nigerian journalist Christine Anyanwu received a
CPJ International Press Freedom Award in 1997 at ceremonies
October 23 in New York and CPJ's pledge to intensify efforts
to free her. She has been in prison in her homeland since 1995.
The 46-year-old mother of two is considered to be one of Africa's
preeminent journalists. But Nigeria's government, headed by Gen.
Sani Abacha, considers her to be an enemy of the state, "an accessory to a treasonable felony." She was sentenced in May 1995
before a closed military tribunal to life in prison for attempting to
do her job as a journalist—to report the news truthfully. Her publication, *The Sunday Magazine*, which she founded and edited, had
reported that Gen. Abacha's claim of having uncovered a plot to
overthrow him was a ploy to trample the opposition. That was the
only evidence used again her.

Although her sentence was reduced to 15 years after an international outcry, that is not good enough. Her health has
deteriorated, and she is in danger of going blind. Held in solitary
confinement under tight security control, she is permitted only
one visitor a month, from a family member who first must obtain
permission and clearance from security officials and prison authorities. Communication with her not possible.

More than 300 journalists, media executives, and human rights
activists who attended CPJ's awards dinner at the Waldorf-Astoria
signed appeals to Gen. Abacha, urging that he release Anyanwu.

Obtaining Anyanwu's freedom and the release of the other 16
journalists imprisoned in Nigeria remains at the forefront of CPJ's
advocacy efforts.

Bill Keller, managing editor of *The New York Times* and a former correspondent in Africa, said in presenting Anyanwu's
International Press Freedom Award:

"Chris Anyanwu is not a firebrand ... Colleagues in Nigeria
describe her as a level-headed professional, competitive, indepen-
dent-minded and strong-willed. But not reckless. But that, of

course, is beside the point. If Christine were an unreliable journalist or a partisan zealot, we would still be appalled by her imprisonment. What inspires us ... is not really her voice, but her refusal to let it be silenced."

On February 16, 1998, Anyanwu was awarded the 1998 UNESCO/Guillermo Cano World Press Freedom Prize. Upon awarding her the $25,000 prize, Claude Moisy, president of UNESCO's Advisory Group for Press Freedom, decried her treatment and faulted Nigeria as "a country where the independent press and freedom of information have almost disappeared."

At the end of the year, Nigeria held 17 reporters and editors in jail—the greatest number of any country in the region. This alarming increase—more than double last year's total of eight—means that Nigeria is now the world's second-worst jailer of journalists, after Turkey. The Abacha government refuses in most cases to permit visitors to these prisoners, who are said to be confined under extremely primitive conditions and subjected to physical abuse.

Please send appeals for the release of Christine Anyanwu and her fellow journalists to:

Gen. Sani Abacha
Chairman of the Provisional Ruling Council
and Commander in Chief of the Armed Forces
State House
Abuja
Federal Capital Territory, Nigeria
Fax: 234-95-232-138

THE AMERICAS

OVERVIEW OF
The Americas
by Joel Simon

With ten journalists murdered in the line of duty, 1997 was an extremely violent year for the Latin American press. While the systematic persecution of journalists has largely abated with the consolidation of democratic regimes, the media's growing independence has exposed journalists to different kinds of danger. Government officials, powerful economic actors, and criminal elements including drug traffickers have responded to efforts to probe their activities by lashing out at the press, often through lawsuits, often through violence.

The changing nature of the threat, coupled with the growing power of journalists in the region, has led CPJ to refocus its mission in Latin America. In 1981, when CPJ was founded, Latin America was the most dangerous place in the world to be a journalist. The military dictators who governed much of the continent were overtly hostile to the press, describing it on occasion as an instrument of international communism. Paramilitary death squads targeted journalists as part of their counterinsurgency strategy.

Despite this fierce repression, journalists throughout Latin America continued to practice their profession, documenting abuses, exposing corruption, and demanding accountability from public officials and elected leaders. In the end, the press played an important role in the collapse of the military juntas.

Today, with the exception of Cuba, the Latin American press is able to report with few restrictions. Throughout the region, journalists pursue stories of official corruption, malfeasance, social injustice, and human rights abuses. In many Latin American countries, such as Argentina, Peru, and Colombia, where the judiciary and legislative branches of government lack independence, the

Before joining CPJ in 1997 as the Americas program coordinator, **Joel Simon** *was a Mexico-based associate editor for Pacific News Service and a contributor to the* San Francisco Chronicle, the Los Angeles Times, The New York Times, *and* Columbia Journalism Review. *He is the author of* Endangered Mexico: An Environment on the Edge *(Sierra Club Books, 1997).*

Research assistant **Marylene Smeets** *worked with the United Nations Mission for the Verification of Human Rights in Guatemala (MINIGUA) until 1997. She is a graduate of the University of Amsterdam and Paul H. Nitze School of Advanced International Relations at Johns Hopkins University.*

Former research assistant **Juanita León** *and intern* **Daniel Shoer-Roth** *also contributed to this report.*

The Robert R. McCormick Tribune Foundation provided substantial support toward CPJ's work in the Americas in 1997. The Freedom Forum funded additional CPJ programming in Mexico.

press has emerged as the institution that inspires the greatest degree of public confidence, according to opinion polls. The growing power of the media has made some Latin American journalists uncomfortable because, they argue, the press is becoming a political actor and thereby compromising its legitimate function of mediating between competing political forces.

In Argentina, the media's strained relationship with President Carlos Saúl Menem turned overtly antagonistic after photojournalist José Luis Cabezas was murdered in January. The brutal murder, and the lack of progress in the investigation, galvanized public support for the media. A series of protest marches throughout the year demanded the arrest of those responsible for the crime as well as greater respect for freedom of the press.

Three Mexican journalists were assassinated in 1997, as a newly aggressive press intersected with deteriorating social conditions. For the majority of Mexican journalists, however, the threat of prosecution is a more immediate concern than the possibility of violent attack. Dozens of journalists have been prosecuted in recent years under Mexico's 1917 libel law, which defined 'defamation' as a criminal offense punishable by up to 11 months in prison. In Colombia, where four journalists were murdered, the situation is even more critical. The government of Ernesto Samper, badly weakened by a series of political scandals, has not only failed to respond to the growing violence against journalists, but has tried to control the media by granting television and radio licenses to the political cronies of the president.

While no journalists were assassinated for their work in Peru, four remain in jail, convicted under that country's draconian anti-terrorism laws. Journalists in Peru allege that the country's shadowy National Intelligence Service (SIN) has launched a campaign against the press that combines legal action, terror, and disinformation. The intention, they allege, is to silence journalists who might produce stories that could damage President Alberto Fujimori's expected campaign for a third term as president.

Rather than intimidating the press, the violence has fueled the formation of journalists' self-defense organizations throughout the region. CPJ has been working closely with a number of them, including the Instituto de Prensa y Sociedad (IPYS) in Peru and Periodistas in Argentina. In November, CPJ hosted a workshop with Mexican journalists in Mexico City to discuss freedom of the press and self-defense strategies in the face of the escalating incidence of attacks. (See "Breaking Away: Mexico's Press Challenges the Status Quo," p. 213.)

The growing network of journalists' organizations in Latin America is playing a vital role in strengthening press freedom. During the 1980s, CPJ was

THE AMERICAS

often the sole source of information about attacks on the press in Latin America because journalists in the region, shackled by repressive regimes, were not in a position to defend themselves effectively. Today, CPJ increasingly relies on local press organizations for information and works with them to lobby their heads of state for press freedom reforms, or to push for justice when journalists are under attack.

In just the last decade, a remarkable region-wide integration has taken place; trade, finance, and immigration have linked North and South America more directly than ever before. The positive impact of this regional integration on efforts to secure press freedom throughout Latin America is manifest. For example, there are now four Spanish-language news networks broadcasting out of the United States into Latin America. Meanwhile, the influx of immigrants into the United States—from places like Mexico, Colombia, Ecuador, and Peru—has provided new impetus for the U.S. media to cover events in places that once seemed remote and of marginal interest. And increased trade has spurred Latin American governments to seek to avoid the negative coverage that flows from press freedom abuses, since they recognize the relationship between their public perception abroad and the level of foreign investment.

The irony is that as Latin American society grows more open, attacks are increasing on journalists pushing the limits of press freedom. Journalists have found, however, that the best defense is to use the power of the press to bring the incidents to the attention of the public. Local press freedom organizations—as well as international groups such as CPJ—are impressing upon Latin American governments that failing to protect this basic freedom carries serious political and social consequences.

In the short term, two trends are clear. The Latin American press will continue to grow more independent, aggressive, and professional. And Latin America will remain a very dangerous place to be a journalist.

Antigua and Barbuda

The press in this tiny Caribbean island nation has long been independent, but recent efforts at more aggressive news coverage have brought journalists into open conflict with the long-ruling Antigua Labor Party, controlled by the Bird family.

For example, L. Tim Hector, a leader of the opposition United Progressive Party and publisher of *The Outlet*, a biweekly newspaper, was served with eight separate court orders prohibiting publication of any information about an alleged scandal linking Prime Minister Lester B. Bird to the Colombian drug cartels. According to stories published in *The Outlet* quoting a Venezuelan businessman and a Colombian government official, Bird was paid a $1-million bribe to allow Antigua and Barbuda to be used as a transfer point for cocaine bound for the United States. Under the country's strict libel laws, Hector could be jailed for publishing additional information.

The government generally relies on subtler means to control the flow of information. Of the three local radio stations, one is government-run and the others are controlled by the Bird family. The sole television station is also run by the state, while a brother of the prime minister owns the cable company. A court decision in December upheld the government's September 1996 closing of a radio station started by newspaper owners Winston and Sammuel Derrick, allegedly for operating without a license.

Strategists in the ruling Antigua Labor Party—which has controlled the government since 1976—blame critical news coverage for their poor electoral showings in the last general elections.

Argentina

The brutal murder of photographer José Luis Cabezas at the beginning of the year rekindled traumatic memories of the persecution of journalists during Argentina's so-called "dirty war" in the 1970s and early '80s. At the same time, it galvanized journalists and the public, who expressed their anger and desire for justice in public demonstrations throughout the year.

After Cabezas' charred, handcuffed corpse was discovered by a fisherman in the town of Pinamar on January 25, journalists and ordinary Argentines took to the streets demanding that the government of President Carlos Menem vigorously investigate the murder and swiftly prosecute those responsible. Over the next few months, they managed to keep the pressure up with horn-honking demonstrations that clogged the streets of Buenos Aires, low-speed caravans to the site of the murder, and vigils that produced moments of eerie silence before soccer matches.

The protests reflect the extraordinary level of cooperation among Argentine journalists and the broad public support for their work. In a country where the congress and the judiciary have been unable to curtail widespread corruption and abuse of power on the part of government officials, the press has taken on the role of public watchdog. In a poll published by the newsweekly *Noticias* in July, the press emerged as the institution enjoying the greatest public support, ahead of the Catholic Church, the military, the congress, and political parties.

This perception may help explain the success of the Association for the Defense of Independent Journalists (Periodistas), a press freedom organization founded in 1995, which not only investigates and denounces attacks on individual journalists, but serves as a public voice for a press that, precisely because of its growing power, is the target of both legal and extra-legal attacks.

President Menem and his advisors have responded to stories about government corruption and malfeasance not with promises to investigate the accusations but with a flurry of litigation. While the lawsuits have been costly for the journalists involved and may have deterred others from publishing investigative stories, the plaintiffs have not prospered in the courts.

Meanwhile, journalists covering the investigation into the Cabezas murder have confronted intimidation of a more violent nature. Many journalists have received physical threats, and the hand of one reporter's sister was slashed. While the inquiry has been slow, the investigating judge in the Cabezas case has made steady progress. With each piece of emerging evidence the explosive nature of the murder has become more apparent.

In 1996, Cabezas' photograph of Alfredo Yabrán, a reclusive businessman with alleged ties to the mafia, was published on the cover of *Noticias*. Yabrán—who, like President Menem, is an Argentine of Syrian descent—had amassed a fortune estimated to be as much as $500 million largely through government contracts and sweetheart deals on state privatizations. His firms are alleged to control half of Argentina's private mail delivery and a large portion of government printing. While Menem initially denied that he knew Yabrán personally, investigators soon found that the elusive tycoon had made dozens of phone calls to Justice Minister Elias Jassan immediately after Cabezas' killing. The revelation led to Jassan's resignation.

On April 9, ex-policeman Gustavo Prellezo was arrested and charged with carrying out the murder. At the time of his arrest, Prellezo was carrying Yabrán's business card, with Yabrán's private phone number scribbled on it in his own handwriting. Nearly a dozen suspects, including Gregorio Rios, Yabrán's head of security, and several ex-police officers have been arrested and charged with carrying out the murder.

Facing intense criticism over the Cabezas investigation and alleged corruption scandals, Menem has lashed out at the press. On June 17, during a press briefing for foreign correspondents, Menem described Horacio Verbitsky, the prominent columnist for the Buenos Aires-based daily *Página/12*, as "one of the biggest terrorists in Argentina." And on September 8, President Menem was quoted as proposing that the Ley de Palos ("The Law of the Stick") be used against journalists (he later said he was joking). In the midst of this climate of open hostility between the media and the government, four men who identified themselves as police officers abducted a former marine named Adolfo Scilingo, who had spoken to the press about his role as an executioner in the dirty war. The assailants carved the letters V, M, and G into Scilingo's face. "For Grondona, Magdalena, and Verbitsky, who are your associates," said the men, naming three prominent journalists with whom Scilingo had spoken. "We're going to kill them; they must be stopped."

By the time U.S. President Bill Clinton visited Argentina in October as part of a trip to three countries in South America, relations between Menem and the press had reached an all-time low. In private meetings with Menem, Clinton expressed his concern. "What I told President Menem is that Argentina is constructing a civil society brick by brick and that freedom of expression is something positive," Clinton explained. During the visit, White House aides also met privately with a group of Argentine journalists and reiterated Clinton's commitment to promoting press freedom. At a briefing with reporters in Buenos Aires, White House spokesman Michael McCurry specifically credited CPJ with bringing the issue of freedom of the press in Argentina to Clinton's attention.

Later that month, Menem's Peronist party lost control of the congress in mid-term elections. Along with unemployment and corruption, Menem's open antagonism toward a press that is both popular and respected may have played a role in the electoral defeat.

January 25
José Luis Cabezas, *Noticias* KILLED

The charred and handcuffed body of Cabezas, a photographer for *Noticias* magazine, was found by a fisherman near Pinamar, a resort where Cabezas had been covering political events. His body was discovered in the fire-gutted hull of a rented car. He was last seen at a celebrity party.

Cabezas, 35, is survived by a wife and three children. President Carlos Menem called Cabezas' death "an act of brutality," but refused to speak to the press after the murder, when crowds took to the streets waving posters and photographs of Cabezas. The investigation has focused on the provincial police in Buenos Aires, a group known for corruption. The method of the killing was similar to the hundreds of assassinations committed by the government-backed death squads in the 1970s.

Argentine and international organizations have called for a complete investigation into Cabezas' death. CPJ wrote a letter to the Argentine government demanding an investigation into the killing.

Cabezas was one of the first journalists to photograph Alfredo Yabrán, a reclusive tycoon described by a prominent politicain as head of the Argentine mafia. On September 3, the Argentine Justice Minister was forced to resign after it became known that he had received phone calls from Yabrán. Numerous arrests have been made in connection with Cabezas'

murder, among them police officers and Yabrán's security chief. Journalists covering the investigation of Cabezas' murder have been threatened.

Numerous arrests have been made in connection with the murders, among them current and former police officers and Yabrán's security chief.

February 5
Fernando Bravo, *Río Negro* HARASSED

Bravo, a correspondent for the regional daily *Río Negro* in General Roca, Rio Negro Province, discovered the car outside his home in flames. According to local journalists, the car was doused with gasoline and set on fire while Bravo slept.

The attack came after Bravo spoke on the radio about the local government's large budget deficit. Bravo hosts a radio show on a station owned by the same company that owns *Río Negro*. Bravo told CPJ that his comments "caused a lot of uneasiness in the ruling Radical Party."

In 1996, Bravo received death threats from people calling his program who told him to stop discussing the deficit. According to Bravo, the callers usually said something like, "Stop fooling around with that issue, we know who you are."

June 17
José Claudio Escribano, *La Nación* THREATENED

An envelope addressed to Escribano, deputy editor of *La Nación*, a daily Buenos Aires-based newspaper, contained a deactivated plastic explosive device, including a small battery and cables. A second envelope delivered to Escribano's office the same day held a typed message warning Escribano, "next time it's for real."

Escribano was out of the country when the letters were delivered. His secretary received and opened them.

CPJ sent a protest letter to President Carlos Menem urging him to conduct an investigation into the circumstances of this threat.

June 17
Horacio Verbitsky, *Página/12* HARASSED

At a press briefing for foreign correspondents, Argentine President Carlos Menem called Verbitsky, a columnist with the daily *Página/12*, "one of the biggest terrorists in Argentina." Menem added, "He is a terrorist who is passing judgment on honest and decent people."

Menem made these statements after Verbitsky wrote a column about the government's intention to promote a military officer charged with torture during the last military dictatorship.

CPJ sent a letter to Menem on July 28 expressing concern that such statements could embolden others to take violent action against the press.

June 23
Antonio Fernández Llorente, Canal 13 THREATENED, HARASSED

Fernández Llorente's sister, María José Fernández Llorente, was attacked by three men who slashed her hand with a razor blade as she was leaving her daughter's nursery school. The attackers warned her, "If your brother doesn't leave [town] in 48 hours, we'll carry on our threats. He's talking too much...."

Fernández Llorente, the Dolores correspondent for TV station Canal 13, had been covering the investigation into the murder of photojournalist José Luis Cabezas, who was found dead in his car on January 25.

CPJ sent a letter on July 28 calling on President Menem to ensure the safety of journalists covering the investigation into Cabezas' murder.

June 23
Ariel Garbarz, *Página/12* THREATENED

Garbarz, a columnist for the Buenos Aires-based daily *Página/12*, explained in a televised interview how police used computer software to trace 17 telephone calls between the Interior Ministry and Alfredo Yabrán, a businessman being questioned in connection with the murder of photographer José Luis Cabezas. Several hours after the show aired, the manager of the company that produced the tracing software received a call from Buenos Aires police officers, who warned that Garbarz would have "trouble" if he continued to tell journalists about the use of the software. The caller also told the manager to tell the reporter to stop writing about the subject.

CPJ sent a letter on July 28 to President Carlos Menem, asking him to ensure the safety of journalists covering the investigation into Cabezas' murder.

June 24
Magdalena Ruiz Guiñazú, Radio Mitre and Canal 9 THREATENED

Ruiz Guiñazú, a prominent journalist with Buenos Aires-based Radio Mitre and Canal 9, received two anonymous death threats. Two callers—a male and a female—phoned the publishing house where the magazine *Noticias* is edited. They warned, "The next is Magdalena." José Luis Cabezas had been working for *Noticias* when he was murdered on January 25.

On July 2, Ruiz Guiñazú's housekeeper found a .38-caliber bullet in the doorway of the journalist's apartment.

Ruiz Guiñazú is the host of one of Argentina's most popular daily radio programs, "Magdalena Tempranísimo," broadcast on Radio Mitre. She also co-hosts "Dos en la Noticia" on Canal 9, in conjunction with Joaquín Morales Sola, and writes for the daily *La Nación*.

CPJ sent a letter on July 28 calling on President Menem to ensure the safety of journalists covering the investigation into Cabezas' murder.

September 11
Horacio Verbitsky, *Página/12*
THREATENED
Magdalena Ruiz Guiñazú, Radio Mitre and
Canal 9 THREATENED
Mariano Grondona, *La Nación* and Canal 9
THREATENED

Former Navy Captain Adolfo Scilingo, who in
1995 revealed the army practice of murdering
those accused of subversion by hurling them
from airplanes, was kidnapped by four men in
downtown Buenos Aires and forced into a car.
Using a knife, the kidnappers carved the initials
M, G, and V on Scilingo's face. "For
Grondona, Magdalena, and Verbitsky, who are
your associates," said the men, naming three
prominent journalists by whom Scilingo had
been interviewed. "We're going to kill them;
they must be stopped."

Verbitsky wrote a book called *The Flight*,
which contains several articles about Scilingo,
who admitted to participating in the murders of
"subversives" during Argentina's "dirty war."

September 21
Carlos Suárez HARASSED

Three men abducted Suárez at gunpoint as he was
entering his apartment building in Buenos Aires.
Suárez was taken with a hood on his head to an
unknown location where he was interrogated for
three hours about a book he is publishing on the
Latin American mafia. He was held overnight and
dropped off on a corner in Buenos Aires.

Suárez's book, *Globalization and the Mafia in
Latin America*, chronicles the reported money
laundering and arms trafficking activities of
Cuban-American businessman Jorge Más
Canosa. Más Canosa, who died in 1997, was
one of the owners of the Argentine newspaper
La República and an investor in Argentine televi-
sion channels and cable networks.

During Suárez's interrogation, he also was
questioned about his relationship with Horacio
Verbitsky, a columnist with the daily *Página/12*.

Bolivia

Working under difficult conditions and
with extremely limited resources, the
Bolivian press has managed to gain the
public's confidence, outpolling the Catholic
Church as the nation's most trusted institution. Bolstered by this support, the media
have been able to wield considerable
influence and successfully lobbied to defeat
a government initiative that would have
made it illegal for journalists to refuse to
reveal their sources.

Under a proposed reform of the Bolivian
criminal code, judges would have been
empowered to order journalists to reveal
their sources if the information was
pertinent to a criminal investigation. After
meeting with media associations and representatives from journalists' associations,
even newly elected President Hugo Banzer
came out against the proposal. Banzer, who
took office in August, has softened his views
about press freedom since he was military
dictator of Bolivia from 1971 to 1978.
Congress eventually came around to his
view, voting on October 15 to scuttle the
proposed legislation.

While press groups hailed the bill's
defeat, journalists are still bound by the
1925 press law, under which it is a criminal
offense punishable by up to two years in
prison to defame or slander public officials
(the sentence can be doubled if the official
in question is the president, vice president,
or a cabinet minister). While physical
attacks on journalists have become increasingly rare, legal action remains a serious
threat. Journalist associations are working
with legislators to update the 1925 press
law and expect the law to be ready in 1998
or 1999.

Brazil

With a reputation for investigative reporting and the resources of huge media conglomerates behind them, Brazilian journalists in major cities such as Rio de Janeiro and São Paulo enjoy widespread public support and growing political power. Their biggest problems are a lack of legal safeguards and increasing collusion between media moguls and Brazilian politicians.

But away from the sophisticated urban media environment, journalists in the poor interior states work under some of the worst conditions in Latin America. Most regional media outlets are owned by political bosses, who use them to advance their own interests. The Collor de Mello family, for example, used its media empire in the impoverished backwater state of Alagoas as a springboard into local politics and, eventually, the presidency. Reporters who criticize regional civilian and military authorities have been threatened, beaten, and even murdered. The assassination of radio journalist Edgar Lopes de Faria, who was gunned down in October in the state of Mato Grosso after denouncing the corruption of local officials, served as a clear illustration to local journalists of the impunity of the regional power brokers.

On a national level, however, journalists often have the upper hand over politicians. Since 1992, when aggressive reporting on corruption forced the resignation of President Fernando Collor de Mello, investigative journalism has become a staple of the Brazilian media. Many journalists view the attempt by Congress to impose legal restrictions on the press as retaliation for aggressive reporting. Press organizations and media owners have banded together to scuttle the most punitive measures, such as jail terms for journalists convicted of libel.

Nevertheless, legislation pending before Congress would expose journalists to fines of up to $100,000 for defamation, and make media owners liable for unlimited amounts in damages. The bill, on which the lower Chamber of Deputies is expected to vote sometime in 1998, would also make it easier for politicians to invoke the "right to reply," under which media outlets are required to give aggrieved parties space or time to respond to allegations made in the press. The bill is expected to be voted on by the lower Chamber of Deputies sometime in 1998.

While journalists support the effort to update the 1967 press law, written under the military dictatorship, they are working to ensure that the new legislation affirms and strengthens the freedom of expression guarantees granted in the 1988 constitution. Journalist's organizations are also concerned that the powerful media conglomerates are dictating coverage and, through their contacts with politicians in Brasilia, setting the country's political agenda. Media owners, for their part, have been unsuccessful in overturning a controversial 1969 law which requires all practicing journalists to have a university degree. They say the law artificially elevates the pay scale and sometimes prevents them from hiring the most qualified person.

January 11
Natan Pereira Gatinho, Ouro Verde KILLED

Gatinho was a correspondent for the television station Ouro Verde, also known as TV Mundial. Until November 1996 he also hosted a program for Radio Cidade, in which he read letters from farmers and workers complaining about their dire conditions. He was fatally shot January 11. He had been receiving death threats because of his radio program. Gatinho was a militant activist of the Worker's Party and had been a candidate in the 1996 municipal elections. A truck driver with whom Gatinho had had a fight two days before his death was arrested for the murder, but he has denied the charges. Brazilian press groups suspect that Gatinho was murdered by local landowners because of his work as a journalist, but some journalists believe he was killed because of a personal feud with the truck driver. Gatinho had accused him of running over and killing a woman who was a colleague at Ouro Verde

October 29
Edgar Lopes de Faria, radio station FM Capital and television station TV Record
KILLED

Lopes de Faria was host of the programs "O Escaramuça" (The Fighter) on radio station FM Capital and "Boca do Povo" (Mouth of the People) on television station TV Record. He was murdered on October 29 in Campo Grando, capital of the state of Mato Grosso do Sul, while on his way to the radio station. Police believe his murder was carried out by trained assassins, who fired with accuracy and left no trail. Lopes de Faria had reported on the hired killers who investigators say are responsible for recent murders in Mato Grosso.

November 13
Mariza Romão, TV Liberal THREATENED

Romão fled Marabá, a town in the northern state of Pará, after receiving a series of death threats.

Romão, who works for Globo Television Network affiliate TV Liberal, reported on the April 1996 massacre in Eldorado de Carajas, a town close to Marabá, in which 19 landless workers were killed. The killings occurred when police tried to clear peasants who were blocking a highway to underscore their demand for land.

Romão testified against 153 police officers implicated in the massacre. On November 12, Judge Otavio Maciel ruled that he found

enough evidence to refer the case of the police officers to a separate court, where a jury will try them for murder. On November 13, Rom‹o began receiving phone calls from a man identifying himself as a friend of the police, who warned her that police officers were planning to kill her. After the calls became more frequent, Romão fled to Brasilia on December 1 with her two young children. Local journalists believe her testimony is crucial for the conviction of the police officers implicated in the Eldorado de Carajas killings.

Chile

Buoyed by continued economic growth and increasingly stable democratic institutions, the Chilean press worked to remove laws established during the military dictatorship of Augusto Pinochet, which impose criminal penalties on journalists convicted of dishonoring the congress, the military, or the flag. Journalists who reveal "state secrets" can also be charged under the State Security Law, and military courts retain the power to try journalists accused of defaming military personnel or of sedition, although the laws have not been enforced in recent years.

Chilean journalists have been lobbying congress to create a uniform legal standard for libel and to eliminate all criminal penalties. The proposed press law has been wending its way through the Congress for several years and is not expected to be voted on until sometime in 1998. Press groups are also working to have a shield law, which would protect journalists from being compelled to reveal their sources, incorporated into the new legislation.

Journalists are also lobbying to overturn a controversial law that allows judges to ban reporting on judicial investigations. In June, Judge Beatriz Pedrals issued an injunction barring journalists from reporting on the

trial of Mario Silva Leiva, an alleged drug trafficker who was accused of bribing court officials and police officers. One newspaper, *La Tercera*, got around the ruling by posting dispatches on the World Wide Web. Judge Pedrals' ban was overturned after 10 days by the Court of Appeals.

Colombia

The assassinations of four journalists cast a pall over Colombia's press, even as the government of Ernesto Samper publicly excoriated the media for perpetuating the violence it covers. While Colombia has long been the most dangerous country in the hemisphere for journalists—45 have been killed in the line of duty since 1986—the Samper government's response has deepened Colombian journalists' sense of isolation and vulnerability.

The irony is that Samper took office in 1994 with broad support from the media, which hoped that the new president would put a stop to the drug-related violence that had decimated the press. But the relationship with Samper soured after *El Tiempo*, Colombia's leading daily, published testimony from a former cabinet minister who alleged that the president had knowingly accepted more than US$6 million in campaign contributions from the Cali cartel. Samper survived impeachment proceedings, but, greatly weakened politically, he has been unable to stem Colombia's slide into anarchy. In this environment, Colombian journalists face myriad and growing risks.

With the power and strength of Colombia's two major guerrilla groups (the Revolutionary Armed Forces of Colombia (FARC) and the National Liberation Army (ELN)) continuing to grow, the military and violent paramilitary groups asserted de-facto political control over large portions of the country. Meanwhile, common crime has reached epidemic proportions and drug-related violence has continued unabated.

Of the four journalists who died in the line of duty, one may have been murdered by local police, another by a paramilitary group, and in a third case, both the paramilitaries and the guerrillas are suspected. In a crime that dispelled the widespread notion that the leaders of the Cali cartel were less violent than their rivals in Medellín, Gerardo Bedoya, the opinion editor of the Cali daily *El País*, was gunned down in front of his home by a professional gunman only days after he wrote a column in favor of extraditing Colombian drug traffickers to the United States. Meanwhile, cameraman Richard Vélez, who recorded soldiers firing on unarmed peasants during demonstrations in 1996, was forced to flee into exile in the United States after he narrowly escaped being abducted.

Despite appeals to Colombian authorities to conduct thorough investigations, no suspects have been detained in any of these attacks. Instead, Samper has tried to turn the tables on the press, declaring, in a speech in August before the Inter American Press Association in Guatemala that, "The news media have been formed by action and violence and what does not march to the tempo is left out."

Rather than publicly affirming the role of a critical press in a democratic society, Samper has tried to limit negative coverage through government regulation and the distribution of media outlets to political cronies. Under a controversial 1996 law, the National Television Commission gained authority to revoke television licenses of news programs that do not conform to standards of "objectivity, impartiality or balance." In October, the commission, packed with Samper supporters, failed to renew the licenses of two newscasts that had broadcast critical stories. In protest over the regulations, Nobel prize-winning author Gabriel García Márquez withdrew his bid to renew the television station he co-owns with journalist Enrique Santos Calderón.

In August, two cabinet ministers were forced to resign after the weekly *Semana* published the transcript of a surreptitiously recorded cellular phone conversation in which they discussed Samper's plan to award radio frequencies to his friends and supporters. The frequencies were supposed to be awarded to the highest bidders at public auction.

The spread of violence and a cynical government effort to control coverage are rapidly undermining one of Latin America's most respected presses. Colombian journalists, who have not flinched from covering the drug trade despite the extreme danger, say they feel at even greater risk in an environment in which physical threat has become more generalized and the government has turned against them. Privately, journalists acknowledge that the new dangers have led to increased self-censorship.

January 30
Néstor Alonso López, *El Mundo* THREATENED
Carlos Salgado, *El Mundo* THREATENED

López and Salgado, reporters for the Medellín-based daily *El Mundo*, received anonymous phone threats after publishing an article in October 1996 about a local security association.

President Ernesto Samper authorized the creation of armed vigilante groups called "Asociaciones Convivir" to allow citizens to defend themselves against criminals. Press reports have linked some Convivir associations to paramilitary organizations.

In their report on one Convivir association in Medellín, López and Salgado revealed the identity of its members and their meeting place. Although Convivir organizations are legal,

the names of members and the location of the offices are kept secret to protect them from attack by such groups as guerrillas, urban militias, and criminals. Several months after the story ran, a bomb destroyed the Convivir office in Medellín that had been identified by López and Salgado. Five people were killed in the blast, and 50 were injured.

The day after the blast, López and Salgado began receiving phone threats from callers who blamed them for publicizing the location of the Convivir association, according to the reporters' written account. López and Salgado were forced into hiding according to local journalists.

March 18
Freddy Elles Ahumada, free-lancer KILLED

Elles was a free-lance photojournalist who drove a taxi to supplement his income. He was abducted by three unidentified individuals in Cartagena on March 17 and found assassinated in his taxi on March 18. He had been shot several times, and his body showed signs of torture. Local journalists believe that Elles may have been assassinated in reprisal for his photographs of police violence published in the Bogotá daily *El Espectador*. Only the spare tire of his taxi was missing, making robbery an unlikely motive for the crime.

March 20
Gerardo Bedoya Borrero, *El País* KILLED

Bedoya, 55, the opinion editor of the Cali daily newspaper *El País* and a harsh critic of drug trafficking, was getting into his car at 8 p.m. when he was shot at least six times by a gunman who fled the scene on a motorcycle. Bedoya had worked for *El País* for five years, after serving two terms in Congress and representing Colombia as an ambassador to the European Community, in Brussels. He recently defended a controversial U.S. decision to decertify Colombia as a recipient of U.S. economic aid because of the Colombian government's alleged ties to cocaine cartels. He had also advocated the extradition to the United States of Colombian nationals accused of drug crimes. His colleagues at *El País* said they believed the murder was the work of drug traffickers.

With the murder of Bedoya, at least 42 journalists have been assassinated in Colombia in the past 10 years, according to information corroborated by CPJ. Bedoya was the most prominent journalist to be murdered in Colombia since the 1986 killing by cartel hit men of Guillermo Cano, publisher of the Bogotá newspaper *El Espectador*.

In a March 21 press release, CPJ called on the Colombian government to take immediate action against those responsible for Bedoya's brutal murder.

March 20
Francisco Santos, *El Tiempo* THREATENED

An anonymous caller telephoned Santos, an editor with the leading Bogotá daily *El Tiempo*, and threatened to kill him. The caller also threatened to "blow up" the newspaper's office. Santos, who in 1990 was kidnapped and held for several months by members of the notorious Medellín cocaine cartel, told CPJ that he believed the threats were made by drug traffickers angry with the newspaper's coverage of the country's internecine drug war.

October 9
Luis Gonzalo "Richard" Vélez, Cadena A, ATTACKED

Vélez, a cameraman with "Colombia 12:30," a news program on television station Cadena A, fled Colombia under the protection of the International Red Cross after he was assaulted by several men who tried to force him into a taxi.

In August 1996, Vélez had filmed soldiers firing on coca growers in the department of Caquetá who were protesting a government-sponsored crop eradication program. He was beaten by three soldiers who tried to confiscate videotape in his camera. Vélez was taken to the hospital for treatment and later transported to Bogotá.

CPJ wrote a letter in August 1996 to the Colombian government denouncing the beating.

Vélez's report of the soldiers' conduct led to a criminal investigation in 1997 of the military officials involved. After a prosecutor called Vélez to testify in August, Vélez began to receive threatening telephone calls and has been constantly followed.

October 24
Alejandro Jaramillo *El Sur* KILLED

Jaramillo last worked in journalism as deputy director of the newspaper *El Sur* in Pasto, southwest of Bogotá from June through August. Before taking that job he had lived in exile in Ecuador, where he fled in 1989 after receiving death threats. Several years earlier, in an incident that may have been related to his work as a police reporter, he was shot and injured while working for *El País* in Cali. He was reported missing on October 24, and his dismembered body was found the following week. Because of the gruesome nature of his murder, involvement by organized crime is suspected.

November 8
Francisco Castro Menco, Fundación Cultural KILLED

Castro was president of the Fundación Cultural, a community foundation which broadcasts daily by radio in the violence-ridden town of Majagual in the department of Sucre. Castro was at home when he was fatally shot by unidentified killers. Although Castro tried to make the Fundación Cultural a neutral forum for community news, it represented an independent voice in a region where both armed guerrillas and paramilitary forces are active.

The Fundación Cultural provided air time for all three mayoral candidates in the October municipal elections without endorsing any. Castro, a community leader and candidate for the departmental assembly in October, hosted a daily program on community topics and often called for an end to the violence. Local journalists believe he was murdered because of his appeals for peace, but are unsure if the guerrillas or the paramilitary are responsible.

CPJ wrote a letter to Colombia's attorney general on November 14, asking that Castro's murder be investigated.

November 20
Jairo Elías Márquez Gallego, *El Marqués*
KILLED

Márquez was director of the magazine *El Marqués*, known for its critical reporting on corruption. He was killed in a drive-by shooting by two gunmen on a motorcycle as he was entering his car on a downtown street in the town of Armenia in western Colombia. Márquez had received numerous death threats in the past two years because of his crusade against corruption in the region.

On November 21, CPJ sent a letter calling for a thorough investigation.

December 13
Carlos Alberto Arredondo, Informativo de Antioquia IMPRISONED
Fredy Ocampo, Informativo de Antioquia IMPRISONED
Carlos Alberto Giraldo, *El Colombiano* IMPRISONED
Jesús Abad Colorado, *El Colombiano* IMPRISONED

Armed members of the Revolutionary Armed Forces of Colombia (FARC) kidnapped Arredondo, Ocampo, Giraldo, and Colorado and released them on December 19.

The four journalists were abducted at a roadblock on the Medellín-Bogotá highway in the Antioquia Province of northern Colombia, while reporting on the abduction of six mayors in the area. FARC claimed responsibility for the kidnapping in a note sent back with the journalists' driver.

One of the four journalists informed CPJ they were detained in a mobile encampment where the mayors were also being held. On December 17, radio station Radionet agreed to air an anti-paramilitary statement prepared by FARC. On December 19, the journalists, along with the mayors, were released.

Costa Rica

The country's long democratic tradition and independent judiciary have created a political environment in which diverse media are able to work with few impediments.

The primary concern among journalists is abuse of the Right to Reply Law, which mandates that those criticized in the media be granted equal time or space to respond to the allegations. For example, after the daily *Al Día* published a series of articles about drug trafficking based on leaked documents from the Joint Center of Antidrug Intelligence, Director Lauriano Orellano Castro demanded space in the newspaper for 10 separate "replies." In another case, a Costa Rican court ordered the garnishment of US$130,000 from the newspaper *Extra* to cover the legal fees of a Right to Reply case stemming from a 1995 article about suspects detained by police in a stolen car. *Extra* quoted the suspects in the story, and it allowed them to publish a "reply" 10 days after the original story ran. But the paper was technically in violation of the law, which mandates that they reply be published within three days. The decision to garnish the legal fees was reversed after more than two months, during which time *Extra* nearly went bankrupt.

Journalists also charge that relations with the government have been strained under the administration of president José María Figueres because he has not made himself available to the press and government agencies have been slow to respond to requests for information.

Cuba

Cuba's fledging independent press survived an extremely difficult year marked by persistent government harassment, periodic crackdowns, and grave financial need. Unrelenting government pressure forced several of the most important journalists on the island into exile; those who stayed face frequent detentions, occasional imprisonment, and the risk of physical harm.

Fidel Castro's communist regime controls all media outlets. Members of the independent press evade the restrictions by dictating stories over the telephone to colleagues outside the country. The stories, which range from political commentaries to reports on human rights abuses, are circulated on the Internet and published in newspapers in Miami and in Europe. While some Cuban journalists identify themselves as dissidents, others perceive themselves as media professionals whose sole interest is to publish their reports.

The independent journalism movement seemed to gain strength until early 1996, when Cuban MIGs shot down two private planes piloted by exiles from Miami. After the U.S. government denounced the attack and imposed economic sanctions on Cuba, the Cuban government began a crackdown on dissidents, particularly independent journalists. Throughout 1997, journalists were detained, arrested, and occasionally beaten, especially preceding major political events such as the Communist Youth Festival in July and the Communist Party Congress in October.

This pattern was repeated in the months leading up to Pope John Paul II's visit to the island in January 1998, but the government backed off as the international visitors arrived.

In order to suppress the flow of information from the island, the Cuban government appears to have created a special task force within the State Security Agency charged with controlling the independent press. A State Security agent, who gives his name as "Aramís," has been involved in nearly every detention of an independent journalist and has been present during nearly every interrogation. He has told journalists that he is in charge of the crackdown.

In August, CPJ sent a letter to President Castro after a number of journalists were detained and interrogated. One such incident took place on July 16, when Luis López Prendes, a reporter with the Independent Press Bureau of Cuba (BPIC) in Havana, was detained by State Security for unspecified "criminal acts." During his three-day detention, authorities interrogated López Prendes three times about why he had reported on five explosions at tourist hotels in July and August soon after the blasts. The case was particularly troubling because López Prendes was released briefly on July 18 and detained again the following night after speaking by telephone to a CPJ researcher.

In many ways, journalists in Cuba are confronting the kind of obstacles that were common throughout Latin America 20 years ago when journalists who published stories critical of the government faced virtually certain reprisal. While there has been a dramatic press opening across the region, state-sponsored repression has thwarted the development of an independent press in Cuba. Although the methods of repression are not as violent in Cuba as elsewhere in

Latin America—no journalist has been murdered in Cuba in the last decade—the effect is the same. Journalists who publish outside Cuba can be prosecuted for a variety of crimes, from defamation to aiding the enemy.

Cuba and Peru are the only two countries in Latin America where journalists continue to be jailed in reprisal for their work. On July 12, journalist Lorenzo Páez Nuñez, was sentenced to 18 months in prison for defaming the National Police. Páez had reported for Radio Martí—the U.S. government's Office of Cuban Broadcasting, which broadcasts to Cuba—that a police officer had allegedly killed a young man during a harvest celebration in Havana Province. He was arrested on July 10 and sentenced after a one-day trial. He was denied legal representation. In another case, journalist Bernado Arévalo Padrón was sentenced to six years in prison for an article that allegedly insulted Fidel Castro.

February 10
Ana Luisa López Baeza, CubaPress HARASSED
Tania Quintero, CubaPress HARASSED
Joaquín Torres Alvarez, Habana Press HARASSED

Approximately 50 members of El Sistema Unico de Vigilancia y Protección, a Cuban vigilante group, organized demonstrations outside the homes of López Baeza, Quintero, and Torres because of their activities with the independent news agencies CubaPress and Habana Press. The rallies, known in Cuba as "actos de repudio," or acts of rejection, were intended to harass and ostracize the journalists. Demonstrators shouted "traitor" and read aloud Article 8 of the so-called anti-Helms-Burton law, passed by the Cuban National Assembly in December 1996.

The Helms-Burton Act, a U.S. law named for its two main congressional sponsors and signed by President Clinton in March 1996,

bolsters the economic embargo against Cuba. Cuba's Article 8 makes it a crime for Cuban citizens to cooperate in any way with news organizations that report American government arguments in favor of the Helms-Burton Act.

February 11
Raúl Rivero, CubaPress HARASSED

Rivero, director of the independent news agency CubaPress, was harassed by dozens of members of El Sistema Unico de Vigilancia y Protección, a Cuban vigilante group tied to the Communist Party. The group organized a rally outside Rivero's home because of his journalistic activities. Such rallies, known in Cuba as "actos de repudio," or acts of rejection, are intended to harass and ostracize people. The crowd taunted Rivero, shouting "traitor."

May 21
Plácido Hernández Fuentes, CubaPress HARASSED

Cuban State Security Police told Hernández Fuentes' father that he would be thrown out of the Communist Party and lose his government benefits if he continued to harbor an independent journalist under his roof. Hernández Fuentes, a writer with the independent news agency CubaPress, has been unable to find a place to live since his father asked him to move out. Housing is exceedingly scarce in Havana.

May 28
Bernardo Arévalo Padrón, Línea Sur 3 HARASSED

Arévalo, a correspondent with the Puerto Rico-based news agency Línea Sur 3, was harassed by leaders of the Federation of Cuban Women. They forced him out of his home and into the street where they insulted him. This type of action has become an increasingly common form of harassment directed against independent journalists.

CPJ strongly denounced the incident in a letter sent to President Fidel Castro on June 17.

May 29
Ricardo González Alfonso, CubaPress HARASSED

Police officials searched the home of González, a reporter with CubaPress, and confiscated a computer, several diskettes, two typewriters, white paper, and articles he had written. Police officials said they were looking for illegal hoarding of peanuts. Although González is a journalist, he has a license to sell roasted peanuts in order to make a living.

May 31, Joaquín Torres Alvarez,
Habana Press ATTACKED

Torres, the director of the independent news agency Habana Press, was attacked by members of El Sistema Unico de Vigilancia y Protección (SUVP), a Cuban vigilante group tied to the Communist Party.

According to Nancy Pérez of CubaPress in Miami, two members of SUVP restrained Torres in his backyard, while others punched him. "Joaquín is full of bruises all over his body," Torres' wife told CubaPress.

May 31
Rafaela Lasalle, OrientePress HARASSED

Members of El Sistema Unico de Vigilancia y Protección (SUVP), a Cuban vigilante group, gathered in the evening at the home of Lasalle, a Santiago de Cuba-based journalist with the independent news agency OrientePress, and shouted insults and threats.

In a June 17 letter sent to President Fidel Castro, CPJ condemned the attacks, pointing out that despite the actions of the SUVP, Lasalle had not violated any Cuban law.

June 2
Tania Quintero, CubaPress HARASSED

Cuban State Security agents with a blank search warrant entered Quintero's home looking for a computer, but were unable to locate one. Quintero is a journalist with the independent news agency CubaPress.

June 12
Marvin Hernández Monsón, CubaPress HARASSED

Members of a Cuban vigilante group called El Sistema Unico de Vigilancia y Proteccion (SUVP) summoned neighbors of journalist Hernández Monsón and yelled insults about her through an amplifier.

CPJ strongly denounced the incident in a letter sent on June 17 to President Fidel Castro.

June 12
Juan Carlos Céspedes, CubaPress IMPRISONED

Céspedes, a Santiago de Cuba-based correspondent for the independent news agency CubaPress was arrested by State Security agents and held for six days, according to journalists in Miami. During an interrogation, agents demanded to know Céspedes' sources for a report on an outbreak of dengue fever which the journalist claimed had caused dozens of deaths.

June 23
Héctor Peraza Linares, Habana Press IMPRISONED

Peraza Linares, co-director of independent news agency Habana Press, was arrested along with his wife, Carmen Ana Fernández de Lara, at their home. Fernández de Lara was released several hours later, but Peraza Linares remained in custody, according to local journalists. No charges were brought against him.

On June 28, State Security agents brought Peraza Linares to his office. While there, he took $160 from a hiding place and gave it to the police. He then signed a document they had given him. Nery Díaz, Peraza Linares' ex-wife who witnessed the event, said Peraza Linares looked like a "zombie"—as if he had not slept for a long time.

CPJ sent a letter to President Fidel Castro on June 30 calling on him to release the journalist and expressing concern over Peraza Linares' health, which was deteriorating. On September 23, Peraza Linares was released. On December 14, he went into exile in Spain, after being granted a visa on humanitarian grounds.

July 1
Ana Luisa Lopez Baeza, CubaPress
HARASSED

Cuban State Security agents detained López Baeza's 22-year-old daughter and told her to tell her mother that she could be imprisoned if she continued to work as an independent journalist.

July 5
Nicolás Rosario Rosabal, Habana Press
IMPRISONED

State Security agents detained Rosario Rosabal, a correspondent for Habana Press. He was released four days later. The agents, who summoned Rosario Rosabal to the police station in Santiago de Cuba, accused him of illegally selling insecticides, Habana Press told CPJ. The agents told Rosario Rosabal that if he continued with his journalistic activities, he would be jailed.

July 12
Lorenzo Páez Núñez, Buró de Prensa Independiente de Cuba (BPIC) IMPRISONED

Páez, a correspondent with the independent news agency BPIC, was sentenced to 18 months in prison for defaming the national police. He was detained on July 10 because of his report about a police officer who allegedly killed a young man during harvest celebrations in the province of Pinar del Río. Páez was convicted after a one-day trial during which he was not permitted legal assistance. On December 19, CPJ sent a letter to the Cuban authorities, asking for information on Páez's legal status. As of press time, no reply was received.

July 16
Luis López Prendes, Buró de Prensa Independiente de Cuba (BPIC) IMPRISONED

López Prendes, a reporter with independent news agency BPIC, was detained by State Security agents who accused him of unspecified "criminal acts." The two agents who searched his home confiscated books, human rights reports, and a book written by Pope John Paul II. During his three-day detention, López Prendes was interrogated about why he had reported on recent explosions in tourist hotels. He was released on July 18 but detained again the following night after speaking with CPJ by telephone. He was released on August 6, but he said State Security agents warned him that if he continued his journalistic activities he would be sent to jail.

July 28
Raúl Rivero, CubaPress HARASSED

Rivero, one of Cuba's leading independent journalists and director of independent news agency CubaPress, was detained and questioned for two hours by State Security agents who apprehended him at his home. During his detention, agents warned Rivero that they were building a case against him and soon might formally arrest him.

On August 4, CPJ sent a letter to President Fidel Castro expressing alarm over the series of detentions of independent journalists in Cuba.

July 28
William Cortés, CubaPress IMPRISONED

Cortés, a correspondent with the independent news agency CubaPress in Pinar del Río, was detained by State Security agents. Family members who tried to visit Cortés in mid-August were told by a State Security agent that Cortés was "under investigation." No charges were formally filed.

According to local journalists, he was released after 27 days of detention.

July 31
Edel García, Agencia Centro Norte del País (CNP) IMPRISONED

State Security agents detained García, director of the independent news agency CNP, after searching his home in Caibarién. No charges were brought against García; he was released after 48 hours.

Local journalists reported that García's detention was part of a crackdown on the independent press, intended to curtail coverage of the communist International Youth Festival, which took place from July 28 to August 5.

July 31
Odalys Curbelo Sánchez, CubaPress IMPRISONED

Curbelo Sánchez, a Pinar del Río-based correspondent with the independent news agency CubaPress, was detained by State Security agents. She was released on August 6, local journalists told CPJ.

August 5
Olance Nogueras Rofes, Buró de Prensa Independiente de Cuba (BPIC) EXPELLED
Lázaro Lazo, Buró de Prensa Independiente de Cuba (BPIC) EXPELLED

Nogueras and Lazo, two of Cuba's best-known independent journalists, were forced to leave the country in order to avoid prison sentences of more than 10 years.

The pattern of harassment that led to their exile began on April 23 when Nogueras was detained by State Security officers while on his way to Lazo's house in Havana. Nogueras had just finished articles on electronic espionage by the Russian government, and on the dangers associated with a nuclear power plant in Cuba.

The officers who detained Nogueras accused him of having contact with former military officers. They told him they were watching him, and threatened him with 15 to 20 years in prison for espionage. Nogueras told CPJ this was the first time he had been accused of that crime; on previous occasions he had been accused of disseminating enemy propaganda, which is punished less severely.

After being held for three days at a military base in Havana, Nogueras was released and forced to return to Cienfuegos Province, where he had been banished in 1995.

On April 30, Nogueras was summoned to a hotel in Cienfuegos to meet with Ramón Pérez Sobre Pera, the chief of military counterintelligence in Cienfuegos. Pérez interrogated Nogueras about his reports on Russian espionage and the nuclear plant.

On May 22, Nogueras was expelled from a press conference and detained for three days. He had come to Havana in spite of his banishment, and was attending a press conference held by the U.S. non-governmental organization Pastors for Peace when State Security officers took him into custody. He was detained again at the military base, and while there went on a hunger strike.

In June, Lazo was summoned to Villa Marista, the State Security headquarters. He was informed that he was going to be tried, and that he could face at least 10 years of prison for enemy propaganda and activities undermining the security of Cuba. In July, Lazo was detained in his home along with Rafael Alberto Cruz, the director of Ciego de Avila-based news agency Patria. A State Security agent questioned both journalists for several hours.

Two days later, Bárbaro Morales, Second Chief of State Security of the province of Cienfuegos, told Nogueras that a trial against him would begin on August 8 on charges of espionage and dissemination of false news endangering world peace. Nogueras was additionally charged with disrespect and dissemination of enemy propaganda, based on his reporting on corruption in Cienfuegos that Nogueras published in *El Nuevo Herald* and aired on Radio Martí.

Given a choice between prison or exile, both Lazo and Nogueras chose exile and left Cuba with their wives. Lazo was not allowed to bring his son, or his wife's two daughters. Each of the exiles had to pay US$600 for medical exams, a pass allowing them to leave, and a passport. State Security officials, including an officer known as "Aramís," saw them off. Aramis has been linked to numerous detentions of journalists documented by CPJ. Airport officials confiscated a radio and a tape recorder Nogueras was carrying.

August 13
Efrén Martínez Pulgarón, CubaPress
IMPRISONED

Martínez Pulgarón, religious affairs correspondent for the independent news agency CubaPress in Havana, was detained by State Security agents while visiting his mother in San Luis, Pinar del Río Province. Local journalists told CPJ that he was taken to National Police headquarters. He was released on September 18. No charges were filed against him.

August 12
Raúl Rivero, CubaPress IMPRISONED

Rivero was detained by three State Security agents who took him to their headquarters in Villa Marista. Agents searched Rivero's apartment in Havana thoroughly for several hours. CubaPress archives, letters, a camera, books, and a typewriter were confiscated. The State

Security agent identified as "Aramís" was responsible for the operation against Rivero. Rivero's wife, who attempted to visit the detained journalist on August 13, was told to return a week later and that a visit might be considered at that time.

CPJ sent a letter to President Fidel Castro on August 12 calling for Rivero's immediate release.

Rivero was released on August 15, and he said he was not mistreated in detention. Some of his confiscated items were returned.

September 4
Jorge Olivera Castillo, Habana Press
HARASSED

Olivera was detained for 12 hours after being expelled from the Military Tribunal in Havana, where he was covering the trial of Maritza Lugu. Lugu was on trial for "bribery" stemming from her attempt to smuggle a tape recorder into the 1580 Prison, where she had hoped to record interviews with political prisoners. Outside the tribunal, Olivera was interrogated by State Security officers, including the officer known as "Aramís."

The officers took Olivera to a small police station, Unit 5b of the Playa National Revolutionary Police (PNR), where he was held for two hours. After being handcuffed, he was taken to a larger station, Unit 5 of the Playa PNR, where he was detained with criminals in a cell without bathroom facilities. He was released at 10:00 p.m. without explanation or charges.

October 16
Ricardo González Alfonso, CubaPress
IMPRISONED

State Security agents detained González, who had reported on a hunger strike by human rights advocates in the province of Santa Clara during the previous week.

González was arrested by two agents who entered his home. One of the agents, who gave his name as "Aramís," told González that he was being detained without cause and would be jailed for a long time. González was taken to a National Revolutionary Police (PNR) jail in Havana known as Territorial Siboney, from which he was released on October 18. No charges were filed against him. During his detention, González was warned that if he did not give up writing for CubaPress, he would have to choose between imprisonment or exile.

October 22
Habana Press HARASSED

State Security and National Revolutionary Police (PNR) officers searched the house of the sister of Habana Press director Joaquín Torres Alvarez, where the agency's archives were kept. The officers confiscated Habana Press documents, calling them "enemy propaganda," as well as a number of books they described as "subversive literature." None of the confiscated items were returned.

October 23
Jorge Luis Arce Cabrera, Buró de Prensa Independiente de Cuba (BPIC) ATTACKED

A retired employee of the Interior Ministry assaulted Arce outside his home on the afternoon of October 23. Arce's relatives report that the man, identified as "Adriano," has been known to carry out assignments for the Interior Ministry.

Adriano again attacked Arce as he was walking on a Cienfuegos street with his wife on the morning of October 29. This time, Adriano hit Arce in the head with a stick. Both Adriano and Arce were arrested by the National Revolutionary Police (PNR).

Prior to his release, Arce was told he would be charged with both the October 23 and 29 assaults.

On October 31, Arce was summoned to the provincial headquarters of State Security, where he was detained for three days in relation to the assaults. On January 12, Arce was fined 250 pesos by the PNR.

November 6
Luis López Prendes, Buró de Prensa Independiente de Cuba (BPIC) HARASSED
María de los Angeles González Amaro, Agencia de Prensa Independiente de Cuba HARASSED

López and González were detained early in the morning near the Provincial Tribunal in Havana, where American citizen Walter Van Der Veer was being tried on charges of promoting armed action against Cuba.

López and González were taken to the Second Police Unit in Old Havana, where they were held for six hours until the trial was over and Van Der Veer had been sentenced to a 15-year prison term.

November 18
Bernardo Arévalo Padrón, Línea Sur 3 IMPRISONED

Arévalo, correspondent with the Línea Sur 3 news agency in the province of Cienfuegos, was detained and jailed on November 18, after having been sentenced to six years in prison on October 31 by the Provincial Chamber of the Court of Aguada de Pasajeros, a town in Cienfuegos. Arévalo was convicted on the charge of "lack of respect" for President Fidel Castro and Carlos Lage, a member of the Cuban State Council. The conviction stems from a story Arévalo published on the leaders' privileges. He reported that a helicopter transported meat from a farm in Aguada de Pasajeros to Havana, despite the fact that the inhabitants there do not have enough to eat.

Arévalo is serving his sentence in Ariza prison in Cienfuegos, where he shares a filthy cell with common criminals. On November 28, the Aguada de Pasajeros Court rejected Arévalo's petition to review the conviction. On December 19, CPJ wrote a letter to Cuban authorities inquiring about Arévalo's legal status. No reply was received.

November 25
Odalys Ivette Curbelo Sánchez, CubaPress
HARASSED
Juan Antonio Sánchez Rodríguez, CubaPress
HARASSED

State Security officers detained Curbelo and Sánchez at 6 p.m. in the town of Pinar del Río as the journalists were visiting Curbelo's grandmother. The officers confiscated Curbelo's camera, which contained film the journalists had shot of vandalized posters of Pope John Paul II, displayed in anticipation of the papal visit to Cuba in January. Curbelo and Sánchez were taken to the State Security headquarters of Pinar del Río, where they were interrogated and threatened for four hours.

Dominican Republic

While there were no major attacks on the press in 1997, a handful of Dominican journalists reported clashes with police while covering demonstrations, such as the general strike in November. Local press groups have denounced telephone death threats against several journalists who were told their reports were "damaging the country's image."

While the Dominican Republic has a vigorous press, many journalists say they are disappointed that relations with the government have not improved since President Leonel Fernández was elected in 1996. Some journalists describe the youthful Fernández as inaccessible and suspicious of the media.

In November, Dominican press groups denounced the detention of sports reporter Kennedy Vargas from the daily *El Siglo*, who was arrested at his home by Dominican Marines. According to Vargas, the Marines beat him and held him overnight in a cave along with 50 other prisoners. The detention took place days before the general strike and Mercedes Castillo, president of the Domincan College of Journalists, denounced the attack as a possible warning to the media. No evidence has been produced, however, showing that the detention of Vargas was carried out in retaliation for his work.

Ecuador

Ecuador's vigorous press, like the rest of the country, spent much of the year recovering from the instability that marked the short term of President Abdalá Bucaram Ortiz, who was forced from office in February.

Bucaram frequently criticized journalists in public speeches and withheld government advertising from newspapers critical of the president. He showed particular disdain for the daily *Hoy*, perhaps because that paper was the first to report the disappearance of funds raised for poor children during a telethon which the president had hosted. At the beginning of the year, a group of journalists protested the growing tensions by marching on the presidential palace.

The media climate has greatly improved since congress removed Bucaram from office for "mental incompetence," but problems remain. In June, Attorney General Leonidas Plaza Verduga brought a nearly US$3 million libel suit against *Hoy* editor Benjamín Ortiz for a story on insurance fraud. The presiding judge dropped criminal charges against Ortiz, but the civil charges are still pending.

In September, the press scuttled an

amendment to the penal code which would have criminalized the publication of images or texts that could "damage the intimacy and personal lives of people, particularly politicians." Also that month, journalists from Ecuador and Peru signed a declaration in Lima promising to report accurately and objectively about the border conflict that had several times brought the two Andean nations to the brink of war. The editors announced that their goal was to nurture peace by "increasing understanding" between the two countries.

El Salvador

While the press in El Salvador has become increasingly professional and political violence has subsided, journalists face new dangers due to a sharp growth in drug trafficking and criminal violence.

On August 25, radio newscaster Lorena Saravia became the first journalist murdered in El Salvador since the end of the civil war in 1992. No motive has been established in the execution-style slaying, and it remains unclear whether Saravia was targeted because of her work, or was merely the latest victim in the capital's crime wave.

Journalists in El Salvador who are reporting on the country's growing drug problem say that gangs moving narcotics from Colombia to the United States have become a visible presence and a potential threat to the press. Several local journalists and foreign correspondents say they have received telephone threats.

While state-directed violence against the press largely ended with the signing of peace accords in 1992, journalists report a tense relationship with the government of President Armando Calderón Sol. Journalists, who say it remains extremely difficult to obtain information about court

cases, were dismayed when the congress passed a new penal code in April which grants judges discretion to limit public access in criminal cases. The law is expected to go into effect in 1998. In July, six reporters covering the arrest of a prominent businessman accused of fraud were injured in a scuffle with police.

August 25
Lorena Saravia, Radio RCS KILLED

Saravia was a prominent newscaster in El Salvador and a news anchor at radio station RCS. She was abducted from her car August 25, murdered with a shot to the head, and found dead in a vacant lot the following morning. Her car was found a week later in Santa Ana, 50 kilometers from San Salvador. Nothing was stolen. The investigation has not produced any leads, and it is not clear why Saravia was killed. Prior to working at Radio RCS, Saravia was a television news presenter. Radio RCS airs political talk shows hosted by ex-military officers and ex-guerrillas.

Guatemala

In the year since a peace treaty ended Guatemala's 36-year-long civil war, the press has become more pluralistic and professional, but is still hindered in its work by a climate of violence and growing tensions with the government of President Alvaro Arzú Irigoyen.

While the government-sponsored death squads that targeted journalists during the civil war have disappeared, political violence continues, especially in the countryside. Jorge Luis Marroquín Sagastume editor of small local monthly called *Sol Chortí*, was one of the victims. He was murdered on June 5 in Jocotán on the orders of Jocotán mayor José Manuel Ohajaca, who was angered by Marroquín's reporting on corruption. At least three other journalists were murdered this year in Guatemala, but against a backdrop of growing crime it was impossible to determine if the killings were motivated by their reporting.

Despite the apparent risks, journalists have reported aggressively on once-taboo subjects such as government corruption, the drug trade, and human rights abuses by the military. Indigenous issues receive increasing attention, not only from regional newspapers but also from Guatemala City dailies like *Siglo Veintiuno*. Cerigua, a news agency that because of the civil war violence once operated exclusively from Mexico but opened a Guatemala office in 1994, provides news from a leftist perspective. Indigenous-language radio stations have proliferated across the highlands.

In August, the Inter American Press Association (IAPA) held its "Unpunished Crimes against Journalists" conference in Guatemala City. The purpose of the event was to focus attention on the lack of progress in the investigations into the murders of journalists throughout Latin America. Six cases were chosen as representative, including two from Guatemala. Speaking to the assembly, President Arzú promised that his government would pursue investigations into the 1993 murder of Jorge Carpio Nicolle, publisher of *El Gráfico*, and the 1980 disappearance of journalist Irma Flaquer.

While Guatemalan journalists applauded Arzú's commitment to investigate the murders, they were taken aback by comments the president made during an official visit to Spain in October. In an interview with a European journalist, Arzú blamed the Guatemalan press for exaggerating its reporting on violent events in order to attract more readers. He was also one of only two Latin American leaders who supported an initiative put forward at the November Ibero-American summit by Venezuelan President Rafael Caldera, which would have affirmed a "right to free and truthful information."

Guatemalan journalists also allege that a publicly funded television news program called "Avances"—ostensibly created to inform the Guatemalan public about government polices—is being used to promote the interests of the governing Partida de Acción Nacional. "Avances" has devoted much of its time to criticizing the press for negative coverage, particularly the daily *Prensa Libre*.

The once-weak Guatemalan press does not seem to have been intimidated. Instead of holding its fire, the press has let fly a fusillade of accusations against the government, calling the president's attacks on the media a smoke screen intended to distract the population from pressing social problems.

June 5
Jorge Luis Marroquín Sagastume, *Sol Chortí*
KILLED

Marroquín was founding director of the local monthly *Sol Chortí*, which has reported extensively about corruption in the mayor's office. He was also a member of the ruling Partido de Avanzada Nacional (National Vanguard Party) in the department of Chiquimula. He was fatally shot in the town of Jocotán on June 5 by two assassins, according to eyewitnesses. Brothers Neftalí and José Gabriel López León, who are being tried for the murder, said that Jocotán mayor José Manuel Ohajaca hired José Gabriel to kill Marroquín. Guatemalan law protects mayors from prosecution for common crimes, but the Human Rights Office of the Archbishop in Guatemala City has petitioned the court to lift the immunity for Ohajaca. The request was rejected by the Sixth Court of Appeals in Jalapa and is pending before the Supreme Court.

THE AMERICAS

July 16
Hernández Pérez, Radio Campesina
KILLED

Pérez was a news reader at Radio Campesina in Tiquisate, Escuintla. He was ambushed by a group of heavily armed men as he was leaving the station on the morning of July 16 and killed instantly by gunfire. Another employee of the station, Haroldo Escobar Noriega, a messenger, was also killed. The motive for the murders is not known.

November 14
Luis Ronaldo De León Godoy, *Prensa Libre*
KILLED

De León was head of the weekend supplement section of the leading daily *Prensa Libre*. He was stabbed November 14 as he was leaving his house in central Guatemala City by an assailant who had been waiting in a nearby car for several hours, eyewitnesses reported. He died after three hours of surgery. Neither money nor personal documents were taken in the attack, local journalists reported, making robbery an unlikely motive.

Haiti

With political violence in Haiti receding in the aftermath of the 1996 democratic elections, the island's once-beleaguered press is working freely, with little fear of government persecution. Rogue police commanders and sporadic street violence accounted for the handful of attacks in 1997. But the virtual demobilization of the military and the disbanding of Duvalier-backed paramilitary groups such as the Touton Macoute have greatly reduced the threat of government-sponsored violence against the press. With their physical safety no longer an overwhelming concern,

journalists began to focus their energy on improving working conditions and access to information. Journalists claim that President René Preval, who took office in early 1996, is remote and inaccessible, generally talking only to hand-picked reporters invited into the National Palace. Faced with limited resources and overwhelming social needs, the Haitian government has not made an effort to get official documents and information into the hands of the public.

Nevertheless, Haitians have access to an increasingly broad range of information and views. The 70-percent illiteracy rate means that radio is the medium of choice, and the number of privately run local stations has doubled in the last few years. Call-in programs give voice to a wide variety of perspectives.

Years of covering Haiti's turmoil and political upheaval have made local journalists extremely proficient at reporting breaking news. But critics say reporters lack the necessary skills to do the analytic and investigative stories that the country's increasingly complex political reality demands. In order to remedy those deficiencies, a group of Haitian journalists who attended a UNESCO-sponsored seminar in December proposed the creation of a "Center for Freedom of Expression" devoted to professional training. While Haiti's overwhelming poverty is likely to limit the professional development of the media, journalists have gained the respect of Haitian society by reporting aggressively and often courageously through the years of political turmoil.

April 26
Rood Cheri, *Haiti Progress* HARASSED

Police officers detained Cheri, a photographer for the U.S.-based newsweekly *Haiti Progress*, while he was covering a protest rally in Port-au-Prince. Police officers, who detained Cheri for several hours, also seized his camera. The authorities later returned Cheri's camera without film, according to Maude Leblanc, *Haiti Progress* editor in New York. Some of the police officers were in plain clothes, according to Leblanc.

May 16
Rodney Jean Baptiste, IBO radio
ATTACKED

Baptiste, a reporter with the Port-au-Prince-based radio station IBO, was beaten by four unidentified individuals while he was covering a student rally in Port-au-Prince. When the police intervened, the attackers, who had struck Baptiste in the chest, fled, taking the reporter's radio, Baptiste told CPJ. No charges were brought against Baptiste's assailants.

June 6
Radio Macaya HARASSED

Police officers carried out an unauthorized search of the office of the Cayes-based radio station Radio Macaya after it broadcast statements by the head of the local police station in which he accused officers in Cayes of drug trafficking.

A reporter from Radio Macaya told CPJ that six armed plainclothes officers threatened the staff of the station as well as its director, Raymond Clerge, while they searched the office for the recording of the statement.

Honduras

The election of President Carlos Flores on November 30—the fifth democratic transfer of power since the end of military rule in 1982—helped solidify democracy in one of Latin America's poorest nations. Violence against journalists remains relatively rare, but the independence of the press has been compromised by political partisanship and allegations of widespread corruption in the media.

While the Honduran press has grown more professional in recent years, journalists in the capital of Tegucigalpa say continued progress is undermined by a system in which politicians pay journalists for positive coverage. In other instances, the measures are more subtle. President Flores, for example, is the owner of one of the country's major dailies, *La Tribuna*, and journalists for rival publications allege that the paper received preferential access during the campaign. They fear these practices will continue during the Flores administration.

Jamaica

Predictions that a 1996 multi-million-dollar libel award against *The Daily Gleaner*, Jamaica's largest daily, would have a chilling effect on the press have not been realized, as the island's diverse media continue to report with characteristic independence.

In one minor incident, a police reporter from CVM TV was roughed up and arrested for disturbing a crime scene. Police later apologized for the incident and agreed to meet with journalists to jointly develop guidelines to allow journalists to cover crime scenes without jeopardizing possible evidence. The press was able to report without incident on the December 18 general elections, during which Prime Minister P.J. Patterson of the People's National Party was elected to a third five-year term.

Meanwhile, The Gleaner Company Limited, owner of *The Daily Gleaner*, continued to appeal the $2.5-million libel verdict, which stemmed from an Associated Press story that ran in 1987. The story contained allegations that former Tourism Minister Eric Anthony Abrahams had accepted bribes.

Mexico

Three journalists were murdered, five were abducted, and dozens were hit with punitive lawsuits, making this the worst year for attacks on the press in Mexico in a decade. While the growing violence is partly indicative of the deteriorating social conditions, it also reflects a positive trend—the growing power and independence of the Mexican media.

Drug trafficking emerged as the primary threat to the press, with one journalist, Benjamín Flores González, murdered in June and another, editor Jesús Blancornelas, badly wounded in a Thanksgiving day attack. Violence against journalists, once largely confined to provincial cities, also invaded the capital city. One journalist was murdered in Mexico City and five others were abducted, apparently by police officials angered by aggressive coverage.

Ironically, the national financial crisis that began in 1995 accelerated the expansion of Mexico's independent press, as the government system that once kept journalists in line through kickbacks, bribes, and state advertising began to break down. As controls have diminished, reporters have begun to probe areas once considered off limits, such as drug trafficking, human rights abuses, and official corruption.

The July 6 mid-term election, during which Mexico's long-ruling Institutional Revolutionary Party (PRI) lost the mayor's race in Mexico City as well as majority control of the congress (and thereby control of the federal budget), rendered the rules that governed interaction between the press and the government obsolete. During the period of transition, with reporters probing the new limits of press freedom, attacks against journalists are likely to remain commonplace.

Even as violence against the press is growing more common, the threat of legal action is the primary deterrent to effective reporting. Mexico's anachronistic libel law—written in 1917—defines defamation as a criminal offense punishable by up to 11 months in prison. At least 74 cases have been filed against journalists in Mexico since President Ernesto Zedillo took office in 1994, according to Citizen Cause, a Mexican civic organization.

President Zedillo publicly affirmed his commitment to press freedom at the Inter American Press Association assembly in Guadalajara in October. Nevertheless, authorities have done little to investigate attacks on journalists and punish those responsible. While two gunmen were arrested for the murder of Flores González, little progress has been made in any of the other investigations. Among the outstanding cases is the 1988 assassination of Héctor "El Gato" Félix Miranda, the co-publisher of the Tijuana newsweekly *Zeta* along with Jesús Blancornelas.

In November, CPJ hosted a one-day conference in Mexico City with 35 top journalists to discuss press freedom and self-defense strategies. (See Mexico special report, p. 213.)

February 3
Jesus Abel Bueno León, 7 *días* LEGAL ACTION
Julio Ayala, 7 *días* LEGAL ACTION
Miguel Cervantes, LEGAL ACTION
Marlén Castro, *Epoca* LEGAL ACTION
Juan Angulo, *El Sur* LEGAL ACTION
Raúl García, *El Sur* LEGAL ACTION
Raphael Solano, *El Sur* LEGAL ACTION

José Rubén Robles Catalán, the former secretary of state for Guerrero, filed a lawsuit for defamation and calumny against seven local journalists—Bueno León, editor of *7 días*, a small weekly; Ayala, director of the same publication; Cervantes, a local radio reporter;

Castro, correspondent from the national news-magazine *Epoca*; and Angulo, García, and Solano, all reporters with the prestigious Acapulco daily *El Sur*. All had reported on serious allegations against Robles Catalán, which were the subject of government investigation: that Robles Catalán had framed his ex-girlfriend on drug charges and that he ordered the murder of her attorney. Rómulo Pacheco González, a former police commander in Guerrero who made similar allegations against Robles Catalán to the National Human Rights Commission, was found dead in his burned car in January, according to local press reports.

April 28
Sam Dillon, *The New York Times*
LEGAL ACTION
Craig Pyes, *The New York Times*
LEGAL ACTION

Jorge Carrillo Olea, governor of Morelos State, filed a criminal and civil libel suit against Dillon, *The New York Times'* bureau chief in Mexico, and Pyes, a Times reporter, alleging that a February 23 article titled "Shadow on the Border: Drug Ties Taint 2 Mexican Governors" contained inaccurate information. Manlio Fabio Beltrones, governor of Sonora State, filed a similar suit on June 9. CPJ sent a letter to President Ernesto Zedillo on June 6, expressing alarm about the criminal prosecution of journalists for defamation. Mexico's Attorney General dropped all charges against Dillon and Pyes on October 4.

May 22
Jesus Abel Bueno León, *7 días* KILLED

Bueno León, the editor of *7 días*, a small weekly newspaper in the Guerrero state capital of Chilpancingo, was shot to death on May 22. His body was found in the wreckage of his charred automobile.

In a letter that Bueno León wrote just before his death, he expressed fear that state officials in Guerrero might have been plotting to have him killed because of his coverage of government corruption.

The letter was retrieved from Bueno León's computer after his death and made public by his widow. A copy of the letter was obtained by CPJ.

Bueno León was one of seven local journalists named in a criminal libel suit filed by a former Guerrero state official. On February 3, José Rubén Robles Catalán, the former secretary of state for Guerrero, filed suit alleging that he had been defamed by published reports that he was being investigated in connection with the murder of a local attorney.

After Bueno León's murder, local journalists in Chilpancingo marched to the governor's palace in Chilpancingo to demand a complete investigation. Governor Angel Aguirre Rivero met with reporters and promised to keep them apprised of new developments.

CPJ sent a letter to Governor Aguirre on May 23 calling for a complete investigation.

May 23
José Tomás Capistrán Ríos, *El Sol del Centro*
ATTACKED, THREATENED, HARASSED, EXPELLED

Based on evidence that Capistrán Ríos faced danger if he returned to his homeland, a U.S. immigration judge granted him political asylum in the United States. Capistrán Ríos, a reporter with *El Sol de Centro* in Cordoba, Veracruz, was detained and tortured by Mexican Judicial Police in 1994 because of his aggressive reporting on the Zapatista conflict in the southern state of Chiapas.

Soon after the conflict began, Capistrán Ríos filed a story based on an interview with a leader of the armed movement who claimed the Zapatista rebels had 2,000 fighters. At the time, the government was claiming there were only a few hundred. A week later, he reported on the existence of a clandestine crematorium where the government was disposing of the bodies of rebels killed in combat.

THE AMERICAS

After filing the second story, Capistrán Ríos was informed that the Mexican Judicial Police were searching for him. Frightened, he secretly returned to Cordoba. On February 8, 1994, Capistrán Ríos was detained by the Judicial Police at the newspaper's office. He was then taken to a empty building where he was beaten and tortured. Solvent was poured down his throat and he was submerged in a tub of water. Police accused Capistrán Ríos of being a Zapatista, but no charges were filed against him. After a week in captivity, he was released.

On February 14, Capistrán Ríos traveled to Mexico City, where he remained in hiding for several months. In May or June of 1994, he filed a confidential complaint with the Mexican Human Rights Commission, a governmental organization charged with investigating human rights abuses. In the complaint, he listed his phone number. Within days, he began receiving death threats.

In September 1994, Capistrán Ríos entered the United States and asked for political asylum. In an advisory opinion submitted by the U.S. State Department to Immigration Judge Robert D. Vinikoor in Chicago, William M. Bartlett, the Director of the Office of Asylum Affairs, wrote, "We are of the opinion that the applicant could well be in danger if he returned to Mexico at this time ... [A]ggressive journalists ... in particular those working in the interior away from the glare of international exposure in Mexico City, are still subject to threats, harassment and illegal detentions."

June 30
Héctor Sánchez de la Madrid, *Diario de Colima* LEGAL ACTION

A criminal judge in the state of Colima issued an arrest warrant for Sánchez de la Madrid, director of the daily *Diario de Colima*, on charges of libel and defamation.

The suit was brought by the president of the Racquet and Country Club in Colima, who filed a suit against Sánchez de la Madrid after his newspaper published a series of articles accusing the club of corruption.

A federal judge granted Sánchez de la Madrid an injunction, which temporarily protected him from arrest.

July 15
Benjamín Flores González, *La Prensa* KILLED

Flores González, editor and owner of the daily *La Prensa* in San Luis Río Colorado, Sonora State, was murdered at 4:30 p.m. as he was arriving at the newspaper's offices. As Flores González opened the door to his pickup truck, a gray Chevrolet Impala pulled up and a gunman jumped out. After firing an entire clip at Flores González, the gunman returned to the Impala and was handed a .22-caliber pistol by an accomplice. He used that weapon to fire three additional rounds into Flores González's head as the victim lay prostrate on the ground. The assassin then got back in the car and drove off.

At the time of his murder, Flores González was facing five lawsuits for criminal defamation, some of them due to his coverage of the drug trade.

CPJ sent a letter on July 16 to the governor of Sonora State calling for a complete investigation and suggesting that the authorities examine whether there is any connection between the criminal complaints and the murder.

Several days later, police arrested two men linked to a jailed drug trafficker who had sued Flores González for libel.

Mexican police believe that Gabriel González Gutiérrez, the brother of the jailed trafficker, organized the plot to murder Flores González. González Gutiérrez is believed to reside in the United States.

July 26
Víctor Hernández Martínez, *Como* KILLED

Hernández, a police reporter for the magazine

Como, died from a traumatic blow to the head. He was attacked the night before, after he went to the federal police station while working on a story. Leaving the station, Hernández was followed by two men. An eyewitness heard a loud noise and then saw the reporter collapse. Hernández died later in the hospital.

Hernández had received several threats, according to *Como* editors. Shortly before his death, someone threw a Molotov cocktail at his car but he escaped serious injury.

CPJ sent a letter to President Ernesto Zedillo on August 29 calling for a complete investigation.

November 6
Miguel Robledo Ramírez, *Expresión*
ATTACKED

Photojournalist Robledo Ramírez was stopped while driving through downtown Matamoros by three men who opened fire with automatic weapons, striking him once in the arm. Robledo Ramírez, who covers police matters for the daily *Expresión*, had recently published a photograph of police apprehending suspects who had shot at the mayor's office, according to an editor of the newspaper.

November 27
Jesús Blancornelas, *Zeta* ATTACKED

Blancornelas, co-editor of the Tijuana newsweekly *Zeta*, was severely injured in an attack that killed his bodyguard, Luis Valero.

At 9:30 a.m., a man standing on the corner of Chula Vista and San Francisco streets in Tijuana opened fire on the red Ford Explorer in which Blancornelas was traveling on his way to *Zeta's* offices. When Valero, who was driving the car, attempted to turn the vehicle around, he was blocked by two cars, a green Pontiac on one side and a white Nissan on the other. Men in both cars began firing on Blancornelas' car with automatic weapons. The first gunman was killed in the crossfire. Blancornelas was hit four

times. He was hospitalized and, on November 29, underwent surgery to remove a bullet fragment that had lodged near his spine.

Federal investigators identified the dead gunman as David Barrón Corona, who went by the alias of C.H. In the week prior to the attack, Blancornelas had published an article in *Zeta* reporting that C.H. was the gunman in the killing of two Mexican soldiers on November 14. Barrón Corona, a U.S. resident who grew up in San Diego, was a reputed member of the "Mexican Mafia," a U.S.-based prison gang that distributes heroin and cocaine in the United States. A few weeks prior to the attack, government bodyguards who had been assigned by Governor Héctor Terán Terán to protect Blancornelas were removed. CPJ sent a letter on December 1 to President Ernesto Zedillo calling for a complete investigation.

At press time, no progress had been made in the investigation of the attack.

Nicaragua

President Arnoldo Alemán, who took office on January 10, promised during his campaign to put an end to the vestiges of Sandinista rule. Critics allege that he has tried to do so by withholding government advertising from Sandinista-controlled media outlets.

Soon after taking office, Alemán announced that, in order to save money, all state advertising would be channeled through five government agencies. Journalists with television station Channel 4 and the newspaper *Barricada*—run by the Sandinista party that ruled Nicaragua until 1988—allege that the agencies are a pretext to justify a government plan to bankrupt them by withholding all advertising.

In 1994, then-president Violeta Chamorro signed the Chapultepec Declaration, affirming her government's

commitment not to use state advertising to punish or reward media outlets for their coverage.

Another relic from the Sandinista era—and one that Alemán has not challenged—is the legal framework that guarantees freedom of expression. The 1987 constitution grants the right to "truthful information" to all Nicaraguans and defines journalism as a "social responsibility" which can be regulated by the state. Article 68 notes, "The media...are at the service of national interests [and] the state will promote access to the people and their representatives to ensure they are not subject to foreign or monopolistic interests." These provisions offer a theoretical legal justification for the government to take punitive measures against journalists or media outlets that publish information deemed to be false, irresponsible, or contrary to the national interest.

Panama

Panama's reputation for respecting press freedom was severely compromised by the government's attempt to expel journalist Gustavo Gorriti from the country in response to his investigative reporting.

Gorriti, who was forced to flee his native Peru in 1992 after being kidnapped by government security forces, joined the staff of the Panama City daily *La Prensa* in 1996. Soon after arriving in Panama, he began reporting on the collapse of the Panamanian Agro-Industrial and Commercial Bank (Banaico). In a series of articles, Gorriti documented how Colombian drug traffickers with close ties to the Panamanian government used the bank to launder money. He also found that a major trafficker with close ties to the Cali drug cartel had made a US$51,000 contribution to President Ernesto Pérez Balladares' campaign fund. After ini-

tially denying the allegation, the president later acknowledged that it was true.

Angered by Gorriti's reports, the government announced on August 5 that it would not renew his work visa in Panama and ordered him to leave the country by August 28. Under Panama's Ley Mordaza (Gag Law) written in 1978 under the military dictatorship of Omar Torrijos, foreigners are banned from holding senior positions in local media. While Labor Minister Mitchell Doens described the decision to expel Gorriti as an attempt to create employment for Panamanian journalists, CPJ, and other international press freedom and human rights organizations, denounced the measure as a transparent attack on press freedom. The attempt to expel Gorriti inspired widespread press coverage in *The New York Times*, *The Wall Street Journal*, *The Washington Post*, and *The Miami Herald*, which reported that the decision was taken after Nicolás Gonzales Revilla, a cousin of the president, complained that the journalist's reporting was interfering with his attempt to gain virtual monopoly control over Panamanian television.

Despite threats to use force if Gorriti refused to leave the country voluntarily, the Panamanian government finally backed down on October 14 and agreed to extend Gorriti's work visa for another year.

While the decision was an important victory for press freedom in Panama, the government has not upheld its commitment to reform the country's gag law. Under provision of that law, the Interior Ministry has discretionary authority to impose sanctions on the print media in the form of fines and to close down print media outlets for such infractions as "publishing facts related to the private life...that can cause moral damage to the person affected." The executive branch exercises discretionary powers to prosecute criminal libel offenses for which it can impose penalties of up to two years in prison.

Moreover, under Panamanian law a defendant can file the same charges with different judges. Tomás Cabal, a free-lance columnist and correspondent for a number of U.S. media outlets, has been sued 34 times by lawyer Hernán Delgado over a 1991 story in which he reproduced statements originally published in *U.S. News & World Report* that linked Delgado to drug traffickers. While Cabal has prevailed in 31 cases, one judge sentenced him to a 12-month suspended sentence, another fined him US$1,000, and a third sentenced him to 15 months in jail. That conviction is under appeal, but Cabal estimates he has shelled out US$10,000 in legal fees.

June 2
Tomás Cabal, *El Siglo* LEGAL ACTION

A Panamanian judge sentenced Cabal, a columnist with the Panama-based newspaper *El Siglo*, to 15 months in jail for libel. The charges were based on a series of reports on drug trafficking and money laundering published in 1991 in the *Panama America* newspaper.

In one of those reports, Cabal quoted remarks by Frank Rubino, a lawyer for two Cuban-American drug dealers, who said there were links between Panamanian lawyer Hernán Delgado and the drug cartels. Rubino's statements were first published in *U.S News & World Report*. Delgado was a former partner in a law firm with President Guillermo Endara.

Under Panamanian law, journalists commit libel or slander if they reproduce information deemed by the authorities to be derogatory or offensive. The sentence was appealed on June 30, and Cabal was not detained.

August 5
Gustavo Gorriti, *La Prensa* LEGAL ACTION

On August 5, the Minister of Labor and Social Welfare, Mitchell Doens, denied a request to renew Gorriti's work visa, which was to expire on August 28. He threatened to deport Gorriti if he had not left Panama by that date.

A prominent journalist who moved to Panama after being jailed and expelled from Peru for his investigative reporting, Gorriti had been working as associate editor of Panama's leading daily *La Prensa* for more than a year. He had quickly established himself as one of the country's top investigative journalists, reporting on corruption, money laundering, and political scandal.

The Labor Minister cited a Panamanian law promulgated under the military dictatorship barring foreigners from holding senior positions in the local media as the legal justification for his refusal to renew Gorriti's visa.

In a letter sent to Panamanian President Ernesto Pérez Balladares on August 7, CPJ noted that expelling Gorriti in reprisal for his reporting would constitute an attack on press freedom. In the months prior to the decision, Gorriti had reported extensively on money laundering and corruption. In 1996, he had reported that a member of the Colombia Cali cartel had made a US$51,000 donation to Pérez Balladares' presidential campaign fund. The *Miami Herald* reported that the decision to expel Gorriti was taken after Pérez Balladares was informed of a secret plan by Peruvian intelligence to murder Gorriti in Panama.

After threatening to carry out the expulsion, the Panamanian government finally succumbed to international pressure on October 14, announcing it would extend Gorriti's work visa and allow him to continue to work in Panama.

THE AMERICAS

Paraguay

Journalists covering Paraguay's borders with Brazil and Argentina confronted a series of attacks and threats from smugglers and drug traffickers who operate openly in the region.

High tariffs in Brazil and Argentina have

turned Paraguay's border towns into a smuggler's haven, where powerful businessmen, working with corrupt local officials, run a lucrative trade in everything from electronics to perfume. In recent years, Paraguay has also become a popular route for drug traffickers moving cocaine from Colombia. Journalists covering the border towns of Pedro Juan Caballero and Ciudad del Este are facing growing risks. In one dramatic example, the former mayor of Ciudad del Este was arrested in March for trying to arrange the murder of the national correspondent for the leading Asunción daily *ABC Color*.

The Paraguay Journalists Union also expressed alarm about a sharp increase in defamation lawsuits, including charges filed by a construction company partially owned by President Juan Carlos Wasmosy. According to reports published in Paraguay and elsewhere, the construction company diverted government funds during the construction of the massive hydroelectric plant in the town of Itaipú.

The Journalists Union has expressed concern that a victory by former general Lino Oviedo in the presidential elections of May 1998 could represent a threat to freedom of expression, given Oviedo's hostile attitude toward the press. Oviedo denounced the press for reporting his involvement in a 1996 coup attempt against President Wasmosy. Despite being ousted as army commander, Oviedo won the 1997 presidential nomination for the Colorado party, which has dominated Paraguayan politics for decades. Former dictator Alfredo Stroessner, who ruled Paraguay for 35 years until 1989, was a member, as is the current president.

January 10
Cándido Figueredo, *ABC Color*
THREATENED

Figueredo, the Pedro Juan Caballero

correspondent for the Asunción-based daily *ABC Color*, began getting anonymous death threats because of his articles about the crash of a plane carrying illegal arms, cocaine, and a suitcase with US$30,000. The plane went down in the Matto Grosso jungle.

Figueredo, who was put under police protection, had previously received death threats from drug cartels in the area. In 1996, his car was hit by gunfire.

The town of Pedro Juan Caballero is 500 kilometers north of Asunción, on the border with Brazil. It is known to be on the route of the drug trade to Colombia.

February 12
Blanca Miño, *Noticias* THREATENED, HARASSED

Two unidentified men attempted to kidnap Miño, the Pedro Juan Caballero correspondent for the Asunción-based daily *Noticias*. Miño was on the street with her three-year-old daughter when a man speaking Portuguese forced her into his car. When she resisted, the would-be abductors fled, apparently out of fear of being apprehended by police. Since then, Miño has received occasional death threats. She told CPJ that she received a letter saying that she would be killed on March 8, "to commemorate International Women's Day." The letter was signed by Fadh Jamil, an alleged drug and arms dealer.

Miño was the first reporter to cover the early 1997 crash in the Matto Grosso jungle of a small plane carrying an illegal shipment of arms. The arms had been stolen from the Paraguayan army. Miño told CPJ that she believes the threats came from drug dealers in the area who are also involved in illegal arms trafficking. Miño reported the incident to the police, who have provided surveillance of her home.

February 15
Antonio Caballero, *ABC Color*
THREATENED

Caballero, San Juan Nepomuceno correspondent

for the Asunción-based daily *ABC Color*, received death threats by phone from an anonymous caller. The next day, unidentified individuals went to his house and threatened to kill him. Caballero had published a series of articles on the illegal trafficking in tropical wood from the Caaguazú National Park and the unlawful occupation of 406,000 kilometers of land in the park by peasants.

March 1

Héctor Guerín, *ABC Color* THREATENED, HARASSED

The former mayor of Ciudad del Este, Niño Giret, was arrested on March 1 for attempting to have Guerín killed. Guerín is the Ciudad del Este correspondent for the Asunción-based daily *ABC Color*. According to *ABC Color* news editor Fabián Núñez, Guerín had been writing about allegations of corruption in the Giret administration for the past year, charges that led to the mayor's resignation.

Giret is alleged to have offered a former convict US$5,000 to kill Guerín, according to reports in *ABC Color*. After receiving a portion of the money, the hit man confessed to Guerín that he had been hired to murder him. Guerín informed the police, and he and the hit man cooperated in gathering evidence on Giret. The evidence included a tape recording of Giret discussing the murder plot with an undercover police official who was posing as an accomplice hired by the hit man to assist in the murder.

Peru

In the aftermath of Peru's hostage crisis, which ended in April with a military raid of the Japanese Embassy compound in Lima, the contentious relationship between the press and the government of President Alberto Fujimori took a turn for the worse. While the Peruvian press is able to report with few restrictions, individual journalists are often subjected to threats, intimidation, and harassment after their stories are published. Many local journalists believe that President Fujimori is trying to muzzle the press in anticipation of his bid for a third term as president in 2000.

The Peruvian military has shown a particularly low tolerance for any sort of public scrutiny. The most alarming example was the campaign directed against muckraking television station Canal 2, known as Frecuencia Latina. Tensions between the station and military authorities began to mount in late 1996 when Canal 2 reported on links between the members of the army and drug cartels. In May, the station aired an interview with a former military intelligence officer who alleged that the army had tortured her and murdered colleagues to prevent them from making public the existence of a secret plan to assassinate several of the country's top journalists. The allegations contributed to a climate of fear among Peruvian journalists, particularly those covering the military.

On July 13, Canal 2 broke yet another major story, airing conversations taped by government security forces who were spying on journalists. The same day the story was aired, Peru's immigration office issued a decree invalidating the Peruvian citizenship of the station's owner, Baruch Ivcher. The government alleged that Ivcher, an Israeli immigrant, had failed to follow the proper administrative procedures when he was granted Peruvian citizenship in 1984. Because Peruvian law precludes foreigners from owning media outlets, Ivcher stood to lose control of the station. After several months of legal wrangling, Peruvian police entered the studio of Canal 2 on September 19 to enforce a court order upholding the Immigration Office's decision and turning over control of the station to the pro-government minority owners.

The move to oust Ivcher as owner of Channel 2 prompted widespread protest not only by journalists, but also among the Peruvian public. Many Peruvians regard the media as a bulwark against government corruption and malfeasance in a country whose legislative and judicial branches are seen as in the thrall of the president.

Peru has an extremely active press organization, the Instituto de Prensa y Sociedad (IPYS) in Lima, which has brought both domestic and international attention to attacks on freedom of expression in Peru.

For the Fujimori government the first step in improving its relations with the media would be the release of the journalists unfairly convicted of subversion under Peru's draconian antiterrorist laws. Four journalists are currently incarcerated, serving sentences of up to 20 year in prison.

April 1
Blanca Rosales, *La República* ATTACKED

Rosales, an editor of the newspaper *La República*, was abducted by three armed men as she parked her car on a main street in Lima just before midnight. The men forced her at gunpoint to drive her car around Lima for 20 minutes. Rosales' colleague, Juan de la Puente, was able to escape and get into a taxi, which followed Rosales' car and a second car belonging to the kidnappers. De la Puente communicated with staff members at *La República*, who contacted the police. Rosales' captors transferred her to another car and took her to an outer district of the city, where they released her uninjured.

After the incident, Rosales has received an anonymous written threat that contained details of where she lives and spends her free time and warned her not to publish any information about the kidnapping or description of its perpetrators.

May 25
Baruch Ivcher, Frecuencia Latina-Canal 2
THREATENED, HARASSED

Ivcher, owner of Lima-based TV channel Frecuencia Latina - Canal 2, was threatened and harassed after his station reported on links between the Peruvian military and drug cartels, Fernando Viaña, managing editor of Frecuencia Latina, told CPJ.

In April, Canal 2 reported on allegations made by Leonor La Rosa, an intelligence officer in the Peruvian military, that she had been tortured by fellow military intelligence officers, who accused her of leaking information to the press. Immediately after Canal 2 aired La Rosa's allegations, military helicopters began to buzz Ivcher's mattress factory.

On May 23, the Joint Command of the Armed Forces issued a press release accusing Ivcher of harming the armed forces' prestige and image. A few days later, a Peruvian magazine published reportsæwhich local journalists believe were based on information leaked by the Peruvian militaryæaccusing Ivcher of selling arms to the Ecuadorian military, with whom Peruvian forces fought a brief border skirmish in 1995. After Canal 2 broadcast interviews with the Ecuadorian generals claiming the documents alleging arms trafficking were false, the Peruvian army paid for television commercials accusing Canal 2 of dishonoring Peru by talking to the Ecuadorian army.

CPJ sent a letter to President Fujimori on July 1 requesting that he provide security for journalists reporting on the military.

May 27
César Hildebrant, Uranio 15 HARASSED, LEGAL ACTION

Hildebrant, director of the Sunday political program "En Persona," broadcast by Lima-based Uranio 15, was the target of harassment and legal action.

Hildebrant was named in two criminal libel

suits brought by members of the ruling party. Local journalists told CPJ that Hildebrant was questioned by government officials about a May 27 broadcast of "En Persona" that featured a secret plan to guarantee President Alberto Fujimori's re-election in 2000. The document outlining the strategy was leaked to the press in December 1996 and later confirmed by an intelligence officer, Leonor La Rosa, on Hildebrant's television program. The army denied the existence of such a plan.

Hildebrant was also named as target of the so-called "Plan Bermuda," reportedly a Military Intelligence Service plan to kill journalists who opposed the government.

CPJ sent a letter to Fujimori on July 1 urging him to thoroughly investigate the existence of such a plan.

June 6
América Televisión Canal 4
THREATENED, HARASSED

An Interior Ministry advertisement in the daily *Expreso* offered a US$10,000 reward for anyone who could identify the hooded man who discussed paramilitary operations on the program "La Revista Dominical," broadcast April 22 on América Televisión Canal 4.

June 15
Gustavo Mohme, *La República* HARASSED

The Peruvian Interior Ministry broadcast an advertisement on several television channels that accused Mohme, owner of the opposition daily *La República*, of lying about the kidnapping of Blanca Rosales, the newspaper's managing editor.

The ads appeared after Rosales, who was abducted in April, identified one of her kidnappers. At the time of the abduction, *La República* reported that the main suspects in the abduction were members of a paramilitary organization with links to the army's intelligence unit.

Mohme also was named as a target of the "Bermuda Plan," reportedly a plot by the army intelligence service to kill certain journalists. The Peruvian government denied the existence of such a plan.

CPJ sent a letter to President Alberto Fujimori on July 1 urging him to guarantee to the safety of Mohme and other journalists who report on the military.

June 18
"En Persona" crew members ATTACKED

Crew members from the Lima-based television program "En Persona," broadcast by Uranio 15, were assaulted at gunpoint, their cameras and videotapes stolen, as they were covering a child abuse case at the Nueva Alianza shelter. Nothing else was stolen.

June 30
Luis Angeles Laynes, *Ojo* ATTACKED

Angeles, the political affairs editor of the daily *Ojo*, was ambushed and assaulted by three armed men. Angeles said the assault could have been a bungled kidnapping attempt.

After unsuccessfully trying to force Angeles into a car, one assailant struck him in the face. He was treated for head injuries at a local hospital.

Angeles, who was critical of the Fujimori government, had received death threats by telephone before the attack.

July 10
Baruch Ivcher, Frecuencia Latina-Canal 2
LEGAL ACTION

The government stripped Ivcher, owner of Lima-based television station Frecuencia Latina-Canal 2, of his Peruvian citizenship. Under Peruvian law, foreigners are not allowed to own media outlets.

The Peruvian government granted Ivcher citizenship on November 27, 1984, in a decree signed by then-president Fernando Belaúnde.

The immigration office invalidated that decree on July 10, saying Ivcher had never renounced his Israeli citizenship. That decision came one hour after Frecuencia Latina broadcast recordings of telephone conversations between journalists, politicians, judges, and businessmen that had been illegally tapped, allegedly by government intelligence services, local journalists told CPJ.

CPJ sent a letter on July 14 to President Alberto Fujimori urging him to reverse the decision. In September, Ivcher's minority partners assumed control of the station. Journalists remained en masse. Since then, Frecuencia Latina has become pro-government in its orientation.

September 3
Tito Pilco Mori, Radio Frecuencia Popular
KILLED

Pilco was owner and director of Radio Frecuencia Popular in Rioja and host of the program "El Pueblo Quiere Saber" ("The People Want to Know"), which frequently criticized public prosecutors, judges, and police officials. He was assaulted August 27 on the outskirts of Rioja as he was returning home from a visit with a cousin. He was found, severely injured and unable to speak, at 5 a.m. on August 28, some distance from his motorcycle. He died September 3 in a Lima hospital. Two witnesses reported seeing assailants in a white car without license plates intercept Pilco on his motorcycle and beat him. But the official report said his death resulted from head wounds received when he crashed his motorcycle because he was drunk. The investigation was initially headed by José Monteverde, a provincial prosecutor whose integrity had been questioned by Pilco on his radio show, according to the local press. After a Lima newspaper published an account of Pilco's death, the case was reopened.

September 19
Ricardo Choy, Associated Press ATTACKED

Peruvian police confiscated Choy's film after he photographed police entering television station Fecuencia Latina-Canal 2 in Lima. Five days earlier, on September 14, the Peruvian Court of Public Law had upheld the Immigration Ministry's decision to strip station owner Baruch Ivcher of his Peruvian citizenship, which was taken after Frecuencia Latina broadcast a series of investigative stories in April. Because only Peruvians can legally own media outlets, control of Frecuencia Latina was transferred to minority owners Samuel and Mendel Winter. Choy had been assigned to photograph the Winter brothers entering the station under police escort.

At the behest of the Winter brothers, police officers at the scene confiscated six rolls of film from Choy, only one of which contained photos of the TV station. After repeated protests, Frecuencia Latina later returned the film. All six rolls of film had been developed. The pictures of the Winter brothers entering the station subsequently went out on the AP wire and were published in Peru and around the world.

December 15
José Arrieta Matos, Frecuencia Latina-Canal 2
LEGAL ACTION

Investigative reporter Arrieta was summoned to appear before the National Board Against Terrorism (DINCOTE) on December 18. With his lawyer present, Arrieta was interrogated for seven hours by Captain Oscar Arriola Delgado about his sources in the Peruvian intelligence services.

Arrieta, former head of the investigative unit at television station Frecuencia Latina-Canal 2, lost his job after the station's owner, Baruch Ivcher, was stripped of his citizenship. That action was taken by Peruvian authorities in response to the station's investigative stories on secret intelligence operations, many of them broken by Arrieta.

Arrieta had produced a series of stories on the paramilitary group Colina, which was allegedly responsible for a dynamite attack on Congressman Javier Díez Canseco in 1990. Arrieta's source for that story was ex-military intelligence officer José Luis Bazán Adrianzén, a former member of Colina. In several interviews, aired in January 1995 and in April 1997, Bazán admitted that he participated in the dynamite attack. He was jailed in April 1997 for eight months for having revealed state secrets. After being released from prison in December, Bazán recanted his testimony.

During his interrogation, Arrieta was told he could be arrested for allegedly bribing Bazán to admit to his involvement in the assassination attempt.

When informed that his arrest was imminent, CPJ wrote a letter to Arrieta inviting him to come to New York to discuss his case. He arrived on January 8, 1998.

Suriname

Press freedom has generally been respected in Suriname, since power was handed over to democratically elected president Ronald Venetiaan of the Nieuw Front party in 1991. As 1997 drew to a close, however, several journalists in Suriname say they received threatening phone calls accusing them of destabilizing the government.

The roots of the current tension date back to 1975, when Suriname was granted independence from The Netherlands. The military has dominated the country since then, holding power during eight of the 23 years since independence. Military repression culminated on December 8, 1982, when strongman Desi Bouterse ordered the execution of 15 political opponents of his regime, among them five

journalists. In response, Suriname lost Dutch development aid, which led to the country's rapid impoverishment.

The 1996 elections brought Bouterse's supporters, now affiliated with the National Democratic Party, back into political power. After the Dutch government issued an international arrest warrant for Bouterse on drug trafficking charges, newly elected president Jules Wijdenbosch appointed Bouterse as Advisor of State, thereby granting him diplomatic immunity.

December 8
Edward Troon, free-lancer HARASSED

Three men abducted Troon in broad daylight and beat him, saying "This is a December 8 gift to you all," in reference to the 1982 massacre carried out on that date.

Troon, a well-known photojournalist, is married to Nita Ramcharan, the editor of *De Ware Tijd*, Suriname's leading daily. He was walking on a Paramaribo street when he was ambushed, blindfolded, and pulled into a car. He was driven around for about 45 minutes and struck repeatedly in the abdomen and face before being pushed out of the car near his house.

Prior to the incident, *De Ware Tijd* had received threatening phone calls, saying the daily would feel the results if it continued to oppose the government, according to local journalists.

Trinidad and Tobago

Prime Minister Basdeo Panday, who has been feuding with the media since taking office two years ago, softened his rhetoric at

the end of the 1997, after journalists banded together to defeat his plan to impose new legal restrictions on the press.

In May, the government published a report entitled "Toward a Free and Responsible Media," which proposed the adoption of statutes requiring journalists to report with "due accuracy and impartiality." The so-called "green paper" also called for the creation of a code of ethics mandating that journalists promote national unity, and economic and social progress. The plan was shelved in response to public outcry.

Panday's war with the media is largely a reflection of Trinidad and Tobago's complex racial politics. The population is equally divided between those of African and Indian descent, but blacks have long held the lion's share of political power. Panday, the first prime minister of Indian descent, has described the largely black-owned media as racist. In 1996, 17 editors left the *Trinidad Guardian* to found a new paper, *The Independent*, after Panday accused the *Guardian* of race-baiting. At one point, Panday called Kenneth Gordon, owner of the daily *Trinidad Express*, a "pseudo-racist," noting, "I do not believe that freedom of the press includes the untrammeled right to publish lies, half-truths and innuendo about anyone."

But Panday began to back down after Roy Boyke, a senior official who has worked for governments throughout the region, advised the prime minister to declare a "unilateral moratorium," and lessen hostilities.

"The press is not racial," insisted new *Guardian* editor Carl Jacobs at year's end. "We want to build readership. We have a vested interest in being even-handed."

United States

President Bill Clinton has made press freedom a focus of U.S. foreign policy during his second term, raising the issue during a White House visit with Turkish Prime Minister Mesut Yilmaz in December, and during a three-country tour of Latin America in October. During his October visit to Argentina, Clinton discussed his concerns during a private meeting with Argentine President Carlos Saúl Menem. Clinton aides also met with a group of Argentine journalists and assured them of the president's commitment to press freedom. The U.S. president's message seemed to have an immediate and dramatic effect. Attacks on the press in Argentina dropped off after the Clinton visit, and President Menem refrained from making menacing statements about the media.

Since its founding in 1981, the Committee to Protect Journalists has, as a matter of strategy and policy, concentrated on press freedom violations and attacks on journalists outside the United States. We do not systematically monitor problems facing journalists in any of the developed industrial democracies. Our resources are limited, and we devote most of our efforts to those countries where journalists are most in need of international support and protection.

While CPJ recognizes that press freedom requires constant vigilance and aggressive defense at home as well as abroad, we are able to rely within the United States on the thorough, professional efforts of organizations with a primarily domestic focus, such as the American Society of Newspaper Editors, the Society of Professional Journalists, the Reporters Committee for Freedom of the Press, the Electronic Frontier Foundation, the American Civil Liberties Union, and the National

Association of Broadcasters, among others. We recommend to journalists and other researchers the bulletins and annual reports of these and similar organizations, as well as the ongoing coverage of First Amendment issues provided by the *American Journalism Review*, the *Columbia Journalism Review*, *Editor & Publisher*, and other specialized publications.

On U.S. policy issues directly affecting the ability of U.S. reporters to work safely and legally abroad, CPJ works with U.S. journalism organizations to effect constructive change.

CPJ's overriding concern in the United States continues to be the cases of journalists who are murdered for reasons related directly to their profession. As a U.S. organization that forcefully urges governments around the world to investigate and prosecute the assassinations of local journalists, we believe that it is essential to hold our own government equally accountable when similar crimes are committed at home.

Since the widely publicized 1976 murder of *Arizona Republic* reporter Don Bolles, at least 11 other American journalists have been murdered because of their work. In all but one case, the victims were immigrant journalists working in languages other than English. Seven of those 10 homicides remain unsolved. Most received little or no national media attention. Limited local police investigations were carried out with only minimal federal law-enforcement assistance—despite strong indications in several cases of possible interstate and even international criminal conspiracies.

In December 1993, CPJ released a 60-page report on these murders titled *Silenced: The Unsolved Murders of Immigrant Journalists in the United States*. The report prompted the Justice Department to reopen investigations into five of the cases, all involving Vietnamese-American journalists. Officials working with a California-based

task force of federal prosecutors and FBI agents said one year later that they were not yet able to report publicly on any progress in the investigation, however.

Uruguay

The kidnapping of journalist Pablo Alfano in January by two armed men was the sole physical attack in a year in which the Uruguayan press continued to report aggressively with few restrictions or reprisals.

Despite calls for reform, the legal environment for the press in Uruguay remains troubling, although few cases result in conviction. A 1989 statute provides up to two years imprisonment for journalists convicted of "knowingly divulging false news" or "insulting the nation, the State, or its powers." Four journalists with the Montevideo daily *La República* were convicted under that statute in 1996 and sentenced to two years in prison based on a critical article about Paraguayan President Juan Carlos Wasmosy. Federico Fasano, *La República*'s editor in chief, and Carlos Fasano, the managing editor, were briefly jailed following the conviction. The case was dismissed in April, but prosecutors have appealed it to the Supreme Court.

January 28
Pablo Alfano, *El Observador* THREATENED, HARASSED

Two unidentified armed men driving a white Fiat abducted Alfano, a journalist for *El Observador*, a Montevideo daily, and drove him around the the side streets of Montevideo for about a half-hour. They ordered him to turn over his sources and terminate his investigation of the Unification Church's activity in Montevideo. Before releasing him, the kidnappers threatened Alfano and

THE AMERICAS

his family with death if Alfano continued his investigation. Later that night, the same men, driving the same car, followed Alfano home. The Uruguayan government and police forces began an investigation into the incident shortly after Alfano was released. To date, no suspects have been named.

Venezuela

After serving five months of a year-long sentence, journalist William Ojeda was released from prison in June. Ojeda became a *cause celebre* in November 1996 after he was convicted of defamation for statements made in a book on corruption in the Venezuelan judiciary titled *How Much is a Judge Worth?*

The decision by President Rafael Caldera to pardon Ojeda came in response to sustained pressure from the Venezuelan media and journalists organizations who were outraged by the jail sentence. But any expectation that the Ojeda pardon represented a thaw in the tense relationship between the press and Caldera was quickly dispelled. In the months prior to the Ibero-American summit (an annual gathering of Latin American, Spanish, and Portuguese leaders) held in November on the Venezuelan island of Margarita, Caldera proposed that the attending governments affirm the "right to truthful and timely information." Behind the seemingly innocuous idea was a plan to regulate coverage and bar journalists from giving opinions.

"Caldera knows that through the dissemination of unlimited information his government will be unmasked," wrote columnist José Vicente Rangel in the daily *El Universal*. Caldera's proposal, vigorously opposed by Venezuelan journalists and Latin American press organizations, was not ratified at the summit.

While the government has been unsuccessful in mandating that journalists report what it defined as the "truth," the practice of journalism in Venezuela requires a license and a college degree under the 1994 Law for the Practice of Journalism. The legislation is opposed by media owners, who have petitioned the Supreme Court to strike it down

The theft of computer and personal files from prominent columnist Alfredo Peña in July raised suspicions that the action may have been taken in response to a series of recent articles about government corruption. The case remains under investigation.

Breaking Away: Mexico's Press Challenges the Status Quo

By Joel Simon

In November 1996, as he was preparing to fly to New York to accept an International Press Freedom Award from the Committee to Protect Journalists, J. Jesús Blancornelas received an unlikely visitor at his Tijuana office. A former Tijuana police chief dropped by—not to offer congratulations, but to warn Blancornelas that if he accepted the award, he was signing his own death sentence.

Almost exactly one year later, the sentence was very nearly carried out. On November 27, Thanksgiving day across the border in San Diego but a normal workday in Mexico, bodyguard Luis Valero was driving Blancornelas to the offices of *Zeta*, the muckraking weekly newspaper he had co-founded in 1980. As Valero drove the red Ford Explorer down Chula Vista Street, a white Nissan cut him off. A pistol-wielding man jumped out and began firing. Valero tried to escape, turning right down San Francisco Street. But a green Pontiac pulled up alongside the Explorer, and four men with automatic rifles raked the car carrying Blancornelas with gunfire. Blancornelas took cover on the floor, while Valero threw the car in reverse, mounting the sidewalk and colliding with an iron fence. Hit by a fusillade of gunfire, Valero lay dying, slumped over on the passenger seat. Blancornelas, who had been struck by four bullets, grabbed the CB radio and called *Zeta*'s offices. "We've been shot!" he yelled into the microphone. By the time reporters and photographers arrived at the scene, Blancornelas was being wheeled away on a stretcher, while one of the assassins, hit in the eye during the crossfire, lay dead, eerily propped up on his own gun.

After nearly two decades as co-editor of *Zeta*, Blancornelas has made his share of powerful enemies, any one of whom could have

CPJ wishes to acknowledge the Robert R. McCormick Tribune Foundation for the generous support which made possible the Mexico City journalism workshop. Additional support was provided by the Freedom Forum.

been responsible for the attack. *Zeta* has run stories about politicians on the take; explored the relationship between drug lords and the state police; and reported on the wave of killings carried out by the Arellano brothers, Tijuana's first family of drug smuggling. Blancornelas has also published stories implicating Jorge Hank Rhon, the scion of Mexico's leading political clan, in the murder of his partner and *Zeta* co-founder Héctor "Gato" Félix, who was gunned down in 1988. Over the years, Blancornelas himself has received numerous death threats. In 1987, *Zeta's* office was riddled with gunfire.

But the air of danger around Blancornelas did seem to heat up after he was honored along with five other journalists at CPJ's International Press Freedom Award dinner on November 26, 1996. In April, gunmen jumped from a car, shooting and killing Héctor Navarro, *Zeta's* former accountant, and Carlos Estrada, Blancornelas' former attorney. Because Blancornelas had been involved in a legal dispute with the two men, Tijuana's tabloid press insinuated that the editor was behind the killings. Soon after the murder of Navarro and Estrada, Blancornelas hired Luis Lauro Valero as his personal bodyguard. Baja California governor Héctor Terán Terán also assigned police protection to Blancornelas. On October 27, 1997, however, the bodyguards Governor Terán had assigned were removed. *Zeta* editors later alleged that the action was taken in response to the paper's aggressive reporting.

CPJ had chosen to honor Blancornelas not only in recognition of his achievements as editor of one of Mexico's most independent newspapers, but also to highlight the dramatic transformation of the Mexican press. *Zeta* was one of the first Mexican newspapers to challenge the decades-old system of bribes, kickbacks, and distribution of government advertising that had been used by the ruling Institutional Revolutionary Party (PRI) to keep the Mexican press in line. *Zeta* reporters were explicitly forbidden to accept gratuities from government officials, and the paper made a concerted effort to cover opposition parties fairly. Partially due to *Zeta's* coverage of the 1989 gubernatorial elections in Baja California, the National Action Party's (PAN) Ernesto Ruffo Appel won the race, ending the PRI's half-century long political monopoly. Today, the kind of journalism that once set *Zeta* apart is becoming more common in Mexico—bribes are no longer routine, and the press has become more aggressive, professional, and independent.

Ironically, as the quality of journalism has improved in Mexico, the risks to journalists have increased, as powerful figures, unaccustomed to public scrutiny, have lashed out violently. Despite Blancornelas' growing sense that he was a marked man in the months after the murders of Navarro and Estrada, *Zeta* continued to cover the dangerous stories. The paper reported extensively on the "Narcojuniors," the children of Tijuana's wealthiest families who had been drawn into the drug trade. *Zeta* reporters also explored the growing ties between the Tijuana cartel and the state judicial police. On November 21, *Zeta* broke the story of how the Arellanos' top assassin was behind the murder of a several police officers. Blancornelas co-authored a report on the gunman, a Mexican who had grown up across the border in San Diego and was known only by his nickname: C.H.

The day after the ambush of Blancornelas and Valero, it became clear that it was Blancornelas' November 21 story that nearly got him killed. A report issued after the autopsy on the gunman killed at the scene revealed that he was covered with elaborate tattoos, including 16 skulls, perhaps representing his victims, and a large "EME," indicating membership in a U.S.-based prison gang called the "Mexican Mafia." Through fingerprints, Mexican federal authorities were able to identify the dead man as David Barrón Corona, better known as C.H.

Only three weeks before the attack on Blancornelas and Valero, editor Raymundo Riva Palacio had addressed a gathering of about 30 of Mexico's top journalists, invited by CPJ to discuss self-defense strategies. "Does someone have to die before we do anything?" asked Riva Palacio. The workshop, titled "¿Cómo se defiende la libertad de prensa?" (How is Press Freedom Defended?), was held on November 7 and 8 in Mexico City.

What Riva Palacio was alluding to was the fractiousness of the Mexican press, which has never had an independent organization to represent its interests. Ideological feuds, personal rivalries, and the insularity of the Mexico-based media have long divided the Mexican press. Many of the journalists at the CPJ-sponsored workshop, for example, had not met the top provincial journalists who were also in attendance. Most of the rivalries and personal differences were put aside, as the journalists found common ground in an issue they were all facing—the rising tide of violence against the press.

Why has the Mexican press been so divided? The PRI is partially to blame. The government has made a concerted effort to undermine and co-opt any press group that challenged the status quo. Yet as Riva Palacio has pointed out, the press has generally been an active participant in the system. "The collusion of the press is so complete that the government does not have to resort to direct censorship to suppress ideas and information," wrote Riva Palacio in an essay published in *A Culture of Collusion*, a book on the Mexican press edited by CPJ executive director William A. Orme, Jr. "The government can exercise control over what it wants published because the press has no desire to give up its share of the bargain; the press can not bear the idea of unbridled competition."

But the mechanisms of state control Riva Palacio described— ranging from free meals and prostitutes to a US$40,000 payment to kill a story—have in fact already begun to break down. The loosening of control began in 1990 under President Carlos Salinas de Gortari. In an effort to sell the virtues of the North American Free Trade Agreement (NAFTA), Salinas employed a sophisticated media strategy, wooing the foreign press and top Mexican journalists with access and inside information. While bribes and threats did not disappear, they were partly supplanted by the introduction of modern "spin control."

The establishment of the Mexico City daily *Reforma* in late 1993 also challenged one of the government's primary strategies for controlling the media—the distribution of state advertising. Many newspapers in Mexico stay afloat with revenue they receive from government ads. And most papers publish *gacetillas*—paid government propaganda disguised as news stores. But *Reforma*, bankrolled by the wealthy Junco family that also owns the Monterrey daily *El Norte*, is one of a handful of Mexican newspapers that has erected a wall between the business side and the news side. Reporters are prohibited from soliciting advertising from the sources they cover, a common practice throughout the rest of the Mexican press corps.

The Mexican media learned an important lesson about the economic value of news in January 1994, when armed Mayan

Indian rebels from the Zapatista Army of National Liberation (EZLN), led by a charismatic, pipe-smoking mestizo who called himself Subcommander Marcos, took over several towns in the southern state of Chiapas. The story had instant appeal, and the Mexican press covered it closely. The left-leaning daily *La Jornada*, which aggressively reported the revolt, found that its circulation doubled, reaching 120,000. The assassination of PRI presidential candidate Luis Donaldo Colosio at a Tijuana campaign rally in March 1994 further fueled the public's appetite for news. Mexicans turned to the press for information and analysis about the violent events that were transforming their country.

At the same time that the print media were being transformed by the growing demand for information, Mexican television was experiencing the birth of competition. In 1993, in accordance with its economic liberalization program, the Salinas government sold a state-owned television station to businessman Ricardo Salinas Pliego (no relation to the president). Few observers expected the new station—christened Televisión Azteca—to pose any real challenge to Mexico's media giant Televisa, whose owner, Emilio Azcárraga, once proudly described his station as "part of the government system." Televisa's nightly newscast—the sole source of news for the vast majority of Mexicans—featured mostly innocuous interviews with prominent politicos and re-heated press releases. While TV Azteca's nightly news program was still favorable to the PRI, it took more risks than Televisa. The station found that its ratings soared when it aired controversial stories, such as an interview with Subcommander Marcos. Within a few years, TV Azteca had siphoned off 40 percent of the prime-time audience. Televisa fought back by upgrading its coverage; Mexico's television war had begun.

By the time Salinas handed over power to Ernesto Zedillo Ponce de León in late 1994, the very ethos of Mexican journalism had changed. Journalists who might have once sought to make a career by cozying up to a powerful politician now built their reputations on exposés of the latest political scandal. Mexicans had access to a wide range of information—two major television networks, cable news programs, several lively and informative radio news shows, and dozens of print outlets spanning the ideological spectrum. A new generation of young reporters—better educated, more independent, and more highly paid—was moving into top editorial positions. Ironically, Salinas found himself the target of forces he had unwittingly unleashed, as an emboldened and sometimes reckless press published stories accusing the ex-president of everything from corruption to murder.

Mexico's press has continued to move toward independence under Zedillo, but for entirely different reasons. While Salinas sought to develop more sophisticated mechanisms for exercising control over the press, Zedillo, who had never held elective office before he became president, seemed to lack both the skills and inclination to manage the media. Even more significant was the near collapse of the Mexican economy in early 1995, which greatly limited the PRI's ability to bankroll journalists. In state capitals where journalists were often paid by the government agencies they covered, budget cuts have ended the practice. The emergence of political competition has also undermined the system, as rival political parties have purged journalists, most of them loyal to the PRI, from government payrolls. The death knell for the old system of media control came with the July 6 mid-term election, in which the PRI lost its majority control of the Congress and, thereby, the purse strings of the nation.

But along with the new opportunities for investigative journalism have arisen new risks. Powerful figures inside and outside the government have come under increased scrutiny; unable to control the press, some have reacted violently. On May 22, for example, the bullet-ridden body of journalist Jesús Abel Bueno León was found in his burnt-out car on a quiet road near Chilpancingo, the capital of the state of Guerrero. Several months earlier, Bueno León, the editor of the weekly newspaper 7 *días*, had published a story on a government investigation of José Rubén Robles Catalán, the former secretary of the state of Guerrero, who had been accused of framing his ex-girlfriend on drug charges and ordering the murder of her attorney. On February 3, Robles Catalán had filed a lawsuit for defamation and calumny against Bueno León and six other local journalists who had covered the investigation. Soon after Bueno León's murder, his wife made public a signed document the journalist had written before his death. "I write these lines to give testimony now that I am no longer alive to the fact that through my journalism I provoked some fights with high government functionaries and even with my journalistic colleagues," Bueno León wrote. "I ask that the first line of investigation be the examination of José Rubén Robles Catalán and his group of corrupt police..."

While journalists in Guerrero organized a series of protest marches to demand a government investigation into the murder, the Bueno León case generated little coverage in Mexico City, where journalists have long considered themselves isolated from the violence that afflicts their colleagues in the provinces. For a long time they have been right—of the 10 journalists murdered in Mexico between 1986 and 1996 only one was from Mexico City. But a series of attacks on Mexico City journalists made it clear that no one was immune to the growing violence.

On September 13, René Solorio, a crime reporter with TV Azteca, was kidnapped by a group of armed men who forced him into a car. A few days earlier Solorio had filmed a segment, aired on the nightly news, which showed criminals working in apparent complicity with the police. The men who abducted Solorio put a plastic bag over his face, fired gunshots near his head, and told him that they had already executed his family. After a seven-hour ordeal, the men released Solorio on the side of a highway. He later learned that his family had not been killed. Earlier that day, one of Solorio's colleagues at TV Azteca was abducted under similar circumstances.

Around the same time, two reporters from *Reforma* and another from the Mexico City daily *El Universal* were also attacked. All had been reporting on crime or police corruption. In July, Víctor Martínez Hernández, a police reporter with the Mexico City magazine *Como*, was murdered. Colleagues from the magazine say Hernández was beaten by several men as he was leaving the Mexico City office of the Federal Judicial Police. They suspect he was killed by police officers angered by his reporting on corruption.

It was in the context of the radical transformation of the Mexican media, and against the backdrop of growing violence against journalists, that the CPJ workshop took place. The objective was both to analyze the risks facing the press and develop ways to make a dangerous job safer. On the morning's first panel on November 8, which focused on attacks and threats, Jesús

Dangerous Profession

The following is adapted from a speech by Jesús Barraza to Mexican journalists at a November 8 workshop on press freedom hosted by CPJ in Mexico City. Barraza took over as editor of La Prensa, *a daily newspaper in San Luis Río Colorado, after editor and publisher Benjamín Flores González was murdered in July:*

D uring the last days of his life, Benjamín Flores González worried about rumors that had begun to circulate in June. It was around that time that he told us that an attack was being organized against *La Prensa*. "What are they capable of doing?" we asked ourselves.

Benjamín was reserved at times about his concerns and, so as not to alarm those of us who worked on the paper, he never mentioned that he carried in his shirt pocket a judicial restraining order forbidding his arrest.

On July 15, nine bullets ended his life. The restraining order in his pocket was useless. We never thought that the system would engender such brutal methods.

Sometimes in a timid manner, and often without taking into consideration libel law or supposed journalistic ethics, some of us journalists have dared to print accusations that we could not completely prove but were supported by interviews with people who were afraid to show their face, or were in difficult circumstances because of a judicial system that is often complicit with those who violate the law.

Our editor, Benjamín Flores, was often obligated to denounce acts of corruption or drug trafficking without having all the details. He was often ironic. After all, his column was called "Unconfirmed."

In one of his columns, Benjamín, the founder of *La Prensa*, explained his suspicions that a judge might have been bought by Jaime González Gutiérrez, who was accused of killing a policeman in San Luis.

After it was published, the judge jailed Benjamín for defamation.

Today, Jaime González Gutiérrez is in jail, accused of ordering the murder of our editor in chief.

When Benjamín Flores fell at the door of the newspaper he had founded five years before, we felt like orphans, overwhelmed by a rage that is difficult to describe.

But July 15 the presses did not stop, and each of us reaffirmed our commitment to Benjamín and his mission. I took immediate control and saw how the reporters wet the keyboards with their tears, and, at times, cried out with impotence, pain, and rage at the image of our editor bleeding to death on the floor.

During the five years that Benjamín ran the paper, we received constant death threats. Of course, we were conscious of the risks we had assumed, but it wasn't until July 15 that we really understood that being a journalist is a dangerous profession.

What class of country is this in which impunity is so great that criminals fear a reporter more than a policeman? At moments, it gets frustrating for those of us who practice this profession to denounce corruption and impunity. Journalists who do so are becoming a kind of people's prosecutor, displacing those who are charged with carrying out justice. In the people's name we should continue to denounce prosecutors, police commanders, judges, and magistrates so they all assume their real responsibility.

More than ever, the organizations that defend our profession should create systems of effective protection and, above all, strive to prevent violence.

From our modest newspaper and through our experience, we have come to sadly demand one single thing: That we all do everything in our power to make sure that blood is never spilled at your newspapers, at it was spilled at ours.

Blancornelas spoke about the deteriorating situation in Tijuana as his bodyguard, Luis Valero, looked on.

Many of the journalists who attended the workshop had, like Blancornelas, traveled from the provinces. For many of the Mexico City journalists, the quality of the work being done by journalists outside the capital came as something of a surprise. Jesús Barraza, who had flown from the border city of San Luis Río Colorado, where he edits *La Prensa*, told how local drug traffickers angered by the paper's coverage had ordered the murder of editor and publisher Benjamín Flores González. (See sidebar, p. 220.). "When Benjamín Flores fell at our door...the presses did not stop," said Barraza, describing the day in June when four gunmen had riddled the editor with bullets as he was arriving at the paper. "I assumed immediate control and saw how the reporters wet the keyboards with their tears...and, at times, cried out, overwhelmed by the impotence, the pain, and the rage of seeing the image of our editor bleeding to death on the floor."

While lawlessness remains an overriding concern, journalists are also threatened by an explosion in defamation litigation. Sam Dillon, *The New York Times'* bureau chief in Mexico, spoke at the conference about the criminal charges that had been filed against him and *Times* reporter Craig Pyes in April. Alleging that they were defamed by a February 11 story titled "Shadow on the Border: Drug Ties Taint 2 Governors," Jorge Carrillo Olea of Morelos State and Manlio Fabio Beltrones of Sonora State filed criminal defamation charges. Under Mexico's libel law—written in 1917—truth is not an admissible defense, public officials are granted a higher level of protection than private citizens, and conviction can mean a sentence of up to 11 months in prison.

In a June 7 letter sent to President Zedillo, CPJ argued that the 1917 Ley de Imprenta represents a serious impediment to the functioning of a free press in Mexico:

> Because a functioning democracy depends on the free exchange of ideas, it is CPJ's position that journalists should never face criminal prosecution because of material they publish. In fact, an honest belief by the journalist that facts contained in a story were correct at the time of publication should be sufficient defense against all legal action. In

instances where a plaintiff can demonstrate malice on the part of a journalist—in other words, that a journalist knew or should have known that the facts in a story were wrong at the time of publication—civil litigation should provide adequate redress for the aggrieved party.

CPJ firmly believes that journalists should have absolute liberty to report on government investigations, particularly those in which public officials are alleged to be involved in wrongdoing. An informed and robust public debate will inevitably expose government officials to caustic criticism. Moreover, in a democracy, elected officials should have less protection under civil libel statutes than do private citizens. Under the terms of the Ley de Imprenta, the reverse is true. Such statutes are the hallmark of an authoritarian society and, therefore, an anachronism in the context of an increasingly democratic Mexico.

The letter also argued that the "appropriate forum in which to settle any dispute regarding an article published in the United States is the U.S. court system. By international convention—and because foreign correspondents do not generally publish in the countries which they cover—foreign correspondents are generally not subject to libel laws of their host country. Holding foreign correspondents accountable to the Mexican defamation statute would therefore represent an extraterritorial application of national law, a practice Mexico has opposed when carried out by other nations." In July, a CPJ delegation traveled to Mexico to meet with officials in the Mexican government to reiterate concerns about the criminal libel proceedings.

In October, Mexico's Attorney General announced the state was dropping the charges against Dillon and Pyes because, under Mexican law, foreigners can not be prosecuted in Mexico for an action which is not illegal in the country in which it was carried out. Since libel is not a criminal offense under U.S. federal law, the case could not be prosecuted in Mexico. This was an important victory for all foreign correspondents in Mexico. But as Dillon pointed out at the workshop, Mexican journalists have no protection from punitive lawsuits brought under the 1917 law. According to Mexican press groups, dozens of journalists have been hit with libel suits in recent years. The most egregious abuse of the libel law was perpetrated by TV Azteca owner Ricardo Salinas Pliego, who has used lawsuits to squelch reporting linking him to a money-laundering scheme.

According to a story first reported in the *Miami Herald*, Salinas Pliego received nearly US$30 million from Raúl Salinas de Gortari, the brother of former president Salinas (Raúl Salinas is currently in jail, accused of money-laundering and murder). When Mexican reporters began to pick up on the story, they were splapped with lawsuits. "Even though Salinas Pliego has no chance of winning, his strategy of using lawsuits to suppress the story has functioned perfectly," said Luis Linares, a columnist for the Mexico City daily *La Jornada* and one of at least a dozen reporters being sued by the businessman. "Today, no one is writing about it."

After analyzing the threats, journalists at the workshop examined the existent press freedom organizations in Mexico, and heard from Peruvian journalists about the creation of Instituto de Prensa y Sociedad (IPYS), a press freedom group based in Lima.

By the afternoon, a consensus had emerged among the conferees that more needed to be done to protect freedom of the press as Mexico enters a new era. Eight journalists were nominated to form a working group. They included Riva Palacio, Rossana Fuentes of *Reforma*; Juan Bautista of the Fraternidad de Reporteros, a Mexico City-based press group; Jorge Zepeda of *Público* in Guadalajara; Razhy González of *Cantera* in Oaxaca; Juan Angulo of *El Sur* in Acapulco; José Santaigo Healy of *El Imparcial* in Hermosillo; and Jesús Blancornelas of *Zeta* in Tijuana.

Less than three weeks later, Blancornelas lay fighting for his life in a Tijuana hospital. While the Mexico City workshop had done nothing to protect Blancornelas from the attack, it was apparent in the aftermath how dramatically public awareness of the importance of press freedom had increased. Many of the top editors who were making decisions about how to cover the Blancornelas attack had met him weeks before. The fact that they felt a personal connection to him, and had been made aware of the dangers and difficulties of practicing journalism in Tijuana, contributed to the extensive coverage.

While the murders of three Mexican journalists earlier in 1997 had received little attention in Mexico, the attack on Blancornelas was covered on television and radio and was on the front page of virtually every newspaper in the country for several days. Heavy play in the Mexican media helped fuel international coverage. In the United States, the Blancornelas attack was covered on national TV news programs as well as in *The New York Times, The Los Angeles Times, The San Diego Union-Tribune*, and on National Public Radio.

That kind of exposure helped fuel a public outcry, showing why the most effective response to an attack on the press is journalism. Mexican authorities, feeling the heat from the news media and the public, were forced to take some concrete actions. The investigation into the attack on Blancornelas, for example, was referred to the federal prosecutor's office, which has greater resources, experience, and independence than state prosecutors, who normally handle such investigations. Federal authorities explained they were taking over the case because the crime was committed by a drug cartel, and trafficking is a federal offense. In a December 1 letter sent to Mexican president Zedillo following the Blancornelas attack, CPJ argued the federal authorities should handle all investigations involving freedom of the press:

> Because of widespread reports of complicity between the State Judicial Police and drug traffickers—some of which have been published in *Zeta*—we support your government's decision to assign the investigation to the Federal Judicial Police. We hope that this will serve as a precedent. In CPJ's view an attack on any journalist which is carried out in reprisal for his or her work should be referred to federal authorities. Under the Mexican Constitution, the right to free expression is guaranteed by the state (Art 6: "el derecho a la información será garantizado por el estado"). Clearly, if a journalist is unable to carry out his or her function because of the threat of physical violence, the Mexican Constitution mandates federal involvement.

In addition, CPJ sent a letter to U.S. Attorney General Janet Reno requesting that the United States cooperate with Mexican officials investigating the crime. The December 4 letter noted:

Mexican investigators have identified the gunman killed at the scene of the crime as David Barrón Corona, a U.S. resident who grew up in San Diego. Barrón Corona, who was known by the alias C.H., was a reputed member of the 'Mexican Mafia,' a U.S.-based prison gang that distributes heroin and cocaine in the United States. In the week prior to the attack, Blancornelas published an article in which he reported that C.H. was the alleged gunman in the killing of two Mexican soldiers on November 14. Because of the possibility that U.S. law enforcement agencies may have information that could be helpful in the Mexican investigation, we are writing to make you aware of the circumstances of this crime. Since there is evidence that that C.H recruited other gunmen from the San Diego area, it is possible that those responsible for the attack on Blancornelas are in the United States.

CPJ received assurances from U.S. officials of their cooperation.

Despite the decision to refer the investigation into the attack on Blancornelas to Mexican federal authorities, Mexican journalists have noted that those responsible for crimes against journalists have rarely been apprehended. For that reason, expectations in the Blancornelas case are limited. Instead, the press is looking inward, coming to terms with its growing power not only to investigate and denounce corruption and malfeasance but also to protect its own interests. Like all of Mexican society, the press is grappling, sometimes awkwardly, with its new freedom. There is little doubt that as journalists continue to tackle dangerous stories they will face reprisals. Nevertheless, the attack on Blancornelas may be remembered in a few years not only as terrible crime, but as the beginning of a new era of independent Mexican journalism.

ASIA

OVERVIEW OF
Asia
by A. Lin Neumann

THE FINANCIAL TUMULT that gripped Southeast and Northeast Asia in the last half of 1997 threatened decades of economic growth and challenged the assumptions of authoritarian leaders who have seen the press as something to be tolerated when docile and punished when independent. In long-suffering Cambodia, a violent coup d'etat disrupted progress toward a free press, while in Hong Kong, observers watched the press for signs of interference by China after the territory was returned to the mainland on July 1.

For South Asia, the challenges to the press were more traditionally repressive and deadly. Seven journalists died in India—the highest total in the world this year. Five members of a film crew were killed by a single car bomb that police said was motivated by a political rivalry directed at a local politician. Elsewhere, the government continued to restrict press access to contested parts of Assam, Kashmir, and Manipur, all of which suffer from separatist violence and stern military responses. In distinct incidents, two journalists for state-owned Doordarshan Kendra TV were killed in Kashmir in attacks police believe were carried out by anti-government rebels.

Sectarian tensions in Pakistan, especially in the Sindh Province, led to frequent clashes, with newspaper offices coming under physical assault by rioting mobs spurred to violence by political leaders. In the Punjab region, the government of Prime Minister Mohammad Nawaz Sharif imposed martial law-style rule in response to factional violence between rival Sunni and Shi'a political groups.

Much of the economic turmoil in the region was the result of cozy relationships between governments and financial institutions that the press did not

A. Lin Neumann *is the program coordinator for Asia.*
Shumona Goel, *research assistant for Asia, provided invaluable help in compiling the documentation for this section and wrote some of the country summaries.*
The Freedom Forum supported CPJ's work in Asia in 1997 with a grant that funded activity in Hong Kong, including the CPJ-sponsored "Freedom of Information and Financial Markets" forum and the "State of the Press in Hong Kong" conference.
CPJ wishes to thank the following organizations for their assistance throughout the year in monitoring press conditions in the region: Institute for the Studies on Free Flow of Information; Bangladesh Centre for Development Journalism & Communication; Pakistani Press Foundation; Sri Lanka Information Monitor; Cambodia Daily; Pacific Media Watch; Pacific Islands News Association; The Nation of Bangkok; Center for Media Freedom & Responsibility; Philippine Center for Investigative Journalism; and the Hong Kong Journalists Association.

report, either because of self-censorship or government prohibitions. Malaysian Prime Minister Mahathir Mohamad, a leading proponent of the idea that so-called "Asian values" encourage obedience over free expression, tried to blame the economic crisis on a conspiracy of international currency speculators and their alleged allies in the Western media. His well-publicized personal attacks on financier George Soros only deepened the malaise in Kuala Lumpur's financial markets. By year's end, Indonesia's President Suharto, who had long suppressed press coverage of his family's vast business holdings and insider access to government-regulated industries, was forced not only to acknowledge the depth of his family's involvement in the country's sagging economy but to publicly pledge to dismantle a portion of his financial empire as a condition of International Monetary Fund assistance. Indonesian journalists were hopeful that the crisis might force open the country's timid media culture. Reporters Ahmad Taufik and Eko Maryadi, both members of the unofficial Alliance of Independent Journalists, were paroled from prison in July. Ironically, Taufik's arrest in 1994 was partly a result of articles he wrote about corruption among the Suharto clan.

Elsewhere, there is evidence of democratic growth in the face of the crisis. In Thailand, a new constitution signed by King Bhumibol Adulyadej in October contains the most sweeping free press provisions in Asia. Efforts by then-Prime Minister Chavalit Yongchaiyudh in June to rein in the press and blame journalists for exacerbating the financial downslide were discredited by the independent Thai press and helped lead to his ouster later in the year.

In both South Korea and Taiwan, political developments seemed to strengthen the hand of free expression. Long-time dissident leader and former political prisoner Kim Dae Jung was elected president of South Korea in December and promptly pledged to protect press freedom at home and promote free expression in the region as a corrective to closed societies and failed economic policies. In Taiwan, the ruling Kuomintang (KMT) lost a landmark criminal libel suit party leaders brought against two reporters for a Hong Kong-based magazine. The verdict was widely seen as expanding the boundaries for press freedom in Taiwan. The KMT's willingness to absorb a stunning political defeat by a pro-independence party in municipal elections in December provides further evidence of the country's democratization and perhaps signals the end of the party's 70-year hegemony.

Hong Kong, meanwhile, returned to Chinese sovereignty on July 1 after 156 years of British colonial rule. Signs of self-censorship and timidity in the Hong Kong press leading up to the transition, coupled with China's dismal record on free expression, caused widespread concern over the future of Hong

ASIA

Kong's media. CPJ monitored the transition and in September issued the first major international report on press freedom under the new dispensation. (See "Press Freedom Under the Dragon," p. 276.) The conclusion: in the first days after the handover, the press remained essentially free, with few signs of overt control by Beijing. Legislative elections in 1998 will be closely watched in Hong Kong for signs of tightening controls that could limit the hopes of democratic opponents against Beijing's hand-picked candidates.

In China, however, the situation remained dismal. The release and forced exile of dissident writer Wei Jingsheng in November did nothing to ease conditions for the press in China. Fourteen journalists remain imprisoned, newspapers are tightly controlled, and China has taken steps to heighten censorship of the Internet. There were stirrings from the dormant dissident community and scattered calls for press freedom in the wake of Wei's release, but no sign yet that President Jiang Zemin would liberalize his one-party rule. Things were no better for Vietnamese journalists. Arrests, harassment, intimidation, and strict regulations on all media including the Internet were staples of government policy toward the press.

The political and social upheaval in Cambodia in the aftermath of Second Prime Minister Hun Sen's coup against his co-premier Prince Norodom Ranariddh in July forced some 40 journalists into exile and resulted in the temporary closure of dozens of opposition newspapers. Although some newspapers later resumed operations, many journalists and editors remained in exile as the ruling Cambodia People's Party issued frequent threats against them. Khmer-Canadian photographer Michael Senior was killed during the coup, and another journalist was slain in political violence leading up to the takeover.

Afghanistan

After nearly two decades of civil war, conditions in Afghanistan are as dire as anywhere in the world. In the absence of a coherent central government or rule of law, there is virtually no press, let alone press freedom. Under the leadership of Mullah Mohammed Omar, the Islamic Taliban movement, which seized the capital, Kabul, in September 1996 and controls 22 of 32 provinces, has put in place the most radical religious government in the world. The Taliban's harsh fundamentalist rule has dismantled civil institutions, closed most schools, and suppressed everything from kite-flying to public entertainment. Women in particular have suffered, becoming virtual prisoners in their own homes because of severe Taliban restrictions on their activities. Public stoning has become commonplace and bands of Taliban thugs roam the streets beating those they deem to be violators of the Sharia, or Islamic legal code.

Cameras are outlawed and any depiction of living creatures is forbidden by authorities, who describe such images as un-Islamic. Patrolling the streets in pick-up trucks, Taliban members, operating under the authority of the General Department for the Preservation of Virtue and the Elimination of Vice, search houses for weapons and in the process destroy television sets, radios, cassettes, and photographs. In late September, the Taliban police detained several journalists, including CNN reporter Christiane Amanpour, and Emma Bonino, the European Union's humanitarian affairs commissioner, when the journalists were photographing women at a hospital in Kabul.

In late August, the Taliban warned resident foreign correspondents that any "biased and false analysis" that referred to the eth-nic, religious, and linguistic differences in Afghanistan would not be tolerated. The Taliban has also threatened to deport foreign reporters if they write unfavorably about the movement. Journalists visiting the capital are required to hire Taliban-approved translators and drivers and must stay in officially sanctioned hotels. There are just three foreign news organizations with offices in Afghanistan. According to Afghan journalists working in the refugee area of Peshawar in Pakistan, the only independent news reaching the portion of the country controlled by the Taliban comes from underground publications smuggled into Taliban areas and short-wave radio broadcasts by the BBC Pushto and Dari services and the Voice of America's Dari service. The Taliban-run Radio Shariat exclusively broadcasts pro-regime news reports and religious programs.

In the northern provinces, where a coalition of anti-Taliban forces have halted the expansion of the Taliban, wartime conditions mean continued risk to local and foreign journalists working in the region.

September 29
Christiane Amanpour, CNN ATTACKED, LEGAL ACTION
Other journalists ATTACKED, LEGAL ACTION

Several journalists, including CNN reporter Amanpour and her film crew, were detained for four hours by Taliban police in Kabul. With them was European Union Commissioner for Humanitarian Affairs, Emma Bonino, and 18 other EU workers. Four journalists were filming and photographing women at a hospital when a doctor telephoned the Taliban authorities. Armed Taliban guards arrived at the hospital and arrested several people; they assaulted an aid worker during the arrest.

Taliban regulations prohibit photographing human beings, particularly women.

EU Commission spokesman Klaus van der

ASIA

Pas said Bonino received apologies for the incident from the Afghan foreign affairs department.

Afghan officials said correspondents had the right to report current events but should avoid any analysis, comments, or stories that referred to ethnic, religious, and linguistic differences in Afghanistan. The Taliban required journalists visiting the capital to hire Taliban-approved translators and drivers and to stay in officially sanctioned hotels.

On August 20, Abdurrahman Hotaqi, the Taliban's deputy minister of information, warned the foreign press that "biased and false analysis" and eyewitness reports would not be tolerated.

CPJ sent a letter on September 30, to the Permanent Representative/Designate of the Afghan Mission to the UN, A. Hakeem Mujahid, deploring the restrictions on foreign or local journalists in practicing their profession freely and safely. CPJ expressed concern that the regulations were intended to discourage investigative journalism.

Since the Taliban ousted President Burhanuddin Rabbani and seized Kabul on September 27, 1996, they have strictly enforced their version of Islamic law on all areas under their control. Taliban regulations include the banning of music, cinema, television, and illustrations (except for pictures of objects and scenes). Taliban strictures prohibit photographing humans, women especially. Though the Taliban promised to lift the ban on television in early February 1997, head of Taliban police Mirza Yousufzai told reporters that programs will have to be approved by Taliban censors. He said, "We banned the programs that used to be broadcast because they went against Islamic principles." He did not say when television would resume broadcasting.

Bangladesh

As Prime Minister Sheikh Hasina Wajed's Awami League enters its second year, the national press in Bangladesh enjoys considerable freedom and continues to play an important role in the transition to democracy. Nevertheless, the frequent political violence has intensified the dangers journalists face in covering national news.

Ongoing disputes between the ruling Awami League and former prime minister Begum Khaleda Zia's opposition Bangladesh Nationalist Party (BNP), however, have sustained political tensions. Hasina's government has refused to allow the BNP and other opposition parties to play a meaningful role in policy formulation. This has led to frequent parliamentary walkouts by the BNP and its allies, resulting in sometimes-violent street protests and general strikes from all parties, and even blocs within parties, called for rallies and demonstrations, using violence and intimidation to enforce general strikes. In separate incidents, two photojournalists were beaten when photographing clashes during street demonstrations. In a third case, a photojournalist was seriously injured when he was hit in the head by a tear-gas shell fired by police attempting to disperse a rally.

In the rural areas, journalists reporting on corruption and government irregularities sometimes face intimidation and harassment. Rural women are becoming increasingly active in a widespread network of non-governmental organizations promoting social development and self-reliance projects. Some conservative Muslim fundamentalists have resisted the increasing political and economic participation of women in Bangladesh and on occasion have threatened journalists covering these issues. However, as one journalist described it, "These represent irritations, not national problems."

Government efforts to fully privatize the print media by closing two state-owned newspapers, *Dainik Bangla* and *Bangladesh Times*, have divided the journalistic community. Some journalists considered the closure of the state-owned newspapers to be a violation of press freedom, claiming veteran journalists sympathetic to those now in opposition have lost their jobs. On the other hand, many journalists applaud the move as a step toward greater autonomy for the news.

February 15
Shawkat Hossain Rubel, *Purbakone* ATTACKED

Rubel, a correspondent and photographer for the daily *Purbakone*, was beaten by activists of the Bangladesh Nationalist Party (BNP) at a polling station in Rangamati. BNP activists beat Rubel on the legs, back, and arms, and stole his camera and a number of personal possessions after he photographed a clash between armed BNP activists and supporters of the opposition Awami League. Rubel required hospital treatment for his injuries.

March 19
Mamun Abedin, *Ajker Kagoj* ATTACKED

Police beat Abedin, a reporter and photographer for the daily *Ajker Kagoj*, as he photographed a clash between police and anti-government demonstators attempting to march on parliament. Police struck Abedin on the head and upper body with batons. He was hospitalized overnight and received stitches for a cut on his head. Police had told journalists to leave the rally and warned them not to take photographs.

August 23
Habibur Rahman, *Dainik Bangla* ATTACKED

Rahman, a photojournalist for the government-owned daily *Dainik Bangla* was seriously injured when he was hit in the back of his head by a tear-gas shell fired by police attempting to disperse a rally. The protest, in front of the National Press Club in Dhaka, was organized by the main opposition Bangladesh Nationalist Party (BNP).

Other journalists rushed Rahman to a hospital, where he underwent surgery. Prime Minister Sheikh Hasina looked into the incident and assigned a deputy police inspector general to investigate the incident. The health minister, the information minister, and the prime minister's press secretary visited Rahman in the hospital.

Reports as of September 14 indicated Rahman was recovering.

September 24
Abul Khair, *Janakantha* ATTACKED

Members of the Fatwabaj, a group of Islamic fundamentalist preachers, assaulted Khair, a journalist for the *Janakantha* newspaper. The men pointed a gun at Khair and severely beat another man who ran to assist Khair.

A group of nearly 100 men hired by the Fatwabaj raided Khair's home in Fultala, ransacked two of his buildings and set a third building on fire. The group threw stones, injuring women and children in the village.

Khair had recently written a story on a flogging sentence handed down by the ruling court—made up of Fatwabaj—against a woman in Fultala who was charged with having had an abortion. The report was carried in various papers including *Janakantha*.

Since the report was published, the Fatwabaj had been threatening Khair. He filed a complaint with the local police, accusing 24 people, including those who issued the flogging sentence against the woman. Police said they would investigate.

Burma

The generals who have run Burma with an iron hand since 1988 tried to soften the image of their authoritarian regime in

ASIA

November when the State Law and Order Restoration Council (SLORC) was given the kinder, gentler appellation of State Peace and Development Council (SPDC). But a junta is still a junta, and the name change did nothing to ease the deplorable state of the press and other forms of free expression.

There are no independent newspapers or broadcast outlets in Burma. It is illegal to own a photocopy or fax machine, computer modems are contraband items, and only a handful of foreign companies, embassies and government agencies maintain legal access to the Internet. Local stringers for foreign news agencies face harassment and are frequently constrained in their reporting. Foreign reporters are often denied visas to the country, especially those whom the generals deem unsympathetic to their rule.

A tiny number of opposition leaflets and newsletters are produced by hand in Burma using silk-screen printing. These publications, seldom numbering more than 1,000 copies, are sometimes distributed on college campuses at great risk to their publishers. Even this activity has been sharply limited by the continuing closure of nearly all universities and colleges following student demonstrations in late 1996. A tiny underground short-wave radio station, the Democratic Voice of Burma, or DVB, operates in the jungles near the Thai-Burma border and carries news of ongoing military campaigns against ethnic insurgents, jailings, and other banned topics. The only other non-official media come from Burmese-language services operated by the Voice of America, British Broadcasting Corporation, and the U.S.-sponsored Radio Free Asia.

The SPDC frequently has continued a long-standing practice of barring visiting journalists from meeting with opposition leader and Nobel Prize laureate Daw Aung San Suu Kyi, whose National League for Democracy (NLD) is virtually the only independent political voice in the country. They also continue to disrupt her phone service, impeding her ability to communicate with journalists outside the country. On the eve of the NLD's party congress in May, the SPDC detained hundreds of NLD aides and party members. Eventually, the two-day event went forward at Suu Kyi's residence, but the military controlled access and barred the press from covering the meeting.

Also in May, the junta asked the government of Thailand to prevent Thai reporters covering a state visit to Rangoon by then-prime minister Chavalit Yongchaiyudh from speaking to Suu Kyi. CPJ joined protests by Thai press groups by writing letters to the governments of both Thailand and Burma denouncing the action. On June 13, five NLD workers were arrested following the release abroad of a videotaped appeal for democracy by Suu Kyi. The five were later given lengthy prison terms and accused by junta member Lt. Gen. Khin Nyunt of having collaborated with "overseas anti-government activists and advocates of destruction within the country."

In July, the Association of Southeast Asian Nations (ASEAN) ignored international protests and an abysmal human rights record and lent legitimacy to one of the world's most repressive regimes by admitting Burma as a member of the association on the strong urging of Malaysia, Indonesia, and Singapore.

May 12
Thai media CENSORED

Burma's ruling State Law and Order Restoration Council (SLORC) sent a letter to the Thai Foreign Ministry requesting that Thailand bar 15 Thai reporters—who were to travel with Thai Prime Minister Gen. Chavalit Yongchaiyudh on an official visit to Burma on

May 15 and 16—from approaching the house of opposition leader Aung San Suu Kyi and from reporting on her activities. The letter also said that Burmese Information Ministry officials intended to closely monitor the Thai journalists.

Burma granted the Thai reporters two-day visas, valid only for the dates of Chavalit's visit, instead of the 14-day visas usually issued on press trips.

Thai officials appeared willing to accept those strictures. Foreign Ministry spokesperson Surapong Jayanaman said, "Each country has its own sovereign right to introduce rules and regulations it deems appropriate to control the media."

CPJ sent letters to both countries urging the governments to relax restrictions on the press.

Cambodia

Second Prime Minister Hun Sen's violent *coup d'etat* on July 5 and 6 ousting his co-premier Prince Norodom Ranariddh raised fears of renewed political terror which could mortally wound Cambodia's emerging free press and civil institutions. In the immediate aftermath of the coup, virtually all of Cambodia's opposition newspapers—especially those identified with Ranariddh's FUNCINPEC party and opposition leader Samuel Rainsy's Khmer Nation Party (KNP)—ceased publishing, while some 40 senior reporters and editors fled into exile in neighboring Thailand. Much of the press eventually resumed publishing, but in late December Hun Sen's government issued a series of verbal threats against the press that heightened feelings of uncertainty among both local and foreign journalists.

Scores of people died in fighting during the July coup, which occurred while Ranariddh was out of the country. Canadian citizen Michael Senior, a 23-year-old photographer of Cambodian descent, was the lone journalist killed. Orphaned during the Khmer Rouge regime, Senior was adopted by a Canadian family and had returned to Phnom Penh in 1995 in hopes of becoming a journalist. He was shot, execution-style, by soldiers loyal to Hun Sen in front of his Khmer wife and infant child as he attempted to photograph troops looting a public market on the Monday after the coup.

After the coup, Hun Sen promised that newspapers would resume operations without sanction, and many Khmer-language newspapers were indeed publishing again by the end of the year. However, a number of journalists remain in exile and in fear: "Yes, my paper is publishing but I cannot go home," said Pin Samkhon, the head of the Khmer Journalists Association and editor of *The Independent*, who is in exile in Bangkok. "I have been told that I will be killed if I return."

Even before the coup, the situation for journalists was deteriorating as relations between the two co-premiers grew increasingly fractious. On March 30, reporter Chet Duong Daravuth of the newspaper *Neak Prayuth* was killed in a grenade attack on a rally staged by KNP leader Samuel Rainsy. Dozens of other journalists were injured and at least 26 people were killed in the incident. On May 4 gunmen fired rocket-propelled grenades at the Sihanoukville office of Cambodia's national television station, TVK, killing one technician and further raising tensions among reporters. Both incidents went unpunished but were widely assumed to be the result of partisan political infighting.

With Hun Sen's Cambodian People's Party in control of the national government, on December 23, Secretary of State for Information Khieu Kanharith, a former newspaper publisher, warned both local and foreign reporters about "unfair" coverage of continuing fighting in some remote areas

ASIA

between forces loyal to Ranariddh and those loyal to Hun Sen. The government, Kanharith said, would take legal action against news organizations whose coverage was perceived as biased against the government. As the year ended, Kanharith threatened to expel reporter Ed Fitzgerald of the television network Asia Business News after Kanharith complained that a year-end ABN report on Cambodia was unfair to the regime.

The coup cost Cambodia much international goodwill, stalled its planned entry into the Association of Southeast Asian Nations, derailed economic growth, substantially reduced foreign aid and effectively isolated Cambodia at a time of worsening economic crisis for the region. If Hun Sen cannot right his ship with a fair election whose results are accepted by the Cambodian people, then the political deterioration seems likely to continue with predictably dismal results for press freedom.

January 2
Leng Samnang, *Kumnith Kaun Khmer*
ATTACKED

Armed men in military uniforms beat Leng Samnang, editor of the Phnom Penh newspaper *Kumnith Kaun Khmer*, and shot him once in the stomach after pulling him from a car as he left a birthday party for co-Premier Prince Norodom Ranaraddh, leader of the FUNCINPEC party. Leng Samnang underwent surgery the following day.

Colleagues speculated that the attack was politically motivated. Cheng Sokna, the publisher of *Kumnith Kaun Khmer*, said the paper is openly critical of co-Premier Hun Sen's Cambodian People's Party (CPP) and that the attack on Leng Samnang followed visits from CPP representatives who had tried to persuade Cheng Sokna to change the paper's anti-CPP stance.

March 30
Chan Mony, *Kampuchea Tgnai Ni* (Cambodia Today) ATTACKED
Zhu Changdu, *Xinhua* ATTACKED
Vong Sopheak, *Moneasekar Khmer* (Khmer Conscience) ATTACKED
Soy Sopheap, Kyodo ATTACKED
Sam Rithy Duong Hak, *Asahi Shimbun* ATTACKED
Sen Sansam Kosal, *Areyathor* (Civilization) ATTACKED
Khieu Bunry, *Serepheap Khmer* (Khmer Liberty) ATTACKED
Um Ly Viroth, *Uddom Gati Khmer* (Khmer Ideal) ATTACKED
Chem Chheng Von, *Khmer Ekreach* (Khmer Independence) ATTACKED
Kung Yuthanea, *Khmer Ekreach* ATTACKED
Kem Punnak, *Koh Santepheap* (Island of Peace) ATTACKED
Chhour Bunna, *Cambodia Today* ATTACKED
Ou Sovann, *Samleng Yuvachun Khmer* (Voice of Khmer Youth) ATTACKED
Vong Rith, *Samleng Yuvachun Khmer* ATTACKED
Kao Prasath Sothea, *Samleng Yuvachun Khmer* ATTACKED
Kimsan Chantara, *The Cambodia Daily* ATTACKED
Mon Try, free-lancer ATTACKED
Oum Sey Hak, *Angkor Thmei* ATTACKED
Chhoy Pisei, *Cambodge Soir* ATTACKED
Keo Phalla, *Neak Prayuth* (The Warrior) ATTACKED
Chet Duong Daravuth, *Neak Prayuth* KILLED

Daravuth, a reporter for *Neak Prayuth*, was killed and 20 journalists were injured in a grenade attack on an opposition rally they were covering led by Sam Rainsy, the leader of the Khmer National Party (KNP), outside the National Assembly building in Phnom Penh.

Those injured were Zhu, a correspondent for the official Chinese news service Xinhua; Sopheak, a reporter for *Moneasekar Khmer*;

Sopheap, a reporter for the Japanese news service Kyodo; Sam Rithy Duong Hak, a stringer for the Japanese daily *Asahi Shimbun*; Sen Sansam Kosal, a reporter for *Areyathor*; Khieu Bunry, a reporter for *Serepheap Khmer*; Um Ly Viroth, a reporter for *Uddom Gati Khmer*; Chem Chheng Von and Kung Yuthanea, reporters for *Khmer Ekreach*; Kem Punnak, a reporter for *Koh Santepheap*; Chhour Bunna, a photographer for *Cambodia Today*; Ou Sovann, publisher and editor in chief of *Samleng Yuvachun Khmer*; Vong Rith and Kao Prasath Sothea, reporters for *Samleng Yuvachun Khmer*; Kimsan Chantara, a reporter *for The Cambodia Daily*; Mon Try, a free-lance photographer; Oum Sey Hak, a reporter for *Angkor Thmei*; Chhoy Pisei, a reporter for *Cambodge Soir*; and Keo Phalla, a reporter for *Neak Prayuth*.

The journalists were among 16 people killed and more than 100 injured when four grenades were thrown into a crowd of about 170 protesters. Two grenades were thrown by two men who escaped on foot, and the third grenade was thrown from a motorcycle that sped past the National Assembly. The origin of the fourth grenade is unknown. A number of the journalists sustained serious injuries: Mony was flown to Malaysia for microsurgery after being struck by shrapnel in both eyes; Zhu's intestines were punctured; Try sustained injuries to his large intestine, requiring extensive surgery; Dapou's spleen was so badly damaged that it was removed; and Rith's right lung was pierced by shrapnel.

The government set up a special committee to investigate the attack, but there is little expectation that the crime will be prosecuted. Rainsy, who was not injured, blamed the attack on Second Prime Minister Hun Sen and his Cambodian People's Party.

May 4
Television of Kampuchea (TVK)
ATTACKED

The Sihanoukville office of Cambodia's national television station, Television of Kampuchea

(TVK), was attacked by gunmen, who killed at least one worker at the station. The seven attackers, dressed in combat fatigues, fired three B-40 rocket grenades before storming the building and firing their AK-47 assault rifles. The station, which contained a studio and a transmitter, was destroyed.

Pich Eam, a technician who was injured in the attack, died the next day. Phan Sopahn, a guard at the station, was shot in the chest.

Information Minister Ieng Mouly immediately labeled the attack as "politically motivated." Mouly believed the attack was instigated by royalist FUNCINPEC (National United Front for an Independent, Neutral, Peaceful, and Cooperative Cambodia) party supporters, telling the South China Morning Post that "government controlled media should prepare to face further political intimidation." The Associated Press reported that on April 22, members of FUNCINPEC took a video tape of a local FUNCINPEC official, Serei Kosal, to the director of the station, Kang Saran, demanding that he air Kosal's speech attacking the rival Communist Cambodian People's Party (CPP). Saran refused to broadcast the speech, and armed men later went to the station chief's house and made the same demand. The station chief again refused.

The staff of TVK, which is aligned with the CPP, had received death threats days before the attack. FUNCINPEC has complained that it isn't given the same amount of air time as the CPP on state-run media.

CPJ sent a letter on May 7 to Cambodia's co-prime ministers expressing concern that the attack was a severe threat to press freedom. The letter stressed that the broadcast media have become victims of political division, as both parties in Cambodia's ruling coalition have accused them of bias.

July 7
Michael Senior KILLED

Senior, a former employee of the *Cambodia*

ASIA

Daily, was shot and killed while photographing looting by soldiers in a public market in the aftermath of the coup that began two days earlier. He was accosted by the soldiers, who were identified with the coup leader, former Second Prime Minister Hun Sen, and shot in the knee. As he lay in the street pleading for mercy, he was shot several times, execution-style, in front of his wife and brother-in-law.

Senior, 23, was a Canadian citizen of Cambodian origin who had been orphaned as an infant during the Pol Pot regime and raised in Canada. He worked as a teacher and part-time newscaster in Phnom Penh. *Cambodia Daily's* editors say that had he been able to submit the photographs he was shooting at the time of his murder, Senior's pictures would have been used as part of their coverage of the coup. His film was confiscated by the officers who shot him.

July 19
Kenichi Kaku, free-lancer MISSING

A Japanese free-lance photographer, Kenichi Kaku, was captured shortly after fighting broke out between soldiers loyal to Hun Sen and the ousted government of First Prime Minister Prince Norodom Ranariddh in northern Cambodia, according to the Japanese Embassy in Phnom Penh. The news reached the capital from a motorbike driver who was in Kaku's employ. According the the embassy report, Kaku was thought to have been captured seven miles north of Samrong, a stronghold of royalist forces.

According to an Associated Press report, witnesses in Samrong told another Japanese freelance photographer, Masaru Goto, that Kaku was caught between rival factions and that he was called by FUNCINPEC soldiers to an army jeep. He approached with his hands up, apparently seeking safety from the fighting.

CPJ wrote a letter on July 21 to Prince Norodom Ranariddh, asking him to confirm the whereabouts of Kenichi Kaku.

According to the Associated Press, Kenichi Kaku was free and safe in northeastern

Thailand as of July 22. While it appears that Kaku was captured by royalist FUNCINPEC soldiers, details remain unknown.

July 22
Khmer Journalists Association
THREATENED

Journalists linked with independent or opposition newspapers in Phnom Penh stopped publishing and fled the country, fearing reprisal after the July 5 coup in which former co-prime minister Hun Sen seized power.

At least eight Cambodian journalists sought refuge in Bangkok after the coup. According to Pin Sam Khon, co-president of the Khmer Journalists Association and one of the journalists who left, said the authorities threatened opposition journalists in Phnom Penh in the wake of the coup.

Pin, editor of the *Khmer Ekareach* newspaper, said the military told his staff that Pin could not return. He had been quoted in the media on the danger facing journalists.

After the coup by Hun Sen's forces, most Khmer-language newspapers linked with the opposition parties and with the regime of ousted First Prime Minister Prince Norodom Ranariddh ceased publication.

CPJ sent a letter on July 22 to Hun Sen urging him to guarantee the respect of journalists' rights in Cambodia.

July 22
Pin Sam Khon, *Khmer Ekareach*
THREATENED, EXPELLED
Khmer-language newspapers
THREATENED, CENSORED
All media THREATENED

Opposition journalists in Phnom Penh have been threatened by soldiers loyal to ousted co-Prime Minister Hun Sen since the July 5 coup. "The military and the police have come to our houses. They know where we live," Pin said by phone from Bangkok.

Pin is one of eight Cambodian journalists who have sought refuge in Bangkok since the coup. Another group is awaiting sanctuary on the border.

According to Pin, statements he has made in the media regarding the dangers facing journalists in Phnom Penh after the coup have drawn fire in Cambodia. "After I spoke out, they (the pro-Hun Sen military in Phnom Penh) told my staff I cannot go back. They said my life is in danger if I go back to Cambodia," said Pin, who is the editor of the *Khmer Ekareach* [Independent] newspaper, said that his experience is not unique. "The houses of many opposition editors have been visited [by the military]. We are fearful for our lives and family."

Since the July 5 coup by forces loyal to Second Prime Minister Hun Sen and his Cambodian People's Party, nearly all Khmer-language newspapers identified with the opposition parties and with the regime of ousted First Prime Minister Prince Norodom Ranariddh have ceased publication. What was recently a vital—if contentious and partisan—press with as many as 50 newspapers has been quickly reduced by fear and uncertainty to a handful of functioning papers.

CPJ sent a letter on July 22, calling on Hun Sen to guarantee freedom of the press in Cambodia and to ensure that reprisals against journalists do not take place. CPJ urged Hun Sen to stand by the statement he made on July 13, when he said, "All press, including formerly critical newspapers, should quickly resume publication, because the voice of the press also plays an important role."

September 9
Prayuth LEGAL ACTION

The Information Ministry ordered a 30-day suspension of the Khmer-language newspaper *Prayuth*, which supported the ousted First Prime Minister Prince Norodom Ranariddh. Authorities said the opposition newspaper had inflated casualty figures in its coverage on September 5 of fighting in northern Cambodia, when the paper reported that 200 troops loyal to Hun Sen had died and another 500 were wounded in recent combat. The Information Ministry said the coverage "seriously affected the Royal Cambodian Armed Forces (RCAF) military operations, political stability and national security." The information ministry reportedly was preparing charges against the newspaper for providing "false information with the intention to incite and demoralize" the RCAF, under a clause in Cambodia's press law that provides criminal penalties for publications that affect national security.

After Second Prime Minister Hun Sen and the Cambodian People's Party gained power on July 5, most Khmer-language newspapers identified with the opposition parties and with the regime of ousted first Prime Minister Prince Norodom Ranariddh ceased publication.

CPJ sent a letter to Hun Sen on September 29, expressing fear that the government's decision to close *Prayuth* was intended to discourage the independent press and silence criticism of the government. CPJ urged him to settle the matter through means other than suspending publication of the newspaper.

October 14
Ou Sareoun, *Samleng Reas Khmer* KILLED

Ou Sareoun, a reporter with *Samleng Reas Khmer* (Voice of the Cambodian People) was shot dead in Phnom Penh's central market. An independent investigation by the Khmer Journalists Association (KJA) determined that the murder was committed by security guards who had been the target of an investigation by the newspaper into an extortion ring operating in the market.

Ou, 21, the son of the paper's editor and owner, was in the market early in the morning distributing *Samleng Reas Khmer* to local vendors when he was assaulted by a group of security guards who dragged him into the street and shot him, according to the investigation. Following the incident, government reports claimed that Ou was killed in a dispute over a card game, and that he was drunk at the time of his death. "Those claims are false. He was killed because the paper reported on the corruption in the market," Pin Samkohn, the chairman of the KJA told CPJ.

According to Pin Samkohn, the guard who shot Ou was initially arrested by police and later released. The family of the slain journalist is afraid to push authorities for a more thorough investigation, according to Pin, because of pressure from armed groups in the market place.

Accounts from witnesses in the marketplace, reporters in Phnom Penh, and other investigators have failed to confirm that Ou was a journalist and that the murder was related to his work.

October 15
Thong Uypang, *Koh Santepheap* ATTACKED

On October 15, two unidentified assailants threw two grenades at the home of Thong Uypang, director of *Koh Santepheap* (Island of Peace), a Khmer-language newspaper, causing damage but no injuries.

December 29
Ed Fitzgerald, Asia Business News
HARASSED

Information Ministry Secretary of State Khieu Kanharith said on December 27 that Ed Fitzgerald, a Canadian correspondent for the television program "Asia Business News" (ABN) in Phnom Penh, would be forced to leave the country because his reporting was too critical of Cambodia's political and economic situation. The expulsion order was to have been signed on December 29, but was not acted upon following an appeal from King Norodom Sihanouk to co-prime ministers Hun Sen and Ung Huot. The king urged the government

"for the sake of democracy" not to revoke Fitzgerald's visa.

In seeking to censure Fitzgerald, Kanharith said that he wanted the reporter to apologize for an allegedly unfair year-end report which aired on ABN. The threat against Fitzgerald followed a more general warning to local and foreign reporters, issued during the week of December 23, in which Kanharith accused some media outlets of biased coverage of the ongoing armed conflict between the government in Phnom Penh and forces loyal to ousted First Prime Minister Prince Norodom Ranariddh.

CPJ sent a letter on December 29 to co-prime ministers Ung Huot and Hun Sen urging them to follow the advice of King Sihanouk and to stop the harassment of Fitzgerald.

On January 7, 1998, Cambodia's Information Ministry dropped the threat to expel Fitzgerald after the journalist said his network was willing to interview a government spokesperson to express his or her view on ABN.

China

President Jiang Zemin's formal consolidation of power after the death of Communist patriarch Deng Xiaoping in February prompted muted calls from within the Communist Party hierarchy for political reform. But while Jiang's program of aggressive economic reform has taken center stage, there has been scant progress toward greater freedom of expression. Pursuing a public agenda of a strong, unified China reaching out to the world, Jiang witnessed China's resumption of control over a prosperous and relatively relaxed Hong Kong in July. In September, the 15th Communist Party Congress offered Jiang a platform to propose further privatization and modernization of China's economy.

Despite his vision of a modern society, Jiang and his Communist Party allies continue to restrict the press and brook little dissent. Chinese newspapers remain distinctly subdued in discussing official events. For example, they published only state-sanctioned reports of Jiang's October visit to the United States, with no mention of the human rights demonstrators who dogged Jiang's every step during the U.S. trip. New press regulations introduced in February forbid the publication of anything that challenges China's constitution, reveals "state secrets," or "harm[s] national security."

In late December, officials announced new restrictions on Internet use, which is growing rapidly in China. Citing the need to control information that might "split the country" or could be seen as "defaming government agencies," the new regulations call for unspecified "criminal punishments" and fines of up to $1800 for violators. In addition, China has pursued a policy of blocking access to World Wide Web sites maintained by news organizations, dissidents, and human rights groups abroad that may carry information critical of the regime.

Beijing's most notable gesture toward human rights and press freedom was the release of dissident writer Wei Jingsheng in November, three weeks after Jiang's summit with President Clinton. The ailing Wei was exiled to the United States as a condition of his release on medical parole, but calls for the release of fellow dissident writer Wang Dan went unheeded. In a disturbing footnote, the White House tried to prevent the Voice of America's television service, which is carried on Worldnet, a television satellite network operated by the U.S. Information Agency, from broadcasting an interview with Wei into China, for fear of offending Beijing. VOA officials reacted angrily to the action, noting that the agency, while government-funded, has a charter guaranteeing

that it make independent news judgments. The interview eventually aired.

Fifteen journalists were in prison in China at the end of the year—the largest number in Asia—including Gao Yu, a reporter serving a six-year sentence for "leaking state secrets" in financial articles written in 1993 for *Mirror Monthly*, a Hong Kong magazine. Denied compassionate medical release despite a number of severe ailments, she was honored in absentia by UNESCO on May 3, World Press Freedom Day, with a $25,000 UNESCO-Guillermo Cano World Press Freedom Prize. An enraged Beijing called Gao Yu "a criminal" and threatened to withdraw from the agency in protest.

Despite official resistance on most press freedom issues, there were signs of growing dissent both inside and outside official circles not heard since the Tiananmen Square massacre of 1989. "The continued rapid development of China's economy is safeguarded by reform of the political structure," a top advisor to Jiang, Liu Ji, told the official Xinhua news agency in September, just prior to the 15th Communist Party Congress, "otherwise the consequences are unimaginable." Liu's words, while not acted upon at the congress, nonetheless seem to indicate an ongoing discussion of press freedom and free expression within party circles. Following Wei's release, China's tiny dissident movement was re-energized as calls for greater press freedom began to circulate. It is too early to say that these signs of a partial thaw in China's official intolerance will lead to greater press freedom, but Jiang's desire for further modernization and reform of the economy may eventually lead to a more open media culture.

January 19
Gao Yu IMPRISONED

Chinese authorities rejected dissident journalist Gao Yu's appeal for bail on medical grounds.

On May 3, Gao Yu was awarded the World Press Freedom Prize by the United Nations Educational, Scientific, and Cultural Organization (UNESCO). The Chinese government attacked UNESCO and condemned its Director General Federico Mayor for supporting the presentation of the award.

In November 1994, Gao, former deputy chief editor of the defunct *Economics Weekly*, was sentenced to six years in prison for "leaking state secrets. " Her lawyers had not been informed that she was being brought to trial. Gao had been held incommunicado by state security officials since her detention on Oct. 2, 1993, just two days before she was to depart for the United States to start a one-year research fellowship at Columbia University's Graduate School of Journalism.

Gao was initially tried on April 20, 1994, at which time the court held that evidence against her was insufficient. Instead of acquitting her, however, the court ordered the prosecutor's office to find additional evidence for its case. According to court papers, she was charged with having obtained classified documents about China's structural reforms from Gao Chao, a Communist Party official and a former university acquaintance. Gao Yu allegedly used the information for political and economic stories published in the *Mirror Monthly*, a pro-Beijing Chinese-language magazine in Hong Kong. Gao Chao was given a 13-year prison term for accepting bribes and providing state secrets to Gao Yu and others.

Gao Yu had previously been jailed for 14 months following the June 1989 Tiananmen Square demonstrations, having been released in August 1990 after showing symptoms of what her family said was a heart condition.

April 28
Juergen Kremb, *Der Spiegel*
IMPRISONED, HARASSED

Kremb, Beijing correspondent for the German magazine *Der Spiegel*, was detained and placed under house arrest by Chinese authorities for conducting "unauthorized news reporting" after he met with the family of jailed dissident Wei Jingsheng. Chinese police detained Kremb, along with Wei Xiaotao, the brother of Wei Jingsheng, in the town of Bazhen, in central Anhui Province, as he had lunch with three other members of the Wei family. Both Kremb and Wei were taken to the Linghu Hotel in nearby Chaohu City and placed under house arrest for two days.

Authorities confiscated Kremb's passport, Chinese residency card, and return plane ticket to Beijing. They demanded he turn over his notes and film and sign a confession admitting that he had conducted illegal interviews. Kremb refused, saying his visit was strictly personal, not part of his work. He was released from house arrest on April 29 and his passport, residency card, and plane ticket were returned. Kremb left the hotel early the next day and traveled to Hefei, the provincial capital of Anhui, where he remained under police surveillance. Kremb returned to Beijing on May 1.

Under Chinese regulations, foreign journalists must obtain a permit from the Chinese Foreign Ministry to travel outside Beijing and are usually assigned an official guide.

November 16
Wei Jingsheng EXPELLED

Wei Jingsheng, among the most prominent dissidents in China and former co-editor of the pro-democracy journal *Tansuo* (Explorations), was released from prison on medical grounds and exiled to the United States. CPJ issued a press release congratulating the Chinese government for finally heeding the many calls for Wei's release. CPJ expressed hope that China's decision will be followed by improved conditions for other writers and journalists still held in prisons. CPJ praised the Clinton administration for its constructive engagement on human rights with China. Credit was also given to the broad coalition of human rights organizations which have consistently pressured Beijing to release political prisoners.

Wei was freed shortly after the visit of President Jiang Zemin to the United States. CPJ assumes the release is a sign of positive linkage emerging from the visit, but nevertheless regards Wei's banishment as an indication of Chinese intolerance of dissent.

Wei, 47, had been convicted on December 13, 1995, by the Beijing Intermediate People's Court of conspiring to subvert the government. Foreign reporters were barred from attending the trial. His 14-year sentence was upheld on December 28, 1995, following a closed appeal hearing. Wei had been held incommunicado since police detained him on April 1, 1994, shortly after meeting with U.S. Assistant Secretary of State John Shattuck. But he was not formally arrested and charged until November 21 of that year.

Wei had been paroled on September 14, 1993, after serving 14 1/2 years of a 15-year sentence for "counterrevolutionary" activities that included writing essays strongly criticizing the goverment and calling for democratic rule. Following his release, Wei wrote several op-ed pieces for publication abroad and concluded a deal with a Hong Kong magazine for the publication of his prison memoirs. These moves prompted an official warning that he was violating the terms of his parole.

In June 1997, Wei was severely beaten by six criminals assigned to guard him in prison. Suffering from several chronic illnesses, he was held in poor prison conditions. Viking Penguin has published a collection of letters Wei addressed to his family and to the Chinese government in *The Courage to Stand Alone: Letters from Prison and Other Writings*. The book includes the text of his famous essay "The Fifth Modernization," which called for democracy and challenged the late Chinese leader Deng Xiaoping.

Federated States of Micronesia

A running battle between the government and newspaper editor Sherry O'Sullivan resulted in her being barred from the country, prompting close scrutiny of the press climate in this tiny Pacific country. Micronesian authorities claimed that O'Sullivan was in the country without a legal work permit and that she failed to understand the culture and traditions of the island nation. O'Sullivan, a Canadian citizen and former editor of the fortnightly *FSM News*, called the government actions against her an attack on press freedom stemming from her exposes of alleged government corruption. The owners of the *FSM News*, then the only independent newspaper in the country, fired O'Sullivan in March when the government began its attacks and closed their doors voluntarily.

With the closure of *FSM News*, virtually all media in Micronesia are government-owned or controlled. In December, however, the first edition of the *Island Tribune*, a new independent weekly newspaper, appeared.

It is hoped that President Jacob Nena, who signed the order barring O'Sullivan, will take no further steps against journalists. In the past, Nena has been active in United Nations human rights organizations and is on record in support of a free press.

June 11
Sherry O'Sullivan, *FSM News* EXPELLED

After a brief business trip to address the Micronesian chapter of the Society of Professional Journalists in Guam, O'Sullivan,

ASIA

former editor of the *FSM News*, was denied reentry into the Federated States of Micronesia on June 11 by immigration authorities as she tried to board a flight for Pohnpei. O'Sullivan was effectively unable to challenge the immigration order in court because she could not get into the country.

The action followed a pattern of harassment against O'Sullivan that began with Congressional Resolution 9-106, passed on March 19, 1997, which called her reporting for the *FSM News* "gross, extreme, careless and...willfully malicious." Without offering specific examples, the resolution sought the approval of the president's office to have O'Sullivan deported.

The resolution did not have the effect of law and it had yet to be acted on by the president's office. Even if the president approved the resolution, its implementation would require court proceedings in which O'Sullivan would have the right to counsel. Instead of allowing for due process of law, it appeared that immigration officials were using O'Sullivan's absence from the country as an opportunity to expel her.

Despite the threat of deportation, O'Sullivan, who no longer works for the *FSM News*, said she intended to return to Micronesia and work on a new publication, *Micronesia News Magazine*.

Ambassador Resio S. Moses, the FSM's permanent representative to the United States, sent a letter to CPJ on June 23 asserting that there was "not now, nor has there been a pattern of harassment of Ms. O'Sullivan by the Government of the FSM."

Fiji

Despite moves by the government of Prime Minister Sitiveni Rabuka toward liberalization and greater democracy, relations between Fiji's government and the press remain tense. Harassment of the country's largest daily newspaper, the *Fiji Times*, continued and harsh press regulations remain on the books and are a potential threat to the media.

Widely hailed constitutional reforms that went into effect in July ended indigenous Fijians' domination of the government and brought to a close a period of military-dominated rule that began when Rabuka led a military coup in 1987 and substantially limited civil liberties for the country's sizable Indian minority. Fiji rejoined the British Commonwealth in September, and Rabuka formally apologized to Queen Elizabeth for ousting her as head of state in the 1987 coup. In this more liberal environment, Fiji's information minister announced in December that proposals for strict media licensing laws were likely to be shelved by the government.

The *Fiji Times*, however, has repeatedly come under fire from the government for its coverage of parliamentary activity. Information Minister Ratu Inoke Kubuabola in February accused the newspaper of breaching parliamentary privilege, which is a crime in Fiji, in its reporting on the debate over the country's new constitution. *Fiji Times* publisher Alan Robinson, editor Samisoni Kakaivalu, and public affairs reporter Jo Nata could be jailed for up to two years under Fiji's Parliamentary Privileges Act. In October, the Fijian Senate again formally threatened to file further breach of parliamentary privilege charges against Robinson and Kakaivulu over a report in the *Times* that questioned the senate's efficiency. In addition, some senators have publicly castigated the *Fiji Times* because it is owned by Rupert Murdoch's News Corporation and is thus a "foreign" entity.

Mike Field, a New Zealand-based correspondent for Agence France-Presse who was briefly detained and denied entry to Fiji in 1996, told CPJ in a telephone interview that he is still on a government "watch" list of allegedly hostile journalists. He has been denied a work permit, which is necessary for foreign correspondents covering Fiji, although he has been allowed into the country on a tourist visa. "There is a deep resentment of the press in Fiji and it's getting worse," Field said.

February 27
Fiji Times LEGAL ACTION

Information Minister Ratu Inoke Kubuabola accused the *Fiji Times* newspaper of breaching parliamentary privilege by reporting proceedings of parliamentary sub-committees reviewing the country's constitiution. Kubuabola said he would conduct a full investigation into the latest leak of what he said were confidential minutes of the sub-committee's deliberations. He said the *Fiji Times'* report was incorrect because nothing had been resolved.

Earlier in the day, the newspaper had published a report of what it described as parliamentary sub-committee recommendations on the future make up of seats in Fiji's House of Representatives. The seats that are currently decided on communal lines guarantee indigenous Fijians more seats than the country's other communities.

On October 3, the Senate had decided to refer the newspaper to the privileges committee over reports and an editorial in the paper saying that the Senate session on September 29 lasted only 20 minutes. The editorial questioned the cost to taxpayers of the 20-minute session and said it called into question the seriousness of the senators' demands for government cost-cutting and improved efficiency.

On October 8, the publisher and editor of the *Fiji Times* appeared before the Fiji Senate Privileges Committee. The committee resolved that one of its members, Senator Afzal Khan, and the lawyer for the newspaper, Richard Naidu, would meet to discuss further the concerns raised in the Senate.

The committee concluded that the three must undergo investigation, and that their case will be taken up at their next meeting, in March 1998. If convicted, the three face a prison term of two years and/or a US$400 fine.

Hong Kong

Because Hong Kong is a center for the regional press as well as the Chinese-language media worldwide, its return to Chinese sovereignty on July 1, was a matter of great concern for press freedom advocates. China's dismal record on freedom of expression sparked fears that Hong Kong's liberal media environment might wither under the stewardship of the mainland. With local journalists warning of a rise in self-censorship in the face of the transition, and Beijing giving conflicting signals leading up to the handover, CPJ followed Hong Kong closely throughout the year. (See "Freedom Under the Dragon: Can Hong Kong's Press Still Breathe Fire?", p. 276) By year's end, however, Hong Kong's press did not seem substantially changed by the turnover, and journalists reported that they were able to go about their business with little sign of intervention from Beijing.

Before the economic meltdown that sent stock markets and currencies tumbling across the region, the biggest Asian story of the year was the July 1 handover of Hong Kong to China, ending 156 years of British colonial rule. In September, the two stories came together, after a fashion, at a CPJ-sponsored forum in Hong Kong timed to coincide with the World Bank/International Monetary Fund annual meetings, the first major international gathering in the territory after the handover. At the session, U.S. Deputy Treasury Secretary Lawrence H. Summers called the preservation of press freedom a key to a healthy economy not only for Hong Kong but for all of Asia. "Hong Kong has an enormous chance to continue to prosper as it has as a financial center, but its success will depend critically on the sense that any and all information can flow freely and accurately, whether it is convenient or whether it is inconvenient," Summers told the forum.

Summers' theme became a familiar refrain as the region's once-prosperous economies faced tough reforms and calls for greater openness. "A free and undisturbed press is important because that is the vehicle through which information is conveyed, and, once conveyed, is trusted," said Summers. "Information is at the center of what makes financial markets work."

The free flow of information through Hong Kong's media has been pivotal as the international focus on the regional economic crisis intensifies. Hong Kong is the center of both media and finance for much of Asia, and if the region is to return to economic vitality, investors and citizens alike will need accurate, timely information on which to base renewed confidence for the future.

India

India's aggressive economic liberalization policies continued as the country celebrated the 50th anniversary of independence from Britain, but so did harassment of the press in some regions. India's claim to being a modernizing democracy was undermined by state-tolerated assaults and intimidation against journalists in areas traditionally troubled by violent secessionist and sectarian movements and other social tensions.

The United Front coalition government of Prime Minister Inder Kumar Gujral was toppled on November 28 when the Congress Party withdrew parliamentary

support for the ruling coalition. The dissolution ended a month-long political crisis prompted by the leaking of the Jain Commission report, which indicted the Dravida Munnetra Kazhagam Party (DMK) for involvement in the 1991 assassination of former Prime Minister Rajiv Gandhi.

On December 4, President K.R. Narayanan announced his decision to dissolve the country's parliament and called for fresh elections to be held by March 15, 1998. Gujral's seven-month-old government had pledged to crack down on widespread corruption, and senior officials, including former Prime Minister P.V. Narasimha Rao, were prosecuted for their roles in various scandals. India's vaunted tradition of press freedom was much on display as national newspapers and broadcast media aggressively pursued the corruption story, hastening the prosecution of tainted officials.

In the northwestern state of Jammu and Kashmir, where a decades-old secessionist movement has captured world attention, journalists are threatened on two fronts. Indian security forces in this officially "disturbed area" are granted sweeping powers to discourage media coverage that could risk national security. Separatist militants, on the other hand, threaten journalists whose reporting might be considered unfavorable. Altaf Ahmed Faktoo, a news reader for the official Indian television network Doordarshan Kendra in the capital city of Srinagar, was shot and killed by militant separatists in January. Two months later, Saidain Shafi, a contributor to programs carried on Doordarshan, was killed by suspected militant separatists. Shafi is the eighth journalist murdered in Kashmir since the armed insurgency against Indian rule erupted in 1989, and the fourth who was targeted because of his work with the state-owned broadcast media.

The restoration of elected government in Jammu and Kashmir in October 1996, after seven years of federal rule and the subsequent appointment of a regional human rights commission, failed to curb state-sanctioned human rights abuses. In late June, Surinder Oberoi, a reporter for Agence France-Presse in Kashmir, was brutally beaten by Indian security forces. Afterward, scores of journalists staging a protest rally on behalf of their colleague were tear-gassed by police. These incidents and the history of unchecked official hostility toward journalists have cowed the local press. Kashmiri journalists report that self-censorship has become routine.

Elsewhere, police in Assam, backed by state and federal officials, engaged in torture, unlawful killings, "disappearances" and other abuses of human rights including violations of press freedom in the region. Ajit Bhuyan, editor of the widely read Assamese-language newspaper *Asomiya Protidin* and its sister paper, *Sadin*, was repeatedly arrested because of the papers' critical coverage of the tense separatist conflict.

January 1
Altaf Ahmed Faktoo, Doordarshan Kendra KILLED

Faktoo, an on-air news reader for the state-owned Doordarshan Kendra television station in Srinagar, Kashmir, was shot to death in the Crown Hotel, reportedly by suspected militant separatists. Three unidentified men entered the hotel, which is owned by Faktoo's family and is in Srinagar's heavily patrolled Lal Chowk area, and fired two shots at the journalist with a silencer pistol. The gunmen immediately fled the scene. No one has claimed responsibility for the murder.

Separatists had threatened Faktoo repeatedly because of his work with Doordarshan Kendra. On the air, Faktoo had read pro-government news reports that were critical of the separatist movement. In 1994, he had been kidnapped and detained briefly by a militant

group. After that incident, he requested and received permission to read the Urdu-language job-listings program "Rozgaar Samachar" (Employment News) instead of regular news broadcasts. Shortly before his murder, however, Faktoo had started reading for a news program about Kashmir that is broadcast by satellite throughout India, but not in Kashmir. Faktoo had told colleagues at Doordarshan Kendra that he felt safe working on the program because it was not being shown in the Kashmir Valley, where the separatist movement is centered.

Unlike other news readers employed by Doordarshan Kendra, Faktoo had declined government offers to provide him an armed escort and other forms of security. In a letter to the Indian government, CPJ called for an investigation into Faktoo's murder.

March 16
Saidain Shafi, Doordarshan Kendra KILLED

Two unidentified gunmen ambushed Shafi, a contributor to programs carried on the official Indian television network Doordarshan, as he was returning to his car from a nearby phone booth in the Narsingh-Garh area of Srinagar, the summer capital of Jammu and Kashmir State. The gunmen fired first at Shafi's personal security officer, Manohar Lal, fatally wounding him, before turning to Shafi and shooting him in the neck. Shafi's mother, who was in the car at the time, was not injured. The gunmen immediately fled the scene in a motorized rickshaw. No one claimed responsibility for the murder.

Shafi had worked as a reporter for two privately produced programs aired nationwide on Doordarshan: "Kashmir File," a weekly news program that was recently discontinued, and "Eyewitness," a five-minute nightly news capsule that is still on the air. "Kashmir File" had been particularly critical of militant separatists in the state, and Shafi had told colleagues and authorities that he had received threats from separatists for what they called his biased

ASIA

reporting. In a letter to Indian Prime Minister H.D. Deve Gowda, CPJ condemned the assassination and called for a thorough investigation.

July 3
Surinder Oberoi, Agence France-Presse
ATTACKED

Oberoi, a reporter for Agence France-Presse in Kashmir, was brutally beaten by Indian security forces.

On the afternoon of June 27, approximately 20 journalists assembled in front of the United Nations military observer office in Srinagar to cover a demonstration by a Kashmiri separatist organization. When police began to beat two women who were chanting slogans for independence, Oberoi asked his photographer, Tauseef Mustafa, to photograph the beating.

According to Oberoi's account of the incident, superintendent of Jammu and Kashmir police Mubariq Ganai asked Oberoi what he was doing at the scene of the demonstration. Oberoi responded, "My professional duty." After ordering Oberoi to "get lost," Ganai struck the journalist with his baton. When Oberoi asked the officer to stop, a dozen lower-ranking policemen joined Ganai in beating Oberoi.

Reporters who were covering the demonstration immediately organized to protest the assault on their colleague and marched toward the district where several news offices are located. Upon seeing the severe bruises on Oberoi's body, other journalists joined in a procession to the office of Kashmir Chief Minister Farooq Abdullah.

About 40 journalists approached the entrance to Abdullah's office, where security officers blocked their entry despite the fact that the journalists displayed their government accreditation cards. When the journalists demanded to see the chief minister, whose office is routinely open to them after 2 p.m., the policeman guarding the main gate fired into

the air to disperse the group. Police Officer Mushtaq and Inspector Ajaz then ordered security forces to fire tear-gas shells. The journalists were tear-gassed, chased, and beaten, leaving at least 20 people injured.

Although Chief Minister Abdullah eventually apologized to the journalists and promised an investigation, he did not arrest Mubariq Ganai, Mushtaq, and Ajaz, the three police officials who had given the order for the attack on the journalists.

The failure of the authorities to press criminal charges against the accused police officers has prompted the Journalists Association in Kashmir to boycott Indian government functions and statements.

CPJ wrote a letter on July 3, to Prime Minister Inder Kumar Gujrall urging that the accused police officers be prosecuted immediately on assault charges. The letter called upon the prime minister's office to publicize the findings of the investigation and asked that he strive to ensure that journalists may work freely, without fear of repression.

July 21
Anindita Ramaswamy, *Asian Age* ATTACKED

Ramaswamy, a journalist for the *Asian Age* newspaper, was attacked in central Bombay by attackers angered by a story that questioned the credibility of the political party Akhil Bharatiya Sena. The story reported that party leader Arun Gawli had not paid his employees' salaries.

The attackers threw stones and other sharp objects at Ramaswamy, cutting the left side of her forehead. She was treated at a hospital.

Gawli had recently entered politics, drawing support from the local community unhappy with the government. He and two of his men were arrested and charged with causing grievous hurt, making threats to Ramaswamy's life, and intending to riot. They were later released on bail.

July 6
Manjunath, *Asian Age* ATTACKED
P.B.R. Srikanth, *Asian Age* ATTACKED

A mob of approximately 40 people stormed into the Bangalore office of *Asian Age* on the evening of July 6, stabbing circulation department employee Manjunath and setting fires, which left office bureau chief P.B.R. Srikanth and the office watchman unconscious from the fumes.

On July 7, M.J. Akbar, editor in chief of *Asian Age*, held a press conference about the attack, and Indian journalist associations protested to the government. Police are investigating the attack.

News editor Kaushik Mitra stated that the office had been receiving threatening phone calls after the newspaper carried a report about an Israeli woman who had put up posters in the West Bank city of Hebron depicting the prophet Mohammed as a pig.

July 27
Habib-ullah Naqash, *Asian Age* ATTACKED
Mukhtar Ahmed, *The Telegraph* and CNN
Arshad Ahmed, free-lancer
Ahmed Ali Fayaz, *Excelsior*

Naqash, photojournalist for *Asian Age*, was beaten by two police officers when stopped at a highway check point on his way to cover Prime Minister Gujral's visit to Kashmir. Several days later, on August 8, Mukhtar Ahmed, a reporter for the Indian daily *The Telegraph* and a correspondent for CNN, and photojournalist Arshad Ahmed were beaten when they were stopped en route to cover the Indian Army's press conference at Badami Bagh in Srinagar.

The Indian Army later raided the residence of Ali Fayaz, bureau chief of the *Excelsior* newspaper in Budgam, near Srinagar.

Local journalists expressed their concern over the repeated attacks in Kashmir, despite assurances from authorities. CPJ sent a letter to the prime minister on August 11, saying the incidents dramatized the dangers faced by reporters covering the separatist conflict in northwestern India. CPJ joined journalists in Kashmir in urging the government to undertake a thorough investigation and to publicize the findings.

August 15
Martin Sugarman EXPELLED

Indian immigration authorities refused to allow Martin Sugarman, an independent U.S. photographer and filmmaker, to enter India on August 13 for the purpose of reporting in the Kashmir Valley.

Sugarman arrived in New Delhi on a flight from London shortly before midnight on August 12. He had been issued a visa on July 16 by the Indian consulate in San Francisco. His passport was seized and then he was detained and questioned by immigration and security authorities at the airport for several hours before being placed on a plane back to London, Sugarman said. "They held me at immigration and asked me if I was a journalist and if I had ever been to Kashmir. Of course, they knew all about my work already," he said. His passport was returned when he boarded a flight back to London.

Sugarman is the author of the 1993 book *Kashmir: Paradise Lost*, a collection of photographs of life in the Kashmir Valley. He is an outspoken critic of the Indian military, which has stationed nearly half a million troops in Kashmir to put down an independence movement that is backed by Pakistan. Sugarman said he told the immigration authorities in New Delhi that he intended to return to Kashmir to update his earlier research.

CPJ wrote a letter on August 15 to Prime Minister Inder Kumar Gujral opposing any restrictions being placed on the ability of journalists to do their jobs. CPJ asked Gujral's government to promptly investigate India's refusal to allow Martin Sugarman to enter the country and make findings of that investigation public.

ASIA

August 25
Ajit Bhuyan, *Asomiya Protidin* and *Sadin*
LEGAL ACTION

Bhuyan, editor of the Assamese-language newspaper *Asomiya Protidin* and its sister paper, the Assamese-language weekly *Sadin*, was arrested.

State authorities linked Bhuyan to the banned United Liberation Front of Assam (ULFA) and accused him of complicity in the kidnapping and murder of social activist Sanjay Ghosh, who died while being held by ULFA members. Since August 25, Bhuyan has been arrested four times and charged with related crimes. On October 1, he was arrested and accused of having ties to the ULFA and charged under the National Security Act with "attempting to wage war against the country."

Bhuyan, who is in very poor health, was hospitalized at the Assam Medical College Hospital under judicial custody.

Bhuyan might have been targeted because of his papers' coverage of the separatist conflict in northeastern India.

CPJ sent a letter to Prime Minister Inder Kumar Gujral on October 22, expressing fear that the arrest of Bhuyan could damage press freedom in India.

In late November, the advisory committee of the NSA concluded that Bhuyan's detention was inappropiate and ordered his release. The central government then immediately dismissed the members of the committee, while Bhuyan was rearrested by the Nagaon Police Station for ties to ULFA.

Bhuyan was finally released from judicial custody on December 3, though he remained in the hospital until December 13. Shortly after returning home, Bhuyan was informed that the owner of his newspapers, Jayanta Barua, had been threatened with arrest under the NSA unless he fired Bhuyan.

Bhuyan has since launched his own newspaper, which he is struggling to print amid government opposition.

November 19
Jagadish Babu, E-TV, KILLED
S. Gangadhara Raju, E-TV, KILLED
P. Srinivas Rao, E-TV, KILLED
S. Krishna, E-TV, KILLED
G. Raja Sekhar, E-TV, KILLED

Five members of a production crew of E-TV (Eenadu Television), a private channel, were covering the making of a film November 19 when they were killed in a car bomb explosion. As they were leaving the Rama Naidu Studios, their vehicle caught the brunt of the massive blast, which police said was caused by a remote-control car bomb parked by the studio entrance. The television crew's driver, P. Chandra Sekhar Reddy, was also killed. At least 17 others died and more than 30 were injured. The attack is believed to have been motivated by political rivalry targeted at the film's producer, Paritala Ravi, a former guerrilla leader pardoned in return for his surrender. Ravi who is a state legislator and member of the governing Telugu Desam party.

Indonesia

As a deepening financial crisis spiraled out of control, attention focused on President Suharto's autocratic leadership. International lenders noted that the absence of a free press has exacerbated Indonesia's turmoil by restricting access to information and allowing widespread corruption to flourish unchecked by the media.

Conditions for the press worsened during the year despite calls for greater transparency as a way out of the crisis. Suharto signed restrictive new broadcast licensing legislation into law in October, adding to already stringent press laws. Many journalists practice self-censorship, while the independent press—especially those allied with the officially unrecognized

Alliance of Independent Journalists (AJI)—risk prosecution and prison sentences. Access to strife-torn East Timor and areas of ethnic conflict in Acheh and Irian Jaya remains tightly controlled, with foreign journalists and unauthorized local reporters generally barred from covering events.

The broadcast bill requires broadcasters to obtain licenses on a five-year renewable basis and also bars foreign ownership of radio and television outlets. While stations may produce their own news programming, they are required to run news bulletins provided by the state-owned Televisi Republik Indonesi. The bill also requires Internet service providers and cable television outlets to obtain similar licenses. Suharto's relatives control three of the five privately owned television stations in Indonesia, while the remaining two are controlled by well-connected businessmen.

Prosecutions of students, political leaders, trade unionists, and journalists for speaking out against the government continued. Andi Syahputra, the printer of the alternative magazine *Suara Independen* (Voice of Independence), published by the AJI, was sentenced to two years and six months in prison for distributing material hostile to Suharto. He had been arrested in October 1996. Two AJI journalists, Eko Maryadi and founding AJI president Ahmad Taufik, were released from prison on parole in July. They had been imprisoned since March 1995 because of their work with AJI and *Suara Independen*.

Taufik, a recipient of a 1995 International Press Freedom Award, was finally able to receive his award in person from CPJ in November during ceremonies coinciding with the Asia Pacific Economic Cooperation forum in Vancouver. Calling his jailers "fascists," Taufik pledged to continue working toward greater press freedom. Taufik later visited San Francisco, New York, and Washington as a guest of CPJ to meet with journalists, scholars, and others interested in press conditions in Indonesia.

In May, a bloody parliamentary election campaign, hailed by the Suharto government as a "Festival of Democracy," resulted in hundreds of deaths in widespread rioting. Due to the 1996 government ouster of Megawati Sukarnoputri as head of the opposition Indonesian Democratic Party (PDI) and other restrictive moves, many government critics urged a boycott of the election. At least five editors were demoted or suspended for election-related coverage, while 20 journalists were beaten or had their film seized by police in the rioting. Leading opposition parties, human rights groups, and the U.S. government criticized the May 29 polls for irregularities that helped the ruling Golkar Party secure 74 percent of the 425 seats.

The Asian economic crisis caused a steep devaluation of Indonesian currency, sparking a banking crisis and sporadic food riots, and prompting the press to push the limits of freedom by tracking the crisis and reporting on allegedly corrupt officials. "No one in the government can control the media totally," said Andreas Harsono, the Jakarta correspondent for the *Nation* newspaper of Bangkok, in a meeting with CPJ in December. "There are too many pockets of resistance. Journalists in Indonesia want to be free."

Concern has deepened over who will eventually succeed Suharto, who has been in power since 1965. Despite growing calls for him to step down and concern over his health, he announced his intention to seek a seventh five-year term in rubber-stamp presidential elections scheduled for March 1998. As pressures mount, the attitude of Indonesian authorities toward the press is epitomized by the deportation of human rights activist Lynn Ann Fredrickson from East Timor in November because she

appeared to be a journalist: she was taking notes and carrying a camera.

April 7
Andi Syahputra IMPRISONED

Syahputra, who manages the printing house that produces the magazine *Suara Independen*, was sentenced to 30 months in prison on charges of defaming President Suharto.

The magazine published an article titled "Suharto in the Process of Becoming a Naked King" in October 1996. Chief Judge Marsel Buchari of the South Jakarta District Court ruled that the article had "clearly" shown intent to defame Suharto.

Syahputra was sentenced to several months in prison after being arrested in a raid of the printing house on October 28, 1996, when police confiscated 5,000 copies of the issue containing the article. They also arrested Nasrul, a press operator.

After the two were taken into custody at a South Jakarta police station, security forces searched Syahputra's home. Syahputra and Nasrul were charged with defaming the president.

Syahputra is a member of Indonesia's only independent journalists' union, the Alliance of Independent Journalists (AJI).

These actions were part of the government's suppression of *Suara Independen*, published by the Melbourne-based Society of Indonesian Alternative Media, and its predecessor, *Independen*, published by AJI.

CPJ sent a letter to Suharto on April 14, condemning the jailing of Syahputra and asked that the president ensure Syahputra's release.

June 11
Muhammad Sayuti Bochari, *Pos Makasar* KILLED ·

Sayuti Bochari, a journalist with the Ujungpandang-based weekly *Pos Makasar*, died in the hospital of head and neck injuries. Sayuti was found lying unconscious on June 9 on a vil-

lage street in Luwu, about 300 miles north of Ujungpandang, the provincial capital. His motorbike, found next to his body, was not damaged. Family members and friends said his injuries indicated he had been beaten.

Sayuti had written several articles about local officials who allegedly embezzled government funds earmarked for alleviating poverty. He had reported also on a theft of timber involving a village chief, a story that made the front page of *Pos Makasar* on June 1. The paper's editor in chief, Andi Tonra Mahie, said Sayuti's death was a result of his reporting on local corruption, but local police said the cause was a traffic accident. The state-sponsored Association of Indonesian Journalists was investigating Sayuti's death.

CPJ sent a letter to President Suharto calling for a thorough investigation.

July 25
Naimullah, *Sinar Pagi* KILLED

Naimullah, a reporter for *Sinar Pagi*, was found murdered. His mutilated body, with stab wounds in his neck and bruises on his head, temples, chest, and wrists, was discovered in the back seat of his car in Pantai Penibungan, about 90 kilometers north of Pontianak, the provincial capital of West Kalimantan.

According to reports in the July 28 editions of the newspapers *Media Indonesia* and *Akcaya*, Naimullah had recently reported on timber theft for *Sinar Pagi* and had been conducting an investigation for the paper into illegal logging in Kalimantan. He was last seen with four men, including one from the company suspected of having been involved with the logging.

CPJ sent a letter to President Suharto on July 28, urging his government to conduct an immediate investigation into the murder of Naimullah and fully disclose the findings.

September 19
Ronald Frisart, Netherlands Press Association
LEGAL ACTION
Step Vaessen, NOS Television
Cable News Network (CNN) HARASSED
Local photographers ATTACKED,
HARASSED

Police arrested the two Jakarta-based journalists at the annual meeting of the officially unrecognized Indonesian Labor Welfare Union, at union headquarters in south Jakarta. They were released on the same day to the Dutch Embassy. Two Australian trade unionists and 10 Indonesian activists were also arrested and later released.

The police also seized film from a CNN camera crew and from a number of local photographers. Reportedly, one photographer was slightly injured by a police baton.

Police raided the meeting after ordering participants to end the meeting. Union chairman Muchtar Pakpahan had been held in detention for more than a year on subversion charges.

October 28
Ezki Suyanto, *Panji Masyarakat* ATTACKED
Satari, *Panji Masyarakat* ATTACKED
Teguh Indra, *Republika* ATTACKED

Police beat three journalists who were covering an anti-government demonstration in Jakarta. Ezki Suyanto, a journalist with *Panji Masyarakat*; Satari, a photographer with the same newspaper; and Teguh Indra, a photographer with the newspaper *Republika* were reportedly threatened and then beaten when officers tried to disperse the crowd. They were taken into custody and released when the officers confirmed that they were journalists.

Malaysia

In the early stages of Asia's economic crisis in the fall, Malaysian Prime Minister

Mahathir Mohamad grabbed headlines by blaming the distress on currency speculators and foreign enemies. Mahathir frequently accused international financier and free press advocate George Soros of fueling the crisis for his personal gain, at one point likening Soros to a drug dealer out to "destroy nations." Many observers believed Mahathir's antics were designed to play to Malaysian media, where self-censorship is routine. Malaysia's Printing Presses and Publications Act (PPA) and Internal Security Act (ISA) encourage a quiescent press through tough licensing requirements and summary detention of suspected violators, respectively.

Mahathir frequently bullies and threatens the media. In April he accused both the foreign and local press of distorting facts and sensationalizing news in order to boost sales and damage Malaysia's credibility. "It is not only the reporters, the sub-editors are also putting the headings (sic) to make it attractive," he told a gathering of journalists. He went on to remind the reporters that they would be subject to penalties if they overstepped the bounds.

Even Mahathir's friends get the message. Wealthy Malaysian tycoon T. Ananda Krishnan drastically reduced locally generated news programming on his recently formed Astro satellite television network, which has aspirations to broadcast regionally. Dozens of journalists he recruited from Australia and New Zealand went home after Krishnan reportedly became concerned that his imported talent was too aggressive in covering the regional economic crisis and Mahathir's war of words with George Soros.

September 4
Murray Hiebert, *Far Eastern Economic Review*
IMPRISONED

A Malaysian court handed down a three-month jail sentence for contempt of court against

ASIA

Hiebert, the Kuala Lumpur bureau chief for the *Far Eastern Economic Review*. It was reportedly the first time a Malaysian court has convicted a journalist of contempt.

The contempt charge was filed by Chandra Sri Ram, the wife of Appeals Court Judge Sri Ram Gopal, following the appearance of an article by Hiebert in the January 23 issue of the *Far Eastern Economic Review* about lawsuits in Malaysia. The article discussed a lawsuit involving Chandra's family, which was later settled out of court. Hiebert reported that the suit moved quickly through the court system and that Chandra's husband was a judge.

Hiebert, a Canadian citizen and veteran reporter, said his story was carefully checked by lawyers for the *Far Eastern Economic Review* before publication. His lawyers argued before the court that there was a potential conflict of interest due to the professional relationship between Low Hop Bing, the judge who tried the case, and Judge Sri Ram Gopal.

CPJ sent a letter on September 4 to Prime Minister Mahathir Mohamad asking for an investigation.

On September 15, Hiebert appealed to the Shah Alam High Court. He also filed a motion at the Court of Appeal against the high court's decision to dismiss his application for release of his passport, which was surrendered as a condition of bail. On October 3, Hiebert failed to get his passport back pending the appeal.

North Korea

Despite a deepening famine that forced the country to seek food aid from abroad, North Korea's isolation has persisted. Few reports of social unrest have emerged from the famine—but few reports of any kind are heard from North Korea, since journalists are seldom allowed to visit the country and never travel without government escorts. Cracks in the facade appeared in February,

however, when Hwang Jang Yop, the chairman of the Foreign Affairs Committee of the Workers Party, defected to South Korea, becoming the highest-ranking official ever to flee the north.

In October, supreme leader Kim Jong Il rose to the post of Secretary General of the ruling Workers Party. The post had been vacant for more than three years, since the death of Kim's father, the country's founder, Kim Il Sung. Official media noted that strange natural events—such as cherry trees blossoming out of season—heralded Kim Jong Il's ascension. "The whole of Korea is replete with great joy and pleasure," the official Central News Agency noted.

The state news agency KCNA continues to post its official Web page, which is virtually the only voice of the North Korean government in the outside world. The site contains articles with such titles as "Independent Economy Hailed," and "Three Pillars in Devotedly Defending Leader," as well as calls for workers in capitalist South Korea to rise up in revolt.

Pakistan

Political crisis, ethnic conflict, and an uncertain future continued to plague the press in Pakistan as regionalism and sectarian movements took their toll on the media.

Although Pakistan's minister of information, Mushahid Hussain Sayed, assured CPJ in a meeting in New York on September 25 that the Pakistani government supports press freedom, Prime Minister Mohammad Nawaz Sharif—elected in February after waging a campaign that led to the ouster of Benazir Bhutto in November 1996 on charges of corruption and human rights abuses—leads a government that hovers on the fringes of repression. Backed by Gen. Jehangir Karamat, Prime Minister Sharif, emerged from a three-month power struggle involving the president and the chief justice, who had moved to oust the prime minister on charges of contempt of court. On December 2, President Farooq Ahmed Leghari resigned and Chief Justice Sajjad Ali Shah was removed by other supreme court justices. Amidst the country's golden jubilee celebrations, on August 14, Sharif enacted the Anti-Terrorism Act (ATA), a harsh martial law-style response to factional violence in the Punjab region between rival Sunni and Shi'a political groups. The new law allows military authorities to arrest "suspected terrorists" without warrant and even, in loosely defined circumstances, to shoot on sight those "committing a terrorist act" or "likely to commit a terrorist act."

In an incident that illustrates the lengths to which Pakistani military authorities can go in prosecuting security "crimes," a military court sentenced Humayun Fur, bureau chief of the Peshawar-based Urdu-language daily *Mashriq*, to five years in prison for relaying state secrets to a foreign diplomatic mission in Islamabad. Fur had been kidnapped by military authorities on June 28, and then held incommunicado for several weeks before he was tried.

Press freedom conditions deteriorated dramatically in Sindh Province, where continued clashes between the provincial government and the United National Movement (Muttahida Quami Movement or MQM), the armed opposition party of Urdu-speaking Indian immigrants, left at least 400 dead in the city of Karachi.

The Sindh National Front party (SNF), headed by Mumtaz Bhutto, former prime minister Bhutto's uncle, repeatedly subjected Sindhi newspapers to attack, harassment, and other forms of intimidation. In one case, SNF party members brutally beat Shakeel Naich, a reporter for the Sindhi-language daily *Awami Awaz*, after he published an article critical of Mumtaz Bhutto. In mid-September, a number of reporters were injured when police broke up a march of more than 300 journalists and media workers who were protesting the escalating attacks on press freedom in Sindh Province.

Journalists also report that in rural areas, where the political structure remains semi-feudal, powerful landlords subject journalists who publish investigative reports that could expose corruption in local governments to intimidation and harassment.

Despite ongoing political, ethnic, and sectarian conflicts, the Pakistani press remains vital. Condemning the escalating attacks on the press, local journalist associations and newspaper unions have demonstrated a firm commitment to protecting the rights of their colleagues and to securing press freedom in the country.

January 18
Z.A. Shahid, *Khabrain* KILLED
Arif Ali, *The News* ATTACKED
Abid Hussain, *Nawa-i-Waqt* ATTACKED
S.A. Raza, *Jang* ATTACKED
Mohammed Riaz, *Akhbar-i-Lahore* ATTACKED
Nadeem, *Pakistan* ATTACKED

Shahid, a photographer for the Urdu-language daily *Khabrain*, was killed, and five other photographers were injured, in a powerful bomb blast outside a courthouse in Lahore.

The bomb at the crowded Sessions Court in Punjab Province's largest city was targeted at two Sunni Muslim leaders of the anti-Shiite Sipah-e-Sahaba Pakistan Party, who were at the court for a hearing. It was concealed in a parked motorcycle.

The journalists injured in the blast were Ali of the English-language daily *The News*, Hussain of the English- and Urdu-language daily *Nawa-i-Waqt*, Raza of the Urdu-language

daily *Jang*, Riaz of *Akhbar-i-Lahore*, and
Nadeem of the Urdu-Language daily *Pakistan*.
A total of 19 people were killed and more than
80 injured.

Police arrested a suspect at the scene who
reportedly confessed to the bombing.

February 16
Assas ATTACKED

Armed men ransacked the Rawalpindi offices of
the Urdu-language daily newspaper *Assas*.
According to staff members, the newspaper had
received a press release the day before from
Raja Ishfaq Sarwar, a candidate for provincial
assembly in the recent elections. The statement
contained allegations against his opponent.
Because the paper could not confirm the allegations, they decided not to publish the report.
The next day, a close friend of Sarwar and more
than one hundred armed supporters raided the
office of the newspaper, held the staff hostage,
and damaged furniture, telephones, and other
equipment. Police arrested eight people for
taking part in the attack.

March 3
Quami Akhbar ATTACKED

On March 3, at around 6 a.m., a homemade
bomb exploded on the first floor of the Karachi
offices of *Quami Akhbar*, a major Urdu-
language daily newspaper, damaging the offices'
premises, equipment, and records at an estimated
loss of one million rupees. No casualties were
reported. Prime Minister Nawaz Sharif, the
Karachi Union of Journalists, and the All
Pakistan Newspaper Employee Confederation
condemned the bomb blast as an attack on the
freedom of press. The Chief Minister visited
the office and assured the press workers that
tight security measures would be adopted for all
newspaper premises so that journalists could
work without fear. There have been no reports
of any arrests yet.

June 5
Zafaryab Ahmed LEGAL ACTION

Pakistan's Federal Investigation Agency arrested
Ahmed without court order or warrant. He was
accused of being an agent of India's Research and
Analysis Wing (RAW), the intelligence agency.
Ahmed was charged with sedition and economic
treason for reserch he had been doing on child
and bonded labor in Pakistan. As a journalist and
a researcher for the Bonded Labor Liberation
Front, Ahmed had reported on the abuses
suffered by children working in the carpet-
weaving industry. Ahmed was released from
prison on health grounds but continued to seek
interim bail every two weeks from the High
Court of Lahore until July 10, when he was
granted permanent bail. The charges, which are
punishable by death, still stood. His case was to
be heard before the High Court on November
16. He was seeking to have the case against him
quashed because the government had not
produced any evidence against him.

July 2
Humayun Fur, *Mashriq* IMPRISONED, MISSING

Fur, bureau chief of the Peshawar-based Urdu-
language daily *Mashriq*, was abducted in
Islamabad. He and his wife were outside their
house when eight men, one of them in police
uniform, approached in two cars. The men
forced Fur into a car and drove away.
Authorities denied involvement in the
abduction. But Fur's wife said Islamabad police
refused to register her kidnapping complaint.

On June 30, Interior Minister Chaudhry
Shujaat Hussain told the National Assembly
that Fur was in the custody of a government
agency, saying the journalist was involved in
anti-state activities. Hussain said Fur was
arrested for providing classified documents to
unspecified neighboring countries.

CPJ wrote a letter on July 2 to Prime
Minister Muhammad Nawaz Sharif asking him

to ensure Fur's immediate release, to make public any charges against Fur, and to uphold his right to due process of law.

On July 20, a Lahore court said Fur was being court-martialed in a secret proceeding. A military panel headed by a Pakistan Army colonel on September 9 found Fur guilty of anti-state activities under a provision of the Pakistan Army Act of 1952. After a 27-day trial behind closed doors, the Defense Ministry said Fur was given a five-year prison sentence for relaying state secrets to a foreign diplomatic mission in Islamabad.

On July 29, CPJ sent another letter to Prime Minister Sharif protesting both the military court jurisdiction for Fur's case and the secrecy surrounding the charges—even the specific law under which Fur is being tried has been kept secret.

On September 10, CPJ sent a letter to Prime Minister Sharif urging him to instruct the appropriate authorities to retry Fur in an open court under civil law. On September 25, CPJ met with Minister for Information Mushahid Hussain Sayed, who said Fur was not being physically harmed and that "this was a case of espionage."

On October 2, Adaila jail authorities brought Fur in fetters to a hospital in critical condition. He was suffering from hepatitis C and jaundice. He slipped into a coma the next day. Fur's health had been deteriorating in jail because he was not provided with medical treatment. On October 7, Fur was released, having been pardoned by the chief of army staff on medical grounds after Fur's wife requested help.

In a phone interview on January 6, 1998, Fur told CPJ that he has been bedridden since his October release from jail and suffers from severe liver damage. His doctors expect another 4-6 months for his recovery. His medical expenses are estimated at more than Rs. 1000 per day (US$22). *Mashriq* has terminated Fur's employment.

July 11
Khaliq Kiani, *The Business Recorder*
ATTACKED

According to unconfirmed reports from Pakistan, Khaliq Kiani, a local correspondent for *The Business Recorder* in Karachi, was attacked by two unidentified motorcyclists near Melody Market while walking toward Aabpara at approximately 9:30 p.m. on July 11. The attackers punched and kicked Kiani, shouting, "Here is one for that piece of news." Kiani's face was seriously bruised and his shirt was torn when he approached the nearby Aabpara police station to register a complaint against the culprits.

According to the same reports, Kiani had been filing investigative stories about bureaucrats who were recently suspended by the government in Pakistan.

The Rawalpindi-Islamabad Union of Journalists (RIUJ) has condemned the attack on Kiani, terming this and other recent incidents of violence against journalists "an attack on the freedom of press" in Pakistan.

CPJ sent a letter of inquiry on July 14 to Minister of Information Mushahid Hussain Sayed, urging him to undertake a thorough investigation into the circumstances of this incident and to share with CPJ any information regarding the attack.

July 16
Sarwat Jamal Asmaia, *Takbeer* HARASSED
Shah Rukh Hasan, *Takbeer* HARASSED
Rafiq Afghan, *Ummat* HARASSED

A group of police officers raided the Karachi offices of the weekly *Takbeer* and attempted to arrest the editor, Sarwat Jamal Asmaia; reporter Shah Rukh Hasan; and Rafiq Afghan, editor of the daily *Ummat*.

Police said the three men were wanted in connection with the killing of two sons of Deputy Superintendent of Police Aziz-ur-Rehman, his driver, and his guard.

Aziz-ur-Rehman said that *Takbeer* had published an article that provoked the killers.

The police deputy inspector general was contacted immediately and intervened. The journalists were not arrested and the raiding police party was suspended.

August 11
Shakeel Naich, *Awami Awaz* ATTACKED

On August 3, Shakeel Naich, a reporter for the Sindhi-language daily *Awami Awaz*, was beaten by Sindh National Front (SNF) party members.

Ayub Shar, a SNF central executive committee member, and six other party members went to the newspaper's office and asked Naich to accompany them for a talk. The group then led Naich to a nearby location where they beat him severely, according to Pakistan Press Foundation reports citing eyewitnesses. Naich suffered head injuries and was hospitalized in a local intensive care ward where he remains in critical condition.

On August 6, journalists protested the attack outside the Karachi Press Club.

Shakeel Naich may have been targeted by the SNF because of his critical reporting. In mid-July, Naich published an article critical of Mumtaz Bhutto, the head of the Sindh National Front. The article was based on an interview with Shehbaz Sharif, chief minister of Punjab, who accused Mumtaz Bhutto, ousted Prime Minister Benazir Bhutto's uncle, of creating political problems by abandoning support for the National Finance Commission Award (NFC) he had initially signed as the interim government's chief minister of Sindh.

CPJ sent a letter on August 7 to Prime Minister Sharif, urging that this incident be immediately investigated and that those responsible be brought to justice.

The SNF has launched an apparent campaign of harassment against *Awami Awaz*. On August 8 and 9, SNF party members obstructed the distribution of the newspaper in several cities including Larkana, Rattodero, Nau Dero, Dharki, and Ubawaro. *Awami Awaz* management told the Pakistan Press Foundation that the SNF instructed its workers to ban the distribution of the paper in Rattodero and ordered the closure of the paper's regional office. News agents and distributors are being victimized and threatened and copies of the paper have been set on fire.

The Pakistan Federal Union of Journalists and the Karachi Union of Journalists met with Liaqat Ali Jatoi, Sindh chief minister, to protest the SNF's violence against the paper. Although Jatoi assured the journalists that those involved in the attack on Naich would be arrested and that the harassment against the paper would be investigated, no arrests have been made so far.

CPJ sent a letter on August 11 to Prime Minister Sharif urging that the attack on Naich be immediately investigated and that those responsible be prosecuted. CPJ urged Prime Minister Sharif to see to it that *Awami Awaz* be permitted to publish and ciruculate freely without fear of reprisal or harassment.

August 27
Pakistan ATTACKED, THREATENED, HARASSED

Police and private security forces raided and seized the Lahore office of the daily *Pakistan*, an independent Urdu-language newspaper. The police then occupied the premises.

The police action was reportedly related to a civil financial dispute between Akbar Ali Bhatti, the newspaper's chief editor and owner, and the Punjab Cooperative Bank, involving the paper's assets—including the building—mortgaged with the bank.

CPJ sent a letter September 23 to Mushahid Hussain, Minister of Information and Media Development, expressing fear that the journalists inside the building would be unable to work freely because of the presence of 51 armed policemen and private security forces.

CPJ urged Hussain to investigate the

circumstances of the occupation and said that civil matters should be addressed in accordance with the rule of law and not by police intimidation.

September 4
Kawish ATTACKED

A group of armed assailants attacked the Larkana bureau of the daily *Kawish*, a Sindhi-language newspaper. The attackers stole computers, a scanner, a fax machine, telephones, and other items.

Kawish might have been targeted because of its extensive coverage of Shakeel Naich, a reporter for the Sindhi-language daily *Awami Awaz* who was attacked by Sindh National Front (SNF) party members, and of the subsequent campaign of harassment by the SNF political party against *Awami Awaz*.

CPJ sent a letter to Prime Minister Muhammad Nawaz Sharif on September 29, joining Pakistani journalist organizations in condemning the attack on *Kawish*. CPJ urged that the attack be immediately investigated and that those responsible be prosecuted.

September 11
Zulfiqar, *Jang* ATTACKED
Khurram, *Assas* ATTACKED
Abidi, *Al-Akhbar* ATTACKED
Raja Iftikhar, *Pakistan Observer* ATTACKED
Afzal, *Pakistan Observer* ATTACKED
Qaiser Shah, *Khabrain* ATTACKED
Majid Ali, *Business Times*
Abdul Hameed, *Jang* ATTACKED

Nine photographers from national daily newspapers were beaten by hospital staff at the Rawalpindi General Hospital. The photographers had been attempting to take pictures of a slain worker of the religious party Tehrik Nifaz-i-Fiqh-i Jaffaria; hospital officials confiscated their cameras. Two photographers, Zulfiqar of the daily *Jang* and Khurram of the daily *Assas* were locked in an emergency room while 200 medical interns attacked the

photographers and smashed their cameras. Those attacked included Abidi of *Al-Akhbar*; Raja Iftikhar and Afzal of the *Pakistan Observer*; Qaiser Shah of *Khabrain*; Majid Ali of *Business Times*; and Abdul Hameed of *Jang*.

The Pakistan Union of Journalists called for the suspension of the doctors involved in the incident. The police superintendent told the journalists that action would be taken against the doctors.

September 15
Zahid Qaimkhani ATTACKED
Zain Daudpota ATTACKED
Arbab Chandio ATTACKED
Haji Rahim Kunbhar ATTACKED
Ghulam Hassan Lander ATTACKED
Aslam Memon ATTACKED
Mehboon Gul Jagirani ATTACKED
Nasir Dad ATTACKED
Abbas Jalbani ATTACKED
Sudhir Jokhio ATTACKED
Zahir Mirani ATTACKED
Shakil Bachani ATTACKED
Altaf Khaskheli ATTACKED
Murtaza Kulhoro ATTACKED
Ismail Khoso ATTACKED
Mehdi Shah ATTACKED
Shakil Ujjan ATTACKED
Ghulam Hussain Fateh ATTACKED
Saleh Billo ATTACKED
Irshad Channa ATTACKED
Iqbal Mallah ATTACKED
Muhammed Ali ATTACKED
Rashid Rajar ATTACKED
Rehman Sammo ATTACKED
Iqbal Saif ATTACKED
Lakhano Siyal ATTACKED

A number of reporters were injured when police charged on a march of journalists and media workers who were protesting the growing number of attacks on newspaper offices in the Sindh Province, including the dailies *Sindh*, *Kawish*, and *Awami Awaz*.

The Council of Sindhi Press, supported by

ASIA

259

the Pakistan Federal Union of Journalists, called together more than 300 journalists in a march toward the chief minister of Sindh's house to hand over a memorandum. Police blocked the procession, assaulted the participants, and snatched their placards and banners. When the journalists tried to proceed, the police charged on the group with their batons. Those injured in the assault included Zahid Qaimkhani, correspondent for *Sindh* and the PPI news agency in Kandiaro and Zain Daudpota, joint secretary of the Hyderabad Press Club.

Some participants managed to reach the house where Badar Channa, an information secretary of the ruling Pakistan Muslim League party, came to receive the memorandum. Press coordinator of the Council of Sindhi Press, Rashid Rajar, refused to hand over the memorandum to Channa because he wanted someone more responsible to handle the matter. He tore up the memorandum and the journalists dispersed.

The police assault against the journalists and media workers was ordered by the sub-divisional magistrate, the deputy superintendent of police, and the station head officer of the area, who were suspended by the Sindh government. An inquiry officer was appointed to conduct a judicial inquiry into the incident.

October 15
Sawal ATTACKED
Kawish ATTACKED
Sindh THREATENED

On October 15, an explosive device was thrown from a moving vehicle at the Hyderabad offices of the Sindhi-language daily *Sawal*, injuring three people, including two of the newspaper's staff members, who were taken to hospital. On the same day, a second explosion targeted the Sindhi-language daily *Kawish*. According to reports from Pakistan, a third Sindhi-language daily, *Sindh*, received a bomb threat by phone

from a man who identified himself as a member of the "Front Tiger."

These latest attacks follow the brutal beating, on August 3, of Shakeel Naich, a reporter for a fourth Sindhi-language daily, *Awami Awaz*. According to the Pakistan Press Foundation, the attack on Naich was carried out by Sindh National Front (SNF) party activists. Awami Awaz and Shakeel Naich may have been targeted by the SNF because of his critical reporting. In mid-July, Naich published an article critical of Mumtaz Bhutto, the head of the SNF.

In September, the SNF announced a boycott of six Sindhi newspapers, including those that have suffereed from recent attacks. In August, SNF party members disrupted the distribution of *Awami Awaz* in several cities, according to the the Pakistan Press Foundation. At that time, *Awami Awaz* newspaper vendors and distributors were threatened while copies of the paper were set on fire.

On September 4, armed assailants entered the Larkana bureau of Kawish around mid-night. The attackers stole computers, a scanner, a fax machine, telephones, and other items. This attack followed the newspaper's extensive coverage of the beating of Shakeel Naich.

In mid-September, a number of reporters were injured when police attacked a group of journalists marching under the banner of the Pakistan Federal Union of Journalists to protest the attacks on newspaper offices in the Sindh province. Those injured include Zahid Qiamkhani, correspondent for *Sindh* and Zain Daudpota, joint secretary of the Hyderabad Press Club. An inquiry officer was appointed to conduct a judicial inquiry into the incident; however, the findings of this investigation have not been made public as yet.

CPJ sent a letter to Prime Minister Muhammad Nawaz Sharif on October 17, stating that CPJ regards the harassment and intimidation of journalists as a violation of the right to "seek, receive, and impart information and ideas through any media and regardless of frontiers," guaranteed by Article 19 of the United Nations' Universal Declaration of Human Rights, of which Pakistan is a signatory. CPJ also mentioned Minister of Information and Media Development Mushahid Hussain Sayed's own words when he visited CPJ in New York on September 25: "We [the Pakistan Government] are strongly commited to the freedom of expression."

CPJ called on his government to launch a prompt and thorough investigation into the attacks on the *Sawal* and *Kawish* offices, with full public disclosure of the findings. CPJ urged the Prime Minister's government to recognize the rights of all journalists to work without fear of government repression.

October 28
Pakistan Television (PTV) ATTACKED

Members of the Jamaat-I-Islami political party ransacked the offices of Pakistan Television (PTV) in Muzaffarabad, Azad Kashmir, to protest the alleged inadequate coverage of their party by the state-run broadcaster. Approximately 40 party activists barged into the PTV office at about 1:30 p.m. and broke window panes, TV sets, tape recorders, furniture, and other items.

The intruders were upset with PTV for not giving coverage to their party chief, Abdur Rashid Turabi, while broadcasting an anti-India rally in Muzaffarabad. They were also angered by PTV's failure to cover a human chain linking different cities of Pakistan on October 24 to express solidarity with the people of Kashmir.

October 28
Lahore Press Club and journalists ATTACKED

Employees of the Lahore Press Club and journalists were beaten by members of the Pakistan Peoples Party (PPP). According to the club secretary, around 200 PPP activists forced their way into the building as the PPP president of Punjab province, Mr. Rao Sikandar

Iqbal, was addressing a press conference after a rally led by him was broken up by police who were wielding batons. One of the PPP activists held a journalist at gun-point while others started beating those inside the building's auditorium. Some PPP workers threw chairs at journalists who were trying to prevent them from entering the auditorium.

December 26
Irfanul Haq, *Lashkar* IMPRISONED
Iftikhar Adil, *Lashkar* IMPRISONED

On December 26, the Baluchistan High Court in Quetta sentenced subeditor Haq and printer/publisher Adil of the Lahore-based Urdu-language evening newspaper *Lashkar* to six months in prison for inaccurate reporting. Despite their written apologies, the two journalists were convicted after publishing an article on the alleged theft of court records. The journalists were also fined Rs. 5000 (US$109).

According to reports from Pakistan, Mohammad Azam Zakroon, a lawyer from Quetta, filed a complaint against the chief justice of the Baluchistan High Court, stating that files and records regarding the Pakistan supreme court's Quetta bench were allegedly stolen from the office of the sub-register of the supreme court. Munir Ahmed, a Quetta-based correspondent of *Lashkar*, reported the story, and the newspaper ran the article titled "Theft Case Against Chief Justice Baluchistan." Munir Ahmed was aquitted of all charges. Haq was released on January 27, 1998, pending appeal.

Papua New Guinea

Fears that Papua New Guinea's generally open media climate might evaporate eased after vigorous protests by press and civil

liberties groups led authorities in February to shelve a proposal for a pair of media licensing and regulation bills modeled on repressive laws in Singapore and Malaysia. The decision handed down by the Constitutional Review Commission said, "It cannot be stressed enough that independence of the media and the communication industry are paramount to ensuring that democratic processes are respected. Freedom of expression and freedom of the press must not be violated or suppressed in any manner or form. These constitutionally enshrined freedoms must be respected as essential elements of a free and democratic society."

It had been feared that the government of then-prime minister Julius Chan would use the proposed bills to shackle the press and help guarantee his reelection. Instead, Chan found himself out of a job after his government was found to have contracted with British mercenaries to aid the army in battling an insurgency on the island of Bouganville.

Journalists had been routinely barred from traveling independently to Bouganville since the strife began in 1988. In February, Defense Minister Mathias Ijape ordered Papua New Guinea security forces to apprehend two foreign journalists, Andrew Marshall, a British citizen on assignment for *Esquire* magazine, and Wayne-Cole Johannes, a free-lance Australian television producer, who had entered Bouganville illegally, and fly them to the capital, Port Moresby, for prosecution, but the reporters escaped.

Following Chan's ouster, Bill Skate took office as prime minister in July and is seeking a negotiated settlement with rebels in a conflict that has claimed some 20,000 lives. As authorities anticipate a negotiated conclusion to the conflict, Bouganville has been reopened to journalists, dispelling some of the mystery surrounding conditions on the island that prevailed during the war.

Philippines

The Philippine press remains among the freest in Asia. Indeed, Manila's 25 often-raucous daily newspapers will print almost anything, including personal attacks on the most powerful figures in the country. Wary of any encroachment on democratic institutions, the press was largely responsible, according to many observers, for the success of a huge public campaign to dissuade President Fidel V. Ramos from pushing through constitutional changes that could have allowed him to seek a second six-year term in 1998. A massive pro-democracy rally in September, led by former president Corazon Aquino, brought an estimated 500,000 people into the streets and quickly put an end to talk that Ramos might not step down.

In rural areas, however, journalists must often negotiate a fine line between military authorities, rebel groups, and powerful business interests. Since democracy was restored in 1986, 31 journalists have been killed in the line of duty in the Philippines, many of them covering local crime or rural insurgencies. The vast majority of such crimes remain unsolved.

While the country has weathered Southeast Asia's economic woes with more aplomb than most of its neighbors, urban crime, much of it drug-related, continues to stir public outcry. Danny Hernandez, a well-known columnist and crime reporter for the tabloid *People's Tonight*, was found in the back of an abandoned taxi with a bullet in the back of his head in June. Hernandez was reportedly working on an investigation linking drug dealers with the police and a well-known Manila politician.

June 3
Danny Hernandez, *People's Journal* KILLED

Hernandez, news editor of the Manila-based daily *People's Journal* and author of the column "Sunday Punch," was found dead in a stolen taxi in Quezon City, a suburb of Manila. His body was found with a bullet in the back of the neck. The taxi, which had been stolen the night before, picked up Hernandez as he left his office at *People's Journal* on Tuesday morning. Colleagues and family said Hernandez had received several death threats in the preceding months by telephone callers angry at his column, which exposed criminal activity and police corruption. At the time of his death, he was writing stories exposing illegal drug and gambling syndicates.

Police arrested three suspects the day after the shooting, and Hernandez's death was subesquently attributed to drug dealers.

The government of President Fidel Ramos has launched a well-publicized investigation into drug-dealing in Manila as a result of public outcry over Hernandez's killing.

Samoa

Samoa's largest daily newspaper rocked the government in April when it uncovered a scandal involving the alleged illegal sale of Samoan passports in Hong Kong. The ensuing political crisis, which has lasted for months, led to public demonstrations against the government and so angered Prime Minister Tofilau Eti Alesana that he called for regulations to license and control the press. Prime Minister Tofilau brought criminal defamation proceedings against Samoa's only independent daily newspaper, the *Samoa Observer* in October. Tofilau then threatened to back legislation allowing the government to close newspapers "for stirring up trouble." The paper, viewed by

most observers as pro-opposition, is no stranger to controversy. Its publisher, Savea Malifa, and Samoan-language editor, Fuimaono Fereti Tupua, face a stack of lawsuits dating back for several years, brought by government officials and business leaders. In 1994, the paper's editorial offices, printing plant, and press were burned down in what many believe was retaliation for the newspaper's reporting on allegations of government corruption. Many earlier suits against the paper have been thrown out by the courts, and the current defamation suit is awaiting appeal on constitutional grounds before it can be heard on its merits.

State-run radio and television deny air time to opposition leaders. In November, a government minister revealed that official discussions were underway aimed at shutting down Radio Polynesia, the country's only independent news radio station. Radio Polynesia carries interviews with opposition party members and anti-government protesters who are banned from the government-controlled radio and television. In May, Liauta Lesifataia, the head of the official Televisi Samoa, confirmed that the station will not allow appearances by opposition politicians.

June 18
Savea Sano Malifa, *Samoa Observer* LEGAL ACTION

Malifa, publisher of the *Samoa Observer*, and Tupua, editor of the paper's Samoan-language section, were accused of defamatory libel after the paper published a letter on June 6 that allegedly exposed Prime Minister Tofilau Eti Alesana's political and personal reputation to ridicule and contempt.

In addition to the libel case, the prime minister was pursuing a separate US$200,000 civil defamation suit against the *Samoa Observer* for its coverage of his family's business activities.

ASIA

The prime minister also threatened in parliament on June 20 to seek legislation to revoke the *Samoa Observer*'s business license.

CPJ wrote a letter on June 24 to the prime minister protesting the use of libel statutes by government officials to shield themselves from critical public scrutiny. CPJ condemned media licensing, which contravenes democratic principles of freedom of expression and information, calling upon the prime minister to drop all charges and legislative actions against the *Samoa Observer*.

On July 18, Seupepe Fuimaono P. Te'o, private secretary to the prime minister, sent a letter to CPJ saying that the libel suits against the *Samoa Observer* would be decided by the courts.

On September 11, a court ordered Malifa and Tupua to pay the prime minister WS500 (US$193) each in court costs.

Singapore

Strict censorship and a tame press continue to characterize the press freedom climate in the city-state, which in October promulgated regulations designed to keep a range of prohibited information from reaching its citizens by the Internet. Using the threat of costly lawsuits, harsh national security legislation, and decades of indoctrination, Singapore's ruling People's Action Party, which has been in power since independence in 1959, has fashioned a predictably bland media culture.

Singapore Press Holdings Ltd., a private corporation with close ties to the government, controls all general-circulation newspapers. The government-linked Singapore International Media PTE Ltd. has a virtual monopoly on broadcasting. Satellite dishes are banned with few exceptions. The government has successfully prosecuted numerous domestic and foreign journalists in the past, and as a result of previous run-ins with the government, many foreign publications have their circulation strictly controlled by the government. Such is the case with *The Asian Wall Street Journal*, the *Far Eastern Economic Review*, and *Asia Week*, the three leading regional news publications.

The new Internet regulations allow unhindered access for commercial users while preventing private users from having access to a wide range of sites. The Singapore Broadcasting Authority (SBA) requires Internet service providers to block sites the government identifies as taboo because of their political or sexual content. The SBA also requires political and religious societies to register their Singapore-based websites. Singapore's government has set a goal of becoming a regional center for both on-line commerce and Internet-control technology. The government considers its Internet controls to be a success and an example to other nations in the region, but the tightly regulated environment for the press at all levels in Singapore is anathema to the promise of unhindered information flow promised by the Internet.

South Korea

The election of long-time human rights campaigner and former political prisoner Kim Dae Jung as president in December should bode well for the continued protection of South Korea's press, which already enjoys considerable freedom. Kim—an outspoken advocate of free expression who was once under sentence of death by a previous military government—seems fully committed to broadening the democracy South Korea has developed since military rule ended in 1987. Shortly after his election, Kim blamed much of the Asian economic crisis on authoritarian governments that "lie" to their people. "Many of the leaders of Asian society have been saying that military dictatorship was the way and democracy was not good for their nations," Kim said in an interview with *The Washington Post.* "I believe that the fundamental cause of the financial crisis, including here in Korea, is because of placing economic development ahead of democracy."

Yet traces of South Korea's authoritarian past are evident. On December 19, just one day after the presidential election, American radio reporter Richard Choi was arrested on criminal defamation charges stemming from a report he filed from Seoul that was broadcast only in the United States. Ironically, it was the *Korea Times/Hankook Ilbo* that pressured prosecutors to jail the reporter. Choi had reported on rumored financial problems at the company. CPJ campaigned vigorously for Choi's release.

Observers in Korea fear that Choi's prosecution, under an old law prohibiting rumor-mongering against corporations, may foreshadow a tougher climate for the media in the face of the worst economic crisis to hit the country in a generation.

Because a formal state of war still exists between North and South Korea, a tough national security law which punishes those who "praise" or "benefit" the north remains on the books and is a potential threat to journalists.

December 19
Richard Choi, Radio Korea IMPRISONED

Choi, 49, a veteran reporter and the vice president of Radio Korea, a Korean-language radio station in Los Angeles, was arrested at the Koreana Hotel in Seoul and charged with criminal slander and defamation on the basis of a story he broadcast from Seoul to Los Angeles. The brief report, which aired exclusively on December 15 on Radio Korea in Los Angeles (KBLA AM-1580), concerned the current economic difficulties of the Korea

Times/Han Kook Il Bo publishing company and its rumored merger with the Hyundai Corporation. The report was not broadcast in South Korea.

According to Jang Hee Lee, the owner of Radio Korea, the report angered the owners of the *Korea Times,* which brought the defamation suit against Choi that led to his arrest. Choi is being detained in the Seoul Jail.

On December 29, CPJ sent a letter of inquiry to the Korean government expressing concern over the incident.

On January 7, 1998, the South Korean government released Choi on his own recognizance, pending trial on January 21, 1998.

Sri Lanka

When President Chandrika Kumaratunga and her People's Alliance (PA) party won power in November 1994, the new administration promised far-reaching reforms to reverse 17 years of United National Party (UNP) aggression against press freedom and civil liberties. After three years in office, however, the PA government earns at best a mixed report card on civil liberties, with some heartening improvements in 1997.

With the bitter civil war between the separatist Liberation Tigers of Tamil Eelam (LTTE) and the Sinhalese majority in its 14th year, the government has tended to restrict press coverage of the conflict through a variety of means, including direct censorship and control of information entering the country. Since the harsh censorship strictures of 1995, local and international activists have pressured the government to relax hard-line restrictions. In the last year, most forms of direct censorship have been lifted. Meanwhile, criminal defamation laws are still used to silence dissent against the governing regime and its policies, while shielding public officials from scrutiny by the media.

ASIA

War correspondents struggled to file independent reports, as they have since 1995 when the Defense Ministry introduced regulations preventing the press from independently visiting specified war zones mostly in northern and eastern provinces.

Local journalists allied with the Free Media Movement in Sri Lanka routinely demonstrated against state-directed and state-tolerated hostility toward the independent media and demanded greater press freedom in Sri Lanka. In May, a landmark Supreme Court ruling declared a controversial Broadcasting Authority Bill unconstitutional. The measure would have given political authorities unrestricted control over the broadcast media. Journalists anticipated an improved media culture as a result of the ruling.

In developments to safeguard the press, in November, three policemen faced charges for the 1990 murder of Richard de Zoysa, an editor and Colombo correspondent for the Rome-based InterPress Service. Though the previous UNP regime denied police involvement in the killing, the PA government reopened the case and has been pursuing investigations since coming to power.

The Sri Lankan press was guardedly optimistic, following President Kumaratunga's appointment of Mangala Samaraweera as Minister of Posts, Telecommunications, and Media in June. Known as a left-of-center liberal, Samaraweera has promised more freedom to the media and, as a gesture of goodwill, approved 13 new radio and television station licenses in mid-June. Among new measures Samaraweera announced are the closure of the state-controlled news agency, Lankapuvath, and the adoption of a code of conduct for journalists in the state-owned media institutions. In addition, after years of censorship, the government asked local television stations not to censor news about Sri Lanka from foreign news broadcasts carried locally.

Samaraweera also promoted the repeal of the infamous Parliamentary Privileges Special Provisions Act of 1978, which empowered the parliament to fine and imprison journalists who allegedly insulted a member of parliament or the procedures of the House. In a related development, parliament appointed a select committee to recommend changes to the laws governing the media, including the repeal or amendment of legislation which poses limitations on freedom of expression. The government has resisted changes in harsh criminal defamation statutes, however, and journalists remain wary of policies which could threaten press freedom.

January 1
Independent Television Network (ITN)
ATTACKED

A camera crew from the state-owned Independent Television Network (ITN) was assaulted by the bodyguards of Reggie Ranatunga, a deputy minister in the government. The journalists were at the scene of a motor accident in the town of Miriswatte, in Gampaha district, when Ranatunga, who was driving in the direction of the scene of the accident, pulled over. His bodyguards then got out of the vehicle and assaulted the ITN crew. The bodyguards stopped when they realized that the crew was from a government station and not, as they had thought, the opposition-allied, privately owned radio and television station Telshan Network Limited (TNL).

Previously, on December 31, 1996, TNL news director Ishini Wickremasinghe Perera was arrested after being summoned to the government's criminal investigation department headquarters in regard to an allegedly incorrect news item broadcast by TNL. Authorities charged her under the Prevention of Terrorism Act in connection with an alleged error in a news broadcast regarding a military operation. The government accused her of inciting racial tension and endangering national security.

July 7
Sinha Ratnatunga, *Sunday Times* LEGAL ACTION

On July 1, Colombo High Court Judge Upali Gunawardena convicted Sinha Ratnatunga, editor of the English-language weekly *Sunday Times,* on charges of criminal defamation brought against him under the penal code and the Press Council Law.

Ratnatunga was indicted for a gossip column item published in the *Times* of February 19, 1995, which spoke about President Chandrika Kumaratunga attending Parliament Deputy Asitha Perera's late-night birthday party at a five-star hotel. The story prompted complaints from the president to the police that the article (which the paper later admitted was incorrect) was defamatory.

A 12-month term was imposed under the penal code and a six-month term was warranted under the Press Council Law provisions. Both sentences were suspended for seven years.

Ratnatunga's suspended jail term discourages him from investigative journalism, because he would have to serve the sentence if he is convicted for another offense within the seven-year period.

Although the recently appointed media minister, Mangala Samaraweera, has promised to promote a democratic and liberal media culture in Sri Lanka, editors of three other newspapers are facing criminal defamation action after criticizing the president.

CPJ sent a letter on July 8 to President Kumaratunga condemning the use of criminal libel statutes and urging the president to use her influence in reversing the indictments against Sinha Ratnatunga. CPJ also appealed to her office to push for the repeal of the existing law on criminal defamation, as the civil law in Sri Lanka is sufficient in the event of any person being allegedly defamed through the media.

July 24
Iqbal Athas, *Sunday Times* (Colombo) HARASSED

Athas, one of Sri Lanka's leading military reporters, is best known for "Situation Report," a weekly column on defense and security issues in Colombo's *Sunday Times.* In early July a group of men conspicuously stationed themselves opposite his home, observing the entrance and upper floors. On July 15, five men walked up to his gate and noted the registration number of a visitor's car. They followed Athas' office assistant and household staff. When neighbors questioned the activity, the men said they were police officers investigating terrorist activity at the Athas residence.

These activities followed Athas' reports on financial irregularities in military and defense operations. "This time it appears that I have disturbed a hornet's nest of corrupt politicians and officials," Athas told CPJ.

Athas wrote to President Chandrika Kumaratunga on July 16, and was subsequently notified by the Minister of Posts, Telecommunications and Media, Mangala Samaraweera, that the surveillance had not been ordered by government security agencies. Samaraweera suggested that Athas make a complaint to the local police station. CPJ wrote a letter to the president on July 24, urging her to conduct a thorough investigation beyond the capacities of the local police and to take appropriate action against those responsible for harrassing or threatening Athas.

An official campaign to discredit Athas began in late November, when several state-run media outlets gave extensive coverage to the story of Selvadurai Senthinathan, a Tamil from the Jaffna Peninsula who surrendered to government security forces and confessed that he had worked as a translator for the separatist Liberation Tigers of Tamil Eelam (LTTE). In a widely publicized videotaped interview with an off-camera interrogator, Senthinathan claimed that he translated several Colombo-based English newspapers into Tamil, and specifically mentioned

ASIA

Athas and "Situation Report." Senthinathan's statement received saturation coverage in Sri Lanka, and was widely interpreted as an attempt to brand Athas and the *Sunday Times* as "anti-national" collaborators who provide useful information to the LTTE. Athas says this is part of a campaign to discredit and forestall criticism of defense and security issues.

Two weeks before Senthinathan's interview was released, Athas had been warned by his sources that a Tamil Tiger who had surrendered to the Air Force was being coached to say that his reports were of assistance to the LTTE.

Sentinathan's alleged confession followed the October 26 "Situation Report," in which Athas reproduced the findings of a presidential committee investigating the crashes of 16 Sri Lanka Air Force planes between April 1995 and May 1997. The committee found evidence of corruption and irregularities in the Air Force; but the government, while embarrassed, appears to have taken no action in response.

CPJ sent a letter to President Kumaratunga on December 4, urging her to take the lead in safeguarding Athas' right to operate as a journalist in an atmosphere free of harassment or intimidation, and asking her to intervene to stop any further attempts to silence Athas.

October 15
Niresh Eliathamby, Associated Press HARASSED

Niresh Eliathamby, a well-known journalist who works for the Associated Press (AP) in Colombo, was held at gunpoint for more than two hours by security personnel following a bomb explosion in Colombo.

Eliathamby was walking in the Colombo Fort area on his way to deliver some rolls of film to his office. He was questioned by two members of the Sri Lanka Navy, who said he had no right to have film with him or take photographs in that area without the written permission of the Secretary of Defense. This requirement had never before been announced by the government, the police, or the security forces.

Eliathamby was taken from Colombo to the Sri Lanka Navy base at Rangalla, several miles away, where he was held at gunpoint and interrogated. His press accreditation card, issued by the government's Director of Information, was ignored. The interrogators also refused to take notice of his National Identity Card, and would not allow him to contact either his office, the Director of Information, the media spokesman of the military, or his colleagues at the AP to verify his identity.

Eliathamby was about to be blindfolded when an officer passing by noticed him. The officer called a senior officer who verified Eliathamby's identity and ordered his release.

Other journalists had taken photographs of the scene of the explosion without incident. It is believed that Eliathamby was questioned and harassed because he belongs to the Tamil community.

Arthur Max, AP's bureau chief in New Delhi, protested Eliathamby's mistreatment.

November 29
S. Surendran, *Virakesari* HARASSED
Sri Gajan, *Virakesari* HARASSED
M. Dunstan, *Virakesari* HARASSED

Reporters Sri Gajan and M. Dunstan and photographer S. Surendran of the Tamil-language daily newspaper *Virakesari*, were harassed and threatened by police officers. The journalists were reportedly covering the transfer of detainees from the Weilikada Prison in Colombo to another detention center in Kalutara. Police officers objected to photographing the detainees, who were being brought to vehicles in order to be transferred, though this took place outside the prison premises in full view of the public. The police threatened the journalists, who had spoken to some of the detainees' family members present at the time. One officer forcibly took the camera from Surendran, removed the film, and exposed it.

November 30,
Sudha Ramachandran, *Deccan Herald*
HARASSED

Sri Lankan police raided the hotel room of Ramachandran, an Indian journalist with the *Deccan Herald* of India, and questioned her for more than an hour about her travels to the Jaffna Peninsula, where the Liberation Tigers of Tamil Eelam (LTTE) are active. Police, who said they were investigating whether Ramachandran had any rebel links, searched her room at Colombo's Taj Hotel. They confiscated and later returned photographs she had taken during her assigment to the peninsula.

As a foreign journalist, Ramachandran had been duly accredited by the Deparment of Information and the Foreign Ministry, and had obtained clearance from the Ministry of Defense to travel to the northeast region, which is under military control, in order to carry out her work there. Journalists traveling to the Jaffna Peninsula must be cleared by the Defense Ministry.

In the past two years, two other Indian journalists have also been similarly searched and interrogated at the Taj Hotel in Colombo during reporting assignments in Sri Lanka.

Taiwan

A dramatic criminal libel suit pitting Taiwan's nascent free press tradition against the once-unchallenged power of the ruling Kuomintang (KMT) ended in acquittal in April. The closely watched case was filed by Liu Tai-ying, the influential business manager of the Kuomintang (KMT), against U.S. reporter Ying Chan and Taiwanese reporter Shieh Chung-liang of the Hong Kong-based weekly magazine *Yazhou Zhoukan* (Asia Week) after an article by the two journalists alleged that Liu had offered $15 million to U.S. President Bill Clinton's re-election campaign fund. CPJ joined an

amicus brief on behalf of the journalists in April, and in October awarded Shieh and Chan a 1997 International Press Freedom Award. Although Liu has appealed the acquittal, the initial verdict was widely hailed as a triumph for the Taiwanese press.

Taiwan's broad criminal libel laws, a legacy of the decades of martial rule that ended in 1987, are frequently used by powerful forces in the government, the KMT, and corporations attempting to curb an otherwise free press. As a result, editors and publishers face the constant threat of costly lawsuits, which may carry criminal sanctions. In August, the government's top intelligence agency filed criminal libel charges against the *Independence Morning Post* newspaper after an article in the paper accused intelligence director Yin Tsung-wen of ordering the phone-tapping of National Assembly deputies. Against the objections of some staff members, the newspaper publicly apologized in order to avoid a court fight.

The government places few direct roadblocks in the way of a lively national press, however, and Taiwan's generally good record on press freedom stands in direct contrast to China, which hopes one day to convince Taiwan to rejoin the mainland under the "One Country, Two Systems" formula being used in Hong Kong. Relations with the mainland could be further complicated due to the overwhelming defeat of the KMT in municipal elections in November by an opposition party that advocates independence from China.

May 20
Ying Chan, *The Daily News* LEGAL ACTION
Hsieh Chung-liang, *Yazhou Zhoukan*
LEGAL ACTION

Liu-Tai-ying, director of the Business Management Committee of Taiwan's ruling Kuomintang, appealed the April 22 ruling that acquitted reporters Ying Chan and Shieh

Chung-liang of criminal libel charges. For the appeal, one member of the three-judge panel was to conduct a full evidentiary hearing much like the first proceeding. The findings of that hearing would then be argued by both sides before the full court.

On October 23, CPJ presented a 1997 International Press Freedom Award to Ying Chan and Shieh Chung-liang for their independent news coverage and viewpoints in the face of arrest and imprisonment.

Liu Tai-ying filed a criminal libel suit against Chan, an American journalist who writes for the *Daily News* of New York, and Shieh, senior editor of the Hong Kong-based *Yazhou Zhoukan*. The suit stemmed from an article the two journalists had written which appeared in the October 25 edition of *Yazhou Zhoukan*. The article said that Liu had offered to donate US$15 million to the Democratic National Committee for U.S. President Bill Clinton's re-election campaign, during an August 1995 meeting with former White House staffer Mark Middleton.

If convicted, Chan and Shieh face up to two years in jail. Liu's decision to sue the reporters was defended by senior members of the Kuomintang. CPJ sent a letter to President Lee Teng-hui condemning the use of seditious libel suits and calling on the government to openly dissociate itself from Liu's suit. CPJ also urged the president to ensure that no government or Kuomintang resources were used in the suit.

A court hearing was held in Taipei on April 15, in which an amicus brief filed by CPJ and 10 other U.S. media organizations in support of the defendants was filed.

A few days later, on April 22, a judge found Chan and Shieh innocent of the criminal libel charges. Judge Li Wei-shin of the 16th Criminal Tribunal in Taipei ruled that Chan and Hsieh had met the requirements of good intent under Taiwanese libel laws. The judge indicated that the *Yazhow Zhoukan* article was a matter of public interest, that the reporters based their report on their investigation and

believed the truth of the story, and that no malicious intent to damage Liu's reputation was intended. The judge also dismissed a civil suit Liu filed asking for US$15 million in damages.

August 12
Independence Morning Post LEGAL ACTION

Taiwan's top intelligence agency is bringing a criminal libel case against the daily *Independence Morning Post*. In the first libel case ever brought by the National Security Bureau against a news organization, the newspaper's top editor and publisher face so-far unspecified jail time. A preliminary hearing in the case was scheduled for August 15.

In a story published on July 22, the newspaper accused Intelligence Director Yin Tsung-wen of ordering the phone-tapping of National Assembly deputies opposed to a series of constitutional amendments to trim the provincial government of Taiwan and expand presidential power. With China claiming that Taiwan is a renegade province, the move to sharply reduce provincial government has been interpreted as a possible step toward formal independence from China. President Lee Teng-hui's government claims the amendments, which passed on July 19, are aimed at trimming bureaucracy.

According to the newspaper, Yin passed on the phone-tapping order at a secret meeting of police and other intelligence agencies on June 28. Yin denied the allegation in the first press conference ever conducted by the head of the secretive agency and demanded that the newspaper print a retraction, which it failed to do. The newspaper's editor in chief, Liu Chung-tse, has said that a number of army generals were the source for the story. "We have the hard proof," Chow Mei-li, a political reporter for the paper, told CPJ, "but we will never reveal our sources."

CPJ sent a letter on August 12 to President Lee Teng-hui condemning the use of criminal libel suits when there are adequate remedies available to aggrieved parties in civil proceedings. CPJ argued that journalists should never be jailed for their writing, and urged President Lee Teng-hui's government to openly dissociate itself from the National Security Bureau's libel suit and ensure that neither Taiwanese government nor Kuomintang resources be used to further the suit.

On September 7, the *Independence Morning Post* published a retraction apologizing for the distress for the National Security Bureau and Director-General Yin caused by the paper's July 22 report. On September 10, General Yin withdrew the libel suit against the newspaper. Yu Yuh-chao, Director of the Information Division of the Taipei Economic and Cultural Office in New York, sent a letter to CPJ on September 22, expressing his opinion that "this outcome reflects the open media environment that has matured in Taiwan."

Thailand

Despite a severe, potentially destabilizing economic crisis and efforts by some in government to rein in the press, Thailand maintained an official commitment to free expression, even deepening constitutional protections for the media. The new Thai constitution signed by King Bhumibol Adulyadej in October contains the most sweeping free press provisions in Asia. The new charter, which has been praised by civil libertarians and human rights advocates worldwide, makes it unconstitutional for the government to censor, ban, license, or restrict print or broadcast media, except by specific legislation in times of crisis. "They cannot ban media, there will be no press licensing," said Kavi Chongkittavorn, the editor of Bangkok's *Nation* newspaper. "The constitution is a very positive development."

In June, Thai media were outraged when the government of then-Prime Minister

Chavalit Yongchaiyudh responded to growing press criticism of the government's economic policies by attempting to track and intimidate the press with an official media monitoring center operated by the Interior Ministry. As the economic crisis worsened in August, and Thailand's once-vibrant economy was shattered, Chavalit lashed out at his critics in the private media and called on government broadcast outlets to put a positive spin on economic news, again generating protests from Thai journalists.

Neither the monitoring center, nor official bluster muted the press; instead, newspapers responded with banner headlines calling on Chavalit to step down. On October 21, the beleaguered prime minister, who had been in office just over a year, reacted to a wave of demonstrations by calling on the military to impose a state of emergency that would have included harsh media censorship and a strict curfew. Reversing a past tradition of often-disastrous armed intervention in Thai affairs, the military refused to go along with the draconian measures. On November 6, Chavalit resigned.

A new prime minister, Chuan Leekpai, leader of the Democratic Party, took office on November 9 with the backing of an eight-party coalition. Thai journalists and the business community praised the appointment of Chuan, who brings a clean reputation to the job, as a sign that the country will attempt to restore its economic luster through constitutional means and sound management.

With the new constitution in place and civilian government assured, the greatest peril to the press, according to some analysts, is economic. The *Nation*'s Chongkittavorn, said, "The government is not a threat. The threat is the economy, and we don't know how bad it will get." He noted that at least 2,000 journalists had lost their jobs through layoffs since the crisis began and there was no end in sight.

ASIA

June 11
All media CENSORED

The News Analysis Center, known in Bangkok as the media monitoring committee, was set up by Interior Minister Sanoh Thienthong and opened on June 11. The action came amid government apprehension of critical economic reporting in Thailand as the stock market reached new lows and negative growth rates were predicted for the first time in 30 years. The center, which houses banks of television and radio monitors and computers, was created to analyze news reports for the prime minister's office to "guarantee accurate reporting."

While Interior Ministry officials were quoted as saying that the News Analysis Center was neither intended to restrict press freedom nor close newspapers or media outlets, the government said the center could urge legal action against reporters and others who were found to be spreading false information.

The Reporters Association of Thailand expressed its concern over the News Analysis Center, calling on the government "not to try and limit the press's freedom by using [this or] any other similar method."

CPJ sent a letter to Prime Minister Chavalit Yongchaiyudh on June 13, warning that it would be closely watching the center for any sign that it was coercing or intimidating journalists.

Tonga

The tiny press community in Tonga is at the center of a struggle in a country whose proud monarchical tradition is often at odds with more democratic voices. Tonga's constitutional monarch, King Taufa'ahau Tupou IV, has the power to appoint the cabinet and prime minister, while half the single-chamber Legislative Assembly is appointed by the island's nobles and the other half is elected by universal suffrage. In this system, dissent has

frequently been unwelcome.

The Tongan government has repeatedly tried to intimidate and restrict the *Times of Tonga*, whose editor in chief, Kalafi Moala, was denied reentry to the country in January on the pretext that he holds dual citizenship. As a result, he is exiled in New Zealand. The paper's business license was held up by Tongan authorities and appeared headed for revocation in February before authorities bowed to international pressure and renewed the permit. Tonga's pro-democracy movement holds six of nine elected seats in the parliament and has proposed a more democratic constitution for the country, but change has been slow. Crown Prince Tupouto'a issued a warning to democracy campaigners in August, telling parliament that those MPs who want democracy would suffer reprisals.

June 23
Filokalafi 'Akau'ola, *Times of Tonga*
HARASSED, LEGAL ACTION

'Akau'ola, deputy editor of the independent weekly *Times of Tonga*, was taken into custody and interrogated by police in Nuku'alofa. He was released the following morning, and has since been charged with sedition.

'Akau'ola had published a letter from a Tongan reader who questioned government claims that Tonga's political system is the best in the world and pointed to Tonga's heavy reliance on foreign aid as evidence of the government's failure. Speaking from New Zealand, the exiled editor of the paper, Kalafi Maola, told Agence France-Press that nothing in the letter was illegal.

Filokalafi 'Akau'ola told Agence France-Presse that police had executed a search warrant on the newspaper offices, looking for the original copy of the letter.

The arrest follows a pattern of government intimidation of 'Akau'ola and *Times of Tonga*. Last year, 'Akau'ola and Maola were jailed for 30 days after Tonga's Parliament convicted them of contempt. They were later released when an appeals court found the Parliament had acted unconstitutionally.

CPJ sent a letter to King Taufa'ahau Tupou IV calling for the immediate and unconditional withdrawal of the charges against Filokalafi 'Akau'ola.

Vietnam

For the Vietnamese press, which has suffered threats, arrests, and tightened regulations, the appointment in late December of a hard-line general to the top Communist Party post signaled even tougher times ahead. Gen. Le Kha Phieu, 66, succeeded economic reform advocate Do Muoi, 80, as general secretary of the party. An advocate of unyielding party control, Gen. Phieu has warned against Western cultural influences in the country as a result of economic liberalization policies put in place in recent years. His appointment was widely seen as heralding a tightening of controls on free expression, especially independent press investigations of official corruption.

A CPJ delegation that visited Vietnam in 1996 found many officials willing to engage in open dialogue about press freedom. Many journalists at the time were pushing the limits of free expression and investigative reporting in the context of state-controlled media. Unfortunately, the mood of relative openness CPJ found in 1996 has been replaced by an official hard-line response toward the nascent independent press.

In early December, the powerful Interior Ministry announced plans to open a new press wing to monitor and control media coverage. The *Quan Doi Nhan Dan* (People's Army) newspaper said the press center would ensure political correctness in news about security matters. Just four days

after the announcement, Huu Tho, head of the Central Committee of Ideology and Culture and the country's top propaganda official, warned news editors to exercise extreme caution in their use of foreign news reports, which he said were potentially dangerous. He was quoted in the *Cong An Nhan Dan* (People's Police) newspaper as telling an Interior Ministry conference, "We have opened the door to the outside world, but we should be alert." Also in December, the *Kinh Doanh Va Phap Luat* newspaper was investigated over unspecified "reporting problems" and journalists at the paper said the publication was under threat of closure for carrying stories "which could be used by outsiders to criticize the country." Officials stopped short of shutting down the paper, however, after issuing a warning shortly after the New Year began.

Journalists were directly threatened on October 8 when Nguyen Hoang Linh, the editor of the state-run business newspaper *Doang Nghiep* (Enterprise), was arrested and charged with revealing state secrets. The arrest and charge—linked to reports Linh wrote in his newspaper exploring questionable business practices by the General Customs Department of Vietnam in the purchase of coastal patrol boats—were widely seen as a warning to reporters who may write about official misconduct.

While anger over government corruption and mismanagement resulted in unprecedented unrest and political demonstrations in some 30 towns and villages in rural Vietnam throughout the year, the local press failed to report on the incidents. In March, the government reacted to reports of defaults and corrupt practices in several banks by imposing sweeping restrictions on coverage of banking and finance. The order compelled domestic news organizations to clear financial stories with censors at the Ministry of Culture's Press Department and gave the official State Bank of Vietnam the power to classify routine financial information as a state secret. In October, the government issued a decree barring domestic journalists from passing information or photographs to foreign journalists without state approval. Foreign news agencies were also banned from hiring local journalists. Instructions were issued to all domestic media in October demanding adherence to Communist Party policy and criticizing newspapers for reporting inaccuracies and revealing state secrets. The official Vietnam News Agency said the directive, issued at politburo level, stressed the media's role in forming healthy public opinion.

The government finally announced plans to allow full-time live access to the Internet from within the country but said that officials would create a fire wall to prevent access to banned information. While officials have not released a list of proscribed subjects, they intend to control access and, with the passage of sweeping Internet censorship laws, they now have that statutory prerogative.

February 13
Radio Free Asia CENSORED

The Vietnamese government announced its decision to jam broadcasts by U.S.-based Radio Free Asia in response to "an American plot of using Radio Free Asia to interfere in Vietnam's internal affairs."

Radio Free Asia, a new U.S. government-financed radio service that broadcasts to Vietnam, mainland China, Tibet, Cambodia, Laos, and Burma, offers information to areas where government censorship prohibits a free domestic news media.

March 1
Internet CENSORED

The government of Vietnam issued a new decree regulating on-line information, to take effect on March 17. Under the new guidelines, the government will manage domestic use of the Internet, supervise all Internet content, and control international links between Vietnamese users and the World Wide Web. In November, the government announced plans to allow "live" Internet access in the country for the first time, under the guidelines passed earlier.

September 2
Nguyen Manh Hung, *Vietnam Investment Review* HARASSED

The Vietnamese government barred Nguyen Manh Hung, news editor of the weekly newspaper *Vietnam Investment Review*, from traveling to the United States for the Dag Hammarskjold Award presented annually by the United Nations Correspondents Association to the world's most promising journalists. Hung was the first Vietnamese journalist to be awarded the fellowship.

According to Sanaa Yousef, the U.N. bureau chief of the Egyptian newspaper *Al Akhbar* and chairman of the fellowship fund, the Vietnamese government would not authorize Hung's trip because the award was not presented through government channels.

A journalist from Barbados has been invited to the United States in his place.

September 18
All Media THREATENED

The government issued a pamphlet on "regulations on cooperation with foreign [media] by the Vietnam press." The government wanted to strengthen control over foreign language radio and television broadcasts, the assignments abroad of Vietnamese journalists, the opening of Vietnamese press offices overseas, and the supply of Vietnamese information and photographs abroad.

On October 6, authorities in Vietnam published a new decree designed to limit contacts between local journalists and foreign correspondents. Vietnamese journalists have been prohibited from providing foreign reporters with information, photographs, and articles without government approval. Under the new rules, foreign news bureaus are not allowed to hire local journalists.

These new measures came shortly after the Vietnamese government barred Nguyen Manh Hung, news editor of the weekly newspaper *Vietnam Investment Review*, from traveling to the United States for the Dag Hammarskjold Award, which is presented annually by the United Nations Correspondents Association to the world's most promising journalists. Hung was the first Vietnamese journalist to be awarded the fellowship. Vietnam reportedly would not authorize Hung's trip because the award was not presented through government channels.

preted as a warning to reporters to stay away from stories about government corruption.

The arrest followed restrictions imposed earlier in the year concerning financial and banking information. President General Le Van Anh's government also barred Vietnamese journalists from giving information to their foreign counterparts without first obtaining state permission.

CPJ sent a letter on October 13 to the president, calling on his government to release Linh and ease restrictions on the press in Vietnam.

October 6
All media THREATENED, LEGAL ACTION, CENSORED

Authorities in Vietnam issued a decree tightening their grip on the media by limiting contacts between local journalists and foreign correspondents. Vietnamese journalists must now obtain the approval of authorities before providing foreign reporters with information, photographs, and articles. Under the new mandate, foreign news offices are not allowed to hire local journalists.

October 8
Nguyen Hoang Linh, *Doang Nghiep* LEGAL ACTION

Hoang Linh, editor of the state-run business newspaper *Doang Nghiep*, was arrested on charges of revealing state secrets. The charges were linked to reports he wrote that explored questionable practices by the General Customs Department of Vietnam in the purchase of coastal patrol boats.

Local journalists said the arrest was inter-

Press Freedom Under the Dragon:
Can Hong Kong's Media Still Breathe Fire?

by A. Lin Neumann

SPECIAL REPORT: Hong Kong

It did not take long for the Hong Kong Journalists Association to serve notice on Executive Secretary Tung Chee-hwa that it would be watching his office closely. On July 10, just days after the handover of Hong Kong to China by the British, the HKJA sent Tung a letter criticizing perceived "favorable treatment" given to official Chinese state news agencies in coverage of the handover.

The group complained that China Central Television was given special access to some of Tung's early official appearances. "If Chinese official media have privileges in reporting, then news and information will very likely be held in the hands of the official media, seriously threatening press freedom," said the letter, signed by HKJA's chair, Carol Lai.

It was the kind of outspoken approach that has become the hallmark of the HKJA. Now in its 30th year, with some 500 members, it is the largest press association in the territory and has lobbied consistently for the continuation of Hong Kong's free press under Chinese rule. The group says it will tolerate no backward movement in the battle for free expression. In their letter, the journalists urged Tung to "make efforts to preserve the existing media coverage system, which is based on fairness for all involved." In response, Tung's office called the incident a misunderstanding.

HKJA vice chairman Liu Kin-ming, a frequent and vocal critic of Beijing, said it is the association's responsibility to remain engaged with the new administration of Tung Chee-hwa and to fight any effort to curb the liberties enjoyed by Hong Kong's reporters and editors. He summed it up this way in an interview with CPJ: "To my colleagues, I ask them to please say no to the censors. To the publishers, I say, without your support we cannot win this battle. And to the outside world: Keep your eyes on Hong Kong."

What's at stake immediately in Hong Kong is the vibrancy not

A. Lin Neumann, Asia program coordinator for CPJ, has covered Asia for 15 years.

just of local media but of the vast network of regional and international press operations based in the territory. Hong Kong has long been East Asia's English-language news media capital and, more important, the principal safe haven for professional, independent Chinese-language reporting about the internal political and economic affairs of the People's Republic. Readers in the vast Chinese diaspora from Taiwan and Malaysia to British Columbia and California have depended on Hong Kong reporters and publications for decades. If this dynamic journalism culture disappears or is significantly eroded, it will have profound repercussions for all of Asia.

Equally important to the region's future is the inextricable relationship between the free flow of information and the strength of financial markets. Hong Kong's robust economy flourished in a climate of free expression that allowed for the rapid exchange of information necessary for the smooth functioning of the regional economy. Investors will still need Hong Kong's free press if they are to understand the dynamics of the changes that are underway in China and the rest of Asia. Without this continual supply of accurate, uncensored economic information, it is hard to imagine Hong Kong retaining its position as the region's premier financial marketplace.

Leaders of the international financial community have begun to articulate this concern. U.S. Treasury Secretary Robert Rubin raised the issue of press freedom during Tung's first official visit to Washington in September.

In a private session with Tung, Rubin linked freedom of information to Hong Kong's continued financial health. "I think Hong Kong can remain and will remain a major market center, a major financial market center, as long as Hong Kong continues to have the free flow of information [and] the rule of law," Rubin told CNN following the closed-door meeting. "I think that's something that we can all be hopeful about but also have to watch very closely."

Hong Kong's new leaders contend such concerns are misplaced. And on the surface, little seems to have changed. After the smoke of fireworks and celebration cleared, Hong Kong businesses resumed their usual frenetic pace, and reporters for the former colony's 16 major daily newspapers continued to file their stories as they had before the handover. Even the most critical dailies have continued to publish without overt reprisals. "The government is functioning as normal," Tung said in early September. "The financial market is moving. Demonstrations are continuing—arguments everywhere.... What has changed is that Hong Kong is now a part of China. There is a sense of pride here that this has happened, and happened without a hitch."

The resumption of Chinese sovereignty in Hong Kong has enormous geopolitical significance, signaling an end to the last vestiges of the British Empire and the emergence of China as an economic and political superpower. The people of Hong Kong have been anticipating this transition for many years, and few seasoned observers predicted dramatic upheaval in the immediate aftermath of the British withdrawal. China's leaders and supporters steadfastly maintained prior to the transition that no major changes would take place. "One Country, Two Systems," the phrase coined by the late Deng Xiaoping to describe the principle that would allow Hong Kong's quasi-democratic, free-market system to coexist with the motherland's one-party communist rule, was supposed to work this way. The Special Administration Region (SAR), as Beijing calls Hong Kong's territory, is meant to be making money, not trouble.

Beneath the calm, however, much has changed. Hong Kong today is a different place than it was before the turnover and a much different place than it was before the reality of the return began to sink in during the last several years. The climate of free expression in Hong Kong has shifted in subtle but distinct ways: In the vibrant Hong Kong press, self-censorship has become a fact of life. Newspapers owned by powerful business leaders with wide-ranging economic interests in China have become less willing to criticize Beijing.

Given China's history of tolerating little, if any, critical reporting or commentary in its national press, Hong Kong journalists have been left to wonder what might really be in store for them. "We don't know the Chinese bottom line yet," said one veteran reporter as she discussed the handover with colleagues inside the cavernous Hong Kong Convention Center press room two days after the fact. "I think Hong Kong journalists will be learning the Chinese bottom line."

Reporter Mak Yin Ting, sitting at the same table, quickly shot back, "Sure, we have to search for a bottom line. But why should there be a bottom line? That is an infringement on freedom. Why is it you can advocate Chinese patriotism but you cannot advocate other ideas?"

What about you, a visitor asked the first journalist, will you challenge the Chinese government's press freedom bottom line once you find it?

"Unfortunately, there is a point beyond which I cannot go and I will not go. Because I do not want to be locked up," she replied.

Tung's Friends

It should come as no surprise that Tung Chee-hwa, a shipping magnate with a history of close ties to Beijing, is more interested in preserving Hong Kong's economic vibrancy than its freewheeling journalism. But Tung's open admiration for Singapore's autocratic leader Lee Kwan Yew may signal more than just disinterest in free expression, presaging harsh treatment of independent journalists. Lee, the architect of Singapore's rise to prosperity through stern governance and laissez-faire economics, is the principal proponent of the view that a free press is incompatible with "Asian values." Lee has been openly critical of Hong Kong's democrats. China is too powerful to be influenced by their calls for democracy, Lee told the Singapore newspaper *Straits Times* in June. "If you don't believe that the Hong Kong people understand that, then you don't understand Hong Kong," he said. "Let's not waste time talking about democracy...If I were a Hongkonger I would think twice before interfering in the political affairs of the mainland."

Under Lee, Singapore offers little space for democracy to flourish, and the notion of modeling Hong Kong on Singapore raises reporters' worst fears. In May 1997, for example, a government critic was ordered to pay senior officials a $5.7 million libel judgment for defaming them. The critic, Tang Liang Hong, called Singapore leaders liars because they had attacked him as an ethnic Chinese chauvinist. Over the years, Singapore has been the bane of journalists. Two Hong Kong-based regional publications, the *Far Eastern Economic Review* and *The Asian Wall Street Journal* have been periodically banned, and their reporters have been sued or barred from the country in disputes with Singaporean officials. In

Singapore, journalists may even be prosecuted not simply for critiques of government leaders, but for the publication of mundane, accurate trade statistics prior to their authorized release by the government.

Tung agrees with Singapore's Lee on the issue of the cultural relativism of rights, supporting Lee's view that Asian countries put a higher value on group harmony and discipline than on the individualism prized in Western cultures. "Human rights is not a monopoly of the West," Tung told reporters in August. "When you talk about this, you have to look in terms of different countries, different historical processes, different stages of development." When asked by reporters for his reaction to Malaysian Prime Minister Mahathir Mohamad's call for a revision of U.N. covenants on human rights to reflect Asian values, Tung said, "I'm sympathetic to this argument. I really am."

Will Tung lead Hong Kong to become a constrained city-state like Singapore, with a tame and timid press? In the rush to please both big business and Beijing, will Hong Kong come to resemble capitalist autocracies like Indonesia and Malaysia, where civil liberties often fall victim to the leaders' whims?

Already, the Beijing-appointed provisional legislature, which supplanted the elected legislature on July 1, has quietly begun to rubber-stamp important pieces of legislation in advance of legislative elections scheduled for May 1998. Hong Kong residency rights have been amended to deny residency to mainland-born children of Hong Kong Chinese residents. This ostensible technicality has great significance in Hong Kong, where mainland-born children of parents with legal Hong Kong residency have long had the right to live in the territory. In a move supported by some business leaders, the appointed legislature also suspended a number of labor laws, passed before Britain returned the colony to China, which gave workers the right to collective bargaining, protected labor activists, and allowed unions to contribute to political campaigns.

A new law governing legislative elections will dramatically limit the extent of popular electoral participation and roll back the near-universal suffrage enacted at the end of British rule. The new proposal allows only 20 of the legislative council's 60 members to be popularly elected. Ten would be named by a Beijing-appointed electoral college. Another 30 would be picked by "functional constituencies," made up of corporate leaders, bankers, and professional groups. The changes virtually ensure that the top vote-getter under the British, the Democratic Party, will have a limited voice in the new legislature. "Tung's new election laws are nothing less than a great leap backward for democracy in Hong Kong," Democratic Party chair and ousted legislator Martin Lee wrote in *The Washington Post* during Tung's U.S. visit.

What is emerging from these changes may be a corporatist model in which an entrenched business elite, backed by a powerful overseer in China and led by Tung, is guaranteed an electoral majority. In such a model, it is not difficult to envision attacks on press freedom or civil liberty easily passing a parliament with only a nominal opposition presence.

Regardless of the promises enshrined in the agreements that govern the handover and the transition to the new Chinese Hong Kong, it seems certain that the press will become less free, more cautious. "The feeling we have is of inevitability," said Daisy Li, a former editor at the Chinese-language *Ming Pao* daily. "Freedom of the press will be cut back."

Li's career reflects many of the changes that some journalists both fear and resist. Widely respected by her colleagues, she has held a number of leadership positions in the Hong Kong Journalists Association. In 1993, worried about the impending transition to Chinese rule, Li led a campaign to reform antiquated British-era official secrecy and sedition laws that could be used to restrict press freedom if they remained on the books. She also helped lead an international campaign to free *Ming Pao* reporter Xi Yang, who was imprisoned in China in 1993 for his reporting on Chinese government gold trading. For her efforts in these campaigns, Li was awarded an International Press Freedom Award by CPJ in 1995.

But Daisy Li sees little future for the mainstream press in Hong Kong. She says her newspaper, once one of the most critical voices in Hong Kong in its coverage of China, has gone soft. Self-censorship is a fact of life in the newsroom, Li says, and she wants no part of it. In August, she left *Ming Pao*, as have three other top staffers and HKJA members in recent months, citing displeasure with editorial changes. "Publishers have ties to big business and to

Beijing," she said. "That just encourages self-censorship." But instead of leaving her home in Hong Kong or her profession, Li has gone to work on the Hong Kong-based online version of the Chinese-language newspaper *Apple Daily*, hoping to find more freedom on the Internet than in the mainstream press. "I'm just leaving my paper," she explained. "I'm not leaving journalism."

The frustration Daisy Li and others feel is captured in a survey of Hong Kong journalists conducted last May by Joseph Chan, a professor at the Chinese University of Hong Kong. Over a third of those surveyed practiced some form of self-censorship in criticism of China or large Hong Kong corporations. More than half of the respondents believed that their colleagues censored themselves. In another survey of journalists undertaken by Hong Kong University in 1995, 88 percent said self-censorship was well-entrenched; 84 percent in that poll expected the situation to deteriorate under China. Eighty-six percent of Hong Kong business executives polled by the *Far Eastern Economic Review* shortly before the handover predicted the press would no longer be free under China.

If the polling data on self-censorship are accurate, the shift to Chinese rule has already had a profound impact on Hong Kong's journalists. The anecdotal evidence of self-censorship is abundant; journalists frequently begin a conversation on Hong Kong's media by conceding that self-restraint now pervades the newsrooms. "It is self-censorship rather than direct intimidation that will undermine the freedom of expression in Hong Kong," said Carol Lai of the Hong Kong Journalists Association. "We are on a dangerous path that can only lead the media to accept greater restraint. So far all the signs do not seem positive but we can only hope."

One of the most respected foreign correspondents in Hong Kong, Jonathan Mirsky, the Asia editor of the *Times of London* and a long-time Hong Kong resident, eloquently described the gradual tightening of controls in a piece for the *Index on Censorship* in January 1997: "This is the way we live now in Hong Kong. Sometimes Beijing barks angrily or just murmurs. More often its likes and hatreds are so well understood that, like the colonial cringe of yesteryear, local collaboration with the 'future sovereign' is automatic and preemptive."

Mirsky has acknowledged, however, that Hong Kong has remained remarkably free. Shortly after the handover, the *Hong*

Kong Economic Times, a Chinese-language business paper, commissioned Mirsky to write weekly pieces for its op-ed pages on China. "They hired me to bash China, and they have allowed that to continue," said Mirsky, who added that he was pleasantly surprised by the continued openness in the press generally. The paper regularly prints other critical voices—including a representative of the Dalai Lama discussing human rights abuses in Tibet—so far without reprisal.

Even before July 1, pessimism was not always the norm among journalists in Hong Kong. L.P. Yau, the editor in chief of the weekly *Yazhou Zhoukan* (Asia Week), a regional Chinese-language news magazine, is well-regarded among Hong Kong journalists. He predicted before the turnover and insists now that Chinese sovereignty presents no direct threat to press freedom. "The Hong Kong press sees no problem of political interference," said Yau. "There is no commissar to tell any publications how to run the newsroom, nor do the readers feel any deprivation of information. There are still all kinds of criticisms of China in the media, as well as those magazines that are specialized in criticizing China."

Yau related an anecdote that he believed offered another positive measure of press freedom. At a recent banquet hosted by Taiwan's Central News Agency's Hong Kong bureau, the bureau's editor in chief declared that his staff has had no problem functioning in Hong Kong since the handover. In contrast, Taiwanese journalists have had a rough time on the mainland, where they are forbidden to set up bureaus and occasionally experience government harassment. So their treatment in Hong Kong is important not only as an indicator of that territory's press conditions, but for what it augurs for China's relationship with Taiwan as Beijing seeks to woo Taiwan into reunification. If "One Country, Two Systems" will work in Hong Kong, the thinking goes, then it should be applied in Taiwan.

"It seems that the SAR government and Beijing are determined to project an image that Hong Kong, unlike China, remains free in the wake of the handover," said Yau. "My personal feeling is that Hong Kong is doing a good job for the time being, yet its destiny is closely related to stability in Beijing. As long as the economy is all right, Hong Kong will relish the good taste of press freedom."

The Case of Jimmy Lai: Hong Kong's Press Freedom Canary?
Those looking to take the measure of China's attitude toward
Hong Kong's outspoken press may not need to wait for macroeco-
nomic changes. Beijing has already expressed its distaste for Hong
Kong's independent journalism in the case of media magnate
Jimmy Lai. The flamboyant millionaire has built a media empire
in a very short time by combining investigative reporting with the
flash of tabloid journalism and a reputation for no-holds-barred
criticism of China. Lai is the sole owner of both the Chinese-language *Apple Daily*, the No. 2 daily newspaper in Hong Kong, and
Next, the territory's leading weekly magazine. His publications
have a combined claimed readership of just more than 3.5 million
out of a potential literate audience of some 5.6 million. Since its
founding in June 1995, *Apple Daily* has revolutionized the newspaper business in Hong Kong. Drawing on feisty politics, sex, crime,
and tabloid tactics, *Apple Daily* became profitable within a year of
its launch.

Jimmy Lai's current troubles with Beijing began in 1994 when,
in a *Next* editorial, he referred to Chinese premier Li Peng as "a
turtle egg" a stinging Chinese insult that questions an individual's
parentage. Soon afterward, Lai's profitable Giordano clothing
chain began to experience financial and regulatory setbacks in
China, which many observers trace to Beijing's official displeasure
with Lai.

Last February, Lai's Next Media Group (which includes a
number of general-interest magazines and a book publishing division) apparently paid a steep financial price for the boss's
brashness. Needing to raise capital to fuel the company's growth,
Lai was poised to list Next Media Group on Hong Kong's stock
market. The much-anticipated Initial Public Offering (IPO)
should have gone smoothly for a company that had surged to a
leadership position among Hong Kong's media businesses.

Instead, Lai suddenly found himself without an underwriter
for his offering when his sponsor, Sun Hung Kai International, a
leading Hong Kong investment bank, withdrew from the deal on
the eve of the listing without explanation. No other sponsor could
be found, and it was widely believed that Beijing had put political
pressure on bankers to torpedo Next's stock offering.

The collapse of Lai's IPO was a major story in Hong Kong,

where business has traditionally been immune to pressure from China. Yet, with the handover just months away, the subject of China's apparent strong-arm tactics was so sensitive that reporters had trouble finding bankers willing to comment. In a chilling coincidence, the Sun Hung Kai pullout came to light on the same day Tung Chee-hwa told CNN that it might be unlawful for Hong Kong people to make "slanderous, derogative remarks and attacks" against Chinese leaders after the handover. Tung's comment echoed a similar threat made by Chinese Foreign Minister Qian Qichen in 1996.

The Chinese government proscribes many subjects considered legitimate grist for news and commentary in the Western press, including the personal lives, financial dealings, and behind-the-scenes political maneuverings of national leaders. Some press freedom advocates fear that this constricted view could eventually prevail in Hong Kong, at least in regard to coverage of the Beijing government. By Beijing's standards, many of the major news stories of the last two decades such as Kurt Waldheim's Nazi past, Watergate, or the scandals that have tarred the ruling elite in Japan would have been inappropriate subjects for media scrutiny. Jimmy Lai is infuriating to China's authoritarian leaders precisely because he refuses to take their cues and yet prospers by printing what his readers want.

Was Jimmy Lai paying the price for insulting Li Peng and covering China with an aggressiveness that had largely disappeared from the Hong Kong press by this time? "I was left scratching my head," said *Next* publisher Yeung Wai-hong, who said the underwriter had originally approached Lai enthusiastically, seeking the business. "They never told us the real reason for pulling out. The pressure that was applied must have been tremendous." After a *Next* editorial criticizing Beijing's role in the deal's collapse, Yeung noted, China's official Xinhua news agency, which during the colonial period functioned as a de facto Beijing embassy in Hong Kong and represented China's interests, countered that it played no role in influencing the bankers. "We never even named Xinhua," said Yeung. "So why are they denying [it]?"

Some analysts believe that Lai is being punished indirectly not by Beijing but by one of Hong Kong's most powerful capitalists, Li Ka-shing. According to this theory, Li, who has vast holdings in

Hong Kong and China, exacted revenge on Lai for publishing exposés about the tycoon's personal life and examining some of his business dealings in China. Publisher Yeung would only note of Li Ka-shing that none of his many companies would advertise with Jimmy Lai's publications.

Despite Lai's failure to launch the IPO and China's refusal to accredit reporters from *Next* or *Apple Daily* there has been no sign that his publications will mute their voices. The companies continue to expand, getting ready to move into a vast new $100-million corporate headquarters. On June 4, *Apple Daily* ran a striking full-page photo of the estimated 55,000 people who showed up in Victoria Park for the annual protest against the 1989 Tiananmen Square massacre. Last May, the paper ran a front-page story trumpeting Chinese President Jiang Zemin's inclusion among CPJ's 1997 Top Ten Enemies of the Press.

"We don't expect anything and we don't try to second-guess what the incoming government will do to us," said Yeung shortly before the handover. "In the greater scheme of things we are low down the totem pole. If they try to jam us up it would be such a violation that they would have to pay a high price. Press freedom is guaranteed in the Basic Law, and we take that as a given. That is the only way we can do business."

Other papers have apparently been more willing than *Next* and *Apple Daily* to acquiesce to Beijing's wishes. The appointment of Feng Xiliang as a "consultant" to the *South China Morning Post* in April sounded alarm bells among those looking for press freedom danger signs. Feng, the founding editor of Beijing's official *China Daily*, has set up shop in an office adjacent to the chief editor of the immensely profitable paper owned by Robert Kuok, a major investor in China and another of the world's wealthiest men.

The *Post*'s editor, Jonathan Fenby, challenged critics at the time to find any change in the paper's coverage, while others denounced the new "commissar" as a sign of things to come. Fenby may be right, at least in the short term the *Post*, never noted as a crusading newspaper even in the best of times, has continued to carry coverage that is critical of Tung and aspects of the transition. "I can say hand-on-heart that since July 1, as far as I'm concerned, there have been no political attempts by the new administration to stop us from doing anything," Fenby said in the pages of his newspaper on

November 6, 1997. "Nobody has rung me up from the Chief Executive's office to say 'do this, do that'."

More disturbing are the changes at *Ming Pao*. Founded in 1959 and long a favorite of Hong Kong intellectuals, *Ming Pao* once broke stories on China's notorious Gang of Four and Beijing's secret military maneuvers. Reporting on Chinese dissidents frequently led the paper, and the official Xinhua news agency often singled out *Ming Pao*'s reporters for criticism.

Then, in 1993, Xi Yang, *Ming Pao*'s Beijing correspondent, reported on a plan by the Chinese government to sell a portion of its vast gold reserve on the world market. The story scuttled the deal by shedding light on the transaction and alerting the markets. Beijing authorities charged Xi with reporting on state secrets; he was tried and sentenced to 12 years in prison.

In 1995, Malaysian-Chinese timber magnate Tiong Hew King bought the paper, and the tone of *Ming Pao* shifted. Stories about China began to emphasize fires, crime, and celebrities; photos got bigger; and the paper began referring to Taiwan as a "province" of China, following the style of mainland papers. An opinion writer from Shanghai who once worked for the Chinese government propaganda department joined the staff. When Xi Yang was released from prison in February 1997, after serving three years, *Ming Pao* thanked China for showing "leniency."

Nothing that has happened at *Ming Pao* could be called direct censorship, but the hand of China or at least the perceived need to please China is manifest in these cases. "Xi Yang broke the law," said Edgar Yuen of the pro-Beijing Hong Kong Federation of Journalists, which was formed in 1996 with China's apparent blessing. "Of course he was punished."

Law-abiding Hong Kong journalists do not need to fear China, said Yuen, whose group was established one year before the handover. "It is a matter of getting to know one another," he said, and of learning about China. "We are not puppets of anyone," Yuen bristled, "and to practice self-censorship would be an insult to the profession."

Yuen and other pro-Beijing commentators argue that China would be foolish to interfere with Hong Kong's formula for success, which generates hard currency and national pride for the mainland. Tsang Tak-sing, a member of the mainland's People's

Congress, is editor in chief of *Ta Kung Pao*, one of two pro-China newspapers in Hong Kong. He told the American Chamber of Commerce in Hong Kong last February that protecting free speech is vital. "We need the free flow of information for Hong Kong to consolidate its position as a regional and international center of financial and economic activities, so as to be useful to the modernization of China." Even so staunch a defender of democratic values as Martin Lee has expressed a sense of cautious optimism a few weeks into the new regime. One month after the handover, in an interview with the *South China Morning Post*, he said, "I hope this is the beginning of building up trust. It takes a bit of time to cultivate. But when they [China] saw a smooth transition, they could say: 'Leave it to Hong Kong'. And the more they do not interfere in Hong Kong, the more we can trust them. So far the climate is right for this trust to grow. If this first month becomes a year, then I'm sure people will feel more comfortable."

If the comfort level for Hong Kong's democrats continues to rise, the Jimmy Lai case may eventually be seen merely as an aberration rather than as the canary in the coal mine, measuring the danger ahead for Hong Kong's press under Chinese rule. But as Martin Lee has often emphasized in advocating for the preservation of democratic institutions in Hong Kong, much more can be gleaned about Hong Kong's future from China's approach to the territory's rule of law.

The Basic Law

If Hong Kong is to remain free, its legal lifeline is the Basic Law, the mini-constitution governing the Special Administration Region. Yet to be fully defined by the courts and open to contradictory interpretations, the Basic Law is the sole guarantor of press freedom and the rule of law for Chinese Hong Kong.

Much of what happens to Hong Kong also may be determined by the attitudes that emerged from the 15th Communist Party Congress held in Beijing in September, the occasion for President Jiang Zemin to formally solidify his hold on power. And as the Congress neared, tantalizing hints of possible political reform in China began to emerge. Early in September, Liu Ji, a senior aide to Jiang, broke with a nearly decade-long moratorium on discussion of reform and called for more political liberalization to satisfy rising popular demand. "The continued rapid development of China's economy is safeguarded by reform of the political structure," Liu Ji said in an interview with the official China news service. "Otherwise the consequences are unimaginable."

Expressing sentiments that have not been heard in official China since the People's Liberation Army violently crushed the democracy movement in June 1989, Liu, who is vice president of the Chinese Academy of Social Sciences, said, "When the people have enough food to eat and enough clothes to keep warm and as cultural standards increase, they will then want to express their opinions. The people wanting to take part in political thinking is a good thing, it is a sign of the prosperity and strength of the nation and is also a tide of the age that cannot be turned back."

Jiang himself hinted at political reform during his speech before the Congress. "As a ruling party, the Communist Party leads and supports the people in exercising the power of running the state, holding democratic elections, making policy decisions in a democratic manner," Jiang said. While hardly a manifesto for free expression, Jiang's remarks were bold by recent Chinese standards. Since 1989, Chinese officials have avoided public discussion of reform because of the assumption that official calls for easing restrictions on expression in the late 1980s contributed to the student uprising in Tiananmen Square.

"For decades, the media sang the praises of the Communist Party. This has become China's cancer," Lin said in his letter, which was made available to foreign reporters. "To remove this cancer, we must come up with a law to protect press freedom."

It is too soon to assess whether such talk of reform will lead to action. And the recent rhetoric of democracy is not likely to erase the cumulative weight of Chinese officials' more typical public pronouncements about the press. For example, Lu Ping, Beijing's Director of China and Macao Affairs prior to the handover, evoked Hong Kong journalists' worst fears about Chinese rule in June 1997 with his warning to the press against "advocating" independence for Taiwan, Hong Kong, or Tibet. That, he said, would be a violation of national security restrictions in China. "It is all right if reporters objectively report. But if they advocate, it is action. That has nothing to do with freedom of the press."

Lu's statements reflect a view of the relationship between

speech and action whose ultimate extension is the massacre of demonstrators in Tiananmen Square. It is a position incompatible with the freedoms that Hong Kong people have enjoyed under the territory's rule of law.

Yet because the Basic Law, hammered out in often-contentious negotiations between Beijing and London after the 1984 Joint Declaration agreeing to the handover, gave half a loaf to each side in the debate over press freedom, there is uncertainty about how the two views will be reconciled in the Post-handover period. Chapter Three, Article 27, of the Basic Law, titled "The Fundamental Rights and Duties of the Residents," provides for "freedom of speech, of the press and of publication." The same article guarantees freedom of association, assembly, procession, demonstration, and the right to strike and form unions; there is also the right of academic freedom, and of literary and artistic creation. Framing these freedoms is Article 39, which promises to comply with the International Covenant on Civil and Political Rights. It also prohibits the introduction in Hong Kong of any restrictions incompatible with the covenant.

But Article 23 seems potentially to contradict Articles 27 and 39. It instructs Hong Kong to pass laws prohibiting "treason, secession, sedition, subversion against the Central People's Government, or theft of state secrets," and prohibits political organizations from establishing ties with foreign political organizations.

The relationship of these three potentially contradictory clauses has never been clarified. This "is the great fascination for me as a constitutional lawyer," Hong Kong legal scholar Yash Ghai said in a wide-ranging analysis published by Dateline: Hong Kong, a Web site devoted to the handover. "It is also the great challenge of the Basic Law."

The Basic Law will be adjudicated both in the Hong Kong courts and by a committee of the Chinese People's Congress, notes Ghai. "You have this one document which is subject to two different regimes of interpretation." Questions about freedom of expression in Hong Kong would ostensibly be handled by the Hong Kong courts, which are to remain independent of Beijing. But Article 23 broadly dictates that certain questions of freedom of expression fall under China's jurisdiction. So, for example, criticism of Chinese authorities might be deemed as within the purview of Article 23.

Hong Kong courts might take the line, consistent with common law, that the Basic Law is binding and creates rights and obligations. But the two bodies could have different approaches to those rights. Ghai said, "I suppose that ultimately the standing committee of the national People's Congress will prevail because it also has a general power of interpretation of all the laws passed in the People's Republic of China."

While such thorny interpretive and jurisdictional issues arising out of the Basic Law may take years to be fully adjudicated, Beijing's decision to dismiss all opposition members of the elected legislature as of July 1 and to appoint a provisional legislature seemed a clear enough sign that civil liberties would suffer. "National security can be anything [Chinese government officials] say it is," noted Robin Munro, the director of the Hong Kong office of Human Rights Watch-Asia, "and that is absolutely worrying."

Will China Rein in Hong Kong's Press?

Will China be able to tolerate an irreverent, independent Hong Kong press climate, in which reporters, writers, commentators, and editors seek to push the boundaries?

With 16 major daily newspapers, two commercial television stations, and two commercial radio stations, in addition to the seven English and Chinese-language outlets of government-owned but independently run Radio Television Hong Kong, the territory's media have flourished under an open system. The city is home to dozens of foreign news bureaus that cover Asia out of Hong Kong because of its ease of transport and climate of freedom. The regional press is also based in Hong Kong, and news magazines such as the *Far Eastern Economic Review, Asia Week,* and *Yazhou Zhoukan* can freely publish objective reports on virtually any topic with little fear of interference.

Hong Kong is one of the few places in Asia where journalists operate with almost no government control. Indonesia, Singapore, Malaysia, and Indonesia require licenses and special visas for journalists. In Hong Kong, anyone can be a journalist. There are no government-issued press cards or journalists' visas. When press rights are threatened elsewhere in the region, Hong Kong is the place of refuge, where regional activists can meet journalists with little fear of apprehension or sanction from local authorities.

China also will have to contend with Hong Kong's role as a center for Internet use in the region. In late December 1997, China unveiled strict new rules governing access to information on the Internet, imposing unspecified criminal punishments and fines of up to US$1,800 for such crimes as using the Internet to leak state secrets, engage in political subversion, and spread pornography and violence. No such regulations exist in Hong Kong, however, and much of the content that Beijing wants banned—such as reports coming from groups advocating human rights in China—originates and is freely available in Hong Kong. Moreover, with the rapid rise of Internet use in China, it may prove impossible for China to accomplish the Sisyphean task of Internet monitoring. Any serious effort to disrupt access in China seems almost guaranteed to bump up against Hong Kong's libertarian media culture.

For its part, Hong Kong's government maintains that China will have nothing to say about the Internet in the Special Autonomous Region. Just after China's new regulations were announced, Anthony Wong, director general of the territory's telecommunications, emphasized that the "One Country, Two Systems" policy also applies to the Internet. "Hong Kong will regulate its own Internet ... and China has its own regulations. The regulations in Hong Kong will not apply in China and visa versa," he told reporters.

Hong Kong remains a media center and a press freedom haven despite the new dispensation. Human rights observer Michael Davis of Chinese University of Hong Kong has said that one important measure of press freedom will be Chinese treatment of dissident publications. "Hong Kong is the one Chinese-language press that regularly confronts Beijing," Davis said. "Watch *China Rights Forum* and other such publications to see how they fare. That will be a test."

China Rights Forum, a small independent magazine published by the group Human Rights in China, has had no trouble, according to director Sophia Woodman. "As far as how things are going here, nothing seems very different," she said in late August. In addition, according to Woodman, *Beijing Spring*, a Chinese dissident magazine produced in the United States, is still on Hong Kong newsstands.

Writing in the *International Herald Tribune* in late August, Philip Bowring, the former editor of the *Far Eastern Economic Review*, said he saw Hong Kong's media little changed after the transition. "Although there was an evident increase in media self-censorship in the months leading up to the handover," Bowring wrote, "the situation has not become worse. Indeed, there are signs of greater determination now to exercise old freedoms and test the new limits. Commentators may be wary of being too rude about leaders in Beijing, but they are familiar enough with many of Mr. Tung's acolytes to feel free to display their views, and sometimes their contempt."

While Hong Kong's journalists may continue to tread lightly on stories about Beijing's power elite, they already regard Tung and the provisional legislature as fair game. Many of the legislators, and certainly Tung himself, have long been subjects of scrutiny by the local media, and they may quickly establish a rhythm in their relationship quite different from that between Beijing and the mainland press.

During the party congress, *Apple Daily* gave front-page play to the full text of a letter signed by former Communist Party leader Zhao Ziyang, who has been persona non grata in China since his ouster just before the Tiananmen Square massacre. Zhao's letter, which called on Politburo leaders to reassess the government's violent suppression of the pro-democracy demonstrators, provoked only stony silence from party officials. But Jimmy Lai's newspaper once again displayed its penchant for airing Beijing's dirty linen in public.

Still, China's record of inflexibility toward the press on the mainland raises the question of how long it will be before China acts to rein in Hong Kong's feisty journalistic culture. With Hong Kong's media often seeping into Southern China, will pledges to leave the broadcast news alone be honored in the longer term? In the event of social or political unrest in China, or other occurrences that could cast Beijing in a less than positive light, how will China's leaders react if Hong Kong reporters cover the story?

Beijing traditionally has been sensitive to the point of paranoia about the reporting of economic information. In 1994, Chinese reporter Gao Yu was sentenced to six years in prison for her reporting on China's economic reforms for the generally pro-Beijing Hong Kong magazine *Mirror Monthly*. Last May, when UNESCO honored Gao in absentia on World Press Freedom Day,

Beijing called her a "criminal" and threatened to close the UNESCO office in China.

It is not hard to imagine a scenario in which powerful economic interests in Beijing bridle at critical reporting about so-called "red-chip" stocks, issued by Hong Kong-based China-owned companies. These red-chip companies have suffered the tumble in Hong Kong share prices that accompanied the economic downturn in Thailand and the rest of Asia. Financial analysts say that many of these companies were wildly overvalued to begin with and that the lack of transparent reporting about the nature of their ownership in China made them inherently unreliable. How will China react if the crisis in Hong Kong's markets deepens, with adverse ramifications for the mainland? Eventually even bullish business writers in Hong Kong could uncover potential scandals in the red-chip market. Would China regard an exposé of a scandal in a Hong Kong-traded, Beijing-owned company as a threat to national security?

Covering the new Tung government has caused some journalists to complain about lack of access and lapse into nostalgia for the public-relations-conscious British administration. "The level of access and the culture of secrecy is already worse," said Stephen Vines, a veteran Hong Kong reporter and editor who has worked in both the local and foreign media. "Something happens when you phone Tung's office and you get no answer. [Former Hong Kong governor] Chris Patten was very media-savvy and media-friendly. Now there is no one you can phone up for a straight answer."

Tung's inaccessibility is symptomatic of an executive-led government that tolerates the press as a necessary evil, Vines said. Patten lobbied long and hard to get the Hong Kong media to believe in his efforts to democratize the territory. Tung doesn't see the press as a partner in the public discourse. "But," cautioned Vines, "it's not as bad as China. Not yet anyway."

Vines' attitude seems to prevail in Hong Kong, where journalists often take to heart the old adage: Hope for the best, prepare for the worst. It is no coincidence that Hong Kong's amazing economic growth—it is the world's eighth-largest trading economy, with a per-capita income that rivals many European countries—has been accompanied by great freedom. It is that freedom to report and challenge and exchange information that has brought the world to regard Hong Kong as Asia's financial and business hub.

If China and Tung Chee-hwa confound the critics and allow the one-country, two-systems philosophy to flourish in Hong Kong, it may open the way toward greater press freedom for all of China. At the 15th Party Congress, Jiang set in motion the further privatization and modernization of the Chinese economy by calling for the sale of state-owned companies to private shareholders. As the Chinese government proceeds with privatization, the last vestiges of a socialist economy will likely whither away, further erasing the barriers between China and the rest of the world. The next aspect of the Chinese system to go should be the apparatus of one-party control over information and the press. No country has built a successful, dynamic modern economy on the scale of China without allowing its people democracy and free access to information. Hong Kong knows how to be free; it can point the way for China.

Success in Hong Kong will be measured in large part by freedom of information and the rule of law. At stake in Hong Kong is the health and vigor of one of the world's great trading economies, a vital cog in the great wheel of Asian commerce and development. In that sense, the whole world will be watching and living with the outcome of Hong Kong's drama.

CENTRAL EUROPE AND THE REPUBLICS OF THE FORMER SOVIET UNION

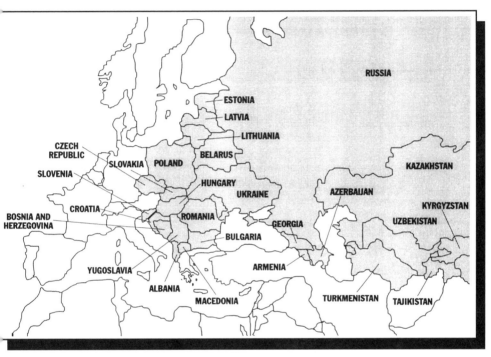

OVERVIEW OF
Central Europe and the Republics of the Former Soviet Union
by Chrystyna Lapychak

W hile the countries that once made up the Soviet bloc now enjoy much greater freedom than they did a decade ago, the status of press freedom and working conditions for journalists in the region vary greatly. With some notable exceptions, overt institutional censorship has largely disappeared, private media have proliferated, and journalists have founded associations to defend their rights. Yet across the region, to varying degrees, journalistic standards are lacking, the role of the media remains ill-defined, and news organizations are still manipulated by and subjected to pressure from governments and burgeoning business interests.

Countries such as Poland, Hungary, and the Czech Republic, which have progressed the most in reforming their political and economic systems, have successfully fostered vibrant, diverse, and free media climates. In some places—Russia is the most important example—government or state monopolies have been replaced by new private media monoliths battling for control of the airwaves. The competition among a handful of powerful media moguls has often proved dangerous, because they still use their media outlets as direct instru-

Chrystyna Lapychak, *program coordinator for Central and Eastern Europe and the former Soviet Republics, has more than 10 years' experience covering the region as a journalist and analyst.*
Irina Kuldjieva-Faion, *research assistant for Central and Eastern Europe, provided extensive assistance for this section and prepared many of the country summaries.*
Catherine A. Fitzpatrick, *former program coordinator for Central Europe and the former Soviet Union, also contributed to the preparation of this section and authored a number of country summaries.*
CPJ's work in Central and Eastern Europe and the republics of the former Soviet Union was funded in part by a grant from the John D. and Catherine T. MacArthur Foundation and the Open Society Institute.
CPJ is grateful for the cooperation of a number of press freedom and human rights groups, professional journalists associations, news organizations, and individuals across the region. These include: the Glasnost Defense Foundation, Internews, the National News Service (NNS), Radio Liberty/Radio Free Europe, the Belarusian Association of Journalists, the Ukrainian Media Club, the Croatian Association of Journalists, Yeni Nesil of Azerbaijan, the Human Rights Center of Azerbaijan, the Yerevan Press Club, the Kyrgyz Committee for Human Rights, the Bishkek Bureau for Human Rights and Rule of Law, and others.

EUROPE

ments of political power. In many countries in the region with developing market economies, the lines between political and business interests are blurred.

In Turkmenistan and Uzbekistan, the media have remained concentrated in the hands of authoritarian rulers, and there are few if any alternative media outlets. Other countries in the region with autocratic regimes, such as the Federal Republic of Yugoslavia, have developed vibrant and varied independent media, which manage to function despite official harassment.

The most alarming trend across the region remains the persistence of violence against journalists, particularly murders linked to their publications or broadcasts. While the overall number of killings, most of which occurred in war zones, has declined since the end of the conflicts in Tajikistan, Chechnya, and the former Yugoslavia, murders and beatings of journalists in nonconflict areas have become routine in such places as the Russian Federation and Ukraine.

Last year, CPJ investigated 10 suspicious deaths of journalists in the region, yet was only able to conclude beyond a reasonable doubt that one journalist, Borys Derevyanko of the Ukrainian daily *Vechernyaya Odessa*, was murdered directly as a result of work. Murky circumstances and contradictory evidence made it difficult to verify the motives in the deaths of two other journalists, Petro Shevchenko of the daily newspaper *Kievskiye Vedomosti* in Ukraine and Valery Krivosheyev of *Komsomolskaya Pravda*, a daily newspaper in Russia. After thoroughly investigating seven other deaths, CPJ concluded that the deceased were evidently victims of crime, accidents, fatal illness, or could not be described as journalists at the time of their deaths.

The number of confirmed assassinations is not the only barometer to measure risk. In and around Chechnya, an epidemic of kidnappings of foreigners, including journalists on assignment, by armed bands seeking ransom have made it the the most dangerous place for journalists in the region. Few if any foreign or Russian journalists venture into the area, which has contributed to its deepening isolation and created a virtual information blackout.

Beatings, death threats, detentions, bombings, arson, and financial pressures have become routine means of intimidating the press, particularly independent and opposition media, across the region. A building housing the state news agency in Dushanbe, the capital of Tajikistan, was bombed, as were the editorial offices of an alternative newspaper in the Serb-controlled area of Bosnia. Bosnian journalists fear crossing borders between the Serb, Croat, and Muslim-controlled areas because they are still often harassed by local police from the other entities, particularly the allies of Radovan Karadzic, the Bosnian Serb opposition leader who is wanted by The Hague Tribunal for initiating wartime atrocities.

EUROPE

Karadzic's hand has been weakened, however, by the loss of control over most of the Bosnian Serb airwaves. In September, NATO returned a confiscated television transmitter to Karadzic's allies on the assurance that they would allow opposition groups to use it. But in Ocober, in a move that sparked international controversy, NATO troops seized four television transmitters from Karadzic's supporters on the grounds that they had violated the Dayton Accords by airing anti-NATO broadcasts. The newly confiscated equipment was then turned over to Karadzic's rival, President Biljana Plavsic (see "Bosnia," p. 321).

News media and journalists were also targets of violent attacks and enforced censorship in Albania during riots protesting the collapse of government-backed pyramid investment schemes. The offices of the opposition newspaper *Koha Jone* were torched, and many journalists were beaten and harassed by police while covering the disturbances. Reporters covering anti-government demonstrations in Bulgaria and Serbia early in the year were also subjected to detentions, beatings, and other forms of intimidation.

Journalists pursuing investigative stories on corruption and organized crime have found themselves at greatest risk across the region, but especially in Russia and Ukraine, where beatings have become routine. These physical assaults have had the expected chilling effect on investigative journalism, frightening some reporters into self-censorship or even quitting the profession, while many have resorted to using pseudonyms. Short-term detention of reporters covering public protests was another ubiquitous means of intimidating them from pursuing such stories. Death threats were used against journalists in Russia, Ukraine, Yugoslavia, Bosnia, Croatia, and Albania.

In his relentless crackdown on Belarus' independent and opposition media, President Aleksander Lukashenko detained, arrested, expelled, disaccredited, and finally banned journalists and news outlets. Conditions for the press are worse than in the final years of the Soviet Union. Lukashenko concentrated his wrath on journalists from Russian television companies whose broadcasts reach a large portion of Belarus. After expelling Aleksander Stupnikov, a correspondent for Russia's independent NTV, he arrested and tried a crew from the Russian ORT company on charges of illegally crossing an unguarded section of Belarus' border with Lithuania. Lukashenko detained and expelled another ORT crew and refused to give anyone from the company accreditation in Belarus. In the fall, the populist leader finally moved to shut down *Svaboda*, a popular opposition newspaper that had endured much official intimidation. His campaign to stamp out all critical coverage culminated in the adoption by his rubber-stamp legislature of new amendments to the country's press law which give him near-total control over the media.

National elections in Yugoslavia and Croatia prompted the leaders of both countries to step up pressure on the independent media. Yugoslav leader Slobodan Milosevic shut down 77 independent radio and television stations in July and August after announcing new and completely convoluted frequency licensing procedures. The stations went back on the air temporarily during elections for the Serbian Parliament only because several political re-alignments at the time seemed to ensure his left-wing coalition would retain dominance. The leaders of Tajikistan and Kazakhstan similarly used their countries' regulatory systems and broadcast licensing procedures to harass independent broadcasters.

Despite a landslide election victory in June, Croatian President Franjo Tudjman continued to exert pressure on independent media, such as the *Feral Tribune* and *Globus* weekly newspapers, with hundreds of seditious, criminal and civil libel suits filed against them by officials.

Although many countries in the region have adopted constitutional guarantees against censorship, their constitutions, media legislation, and criminal codes limit criticism of government officials by penalizing so-called false and dishonoring comments, insults, and criticism of the president. Criminal libel statutes are frequently misused by public officials to suppress journalistic investigation and shield themselves from public scrutiny.

There are also many contradictions and restrictions within national media legislation throughout the region that effectively limit press freedom. Many countries have incorporated Article 10 of the European Convention on Human rights guaranteeing freedom of expression, but not without qualification: The constitutions and media laws of many countries, from Armenia to Ukraine, list vague restrictions on free expression in the interest of national security, public order, and the protection of reputations which are open to broad interpretation and abuse.

EUROPE

Albania

In January and February, a violent crisis erupted in the country, sparked by the collapse of several pyramid investment schemes, costing many Albanians their life savings. US$1.5 billion was lost. The northern and southern regions of the country descended into anarchy as thousands of angry Albanians looted military and police arsenals, and the government lost control of many areas. Most Albanians blamed their financial ruin on the increasingly autocratic administration of President Sali Berisha and his ruling Democratic Party, who had failed to institute economic reform or warn citizens against the dubious pyramid schemes. On January 26, thousands of protesters clashed with riot police in central Tirana and government buildings were set ablaze across the country. On March 2, Berisha declared a state of emergency in the north, instituted a curfew in Tirana, and imposed blanket censorship on the media.

These conditions created tremendous obstacles for the newly independent media, as well as for state-controlled television and radio broadcasts, which were closely monitored by Berisha and his government. With the introduction of censorship, no independent newspapers were published for almost a month. Before they could publish, newspapers had to be scrutinized by the State of Emergency Staff, established in the respective districts. The only papers that managed to circulate in March were *Rilindja Democratike*, the organ of the Democratic Party, and the *Albanian Daily News*, which submitted to censorship.

Journalists faced threats and beatings for reporting on anti-government rallies in Tirana and elsewhere, while media organizations were targets of looting and robberies of computer equipment and cars.

The offices of the largest independent newspaper, *Koha Jone*, were torched by Berisha loyalists. The newspaper's archives and computers were destroyed, with damages amounting to US$220,000. Zamir Duke, *Koha Jone*'s chief crime reporter, was abducted from the office during the incident. He was beaten and released the next day. The paper's top legal correspondent, Alfred Peza, was arrested, interrogated, and tortured for three hours by police in Fier. The nationwide curfew was strictly enforced upon journalists, which enormously hampered the news-gathering process and created distribution restrictions on the print media, especially in the south.

The government and Berisha targeted foreign media (BBC and Reuters, in particular), along with the opposition Socialist Party, blaming them for the crisis.

Newspapers began to publish once the declaration of the state of emergency and the curfew were formally lifted in April, but not without risks for journalists and newspaper owners. Occasional attacks on *Koha Jone* journalists occurred as late as August.

Berisha conceded to demands for new general elections in June. During the election campaign, the print media were split into two main political camps supporting either the former coalition government or the left-wing opposition. The dailies with the largest circulation were either political party publications or independent papers that nevertheless displayed some political bias. State television and radio needed to comply with the electoral law, which required them to provide access only to leaders of the major political parties. Only independent Shijak TV, a station situated between Tirana and Durres, provided comprehensive election coverage and equal access to all parties.

The Socialist victory in June brought some stability to Albania. But many of the press' problems have persisted. Poor distribution systems, as well as occasional attacks on reporters and theft of equipment, still plague the media. Limited printing facilities, financial constraints, and an underdeveloped advertising market exacerbate the problem. A number of qualified journalists have either left the country or have quit the profession. The remaining journalists require training in the traditions of independent media. But the Albanian media have grown more diverse since the June elections.

In September, the parliament adopted a new press law that states simply that "the press is free" and "freedom of the press is protected by law." The 1993 press law had listed numerous restrictions, which allowed authorities to confiscate publications on vague grounds, limited journalists' access to information, and established large fines on editors publishing anything arbitrarily deemed illegal.

The new law also amended the statutes governing state radio and television, allocating broadcast time between the president, government, and opposition and guaranteeing political parties the right to define the content of their air time.

On September 2, the Albanian legislature also amended the broadcast law to provide for more air time for presenting "alternative" views. But Albania still lacks clear guidelines for the licensing of private television and radio stations, which allows for the arbitrary denial of licenses on political grounds. Nevertheless, a number of private regional and local broadcasters exist; six private television stations broadcasting locally, most of them focusing on local issues. Two stations, TV Arberia and Shijak TV, broadcast evening news programs.

A four-day strike by nine of the country's largest papers in November highlighted the serious financial dilemmas faced by print media. The government rejected their demands for a cut in the value-added tax on

newspapers, which it had raised to 22 percent in September, but made cuts in import duties on newsprint, ink, and spare parts, and eliminated the tariff on new printing equipment.

January 26
Roland Beqiraj, *Koha Jone* IMPRISONED

Police detained Beqiraj, a correspondent for the independent daily *Koha Jone*, in the southeastern Albanian city of Korca. That day, Beqiraj had published a story in the newspaper headlined "Protesters Burn Portrait of President Sali Berisha." Beqiraj had been covering demonstrations by Albanians who lost money in failed pyramid schemes backed by the government.

A source told the editor of *Koha Jone* that Beqiraj was severely beaten. The source believed authorities were delaying Beqiraj's release to allow time for his wounds to heal. CPJ appealed to President Berisha to ensure Beqiraj's immediate release. He was freed on February 7.

January 29
Muharren Meko, *Zeri i Popullit* IMPRISONED

Plainclothes police officers detained Meko, a correspondent for the Socialist Party paper *Zeri i Popullit*, in the southeastern Albanian city of Korca. Meko had just published an article in his paper about widespread demonstrations by Albanians who lost money in failed pyramid schemes backed by the Albanian government. The officers said they wanted to ask Meko questions about the demonstrations.

The Association of Professional Journalists of Albania (APJA) received notice from the Korca district attorney's office that Meko had been accused of "violent activity against common property" under Article 231/25 of the Albanian Penal Code. *Zeri i Popullit*'s editor has confirmed, however, that Meko was at the demonstrations only to report on the event for the newspaper. CPJ appealed to President Sali Berisha to ensure Meko's immediate release.

February 1
Anilda Ibrahami, *Koha Jone* HARASSED

Ibrahami, a correspondent for the independent daily *Koha Jone*, was expelled from a meeting of the ruling Democratic Party in Vlora. According to the newspaper's editor, after Ibrahami entered the meeting, which other journalists were attending, party members immediately began deriding her and her newspaper. At that point, the vice premier of the ruling party, Sehu Tritan, called a vote to decide whether Ibrahami should be permitted to stay and report on the meeting. The members voted to expel her, and security guards then escorted her from the building. CPJ appealed to President Sali Berisha to cease such harassment of journalists.

February 5
Koha Jone CENSORED

Police prevented distribution of the independent daily *Koha Jone* during widespread demonstrations by Albanians who lost money in failed pyramid schemes. The action was probably a response to the papers coverage of the demonstrations. The police blocked a truck carrying copies of *Koha Jone* from entering the town of Vlora, where demonstrations were scheduled to take place. Delivery trucks carrying other newspapers were permitted to enter, and those publications were distributed.

That day's edition of *Koha Jone*, as well as the previous day's edition, appeared with blank spaces where censors had blocked stories. CPJ appealed to President Sali Berisha to cease such censorship of the press.

March 2
Koha Jone ATTACKED
VOA Albanian Service CENSORED
BBC CENSORED

Police ransacked the office of Tirana's largest daily, *Koha Jone*, and arsonists set fire to the building a few hours later.

Police pushed past the security guard and broke down the door during the late-night raid. No editorial staff were present, and there were no reports of injuries. The newspaper's offices and equipment were extensively damaged.

The action followed parliament's declaration of a state of emergency on March 2, in response to widespread rioting.

The Voice of America's Albanian-language Service was taken off the air in Tirana. FM Radio 107.4, which alternates VOA programming in English and Albanian, had its license suspended on March 2. Three other local affiliates with agreements to rebroadcast VOA—in Gjirokaster, Shkoder, and Kukes—were also suspended. The British Broadcasting Corp. (BBC), which leases a transmitter to Radio Tirana, also had its programs silenced. Foreign broadcasting could only be heard over shortwave radio.

CPJ wrote to Albanian President Sali Berisha on March 3, strongly condemning the censorship of the news media.

March 2
All media CENSORED

The Albanian parliament declared a state of emergency in response to widespread rioting. The resulting crackdown on the media followed weeks of beatings, short-term detentions, and harassment of reporters who covered the collapse of Albania's pyramid schemes—the source of a massive public protest that led to early general elections in June. Parliament ruled that all local broadcast and print media must submit their materials to government censors prior to publication or broadcast.

March 25
Nikoll Lesi, *Koha Jone* ATTACKED,
THREATENED

Lesi, publisher of the opposition daily *Koha Jone*, was attacked at a Tirana hotel by a man believed to be a member of the state security police. The assailant punched Lesi in the face several times and made verbal threats.

The hotel where the attack occurred is a gathering place for local and foreign journalists. It was feared that this incident and others were intended to discourage the press corps from meeting there.

On March 28, CPJ wrote to President Sali Berisha about the attack on Lesi and other threats to journalists.

August 21
Mujo Bucpapaj, *Rilindja Demokratike*
ATTACKED

Bucpapaj, a journalist with *Rilindja Demokratike* (the official newspaper of the opposition Democratic Party), was shot and seriously wounded. According to the Bucpapaj family and a Democratic Party press statement, individuals in a police car fired at Bucpapaj, striking him in the leg. The Democratic Party said the attack was politically motivated. Police said that Bucpapaj was caught in a gun battle between two armed gangs.

Because of past threats and attacks against Albanian journalists, including others associated with *Rilindja Demokratike*, CPJ was concerned that the shooting was related to Bucpapaj's profession.

Armenia

Compared to 1996, a record year for press freedom violations in Armenia, 1997 did not bring any major new encroachments upon the rights of journalists and media freedom. But the ongoing tension between Armenia and neighboring Azerbaijan over Nagorno-Karabakh, the Armenian-populated enclave within Azerbaijan's borders, continues to provide an impetus for the government to tightly rein in the press. Even the resignation

on February 3, 1998, of President Levon Ter-Petrossian, who reigned over the media crackdown of the past two years, under pressure from hard-liners in the government, is unlikely to bode well for press freedom, at least in the near future.

On June 18, the Ministry of National Security summoned three journalists from the independent Noyan Tapan news agency for questioning about the sources of an article on the Organization for Security and Cooperation in Europe (OSCE) effort to mediate a settlement between Armenia and Azerbaijan. Interrogators suggested that the journalists, whose agency exchanges information with the Azerbaijan News Service in Baku, were harming national interests by revealing confidential information on the delicate negotiations. Presidential Press Secretary Levon Zourabian, in a letter to CPJ, asserted that the security service was only doing its duty in trying to plug a leak, since the Armenian government had agreed to strict confidentiality about the mediation effort. Zourabian stated in the letter that the reporters were not criminally charged and could have walked out of the meeting at any time. The journalists, however, felt intimidated.

Despite its professed support for freedom of expression, the Armenian government has frequently betrayed a desire to restrict the media. Journalistic freedoms are regulated by a Soviet-era media law, adopted in October 1991. The law bans censorship, but outlines a list of restricted topics, such as incitement to violence and hate speech. While those restrictions reflect standards within the European Convention on Human Rights, the law also limits "false and unverified information," a vague phrase that can readily be twisted by authorities. In recent years, a new media law was drafted and rejected. The Yerevan Press Club and other new press associations drafted a model press law, published in January in the newspaper *Azg*, which they submitted to the National Assembly for consideration. The draft emphasized media independence from government and forbade prior restraints.

Armenia has no law regulating television and radio broadcasting, but lawmakers have drafted legislation which reflects the spirit of the 1991 press law, banning censorship, while repeating its restrictions. Additionally, the proposed bill required broadcast media to give immediate air time to government officials in emergencies. Press freedom advocates faulted the legislation for failing to create an independent television authority to regulate state television and radio, and for requiring all programs (including foreign films) to be broadcast in Armenian.

The main source of news and information about Armenia comes to Armenians through the nationwide state-owned television, which the government oversees closely. Although there is no official censorship in Armenia, television is regulated by a loyalty system, which is censorship in all but name. Many of state broadcast media employees still believe that their role is to assure and defend presidential power and the president's policies. As a result, self-censorship is a widespread phenomenon among television and radio journalists.

Eighteen independent radio and television stations are in operation across the country, including A1+, a private company in Yerevan that made a name for itself with its courageous reporting on the opposition's raid on the parliament following the disputed presidential election of 1996.

As in many other East European countries, the print media are officially free, but enormously dependent on economic reforms, an underdeveloped advertising base, centralized distribution and printing facilities, underpaid journalists, and the meager purchasing power of the population. Editors faced daunting challenges. They have complained that 34 percent of their newspapers' revenues are spent on a variety of taxes and another 25 percent cover fees to the state distribution agency, Haimamul.

The state publishing house Periodica has been another source of contention. On some occasions it has refused to publish opposition newspapers, usually for political reasons. Periodica gained control of the market by offering attractive prices for newsprint, but has gradually increased them to burdensome levels.

Beleaguered by such pressures, on December 3, nearly all major newspapers, nine news agencies, and one radio station staged a day-long strike to demand tax and rent exemptions, the restructuring of the state distribution monopoly, and more competition in the publishing industry. Prime Minister Robert Kocharian agreed to meet with the editors and directors of these news organizations to discuss their demands. In a conciliatory gesture, Kocharian fired Garegin Chookaszian, the head of the government information department, whom he blamed for not solving the press' problems.

The president's office, the parliament, the Foreign Ministry, and the other government agencies require accreditation as set out by the current law on mass media. Some journalists complained they were denied accreditation for no clear reason other than suspicion that they are "unfriendly" or "incompetent." The Armenian law is vague on removal of accreditation. It does not include criteria for barring a reporter from a government agency, but it provides for removal of accreditation of foreign reporters if they violate the Armenian legislation. Press access to Defense Ministry functions, ranging from press conferences to visits to military bases, are tightly controlled and usually require the personal permission of the defense minister. At photo opportunities, press officials frequently try to instruct the media about whom, how, and where to shoot.

In April, Nicholas Daniloff, a former Moscow bureau chief for *U.S. News & World Report* who now directs the journalism program at Northeastern University, undertook a three-month fact-finding mission to Armenia and Azerbaijan for CPJ. The resulting report, "Mixed Signals: Press Freedom in Azerbaijan and Armenia," appears on p. 358.

March 7
Mikael Hayrapetian, *Erevanian Orer*
ATTACKED

Two unknown individuals entered the Yerevan office of Mikael Hayrapetian, editor in chief of the independent newspaper *Erevanian Orer*, and demanded that he stop publishing the newspaper. When Hayrapetian refused, one of the men assaulted the editor, hitting him repeatedly in the head, while the other blocked the entrance to his office. The assailants then threw the journalist to the ground before leaving. Hayrapetian was admitted to a hospital two days later as his condition worsened, with cerebral shock, serious damage to his eyesight, and cuts on his forehead.

June 18
Zhanna Krikorova, Noyan Tapan
HARASSED
Gayaneh Arakelian, Noyan Tapan
HARASSED
Tigran Harutiunian, Noyan Tapan
HARASSED

Harutiunian, general manager of the Noyan Tapan news agency; editor in chief Arakelian; and Krikorova, a reporter, were summoned to the Ministry of Interior and National Security. Ministry officials pressured the journalists to reveal the source of a June 16 article about the Minsk Group of the Organization for Security and Cooperation in Europe, regarding the settlement of the Nagorno-Karabakh dispute between Armenia and Azerbaijan.

Harutiunian told officials that Krikorova was the author of the dispatch; a Noyan Tapan official told CPJ that the agency does not conceal authors' identities. Harutiunian and Arakelian spoke with ministry officials for several hours but refused to reveal the source of the news. Krikorova, who was detained in the ministry for about seven hours, suffered physical and mental distress.

On June 27, CPJ sent a letter to Armenian President Levon Ter-Petrossian condemning administrative pressure on journalists to reveal sources of information.

Azerbaijan

International interest in Azerbaijan and its vast Caspian Sea oil reserves grew again this year, and its leaders have stepped up efforts to improve the country's image among potential investors. But President Heydar Aliyev's drive to woo the West changed little for Azerbaijan's independent media, which routinely confronted official censorship and harassment.

The Azerbaijani government continues to practice Soviet-style censorship over the print media, although constitutional and legal safeguards exist on the books. Despite a 1996 presidential decree removing military censorship, instituted during the conflict with Armenia over the Armenian-populated enclave of Nagorno-Karabakh, journalists and media-watch groups reported that the practice has persisted along with political censorship. The country's 1995 constitution and its criminal code contain provisions that effectively ban criticism of the president and make libel a criminal offense.

On January 25, Azerbaijan enacted a comprehensive law on official secrets, which holds journalists, as well as officials, responsible for leaks of classified material, which it groups into four categories: military, economic, foreign policy, and intelligence. Some subjects that were banned during

Soviet times, such as the health of officials, accidents, and environmental problems, are now declassified.

Leading independent and opposition newspapers had dozens of articles, commentaries, and even letters to the editor censored throughout the year, forcing them to fill the blank spaces chiefly with cartoons. The primary targets of censorship were articles about human rights violations in Azerbaijan, interviews or statements by opposition politicians, reviews of the political situation, Armenian-Russian relations, the plight of refugees in Nagorno-Karabakh, environmental damage linked to offshore oil drilling, any information about ex-president Abulfaz Elchibey, and even coverage of President Aliyev's official visit to the United States in July. Earlier in the year, journalists returning from the Nakhchivan region, where former president Elchibey was based, were routinely detained and searched for materials about him.

The government maintains strong control over state television and radio, the only outlets that reach the entire nation. But officials allow one private television broadcaster, Azerbaijan News Service (ANS), to operate and broadcast news almost without censorship, chiefly because the station reaches less than 13 percent of the population. The authorities also do not jam foreign television and radio broadcasts, although they did censor some programs broadcast by the private Russian television company NTV in May, two weeks after NTV began broadcasting in Azeri for viewers in several regions in Azerbaijan. The government said it found some of the NTV programs "harmful to public morals."

Journalists continue to suffer beatings and violent threats, as well as police harassment while on assignment. The number of violent incidents fell when compared with 1996. Local media watchdog groups such as Yeni Nesil, however, attribute the decrease

to self-censorship by journalists hoping to avoid such retribution.

In April, Nicholas Daniloff, a former Moscow bureau chief for *U.S. News & World Report* who now directs the journalism program at Northeastern University, undertook a three-month fact-finding mission to Armenia and Azerbaijan for CPJ. The resulting report, "Mixed Signals: Press Freedom in Armenia and Azerbaijan," appears on p. 358. CPJ also issued an open letter to President Aliyev during his official visit to Washington in July, calling on him to immediately lift censorship restrictions on the media in Azerbaijan.

February 7
Gunduz Tairli and Kenan Aliyev, *Azadliq,*
HARASSED
The chief prosecutor summoned Gunduz Tairli, editor of the opposition newspaper *Azadliq,* and one of his reporters, Kenan Aliyev, to answer questions about publication of an investigative piece on government corruption between 1992 and 1994. During the interrogation, the prosecutor demanded that the journalists deny that Deputy Prime Minister Abbas Abbasov was involved in the wrongdoing. When the journalists refused, he warned that the next time they published anything similar they would be prosecuted under Article 36 of the Law on Mass Media.

February 13
Jumkhurriyet CENSORED

Authorities suspended publication of the weekly newspaper of the opposition Party of the Popular Front for four weeks. The executives of the printing house did not give any explanation for their refusal to publish the paper. *Jumkhurriyet* resumed printing on March 8.

February 20
Leila Ismailova, Turan Information Agency
ATTACKED

L. Muradov, director of the Ganjlik summer

youth center near Baku; S. Guseinov, a Ministry of Youth and Sport official; and U. Abdullaev, a participant in a world checkers tournament being held at the youth center, attacked Leila Ismailova, a correspondent for the Turan Information Agency, on the grounds of the center. When Ismailova, who was covering the tournament, asked Muradov, Guseinov, and Abdullaev about allegations that they were cheating, they started to beat her. Guseinov, who was visibly drunk, kicked Ismailova. After the beating, the assailants forced Ismailova off the center grounds. She did not file charges.

April 11, 1997
Avrasia HARASSED
The Azeri ambassador to Iran said the newspaper *Avrasia* "misinterpreted" his trip to Iran. He threatened to file suit against the newspaper. He did not follow through with his threat.

April 18
Mustajab Mutalimoglu, *Yeni Musavat* HARASSED
Mutalimoglu, a regional correspondent for the opposition newspaper *Yeni Musavat*, was fired by Astara authorities from his job at the local newspaper *Astara*. The journalist said he was fired and harassed because of an article he wrote and published in the March 4-6 issue of *Yeni Musavat* that was critical of regional authorities. He said he received several threats from supporters of the head of the regional administration. *Yeni Musavat* published an appeal signed by a group of opposition Popular Front members demanding an end to the harassment of the journalist.

April 23
525t-chi Gezet CENSORED
Government Censors removed an article about human rights violations in Azerbaijan from this independent newspaper. A cartoon replaced the article.

April 25
Press-Fakt CENSORED
Government Censors cut an interview with ex-president Abulfaz Elchibey.from this independent newspaper.

May 4
Elchin Seljuk, *Azadliq* IMPRISONED
Police arrested Seljuk, a correspondent for the opposition newspaper *Azadliq*, in the Nakhchivan airport on charges of being "a suspicious person." The journalist was detained upon his return to Baku from a village in the Nakhchivan Autonomous Republic, where the former president, Abulfaz Elchibey, lives. After a one-day investigation, Seljuk was accused of "ill-treatment of the police." A judge fined him 22,000 manat (around US$5) and he was allowed to return to Baku.

May 13
Irena Seidova, *Panorama* THREATENED

Seidova, a journalist from the *Panorama* newspaper in Baku, was in the Baku airport on her way home from Tbilisi, Georgia, when she decided to write a story about the work of Baku airport customs. After she had taken several photographs of a crowd of people standing in line waiting to go through customs, police asked Seidova and other journalists who were returning with her from an international media seminar in Tbilisi to talk with the head of criminal police of the airport. He demanded that Seidova expose the film, but she refused. Police dropped the demand after pressure from the other journalists present.

May 15
Israfil Agayev, *Lenkaran Hayaty* IMPRISONED, LEGAL ACTION

The district court of the Yasamalin region sentenced Agayev to three years in prison for "spreading libel against public officials of the region." During the three months he worked for the regional newspaper, Agayev published several articles about the former prosecutor of the region, Nazim Tagiyev, who was then working in the national prosecutor's office. The court called Agayev's articles libelous.

Agayev was freed on appeal on October 4, after spending four months and 19 days in prison.

June 6
Kamal Ali, *Ayna-Zerkalo* ATTACKED
***Khalg* correspondent** THREATENED
Bakinsky Rabochii THREATENED
Other reporters THREATENED

During a session of the Azeri parliament, a guard with the State Agency for Security slapped Ali, a correspondent for the newspaper *Ayna-Zerkalo*, in the face. "The journalist was speaking too loudly with his colleagues," the guard said. The unidentified guard threatened to use physical force against other journalists who defended Ali. The guard did not stop his harassment until parliament members and the Security Service chief intervened. The guard was forced to apologize. On the same day, the guard also threatened correspondents from the newspapers *Khalg* and *Bakinsky Rabochii*.

June 10
Talekh Zafarli, *Chag* ATTACKED

Natik Aleskerov, a member of the opposition Party of the Popular Front, insulted and beat Zafarli, editor of the newspaper *Chag*. Zafarli said that a few days earlier, former prime minister Panakh Gusseinov, one of the leaders of the Popular Front, had threatened him. According to Zafarli, the attacks likely stemmed from a series of critical articles he wrote about a split within the Party of the Popular Front.

June 22
Iranian state television CENSORED

Officials suspended retransmission of Iranian television programs in Azerbaijan on June 22.

Nizami Khudiev, the chairman of Azerbaijan's State Television and Radio, said that it was a temporary measure aimed at preventing the broadcast of provocative anti-Azerbaijani programs which distort historical truth and incite inter-ethnic division. Khudiev said that the Iranian broadcasts would remain off the air until Iran and Azerbaijan reached agreement on a treaty ensuring reciprocal broadcasts of Azerbaijani television in Iran.

June 30
Jeihun Nasibov, *Ayna* HARASSED, CENSORED
Azer Rashidoglu, *Azadliq* HARASSED, CENSORED

Police confiscated tape recorders from Nasibov and Rashidoglu, who were covering the congress of the Azerbaijan Communist Party. The journalists then were pushed out of the congress hall.

Police returned the equipment the same day but the recorded cassettes had been removed. Afig Shukyurov, deputy chief of administration of the Sabunchi region, said that the regional prosecutor's office would study the tapes and if they did not contain "anti-state speeches," they would be given back to the reporters. The tapes were not returned.

July 1
Azadliq HARASSED

Military censors at a special agency in the president's administration demanded that Gunduz Tairli, editor of the opposition newspaper *Azadliq*, provide them with the addresses and home telephone numbers of all the newspaper's staff, or they would ban the newspaper. Tairli refused to obey the order. No reprisals followed.

July 8
All media CENSORED

Minister of Internal Affairs Ramil Usubov ordered all police staff in Azerbaijan not to provide any information to the media without the permission of the ministry's press center. The official explanation for the order was that "recently a number of low-quality criminal stories were published in provincial newspapers."

July 12
Irena Lasota, *Uncaptive Minds* HARASSED
ANS television CENSORED

Lasota, an editor of the Washington, D.C.-based quarterly *Uncaptive Minds*, was traveling to Nakhchivan, an exclave of Azerbaijan. As Lasota was preparing to board a plane to Baku, several uniformed men approached her and asked what she was doing in Nakhchivan. She replied that she was visiting former President Elchibey in the village of Kelaki. The men asked whether Lasota had any video or audio cassettes or rolls of film with her, which she denied. They took her to a room where a police inspector told her that her bags would be searched for interviews or photographs of the former president. After failing to find anything in her baggage, the inspector said: "We will find the people who are bringing the cassettes to you and we will get them." Lasota was then permitted to board the plane.

July 25
Ali Hajikuliyev, *Jumkhurriyet* ATTACKED

Police beat Hajikuliyev, the executive secretary of the opposition newspaper *Jumkhurriyet*, on a subway platform in Baku.

Hajikuliyev said the incident began when policemen stopped him in the subway and demanded to see his identification. The officer was rude and Hajikuliyev said he asked for more polite treatment. In response, the officer slapped him several times and tore his shirt. A few more police officers joined their colleague and threw Hajikuliyev's press card to the floor. He demanded the policemen identify themselves and told them he would file a complaint with police, the Interior Ministry, and the Azeri pres-

ident. The police swore at him and used foul language about journalism and the president.

Hajikuliyev filed a complaint with the Interior Ministry. The ministry refused to investigate the case.

August 4
Mustajab Mutalimoglu, *Yeni Musavat* HARASSED

Mutalimoglu, a regional stringer for the opposition newspaper *Yeni Musavat*, was fired from his staff job at the local newspaper *Astara*. The journalist said he was fired and harassed because of an article he wrote and published in the March 4-6 issue of *Yeni Musavat* that was critical of regional authorities. He said he received several threats from supporters of the head of the regional administration. *Yeni Musavat* published an appeal signed by a group of opposition Popular Front members demanding an end to the harassment of the journalist.

August 4
Elchin Seljuk, *Azadliq* IMPRISONED

Police arrested Seljuk, a correspondent for the opposition newspaper *Azadliq*, in the Nakhchivan airport on charges of being a suspicious person. The journalist was detained upon his return to Baku from a village in the Nakhchivan Autonomous Republic, where former president Abulfaz Elchibey lives. After a one-day investigation, Seljuk was accused of ill-treatment of the police. A judge fined him 22,000 manat (around US$5) and he was allowed to return to Baku.

August 4
Chag CENSORED

Censors removed an article about the activity of Speaker of Parliament Murtuz Alesqerov from the newspaper.

EUROPE

August 4
Jeihun Nasibov, *Ayna-Zerkalo* HARASSED
CENSORED
Azer Rashidoglu, *Azadliq* HARASSED
CENSORED

Police confiscated tape recorders from Nasibov and Rashidoglu, who were covering the congress of the Azerbaijan Communist Party. The journalists then were pushed out of the congress hall.

Police returned the equipment the same day but the recorded cassettes had been removed. Afig Shukyurov, deputy chief of administration of the Sabunchi region, said that the regional prosecutor's office would study the tapes and if they did not contain anti-state speeches, they would be given back to the reporters. The tapes were not returned.

August 4
Jumkhurriyet CENSORED

Censors removed an interview with Ali Kerimov, deputy chairman of the opposition Popular Front of Azerbaijan, from the newspaper. Information about President Heydar Aliyev's political opponents is routinely blocked by the government.

August 4
Ali Hajikuliyev, *Jumkhurriyet* ATTACKED

Police beat Hajikuliyev, the executive secretary of the opposition newspaper *Jumkhurriyet*, on a subway platform in Baku.

Hajikuliyev said the incident began when policemen stopped him in the subway and demanded to see his documents. The officer was rude and Hajikuliyev said he asked for more polite treatment. In response, the officer slapped him several times and tore his shirt. A few more police officers joined their colleague and threw Hajikuliyev's press card to the floor. He demanded the policemen identify themselves and told them he would file complaints

with police headquarters, the Interior Ministry, and the Azerbaijani president. The police swore at him and used foul language about journalism and the president.

Hajikuliyev filed a complaint with the Interior Ministry. The ministry refused to investigate the case.

November 2
Millet THREATENED

The Ministry of Information and Press warned the opposition newspaper *Millet* that it was in danger of suspension of its publication license because it had violated Article 4 of the Law on Mass Media. Nazir Akhmedli, editor in chief of the paper, said that the warning stemmed from an article published in the paper on October 29 titled "Mass Famine in Azerbaijan."

December 22
Savalan Mamedov, *Istintag* IMPRISONED

Mamedov, editor of the Baku weekly *Istintag*, was arrested and imprisoned on charges of libel (Article 121 of the Azerbaijani penal code) against the former prosecutor of the Lenkoran district, Nazim Tagiev. In a number of articles Mamedov claimed that Tagiev had cooperated with Alikram Gumbatov, who was convicted of treason and attempting to stage an uprising. Mamedov was released from police custody on January 23, 1998. Court hearings have not yet been scheduled. Mamedov could serve a sentence of up to five years if he is found guilty.

Ayna-Zerkalo CENSORED
Government censors removed and cut articles from the independent newspaper *Ayna-Zerkalo* on several occasions in 1997. For example:
April 5 – Censors cut an article about the arrest of former prime minister Suret Husseinov.
April 12 – Censors removed part of an article on Armenian-Russian relations.
April 26 – Censors cut information about the

state importing products of inferior quality from Austria.

May 17 – Censors cut an article about leaders of the opposition National Independence party.

Azadliq CENSORED

This opposition newspaper suffered from government censorship on many occasions in 1997. For example:

April 2 – Censors removed part of a statement of the Democratic Congress condemning attacks on the opposition by the authorities.

April 3 – Censors removed an article on the facts of human rights violations in Azerbaijan, running a cartoon instead.

April 24 – Censors removed four articles.

April 30 – Censors cut a political commentary.

May 14 – Censors cut part of an article about the problems of foreign students studying in Azerbaijan.

May 17 – Censors cut a statement by the Popular Front of Azerbaijan (PFA) about a violation of the presumption of innocence by the State Radio and Television.

May 20 – Censors removed a statement by the PFA on the occupation of Shusha and Lachin cities.

May 22 – Censors cut an article on the investigation of an explosion in a military unit of the Azeri army. An article on a parliamentary session also was cut.

July 1 – Censors cut two articles, one on the occupation of the Fizuli region by Armenian troops and one on the death of PFA member Shahmardan Jafarov.

July 3 – Censors cut a report on a press conference held by the leader of the opposition party, Isa Gambar.

July 5 – Censors cut an article on the ecological damage caused by offshore oil production.

July 16 – Censors cut an article about the country's socio-economic condition.

July 19 – Censors cut large parts from an interview with former president Abulfaz Elchibey.

July 29 – Censors cut an article about President Aliyev's visit to the United States.

September 26 – Censors cut two stories.

October 12 – Censors cut a letter from a refugee and an article describing numerous details of illegal sales of military property and construction.

November 7 – Censors substantially cut an article about the work of Parliament deputies.

November 15 – Censors cut an article about the visit of President Heydar Aliyev to Nakhchivan and an interview with one of the leaders of the Party of the National Front, Ali Kerimov.

November 16 – Censors cut an article about Boris Berezovsky.

Khurriyet CENSORED

Government censors repeatedly removed or cut articles in the opposition newspaper *Khurriyet* in 1997. For example:

April 15 – Censors cut an article about the arrest of Gamidov.

April 28 – Censors cut an interview with a parliamentary deputy, Shamil Yusifov.

Millet CENSORED

Government censors repeatedly removed articles and cut material from this opposition newspaper during 1997. For example:

April 12 – Censors cut material concerning the situation in the media in Azerbaijan.

April 18 – Censors removed an article describing persecution of the leader of the opposition National Independence party.

April 24 – Censors removed two articles—parliament and on the persecution of opposition leader Etibar Mamedov—and replaced them with cartoons.

April 26 – Censors removed an article on the country's socio-economic woes.

May 17 – Censors cut an article about the political situation in Azerbaijan.

Mukhalifat CENSORED

Government censors repeatedly subjected this opposition newspaper to cuts and removal of articles during 1997. For example:

April 2 – Censors cut four articles about

EUROPE

Azerbaijan's political situation and persecution of the families of veterans of the Nagorno-Karabakh war.

April 12 – Censors cut an article about sales of Russian arms to Armenia. They removed two letters to the editor on Azerbaijani politics from the same issue.

April 15 – Censors removed part of an article on the arrest of former prime minister Suret Husseinov.

April 20 – Censors removed an article about politics and human rights violations in Azerbaijan.

April 22 – Censors cut two articles on politics.

April 23 – Censors cut three articles—on the plight of refugees; the army at the Nagorno-Karabakh front; and on misinterpretation of historical facts.

April 30 – Censors cut an article on the history of the Azerbaijan Democratic Republic.

May 7 – Censors cut part of an investigative report on the occupation of the Azeri town of Shusha in May 1992 by Armenian troops.

May 14 – Censors cut three articles on the situation in southern Azerbaijan (North of Iran) and Azerbaijani politics.

July 3 – Censors cut an article about Azerbaijan's domestic situation.

July 12 – Censors cut letter's to the editor and an article about the results of the NATO summit in Madrid.

Yeni Musavat CENSORED

Government censors repeatedly cut materials for articles or removed articles in their entirety from this opposition newspaper during 1997. For example:

April 4 – Censors cut an article about the arrest of the former speaker of Milli Mejlis Isa Gambar and two articles about Azerbaijan's political situation.

April 25 – Censors removed part of an article on parliament.

July 1 – Censors cut three articles about Azerbaijan's political situation and about state television activity.

July 8 – Censors cut an interview with Salakhaddin Alkperov, the deputy chairman of the Musavat party.

7 Gün CENSORED

Government censors repeatedly cut material and removed articles from this opposition newspaper in 1997. For example:

April 26 – Censors removed an article citing various criticisms by opposition politicians on the eve of Azerbaijan's 1992 presidential elections.

May 1 – Censors cut part of an article on the investigation into the murder of parliamentary deputy Ziya Bunyatov.

May 9 – Censors cut an article on the occupation of the town of Shusha in Nagorno-Karabakh.

July 5 – Censors cut two articles about the liquidation of the Trade and Foreign Economic Relations ministries.

July 8 – Censors removed an article about the plight of the poor in Azerbaijan.

Belarus

In a drive to consolidate his rule and eradicate all sources of opposition, the authoritarian Belarusian president Aleksander Lukashenko waged an all-front war on the press. Lukashenko, whose ambition it is to lead a Soviet-style union with his Slavic neighbors, especially Russia, stepped up his earlier efforts to harness independent and opposition news organizations, formally institutionalizing his control over the media. On top of his systematic extra-judicial attacks and use of economic pressures against critics and independent journalists both domestic and foreign, Lukashenko pushed through an amended press law that boosted his powers and tightened his legal grip on the press.

In the weeks before the April 2 signing

of an integration treaty with Russia, Lukashenko ordered a crackdown on opponents of the union as well as on media coverage of opposition rallies. His methods of intimidation included detention, arrest, beating, and harassment of correspondents attempting to cover mass protests against the union treaty in mid-March and early April in Minsk.

The first quarter of the year also featured Lukashenko's renewed attempts to silence critical coverage by foreign news organizations, notably Russian television. Because of the limited reach of domestic opposition and independent news media, the Russian television companies ORT, NTV, and RTR had become the only alternative to state television for most Belarusians. Lukashenko grew progressively angrier at critical coverage by the Russian news programs and their Minsk-based correspondents, whom he accused of biased reporting intended to subvert his regime and its fraternal relationship with Russia. Throughout the year, the Belarusian government hit Russian correspondents with a variety of reprisals for these imagined slights, including disaccreditation, arrest, and expulsion.

Lukashenko moved to introduce new media restrictions, aimed in particular at foreign news media. After briefly barring all foreign television companies from the state satellite transmission center in late March, the administration announced new rules for access to the center, requiring among other things, prior censorship of all broadcast materials and the presence of a censor during transmission. Authorities also announced plans to review the credentials of all foreign correspondents in the country and repeatedly threatened to withdraw the press credentials of foreign and local reporters if their work was deemed harmful to state interests.

The president also took measures to further restrict the beleaguered domestic private press, especially newspapers that were forced to publish in neighboring Lithuania because the state-controlled publishing house refused to publish them. On March 18, the Council of Ministers issued a decree restricting the import and distribution of any printed material that could be construed as "a threat to national security, the rights and freedoms of individuals, health and morale of the population, and environment." The measure also banned the import of audiovisual or printing equipment, as well as other instruments "that contain information," which could "represent a threat to the country's political and economic interests."

On April 3, Foreign Minister Ivan Antonovich criticized journalists and foreign news outlets for allegedly "leading an information war against Belarus" and blamed them for causing public unrest. He said the government could not guarantee their safety if they continued to cover unsanctioned public demonstrations. He added that new rules could bar Belarusian citizens from working as correspondents for foreign news agencies, which would deprive a large number of Belarusian journalists from their chief source of livelihood.

The government announced on July 12 that it would begin a two-month process of re-accrediting all foreign media, as it had threatened to do several months before. Government Resolution 869 barred Belarusian journalists from obtaining accreditation as correspondents for foreign media outlets. The Foreign Ministry could unilaterally withdraw accreditation and expel any journalist or news organization it deemed to be biased, according to the measure.

The lower house of the parliament on October 15 adopted several potentially restrictive draft amendments to the country's press law. The amendments, which were an attempt to codify the March 18 decree, provided for considerably more intervention by the executive branch's State Press Committee and established heavy penalities for libel, especially regarding the president. The changes also threatened small publishers with stringent economic and administrative restrictions.

On October 29—hours after Lukashenko promised press freedom advocates that he would take their concerns about the amendments into consideration—the upper chamber surprised many by refusing to confirm the amendments, and sent them back to the lower house. A visiting delegation from the International Federation of Journalists (IFJ) had presented Lukashenko with a petition from the Belarusian Association of Journalists and the Belarusian Union of Journalists asking him to refrain from signing the restrictive measures into law. Lukashenko's response to the Western visitors, albeit cosmetic, was unprecedented.

The lower and upper chambers of the parliament, on December 17 and 20 respectively, gave their final approval to the restrictive press law amendments. The changes, which had not yet been signed into law by President Lukashenko, varied somewhat from the original draft, but still greatly boosted the executive branch's powers to interfere with and control the media.

On November 24, the Supreme Commercial Court ruled to shut down *Svaboda*, one of the country's largest and most popular independent newspapers. Its staff continued to publish the paper on its Web site, until its Web provider cut off service. Radio Liberty posted the paper on its Web site.

February 10
Ihar Hermianchuk, *Svaboda* HARASSED

An attacker fired shots at the home of Ihar Hermianchuk, editor in chief of the indepen-

dent daily *Svaboda*. Hermianchuk, who was not home at the time, said gun shots shattered the double-glazed windows of his kitchen.

The editor lives in the village of Kolodishi, outside Minsk, and he said he often works on *Svaboda* material at night in his kitchen. He said the incident was a warning from the Belarusian authorities to stop his newspaper's critical coverage of the government. Hermianchuk said he did not know why he was harassed at that particular time because the newspaper was not doing anything that differed from its past work.

March 13
Ihar Rynkevich, Belarusian Association of Journalists HARASSED
Oles Doshinsky, Radio Liberty HARASSED
Sergei Grits, free-lancer HARASSED
Pavel Karnazytsky, *Zdravy Smysl* HARASSED
Irina Khalip, *Imya* HARASSED
Oles Khmelnitsky, Radio Liberty HARASSED
Svetlana Kurs, free-lancer HARASSED
Sergei Malinovsky, *Svabodniye Novosti Plus* HARASSED
Alexander Mikhalchuk, *Belarusskaya Gazeta* HARASSED
Algerd Neverovsky, *Svaboda* HARASSED
Galyazh Potopovich, *Svaboda* HARASSED
Roman Yakovlevsky, *Belarusskaya Gazeta* HARASSED
Sabian Frenzel, student newspaper in Berlin HARASSED
Tim Kokhler, student newspaper in Berlin HARASSED

Police detained at least 12 journalists in Minsk on March 13 and 14 before a planned opposition rally. Ihar Rynkevich, executive director of the Belarusian Association of Journalists, was held and questioned by police on charges of taking part in an unauthorized picket line on March 10. Police said they had a film showing Rynkevich at the demonstration. Rynkevich said he was there in a journalistic capacity but had not carried a camera, remained on the sidewalk, and had not had any interaction with police. He refused to sign a record of his detention because the authorities offered no proof of an infraction. After one court session, a hearing in Rynkevich's case at the Moscow District Court in Minsk was postponed, and he was released on his own recognizance.

Roman Yakovlevsky of the independent *Belarusskaya Gazeta* and a board member of the Belarusian Open Society Foundation, was also held and fingerprinted by police. His detention occurred at a time when the country's general prosecutor was investigating the foundation, which has provided grants to independent media organizations. The government had recently barred the foundation's executive director from re-entering Belarus.

The other 10 detained journalists, including two Germans from a Berlin student newspaper, were released.

March 18
All media CENSORED
Belarusskaya Gazeta CENSORED

The Belarusian Council of Ministers restricted the import, circulation, or distribution of any materials deemed a threat to "national security, the rights and freedoms of individuals, health, and morale of the population, and the environment."

The measure banned the transfer or import of technical equipment used by the media that could threaten the country's "political and economic interests." That included audiovisual equipment, printing presses, and other equipment "containing information."

On the same day, Belarusian customs officials at a border crossing with Lithuania intercepted all copies of the independent daily *Belarusskaya Gazeta*, which had been printed in Lithuania to avoid government harassment. The Belarusian officials inspected the newspapers before returning them, delaying distribution of the issue.

March 27
Alexander Stupnikov, NTV EXPELLED
CENSORED
All broadcast media HARASSED, CENSORED

Belarus' Interior Ministry ordered Alexander Stupnikov, a correspondent for Russia's independent NTV station to leave the country within four days. The expulsion stemmed from Stupnikov's alleged violations of the country's press law. Officials also warned NTV that if Stupnikov's name or voice were used in any future broadcasts, the Russian station would be banned from Belarus.

Threatened and harassed by government officials for months, Stupnikov had been stripped of his accreditation a few days before he was expelled. The actions appeared linked to NTV's coverage of a March 23 opposition rally in Minsk that riot police had violently dispersed.

The government barred foreign television journalists from accessing the state television's transmission center—the country's only direct satellite link—from March 24-26. The government restored access only after it issued new rules requiring prior censorship of broadcast materials and the presence of a censor during transmission.

April 2
Pavel Bykovsky, *Belarussky Rynok* ATTACKED, HARASSED
Irina Khalip, *Imya* ATTACKED, HARASSED
Vladimir Khalip, free-lancer ATTACKED, HARASSED
Tamara Khamytsevych, *Vecherniy Minsk* HARASSED
Pavel Kornazytsky, *Zdravy Smysl* IMPRISONED, ATTACKED
Vladimir Kostin, Belarusian Independent TV ATTACKED, LEGAL ACTION
Sergei Malinovsky, *Svobodniye Novosti* HARASSED
Valery Shchukin, *Tovarishch* ATTACKED, HARASSED

At least eight journalists were beaten and

EUROPE

detained by the OMON special police forces while covering a rally in Minsk. The demonstrators were protesting the signing of an integration treaty between Belarus and Russia. Riot police injured several people during violent clashes with protesters.

Police held the journalists for a few hours before releasing all of them except for Pavel Kornazytsky, a correspondent with *Zdravy Smysl*, who was sentenced to 10 days in jail for violating Presidential Decree No. 5 on unauthorized assemblies. The authorities reportedly view his newspaper as more radical than others.

June 25
All media CENSORED

The lower house of the Belarusian parliament approved several restrictive draft amendments to the country's press law. A final version of the amendments, with some revisions, passed both the lower and upper houses of parliament in December and is expected to be signed into law by President Aleksander Lukashenko in 1998.

The new regulations greatly enhance the executive branch's power to interfere with and control the media. Under the legislation, the State Press Committee may exercise judicial functions by declaring the registration of any media outlet invalid after two official warnings to the news organization that it violated the press law. The bill shortens the time period for which publications may be suspended upon violating the law from one year to three months, but adds a clause barring editors of suspended media units from registering new ones for two years.

Although the new bill forbids formal censorship, the press committee may require new publications to submit detailed information on target audience and editorial focus for registration purposes; it may even demand evidence that local authorities do not object to the establishment of the news outlet in their district. The press committee also must approve of the distribution of foreign-based periodicals; for-

eign reporters are to be accredited through the Ministry of Foreign Affairs, which will have the right to limit accreditation in cases of journalists coming from countries where restrictions are imposed on Belarusian reporters.

July 2
Pavel Sheremet, ORT and *Belarusskaya Delovaya Gazeta* CENSORED

The Belarusian Foreign Ministry suspended the special events accreditation of Pavel Sheremet, the Minsk bureau chief for ORT (Russian public television). The suspension was evidently an effort to prevent ORT from covering public gatherings on July 3, the new national independence day and the 930th anniversary of the founding of Minsk.

Officials told Sheremet that he had insulted the president and the nation of Belarus in a June 28 broadcast in which he characterized the new date to celebrate independence as "President [Aleksander] Lukashenko's idea", and said that despite heavy rains that had killed five people, preparations for the holiday were still underway.

On July 3, the Foreign Ministry sent an official note of protest to ORT management in Moscow, saying that unless the station apologized, Sheremet would be stripped of his full accreditation. ORT management did not make apologies, so, on July 7, the Foreign Ministry permanently revoked Sheremet's accreditation.

CPJ sent protest letters to Lukashenko on July 3 and July 9, urging the president to restore Sheremet's credentials.

July 12
All foreign media CENSORED
All media CENSORED

Belarus authorities passed Resolution 869, requiring all foreign media to be re-accredited, a process expected to take two months. The resolution also bars Belarusian journalists from gaining accreditation as correspondents for foreign media, and gives the Foreign Ministry power to withdraw accreditation and expel any journalist or news organization it deems biased.

July 22
Pavel Sheremet, ORT IMPRISONED, LEGAL ACTION
Dmitriy Zavadsky, ORT IMPRISONED, LEGAL ACTION
Yaroslav Ovchinnikov, ORT IMPRISONED, LEGAL ACTION

Belarusian border guards detained an ORT film crew led by Minsk bureau chief Sheremet. The crew was investigating security at the Belarus-Lithuania border, which the government said it had increased. Sheremet, his cameraman Zavadsky, and driver Ovchinnikov had requested permission to film, but received no reply. Sheremet and his crew went to the border and found an unguarded section, which they filmed before proceeding to a checkpoint. There, guards detained them, took their videotapes, and released them that day.

On July 26, border guards detained Sheremet and Ovchinnikov at the Minsk airport and took them to Grodno near the Lithuanian border for questioning about the July 22 incident. Border agents also went with a warrant to Zavadsky's home in Minsk and said that unless he agreed to appear as a witness in the case, he would be taken into detention. Agents then took him to Grodno.

The crew was held in a Belarusian KGB investigation cell in Grodno on charges of illegally crossing the border, which carries a maximum sentence of five years. Ovchinnikov was released, but faced the same charges. He was formally charged on August 6.

Police searched the ORT bureau, as well as the homes of Sheremet and Ovchinnikov. Police seized Sheremet's accreditation card (although the government had stripped him of his accreditation on July 9), his passport, and several documents.

On September 4, Zavadsky was released on his own recognizance but remained in Grodno to take part in the investigation. Sheremet refused to confess guilt. President Lukashenko said that Zavadsky had requested to be released, but Sheremet must like it in his cell.

President Aleksander Lukashenko's promise that Sheremet would be released before a summit with Russian President Boris Yeltsin was not honored.

On September 25, prosecutors announced they had extended by 30 days their investigation into the case. Their announcement occurred just before the legal deadline for pre-trial detention expired. The Belarusian KGB said the trial would begin as soon as the lawyers in the case were ready.

Also on that day, the Foreign Ministry again denied permanent accreditation to Sheremet and his crew.

On October 8, Sheremet was released from prison pending trial. He was taken home in handcuffs under police escort. His release was on condition that he not leave Minsk.

The documents pertaining to the case were submitted to the prosecutor of Grodno by Judge Boris Raguimov on November 25. The prosecutor speedily transferred the case to the court in the small border town of Oshmiany. Observers and journalists were unable to attend the hearing, which opened on December 17, because they needed to get border permits. The court postponed the hearing until December 23 for technical reasons—the defendants were not provided with readable copies of the charge.

The court resumed its work on the Sheremet case on December 23. Sheremet, Zavadsky, and their lawyer appealed to the court to drop the charges for lack of evidence. They also asked permission to present new witnesses but the judge refused. The court decided to postpone the hearing until December 29.

The trial was subsequently postponed until January 5 because Sheremet's lawyer became ill. It resumed on January 8 after another postponement.

On January 28, Sheremet and Zavadsky

were found guilty of illegally crossing the border and were given suspended sentences of two years and 18 months respectively, by Judge Vitaliy Kazakevich. The resolution came after Lukashenko and Yeltsin reached a compromise on the case during a summit meeting in Moscow the previous week.

Although the two were freed, Sheremet was barred from working as a journalist for one year.

August 15
Anatoliy Adamchuk, ORT IMPRISONED
Aleksandr Oganov, ORT IMPRISONED
Valeriy Astashkin, ORT IMPRISONED
Vladimir Kostin, ORT IMPRISONED

Three members of an ORT television crew, all Russian citizens, were detained and held in Lida. They were freed on August 22 and returned to Moscow that day. A fourth member of that crew, a Belarusian citizen, was released three days later.

Adamchuk, Oganov, Astashkin, and Kostin were detained by Belarusian border guards as they gathered footage of unguarded sections of the frontier between Belarus and Lithuania. Belarusian officials reportedly elicited a "confession" from Adamchuk, who read his statement on state television, claiming ORT management had threatened to fire him if he refused the assignment. Belarus claimed ORT orchestrated the incident to undermine Belarus' union with Russia.

The crew had retraced the footsteps of another ORT crew, led by Minsk Bureau Chief Pavel Sheremet, whose members were arrested on July 22 for filming at the border without permission.

August 20
ORT CENSORED

The government of Belarus annulled ORT's accreditation and accused ORT management of organizing "a political provocation against the country's leadership." Belarus revoked ORT's accreditation after two ORT television crews were charged with illegally crossing the Belarus-Lithuanian border. The crews had been investigating security issues at the border.

On September 25, the Foreign Ministry refused to grant permanent accreditation to the crew of ORT's Minsk bureau chief Pavel Sheremet, who remained imprisoned on charges of illegally crossing the Belarusian-Lithuanian border while filming.

August 22
Vladimir Foshenko, ORT HARASSED, EXPELLED

Authorities expelled Foshenko, an ORT special correspondent in Voronezh, accusing him of biased reporting on Belarus. Foshenko had been detained on August 18 in Minsk and questioned in connection with the activities of an ORT television crew that had been filming on the Belarusian-Lithuanian border.

On September 25, the Belarusian Foreign Ministry denied Foshenko temporary accreditation.

November 24
Svaboda CENSORED

Maya Klimenkova, a justice of the Supreme Commercial Court ordered the immediate shutdown of the thrice-weekly paper during a November 24 court hearing. The State Press Committee had charged *Svaboda* with violating the country's press law by inciting social discord. The judge also canceled the newspaper's registration and ordered *Svaboda* to pay about US$30 for court expenses.

Judge Klimenkova ruled that the State Press Committee had acted in accordance with the Law on the Press and Other Mass Media when it filed suit against *Svaboda* after issuing four warnings to the newspaper. The newspaper's attorney argued that the charges were not commercial in nature and so did not fall under the Supreme Commercial Court's jurisdiction. Judge Klimenkova disagreed, claiming her court's jurisdiction over the case had the backing of the Supreme Civil Court.

Svaboda filed an appeal and editor Ihar Hermianchuk said that the charges against his newspaper were "absurd" and unfounded. He said the closure of *Svaboda*, which averaged a circulation of 50,000 copies among its three weekly issues, was meant as a warning to other independent and opposition publications.

Bosnia-Herzegovina

Two years after the Dayton peace accords, Bosnia-Herzegovina remains divided along ethnic lines, with state-run media used by all sides as tools for spreading nationalist propaganda and retaining power. Further complicating media issues in the region was the direct intervention of NATO forces in the control and management of state broadcasting facilities, raising troubling questions about media independence and the appropriate mechanisms, if any, for combating ethnic propaganda in a volatile post-war environment.

The ruling nationalist factions in each ethnic community exercise direct or indirect control over local news broadcasting. The news media is more lively and diverse in Sarajevo and other areas of the Muslim-Croat Federation. In the Serb Republic, there are few independent publications or broadcasters. Most Bosnian Serb news outlets operate on behalf of one of the two rival centers of political power. Although the Western-backed Bosnian Serb president Biljana Plavsic serves as the duly elected leader in Banja Luka, wartime Bosnian Serb leader Radovan Karadzic, an indicted war criminal, controls much of region from his base in Pale.

Newsgathering throughout the country is hampered by police harassment, poor telecommunications, and restrictions on transit between the Serb Republic and the Muslim-Croat Federation and between Muslim- and Croat-controlled areas. The development of independent media has been hurt further by the loss of the many journalists who were killed in the war, emigrated, or left the profession for more secure employment.

The Dayton peace accords addressed the need to safeguard both the security and independence of journalists, but those promises have not been vigilantly enforced. In a memorandum to U.S. Secretary of State Madeleine K. Albright in May, before she traveled to Bosnia, CPJ recommended measures to secure the safety of journalists and to aid the growth of independent media before the fall local elections. The memorandum urged that Stabilization Force (SFOR) troops be authorized to safeguard not only transmitters or media offices, but also the journalists themselves—with the use of force if necessary. CPJ called for the prosecution of police officers who attack journalists. Because regionally differentiated license plates were used to identify traveling reporters by their ethnicity, exposing them to local police and paramilitary harassment, CPJ asked the Organization for Security and Cooperation in Europe (OSCE) to offer shuttle buses to journalists covering the election across inter-entity boundaries until the entities adopted a universal license plate. CPJ also appealed for SFOR adjudication of broadcasting regulatory disputes, such as the case of Radio Zid, an independent Sarajevo station whose signal was overpowered on the same frequency by the Karadzic family's Radio Orthodox St. John in Pale.

In May, Albright pledged that by year's end all Bosnians would have access to independent television or radio reporting. She announced plans to expand broadcasts of

EUROPE

Radio Free Europe and the Voice of America to counter "misinformation designed to fuel hate" by official media. The NATO powers authorized High Representative Carlos Westendorp, the top peace envoy in Bosnia, to take action against media deemed to be working against the peace process. In August, the television studio in Banja Luka, controlled by Plavsic supporters, cut links with Karadzic-backed Serb Radio and Television (SRT) in Pale, citing its "primitive propaganda," and broadcast its own news program. Plavsic demanded the resignation of SRT's pro-Karadzic editorial managers. In August, when SRT's Pale TV intercut footage of Nazi tanks with footage of NATO troops deployed in Bosnia, NATO deemed the programming to be in violation of the Dayton accords. On September 1 nearly 300 U.S. SFOR troops interceded to block armed pro-Pale Bosnian Serbs from illegally taking control of a television transmission tower in Udrigovo that new non-governmental broadcasters had hoped to use. After a day of Bosnia Serb protests and mob attacks, the U.S. troops withdrew. SFOR returned the transmitter to the Karadzic loyalists, who pledged to tone down anti-NATO editorializing and provide an hour of prime time to rival factions. Pale TV denounced the move, saying NATO had engaged in censorship by seizing the transmitter and dictating the terms of its return. In a letter to Secretary Albright, CPJ objected to NATO's decision to turn the Udrigovo transmitter over to the Karadzic forces, noting that it would curtail promised opportunities for independent broadcasters. The letter reiterated CPJ's position that NATO should enforce the Dayton accords' "ample guarantees for press freedom" and "ensure that a variety of viewpoints—including criticism of the actions of NATO—can be expressed in the local media."

On October 1, Westendorp condemned SRT for its alleged "persistent and blatant contravention" of the Dayton accords and "insulting language and highly biased reportage," and authorized SFOR's seizure of four transmitters used by Pale TV.

The transmitters were turned over to Plavsic's state broadcasting service in Banja Luka. Miroslav Toholj, the general manager of Pale TV, called the seizure of transmitters "violence against freedom of the media." Journalists from the Pale studio went on strike, proclaiming themselves victims of press attacks initiated by NATO.

While CPJ took no position on the NATO seizure of the transmitters, which had been at the service not of a news organization but of the propaganda arm of an unrecognized government run by indicted war criminals, the Board of Directors voted later to oppose any NATO intervention which would reduce rather than increase the availability and diversity of published and broadcast news and opinion. CPJ urged Westendorp to ensure that the transmitters would be used for balanced, impartial news coverage. In October, former CPJ chairman Kati Marton traveled to Bosnia and Serbia with *New York Times* columnist and fellow board member Anthony Lewis. During their week-long visit to Sarajevo, Banja Luka, Doboj, and Belgrade, they met with Bosnian and Serbian journalists and political leaders, seeking stronger press freedom guarantees and support from the international community for independent broadcasting. They urged that any new regulatory agencies be supervised by professional journalists, not politicians.

The Bosnian Serb broadcasters were not the only ones accused of violating the Dayton agreement by airing biased and inflammatory programs. Banja Luka TV broadcast an inflammatory anti-Croatian program at year end, prompting Westendorp to announce that he would appoint a foreign "supervisor" for the Bosnian Serb station. Croatian Television

Mostar, HTV, in Croat-controlled western Mostar, was warned on three separate occasions in 1997 by the OSCE media commission and NATO to stop broadcasting allegedly racist denunciations of Bosnian Muslims. The OSCE ordered HTV to apologize during their evening news broadcasts, under threat of punitive NATO action. The station acquiesced, but two general managers resigned in protest.

The print media also became a target in the Bosnian Serb power struggle, with the bombing in September in Doboj of *Alternativa*, the only pro-Plavsic newspaper in the Karadzic-controlled town. *Alternativa*'s offices had been machine-gunned a month earlier at a time when its publisher was held in custody by pro-Karadzic police. In a troubling development for Sarajevo's independent press, Bosnian President Alija Izetbegovic attacked *Dani* and other leading magazines for reporting on Muslim atrocities against Serbs in the Bosnian capital. Izetbegovic called the journalists anti-Muslim traitors "financed by foreign sources."

January 27
Two journalists, *Stern* HARASSED, CENSORED

Police detained two unidentified journalists from the German magazine *Stern* for more than an hour in Vitez in Croat-controlled territory. Police told the journalists that they required prior permission to conduct interviews and photograph. Police confiscated notes and film.

February 12
Crew, RTV-TPK HARASSED

Bosnian Serbian police confiscated a television camera and equipment from a Tuzla-based RTV-TPK television crew at a border between the Serbian and Muslim-Croat entities in Bosnia. The camera was returned in May after repeated requests by the Media Experts Commission of the Organization for Security and Cooperation in Europe.

February 13
Ivica Milesic, Radio Herze Bosna ATTACKED, THREATENED

Milesic, a free-lance reporter for Radio Herze Bosna, was knifed outside his home in Zenica, in the Croatian area of Bosnia. The radio station filed a formal complaint with the Media Experts Commission of the Organization for Security and Cooperation in Europe. Before the incident, Milesic had received several threatening phone calls and his car had been vandalized. A journalist for 30 years, Milesic said he believed he was a target because of his position and reputation. He could not identify his attacker.

March 12
Two journalists, Studio Pirej HARASSED, CENSORED

Police from the Muslim-Croat Federation detained a two-man television crew from Studio Pirej, a station based in Skopje, Macedonia, in Jajce. Police warned that the crew members required permission for filming. Later, the crew was stopped again in Drvar, also on federation territory, and were again informed that they needed permission before filming.

March 12
Canadian Broadcasting Corporation (CBC) crew HARASSED, CENSORED

Serb entity police detained SFOR spokesman Maj. Tony White and a CBC crew for more than two hours. Police said the crew needed prior permission for filming and demanded it turn over its equipment. A police escort was imposed on the crew members after they were released. When the journalists stopped at a station manned by the International Police Task Force to report the

EUROPE

incident, the Serbian escort tried to force them to return to the Serbian police station.

September 27
Alternativa ATTACKED

An explosion ripped through the editorial offices of *Alternativa*, the only opposition newspaper in the Bosnian Serb town of Doboj.

No one was injured, but the explosion destroyed the newspaper's offices, started a fire, and damaged several adjacent apartments. Local authorities did not identify the cause of the explosion.

The blast was the second attack in a month on *Alternativa*, which is owned and edited by Milovan Stankovic, a retired Bosnian Serb army colonel and an opponent of ultra-nationalist leaders in Pale.

On August 28, the offices of *Alternativa* were sprayed with bullets by a gunman with an automatic weapon. The assailant also threw a hand grenade into the newspaper's offices.

Bulgaria

The year opened with mass public strikes and rallies—the first in Bulgaria since the collapse of communism in 1989—demanding reforms and new elections. Several journalists from the influential private radio station Darik, *Kapital*, and other newspapers, were beaten by police while covering demonstrations in Sofia. The protests succeeded in ousting the Bulgarian Socialist Party government of Zhan Videnov, widely blamed for the country's deep economic, financial, and political crisis. The March elections brought the victory of the United Democratic Forces (UDF) and their majority in parliament. A new pro-reform and pro-Western government was formed, headed by the former finance minister, Ivan Kostov.

The raging economic crisis resulted in low sales for most newspapers in Bulgaria, which rely heavily on circulation because advertising remains underdeveloped—a legacy of the previous government's resistance to privatization. Dailies and weeklies are a luxury for average Bulgarians; 74 percent of those polled reported that they rely on state-controlled National TV programs for news. Ten percent said they relied on state radio, while only nine percent of the population considered print media as their primary information source. Bulgaria still has no privately owned national television station, although debate over the issue resumed some months after the new government took office. The new government announced it would privatize one of Bulgaria's two national television channels, the Efir channel, but has not made good on its pledge.

The ruling parties in the UDF coalition, have little incentive to break the government television monopoly and the parties' influence on programming. Even the new amendments to the highly restrictive 1996 Law on Radio and Television, approved in December, allow the ruling political parties to maintain some control over television and radio. According to the amendments, the National Council on Radio and Television, the chief broadcast regulatory body in Bulgaria, will continue to appoint the heads of state radio and television. The parliament appoints a majority of council members and the president selects the rest, ensuring control over the body by the ruling coalition. The council will no longer be allowed to interfere in editorial policy, however, and it will be authorized solely to oversee the press' adherence to regulations in the media law. Overall, the amendments appear to be vague and minor.

There are some 10 private radio stations in Sofia and a few scattered throughout the country. Most devote the bulk of their air time to music and entertainment programs. Only the Darik radio station in Sofia has earned a reputation for independent news reporting. Its coverage of the demonstrations early in the year, the only source of news about the events, made Darik the most popular radio station in the capital.

Press freedom in Bulgaria is guaranteed and regulated by the constitution (Articles 39, 40, and 41), the penal code (Articles 146, 147, and 148) and ratified international human rights agreements. Provisions of the penal code, which place the burden of proof on the journalist, criminalize libel and defamation; convictions under these statutes are punishable by up to three years' imprisonment. The number of new criminal and civil libel suits against journalists apparently decreased once the new government took office, but both criminal and civil libel statutes continue to be used by public officials and businessmen as an instrument of harassment against investigative reporters and editors.

January 11
Velko Angelov, *Capital* ATTACKED
Raly Marinov, *Zemedelsko Zname* ATTACKED
Assen Tonev, free-lancer ATTACKED
Irina Alexieva, Darik ATTACKED
Sava Dinev, Radio France International (RFI)
ATTACKED

Police attacked five journalists who were covering a mass demonstration by opponents of the ruling Bulgarian Socialist Party outside the Bulgarian Parliament. Angelov, a photojournalist with the weekly *Capital*, received serious head injuries; Marinov, a reporter for the newspaper *Zemedelsko Zname*; and Tonev, a free-lance cameraman; were beaten. Alexieva, a reporter for the independent radio station Darik, and Dinev, a correspondent for Radio France International, were assaulted with police clubs.

January 17
Ivo Momtchev, 7 Dni ATTACKED

Unknown assailants attacked Momtchev, a reporter with the independent radio station 7 Dni (7 Days), while he was covering an opposition demonstration in Sofia, breaking his nose and injuring his head and left eye.

March 21
Yovka Atanassova, *Starozagorsky Novini*
HARASSED, LEGAL ACTION

Yovka Atanassova, owner and editor of the daily newspaper *Starozagorsky Novini* in Stara Zagora, was found guilty in four separate cases of seditious libel. She was given four consecutive sentences under Articles 147 and 148 of the Bulgarian penal code, adding up to a three-year prison term and a fine of about US$410. If Atanassova fails to pay her fine, the court can seize some of her property. She appealed in the higher regional court and remains free pending appeal and a confirmation of the sentence by the regional court.

By the end of 1997, there were 12 civil and criminal libel cases pending against her. The charges against Atanassova stemmed from articles reporting that several politicians and security specialists had served in the past as informants in the Bulgarian secret police.

January 11
Velko Angelov, *Capital* ATTACKED
Raly Marinov, *Zemedelsko Zname* ATTACKED
Assen Tonev, free-lancer ATTACKED
Irina Alexieva, Darik ATTACKED
Sava Dinev, Radio France International (RFI)
ATTACKED

Police attacked five journalists who were covering a mass demonstration by opponents of the ruling Bulgarian Socialist Party outside the Bulgarian Parliament. Angelov, a photojournalist with the weekly *Capital*, received serious head injuries; Marinov, a reporter for the newspaper

Zemedelsko Zname; and Tonev, a free-lance cameraman; were beaten. Alexieva, a reporter for the independent radio station Darik, and Dinev, a correspondent for Radio France International, were assaulted with police clubs.

January 17
Ivo Momtchev, 7 Dni ATTACKED

Unknown assailants attacked Momtchev, a reporter with the independent radio station 7 Dni (7 Days), while he was covering an opposition demonstration in Sofia, breaking his nose and injuring his head and left eye.

March 21
Yovka Atanassova, *Starozagorsky Novini* HARASSED, LEGAL ACTION

Yovka Atanassova, owner and editor of the daily newspaper *Starozagorsky Novini* in Stara Zagora, was found guilty in four separate cases of seditious libel. She was given four consecutive sentences under Articles 147 and 148 of the Bulgarian penal code, adding up to a three-year prison term and a fine of about US$410. If Atanassova fails to pay her fine, the court can seize some of her property. She appealed in the higher regional court and remains free pending appeal and a confirmation of the sentence by the regional court.

By the end of 1997, there were 12 civil and criminal libel cases pending against her. The charges against Atanassova stemmed from articles reporting that several politicians and security specialists had served in the past as informants in the Bulgarian secret police.

Croatia

President Franjo Tudjman consolidated his control over the media after landslide presidential elections in June which ensured his ruling party's hold over the appointment of executives and editors in the state-dominated media. Some visible gestures of conciliation to the media such as granting independent Radio 101.2 FM a long-term license after prolonged resistance, mixed with the president's new legal restrictions added uncertainty to Croatia's outlook for press freedom.

Croatia was admitted into the Council of Europe in November 1996 on a one-year conditional basis. European leaders linked Croatia's full membership to its progress in various human rights areas, including conditions for press freedom. After the trial year ended in October, the United States demanded that Croatia's membership in the council be suspended due to human rights concerns, including continued harassment of the independent press. Despite the U.S. government's lobbying effort, Croatia obtained full membership in November. The largest state-owned newspapers and Croatian radio and television remained under the control of the ruling Croatian Democratic Union, causing Council of Europe officials to voice concern after a summit in Strasbourg on October 11.

The international community's protests, as well as a pending International Monetary Fund loan tranche, no doubt motivated President Tudjman to take a number of steps to polish his image. In addition to hastily rounding up war crime suspects and turning them over to the Hague Tribunal, the president backed away from direct suppression of the leading independent media outlets. While granted only a temporary license to operate until October 31, managers of the popular Radio 101.2 FM, whose closure sparked mass demonstrations last year, finally received a long-term license on November 4—achieved through complex financial negotiations with municipal authorities.

Some two dozen prominent reporters from the state-run HTV television and radio company formed an association, called Forum 21, to press for reforms within the public television network. The journalists called for greater editorial freedom and balance of political viewpoints on national television. Although it is unclear whether the initiative will reap any results, the establishment of Forum 21 was notable because it represented a call for change from inside Croatian state television, which remains the chief source of news for most Croatians.

The satirical weekly *Feral Tribune* suffered its most severe threats in years, with several police raids in May and anonymous death threats to editor in chief Viktor Ivancic in September after he ran the confessions of a wanted war criminal in the Split-based newspaper. In May, Ivancic and co-defendant Marinko Culic were informed that their September 1996 acquittal on charges of insulting President Tudjman had been overturned. The state vowed to prosecute them once more at a court hearing on October 20. CPJ chose Ivancic as one of its International Press Freedom awardees, and he accepted the award at the October 23 ceremony in New York. A judge officially granted Ivancic permission to postpone his court appearance until after the ceremony, but ruled that his co-defendant had to be present. Once again, the court postponed the hearing until December 22.

At that hearing, lawyers for *Feral Tribune* discussed the contents of the article that prosecutors claimed had defamed President Tudjman by comparing his plan to bury the bones of Croatian fascists alongside their victims at the site of a World War II death camp to a similar plan by the late Spanish dictator, General Francisco Franco. The judge ruled that his lack of expertise in the policies of the late Spanish ruler would require him to call an expert witness of his own by petitioning the Spanish Justice Ministry for their expert legal assessment. He adjourned the trial until the court received a response from the Spanish government. A final resolution of the seditious libel case against *Feral Tribune* will likely face a long delay.

The farcical resolution bodes better for Croatia's judiciary than for the newspaper which sought an acquittal as a legal precedent for future seditious libel cases against journalists. It underscores the need for Croatia to eliminate all statutes in its penal code that criminalize criticism and satire of public officials as inconsistent with the country's professed desire to integrate with the West. *Feral Tribune*, and other independent newspapers, such as *Globus*, also face hundreds of civil libel cases, filed primarily by public figures to pressure them to refrain from pursuing journalistic investigations. Lawsuits, such as one filed by President Tudjman's daughter, Nevenka, against *Feral Tribune*, for damages worth about US$560,000, often aim to deal a crushing financial blow on independent publications.

On October 1, Croatia adopted a revised penal code that would allow the prosecution of journalists for reports considered "insulting" even if factually correct, which would take effect in January. "Journalists will have to prove their intention was to inform the public in good faith and objectively and not to insult or slander," said Zeljko Horvat, a government legal advisor who is one of the new code's authors. While technically consistent with the judgments of the European Court of Human Rights, Croatian journalists feared that in Croatia's repressive climate, the code could be used to prosecute them.

As with other countries in the region known for curbing press freedom, while taking away journalists' liberties with one hand, the state feigned concern about their attackers by making it a crime for anyone to deny the right to freedom of speech and the press or to refuse to divulge unclassified official information—offenses that are

EUROPE

extremely difficult to investigate and prosecute.

Domestic and foreign criticism of Croatia's press freedom record also apparently prompted Tudjman to invite two leading professional journalists back to Croatia from Parisian exile. Goran Milic, a Serb and former prime-time news editor at Yugoslav Radio Television before the war, who worked as the Paris correspondent for the official daily *Vjesnik*, was appointed to head HRT. Branko Salaj, a respected Croatian emigre journalist, was serving as Croatia's envoy to France when he was called back to head HINA, the Croatian state news agency.

May 5
Victor Ivancic, *Feral Tribune*
LEGAL ACTION
Marinko Culic, *Feral Tribune* LEGAL ACTION

Ivancic and Culic, who were acquitted of criminal libel charges by the Zagreb Municipal Court on September 26, 1996, face another trial on charges of slandering President Franjo Tudjman, because an appeals court on May 5 overturned the acquittal. The state appealed the acquittal by Municipal Court Judge Marin Mrcela, and scheduled another court hearing on October 20, 1997. Judge Mrcela's acquittal was overturned on a technicality, while the substance of the case was ignored.

Ivancic received an International Press Freedom Award from CPJ on October 23, and the judge granted him permission to postpone the hearing until December 22.

The new trial takes up the same charges of insulting the president in an article titled "Bones in the Mixer" and a photomontage titled "Jasenovac—The Largest Croatian Underground City."

The journalists were charged with seditious libel under Articles 71 and 72 of the penal code for defaming President Tudjman by criticizing his plans to build a single monument in the former World War II concentration camp of Jasenovac and bury the bones of Croatian Fascists alongside with those of their Jewish, Serb, Roma, and Croat victims.

At the new hearing, *Feral Tribune* lawyers discussing the contents of the article which criticized the above-mentioned Tudjman plan, compared it to a similar plan by the late fascist leader of Spain, Generalissimo Francisco Franco. Judge Mrcela ruled that he would need an expert legal assessment on the policies of the dictator by the Spanish Justice Ministry. He adjourned the trial until receipt of a response from the Spanish government.

May 29
Heni Erceg, *Feral Tribune* HARASSED

Interior Ministry investigators went to the home of Heni Erceg, an editor of the *Feral Tribune*, questioning her about the newspaper's staff. At the same time, two police officers appeared at the newspaper's office with a warrant to obtain information about another *Feral Tribune* journalist. The investigators asked about the size of the newspaper's staff, their whereabouts, how they communicate with each other, whether Erceg traveled abroad, how often, and for what purpose. The police inspectors tried to question another editor, but he was not at home. The investigation followed other legal actions—both criminal and civil—designed to harass the independent weekly.

September 1
Victor Ivancic, *Feral Tribune* THREATENED
Staff, *Feral Tribune* THREATENED

Ivancic, editor in chief of the *Feral Tribune*, said his paper received about 20 threatening telephone calls the day he ran an interview with a police officer who admitted to killing 72 people during the civil war. The paper reported that Miro Bajramovic confessed to killing the 72 people, mostly ethnic Serbs, at the beginning of the war in 1991.

Ivancic said the anonymous callers threatened to kill him, his son, and other *Feral Tribune* staff members. He said there were several more threatening calls in the days that followed.

Although the *Feral Tribune* had received numerous threats for its hard-hitting reporting in the past, Ivancic said these death threats were more troubling.

Soon after the interview was published, Croatian police arrested Bajramovic and three other members of a wartime paramilitary police unit who Bajramovic claimed had carried out ethnic cleansing in the Croatian countryside. But other former unit members Bajramovic implicated remained free, Ivancic said.

Local police responded swiftly to Ivancic's complaint about death threats. Officers reportedly were cooperative and promised to watch the newspaper's premises.

Georgia

There has been a progressive trend toward press freedom in Georgia. One of the best examples of that trend was the legal victory of Rustavi-2, the leading independent Georgian TV station, which had been forced off the air in July 1996 when the Georgian Ministry of Communications revoked its broadcast license. On November 4, 1996, the Georgian Supreme Court ruled that the denial of Rustavi-2's license was unlawful and ordered its restoration. The Ministry, however, delayed its return. Rustavi-2 finally obtained its license and resumed broadcasting April 28.

The victory came after protracted legal battles and international pressure on the government and ministry to restore Rustavi-2's license. Many independent observers viewed the silencing of the station as an attempt to pressure independent broadcasters and to stop Rustavi-2's

coverage of controversial news on political and ethnic issues, as well as on organized crime.

Georgy Akimidze, the co-founder and artistic director of Rustavi-2, said the decision to revive the Rustavi-2 broadcasts "gave hope for an improvement in the situation between mass media and regulatory agencies and was a positive step for the development of the independent media in Georgia." He thanked CPJ and other press freedom advocacy groups for their support.

Another positive achievement was the dismissal of Security Minister Shota Kviraya, who had ordered the tapping of opposition journalists' telephones.

Reporters nevertheless still face obstacles to practicing their profession freely. For example, journalists were barred from the courtroom during the high-profile trial of 15 people accused of "acts of terrorism," including an alleged attempt to kill President Eduard Shevardnadze.

This year again the parliament debated altering some clauses in the 1991 Law on the Press and Other Mass Media. After failing to make some restrictive changes in 1996, lawmakers proposed separate laws on television, radio, and the press. Independent reporters, editors, and broadcasters protested, arguing that the absence of press laws was the best strategy to guarantee press freedom. At the end of December, the speaker of the parliament announced that parliamentary media submissions were working on new bills on television, radio, and the press. The parliament did, however, approve a new Law on Freedom of Information that contains brief, vague provisions meant to guarantee the right to freely receive and impart information.

The Law on the Press and Other Mass Media allows journalists and media outlets to file appeals in disputes with government agencies over licensing and accreditation, as in the case of Rustavi-2. Although it forbids censorship, as well as the existence of any media or distribution monopoly—including by the state—the law contains some limits on disclosing "state secrets," hate speech and inflammatory language, and infringement on "the honor and dignity" of citizens, which can easily be misinterpreted and misused. The law also leaves no doubt that state-run media remain under strict government surveillance. For example, television and radio news coverage of political developments has to follow "official guidelines." Top management at state television and radio, and at the official information and publishing corporation, Sakinform, is appointed by the parliament and the president.

Kazakstan

President Nursultan Nazarbayev continued to consolidate his control over the media in anticipation of the presidential elections scheduled for 2000, upgrading the national press agency to the status of a ministry after a government reshuffle in October. Most disturbing, a highly controversial tender of broadcasting frequencies dealt a shattering blow to the burgeoning independent electronic media in the Central Asian nation receiving the most Western economic aid.

Starting in November 1996, communications officials used a variety of crude tactics (such as claiming "interference with air traffic control") to force unfavorable independent radio and television channels off the air in the capital. These tactics were replicated in the provinces, as provincial officials conducted hostile inspections of some broadcasting studios.

In December 1996, the government announced that it would hold a tender for broadcasting frequencies. The tender was not an auction, where the frequency was awarded to the highest bidder. Instead, the government Frequency Commission accepted applications and met with individual broadcasters to hear their arguments as to why they should be granted the frequencies. The cost of the license and the annual fees were extremely high by local standards, and substantially higher than equivalent fees in the region or indeed the world. Yet even those independent broadcasters who mustered the amounts required were denied licenses.

Not surprisingly, stations like TV M, which aired a popular political program called "Open Zone" providing a platform for the political opposition, were forced out of business by the tender. Independent station managers united in ANESMI, the Association for Independent Electronic Mass Media, called the tender unfair, unlawful, and politically motivated. They said it was designed to sweep the stage clear of any broadcasters who supplied critical news coverage and allowed commentary from opponents to President Nazarbayev—or for that matter, any who provided more professional public service and entertainment programs than state television and hence were more popular. ANESMI's charges were substantiated by the Prosecutor General and other officials concerned about the abuse of anti-monopoly laws and constitutional guarantees of equal rights for state and private property.

Following the government's success in clamping down on broadcasters in the capital, officials turned their sights to the provinces. In April, three popular channels in Akmola were suddenly told to shut off their transmitters. Startled viewers showered the stations—Efir, TSPR, and NTV-6 (which rebroadcast Russian-based programming)—with letters and telegrams, and station managers protested to the Prosecutor General of Kazakstan, who replied that an appeal of the administrative decision would be justified. In May, the Minister of Transportation and Communications held a tender for regional radio frequencies in seven provincial cities. Yet even in areas where only one commercial station applied to take part in the tender, the licenses were not awarded to independent broadcasters.

The effect of the tender has been to leave only four nominally non-state television channels in the capital of Almaty, where once eight feisty private channels flourished, and JUST three ostensibly independent radio stations. The winners of the tender included President Nazarbayev's daughter, Dariga Nazarbayeva (owner of a partially state-run television company, Khabar, and a nominally private station, NTK), as well as other individuals related to the President by marriage or through political loyalties.

Independent broadcasters who rebroadcast Voice of America programs, have been silenced. Some stations have been able to make do with the UHF stations and retain a limited audience at considerable expense; others have begun to broadcast their programs over their still-existing radio stations.

Because of the high cost of print production and distribution, and the related low circulation, newspapers and magazines have far less influence than television. In some cases, print journalists have resorted to self-censorship—the result of criminal libel suits and other official harassment in the past.

Today, news stories on sensitive topics such as the disappearance of the former prime minister and the appointment of his replacement; coverage of considerable labor unrest and agitation for social rights; and the activities of Kazakstani and foreign oil companies are either absent from the news or covered in a biased fashion.

In January, Chris Gehring, a United States Agency for International Development contractor based in Almaty who directed the Central Asian programs of Internews, was murdered. Internews—a nonprofit organization supported by the U.S. government and private foundations such as George Soros' Open Society Institute—is devoted to increasing the broadcast capabilities of the independent television broadcasters of the former Soviet Union. Gehring had been assisting independent broadcasters who were contemplating a legal challenge to the tender. He was slain in his apartment on January 9, apparently the victim of a burglary. CPJ conducted an exhaustive investigation of the murder and concluded, as did Internews, that Gehring's death was not related to his work as a journalist or as a media trainer, nor to the political and legal issues surrounding the tender. Nevertheless, CPJ noted in appeals to U.S. government and Kazakstani officials that the murder had sent a shock wave through the foreign and domestic journalism communities, and continued to have a chilling effect on their work. CPJ urged that both governments make forceful public statements regarding the murder and the conviction of the suspects in order to dispel the rumors surrounding the case. Three suspects were subsequently arrested—with remarkable alacrity, as journalists' murders in the region often go unsolved. In an unusually speedy trial, the three were convicted and sentenced to the maximum 15-year prison term.

Kyrgyzstan

Kyrgyzstan clings to its reputation as an island of democracy in a sea of authoritarian Central Asian states. President Askar Akayev took steps several times this year to salvage his reputation for tolerance of independent and opposition media. But his steps were merely gestures to accommodate

EUROPE

Western opinion and investors, and attempts to mask a pattern of attacks against the press.

The attacks ranged from the appointment of a former Communist Party ideology secretary as head of state radio and television to sanctioning criminal charges against journalists for insulting the president. A number of newspapers were refused registration or were shut down because of articles offensive to the government.

Res Publika, the leading opposition newspaper, has suffered the brunt of the crackdown, in part from a criminal libel suit filed by a state-run gold-mining company. Ultimately, the paper was forced to suspend operations after four of its journalists were convicted in May on criminal libel charges, for which the penalties included forced labor and a ban on practicing journalism for up to 18 months. Three of the convictions were ultimately overturned, and in the fourth case the sentence was suspended.

The case of Yryspek Omurzakov, a reporter for *Res Publika*, was especially disturbing. After several warnings for his satirical writings, he was arrested on March 24 on a criminal libel charge. CPJ and international human rights organizations protested the prosecution. He was convicted in October and sentenced to three years in jail.

At a press conference in New York in July, Akayev spoke of the value he attributed to the development of a free press as the cornerstone of the democratic development in his country. He mentioned that the opposition newspapers were "free to criticize the leadership of the country," but did not elaborate on the penalties for such actions. CPJ used the occasion to confront Akayev about the prosecution of the *Res Publika* reporters and editors and the use of criminal libel statutes against journalists. Although the president agreed that "there were certain problems," he said

"not much can be done until a new civil code is adopted." He added that although its laws were not ideal, Kyrgyzstan needed to "adhere to the rule of law." When CPJ's representative urged the president to use his authority to stop attacks on the media, Akayev said he could not interfere with the independence of the judiciary. In reality, however, the suits against the journalists were brought by the prosecutor's office, an institution which has retained the Soviet-era powers of investigating, prosecuting, and overseeing criminal cases. Local journalists and foreign observers said the president has a significant impact on decisions of prosecutors and judges concerning journalists.

On November 12, the parliament adopted several amendments to the existing media law. The amendments affect 47 articles regulating citizens' freedom to gather and impart information, as well as journalists' rights and obligations. According to the bill, "moral damage inflicted on a citizen or legal entity which discredits a citizen or blackens the business' reputation" would have to be compensated both by the journalist and by the media unit "on a scale to be established by the court."

On December 8, President Akayev vetoed the amendments, chiefly because he opposed Article 12 of the bill, which he said "considerably curtails media rights and freedoms." Akayev suggested deleting the clause barring journalists from reporting on ongoing criminal investigations. He proposed a law guaranteeing the protection of journalists' professional activities, which was adopted by the legislative assembly. It forbids censorship and makes public officials liable for preventing journalists from exercising their professional responsibilities. The law also includes a provision replacing criminal penalties for libel with fines and damages.

February 25
Kriminal LEGAL ACTION

Prime Minister Apas Dzhumagulov filed a libel suit against the new independent weekly *Kriminal*, asking for the equivalent of about US$6,000 in damages. *Kriminal* published a story in the paper's first issue on January 10, claiming that Dzhumagulov had built a mansion on the site of a former cemetery. On March 7, Dzhumagulov met with Beken Nazaraliev, the editor in chief of *Kriminal*, who agreed to publish a response from the prime minister. The lawsuit is still pending.

March 12
Kriminal CENSORED

A court order suspended publication of *Kriminal*, a new independent weekly newspaper, for "publication of unverified or false information" in violation of the civil code. The court dropped two charges of "insulting" public officials. *Kriminal*'s first issue, on January 10, was critical of the Kyrgyz authorities.

Deputy Justice Minister Cholponkul Arabayev sent a letter to the state-owned Uchkun Publishing House on January 17, instructing it to stop printing *Kriminal*. A parliamentary commission on information and media reviewed the case on January 30 and persuaded the Justice Ministry to reverse its order. On February 6, however, a district court judge in Bishkek temporarily suspended publication of the paper.

In February, Prime Minister Apas Dzhumagulov filed a libel suit against *Kriminal*.

In the March 12 hearing, the judge ordered *Kriminal* banned. *Kriminal*'s editors then appealed to the Bishkek municipal court, which on May 7 upheld the ban. The editors appealed to the Supreme Court.

March 24
Yryspek Omurzakov, *Res Publika*
IMPRISONED, LEGAL ACTION

Omurzakov, a reporter for the opposition weekly *Res Publika*, was sentenced to three years in prison for libeling the manager of a state-owned factory.

Mikhail Paryshkura, the manager of the Frunze Machine Factory, filed criminal libel charges against Omurzakov on February 7 for an article published in *Res Publika* that reported on poor conditions in the factory's hostel.

He was arrested on March 24 and freed on bail on June 10 pending a court review. The criminal trial against Omurzakov that began on May 19 was suspended two days later when the judge returned the case to the prosecutor for further investigation. The trial resumed on September 18, when a judge ordered Omurzakov to serve two and a half years in a minimum security penal colony, counting his six months in detention as time served. Omurzakov said he would appeal to a higher court. The Kyrgyz government extended the amnesty to Omurzakov in October.

Before the trial, Omurzakov had met with Paryshkura to show him a petition signed by 108 plant workers complaining about their living quarters. Paryshkura then agreed to drop the suit, but did not do so. The prosecutor refused to release Omurzakov after the newspaper's editor, as well as other journalists, sent copies of the workers' petition to his office.

Two factory workers who had signed the petition testified at the trial that Omurzakov's article was correct. After that testimony, the prosecutor filed charges against the two for disseminating false information and named them as co-defendants. The two were convicted and later pardoned.

Before his arrest, Omurzakov had been the target of repeated warnings from law enforcement officials regarding his work. In February, the prosecutor warned Omurrzakov of criminal punishment if he did not stop publishing articles critical of public figures.

In July 1996, Omurzakov had been given a two-year suspended sentence for insulting the president.

May 23
Zamira Sydykova, *Res Publika* IMPRISONED, CENSORED
Aleksandr Alyanchikov, *Res Publika* IMPRISONED, CENSORED
Bektash Shamshiev, *Res Publika* LEGAL ACTION, CENSORED
Marina Sivasheva, *Res Publika* LEGAL ACTION, CENSORED

According to Radio Liberty and the Bureau on Human Rights and Rule of Law in Bishkek, Zamira Sydykova and Aleksandr Alyanchikov, editor and journalist, respectively, of the newspaper *Res Publika*, were sentenced on May 23 to 18 months in a labor colony for slander and libel. Sydykova and Alyanchikov as well as two other *Res Publika* editors, Bektash Shamshiev and Marina Sivasheva, were barred from practicing journalism for 18 months. The latter two were also fined about US$115 each in damages.

The charges stem from articles published in *Res Publika* from 1994 to 1996, detailing alleged corruption by Dastan Sarygulov, president of Kyrgyzaltyn, the state-owned gold-mining company.

On June 10, a municipal court in Bishkek reviewed the May 23 ruling, reducing Alyanchikov's 18-month sentence to a one-year suspended sentence. Sydykova's 18-month sentence was upheld, but to be served at a more lenient labor colony. The new ruling upheld the ban on their work, however. The court also overturned the May 23 convictions of their codefendants in the case, *Res Publika* editors, Shamshiev and Sivasheva.

Sydykova received a reprieve on August 6, when the Supreme Court overturned her libel convictions.

Poland

In a nationwide referendum in September, Poland adopted a new constitution which forbids censorship and guarantees "freedom to express opinions, to acquire and disseminate information." This assurance is qualified, however, by vaguely worded exceptions "to protect the freedoms and rights of other persons and economic subjects, public order, security or important economic interests of the state." Caveats of this sort are typical for the region and easily misused by governments, although such abuses are generally the exception rather than the rule in Poland's open media climate.

Prime Minister Jerzy Buzek's center-right government, elected in September, has not expressed any intention of repealing provisions of the country's penal code on criminal and seditious libel, despite assurances made by President Aleksander Kwasniewski in 1996 that Poland would remove them. Of particular concern is Article 236, which makes insulting a public official punishable by up to two years in prison. While there were no criminal defamation cases filed against journalists in 1997, CPJ continues to monitor the case of Tadeusz Rydzyk, a priest who hosts a program on Radio Maryja. He is under investigation for allegedly insulting members of the Sejm who voted to liberalize the country's abortion law. The possible application of Article 236 in the case would clearly tarnish Poland's otherwise improved press freedom record.

There are still many complaints that the National Radio and Television Broadcasting Council, the chief regulatory body for broadcast media, lacks sufficient independence. Some observers have noted that state-run television and radio news broadcasts are still susceptible to the influence of political parties and lack balanced coverage of events.

Despite these outstanding issues, however, Poland's media remain among the most free, diverse, and professional in the region. Successful media outlets, such as *Gazeta Wyborcza*, have begun to provide professional and technical training to journalists from media trouble spots around Eastern Europe.

Romania

The election of Emil Constantinescu as president and the multi-party Democratic Convention in November 1996 held good prospects for press freedom and independent media in Romania. Along with a promise to speed up privatization and reforms, Constantinescu's centrist, pro-Western administration pledged changes in the penal code and broadcasting law, which criminalize defamation of public officials and prohibit the spread of false information allegedly aimed at harming state interests. Officials in the previous administration of Ion Iliescu had used the vague language of these restrictive articles to prosecute journalists investigating corruption and scrutinizing public officials.

Fewer Romanian journalists were convicted under Article 206, which penalizes calumny, as Romanian courts doled out fines rather than jail terms. Articles 205 and 239 of the criminal code make insulting a public official a crime, although there were fewer such cases last year. Article 207 lays the burden of proof in such cases on journalists. They cannot use the standard of good faith nor the public interest for their defense as afforded to journalists in most Western democracies.

In December, Marius Avram, a reporter for the newspaper *Stirea*, was convicted of calumny against Georghe Funar, the mayor of Cluj. Avram was ordered to pay damages of 100,000 lei (about US$800).

By year's end, Constantinescu had failed to keep his promise to amend the penal code. This fact, as well as Avram's conviction, sparked several public protests in Cluj in early December. More than 50 journalists from local media issued protests and set up a fund to cover Avram's fine—an unprecedented act of solidarity for Romania's journalistic community.

Romania has more than 50 private television stations and about 110 private radio stations, in addition to cable television, which offers viewers access to foreign broadcasts. Most of these stations are regional, while for a large number of rural areas, the only source of information remains the state-owned Romanian Radio and Television Company, which is heavily regulated. Public radio and television continue to rely heavily on state subsidies, which leaves them vulnerable to political pressures.

The 1996 Law on Television and Radio established the National Audio-Visual Council, the agency charged with distributing broadcast licenses and regulating the airwaves. The law has been criticized for failing to guarantee the council's independence from political interests.

Private newspapers have mushroomed. Nevertheless, the print media must contend with high printing costs, the decline in state subsidies, and the lack of advertising revenue. Distribution of newspapers and journals suffers from the lack of efficient private networks to replace the old state-run system. Currently, the state newspaper distributor Rodipet is the only company capable of national distribution. Compared to other countries in the region, however, Romania has made significant strides in achieving pluralistic and diversified media.

March 1
Sabin Orcan, *Opinia* HARASSED, LEGAL
ACTION
Florian Angelo, *Opinia* HARASSED, LEGAL
ACTION
Corneliu Stefan, *Opinia* HARASSED, LEGAL
ACTION

Stefan, an editor, and Orcan, and Angelo,
reporters with the independent daily *Opinia* in
Buzau, were convicted of calumny by a Buzau
municipal court on March 21. They were
charged in connection with an article about the
private business dealings of a former prosecutor. Each was given a one year suspended
sentence and ordered to pay damages of
140,000,000 lei (about US$17,000). An appeal
filed at the Buzau district appellate court was
still pending at the time of this writing.

Russia

In a March radio address, President Boris
Yeltsin claimed that "one of the chief victo-
ries of the new Russia, undisputed even by
its opponents, is freedom of the press, and
its independence from yelling bosses and
ideological pep-talks...we will no longer
have political or ideological censorship."

Most investigative reporters, especially in
provincial areas, begged to differ. Yet soon
after his speech, leading Russian journalists
were quoting Yeltsin's words back to him in a
paradoxical cry for his intervention. A group
of editors and prominent cultural figures
appealed publicly to Yeltsin to intervene and
protect editorial integrity in the face of
mounting pressure from commercial interests. They shared the concerns outlined in a
government-sponsored report on the media
which bemoaned the "intensive monopolization of the press, its concentration in the
hands of certain individuals and financial
giants, and the creation of multimedia con-

cerns which conducted their own information
policy." Yeltsin met in September with six of
Russia's biggest financial and media magnates, urging them to stop "slinging mud" at
each other and his cabinet members through
their media outlets.

The "clash of titans"—the war over
media properties by Russia's top bankers
and industrialists—had a pervasive effect on
Russia's press throughout the year. Editors,
reporters, and foreign observers agree that
press freedom has been the loser as frenzied
battles for ownership and control of influential media outlets led to the resignation
or dismissal of a number of prominent editors and columnists, and to the muting of
criticism of certain public officials.

The new media moguls do not acquire
newspapers or television stations because of
their profitability, given the still relatively
weak advertising sector, but to increase
their political influence. Encroachment of
big business interests has not only affected
reporting on the Kremlin; coverage of the
opening of the Caspian Sea oil pipelines,
one of the biggest stories of 1997, and other
Caucasian affairs, were also distorted. For
example, Vagit Alekperov, the head of the
oil company Lukoil, which owns a large percentage of the newspaper *Izvestia*, was
reported by rival media to have forbidden
the paper to criticize Azerbaijan in its conflict with Armenia, or to investigate oil deals
emerging from a state visit to Russia by
Azerbaijani President Heidar Aliyev.

Media revelations of government scandal
could be read in terms of their owners'
agendas. In October, reporter Alexei Minkin
of *Moskovskiy Komsomolets*, broke the story
of large payments for a book contract
received by Vice Premier Anatoly Chubais,
who has led the effort to privatize government properties. The media owned by
Vladimir Gusinsky gave the story full play—
a response some observers said was related
to Gusinsky's failed bid for shares in

Svyazinvest, a telecommunications company, which was won by Oneksimbank, which is perceived to be as close to Chubais. *Moskovskiy Komsomolets*, which claims to exist on advertising revenue, is believed to be more independent than other papers with large investments by financial concerns, but reportedly receives backing from Moscow's Mayor Yuri Luzhkov (who receives favorable coverage in the paper).

Charges of reprisal killings of journalists are common in Russia, although usually unsubstantiated. The murder of several prominent investigative journalists in the last five years remain unsolved. Some unsolved cases, such as the murder of Vadim Biryukov, formerly of the leading government wire service ITAR-TASS, deputy director of the publishing concern Press-Kontakt, and founder of the magazine *Delovyye lyudi* (Business People), straddled a gray area between journalism and commerce, where the commingling of news and business interests made it particularly difficult for outside observers to determine the motive in the killings.

Still, journalism was aptly dubbed Russia's "most dangerous profession" by newscasters, not only because of physical attacks, but due to a world record of 21 journalists kidnapped in or near the secessionist republic of Chechnya. NTV war correspondent Yelena Masyuk—one of CPJ's 1997 International Press Freedom awardees—was kidnapped with her crew in May by Chechen rebels, and held for three months. At year's end, all the abducted journalists except two Polish free-lancers had been freed, but only after complicated and prolonged negotiations and in most cases, the payment of huge ransoms. The epidemic of kidnappings led to severely curtailed news coverage of the troubled region and a virtual information blackout. The brief seizure of seven Chechen reporters in neighboring Dagestan in late December reinforced the conventional edito-

rial wisdom that Chechnya should remain off-limits for reporters.

Vicious beatings of Russian journalists continued apace. The incidents stemmed from coverage of alleged corruption among government officials and organized crime.

Yeltsin's chief political rivals, the Communists and nationalists in the Duma (the federal parliament) were certainly no kinder to the press. In February and March, the Duma first ruled to strip an ORT parliamentary correspondent of his accreditation for critical coverage of debates on laws to curb pornography, then barred ORT from entering the parliament. Although the Judicial Chamber for Information Disputes called the parliament's action a violation of the Law on the Media and the Constitution, this body and other executive agencies were helpless to control parliamentary censorship. After further acrimonious debates and appeals, the parliament banned all television coverage of its sessions and ruled to ban journalists from corridors near the chambers where debates took place, a move condemned by reporters as an unacceptable restriction on their access to legislators. Generally, libel suits and hostile tax inspections were the preferred methods of harassment, leading to hundreds of court cases.

January 19
Roman Perevezentsev, ORT IMPRISONED
Vyacheslav Tibelius, ORT IMPRISONED

Perevezentsev and Tibelius, two Russian correspondents from ORT, the Russian public television channel, were reported missing in or near Chechnya while on assignment covering the Chechen presidential election campaign. The pair were traveling from Grozny, the capital of the secessionist republic, to Nazran in the neighboring republic of Ingushetia to file their report to Moscow. They never reached Nazran.

Perevezentsev and Tibelius were freed on February 18 and allowed to return to Moscow. Russian and Chechen officials were involved in negotiating their release, but declined to provide details about who was holding them and how and where they were released.

February 21
Albert Musin, free-lancer IMPRISONED, LEGAL ACTION

Musin, an Uzbek free-lancer, was detained for a personal documents check by Moscow police on the evening of February 21 at a market in a Moscow suburb. The police had stepped up their campaign of stopping dark-skinned people for document inspection after a series of bombings in Moscow were blamed on Chechen separatists. He was taken to a police station in the Tyoply Stan neighborhood where police discovered he was living in Moscow without proper registration. Police later learned that Musin was wanted by authorities in Uzbekistan, where a criminal case had been instituted against him in March 1996 for "illegal collection, divulging and use of information" (Article 191 of the Uzbekistan criminal code). Moscow police reported that the general prosecutor was reviewing the possibility of extraditing Musin to Uzbekistan.

Musin left his native Uzbekistan in 1992 to escape harassment by authorities for his work editing a human rights bulletin. He took Kazakstani citizenship, but then left behind that country's similarly repressive regime in 1993 for Moscow, where he eventually obtained refugee status. He has since been working as a free-lance correspondent for *Nezavisimaya Gazeta*, *Komsomolskaya Pravda*, *Express-Chronicle*, and the radio station Ekho Moskvy.

On March 3, the Uzbek Embassy in Moscow announced that the Uzbek government had dropped all charges against Musin. He was released from the custody of Moscow police on March 6.

February 23
Mauro Galligani, *Epocha* and *Panorama* IMPRISONED
Francesco Bigazzi, *Il Giorno* HARASSED

Four armed, masked men stopped Galligani, a photographer for the Italian weeklies *Epocha* and *Panorama*, and Francesco Bigazzi, a correspondent for the Italian daily *Il Giorno*, along with their driver and interpreter, in Grozny, the Chechen capital. Bigazzi and the others were allowed to proceed, but Galligani was taken, forced into a car without license plates.

Galligani was freed on April 13, but the circumstances of his kidnapping and release were unclear.

March 4
Nikolai Zagnoiko, Itar-Tass IMPRISONED
Yuriy Arkhipov, Radio Rossiya IMPRISONED
Nikolai Mamolashvili, Radio Rossiya IMPRISONED
Lev Zeltser, Radio Rossiya IMPRISONED

Chechen gunmen seized Zagnoiko, an ITAR-TASS staff writer; Radio Rossiya reporters Arkhipov and Mamolashvili; and Zeltsin, a satellite communications technician for Radio Rossiya, in Grozny, Chechnya. Two of the hostages contracted pneumonia during their three-month imprisonment without light, fresh air, or exercise.

The hostages were freed on June 6.

April 2
Aleksandr Utrobin, *Satkinskiy Rabochiy* IMPRISONED
Olga Bagautdinova, *Satkinskiy Metallurg* IMPRISONED

The Chelyabinsk Union of Journalists reported two journalists missing from the city of Satka in the southern Ural Mountains area. Utrobin, a photojournalist for the newspaper *Satkinskiy Rabochiy*, and Olga Bagautdinova, a correspondent for the newspaper *Satkinskiy Metallurg*, had traveled to the Chechen capital of Grozny by car, bypassing Chechen government restrictions, for a story on a missing soldier from their city.

The mayor of Satka received an anonymous telephone call demanding ransom for the two journalists, and local officials negotiated with the Chechen government for the hostages' release.

On May 6, the Chechen Interior Ministry said Utrobin had escaped his captors and contacted police, who then stormed the apartment where Bagautdinova was being held, securing her release.

April 17
Irina Chernova, *Komsomolskaya Pravda* ATTACKED

Chernova, a Volgograd correspondent for the national daily *Komsomolskaya Pravda* and head of the Press Club, a local independent journalists organization, was attacked by two assailants on the street. They beat and kicked her, breaking bones in her face. She was not robbed.

Chernova said the attackers had been following her for several days. The motive for the attack might have been related to Chernova's investigation into corrupt practices at a local oil business. Chernova also said that vindictive officials from the Volgograd Interior Ministry might have been responsible, because she recently filed a lawsuit against the ministry.

CPJ protested the attack on April 18 in a letter to the Russian Federation Interior Ministry.

April 22
Kachara Guseynayeva, *Ilchi* ATTACKED

A bomb was planted under the apartment door of Kachara Guseynayeva, editor in chief of *Ilchi*, a newspaper based in Mkhachkala, the capital of Dagestan. Doors and windows were shattered, and neighbors' apartments were damaged.

Guseynayeva's daughter suffered shoulder lacerations from shards of glass.

Officials from Russia's Federal Security

Service said the attack was probably in revenge for unspecified articles in the newspaper.

May 8
Yulia Olshanskaya, 2x2 ATTACKED
Valery Ivanov, 2x2 ATTACKED

Vladimir Zhirinovsky, the ultranationalist Duma deputy and leader of the Liberal-Democratic Party of Russia, assaulted television correspondent Yulia Olshanskaya and cameraman Valery Ivanov of Moscow's television channel 2x2.

Russian television broadcast video footage of Zhirinovsky attacking the journalists, who were filming him being denied entry to a World War II commemoration ceremony at the Tomb of the Unknown Soldier. Policemen stood by as an enraged Zhirinovsky grabbed Olshanskaya's microphone and threw it to the ground. He twisted Olshanskaya's arm, then threw her into his car, where his bodyguards tried to seize her documents. She managed to break free and escape. Olshanskaya later said she had feared Zhirinovsky would abduct her.

Zhirinovsky's guards also shoved and punched Ivanov as he tried to film the violence.

The Moscow-based Glasnost Defense Foundation and the Russian Journalists' Union issued a statement condemning the attack and police negligence and lack of action.

The Moscow city police began a criminal investigation of Zhirinovsky for hooliganism, Interfax reported on March 20. The State Duma would have to lift Zhirinovsky's parliamentary immunity from criminal prosecution before he could be charged.

May 10
Yelena Masyuk, NTV IMPRISONED
Ilya Mordyukov, NTV IMPRISONED
Dmitry Olchev, NTV IMPRISONED

Masyuk, her cameraman Mordyukov, and sound technician Olchev were abducted near the village of Samashki in western Chechnya on their way to neighboring Ingushetia in the Russian Federation.

Six masked gunmen ambushed the car in which the NTV journalists were traveling, then forced the journalists to another car and drove away. The driver was allowed to escape. At the time of the abduction, the crew had just finished filming a public rally and had interviewed rebel leader Salman Raduyev in central Grozny. They were leaving Chechnya with their videotapes. The kidnappers did not publicly demand ransom.

CPJ repeatedly issued appeals to Russian, Chechen, and U.S. officials. NTV executives and Russian government officials traveled to Chechnya to negotiate with the Chechen government, which at first claimed to have no knowledge of the journalists' location, then said on June 5 that the crew was being held in Grozny and periodically moved to different places.

Masyuk is a special correspondent for NTV known for her war coverage in Chechnya.

Masyuk, Mordyukov, and Olchev were released from captivity on August 18, just hours before a Moscow summit between the Russian and Chechen presidents. The journalists returned to Moscow that day. The circumstances around their release were unclear; both Chechen and Russian authorities claimed responsibility for their release. NTV chief Igor Malashenko said he paid several million dollars in ransom to obtain the journalists' release. Chechen leaders said they carried out a rescue operation that left one soldier dead, but NTV denounced that claim.

On October 23, Masyuk received an International Press Freedom Award from CPJ in New York.

June 11
Ilyas Bogatyryov, "Vzglyad" IMPRISONED
Vladislav Chernyayev, "Vzglyad" IMPRISONED

Bogatyryov, a correspondent for the Moscow-based television program "Vzglyad," and

Chernyayev, his cameraman, were kidnapped at gunpoint in Grozny by masked men. The pair were traveling in Chechnya in a rented car when they stopped to make a phone call. Two cars approached them, and masked men jumped out of one car, shooting into the air. They struck the journalists, pushed them into the second car, and disappeared.

In May, Bogatyryov had videotaped four kidnapped journalists from Radio Rossiya and ITAR-TASS while they were being held by Chechen rebels. The four were released June 6 after negotiations involving officials from Chechnya, neighboring Dagestan, and the Russian Federation.

"Vzglyad," a current affairs program produced by the independent production company VID and aired on ORT, Russia's public television station, recently broadcast an interview with a Chechen man who said he belonged to a gang trying to profit from kidnapping journalists. Lecho Khultygov, deputy head of Chechnya's security service, said his agency had wanted to question Bogatyryov about a suspected scheme that used his reporting to pressure Russian and Chechen officials to pay ransom for captive journalists.

Glasnost Defense Foundation, a Moscow-based press freedom organization, reported that in February 1996, Bogatyryov had been detained by security agents of Gen. Jokhar Dudayev, the Chechen president who was killed last year by Russian troops. Bogatyryov and Chernyayev were released after a few weeks.

June 11
Aleksandr Postnov, *Express-Chronicle*,
THREATENED

Postnov, a correspondent in Kazan, Tatarstan, for the weekly *Express-Chronicle*, was threatened by callers who urged him to stop writing articles about arms shipments to Afghanistan.

Express-Chronicle said Postnov had been investigating the involvement of the Aerostan Company, a Russian aviation concern, in weapons shipments to the Rabani government in Afghanistan. The Aerostan Company reportedly had provided the Afghan government with airplanes and pilots to transport weapons. The rebel Taliban forces had captured some of the company's pilots and held them as prisoners for many months. They eventually escaped.

Aleksandr Podrabinek, editor in chief of *Express-Chronicle*, has appealed to the prosecutor general of the Russian Federation to take immediate steps to protect Postnov. CPJ appealed to Russian authorities in a letter on June 17 to investigate the threat.

December 17
Krzysztof Galinski, free-lancer IMPRISONED
Marek Kurzyniec, free-lancer IMPRISONED

Galinski and Kurzyniec and three other Polish citizens were kidnapped in Chechnya by unknown assailants while trying to deliver a shipment of food aid. All five undertook the mission on behalf of the National Federation of Anarchists in Poland, of which they are all members.

Galinski is an editor with the Gdansk-based *Mac Pariadka*, the country's largest national anarchist monthly magazine. Kurzyniec edits his own small political bulletin *Marscho*, also in Gdansk.

Although their primary mission was the delivery of food aid, both men carried press credentials from *Zycie*, a national daily newspaper in Gdansk. They had agreed to a request from the editor to write free-lance articles about the situation in Chechnya upon their return.

The National Federation of Anarchists reported that all five hostages were safe as of mid-January 1998. Rumors that the hostage-takers had demanded ransom from *Zycie* and the anarchists' group could not be confirmed.

September 6
Valery Krivosheyev, *Komsomolskaya Pravda* KILLED

Krivosheyev was a special correspondent for the national daily *Komsomolskaya Pravda* in

Lipetsk in central Russia. He was found dead from skull trauma, near a coffee shop where the reporter frequently met his sources. Colleagues at the newspaper and at the Glasnost Defense Foundation claim that Krivosheyev's killing was related to his work as an investigative journalist covering local and national public figures. Later reports indicated that he was killed in a brawl during a wedding reception at the café. The day before his death he told friends at *De-Fakto*, the newspaper where he had formerly worked, that he had scheduled a meeting with a source on a story he called "a bombshell of national proportions." By year's end, CPJ could not confirm that Krivosheyev's death was connected with his work as a journalist.

December 24
Ruslan Musayev, Associated Press (AP) IMPRISONED
Arbi Zubairaev, NTV IMPRISONED
Umar Magomadov, ORT IMPRISONED
Aslambek Dadayev, WTN IMPRISONED
Alkha Tasuyev, Reuters IMPRISONED
Ayub Vedzizhev, Reuters IMPRISONED
A seventh journalist is unidentified, reported to be working for a Chechen Press Agency IMPRISONED

Seven Chechen reporters who work for Russian and Western news organizations were seized after crossing into Dagestan to cover attacks on Russian military outposts by Chechen guerrillas and Dagestani Muslim fundamentalists. A group calling itself the People's Volunteer Corps of Dagestan claimed responsibility for the kidnappings. They said the journalists would be freed in exchange for seven Dagestani police officers taken prisoner during recent clashes and believed to be held in Chechnya. The journalists were kept in the basement of a house and treated well, according to Ruslan Musayev, an AP reporter and one of the seven hostages. The kidnappers blindfolded the journalists, tied their hands, and dropped them off at a construction

EUROPE

site in the Dagestani capital Makhachkala. They were picked up by Dagestani authorities and released on December 31. The seven Dagestani police officers were reportedly released in subsequent weeks, but both Dagestani and Chechen officials have denied any connection to the release of the journalists.

Slovakia

While attempting to maintain the appearance of growing democratization, the coalition government of Prime Minister Vladimir Meciar boosted its efforts, both surreptitiously and overtly, to subdue independent and opposition media.

The government has frequently boasted that most of Slovakia's diverse media venues are privately owned and therefore independent. The ruling Movement for a Democratic Slovakia (HZDS) has repeatedly denied influence on editorial policies, despite evidence that firms with close ties to the HZDS have been favored in privatizations or purchases of news organizations or related companies.

In anticipation of parliamentary and presidential elections in 1998, the HZDS moved to covertly seize control of media outlets through privatization of state-owned enterprises. For example, the state publishing house Danubiaprint, which prints many of Slovakia's largest dailies, was privatized in 1997 and is now run by individuals affiliated with the HZDS. Party cronies also took over management of the H-Press Joint-Stock Publishing Company, which has tried to buy out a number of independent regional dailies, sometimes by coercive means. In June, the Slovak legislature voted to prevent the privatization of the second channel of Slovak Television (STV), the state-owned national television company, after the Slovak Council for TV and Radio Broadcasting

approved a license for the HZDS-affiliated Pro-TV company.

Although the government maintains control of STV (comprised of the only two channels that reach a national audience), its rigid and unprofessional programming has caused it to fall in ratings behind the private Markisa TV. The company—partially owned by U. S. investors—has become the most popular television station in Slovakia as its programs, especially news shows, have gradually grown bolder and more independent. Although its signal only reaches a little over half of Slovakia, Markisa TV has drawn authorities' ire in the form of verbal attacks, threats, and harassment.

Hard-hitting reporting on government activities may have prompted the authorities to retaliate against the independent station Radio Twist by suspending it from its main frequency in Bratislava for 25 hours on October 13. The state-run telecommunications company, Slovak Telecom, cut off the popular radio station from most of its listeners in the capital city citing unpaid bills for the use of the transmitter. The station's owner said Radio Twist was singled out for its critical news coverage. He said STV, public radio and the privately owned—though government-linked—VTV company, all owed vast amounts in arrears to Slovak Telecom, but remained on the air.

In addition to these oblique attacks, Slovakia's press came under frequent verbal assault from Prime Minister Meciar, whose government repeatedly demonstrated its antipathy toward the independent and opposition media.

On March 26, following protests by CPJ and other press freedom advocates, the Slovak parliament rejected the so-called Law on the Protection of the Republic, which would have severely restricted press freedom in Slovakia. The proposed amendment to the country's penal code, which would have made it a crime to "spread false information abroad," was defeated by a very narrow margin.

The Culture Ministry barred journalists from non-state media from its news conferences in March, and in October the government proposed raising the value-added tax from 6 percent to 23 percent on publications that devote more than 10 percent of their space to advertisements. This was widely viewed as an attempt to squeeze independent and opposition media, which rely heavily on advertising revenue. Bratislava's leading newspapers carried blank spaces on their front pages for a week in November to protest the proposal. They called off their protest after Slovak lawmakers suggested they would not approve the measure.

Meciar suspended weekly government press briefings on December 3 to punish journalists for questioning him about a mysterious trip he took to Russia with the head of the Slovak Intelligence Service on November 28, and about the role of an increasingly visible government advisor. After lashing out at journalists as well as lawmakers for their inquiries, the prime minister said that he and other members of his cabinet would no longer brief reporters during visits by foreign dignitaries to Slovakia unless provided for by diplomatic protocol.

Acts of violence and intimidation targeting the press punctuated the year. Reporter Adriana Hostovecka of the Paczelt news agency and a camera crew were beaten by guards and HZDS supporters while covering an HZDS rally in Bratislava on March 18. Peter Licak, editor of the *Presovsky Vecernik* daily in Presov, and Peter Toth, a reporter for the popular *Sme* newspaper in Bratislava, had their cars destroyed by arson. Licak believed the incident was related to attempts by an HZDS-affiliated firm to buy out his popular regional paper. Toth's has been the target of numerous libel

suits and attempts at intimidation for his investigative reports.

The Bratislava offices of the first independent Slovak news agency, SITA, were burglarized only days before the new agency was scheduled to launch its new operation. The robbery of SITA's computers, fax machines, photocopiers, and satellite equipment hampered the agency's ability to compete with TASR, the state-run Slovak Press Agency.

Libel and slander cases filed by officials against journalists and media outlets, already burgeoning last year, continued to mount. Slovakia does not have a criminal defamation law, but it does have a statute giving special civil protection for defamation of state officials.

June 7
Slovak Information & News Agency (SITA) HARASSED

The Bratislava office of Slovakia's first independent news agency, SITA, was burglarized a week before it was scheduled to open. SITA's director, Pavol Mudry, said that despite the building's security system, most of the agency's technical equipment was stolen. The agency lost several dozen computers, fax machines, photocopiers, and its satellite equipment.

SITA competes with the state-run Slovak Press Agency (TASR) in coverage of economic and domestic political news.

October 13
Radio Twist CENSORED

The state-run telecommunications company cut Radio Twist off from its main frequency for 25 hours, citing unpaid bills for the use of its transmitter in the capital. Andrei Hric, the station's owner and general manager, said Radio Twist was switched off without notice after its midday news show. Telecom officials told Hric the move resulted from his station's failure to

EUROPE

pay 170,000 crowns (US$5,600), in overdue debts since September 13. Hric said he paid the overdue debt on October 13, but the signal was still shut off. He believed the decision was politically motivated.

Hric said Slovak state television and public radio together owe Slovak Telecom some 550 million crowns in overdue debts, while VTV, a private television station linked to the government, owes 400 million crowns. None of these stations was shut off for their arrears. Hric concluded that Radio Twist had been singled out for its hard-hitting reporting on government activities. He said Prime Minister Vladimir Meciar, in a television interview aired the previous week, threatened unspecified retaliation against his station and the independent Markisa-TV for reporting on his recent trip to Croatia. Hric complained that Radio Twist has been subjected to repeated verbal attacks and harassment by Slovak officials over the past few years.

Radio Twist managed to stay on the air for the full 25 hours, but for only part of its audience. The station switched its signal to its privately owned transmitter in Banska Bystrica, in central Slovakia, and moved all of its programming to its studio there. Listeners in Bratislava, however, where Radio Twist enjoys the greatest market share, were cut off due to distance, which prompted many public protests. The signal was switched back on after 2 p.m. the next day, which Hric attributed to public pressure.

Tajikistan

After four years of civil war, which claimed the lives of at least 29 journalists, autocratic president Imomali Rakhmonov and United Tajik Opposition leader Said Abdullo Nuri concluded a peace accord in June. The rivals began to work out a power-sharing agreement through the National Reconciliation Commission in anticipation of parliamentary elections in 1998. But sporadic fighting in and around Dushanbe and other cities continued to create difficulties for both local and foreign (mainly Russian) journalists. When the conflict was at its worst, Tajik and Russian officials discouraged or condemned the coverage by the foreign press corps.

For the first time since 1992, no journalists were killed, but no action was taken to advance the investigations into the still-unsolved murders or to prosecute the perpetrators of killings from previous years. According to the Glasnost Defense Foundation, some 30 independent publications were shut down during the civil war, and at least 100 journalists fled the country in fear of reprisal; none have returned to date. Death threats to correspondents continue unabated, and Tajikistan joined the breakaway Russian republic of Chechnya as the most dangerous areas of the former Soviet Union for journalists, owing to the insidious practice of hostage-taking.

While often accused of inaction by desperate journalists, Russian consular officials did at times intervene on their behalf. But Russian officials were powerless to prevent such incidents as the blocking of press accreditation for Moscow's former Communist newspaper, *Pravda-5*, or the abduction of four Russian journalists for 11 days in February.

The Charter of the National Reconciliation Commission promises regular press briefings by the commission, and includes language supporting equal access for government and opposition mass media to its activities. But the commission has not been as forthcoming with information as promised, and the notion of unbiased professional media coverage has not yet taken root—as evidenced by a death threat against Radio Liberty correspondent Jovid Mukimov.

On September 25, a bomb exploded in the building that houses Khovar, the state news agency, and other state-sponsored publications, reportedly causing minor injuries to journalists. The attack fit a pattern of a dozen such bombings of visible targets in September and October, designed to discourage the opposition's return to Dushanbe. While not directed at journalists as such, the bombing did serve to highlight the continued vulnerability of reporters who work for the state.

An electronic broadcasting law passed in December 1996 held out the promise of more opportunity for Tajikistan's fledgling independent media. But in July, President Rakhmonov ordered the temporary closure of non-state television and radio companies until they were licensed, and the appropriation of technical equipment from some local stations for use by state television, ostensibly to improve its quality. Except for national and regional state television, no stations could continue broadcasting until the government officially set the price for a license.

In August, the Ministry of Culture and Information was divided into the Ministry of Culture and Press, and the State Committee on Television and Radio Broadcasting. The new broadcasting body was placed directly under the president's control, and was supposed to form a subcommittee to issue licenses. That month, the government told officials from the Organization for Security and Cooperation in Europe (OSCE) that applications would not be reviewed until the national reconciliation process was further advanced, but offered no specifics.

Despite repeated attempts, journalists, foreign embassies, and human rights organizations were unable to obtain a copy of the president's closure order. Apparently, some stations which began broadcasting before 1994 received temporary permission to operate, but procedures for the majority of stations to get new licenses remained unclear. Several local stations that submitted documents to authorities were ignored.

As in other countries in the region, politics and the media remain closely intertwined. The president's order should have closed Poitakt, a television station in Dushanbe, but it remained in operation, apparently because the city's mayor owns a majority stake in the station. Stations were also ordered shut down in Isfara, Kanibadam, Ura Tube, and Pendjikent, but they continued to broadcast, because of their close relationships with local officials. On the other hand, three local stations in Tursanzade, Vose, and Khojand were closed by those cities' mayors—and the station in Vose had already paid a fee of US$1,500 to the Ministry of Communications for a channel.

On December 3, the State TV and Radio Committee finally issued the first long-term license, to the private TV Studio "Mavchi ozod." The studio was awarded a five-year license to produce and broadcast television programs in the Vose region for 18 hours a day every other day on odd days. The move was viewed as a victory for private broadcasters, as another dozen private stations were expected to get licenses in the ensuing months.

Yet the licensing process remains unfair. State-run television should not be empowered to license or restrict the operation of its competitors. The "Mavchi Ozod" TV Studio was denied rights to rebroadcast foreign programs, and was limited to broadcasting only on odd days. The local government in Vose has set up its own transmitter on the same frequency as the station. All these are clear efforts by the authorities to squeeze out private competitors.

February 5
Bobjan Tuganov, NTV IMPRISONED
Odiljan Ashurov, NTV IMPRISONED
Galina Gridneva, ITAR-TASS IMPRISONED
Suraye Sobirova, Interfax IMPRISONED

Gunmen from a rebel group led by Bahrom Sadirov seized the four journalists and their driver near Obi-Garm, about 50 miles from Dushanbe, the Tajik capital. Cameraman Tuganov and correspondent Ashurov, both from NTV; Gridneva, a reporter with the Russian government wire service ITAR-TASS; and Sobirova, a correspondent in Dushanbe for the Russian news agency Interfax, were on their way to a rebel stronghold to interview Sadirov about his capture of five U.N. military observers on February 4.

In exchange for the release of the hostages, the insurgent group was demanding that Sadirov's brother, Rizvon Sadirov, and a band of guerrilla fighters under his command in neighboring Afghanistan, receive safe passage to Tajikistan.

Sobirova had received an anonymous death threat on January 9 in a note sent to her home. She pleaded with the Russian consulate in Dushanbe to intervene on her behalf with Tajik authorities, but she received no response.

Russian and Tajik officials negotiated for two weeks for the release of the hostages. Russian Prime Minister Viktor Chernomyrdin then sent Defense Minister Igor Rodionov to Tajikistan to negotiate; Tajikistan Defense Minister Saidamir Zukhurov, who traveled to Obi-garm to negotiate with the rebels, was himself taken hostage.

After further negotiations, the rebels on February 15 handed over Gridneva, Sobirova, and the NTV crew's driver to Russian representatives in Dushanbe. The next day they released Tuganov, Ashurov, and three other hostages. The journalists were flown to Moscow and later said they would not return to Tajikistan for fear of retaliation.

August 24
Jovid Mukimov, Radio Free Europe/Radio Liberty THREATENED

Mukimov, the Dushanbe correspondent for the Tajik Broadcast Service of Radio Free Europe/Radio Liberty, was threatened by an official he quoted in an August 22 broadcast.

Commenting on clashes outside the capital, Mukimov quoted Jaloliddin Mahmudov, co-chairman of the Joint Ceasefire Commission, as saying that Sayid Abdulloh Nuri (leader of the United Tajik Opposition) had called for an end to cease-fire violations. Mukimov quoted Mahmudov as saying that the UTO would act in concert with government forces to prevent such incidents in the future.

On August 23, Mahmudov called Mukimov at home and angrily demanded another interview in which he could retract the previous statement.

On August 24, Mahmudov telephoned again and threatened Mukimov, saying that he "would execute" him. The Tajik Broadcast Service condemned the threat in a letter to Nuri, copied to the UN office in Tajikistan and the U.S. Embassy. In a letter dated August 29, Nuri replied that Mahmudov's behavior was "incorrect" but denounced Mukimov's report as "incorrect and inflammatory."

Turkmenistan

The poorest of the former Soviet republics and the Central Asian nation with the lowest level of press freedom, Turkmenistan has recently been the focus of considerable international media scrutiny. Yet more exposure has not spelled more freedom for the intimidated corps of state scribes who crank out the propaganda in the only former Soviet republic to retain a leader who came to power before perestroika.

Ruled by the despotic Saparmurad Niyazov, or "Turkmenbashi, father of all Turkmen people," land-locked Turkmenistan has the fourth-largest natural gas reserves in the world, and has only lacked a secure pipeline to Western markets to unleash its riches. Oil magnates in Russia, the United States, and Iran have been courting Niyazov assiduously in an

effort to tap those reserves. The frenzied bidding for various pipeline projects captured the attention of Russian and Western journalists, who reported about such scandals as the squeezing out of an Argentinian company which had originally purchased the rights to the gas deposits at a far lower cost. By the end of the year, Iran succeeded in clinching a deal with Niyazov, and a pipeline was opened between the two countries.

Yet all the visits to Turkmenistan by reporters and officials did not lead to coverage of the country's social and political ills, and local journalists had no access to details of the large gas deals. Following what he terms "an Asian path," President Niyazov has welcomed joint ventures to fuel government revenue-generating schemes, but has maintained absolute political and social control. Marat Durdiyev, a prominent educator and historian, once a journalist for official local papers as well as Russia's *Pravda*, lost his privileged positions on editorial boards when he let comments slip such as, "We have an authoritarian country," and "Only one person does all the thinking."

Few foreign correspondents venture beyond the official dimensions of the oil and gas story to investigate Turkmen society. Small wonder, given the country's forbidding press climate, in which officials confiscate foreign newspapers from airplanes as soon as they land, secret police tail reporters if they stray from the officially prescribed itinerary, and border guards are known for their thorough searches. Zealous customs agents detained Youshan Anna Kurbanov, a Radio Liberty stringer and one of the few independent journalists in the country, as he tried to board a plane for Prague on October 30. They held him for two weeks without charge and confiscated his audio tapes, which contained mostly folk music.

Every morning the television broadcasts school children singing "for the slightest slander, let my tongue be lost/at the moment of my betrayal to my motherland, to her sacred banner, to my president, let my breath stop." This macabre pledge of allegiance is emblematic of the culture of fear. Unlike other Central Asian countries with similar authoritarian regimes, Turkmenistan has failed to develop even a tiny community of dissidents, human rights activists, or intrepid journalists in its Soviet and immediate post-Soviet periods—people who could challenge the president's absolute power. Some independent environmental, cultural, and women's organizations do manage to survive despite the odds, especially outside of the capital of Ashgabad, but their publications do not attempt to challenge or investigate the regime.

According to Greg Myre of the Associated Press, one of the few Westerners to penetrate Turkmenistan, the abrupt switch from the Russian Cyrillic alphabet to the Latin alphabet has left many adults functionally illiterate and unable to read the state-run newspapers. At the state-run national library, no new books have been purchased since independence, and the only periodicals from the outside world are dated magazines and newspapers donated by Western embassies. Foreign aid groups and embassies who offered to connect the library to the Internet and computerize its card catalogue free of charge were rebuffed, since official policy requires Turkmenistan to be self-sufficient. Librarians told Myre that instead of buying books and linking the library to the Internet, the government was building a multi-million dollar presidential palace.

Ukraine

Over the past few years, press freedom conditions in Ukraine have gone from promising to precarious, if not dangerous. Although the number and variety of media outlets has continued to grow, attempts to manipulate their content by the administration of President Leonid Kuchma, his political rivals, local officials, and related business interests have caused a profound erosion of press freedom in the country.

The most serious symptom of the decline has been the rising tide of violence against journalists, most notably the murders of reporters and editors for their professional activity. Beatings of journalists have become routine. Few of these cases are investigated properly by police, and they generally go unsolved and unpunished.

On August 11, the veteran editor of a popular newspaper in Odessa, Borys Derevyanko of *Vechernyaya Odessa*, was shot and killed on a city street in broad daylight. The regional prosecutor swiftly concluded that Derevyanko was assassinated because of his editorial work. Derevyanko's murder generated considerable publicity and outrage because of his prominence as a journalist and critic of Odessa Mayor Eduard Gurvits. Police arrested a suspect who confessed to the contract killing of Derevyanko. Reflecting a long-standing rivalry, city and regional officials exchanged accusations, each group attempting to link the other to the murder.

Derevyanko's murder was typical of many violent incidents against journalists, but atypical in that it produced an arrest. Following Derevyanko's murder, Ukraine's acting general prosecutor Oleh Lytvak acknowledged that violent crimes against journalists were on the rise. He said 29 journalists reported they were victims of assault between April 1996 and October 1997, but insisted that most cases were random muggings and reflected the overall spread of crime in Ukraine. Lytvak accused journalists of seeking sensational stories, implying that reporters may provoke such incidents. Journalists groups protested his

remarks and contested his statistics, blaming the authorities' poor record of prosecuting attackers for journalists' reluctance to report crimes against them.

CPJ investigated the suspicious death of Petro Shevchenko, a correspondent in Luhansk for the popular tabloid, *Kievskiye Vedomosti*, who was found hanged in an abandoned building outside Kiev in March. Although police said they found a suicide note at the scene, Shevchenko's colleagues hesitated to accept this explanation, citing the reporter's recent troubles with local security service officials in Luhansk. Shevchenko had complained of pressure from officers from the local branch of the Security Service of Ukraine (SBU) who were angered by his articles about their conflict with the mayor of Luhansk. His case, as well as a number of assaults against journalists documented by CPJ last year, revealed a disturbing trend of reporters and editors in the perilous midst of political and commercial rivalries.

Independent and opposition news organizations faced other forms of intimidation as well, and they fear more such harassment in the run-up to parliamentary elections in March 1998. Libel suits filed against publications and journalists by political and business figures have proliferated. Most are civil cases punishable with fines, but the officials and business people often seek huge amounts of damages to bankrupt and silence media outlets. Perhaps the most visible case last year was a libel suit filed by Interior Minister Yuri Kravchenko against *Kievskiye Vedomosti*, which bore the brunt of official harassment for its investigations of corruption and organized crime. The minister is seeking damages worth about US$4.5 million from the newspaper, and about US$1 million each from two reporters, Serhiy Kiselev and Henadiy Kirindyasov, for a series of articles alleging impropriety and corruption. The trial has repeatedly been postponed. The paper lost another civil suit in the spring filed against it by the Kiev city administration, paying about a half million U.S. dollars in damages. The paper's publisher, Mykhailo Brodsky, a wealthy entrepreneur and critic of President Kuchma, claimed the cases were politically motivated. Many journalists, particularly those working for struggling publications outside major urban areas, have resorted to using pseudonyms to avoid prosecution.

Kievskiye Vedomosti and a host of other opposition and independent newspapers also suffered a series of random tax and fire inspections throughout the year. A number of Brodsky's bank accounts were frozen in the process.

The struggle for control of Ukraine's airwaves intensified in the run-up to the national elections. The leftist-dominated Ukrainian parliament voted in November to regain some air time for itself by setting up a public television network under its control. Most of Ukraine's national airwaves have been split up among pro-Kuchma State Television and private broadcasters viewed as loyal to the president, and little time has been available to the president's political rivals. Most Ukrainians still rely on television as their chief source of news because they cannot afford subscriptions to periodicals. Private broadcasters loyal to the president, such as Studio 1+1, viewed the parliament's decision to establish its own Public Broadcasting of Ukraine as an attack on independent broadcasting because it would ultimately take air time away from them. The lawmakers claimed they were in effect breaking a monopoly because top officials in the presidential administration and government held financial stakes in Studio 1+1 and other private broadcasters as well as controlling State TV. But the deputies failed to indicate how they would pay for their public television programs, especially as the cash-strapped government owes months' worth of back

wages to workers in the still-huge public sector.

The privately produced popular weekly news magazine show "Pislyamova" was taken off the air by Studio 1+1 on two occasions last year for segments deemed inappropriate. Private program producers are expected to censor themselves on politically sensitive topics if they want even private broadcasters like Studio 1+1 to air their shows.

March 13
Petro Shevchenko, *Kievskiye Vedomosti*, KILLED

Shevchenko, correspondent for the daily newspaper *Kievskiye Vedomosti*, was found dead hanging from a rope in an abandoned building in Kiev. Shevchenko, the popular tabloid's correspondent in the Luhansk region, had co-authored a series of articles published in recent weeks about disputes between the Luhansk mayor and the local branch of the Ukrainian Security Service (SBU), successor to the KGB.

According to colleagues, Shevchenko had phoned the paper's headquarters in Kiev in early March to express his fear of reprisal from the SBU in Luhansk, a town near the Russian border thriving with privatization ventures. Local SBU officers had held a press conference in February to denounce the newspaper's series as biased.

A *Kievskiye Vedomosti* editor told CPJ that Shevchenko arrived in Kiev by train on March 12 and was met by the newspaper's messenger. Shevchenko told him he planned to go to the paper's offices later that day.

His body was found the evening of March 13 in an empty boiler room by children playing nearby. Police said Shevchenko had died the morning before. There were no signs of a struggle, and he had not been robbed.

The editorial board of *Kievskiye Vedomosti*, other Ukrainian journalists, and a local press freedom group said that Shevchenko's death might have been murder. At a press conference

EUROPE

in Kiev on March 13, journalists asked President Leonid Kuchma to investigate the death of Shevchenko and other unexplained deaths of journalists in Ukraine in recent years.

The prosecutor's office, which has opened an investigation into the hanging, claimed it found a suicide note with a farewell to Shevchenko's family and an indication that he was under SBU pressure. But the office has not allowed Shevchenko's colleagues to see the note.

Kievskiye Vedomosti has been covering disputes between Luhansk Mayor Alexei Danilov, a reform-minded young businessman, and the local SBU department. An editor said the newspaper, which frequently features crime and political scandals, has also reported incidents of alleged SBU harassment of the mayor. At year's end, CPJ was unable to confirm whether Shevchenko's death was a suicide or murder.

June 6
Taras Moskaliuk, Ukraine TV and Radio Broadcasting Company ATTACKED

The host of the popular "Ranok Vechora" television news program produced by the Ukraine TV and Radio Broadcasting Company was abducted in front of his home in Donetsk, Ukraine. Moskaliuk was forced into a car and taken at gunpoint to an empty lot. The assailants demanded that his program immediately stop broadcasting in the Russian language and begin using Ukrainian.

The kidnappers released Moskaliuk several hours later, warning that if Ukrainian-language broadcasts did not begin immediately, they would blow up the television studios later that day. The company evacuated the building, but a police search did not turn up any explosives.

The identity of the abductors and their motives were not known. Law enforcement agencies and the Security Service of Ukraine launched official investigations.

July 9
Aleksander Anishchenko, *95 Kvartal*
ATTACKED

Anishchenko, the deputy editor of *95 Kvartal*, a private weekly newspaper in the city of Kryvyi Rih, was attacked July 9 by three masked men wearing camouflage uniforms. Anishchenko said the men jumped him on the stairwell in the paper's offices and beat him with police truncheons, shouting, "This will teach you how to write about the police." Hearing Anishchenko's calls for help, Serhiy Yakymenko, the paper's owner and editor, ran to the scene and the attackers fled. Eyewitnesses said the assailants jumped into a car and drove away. Anishchenko was hospitalized for two weeks.

Anishchenko said local and regional authorities were investigating. The journalist said police treated the attack as a random mugging. Because the attack took place near the newspaper's office in broad daylight—and close to police headquarters—Anishchenko said the assault was deliberately aimed at *95 Kvartal*, which covers local crime and government scandals.

August 8
Kostiantyn Serdiuk, *Chernigovsky Poldin*
ATTACKED

Serdiuk, editor of the independent Russian-language newspaper *Chernigovsky Poldin*, was attacked by three assailants in an alley in Chernihiv. The attackers called out his name before grabbing him and kicking him repeatedly in the head. Serdiuk suffered brain damage and heavy internal bleeding. Colleagues from the Chernihiv Media Club said police were investigating the incident. In a petition to local and regional authorities, the journalists linked the assault to a recent article Serdiuk wrote that criticized local government policies.

Journalists say that regional officials, dominated by old-style communists, often intimidate independent and opposition journalists. Recently, authorities banned the screening of a film critical of Belarusian President Aleksander Lukashenko, saying the screening interfered in the internal affairs of a neighboring country.

August 11
Borys Derevyanko, *Vechernyaya Odessa*
KILLED

Derevyanko, editor in chief of *Vechernyaya Odessa*, was shot twice in the heart and stomach.

Vasily Ivanov, chief regional prosecutor, declared Derevyanko's murder a contract killing and launched an official investigation. Ruslan Bodelan, governor of Odessa Region, called the murder "an act of political terror."

Colleagues of Derevyanko, a veteran newsman who served 24 years as the editor of *Vechernyaya Odessa*, believe his killing is related to the newspaper's opposition to city hall. Derevyanko was not known to be involved in any investment dealings. The newspaper is supported by advertising revenue, as well as by its founding sponsors, who include government and industrial figures. Its editorial position is left of center and it has been particularly critical of the policies of Odessa Mayor Eduard Gurvits. Derevyanko, a former member of the USSR Supreme Soviet, was a deputy to the Odessa city council.

Local reporters cited several previous attacks on journalists at the newspaper as evidence that Derevyanko's killing could be related to his editorial position. On August 3, 1995, Sergei Lebedev, a correspondent for *Vechernyaya Odessa*, survived three shots from an attacker who was later arrested and tried but was sentenced to only 18 months. In 1996 and again in the spring of 1997, another journalist at the paper, Vitaliy Chechik, was beaten; last year the alleged attacker told him to "stop writing articles about the mayor."

Derevyanko was beaten once in 1994, but was not known to have received any threats nor to have published any unusually sharp editorials recently. Local authorities announced in September that they had arrested a suspect,

described as a professional assassin, who confessed to killing Derevyanko, but they gave no details about his confession.

Uzbekistan

Uzbekistan's abysmal record on press freedom has not changed much since it gained independence in 1991. Claims by the autocratic president Islam Karimov about freedom of speech and the lack of censorship in the large Central Asian nation carry little substantive meaning or connection with reality. Karimov and his government maintain a tight grip on State Television and Radio, whose broadcasts are thoroughly censored, sterile, and devoid of open debate and comment on the politics and the economy. The state limited the number of Russian television programs broadcast in the country to a minimum, dooming the 23 million Uzbeks to a diet of Karimov's speeches, political propaganda, and other sanitized broadcasts. The one non-government channel in Tashkent, launched in March, was allowed to rebroadcast only the entertainment and family programs of the Russian ORT. As proof of the seriousness of the president's call for democratization, the BBC and Radio Liberty were allowed to open offices in Tashkent in this otherwise closed country.

The print press is also heavily controlled and censored. In the Soviet tradition, front pages of state-run newspapers such as *Narodnoe Slovo* and *Pravda Vostoka* regularly feature the president's photograph and unabridged speeches. Liberal Russian newspapers are banned, as are Uzbek independent and opposition papers published abroad. Underground opposition newspapers smuggled in from Russia introduce some criticism of the government into the country.

Karimov recently has professed a "commitment to democratic media and reform,"

which he attempted to prove with the passage of a Law of the Republic of Uzbekistan on the Mass Media in the last week of December. The draft law was published in November in *Narodnoe Slovo* and passed during the December session of the Oli Majlis, the national legislature. Article 2 of the law states that censorship of mass media is "inadmissible," and yet the Republican Committee on Mass Media, appointed by the government, completely controls the registration process of media outlets.

Yugoslavia

As the year began, then-Serbian President Slobodan Milosevic's ruling socialists continued to resist ceding control of municipal councils and media outlets in 14 cities around the republic, where members of the democratic Zajedno coalition had won majorities in elections on November 17, 1996.

For three months last winter mass demonstrations brought unprecedented numbers of protesters into the streets to demand that Milosevic enforce the election results and hand over city-owned television and radio stations to his opponents. By January, it was clear that he would be forced into relinquishing his control over the local councils and broadcast media. He had already given up jamming the popular independent B-92 radio station in Belgrade in the face of mass rallies and international protests, including a plea in person by CPJ's Kati Marton during a special mission to Serbia in December 1996.

The pro-Milosevic, state-run press lost a large number of readers throughout the year to the independent print media. By December, the overall circulation of the independent press had surpassed that of all the state-owned publications. Diverse independent newspapers such as *Blic*, *Nasa Borba*, and *Danas* had become serious competition for established state-run dailies like *Politika*, while independent news agencies such as Beta and Fonet outpaced the official Tanjug as important news sources for the opposition-controlled municipal broadcast media.

The loss of the municipal broadcast media and the growing popularity of the independent press were clearly unacceptable to the ruling party, which faced parliamentary elections in the fall. Milosevic himself was legally barred from running for re-election as president of Serbia in the fall election and had become a candidate for president of Yugoslavia, to be elected by the Federal Assembly in July. The urgency for a socialist victory prompted his government to launch a two-pronged attack on the independent and opposition media that continued throughout the year.

The first line of attack involved the introduction of a new draft law on information in March by the Serbian Minister of Information, Radmila Milentijevic. The bill was clearly designed to restrict the independent media, by limiting the maximum broadcast audience for all non-public television and radio stations to 25 percent of the population and prohibiting any private person or organization from owning more than 20 percent of the media market.

Milentijevic boasted that the provisions were aimed at preventing the growth of monopolies. Critics, such as the Independent Association of Journalists (NUNS) and the Independent Media Union, pointed to the fact that the bill failed to address the state's monopoly on national broadcasting and its control of the three national television channels. The draft also required private newspapers to regularly declare on their front pages or covers any foreign funding or assistance they received.

Milosevic also pressed independent

broadcasters on the murky issue of broadcast licenses. In early June, telecommunications officials announced a June 30 deadline for private broadcasters to submit the required documents to receive a temporary operating license, good only until the Federal Assembly adopted a new broadcasting law. As a warning to so-called "pirate" radio stations, the ministry banned most radio stations without permits during the week of June 2-6. A crisis ensued as broadcasters faced what they viewed as an impossible deadline with a procedure that was confusing and contradictory.

By June 30, not one license application was complete and soon federal authorities began shutting down radio and television stations. They confiscated broadcasting equipment and closed stations despite independent broadcasters' attempts at compliance with official demands. As of August, 77 radio and television stations had received notices that they were banned.

After Milosevic was elected and sworn in as president of Yugoslavia in July, the leader met with some opposition leaders concerned about the mass shutdown of local radio and television stations. The leader promised them equal access to media during the election campaign. On July 26, his government announced that a settlement of the licensing crisis would be postponed until after the September 21 elections for the Serbian legislature. However, station closures continued and tensions remained high over seized equipment. Eventually, all the stations managed to resume broadcasting through the elections, including Radio Boom 93 in Pozarevac, which had been banned since December 1996.

Political re-alignments may have played a greater role than international and domestic pressure in the Yugoslav leader's decision to temporarily back down from his campaign against independent broadcasters.

After the elections, broadcasters were given a new deadline of October 31 to sub-mit all license documents. The deadline was moved again until after the Serbian presidential run-offs in December. By the end of the year, there was no word about a new deadline. But the Information Ministry announced that the government was drafting a new telecommunications law to resolve the matter and pledged that licenses would not be withheld from anyone for political reasons.

A struggle for control of republican and municipal broadcast media took place in Montenegro between outgoing president Momir Bulatovic and president-elect Milo Djukanovic, who served as the republic's premier. Following his victory in the October presidential elections, Djukanovic, viewed as a democrat, made personnel changes at RTV Montenegro, the republican channel. The new managers and editors have diversified their news sources to include independent and international agencies, and have given more air time to the opposition. The news now has a pro-Djukanovic slant and journalists tend to demonize Bulatovic. Most of the independent media in Montenegro, including the popular Radio Antenna M and Montena Fax news agency, who were often harassed by the Bulatovic administration, have taken a pro-Djukanovic line. Only the independent weekly newspaper *Monitor* seems to be independent. The regional state-run radio station, as well as the Serbian official press, have remained loyal to Bulatovic, who continued to refuse to recognize the election results and hand over power to his rival at year's end.

Montenegrin media have voiced concerns that any new federal telecommunications legislation that may transfer distribution of frequencies from the republican to the federal government will be discriminatory and take away their autonomy.

In the volatile, predominantly ethnic Albanian province of Kosovo, the federal

EUROPE

authorities continued to restrict private Albanian broadcast media. There is no local Albanian radio or television, but Kosovo has a variety of newspapers, chiefly Albanian-language, and some local Serbian publications.

January
Trstenik TV station HARASSED
Kanal 4 TV station CENSORED
All radio and TV stations in Kragujevac CENSORED

Early in the month, a Socialist former manager of a TV station in the town of Trstenik, apparently angered by the loss of his post, reportedly stole the station's van, high-range transmitter, and other technical equipment. The station's new management from the Zajedno coalition replaced the equipment, but operations were again disrupted on January 18, when its offices were vandalized. Several cameras and telephones were stolen.

On January 24, the Transportation and Communication Ministry told Kanal 4 in the town of Bajina Basta that it would suspend the station's broadcasts. Kanal 4 had been broadcasting daily reports about demonstrations in Belgrade against the ruling Socialist Party.

In Kragujevac, local TV and radio stations were barred from broadcasting all news and political programming until a court decided which party would run the station. The Socialist Party refused to yield control of the local radio and television offices to newly elected opposition politicians. The party instead integrated the town's radio and television stations into its national Serbian Television Network, and it sent 200 police to Kragujevac's media offices to prevent the opposition from taking over.

January 23
Srdjan Nedeljkovic, Associated Press Television (APTV) ATTACKED HARASSED
Dejan Mladenovic, APTV THREATENED HARASSED

Police assaulted Nedeljkovic, a soundman from

APTV, and threatened Mladenovic, an APTV cameraman, at a demonstration near Kragujevac. The camera crew was stationed at barricades outside the city, where they were filming opposition supporters blocking entry to the city center. The demonstrators were protesting the Socialist Party's refusal to allow newly elected opposition leaders to take over Kragujevac's media offices.

Police yelled at the crew to stop filming. When they did not comply, police struck Nedeljkovic in the stomach with a baton and threatened Mladenovic by waving a baton in his face. The officers then confiscated the journalists' videotape and drove them to the local Kragujevac police station where they were detained for 45 minutes. They were released unharmed, but without their video.

January 23
Kragujevac media CENSORED

The ruling Socialist Party of Serbia (SPS) refused to yield control of the local radio and television stations in the central industrial city of Kragujevac to newly elected opposition city council members. The SPS instead integrated Kragujevac's radio and television stations into the SPS-controlled national Serbian Television Network (RTS). When the RTS sent 200 police into Kragujevac's media offices to prevent an opposition takeover, thousands of opposition supporters flocked to the stations' building in protest and blocked entrance to the city's center.

February 2
Maria Fleet, CNN ATTACKED
Serhii Karaziy, Reuters TV ATTACKED
Maja Vidakovic, BK Telecom ATTACKED
Savo Ilic, BK Telecom ATTACKED
Predrag Vujic, Beta News Agency ATTACKED
Marko Petrovic, *Blic* ATTACKED
Reiner Herscher, Associated Press Television ATTACKED

Rastko Kostic, student media ATTACKED
Vanja Lazin, BK Telecom ATTACKED

Several journalists were attacked during an opposition demonstration in Belgrade. Police attacked Fleet, a CNN camerawoman, and broke her equipment, although she was not injured. Police also beat Karaziy, a Ukrainian cameraman working for Reuters Television, and smashed his camera. Karaziy, who sustained injuries to his back, legs, and head, was treated at a clinic and released. BK Telecom reporter Vidakovic, cameraman Ilic, and assistant Lazin were also attacked and their camera was damaged. Vujic, a reporter for the news agency Beta, and Petrovic, a reporter for the independent daily *Blic*, were also beaten despite showing police their press cards. Police pummeled Herscher, a German cameraman for Associated Press Television and pushed him to the ground. Wielding clubs, police beat Kostic, a reporter for the student media, and knocked out two of his teeth.

CPJ wrote Serbian President Slobodan Milosevic condemning the brutal attacks.

March 5
BK Telecom CENSORED

Radio-Television of Serbia (RTS) sent notice to BK Telecom, an independent television company in Serbia operating BK Television, that its lease for use of transmitter sites in Misenluk, Venac, Jastrebac, Crni Vrh, and Goles would expire in 15 days, and that the agreement to use frequencies at Jastrebac, Crni Vrh, and Goles was terminated.

According to BK TV's editorial board, BK Telecom had a valid agreement with RTS to relay its programs and had regularly paid high leasing fees. BK TV said it was the only station that had received such a cancellation, ostensibly dictated by RTS's need for technical expansion. The RTS cancellation also ignored the terms of the lease, which called for a six-month advance notice for such termination.

BK Telecom, owned by Serbian entrepreneur Bogoljub Karic, has the capacity to reach an estimated 60 percent of Serbia's population. It recently had intensified its criticism of President Slobodan Milosevic.

May 8
BK TV Pec CENSORED

Miladin Ivanovic, a local official of the ruling Socialist Party, shut down the BK Telecom television affiliate in the town of Pec on May 8 by sealing the independent station's studios, BK management in Belgrade said.

The station had refused Ivanovic's demand that BK TV stop airing news programs, so the official locked up BK's rented studios, forcing the station to stop broadcasting.

A crowd gathered on May 16 outside the studios to protest the move, flouting a local interior ministry ban on such demonstrations.

Station Director Nebojsa Radunovic pleaded with the crowd to disperse, but police detained and questioned him for two hours. Police dispersed the rally and confiscated BK TV's videotape of the protest as well as film taken by several other photographers.

Station managers said that BK TV's parent company has been leasing a space for its transmitter for nearly a year, but the state-run Serbian Radio-Television (RTS) has prevented BK engineers from installing the necessary equipment.

May 11
Radio-Television Kragujevac HARASSED

Serbian Information Minister Radmila Milentijevic threatened punitive actions against the opposition-run Radio-Television Kragujevac for making on-air statements asserting that the state-supplied news bulletins are not truthful. Radio Kragujevac had apologized to its audience "for having to make them listen to lies," a reference to state-run news that the government forces it to broadcast.

Milentijevic said the management of Radio-Television Kragujevac "should pay for" routinely telling radio listeners that the official news bulletins are fallacious. She urged the state-run television station to "take control of Kragujevac Radio-Television and bring its management to justice."

The Zajedno opposition coalition, which controls Kragujevac's town council, took over the station's television operations in January following mass demonstrations. But its radio division is still forced to air state-produced news announcements twice daily.

CPJ wrote a letter to Serbian President Slobodan Milosevic on May 20, strongly protesting the government's harassment of opposition television and radio.

June 11
Nasa Borba HARASSED

Government revenue inspectors ordered Fininvest, the publisher of *Nasa Borba*, to pay the dinar equivalent of US$76,000 in back taxes. Fininvest said the authorities were misusing the tax police to put pressure on the independent newspaper.

Fininvest said the taxes had been paid in full and showed corroborating documentation. *Nasa Borba* officials said the tax order was a form of harassment in retaliation for the paper's opposition stance.

In a June 26 letter to Serbian President Slobodan Milosevic, CPJ expressed concern that the tax inspection was a pressure tactic, noting that the action came only a few days after *Nasa Borba* was awarded the Golden Pen of Freedom by the World Association of Newspapers.

July 23
77 radio and TV stations in Serbia CENSORED

In late July and early August, the government closed 77 small independent radio and television stations throughout Serbia, including many that broadcast alternative news and commentary unavailable from state broadcasters.

The Yugoslav Ministry for Transport and Telecommunications on June 2 had announced a June 30 deadline for the submission of the documentation necessary to receive an operating license. Broadcast journalists complained to CPJ that the new procedure was confusing and contradictory and the deadline impossible to meet. Authorities then confiscated broadcasting equipment and closed stations despite attempts at compliance with official demands.

The government in late August allowed the stations to temporarily resume broadcasting in the run-up to the autumn national elections, but it did not change the new regulations.

September 30
Studio B TV CENSORED

Zoran Ostojic and Lila Radonjic were fired as the director and editor in chief, respectively, of Studio B TV, the municipal television station in Belgrade. Their dismissal in effect silenced the capital city's only alternative, pro-democratic voice on television.

After ousting opposition Mayor Zoran Djindjic, the combined forces of the Serbian Socialists, Radicals, and the Renewal Movement moved to sack the top management at Studio B TV and replace them with their own supporters.

The Socialists replaced the two executives with former station manager Dragan Kojadinovic, whose policies favoring the Serbian war lobby had prompted more than 100 employees to quit the station in 1993. Before losing control of the station, the staff of Studio B TV broadcast live footage of the unfolding events, and called on citizens to attend an evening opposition rally.

The station's entire board of directors was also fired and replaced by members of the Serbian Renewal Movement and the Radical and Socialist parties.

Several thousand Belgrade residents demonstrated that night. Scores of police beat and detained protesters. The Association of Independent Electronic Media (ANEM) in

Serbia protested the overthrow of Studio B TV's management, whom they regarded as impartial and professional. ANEM leaders said the television officials were dismissed without public knowledge and said they feared the new managers would place party interests before the public interest.

October 1
Dragutin Rokvic, Independent Union of Journalists of Serbia ATTACKED

Belgrade police beat Rokvic, the general secretary of the Independent Union of Journalists of Serbia, during a mass demonstration on October 1.

According to Rokvic, police intentionally targeted journalists who were covering the demonstration, protesting the recent dismissals of opposition Mayor Zoran Djindjic and the managers of the popular Studio B TV station by ruling coalition officials.

Rokvic was attacked by police wielding batons as he stood with a group of colleagues near the demonstration. He was hit repeatedly with the batons and kicked in the legs. The officers threw Rokvic to the ground and handcuffed him. He and several of his colleagues were taken to police headquarters, where they were questioned. Police told them they would face criminal charges for throwing stones and insulting police officers. Rokvic suffered a broken hand.

During a news conference the next day, Rokvic called on all journalists who were harassed by police to file complaints to his organization so that it could initiate legal action against police officers responsible for excessive use of force.

October 15
Gordana Igric, free-lancer THREATENED

Igric began receiving threatening phone calls after Serbian, Bosnian, and European media broadcast excerpts of her conversation with Janko Janjic, a Bosnian Serb soldier known as "Tuta," who was wanted for rape. The segments originally aired on the CBS program "Public Eye with Bryant Gumbel" on October 15. On hidden camera, Janjic told Igric and CBS News producer Randall Joyce that for about US$2,800 he would describe how he killed and raped hundreds of Bosnian Muslims in Foce. He boasted no fear of being caught by NATO soldiers, who were shown sitting in an adjacent restaurant.

The telephone calls Igric received at her Belgrade apartment featured the sounds of gunfire and the ticking of a time bomb. The journalist, who is writing a book about war crimes in Foce, took refuge at a location outside Belgrade. But the threatening telephone calls followed her to this hiding place, forcing her to move again with her two children.

Igric received death threats for her reporting on war criminals in Foce once before. One of her articles, which appeared in the *Sunday Times* and was reprinted in Bosnian Federation newspapers in July 1996, prompted threatening phone calls.

On October 28, CPJ sent a letter to President Slobodan Milosevic urging him to ensure a swift and thorough investigation into the threats against Igric.

EUROPE

Mixed Signals: Press Freedom in Armenia and Azerbaijan

By Nicholas Daniloff

The persistence of political and military censorship, restrictive media legislation, and violent attacks against journalists and media organizations in Azerbaijan and Armenia prompted CPJ to undertake a research project in 1997 focused on the media climate in the two states. With the support of the Open Society Institute, CPJ commissioned Nicholas Daniloff, a specialist on the media in the Caucasus who directs the journalism program at Northeastern University in Boston, to conduct a three-month fact-finding mission to the two countries beginning in April 1997. While on sabbatical in 1997, he lectured on democracy and the role of the independent press at Garb University in Baku. He conducted extensive interviews with local editors, reporters, media and human rights groups, professional associations, and government officials in Armenia and Azerbaijan.

This report is adapted from CPJ's full-length special report, "Paradoxes in the Caucasus." For the complete report, visit our website at http://www.cpj.org or call 212-465-1004.

Oil Flows More Freely Than Ideas in Azerbaijan

At 25, Gunduz M. Tairli is a chain-smoking, ink-stained journalist. His face is angular; his expression intense. He is chief editor of *Azadliq*, one of Baku's most popular newspapers, and the organ of the opposition Popular Front party. Putting out *Azadliq* is a daily struggle for Tairli, who labors 12 hours a day, six days a week for the equivalent of $50 a month.

Every night, Tairli's colleagues run the tabloid's eight pages across town to the headquarters of the Main Administration for the Protection of State Secrets (also referred to as Glavlit, the acronym for Soviet censorship) to get the censor's stamp of approval before it is published in the Azerbaijan Publishing House. There are no private publishing houses available to newspapers; presses for large print runs are expensive, as are newsprint and electricity.

Approval comes only after the censor ponders each page and

cuts material deemed undesirable as the *Azadliq* journalists wait. Explanations for cuts are not offered, and when journalists ask, they get evasive answers. *Azadliq* (the Azeri word for "liberty") keeps a collection of cartoons to fill in the holes, because censors don't like blank spaces. Nevertheless, they sometimes appear in the newspaper. If the gaps are too large, the censors may ban the entire edition. Tairli maintains a remarkable equanimity about it all and reveals that, from time to time, the newspaper gets telephone calls of approval from secret admirers within the official establishment.

Between 1992 and 1997, censorship in Azerbaijan has waxed and waned, depending on the administration in power. In the first months of Abulfaz Elchibey's Popular Front government in 1992, censorship was all but abandoned, only to be revived as a result of the 1992-94 war between Armenia and Azerbaijan over Nagorno-Karabakh, an Armenian-populated enclave within Azerbaijan's borders. On coming to power in 1993, President Heydar Aliyev continued the military censorship of his predecessor and added two other layers of constraint: political censorship and military censorship by the Baku commandant.

During the parliamentary elections of November 1995, Aliyev eased censorship and allowed the media to report instances of election fraud. The Baku commandant no longer reviews materials for publication, but there have been recent complaints that military censorship persists despite its formal abolition last year. These days, censors focus mostly on guarding Aliyev and family members from embarrassment.

One of the difficulties of living with censorship has been the absence of an official "taboo list." Censors get oral instructions from the chief censor and his colleagues. They also keep a log book of what they have cut and pass notes among themselves.

While censorship is occasionally acknowledged, officials mention it as little as possible. The official calling card of chief censor Jahangir Ildrimzade gives only his name, not his job.

Subjects routinely excised include human rights in Azerbaijan; criticism of government policy; criticism of the defense, security, police, and other law-enforcement agencies; and accounts of opposition leaders. According to the New Generation Group of the Union of Journalists, known by its Azeri name, Yeni Nesil, which keeps a tally of incidents, censorship of opposition and independent newspapers continued throughout 1997. (See p. 307 for list of Azerbaijani cases).

The primary statute regulating the Azerbaijani press since independence in 1991 is the Law on Mass Media, derived from the Soviet Union's press law, and adopted by Azerbaijan on July 21, 1992. While the law explicitly prohibits prior censorship, when Azerbaijan went to war with Armenia over Nagorno-Karabakh, the government declared a state of emergency and reimposed censorship in violation of the constitution. Parliament subsequently modified the law in December 1993, to allow military censorship.

The law's formal ban on censorship is further eroded by so-called "take-away" clauses, adopted directly from Soviet law, that prohibit the publicizing of state secrets; classified materials; calls for the forcible overthrow of the government; war propaganda; violence and cruelty; hatred and intolerance of ethnic, social, or class groups; pornography; invasions of personal privacy; and assaults on the honor and dignity of citizens. These vaguely defined subjects are open to interpretation.

The law contains several other restrictions, such as the requirement to register with the authorities, and not to disclose developments in criminal investigations without written permission from the prosecutor. The law provides for the closure of mass media in some cases and even contains a list of dos and don'ts for journalists, in a section titled "Rights and Obligations of the Journalist."

The criminal code, virtually unchanged from Soviet times, limits criticism of government officials, punishes "false and dishonoring" comments; and specifically prohibits "critical comments on the activity" of the president of the republic.

The new Azerbaijani constitution, drafted under President Aliyev, was adopted by referendum on November 12, 1995, four years after independence, and imposed upon Soviet-era legislation, which has yet to be revised. This 154-article constitution contains all the standard freedoms of a fundamental law on democracy, including popular elections of president and parliament, separation of powers, rights of the individual, an independent judiciary, and judicial review by a constitutional court. There are articles banning state censorship and guaranteeing freedom of expression, speech, religion, and assembly. Citizens may petition the state for the redress of grievances.

But along with these freedoms come potentially restrictive clauses. The constitution pays particular attention in Article 46 to protecting the honor and dignity of citizens—a traditional issue in the Caucasus. Article 106 protects the honor and dignity of the president; Article 75 guarantees respect for state symbols. Together, these articles effectively ban criticism of the chief executive.

On January 25, 1997, Azerbaijan enacted a comprehensive law on official secrets, which holds journalists, as well as officials, responsible for leaks of classified materials. Critics assailed the bill for ushering in such a wide range of forbidden topics that journalists would be unable to write anything. The statute, inspired by the Russian law on official secrets, groups sensitive subjects under four headings: military, economic, foreign policy, and intelligence. Nevertheless, it officially places some issues that were secret during Soviet times—such as the health of high officials, accidents, and the state of the environment—within the public domain.

The Azerbaijani parliament is slated to consider further legislation affecting the press. Draft bills on freedom of information and on financial support of the press have been forwarded to the parliament by Yeni Nesil. Parliamentary sources report that the legislature is drafting its own versions of these bills.

No law currently regulates television or radio, although the spirit of the Law on Mass Media prevails in broadcasting. Television journalists are drafting a model law which would deal specifically with broadcasting, allocation of frequencies, and the status of independent stations.

The government maintains strong control over Azerbaijani State Television and Radio, the only medium that reach the entire nation, and that are the only source of information in some rural areas. Control is exercised through the loyalty of key personnel, verified by a censor's office located at television headquarters, and monitored by the presidential office.

State television broadcasts on two channels, Az/TV-1, and Az/TV-2. Channel 1 devotes large segments of its newscasts to coverage of President Aliyev, including repeated clips of his pilgrimage to Mecca and his kissing of the Azeri flag. Az/TV-2 concentrates more on entertainment.

Strict control on both channels induces self-censorship among editorial employees. "After you've been censored three times," says one TV journalist, "you either think, 'I must do this or that to make the piece acceptable or it won't go, and I won't get my honorarium.' If you are not able to accept that, you leave."

Paradoxically, however, the government allows one private television broadcaster, Azerbaijan News Service (ANS), to operate and broadcast news almost without censorship; it is something of a showpiece with which to court the West. ANS is not considered a threat because it reaches less than 13 percent of the population, mostly located in the Baku area where the opposition press operates. But the ANS management has plans to extend the reach of its signal and so could become more threatening in the future.

Despite controls on television, Baku residents do not feel isolated from the outside world. The government does not jam foreign television broadcasts. Two Russian channels—ORT and RTR—are widely available, as are two Turkish channels—TRT and one private Turkish channel. In May, NTV, a leading Russian private television company, began broadcasting in Azeri, reaching viewers in Baku, Sumgait, and Absheron Peninsula. Just two weeks after NTV went on the air in Azerbaijan, however, some of its programs were censored—instead of the scheduled programs, still shots occasionally appear. Evening movie broadcasts have been stopped altogether. These measures resulted from a decision by "the relevant body responsible for ideology," as Vahif Musayev, an official of the Communications Ministry, explained, "because NTV's programs are harmful to public morals."

For the vast majority of Azerbaijan's population, however, the main source of news and information remains the two state channels. President Aliyev's office makes sure that these channels project constant and upbeat views of his activities. Az/TV-1 lavishes air time on press conferences, airport arrivals and departure statements, and visiting foreign VIPs. (The newspapers *Bakinskii Rabochii* and *Khalq Gazeti* do the same in print). One joke currently circulating in Baku portrays the televised Aliyev personality cult this way:

A frustrated viewer calls the television repair man to his apartment. The repairman examines the television set which is producing a distorted image on the screen. He offers this explanation: "I can fix Channel 1 pretty easily, but I'll have to go back to the shop to get some parts for Channel 2. Will that be all right?" The owner, anxious to restore reception, agrees. The repairman writes down on a piece of paper what parts he needs to fix Channel 2. As for Channel 1, he takes a portrait of President Aliyev out of his pocket and tapes it over the screen.

State television has apparently succeeded in convincing the population that Aliyev is the man of the hour. Ask people on the street what they think of the president and they will tell you: He is a strong leader, which is what we need at this moment. He knows the world. After all, he rose to the top of the political establishment of the Soviet Union and became a Politburo member. He, if anyone, can solve our greatest problem, returning the lost land of Nagorno-Karabakh to Azerbaijan and sending the one million refugees back to their homes. (Azeri intellectuals have more critical views, but carry less weight in the Azerbaijani political world.)

The chief television censor's office is in Room 46 on the second floor of the State Television and Radio building. All broadcast material must receive the censor's approbation as well as the approval of editors. Because of the length of the approval process, state television is often behind the curve with important breaking news. When a major event occurs, like the explosion in the Baku metro in the fall of 1995, state television was days behind the ANS reports.

One former state television employee questions whether the censor is really necessary. "On Azeri television you can't have free opinions," he says. "Government television workers are like birds who have grown up in a cage. They don't know what freedom is. If they step out of line, they soon find themselves out of work."

The management considers it inappropriate to allow political opponents access to state television, other than at times stipulated by election laws. Furthermore, the president's control of the airwaves gives him carte blanche to smear his opponents.

At present, the authorities have not addressed the issue of freedom of information on the Internet. Some observers believe that the Azerbaijani government has not developed sufficient computer literacy to appreciate the possibilities of the Internet, or to know how to block pornographic or dissident materials. Free access to the Internet is limited and available only at the Academy of Sciences and a few other academic institutions. Private subscribers can gain access by subscribing for a fee through two companies, Intrans and Compuserve.

D espite censorship, Azerbaijani print journalism shows signs of vitality. Until 1995, the country had only one daily newspaper, *Azerbaijan*, but today it has more than a dozen dailies. These newspapers, and other sheets which appear one or more times a week, supply a wide variety of domestic news and political views—diversity of information unheard of in Soviet times.

Newspapers are inherently vulnerable in the economic conditions prevailing in Azerbaijan. They depend on additional revenues from sponsors such as political parties, wealthy individuals, or Western nongovernmental organizations such as the Westminster Fund (United Kingdom), The Soros Foundation (United States), or The Nauman Fund (Germany). The government occasionally plays on this vulnerability. *Azadliq* says it is losing advertising revenue because government officials have warned some clients to remove their ads. Facing severe financial constraints, corruption in the form of payments for puff pieces or withholding information sometimes occurs.

The government holds another card: control of premises. The Turan news agency and *Azadliq* are both housed in a building on Hagani Street in central Baku belonging to the city. Neither pays rent, but neither feels secure about the long-term future.

The government also monopolizes printing. All dailies are published by the Azerbaijan Publishing House, accountable to the president's office. This presidential link is occasionally exercised. In August 1996 the printing house refused to print the newspaper *Avrasiya* for several weeks because of critical articles it had published; and in February 1997, it declined, without explanation, to publish the opposition newspaper *Jumkhurriyet*.

The Azerbaijan Publishing House can also inflate the price of newsprint. During the mid-1990s, when there was a newsprint shortage, the publishing house charged $1,500 a ton. *Zerkalo* editor Rauf R. Talishinsky says he now pays $750 a ton by importing newsprint from Russia.

Newspapers in Baku and Azerbaijan are distributed principally through the state distribution service, Metbuat Yaiymy. Their charge for this service is extravagant: 48 percent of sales. Recently, this service imposed a new financial burden on newspapers by requiring them to pay in advance and delaying the forwarding of receipts to editorial offices.

As Azerbaijan finds its way in the post-Soviet era, powerful officials accustomed to an obedient press have taken matters into their own hands when censorship has failed them. In May 1997, police stopped *Azadliq* correspondent Elchin Seljuk while he was on assignment in Nakhchivan to report on the political intentions of former president Elchibey. They accused him of disorderly conduct and held him overnight. A local court rejected a prosecutor's demands for a guilty verdict and 15 days' imprisonment, but fined Seljuk 22,000 manats (about $5.50). *Azadliq* editor Gunduz Tairli said the police action did not surprise him. "The authorities are not anxious for us to report on Elchibey's plans," he said.

On June 6, 1997, a security guard slapped *Ayna-Zerkalo* correspondent Kamal Ali in the face while Ali was conducting an interview in parliament. The guard claimed that the interview had gone on too long. When Ali and fellow correspondents refused to leave, the guard began striking the others. In the aftermath of the incident, the parliament's security chief acknowledged the misbehavior and both he and the guard apologized for the attack.

Azerbaijani press critics say there have been fewer physical attacks on journalists in the last two years, prompting some to assert that media conditions in Azerbaijan are improving. Others disagree. "Not so," says one journalist for *Ayna-Zerkalo*. "What's really happening is that we have learned what irritates the authorities and we are censoring ourselves."

Despite difficulties, the Baku journalism community is productive and feisty. One indicator is the determination of Yeni Nesil to keep a detailed list of censorship abuses. It has been difficult to compile, however, because some editors prefer to avoid attention. Government officials do not relish publicity for the dark side of state control. Nevertheless, Yeni Nesil publishes these incidents in Azeri, Russian, and English in its monthly bulletin, "Principles and

Reality," which circulates in Baku and among human rights and press freedom organizations in the West.

Another initiative by Yeni Nesil was to organize top editors to protest the new licensing regulations adopted at the end of 1996. This protest was also published in "Principles and Reality" but produced no results. Another journalistic protest, however, proved more successful. In June 1996, the Special Department of the president's office asked all newspapers to supply lists of their reporters with home addresses and home phones. The editors of *Zerkalo*, *Azadliq*, and *7 Gün* pointedly refused. In view of public indignation over the issue, the request was dropped.

Editors are coming up with new initiatives. *Günay* and the Assa-Irada news agency decided independently to publish two English-language weeklies, *Günay* and *Azernews*, for the growing international community. *Azaliq* recently inaugurated a weekly Russian edition to make its news available to the long-time Russian community of Baku.

One of the more imaginative developments is *Monitor*, a glossy monthly magazine, which avoids Azerbaijani censors by being published in Turkey. The magazine recently ran such pieces as "Do We Need Censorship?" "Freedom of Speech in Azerbaijan," and "The Great Sexual Revolution"—topics inconceivable during Soviet times. Officials could stop *Monitor* at customs, but so far this has not happened.

"There are two views of the Azeri press today," says Arif Aliyev, president of the Yeni Nesil. "The view from the trenches is that there are too many restrictions. But the longer view is that there has been a big change and there is hope it will develop some more."

Soviet-Era Legacy Constricts Armenia's Media

Seeking to build a democratic society in which media play a major role, Armenia, unlike Azerbaijan, has given free rein to the press. Journalists concede that the new era has, on occasion, bordered on license. "Some of our journalists attack the president like hooligans," says one editor. The bitter truth is that editors and reporters have discovered that a high level of liberty combined with inexperienced, opinionated, young reporters who are careless about verifying facts has led to errors, denials, corrections, and general loss of credibility in the media.

An unhealthy confrontation between press and government has arisen in recent years in which officials have on more than one occasion taken revenge.

Armenian journalists are caught in a vicious circle: They bear the wrath of government officials who say reporters are neither fair nor balanced; at the same time, they often find it impossible to present the full picture because officials withhold information. Because of war and blockade, Armenia has been relatively isolated from the outside world. Journalists clearly need more contact with Western practice which seeks to present all sides of a story. Officials need to learn that in a democracy, honesty rather than evasion or cover-up is the best policy. Unfortunately, Western journalists have largely by-passed the Caucasus, preferring to offer their advice on how independent journalists operate to the new democracies of Eastern Europe.

Government pressure on journalists has produced contradictory reactions in the journalistic community. Some journalists assert that the attacks only feed their contrariness. Others admit to reacting with caution and self-censorship.

Intimidation persists, in the view of reporters. On June 18, 1997, the Ministry of National Security summoned three journalists from the independent Noyan Tapan News Agency for questioning about the sources of an article on the OSCE effort to mediate a settlement on Nagorno-Karabakh. Interrogators suggested the journalists, whose agency exchanges information with the Azerbaijan News Service in Baku, were harming national interests.

Presidential Press Secretary Levon Zourabian put a softer spin on the incident. In a letter to CPJ, Zourabian asserted that the security service was only doing its duty in trying to plug a leak, since the Armenian government had agreed to strict confidentiality about the mediation effort. The journalists, on the other hand, felt intimidated. Zourabian asserted in his letter that the journalists were not being criminally charged and could have walked out of the meeting at any time.

In the absence of censorship, Armenian officials resort to verbal pressure and sometimes physical retribution to knock journalists into line.

Ruben A. Satyan, editor in chief of the Russian-language newspaper *Vremya*, recounts a run-in with officials. In describing a military parade in 1994, he reported that one Armenian general was wearing non-regulation trousers. Because of a shortage of uniforms, the general had sewn red stripes on pants intended for a private.

Satyan was summoned to the military prosecutor's office, and given a dressing down. He was warned to be more careful in the future. "How old are you?" demanded the prosecutor, Satyan recalls. When Satyan answered, "I'm 48," the prosecutor retorted, "It's good you're not 45, otherwise, I'd have you sent to fight in Karabakh."

The view of the press from the presidential office is equally harsh. An advisor to President Levon Ter-Petrossian* recalls the case of an elderly survivor of the 1915 genocide who asked him to inquire into the fate of his grandson whose release from prison on good behavior was being held up. A prison official was demanding a US$300 bribe. The advisor says he referred the matter to a presidential commission which oversees prison sentences. The commission identified the extortionist and fired him; the young man was released. But the presidential advisor says that journalists, reporting the incident in the press, accused him of abuse of power without seeking his side of the story.

"They never even bothered to call me to find out the facts. They were afraid that they would be proved wrong," the advisor recalls. And he continued, "The press is absolutely free here. Things are written which can't be written in Europe—I mean the degree of hatred and disrespect I see. I seldom feel that what is written in our press is opening a new thought or adding a dimension to my thinking. I'm not satisfied."

Armenia declared its intention to become independent in 1991, before the collapse of the Soviet Union. Yet its new constitution, proclaiming Armenia to be a democratic, sovereign state based on the rule of law, was adopted only on July 5, 1995, by referendum. A laborious process is now underway to redraft Soviet-era legislation to conform with the new order.

* NOTE: In the first week of February 1998, as this book went to press, Ter-Petrossian resigned under pressure from political leaders who had become increasingly disenchanted with what they perceived as the president's surrender of Nagorno-Karabakh to Azerbaijani control.

Journalistic freedoms, meanwhile, are regulated by a Soviet-era media law, adopted on October 8, 1991, which is considered out of date by most political and journalistic leaders except the communists. A new media law was drafted but rejected as inappropriate. Yerevan journalists have submitted a draft law of their own, which has yet to be debated in the National Assembly.

As in Azerbaijan, the operative law on the press and other mass media derives from Soviet law and stresses restrictions at the expense of liberty. Article 2 of the Armenian law, for example, forbids censorship, but qualifies that ban with Article 6: a list of vaguely worded prohibitions against appeals to war or illegal acts, violence, religious hatred; against publication of pornography, against promotion of drug usage, or disclosure of details of discreet adoption of children, or facts about a person's sexual life. Questionable from a Western point of view (which holds that errors are inevitable in journalism) is a clause prohibiting the publication of "false or unverified information." Article 11 permits the closure of media outlets that violate the law, although it allows appeals.

A separate section of the law outlines the rights and responsibilities of the journalist. Troublesome from a democratic point of view is Article 28.2, which requires publication only of "verified and reliable information." Another article obliges journalists to name sources "if required" without specifying the circumstances.

The Yerevan Press Club and other new press associations drafted a model law published in January 1997 and forwarded to parliament. This draft emphasizes media independence from government and forbids prior restraints. It addresses such issues as the need for protection of anonymous sources, the permissible use of hidden cameras and recordings and the possibility, within certain guidelines, of publishing or broadcasting erotic material.

Even the press club draft, however, reflects what could be called a "Soviet mentality." Article 4 of the draft repeats the prohibitions of the Soviet press law and retains a requirement to register a journalistic operation with the authorities. It outlines the rights and responsibilities of journalists and calls on the state to safeguard journalists, a clause intended to counter a rash of beatings of journalists.

Article 29 of the journalists' draft also preserves a procedure for closing down a journalistic operation. For Armenian journalists, creating a process for closure may be a lesser evil: In December 1994, 13 newspapers and presses associated with the Dashnak party were closed without due process when President Ter-Petrossian decreed a temporary ban on the party's activities.

The new Armenian constitution is cautious about media freedom. Article 24 guarantees freedom of expression: "Everyone is entitled to freedom of speech, including the freedom to seek, receive, and disseminate information and ideas through any medium of information, regardless of state borders." But media censorship is not explicitly banned. Furthermore, in a borrowing from the Russian constitution, Articles 44 and 45 allow temporary suspension of media liberties to protect "state and public security, public order, public health and morality, and the rights, freedoms, honor, and reputation of others."

In 1996, a restrictive law on state secrets was adopted. As in Azerbaijan, the terms of this law are derived from the Russian Official Secrets Act.

Currently, Armenia has no law regulating television or radio broadcasting, although one is being developed. The draft of March 18, 1997, has been forwarded to parliament's Standing Committee on Science, Education, Culture, and Youth. In several respects, this bill reflects the spirit of the Law on the press and other mass media: It bans censorship and repeats the restrictions found in the print law. Additionally, it requires broadcast media to give immediate air time to government officials in emergencies. The draft has been criticized for not creating an independent television authority to run state television and radio, and for requiring all programs (including foreign films) to be in Armenian.

Despite its professed support for freedom of expression, the Armenian government betrays a disinclination to allow an open approach to media freedoms. As Vano Siradeghian, Minister of Internal Affairs, has warned, "To give democracy in its full extent, in its Western form, to a society that has never known what democracy is, is to destroy that society. I am convinced that the transition to democracy should be accompanied by a certain demonstration of authoritarianism."

The main source of news and information about Armenia comes to Armenians through nationwide television. As in Azerbaijan, television is the one medium capable of reaching the vast majority of citizens and for that reason the government oversees it carefully. Although there is no official censorship in Armenia, television is regulated by a loyalty system that is censorship in all but name.

Alex Iskandarian, a television journalist with long Soviet experience, is the chief of the Television Analytic Information Agency, which puts together the "Lhraber" program. At the downtown offices of state television, he creates and coordinates each day's program, as he frantically tries to answer telephone calls.

"We work by government order," he says candidly. "We decide by smell what to put on. We don't give the opposition view, but we don't always put on what the ministries want, either." He explains that ministries sometimes give him materials to air, but he has the right to object, and he exercises it. He justifies government control by appealing to the difficulties of the transitional economy. But he says he foresees a freer era "if we have peace."

"For now, we need to have television in the hands of the state to tell people that we are in a tough situation. It's difficult to come from a socialist past and go to real democracy."

Armenia's television operation is overseen by Perch Stepanian, who joined state television in 1967; he was named chief in 1995. This white-haired administrator, like so many other officials, seems to be struggling to adapt to Armenia's new ways. Asked what he considers to be the main goals of contemporary television, he replies, "One of our major goals is to present the government's programs. But we must also give time to the political opposition."

He explains that opposition figures are invited to participate in discussion shows such as "Orenk yev ishkhantyun" (Law and Power), "Dem ar Dem" (Face to Face), or "Hingshabti" (Thursday). They don't always accept, though. "We have lots of live coverage where people can proclaim what they want," he says. But he concedes that the lion's share of air time goes to the government. "That's dictated by our status."

During the 1996 presidential elections, President Ter-Petrossian appeared so often on Channel 1 that many Yerevaners say they tired of his appearances.

Stepanian acknowledges that many television programs do not elicit the kind of interest he would like to see. "Our workers come with Soviet experience," he explains. "It is difficult for them to forget Glavlit [censorship] and self-censorship and to teach them freedom. Mostly the fault is with the journalists, rather than the government."

Presidential Press Secretary Levon Zourabian says Channels 1 and 2 might be privatized by auction, although there is concern about keeping them out of the hands of business interests who might ignore the public trust and use them to promote their own selfish, commercial interests.

Officials are studying control of television in Britain and France even as the National Assembly prepares to debate the draft law on television, possibly this fall. Director Stepanian is not enthusiastic about the bill. He says it does not provide the mechanism needed to put television under mixed government-private control.

Of course, an administrative reorganization would be only a first step toward improving the credibility and popularity of state television. The focus of programming should shift to issues relevant to ordinary citizens and away from the activities of officials. And Armenian television journalists would profit from training and on-the-job experience in Europe or the United States.

The state's Channels 1 and Channel 2 (the second channel is also known as Nork) are only part of the picture of television in Armenia. Eighteen independent stations have cropped up across the country, including A1+, a private company in Yerevan. This station, run by journalistic entrepreneur Mesrop Movsesian, has made a name for itself with its courageous reporting. It aired two-and-a-half hours of coverage of the opposition's raid on parliament following the disputed presidential elections of 1996, reaching an audience of 150,000 (about 15 percent of Yerevan's 1 million population). Another independent station, Ashtarak TV, also sent a reporter to cover the event, which was minimized by State Television and Radio. Afterwards, the Ashtarak station director was beaten up.

Movsesian got the message and has moderated his broadcasts by giving access to government views. He hired Aram Abramyan, a former presidential press secretary, to host a Sunday analysis program.

A1+ is located in eight dingy rooms in an Academy of Sciences building in central Yerevan. On May 31, 1997, the station broadcast a critical piece about the judicial system in Armenia on its 9:45 p.m. newscast. The previous night it had aired a segment on the slow city clean-up after the traditional, all-night celebration of high school graduation.

Internews, the California-based foundation, is encouraging the creation of a network of independent television stations in Armenia.

Another source of independent news is the Internet. So far, access for the public in Yerevan is limited but available at the Institute of Physics, the U.S. Information Service, and IREX, the American exchange agency for scholars. Two Internet providers, Arminco and Infocom, provide service to a few wealthy subscribers. In the city of Gyumri, access is available at the non-governmental organization center.

The government did not try to interfere directly with the Internet during the controversial presidential elections of 1996, but journalists noted that telephone lines were sporadically cut, complicating access.

The newly created Chief Directorate for Information and Book Publishing has replaced the Ministry of Press and Information, which was disbanded under Prime Minister Armen Sarkissian. The agency will bear watching to see if it promotes access to the Internet for all citizens, or seeks to limit its informational possibilities when they include critical views of the government.

The print media are free in Armenia, but they are financially dependent and vulnerable to outside pressures. Because of the poor state of the economy, there is an inadequate advertising base. Newspapers cannot sustain themselves by sales and revenues from classified and general advertising.

Today in Yerevan, a plethora of government, independent, and opposition newspapers vie for readers. This competition promotes sensationalism and discourages badly needed cooperative ventures in the journalistic community.

The economics of newspapering in Armenia today are forbidding. Newspapers sell for 30 drams (7 cents) for government broadsheets and up to 100 drams (22 cents) for independent or opposition newspapers. For a wage-earner who is bringing in the equivalent of US$40 a month, these prices are high. That means few Armenians can read all of the capital's newspapers, and most will read only one or two on an irregular basis. Thus, the new pluralism of views is lost on the individual.

Editors face daunting challenges—they say 34 percent of income goes to pay a variety of taxes, and another 25 percent is spent on the state distribution agency, Haimamul. Yerevan newspapers are obliged by law to rely on the agency. Outside of Yerevan, regional newspapers suffer similar financial difficulties, which force them to publish irregularly and in very small editions. There is some talk among officials about privatizing this agency.

Another source of contention is Periodika, the state publishing house, which publishes all major Yerevan dailies. On occasion, Periodika has refused to publish opposition newspapers for reasons which are often unclear but appear to be political. While Periodika is not the only press available, it has established a firm hold on the market by offering attractive prices. Nevertheless, editors complain that Periodika overcharges for newsprint and believe that competition could force a reduction in rates.

Currently, the U.S. Embassy and government officials are discussing the possibility of financing an alternative publishing house for daily newspapers.

President Ter-Petrossian professes admiration for a free press, but his administration has set a negative tone in relations with the media—rarely, if ever, allowing interviews with the president. His aides give three explanations: First, the president is not a populist and does not seek to curry favor by frequent appearances. Second, frequent appearances would only debase the currency of his pronouncements. Third, the president feels the new Armenian media are immature and unprofessional.

Since coming to office in 1991, Ter-Petrossian has held only two official news conferences for the Armenian press, although he has made himself available for "protocol" press conferences when receiving foreign dignitaries. During the spring visit of Kyrgyzstan's president Askar Akayev, Ter-Petrossian took questions from journalists for about 40 minutes. The president seems to prefer to speak with experienced foreign correspondents. Consequently, some important disclosures relating to Armenian policy have come from abroad, clearly offending home-grown media.

Ministerial officials, taking their cue from the president, have felt free to adopt restrictive policies on access. The president's office, parliament, the Foreign Ministry, and other government agencies require journalists to be accredited according to the procedures set out in the Law on Mass Media. Usually, an editor's letter of recommendation is required for accreditation, but some journalists say they have been denied accreditation for no clear reason other than a suspicion that they are "unfriendly" or "incompetent." In addition to accreditation from the relevant ministry, journalists need to be accredited by the Foreign Ministry and an identification card from the media outlet with which they are affiliated.

The Armenian law is vague on the removal of accreditation. The law does not include criteria for barring a reporter from a government agency. But it does provide for the removal of foreign correspondents' accreditation if they violate the laws or constitution of Armenia.

Government ministries have established press offices, but journalists report that their aim is more to protect the agency and the minister than to facilitate the flow of information. Furthermore, there is a tendency on the part of government press officials to supply news first to the official news agency, Armenpress, or to government media and friendly journalists. A number of Yerevan journalists said they were surprised to see that visiting German foreign minister Klaus Kinkel included on his plane a handful of journalists critical of German policy. That kind of access for the opposition press is inconceivable in Armenia.

Even an open body such as the National Assembly is reluctant to share information with independent journalists. "I try to explain to them that it only advances their interests to share with me the bills that they are working on. But they don't seem to understand. They seem to fear what we journalists are going to seize on," says reporter Naine Mkrtchian of the newspaper *Azg*.

Press access to Ministry of Defense events are highly controlled and usually require the personal permission of the defense minister. During a visit by Alexander Lebed, the former Russian general and politician, ministry press officials ordered the media not to film Defense Minister Vazgen Sarkissian alongside Lebed. Officials said the political ramifications of showing them together were too complicated.

The collapse of Soviet-style journalism has brought a new type of writer to the fore—youthful, enthusiastic, but often without training or experience. Some experienced editors say the new journalists fail to differentiate news from views; are insufficiently concerned about accuracy; lack historical and political knowledge; and are unskilled in interviewing and developing sources. As a result, young journalists are sometimes inept at digging out facts, and can be thrown off the scent by clever officials.

Senior members of the Yerevan Press Club tend to confirm this assessment. "We don't yet have a critical mass of good journalists," says one officer. "There are only about a handful who really can go after information and dig it out, and those are usually working for foreign news agencies."

Naine Mkrtchian, a youthful reporter for *Azg*, rankles under such charges. She asserts that government officials are largely to blame for placing obstacles in the way of all but friendly reporters. President of the newly formed National Press Club, this young woman feels the Soviet heritage of press controls still weighs too heavily in Yerevan. She opposes the draft press law, developed by the Yerevan Press Club, which she considers insufficiently democratic. "A press law in itself means regulation; the fewer rules, the better," she says.

One experienced journalist sums up the mood in Armenian journalism today: "You work without the feeling of hope that your work is going to be useful to someone. Yes, there is pluralism of views, but that pluralism is pushed into a small box. There is pluralism but not that much objectivity. The government tolerates this, but we get the impression that this is a gesture to the West."

Efforts are being made to train the new generation of journalists and to develop a general code of ethics. Both the Yerevan Press Club (60 members) and the Union of Journalists (1,500 members) have held training seminars for journalists, supported by several Western foundations. The independent television station A1+

received a grant for short-term instruction of television journalists which was deemed to be successful. Several new private colleges are reported to have opened journalism departments.

The Yerevan Press Club has developed a 12-point declaration of support for independent media. But this document is concerned principally with the management of media rather than the ethical conduct of journalists. The newly formed, 20-member National Press Club reports that it has created a committee to develop a code of ethics.

e/oe/oe/oe/oe/oe/o

CPJ recommends that:

- The governments of Armenia and Azerbaijan respect freedom of the press and provide guarantees so that journalists may work freely and safely, without fear of reprisal. The notion that free media are in any way a destabilizing factor or harmful to national or public interests contradicts all universally recognized principles of democracy;
- The governments of Armenia and Azerbaijan must ensure that all cases of violence and crimes against journalists and media organizations be thoroughly investigated and that the perpetrators are brought to justice. The lack of due justice on behalf of victimized journalists fosters a climate of fear and intimidation that inhibits freedom of expression;
- Despite constitutional guarantees against censorship, the criminal codes in both countries limit criticism of government officials through various statutes penalizing "false and dishonoring" comments, insults, and criticism of the president. CPJ opposes the use of criminal statutes to address libel suits and condemns the misuse of libel statutes by public officials to suppress journalistic investigation.
- The government of Azerbaijan should immediately and unconditionally lift all political and military censorship of the media. Despite a 1996 presidential decree removing military censorship, journalists and media-watch groups report that the practice persists along with political censorship in violation of all international norms of press freedom and free speech.

- As a matter of foreign policy, CPJ calls on the U.S. government to stress the importance of free media in its dealings with both Armenia and Azerbaijan. It is the view of independent journalists in the region that greater support for professional training could contribute greatly to the development of an independent press community. CPJ encourages the U.S. government to establish regular opportunities for journalists in Armenia and Azerbaijan to travel to the United States and participate in media conferences and training programs. We note the effectiveness of the United States Information Agency exchange program for journalists from Bosnia-Herzegovina in particular, where Bosnian Muslims, Serbs, and Croats jointly participated in meetings in the United States. Similar efforts must be made to engage Armenian and Azerbaijani journalists in such joint programs, whereby the U.S. host organizations would provide a neutral ground for discussion and debate on relevant issues in the Caucasus.

THE MIDDLE EAST AND NORTH AFRICA

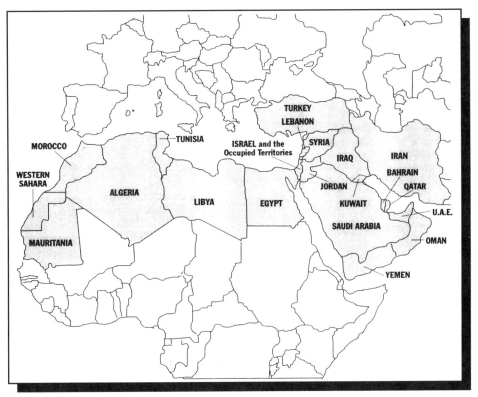

OVERVIEW OF
The Middle East and North Africa
by Joel Campagna

Across the region, from Mauritania to Iran, governments sought to control or silence independent and dissenting voices in the media. Political violence provided the backdrop for government restrictions on the press in Algeria and Turkey, where authorities continued efforts to quash independent reporting of two of the region's bloodiest conflicts. In Algeria, the press routinely reported on the horrific massacres of innocent civilians, but fear of reprisal and the sheer difficulty of gathering information kept journalists from identifying the perpetrators. Indeed, the government's grip on "security"-related information and its restrictions on the local and foreign press have kept most news about the Algerian conflict out of the public's reach and have shaken confidence in the state. "Censorship and the manipulation of the press creates a climate of suspicion," wrote Algerian political scientist Lahouari Addi in late 1997. "People have lost confidence in the forces of law and order; they openly accuse the government of complicity with those who slit the throats of small children. Only freedom of information will restore the credibility of the police and army and prevent further massacres of innocents."

Calls for greater freedom of information could also be heard in Turkey among critics of the 13-year military conflict with Kurdish insurgents in the southeast. Like their Algerian counterparts, Turkish journalists faced ongoing state efforts to silence independent coverage of the costly conflict. The threat of prosecution under Turkey's press laws as well as restrictions on the freedom of movement of journalists in the southeast and in northern Iraq continued to deny the public alternative news and opinion about the state's counter-insurgency campaign.

In Saudi Arabia, Libya, Tunisia, Iraq, and Syria, the state is in total command of the broadcast media and press, allowing no outlets for dissenting voices, while the Palestinian press, in its fourth year under Palestinian Authority

Joel Campagna *is program coordinator for the Middle East and North Africa.*
Marie Daloz, *an intern at CPJ, researched the Morocco country summary. Special thanks to Saleh Hassan and Muhammad Najuib, who contributed valuable research to this chapter.*
This chapter is dedicated to the memory of Hisham Mubarak (1963-1998).
The John S. and James L. Knight Foundation supported CPJ's work in the Middle East and North Africa in 1997 with a challenge grant that funded CPJ mission activity in Turkey.

rule, has become steadily more submissive to the heavy-handed practices of authorities. In countries where privately owned and independent media push the limits of government-sanctioned views, they faced direct pressure from the state, in the form of legislation and executive decrees. In May, Jordan's King Hussein put his stamp of approval on a draconian press law that virtually eliminated the country's burgeoning and often-raucous weekly newspapers, increasingly known for their independent reporting on government policies and other sensitive political issues. In Lebanon, the government of Prime Minister Rafiq al-Hariri instituted prior censorship of news and political programs broadcast abroad by satellite, while the media remain subject to broadcast and press laws that restrict news content. Press laws in Iran, Egypt, Lebanon, and Yemen enable authorities to prosecute journalists for reporting on alleged government corruption and other controversial domestic issues.

International and Arabic satellite networks have become an increasingly popular alternative for news and information for residents of Tehran, Damascus, and Algiers, providing a means to circumvent government-imposed restrictions on the flow of information. Internet use has begun to spread gradually in many countries throughout the region despite government efforts to limit its use. Although the Internet remains largely beyond the reach of most people because of factors such as cost and literacy, independent daily and weekly newspapers in Egypt, Jordan, Lebanon, and Yemen have gone online. The Internet has also allowed people throughout the region to read daily European and U.S. newspapers, offering them a window to see the world beyond their borders. In several countries, however, Internet access is banned, unavailable, or closely monitored by the state. Efforts now underway by member states of the Gulf Cooperation Council to restrict Internet access to politically "subversive" information—similar to tactics adopted recently in Singapore—signal a troubling trend.

Still, journalists, concerned citizens, and political opposition groups continue to challenge government attempts to muzzle free expression. In Jordan, when opposition parties boycotted the country's parliamentary elections in November, their complaints included the restrictive new press law. In December, Lebanese university students and professionals took to the streets to protest the government's censorship of political programming on television. And throughout the region, freedom of expression remained high on the agenda of the blossoming human rights movement.

CPJ and other international organizations have sought greater collaboration with local nongovernmental organizations to pressure the region's governments for change. In July, CPJ led a group of international press freedom organiza-

MIDDLE EAST

tions and local journalists groups in three days of talks with the new Turkish government of Prime Minister Mesut Yilmaz to urge the government to release the country's imprisoned journalists and end state harassment of the press. Yilmaz pledged that his government would make press freedom a priority and would initiate reform of the country's harsh laws that govern the press. In perhaps the year's most positive development, following the mission, the parliament passed a limited amnesty bill that resulted in the release of seven jailed editors, including Ocak Isik Yurtçu, a 1996 winner of CPJ's International Press Freedom Award. (For more on CPJ's mission to Turkey, see the special report on p. 82.)

Algeria

Violence against journalists has taken a back seat to the military-backed regime's monopolization of news coverage of Algeria's brutal, six-year-long civil conflict. Strict government censorship, long-term suspension of newspapers, and the fear of state prosecution for coverage of "security" matters contribute to making the political violence in Algeria one of the most underreported conflicts in recent history.

The bloody, three-year assassination campaign against journalists, which has claimed the lives of 59 members of the media since May 1993, appears to be in recess; no murders of journalists were reported this year. Although the reasons for the hiatus remain unclear, some journalists attribute it to disarray among militant Islamist groups, who are presumed responsible for most of the deaths between May 1993 and August 1996. Whatever the explanation, the lull in assassinations has failed to comfort journalists. Many still live in constant fear for their lives and continue to take precautions in their daily activities. "We still sign our articles with pseudonyms and do not publish our own photographs in the newspapers," said one independent reporter. "There are no guarantees that the assassinations will not resume in the future." Because of such fears, many journalists remain holed up in hotels or isolated compounds in Algiers, such as the one at Al-Manar Sidi Faraj, attempting to carry out their work under siege-like conditions.

But it is the state's iron grip over the flow of information on the civil conflict that has proven the year's dominant theme. Independent news reporting on acts of political violence or government counter-insurgency operations remains virtually impossible because of severe government restrictions. A March 1994 interministerial decree, circulated to the national media, forbids newspapers from publishing any news on "security" matters except for that provided by the official Algerian Press Service (APS). Since 1993, CPJ has documented 24 cases of newspapers suspended for reporting on security-related topics—a broad category which authorities interpret to encompass guerrilla attacks on security forces, government human rights abuses, and the reporting of Islamist viewpoints. CPJ has also documented at least 19 prosecutions of journalists under the information code or related statutes for reporting on proscribed topics. Most newspapers have adopted a strict regime of self-censorship on security-related issues thus allowing the state in December to abolish "reading committees" it had established in February 1996 to ensure that stories about civil strife conform to official accounts.

The state also employs less direct means of reining in the press: It controls the supply of newsprint, the distribution of newspapers, and owns the printing presses. The government also uses its control over the distribution of advertising to reward newspapers whose editorial line on the conflict most closely resembles the state's.

Authorities this year launched a new weapon against the independent press—the closure of newspapers that have outstanding debts—to silence publications which criticized or contradicted the government's position on the conflict and other domestic issues. Between January and April, state actions forced the closure of four leading independent newspapers—*La Nation*, *Al-Hourria*, *Eshourouk al-Arabi*, and *Al-Ouma*. On April 11, two of them—the French language daily *El-Ouma* and the Arabic weekly *Eshourouk al-Arabi*—ceased publication following the government closure of Sodipresse, the newspapers' printing press. Sodipresse, Algeria's first privately owned printing press, which began operation in March, had been launched by a group of Algerian investors in response to the state's printing monopoly and its use of economic pressure against independent newspapers.

Several other newspapers have remained closed since civil strife erupted in 1992, including the Arabic-language weeklies *Al-Wajb al-Akhar*, *Essah-Afa*, and *Ennour*, and the daily *Al-Djazair al-Youm*. Each of these newspapers was known for its critical stance on the military's intervention in the electoral process and on government human rights abuses throughout the conflict. Although Algerian law stipulates that news publications may not be suspended for more than six months, the state printing house refuses to resume printing these newspapers.

Foreign correspondents who report on forbidden subjects are also vulnerable to state reprisal. In September, authorities refused to renew the accreditation of an Agence France-Presse correspondent in Algiers, in apparent retaliation for his reporting figures which contradicted the official death toll in massacres that took place in the Algerian countryside. Citing security concerns, the government has prohibited foreign journalists from traveling around the country without escorts, which severely inhibits investigative reporting. Although authorities describe these escorts as optional, they ignore journalists' requests to go it alone. In one instance, security agents detained *Newsweek* reporter Mark Dennis overnight after he ditched his escort to interview Islamic Salvation Army military commander Ahmed Benaicha in the field. Dennis was subsequently expelled from the country.

There was no new information in 1997 about the case of Djamel Fahassi, a reporter with the government-run French-language radio station Alger Chaine III and a former contributor to the now-banned *Al-Forqane*—a weekly organ of the Islamic Salvation Front—who was arrested by security forces in 1995. Although witnesses to his abduction say that Fahassi had been apprehended by security forces, authorities continue to deny knowledge of his arrest. In what appears to be a new case of government-inspired "disappearance," gunmen identifying themselves as security agents abducted Aziz Bouabdallah, a journalist for the Arabic daily *Al-Alam al-Siyassi*, from his home in Algiers. Despite government denials of any knowledge of the incident, CPJ received reports in July that Bouabdallah was being held in the Chateneuf detention facility in Algiers, where he was reportedly tortured. On July 25, CPJ sent a letter to President Liamine Zeroual urging that authorities locate Bouabdallah and bring him to safety.

January 1
La Nation CENSORED
Al-Hourria CENSORED

The state-owned printing press, Societé d'Impression d'Alger (SIA), refused service to the independent French-language weekly *La Nation* and its sister publication, the Arabic weekly *Al-Hourria*, due to outstanding debts, in late December 1996. Both papers had been vocal in their calls for a negotiated settlement to Algeria's civil conflict, and were known for their critical coverage of the military-backed regime. In late March, *La Nation* and *Al-Hourria* settled their debt with SIA, but the printing house refused to resume printing the papers. In a joint letter to Algeria's President Liamine Zeroual on May 21, CPJ and the London-based ARTICLE 19 protested the closure of *La Nation* and *Al-Hourria*, expressing concern about the government's apparent use of debt obligations to silence newspapers with a critical editorial line toward the state. Both organizations pointed out that other indebted newspapers have been allowed to continue publishing in Algeria and that no clear legal guidelines exist for authorities to close newspapers because of debt.

January 15
Al-Mouad CENSORED

Authorities seized copies of the weekly *Al-Mouad* from the state-owned printing press in Algiers. Observers believe the confiscation was the result of an article about the venerated Algerian nationalist leader Emir Abdelkader. The article reported that Abdelkader's former residence in exile in Syria had recently been converted into a nightclub. The incident marked the third time in three years that authorities prevented the distribution of *Al-Mouad*.

April 11
El-Ouma CENSORED
Eshourouk al-Arabi CENSORED

Two newspapers—the French-language daily *El-Ouma* and the Arabic-language weekly *Eshourouk al-Arabi*—were forced to cease publication after authorities closed Sodipresse, the newspapers' printing press. Sodipresse, the first privately owned printing press in Algeria, was established in July 1996 by a group of Algerian investors in response to the state's printing monopoly. Algerian authorities cited a bounced check issued to the state printer by Saad Lounes, president of Sodipresse and director of *El-Ouma*, for money *El-Ouma* owed to the printer. On April 28, Lounes was convicted and sentenced to 30 months in jail.

El-Ouma said the state had no legal basis for its action, because Sodipresse was a private enterprise with no formal links to *El-Ouma* and, more important, because Sodipresse had not committed any offense under Algerian law. Spokesmen for the newspaper said the authorities' motivation might have been *El-Ouma's* increasingly critical editorial line against the state. One week before Sodipresse's closure, a column in the April 5 issue of the newspaper

titled "The Party of National Shame" strongly criticized the National Democratic Rally (RND), the newly formed political party supportive of Algerian President Liamine Zeroual. The other newspaper that used Sodipresse, the weekly *Eshourouk al-Arabi*, was also forced to cease publication. Like *El-Ouma*, it had criticized the RND.

April 12
Aziz Bouabdallah, *Al-Alam al Siyassi* MISSING

Bouabdallah, a journalist who writes frequently on political affairs for the Arabic-language daily *Al-Alam al-Siyassi*, was abducted from his home in Algiers by three armed men. The men identified themselves as Algerian security agents and forced Bouabdallah into a waiting car. CPJ later learned that Algerian authorities were holding Bouabdallah in an Algiers detention center. He was said to have been tortured repeatedly.

CPJ wrote to Algerian President Liamine Zeroual on July 25, calling for Bouabdullah's immediate and unconditional release.

November 5
Omar Belhouchet, *El-Watan*
LEGAL ACTION

Belhouchet, editor of the French-language daily *El-Watan*, was sentenced to one year in prison under several provisions of Algeria's penal code, including a statute criminalizing the "harming of state institutions." The case against him stemmed from a November 1995 interview he gave to the French television stations TF1 and Canal Plus, during which he speculated that the state may have been involved in some of the assassinations of journalists that have occurred since May 1993. Belhouchet and his lawyer have appealed the decision.

Shortly after the verdict, police summoned Belhouchet and questioned him for four hours about an opinion column published in *El-Watan* on October 29. The column, by columnist Yasser Ben Miloud, strongly criticized Algerian President

Liamine Zeroual in the aftermath of municipal elections which were stained by charges of fraud. On November 6, Belhouchet was again summoned for questioning at police headquarters, where he was kept for nearly six hours.

In a November 6 letter to President Liamine Zeroual, CPJ condemned the court decision and urged the Algerian leader to end state harassment and prosecution of journalists in retaliation for their work.

Egypt

Despite explicit constitutional guarantees of a free press, Egyptian authorities use a variety of tactics to hinder investigative journalism and muzzle reporting on sensitive domestic issues. Government officials and their family members often bring seditious libel and other lawsuits against newspapers in response to allegations of corruption. In one noteworthy example, Magdy Hussein, editor in chief of the biweekly *Al-Sha'b*—a muckraking journal which has led a crusade against official impropriety—was the target of several suits brought by Interior Minister Hassan al-Alfi and his sons. On September 10, a court suspended the publication of *Al-Sha'b* for three issues because of its coverage of a pending libel suit initiated by the minister against five *Al-Sha'b* journalists. The move reportedly marked the first time in Hosni Mubarak's 16-year presidency that authorities closed an Egyptian newspaper.

The prosecutions of Hussein and *Al-Sha'b* underscore the threat Egyptian law poses for the opposition press. Despite the government's revocation of a draconian press law in 1996, journalists remain vulnerable to prosecution under a host of highly interpretive charges—including "inciting hatred," "violating public

morality," "harming the national economy," and offending a foreign head of state. These charges carry prison sentences of one to two years. Individuals charged with libel offenses face a maximum prison sentence of one year, and in cases where public officials are involved, journalists are subject to up to two years in prison. Fines reach as high as 20,000LE (US$5,900) for each offense.

Officials imposed three media blackouts in September and October: the first banning all local and foreign coverage of the libel suit between al Alfi and *Al-Sha'b*; the second, the military prosecution of individuals implicated in a deadly attack on tourists in Cairo; and the third quashing reports on the investigation of a Cairo prostitution ring allegedly involving noted Egyptian actresses.

Authorities continued a long-standing pattern of harassment and censorship of the English language-weekly *The Middle East Times*. Thomas Cromwell, the paper's editor and publisher, was expelled from the country on August 22, after Egyptian police detained him for three hours upon his arrival at Cairo International Airport and informed him that he could not re-enter the country. The Ministry of Information censored at least nine stories in the paper that dealt with such topics as discrimination against the Coptic Christian minority and the activities of outlawed Islamist groups. In recent years, CPJ has documented numerous instances of government harassment of the newspaper, including censorship of news articles and the outright confiscation of issues in response to what the government has viewed as unfavorable reporting on domestic issues in Egypt.

January 27
Madgy Hussein, *Al-Sha'b* IMPRISONED, LEGAL ACTION

A Cairo criminal court convicted Hussein, editor in chief of the biweekly opposition paper *Al-Sha'b*, of libeling the son of Interior Minister Hassan al-Alfi and sentenced him to three years in prison. The case was filed by Ala'a al-Alfi in response to an article that reported al-Alfi had exploited his father's position to profit from business deals. The day after the conviction, Egyptian police arrested Hussein at his home, attempting to enforce the sentence before he could appeal. Hussein was released later that evening, after the court had received a formal request for an appeal.

July 20
Magdy Hussein, *Al-Sha'b* LEGAL ACTION
Muhammad Hilal, *Al-Sha'b* LEGAL ACTION

A Cairo criminal court convicted Hussein, editor in chief of the biweekly *Al-Sha'b*, and Hilal, a reporter for the newspaper, of libeling the sons of Interior Minister Hassan al-Alfi. Ala'a and Adel al-Alfi accused the journalists of defamation because of an article in *Al-Sha'b* which reported the two men were involved in improper land purchases, in which they had taken advantage of their father's position. On July 20, Hussein was sentenced to two years in prison and fined 2,000LE (US$600), while Hilal was sentenced to one year in prison and fined 1,000LE (US$300). Both men have appealed their convictions.

August 16
Magdy Hussein, *Al-Sha'b* LEGAL ACTION
Salah Badawi, *Al-Sha'b* LEGAL ACTION
Hoda Mekawi, *Al-Sha'b* LEGAL ACTION
Hamdy al-Shamy, *Al-Sha'b* LEGAL ACTION
Essam Sherkawy, *Al-Sha'b* LEGAL ACTION

Hussein, editor in chief of the biweekly *Al-Sha'b*; Badawi, Mekawi, and Al-Shamy, journalists for the newspaper; and cartoonist Sherkawy were implicated in a libel suit brought by Interior Minister Hassan al-Alfi.

The suit stemmed from a series of articles and caricatures in which *Al-Sha'b* implied the interior minister's involvement in massive corruption. In one article, the paper reported that Al-Alfi had profited through business deals with a former government minister jailed on corruption charges. In one of the cartoons, al-Alfi was depicted wielding a wooden club, leading a pack of thieves.

August 22
Thomas Cromwell, *The Middle East Times* EXPELLED

Police detained Cromwell, the editor and publisher of the Cairo-based weekly *The Middle East Times*, for three hours after he arrived at Cairo International Airport. They told him he could not re-enter Egypt. The officers forced him that day to leave on a flight to Jordan.

After the incident, Cromwell wrote to the Information Ministry requesting an official explanation for the authorities' action, but he did not receive a reply.

September 2
All journalists CENSORED

Prosecutor General Raga' al-Arabi announced a ban on all media coverage of a libel suit involving Egyptian Interior Minister Hassan al-Alfi and the newspaper *Al-Sha'b*. The national, partisan, local, and foreign press were not allowed to publish reports of any fruther developments connected with Interior Minister Hassan al-Alfi's libel charges against the editor in chief and some reporters of the opposition newspaper *Al-Sha'b*, Al-Arabi said in a statement.

The interior minister filed a libel suit on August 16 against *Al-Sha'b*'s editor in chief, Magdy Hussein, and four other journalists who allegedly had implied Al-Alfi's involvement in massive corruption schemes.

MIDDLE EAST

The authorities rescinded the ban on September 23.

September 7
Ahmed Musa, *Al-Ahram* LEGAL ACTION
Magdy Hussein, *Al-Sha'b* LEGAL ACTION

The public prosecutor summoned Musa, a journalist with the semi-official daily *Al-Ahram*, and Hussein, editor in chief of the opposition biweekly *Al-Sha'b*, for questioning about their alleged violation of a government ban on news coverage of a pending libel suit filed by Interior Minister Hassan al-Alfi against the *Al-Sha'b* newspaper. The ban was imposed on September 2.

September 8
Magdy Hussein, *Al-Sha'b* HARASSED

Egyptian security authorities prevented Hussein, editor in chief of the opposition biweekly newspaper *Al-Sha'b*, from leaving the country. Hussein was on his way to board a flight to Lebanon when he was turned back at the airport. The authorities gave no explanation for their action.

September 10
Al-Sha'b, LEGAL ACTION, CENSORED

A court banned publication of three issues of the biweekly newspaper *Al-Sha'b* as a result of its coverage of a libel suit against *Al-Sha'b's* editor in chief, Magdy Hussein, and four reporters.

The move followed Prosecutor General Raga' al-Arabi's decision on September 2 to prohibit the news media from covering proceedings of the case, which was initiated by Interior Minister Hassan al-Alfi. That suit had been filed because of articles about the minister's business dealings with an Egyptian government minister jailed on corruption charges. The court's decision to ban *Al-Sha'b* was based on an obscure article in Egypt's penal code that prohibits newspapers from reporting on legal actions in

which they are defendants. The court's decision reportedly marked the first time that an Egyptian newspaper was suspended during the 16-year presidency of Hosni Mubarak.

CPJ protested *Al-Sha'b's* suspension in a September 17 letter to President Mubarak.

September 14
Hisham Hafez, *Al-Sharq al-Awsat*
LEGAL ACTION
Muhammad Ali Hafez, *Al-Sharq al-Awsat*
LEGAL ACTION
Othman Al-Omeir, *Al-Sharq al-Awsat*
LEGAL ACTION
Fawaziyya Salameh, *Al-Jadida* LEGAL
ACTION
Gamal Ismail, *Al-Jadida* LEGAL ACTION
Sayed Abdel Ati, *Al-Jadida and Al-Wafd*
LEGAL ACTION

A criminal court convicted six journalists employed by publications published by H.H. Saudi Research & Marketing (UK) Ltd. of libel in connection with an advertisement which appeared in the newspaper's May 28 issue. The ad announced an upcoming issue of the newspaper's sister publication, *Al-Jadida* magazine, which was to contain an exposé of the allegedly corrupt business dealings of Egyptian President Hosni Mubarak's two sons, Ala'a and Gamal Mubarak. Hisham and Muhammad Ali Hafez, publishers of Al-*Sharq al-Awsat* and *Al-Jadida* magazine; Al-Omeir, editor in chief of *Al-Sharq al-Awsat*; Salameh, managing editor of *Al-Jadida*; and Ismail, a copy editor for *Al-Jadida*, were each sentenced in absentia to one year in prison and fined 20,000LE (about US$6,000). Also convicted was Sayed Abdel Ati, a journalist for both publications who wrote the article. He was sentenced to six months in jail and fined 15,000 LE (about US$4,500). Ati is also a journalist for the Egyptian daily *Al-Wafd*.

The court ruled that Ala'a and Gamal Mubarak's reputations had been harmed as a result of the advertisement, although the *Al-Jadida* article was never printed.

On September 17, CPJ wrote to President Mubarak urging that the court rulings against the journalists be reversed.

On December 2, Ala'a and Gamal Mubarak dropped the lawsuit, which was under appeal. This followed a private meeting between Gamal Mubarak and *Al-Sharq al-Awasat's* publishers the previous day.

September 24
All journalists, CENSORED

Prosecutors ordered a ban on all media coverage of the military investigation of 16 suspects in a September 18 attack against tourists in downtown Cairo. The government banned all Egyptian and foreign media based in or visiting Egypt from covering or publishing any items related to the military court's investigations of the attack.

The ban was the second such action taken by Egyptian authorities in the space of a month. In early September, Egypt's prosecutor general banned media coverage of a libel suit brought by Interior Minister Hassan al-Alfi against the biweekly newspaper *Al-Sha'b*.

Iran

The Iranian press continued to suffer severe restrictions. Criticism of prominent government officials and the ideals of the Islamic revolution remain forbidden topics for journalists, and transgressors face swift reprisal, including prosecution or banishment from their profession. The sweeping provisions of the press law empower the state to fine, censor, or imprison outspoken journalists for publishing "false information" or news that "harms national interests." The Ministry of Culture and Islamic Affairs actively monitors publications to ensure that journalists abide by the law.

Still, the May election of reformist cleric Mohammad Khatemi as president was cause for a modest degree of optimism. After taking office, Khatemi called for an end to censorship of books, newspapers, and other publications. Initial reports indicate the government has in fact eased the practice and has also granted licenses to dozens of new publications while allowing previously banned publications to resume publishing. To what extent Khatemi's liberal ideals can effect change remains to be seen in 1998.

Faraj Sarkoohi, the imprisoned editor in chief of the monthly literary magazine *Adineh*, was freed on January 28, 1998, after serving a one-year sentence imposed in September for "spreading propaganda." The charge stemmed from a letter he smuggled out of Iran, describing his detention and torture in 1996. Sarkoohi's release was the culmination of a 13-month ordeal that began with his "disappearance" at Tehran airport on November 3, 1996, while on his way to Germany. In 1994, Sarkoohi had been one of 134 writers and intellectuals who petitioned the Iranian government for an end to censorship and for official efforts to foster greater free expression.

February 22
Ebrahim Zalzadeh, *Mayar* KILLED

Zalzadeh, former publisher of the now-defunct monthly magazine *Mayar*, disappeared on February 22. His body was identified at a Tehran morgue on March 29. According to the coroner's report, unknown individuals delivered the body to the morgue after finding it alongside a road in Yaft-Abad, near Tehran, on or about February 24. Zalzadeh's body had several stab wounds in the chest.

Mayar had persistently criticized government censorship of the media before authorities closed the magazine in 1995. When Abbas Maaroufi, editor of the monthly magazine *Gardoon*, was sentenced in January 1996 to six months in prison and 35 lashes for his criticism of the

MIDDLE EAST

Iranian government, Zalzadeh was one of several Iranian writers and publishers who volunteered to share Maaroufi's punishment by taking some of the lashes. Maaroufi eventually left Iran, and the government never meted out the punishment.

CPJ wrote to Iranian President Hashemi Rafsanjani on April 7, urging the government to immediately launch an investigation into Zalzadeh's death.

April 1
Muhammad Sadeq Javadi-Hessar, *Tous* LEGAL ACTION

Javadi-Hessar, editor of the weekly magazine *Tous*, was fined 5 million rials (US$1,000) in April and banned from practicing journalism for 10 years after an Iranian court found him guilty of publishing false information. The charge stemmed from an article that appeared in *Tous*, which reported that universities in Iran were more religious than Islamic seminaries. Javadi-Hessar said he believed the conviction was political in nature and came as a result of his magazine's support for liberal presidential candidate Muhammad Khatami. Javadi-Hessar appealed the verdict.

July 19
Mehdi Nasiri, *Sobh* LEGAL ACTION, CENSORED

A Tehran court found Nasiri, managing editor of the monthly magazine *Sobh*, guilty of insulting Communications Minister Muhammad Gharazi. Nasiri was fined 5 million rials (US$1,700) and *Sobh* was suspended from publishing for one month. Gharazi initiated the suit against Nasiri after *Sobh* published an article reporting on corruption within the Ministry of Communications. The court acquitted Nasiri of the charge of publishing false information.

August 16
Iran e Farda ATTACKED

Unknown assailants forcibly entered the Tehran office of the monthly magazine *Iran e Farda*. The assailants beat two employees and vandalized computers and files. The motivation for the attack remains unclear. Officials from the newspaper presented police with the license plate number of the assailants' automobile, however, no arrests have been made.

September 18
Faraj Sarkoohi, *Adineh* IMPRISONED

Sarkoohi, editor in chief of the monthly literary magazine *Adineh*, was sentenced to one year in prison for "spreading propaganda," a charge which stemmed from a letter he smuggled out of Iran in January describing his detention and torture at the hands of Iranian authorities in 1996. Previously, in 1994, Sarkoohi had been one of 134 writers and intellectuals who petitioned the Iranian government to end censorship and launch official efforts to foster greater freedom of expression. Sakoohi was freed on January 28, 1998, after completing his sentence.

November 9
Morteza Firouzi, *Iran News* IMPRISONED

The official Iranian daily *Joumhouri Islami* reported that Firouzi, editor in chief of the English-language daily *Iran News*, was arrested on charges of espionage. Prior to *Joumhouri Islami's* announcement, Firouzi had been rumored "disappeared" since about the time of the presidential election in May. Authorities have provided no further details about his case, but CPJ has received reports that Firouzi's arrest was related to articles published in *Iran News* calling for the release of foreign nationals from Iranian prisons, and for warmer relations with the United States. The charge of espionage is frequently brought against individuals viewed as threats to the regime. The charge has also been used by political factions within the government to attack their opponents' allies.

Iraq

Saddam Hussein continues to hold uncontested power in Iraq, and thus his notoriously ruthless Ba'th regime maintains its stranglehold on the media. News outlets are under the control of the Ministry of Information, whose functionaries compose all "news." The country's daily newspapers offer a steady diet of articles extolling Hussein's virtues and the blessings of his rule. Virtually no news of events outside of the capital, Baghdad, reaches Iraqis, and when the media report on international events, the content is highly restricted. One of Saddam's sons, Uday, unofficially serves as the head of the Ministry of Information and owns the nation's only "private" and most influential newspaper, *Babil*.

Iraqis have virtually no alternative sources of information. The government has banned satellite dishes, and the seven-year-old United Nations embargo keeps foreign publications beyond reach. The government also reportedly jams radio broadcasts from abroad. "Most Iraqi citizens know very little about what is happening inside their country, or for that matter around the world," observed a reporter from National Public Radio.

Foreign journalists who travel to Iraq continue to face constraints on their freedom of movement. Authorities require foreign reporters to travel with government escorts, who restrict their access to certain areas and often compromise their ability to conduct interviews.

Israel and the Occupied Territories

Severe restrictions on movement and violent attacks by the Israeli Defense Forces (IDF) and Jewish settlers continue to hamper Palestinian journalists in Israel and the Occupied Territories. For most West Bank Palestinian journalists, gaining access to Jerusalem remains a tedious endeavor, requiring special permits which are often withheld. Israel's closure of the West Bank in July and again in September following suicide bombings in Jerusalem, exacerbated the situation. Most West Bank journalists chose to circumvent official military checkpoints, entering the city illegally through alternate routes. From Gaza, meanwhile, access to Jerusalem and the West Bank is almost impossible except for the handful of reporters who possess the required paperwork. "There is no way for us to leave Gaza," said one Palestinian reporter. "It's impossible for us to go to Jerusalem."

The long-standing pattern of unpredictable and often-volatile behavior of IDF soldiers and Jewish settlers in the West Bank continue to pose threats for Palestinian reporters. As in previous years, they were subject to assault or the threat of violence from soldiers and settlers while trying to cover stories. In one particularly disturbing incident, four journalists were wounded by rubber bullets fired by IDF soldiers in Hebron on July 13 while covering a group of Palestinian demonstrators burning an Israeli flag. Eyewitnesses were dismayed by the incident, given the considerable distance of at least three of the four journalists from the demonstrators and their conspicuous camera equipment, clearly identifying them as members of the media.

MIDDLE EAST

Israeli military censorship remains in effect for print and broadcast media in Israel and the Occupied Territories, requiring editors to submit news deemed to threaten national security for review. In September, authorities restricted coverage of the Mossad's failed assassination attempt on Hamas political leader Khaled Meshaal in Amman, Jordan—a move that forced editors to attribute much of their reporting to "foreign sources" in order to avoid breaking the law. In September, a Tel Aviv court cited threats to national security when it banned distribution of Israeli author and journalist Michael Eldar's latest book, *Dakar*, which examines the 1968 disappearance of an Israeli submarine in the Mediterranean Sea.

In south Lebanon, where Israel occupies a nine-mile swath of territory, the IDF and its proxy, the South Lebanon Army, continue to operate above the law in handling the local press. On July 3, IDF soldiers detained Roger Nahra, a cameraman for Murr Television (MTV) and correspondent for the Arabic daily newspaper *Al-Liwaa*, after storming his home in the town of Qlaiaa. Nahra was held incommunicado in Khiam Prison until his release on August 6. The motivation for his detention is unclear, but representatives from *Al-Liwaa* believe the move may be tied to an article Nahra wrote on July 2, which strongly criticized Israel's occupation of southern Lebanon.

A March 18 story in the Israeli newspaper *Ha'aretz* raised suspicion that Israel may be holding Iranian journalist Kazem Akhavan, a photographer for Iran's official news agency IRNA who had been believed killed in Lebanon in 1982. The story, written by Israeli journalist Yousef al-Ghazi and based on information provided by the Israeli prison service, reported that three Iranian nationals are currently imprisoned in Israel. Akhavan, who disappeared in Lebanon on July 4, 1982, along with two officials from the Iranian

embassy in Beirut, was believed to have been kidnapped and later executed by Phalangist militiamen at a checkpoint near the northern city of Byblos. CPJ wrote to Israeli Prime Minister Benjamin Netanyahu on April 15, requesting the names of the imprisoned Iranians, but received no response.

January 18
Mazen Dana, Reuters ATTACKED

Dana, a cameraman for Reuters, was assaulted by a Jewish settler at a checkpoint between the town of Harsina and the Jewish settlement of Kiryat Arba in the West Bank. He and a colleague were transferring camera equipment between cars when the settler, Avraham Hassoon, approached the two men and began shouting at them. Hassoon, who objected to the presence of a camera crew in the area, attacked Dana, striking him several times with a rifle butt. Dana sustained injuries to his hand and back.

February 16
Challenge CENSORED
Al-Sabar CENSORED

Israel's Government Press Office (GPO) denied the English-language bimonthly magazine *Challenge* and its sister publication, the biweekly Arabic-language magazine *Al-Sabar*, their request for seven press cards for reporters. Among the reasons cited by the GPO for its decision was that some of the journalists who had applied for the documents had been convicted in 1989 of membership in a hostile organization—the Democratic Front for the Liberation of Palestine—and that they opposed the Israeli-Palestinian peace process outlined in the Oslo accords. The GPO also noted state security concerns for denying the accreditation. *Challenge* reported that the GPO's decision to deny press cards came as the result of a directive from Israel's General Security Services (GSS).

Press cards are essential for Israeli journalists to gain access to areas in the West Bank and

Gaza Strip under the control of the Palestinian Authority. Officials from *Challenge* said that since Palestinian self-rule was instituted in 1994, not one of their journalists has been permitted to enter the Gaza Strip.

On September 25, CPJ wrote to Israeli Prime Minister Benjamin Netanyahu requesting that journalists from both publications be granted government press cards.

July 3
Roger Nahra, Murr Television and *Al-Liwaa*
IMPRISONED

Israeli military forces stormed Nahra's home and detained him, his two brothers, and a cousin. Nahra, a correspondent in south Lebanon for Murr TV and the Arabic daily *Al-Liwaa*, was taken to Khiam Prison in Israeli-occupied south Lebanon where he was held for 34 days. Officials from *Al-Liwaa* said the action might have been prompted by an article Nahra wrote for *Al-Liwaa* published July 2, which strongly criticized Israel's occupation of southern Lebanon.

July 13
Imad al-Said, Associated Press Television
ATTACKED
Mazen Dana, Reuters ATTACKED
Amer Jabari, ABC ATTACKED
Diya Juabi, Abu Dhabi Television
ATTACKED

Israeli Defense Forces soldiers shot rubber bullets at Al-Said, Dana, Jabari, and Juabi—cameramen for APTV, Reuters, ABC, and Abu Dhabi TV, respectively. The journalists were covering a demonstration where Palestinians were burning an Israeli flag. Eyewitnesses said the soldiers intentionally fired on the journalists, most of whom were at a considerable distance from the demonstrators and carried conspicuous camera equipment which clearly identified them as media.

CPJ on July 23 wrote to Israeli Prime Minister Benjamin Netanyahu, urging an

immediate investigation. The next day, the IDF said a special investigation would be conducted.

July 31
Voice of Palestine (VOP) THREATENED
Palestine TV ENED

The Israeli cabinet, in an emergency session following a double suicide bombing in west Jerusalem, passed a resolution to jam transmissions of the VOP and Palestine TV, the official radio and television stations of the Palestinian National Authority. Israeli government officials cited the station's reported role in inciting Palestinian violence against Israelis as justification. The government was prevented from carrying out its wish when the Israeli Broadcasting Authority refused to jam VOP and PTV transmissions.

On August 4, CPJ protested the cabinet's decision in a letter addressed to Prime Minister Benjamin Netanyahu.

August 2
Kawthar Salam, *Al-Hayat al-Jadida*
ATTACKED
Mazen Dana, Reuters ATTACKED

Salam, a reporter with the Ramallah-based newspaper *Al-Hayat al-Jadidah*, was detained by members of the Israeli Defense Forces while she was attempting to photograph Israeli soldiers at the Halhoul checkpoint near Hebron. Dana, a photographer for Reuters, was attacked by IDF soldiers, apparently in reaction to his attempt to film Salam's arrest. Photographs of the incident, which were published in the August 3 issue of the London-based daily *Al-Hayat*, showed IDF soldiers attacking Dana and placing him in a choke hold. Both journalists were held for nearly eight hours at a police station in Kiryat Arba and released.

The IDF responded by claiming that Salam and Dana had disturbed the soldiers' work. CPJ protested in a letter to Israeli Prime Minister Benjamin Netanyahu on August 4 and called on the Israeli government to take all necessary measures to ensure that journalists do not face reprisal for reporting the news.

September 18
Michael Eldar, free-lancer CENSORED

A Tel Aviv court temporarily banned distribution of *Dakar*, a newly released book by Eldar, a former navy captain who is now an author and free-lance journalist. Hundreds of copies of the book were seized from bookstores in Israel after the court ruled that its content threatened national security. The same day, police raided Eldar's home, confiscating his passport, some files, and his computer, which contained detailed information of his research and the names of many of his sources. The cause of the raid, police claimed, was Eldar's purported involvement in espionage. He was eventually taken to the Batyam police station for questioning and was later released.

In his book, Eldar describes the case of the Israeli submarine Dakar, which disappeared in the Mediterranean Sea without a trace in 1968. Relying on testimony obtained from confidential sources, Eldar criticized the Israeli government for failing to conduct a serious investigation into the incident.

In November 1996, authorities had banned the distribution of *Flotilla 11*, a book written by Eldar describing his experience in the Israeli navy. Authorities also charged that the book, which cast a negative light on some aspects of the navy's operations, was a threat to national security.

In a letter to Israeli Prime Minister Benjamin Netanyahu on September 30, CPJ urged him to lift the distribution ban on *Dakar*.

September 19
Nasser Shiyoukhi, The Associated Press HARASSED

Shiyoukhi, an AP reporter, was told by an Israeli soldier that he could not enter a Jewish area in the town of Hebron because he was an Arab. The soldier told two of Shiyoukhi's colleagues, who were traveling with Shiyoukhi, that the three journalists could not park their car near the enclave because they had an Arab in the car. After Shiyoukhi explained he was a journalist, the soldier punched him in the head, knocking him to the ground. Shiyoukhi later filed a complaint with the police, at the behest of Israeli border guards who witnessed the incident.

On September 25, CPJ protested the incident in a letter to Israeli Prime Minister Benjamin Netanyahu and called for an immediate and vigorous investigation into the case.

Jordan

Independent print media received a near-fatal blow in May when the government introduced "temporary" amendments to the 1993 Press and Publications Law. The press amendments, which were ratified by King Hussein on May 17 without public or parliamentary debate, prescribed sweeping restrictions on the press, granting authorities wide berth to suspend, fine, and permanently close newspapers found to be in violation of the law's broad and ambiguous content bans. By late September, just weeks before parliamentary elections on November 4, 13 weekly newspapers were suspended by the Ministry of Information for their failure to meet one of the law's more controversial provisions requiring weeklies to raise their capital base twenty-fold, from 15,000JD (US$21,135) to 300,000JD (US$422,700). By mid-November, 12 of the 13 papers had their licenses permanently revoked for noncompliance. (See the special report on Jordan, p. 413.)

Indeed, following their implementation, the press amendments had a chilling effect on the daily and weekly press. "Before the

new law, we would never talk about the King but we would criticize the government for its concessions to Israel," said the publisher of a now-suspended weekly newspaper. "Now after the new law we can't say anything." The amended version of Article 40, for example, banned any "news, views, opinions, analysis, information, reports, caricatures, photos or any type of publication" that violates the already ambiguous provisions of the 1993 law. These include bans on information that "offends the King or the Royal Family," "damages national unity," "foments hatred," or insults the "Heads of State of Arab, Islamic or friendly countries." A new provision of Article 40 prohibited the publication of "false news or rumors that offend public interests or state departments," effectively granting authorities even wider latitude to haul outspoken journalists to court and to further shield government officials from criticism. "Article 40 basically means that newspapers should be a copy of the official government line," said Taher Adwan, editor in chief of the recently formed independent daily *Al-Arab al-Youm*. "This provision is tantamount to brandishing a sword over the heads of journalists."

Newspapers and other publications deemed by authorities to be in violation of the provisions of Articles 40 and 42 (which ban publication of court proceedings prior to final rulings) were also subject to suspension by the courts and can only resume publication at the discretion of the Minister of Information. Newspapers that violated the law for a second time within a five-year period were subjected to suspensions ranging from three to six months, and third-time offenders within the span of five years can have their license revoked by court order. Newspapers charged with violating Articles 40 and 42 were subject to harsh fines that range from JD15,000 (US$21,135) to JD25,000 (US$35,225) for

each offense—a four-fold increase in the maximum fine decreed under the original law. In a move that some journalists interpreted as yet another manifestation of the government's desire to control the press, the amendments also abolished a provision in the previous law that required the state to divest its equity in the country's two leading daily newspapers, *Al-Dustur* and *Al-Rai*, by 1997.

In the months leading up to the amendments' introduction in May, the state displayed mounting intolerance for the weeklies, prosecuting and convicting a number of their editors and reporters. On January 16, Abdullah Bani 'Issa, the former editor of the weekly *Al-Hiwar*, was convicted and sentenced to six months in prison for "offending" King Hussein and Crown Prince Hassan and for publishing "inaccurate news"—charges that stemmed from *Al-Hiwar's* publication of a 1995 interview with Ata Abu al-Rishtah, a spokesman for the outlawed Islamic Liberation Party who criticized the Jordan-Israel peace agreement. Although 'Issa was eventually acquitted on appeal, the court's decision reportedly marked the first time in Jordan's history that a journalist was sentenced to prison for a publications offense.

Authorities also stepped up censorship against the foreign press, preventing the distribution of newspapers including the London-based dailies *Al-Hayat* and *Al-Quds al-Arabi*. In October alone, 15 issues of the daily *Al-Quds al-Arabi* were seized in 18 days, presumably for the paper's coverage of the Israeli Mossad's failed assassination attempt against Hamas political leader Khaled Meshaal in Amman in September.

January 16
Abdullah Bani 'Issa, *Al-Hiwar*
LEGAL ACTION

'Issa, former editor of the weekly *Al-Hiwar*, was

sentenced to six months in prison and fines of JD500 (US$700) for libeling King Hussein and Crown Prince Hassan and publishing inaccurate news, under both the Press and Publications Law and the penal code. The charges stemmed from a December 1995 interview in *Al-Hiwar* with Ata Abu al-Rishtah, a spokesman for the outlawed Islamic Liberation Party. In the interview, Abu al-Rishtah indirectly criticized King Hussein and the Jordan-Israel peace agreement. The court's decision reportedly marked the first time in Jordan's history that a journalist was sentenced to prison for a publications offense. CPJ wrote to King Hussein on March 28 in advance of his Washington visit with President Clinton, urging the Jordanian leader to play a vigorous role in reversing the erosion of press freedom in Jordan. On April 9, the Court of Appeals overturned the verdict against 'Issa, arguing that the content of the published interview was neither criminal nor libelous.

January 23
Nael Saleh, *Al-Haqiqah* LEGAL ACTION

The Court of First Instance convicted Saleh, the editor in chief of the weekly *Al-Haqiqah*, to a total of nine months in prison and JD15,000 (US$21,000) in fines for "spreading false news and publishing pornographic material" under provisions of the Press and Publications Law and the penal code. The basis for the charges against Saleh were articles published in *Al-Haqiqah* in July 1996 that reported on prostitution in Amman. Saleh appealed the court's decision and remains free, pending the court's ruling.

January 24
Omar al-Nadi, **Yusuf Gheyshan**, *Abed Rabbo* IMPRISONED, LEGAL ACTION

Police arrested Al-Nadi and Gheyshan, editors for the satiric weekly *Abed Rabbo*, on January 24 and January 28, respectively, by order of a state

prosecutor. Their arrest followed the publication of an article and a cartoon that ran in separate issues of the newspaper in December and January. The article described Ibrahim Zayyid al-Kilani, a parliamentary deputy, as a "hypocrite, " while the cartoon accused Minister of Public Works and Housing Abdel Hadi al-Majali of using his status as a government official to profit from the sale of automobiles in Jordan. Both were charged with "publishing inaccurate news" and "soiling the image" of state officials under the Press and Publications Law. They await trial in the Amman Court of First Instance. On March 28, CPJ raised the case in a letter to King Hussein, protesting the erosion of press freedom in Jordan.

May 6
Fahd Rimawi, *Al-Majd* ATTACKED

Rimawi, editor in chief of the Arabic weekly *Al-Majd*, was summoned to the headquarters of Jordanian Intelligence. Rimawi said, "As soon as I entered the office, two security officers cursed me and began to slap me on the face." The officers never informed Rimawi why they had summoned him. In recent years Rimawi's newspaper has been a favorite target of the Jordanian authorities due to its vocal opposition to the peace treaty between Israel and Jordan.

May 17
All media LEGAL ACTION

A royal decree ratified amendments to the 1993 Press and Publications Law, imposing new restrictions on the press. Under the amended law, decreed without public or parliamentary debate, the state assumed broad powers to suspend, fine, and permanently close newspapers that violate the press law.

The changes broaden bans on publications that offend the royal family, damage national unity, foment hatred, or insult other heads of state. Authorities are also empowered to suspend and close publications that violate the law and levy large fines that range from JD15,000 (US$21,135) to JD25,000 (US$35,225) for each offense—a four-fold increase in the maximum fine. A new provision increases capital requirements for newspapers—a move that forced most opposition weekly newspapers to close.

On June 11, CPJ and the London-based ARTICLE 19 wrote to King Hussein, urging an immediate repeal of the new law.

June 14
Abed Rabbo HARASSED

Abed Rabbo, a satirical Arabic-language weekly, closed. The newspaper cited fears of heavy financial penalties outlined in the newly ratified amendments to the 1993 Press and Publications Law. "The new law is very elastic, and it can be applied to almost any article we publish," said editor in chief Yousef Gheishan. *Abed Rabbo* was the first newspaper to close because of Jordan's new press law.

September 2
Al-Bilad LEGAL ACTION

A court convicted the Arabic-language weekly *Al-Bilad* of violating Article 40 of the Press and Publications Law, which criminalizes the publication of news pertaining to security forces. The charge followed an article, which ran on an unspecified date during the summer, reporting that the Jordanian government had handed over to Israel the husband of Sonia Rai, a member of the Popular Front for the Liberation of Palestine who had shot and killed an Israeli soldier earlier in the year. The newspaper was fined 15,000JD (US$22,600).

Officials from *Al-Bilad* said they were not informed that the legal case had been filed against them, and only learned of it after the court issued its decision.

It was the first conviction of a Jordanian newspaper since King Hussein ratified stricter amendments to the Press and Publications Law in May. *Al-Bilad* was appealing the ruling.

Lebanon

The government continued to use its regulatory system to restrict Lebanon's broadcast media, a practice it relied on last year. In July, the cabinet handed out licenses to one television station and eight radio stations, including Hizballah's Al-Manar TV, Voice of Lebanon (formerly owned by the Phalange party), and Voice of the People (Communist Party). The sectarian and political groups that received approval had been excluded during the previous round of licensing in September 1996. Only four television stations and 11 radio stations were licensed at that time, drastically reducing the number of broadcast outlets that had proliferated during the 1975-1990 conflict. Of the newly licensed radio stations, only three were authorized to broadcast programs with political content. Stations that were denied licenses in July included the Independent Communications Network (ICN) and New Television (NTV), both widely recognized for their independent broadcasting.

In a more direct threat to free expression, the Ministry of Information in February implemented prior censorship of television news broadcasts and political programs that are beamed abroad via satellite. Government officials defended the move as necessary to preserve relations with friendly Arab regimes. "The Arab regimes are different from the regime in Lebanon," Prime Minister Rafiq Hariri said in a January interview with the daily *Al-Sharq al-Awsat*. "So, out of concern for our Arab relations, we will not allow any private station to transmit news or political programs detrimental to our ties with the Arab states." Critics assailed the move, maintaining that the real intent was to stifle unfavorable coverage of political allies Syria and Saudi

Arabia. Broadcasters complained that the government continued to censor them throughout the year, despite a ruling in April by the country's highest court that the practice was illegal.

As the year came to an end, the government stepped up its interference with private news programming. On December 11, the station Murr TV (MTV) was forced under government pressure to cancel a live interview with exiled former army commander Gen. Michel Aoun, a leading opponent of the Lebanese government and of Syria's ongoing military presence in Lebanon. Information Minister Bassem Sabaa had warned MTV officials that if the Aoun interview went ahead it would harm "public order and national reconciliation." Sabaa later added that he would not tolerate programming that "aims to destroy relations with Syria." Weeks earlier in November, state prosecutors had initiated an investigation into the Lebanese Broadcasting Corporation International (LBCI) after the station had aired an interview with Roger Tamraz, an exiled Lebanese financier who was convicted in absentia for "collaborating" with Israel. LBCI's chairman and a journalist from the station were summoned for questioning in front of a judge. The case was eventually dismissed.

Government officials responded to the media's more daring approach to news coverage by issuing alarming public warnings. On December 10, following a meeting of the Central Security Council (CSC), Interior Minister Michel al-Murr stated that the government "will not allow unrestrained political views to be voiced during televised interviews which include attacks on officials and the public." Al-Murr added that the government would "no longer allow television to be a place for some people to voice whatever they feel like talking about, especially as it might influence public opinion."

Both the broadcast media and the press

continued to face the threat of prosecution under a plethora of statutes that allow the state wide latitude to haul journalists to court for their reporting of news and opinion. Decree 7997 (enacted in 1996), for example, bans stations from broadcasting news that seeks to "inflame or incite sectarian or religious chauvinism," or which contains "slander, disparagement, disgrace, [or] defamation." The Audiovisual Law (1994) empowers the Ministry of Information to close stations that violate these and other equally ambiguous statutes. A favored tool of the state against outspoken journalists has been the infamous Decree 104 (1977), which criminalizes "fomenting sectarian strife and defaming officials or foreign heads of state." Walid Husseini, editor in chief of the now-daily *Kifah al-Arabi*, was convicted on December 26, 1996, for an editorial he wrote denouncing Saudi Arabia's King Fahd. He was sentenced to two months in prison and fined of LL50 million (US$32,726). In a separate suit, Husseini was also charged under the decree for allegedly defaming Prime Minister Hariri and the Saudi government in a second editorial.

Syria's ongoing military presence in Lebanon continued to compromise Lebanese media coverage of Syrian affairs. Ever since Syrian troops occupied and temporarily shut down the offices of several newspapers in late 1976, the press has refrained from any meaningful criticism of Assad's regime and its controversial presence in Lebanon. The fear of reprisal for critical reporting among journalists is well-founded. In the years following the Syrian intervention, a number of journalists were assassinated in Beirut—presumably by Syrian agents for their critical coverage of Assad's military initiative in Lebanon. Syria's continued dominant political and military influence in Lebanon, along with the notorious activities of its intelligence services in certain parts of the country, further enforce self-censorship among the Lebanese press.

April 13
Muhammad al-Asad, Al-Sharq News Agency HARASSED
Ghassan al-Zaater, *Nida al-Watan* HARASSED
Muhammad Saleh, *Al-Safir* HARASSED
Abdel Ghani al-Jardali, Al-Sharq News Agency HARASSED
Ahmad Montash, *Al-Nahar* HARASSED, MISSING
Nazih al-Naqouzie, Reuters, LBC, *Al-Anwar* HARASSED
Khaled al-Ghourabi, *Al-Bayraq* HARASSED
Haitham Zouaiter, *Al-Liwa* HARASSED
Muhammad al-Qabrushi, MTV HARASSED
Abdel Mullah Khaled, Tele Liban HARASSED
Hassan Hanqir, Reuters Television HARASSED
Muhammad al-Zaatari, The Associated Press HARASSED
Mahmoud al-Boubou, LBCI HARASSED

Lebanese police in Sidon arrested a group of 13 reporters, photographers, and cameramen. The journalists were covering elections of the General Confederation of Lebanese Workers, Lebanon's independent umbrella organization for trade unions. The arrests occurred amid skirmishes between competing trade union factions. At least 25 union activists were also arrested. The 13 journalists were taken to local police headquarters in Sidon, where they were held for nearly five hours. Police confiscated their cameras and film.

November 11
LBCI LEGAL ACTION

State prosecutors announced that they would initiate an investigation into the Lebanese Broadcast Corporation International (LBCI) after the station aired an interview with Roger

Tamraz, an exiled Lebanese financier (now a U.S. citizen) who was convicted in absentia of embezzlement and alleged collaboration with Israel. LBCI chairman Pierre Daher and talk show host Marcel Ghanem were later summoned for questioning in front of a judge, although the case was eventually dismissed.

December 11
MTV CENSORED

The private television station Murr TV (MTV) was forced under government pressure to cancel a live interview with exiled former army commander Gen. Michel Aoun, scheduled to be aired on December 14. The station's decision to cancel the interview followed a meeting on the same day between representatives of MTV and Information Minister Bassem Sabaa, who reportedly expressed a "wish" that MTV not broadcast the program. Sabaa stated that if the Aoun interview were to take place it could cause harm to "public order and national reconciliation."

Mauritania

The Ministry of Interior continued its practice of banning outspoken newspapers with impunity. The infamous Article 11 of Mauritania's 1991 press ordinance grants authorities the power to ban the distribution and sale of any newspaper or periodical that is likely to harm Islamic principles or state authority, or that jeopardizes public order. Such broad proscriptions have been employed to silence newspapers that publish news or commentary on issues such as the practice of slavery in Mauritania, the improper activities of public officials, or internal power struggles within the regime.

The independent weekly *Mauritane Nouvelles* was again the target of repeated and unexplained government censorship. It

was suspended for one month in April and later slapped with a three-month ban in October, prior to the presidential election in December. In both instances, authorities alleged that the newspaper had threatened "national security." Thirteen other issues of the paper were seized throughout the year.

Morocco

Although the government is generally tolerant of political satire and criticism of state policy in the opposition press, journalists are aware of certain lines they cannot cross. Two subjects that are off-limits are criticism of the monarchy and any questioning of the country's territorial sovereignty over Western Sahara.

In recent years, authorities have responded to undesirable news about the king and reports on official corruption by confiscating newspapers, or temporarily banning their publication or distribution in the country. Foreign publications, including the French-language daily *Le Monde* , were subject to distribution bans throughout the year stemming from unfavorable articles about the government.

The country's press code further deters critical journalism, decreeing stiff prison penalties and heavy fines for journalists deemed to have offended the king and royal family, and defamed political officials. The press code also grants the Interior Ministry the power to confiscate newspapers that are a "threat to public order."

The Palestinian National Authority

Fear and self-censorship marked the situation of the local press under Yasser Arafat's Palestinian National Authority (PNA). Just four years after the PNA assumed control over areas of the West Bank and Gaza Strip, journalists have learned that criticism of the Palestinian leader and official PNA policy is risky business.

Arrests of outspoken journalists and the closure of newspapers in the initial months of Arafat's rule has had a chilling effect on the Palestinian press. So too have the erratic and heavy-handed practices of Arafat's security forces, who have demonstrated little tolerance for independent journalism. "They don't think that people can hold other opinions and ideas. You must go with the flow," one Palestinian reporter said when describing a run-in with security forces over a news report. "It is very lamentable when a 15-year-old boy who can't even read or write asks you about press etiquette and how you should behave as a journalist. But he has a gun, a military uniform, and [Palestinian security chief] Jibril Rajoub behind him."

Police and security forces have also employed more subtle tactics to keep journalists in check. Both local and foreign journalists complained of daily harassment in the form of telephone calls from security agents, inquiring about news articles and requesting information. Such measures serve to remind journalists that their actions are being closely monitored. "I avoid writing stories which I feel I will be questioned about," said one veteran journalist. Some Palestinian journalists working with the

Western media seek clearance with the security forces before filing a story, illustrating the pervasive fear among the press.

The upshot is a largely supine press that rarely provokes the authorities. Newspapers steer clear of sensitive issues such as corruption, political nepotism within the PNA bureaucracy, and any reporting that might be viewed as critical of Arafat. News stories pertaining to PNA policy tend to mirror the accounts of WAFA, the official Palestinian news agency.

In one highly publicized incident, authorities detained Daoud Kuttab, founder and director of the Modern Media Institute at Al-Quds University, for seven days in May after he stated in an article in *The International Herald Tribune* and *The Washington Post* that the Palestinian Broadcasting Company (PBC) had been jamming his live coverage of Palestinian Legislative Council sessions. Kuttab, through a project of Al-Quds Educational Television, had secured a contract with the Palestinian Authority to broadcast the council's proceedings, but the transmissions had been repeatedly blocked. Kuttab said Palestinian officials were disturbed about the content of debates, during which legislators often criticized Arafat and his policies. After CPJ and several other international human rights organizations conducted a sustained campaign for his release, Kuttab was freed on May 27. In a separate incident, Palestinian Security Service (PSS) agents detained Khaled Amayreh, a free-lance journalist based in the West Bank, after he published an exposé on torture in a Palestinian jail in the weekly *Sawt al-Haq wal Huriyya*. Amayreh spent more than 24 hours in PSS custody and was released after he signed a piece of paper stating that he would be observe "objectivity" in his writing.

March 23
Khaled Amayreh, Sharja Satellite TV
HARASSED

Four agents of the Preventive Security Service (PSS) visited the home of Amayreh, a correspondent for the United Arab Emirates-based Sharja Satellite TV, and summoned him to PSS headquarters in Dura for questioning. Amayra was interrogated for two hours about a broadcast that aired the same day in which he reported on a recent meeting between the head of Israeli intelligence, Ami Ayalon, and the head of PSS, Jibril Rajoub. According to the report, Ayalon had requested during the meeting that Palestinian security forces begin to arrest activists from the Islamic Resistance Movement (Hamas), which claimed responsibility for a March 21 suicide bombing in Tel Aviv.

During the interrogation, PSS agents alleged that Amayreh's news report represented an attempt by Israel to "distort" the image of the Palestinian National Authority and threatened to jail him for 48 hours. Just before his release, Amayreh was ordered to sign a written statement, affirming that he "did not intend to libel anybody or place [anyone] in a bad light" as a result of his report.

March 25
Muhammad Ali Assad, Cable News Network (CNN) ATTACKED

Assad, a cameraman for CNN, was struck in the head by a stone, apparently thrown by a Palestinian demonstrator in Bethlehem. Assad had been covering clashes between Palestinians and the Israeli army following the Israeli government's decision to build a controversial settlement near Bethlehem. Assad received four stitches in his head as a result of his injury.

March 26
Emad al-Sayyed, Associated Press Television (AP TV) ATTACKED

Al-Sayyed, a cameraman for AP TV, was struck

in the head by a rock thrown by Palestinian demonstrators in the town of Hebron. The attack occurred while Al-Sayyed was filming clashes between Palestinians and the Israeli army. The journalist was knocked unconscious for about 10 minutes.

Clashes between Palestinians and the Israeli army erupted following the Israeli government's decision to build a controversial housing settlement.

April 11
Several journalists ATTACKED, THREATENED

Palestinian demonstrators in Hebron pelted a group of 10 local and foreign journalists with stones while they were covering clashes between Israelis and Palestinians in Hebron. The incident occurred after Palestinian police officer Wasfi Abu Ayman publicly provoked the demonstrators to attack the journalists, whom he referred to as collaborators. Ayman also attacked an unidentified cameraman, punching him in the head, and threatened to break the camera of AP correspondent Nasser Shoukhi.

Some journalists said Ayman might have been angered by photographs published in the Palestinian press the previous day that showed a Palestinian policeman throwing stones at Israeli troops.

Later that day about two dozen Israeli, Palestinian, and foreign journalists held a sit-in protest in front of the Palestinian police checkpoint in the area to protest the Palestinian officer's incitement against the reporters.

April 24
Majed Arouri, The Associated Press (AP) ATTACKED

Arouri, an AP cameraman, was ordered by Palestinian police to stop filming a teachers' strike in the town of Al-Bira in the West Bank. He was detained for an hour and police confiscated his film.

May 16
Hisham Sharabati, free-lancer HARASSED

Sharabati, a free-lance cameraman, was ordered by Preventive Security Service agents to stop filming the arrest of two stone-throwers in Hebron by Palestinian forces. One of the agents threatened to break Sharabati's camera if he continued filming, and he subsequently confiscated Sharabati's film.

May 20
Daoud Kuttab, Al-Quds Educational Television IMPRISONED

Kuttab, a Palestinian journalist and director of the Modern Media Institute at Al-Quds University, was detained by Palestinian authorities in Ramallah in the West Bank. His detention followed the publication of an article in the *International Herald Tribune* and *The Washington Post* in which Kuttab described efforts of the Palestinian Broadcast Company to jam his live television coverage of the Palestinian Legislative Council.

Kuttab, through a project of Al-Quds Educational Television, had a contract with the Palestinian Authority to broadcast the council's proceedings. In the weeks before his arrest, however, the transmissions had been repeatedly blocked. Kuttab blamed Palestinian officials, who he said were disturbed by legislators' criticism of Palestinian leader Arafat and his policies during the sessions.

After CPJ spearheaded a seven-day international campaign, including appeals to Yasser Arafat and the U.S. government, Kuttab was released on May 27 without charge.

June 4
Muhammad Najuib, free-lancer HARASSED

Najuib, a free-lance journalist working in the West Bank, was approached by a Palestinian intelligence officer while covering a Ministry of Information press conference in Ramallah. The officer questioned Najuib about why he was attending the press conference, confiscated his press card, and ordered him to appear at intelligence headquarters the next day. When Najuib appeared the next morning, his press card was returned and an intelligence officer advised him not to cover news about the Palestinian Authority.

October 26
Khaled Amayreh, *Sawt al-Haq wal Huriyya*
IMPRISONED

Agents of the Palestinian Authority's Preventive Security Service (PSS) detained Amayreh, a free-lance journalist and member of the board of trustees of the Palestinian Human Rights Monitoring Group, after summoning him to the PSS office in Dura. The move followed an article Amayreh wrote for the October 26 issue of the Israeli-Arab weekly *Sawt al-Haq wal Huriyya*, describing testimony of suspected members of the Islamic Resistance Movement (Hamas), who claimed that they were severely tortured by PSS agents at Dahiriyya Prison.

After he reported to the PSS office in Dura, Amayreh was taken by jeep to the PSS Academy in Jericho, where he was brought before PSS head Jibril Rajoub, who verbally abused him and threatened to bring him before a state security court.

Amayreh was later transferred to a hospital after complaining of hypertension. He was released from custody at midnight on October 27 after signing a paper affirming that he would "observe objectivity in [his] writing."

Saudi Arabia And Other Members Of The Gulf Cooperation Council

The member states of the Gulf Cooperation Council (GCC)—Saudi Arabia, Bahrain, Kuwait, Oman, Qatar, and the United Arab Emirates (UAE)—remain hostile territory for independent journalism. The print media are mostly privately owned and often enjoy the benefits of cutting-edge technology, but journalists operate under severe constraints in providing independent or critical reporting on the domestic affairs of their respective countries.

Saudi Arabia, the largest and most influential member of the GCC, has perhaps the most tightly controlled press in the Middle East. The Ministry of Information approves the hiring of editors and may dismiss them at will. Criticism of the government or the royal family is taboo, as is discussion of controversial political issues. At the very least, transgressors will be punished with dismissal from their jobs. The state tightly monitors foreign publications entering the kingdom, weeding out news that touches on sensitive internal political issues, criticizes Islam, or discusses the country's dismal human rights record. Foreign journalists continue to face impediments in gaining entry to the country.

Saudi Arabia's tight control of the media also extends beyond the kingdom's national borders. In the 1990s, businessmen with close ties to the royal family invested heavily in the expanding pan-Arab media and now exercise tremendous leverage over its content and programming. Among Saudi-owned publications are the influential Arabic daily newspaper *Al-Hayat* and the magazine *Al-Wasat*, both based in London and owned by Prince Khaled Bin Sultan, a nephew of King Fahd. Another influential pan-Arab paper, the London-based daily *Al-Sharq al-Awsat*, is owned by Prince Ahmad Bin Salman. And the popular Middle East Broadcasting Corporation (MBC), with a region-wide viewership in the tens of millions, is owned by the prominent Saudi businessman Sheikh Walid al-Ibrahim, a brother-in-law of King Fahd. The other main broadcasting networks which service the region, such as Arab Radio and Television (ART) and Orbit, are also Saudi-owned. News and programming from these sources rarely, if ever, disseminate criticism of the Saudi regime or report on sensitive political issues vis-à-vis the kingdom.

Despite their ostensible editorial independence, some Saudi-owned publications have made a financial decision to censor themselves. "Our main concern is not to be banned in Saudi Arabia because most of the advertising comes from the Saudi market," said one editor from *Al-Hayat*. "From time to time, we have taken into consideration Saudi censorship."

The Saudi government exerts considerable influence over the local press in other Arab countries. Across the region, media criticism of Saudi human rights abuses or official corruption has prompted strong official responses. Some journalists contend that the Saudi government has signed "media protocols" with the ministries of information in several Arab countries which, in effect, obligate them to censor any news that discusses internal Saudi politics or criticism of state officials. CPJ has documented instances of censorship or state prosecution of newspapers and journalists in Jordan,

Lebanon, Egypt, and GCC countries for unfavorable coverage of Saudi affairs. One example is that of Walid Husseini, the editor of the Beirut-based daily *Kifah al-Arabi*, who was convicted and sentenced to 60 days in prison in 1996 for an editorial allegedly defaming King Fahd. He also faces criminal charges filed by Lebanese authorities in retaliation for another editorial that criticized King Fahd and Lebanon's close relations with Saudi Arabia. "[For] anything bad you say about Saudi Arabia...they will take you to court," commented one Arab journalist. The fear of such backlash has forced some Arab journalists outside of Saudi Arabia to censor themselves on Saudi issues.

In Kuwait, the press enjoys a considerable degree of freedom. Privately owned newspapers carry stories on a wide variety of socio-political issues, providing critical coverage of the government and state policies. Nonetheless, journalists engage in self-censorship, particularly with regard to criticism of the Emir, and avoid commentary that might be viewed as offensive toward Islam. In a welcome development, the government released six journalists from prison in February as part of a general amnesty. They had been tried and convicted by state security courts and martial law tribunals after the liberation of Kuwait for "collaborating" with the Iraqi occupiers— charges that stemmed from their employment with the newspaper *Al-Nida*, which was published in Kuwait during the Iraqi occupation. Some of those who were released reported that they had been tortured during their incarceration. Seven journalists from *Al-Nida* remain in Kuwait Central Prison.

In Bahrain, the government pressured the media for its coverage of political unrest, which has entered its third year. On July 1, authorities expelled *Deutsche Presse Agentur* correspondent Ute Meinel because of a news report in which she quoted an opposition group. Other foreign news agencies, meanwhile, reported harassment and intimidation by authorities. The local private press, which functions under legal restrictions that prohibit criticism of the Emir and allow authorities to ban publications that offend the state, has increasingly engaged in self-censorship, particularly regarding local unrest.

Collectively, GCC states have stepped up their efforts to restrict Internet access on information deemed immoral or politically subversive. In 1997, the UAE announced that the country's sole Internet service provider, Etisalat, would block access to websites it deemed morally offensive. Saudi Arabia is expected to follow a similar model when it officially launches Internet service in the kingdom in 1998.

April 6
Al-Ahram al-Arabi CENSORED

Saudi authorities banned distribution of the April 5 issue of the Cairo-based, Arabic-language weekly *Al-Ahram al-Arabi*. Although no official explanation was given, officials at *Al-Ahram al-Arabi* believed the ban came as a result of an article in that issue, which discussed the activities of Saudi dissident and Islamist militant leader Osama Bin Laden.

May 12
Al-Hayat CENSORED

Saudi authorities banned distribution of the May 12 issue of the London-based Arabic daily *Al-Hayat*. The apparent reason behind the move was the newspaper's publication of statements made by Saudi dissident and Islamist militant leader, Osama Bin Laden, during a highly publicized interview with CNN.

July 1
Ute Meinel, Deutsche Presse Agentur (DPA) EXPELLED

Authorities expelled Meinel, a correspondent for DPA in Bahrain. The official Gulf News Agency said that one of Meinel's reports included falsehoods and insults to the State of Bahrain.

Meinel had quoted the Bahrain Freedom Movement, a London-based opposition group, as saying that the government planned to bomb Shiite villages. Authorities questioned her about the article for several hours and temporarily confiscated her passport before forcing her to leave the country.

Syria

As President Hafez al-Assad completed the 27th year of his authoritarian rule, the press remained firmly under state control. The absence of independent media is testimony to the regime's dominance over civil society, unabated since Assad eradicated his political opposition in the early 1980s. The fear of arrest, torture, and prolonged imprisonment—treatment that has become the hallmark of much of Assad's rule—keeps journalists in check and hinders the emergence of nonpartisan media. Although in recent months, newspapers have been able to run stories about official corruption, the Ministry of Information closely supervises the country's state-run dailies and provides strict content guidelines for editors and journalists.

Those foreign publications that are allowed into the country offer some independent news coverage, but they must first run the gantlet of state censors. For example, the London-based daily *Al-Quds al-Arabi*, which began distribution in Syria in July, says that distribution of the paper was banned on an average of four times a month during the year for its coverage of Syrian affairs. Because of restrictions on the domestic print media, satellite dishes have proliferated, and Syrians increasingly rely on television programming beamed in from abroad.

At year's end, five journalists remained in prison in Syria. Between 1992 and 1994, they were convicted by the Supreme State Security Court and sentenced to anywhere from three to 15 years for a variety of alleged offenses, including their involvement in political organizations and their affiliation with the leading Syrian human rights group, the Committees for the Defense of Democratic Freedoms and Human Rights in Syria (CDF). Nizar Nayouf, an activist with the CDF who received a 10-year sentence in 1992, has remained in solitary confinement at Mezze military prison in Damascus since 1993.

Tunisia

Since Zine Abdine Ben Ali assumed the presidency nearly 10 years ago, the Tunisian press has become among the most restricted in the Arab world. Journalists who exhibit any independence in this police state suffer censorship, harassment, and imprisonment. The result is a climate of fear for local and foreign journalists, resulting in widespread self-censorship on a variety of social and political issues.

Although private newspapers exist, they avoid meaningful social or political commentary for fear of state reprisal. In recent years, the state has actively targeted journalists and newspapers critical of official policies—part of its all-out assault on political opposition groups. Attempts to report on such sensitive topics as human rights and the activities or viewpoints of the political opposition have provoked swift official responses, including the prosecution, imprisonment, and intimidation of reporters. Journalists have been dismissed from their jobs, denied accreditation, or have been prevented from leaving the country. The state has also exerted economic pressure on newspapers it deems undesirable by withholding vital revenue-producing advertising. As a result of these policies, Tunisian authorities have little reason to actively harass and censor journalists; privately owned newspapers refrain from reporting on even the most benign political issues and have become virtual carbon copies of the state-controlled press on policy issues.

Foreign correspondents have also experienced the Tunisian government's intolerance for independent coverage of domestic issues. Since 1991, four correspondents have been expelled from the country as a result of their reporting. One of them, BBC correspondent Alfred Hermida, was expelled in February 1994 for his coverage of Tunisian human rights activist Moncef Marzouki, who was then a self-declared candidate for president. Authorities have used threats of expulsion against correspondents or the closure of their news agencies' offices to discourage unwanted news coverage.

Beyond intimidation, authorities have maintained their control over the flow of information through systematic censorship of foreign publications entering the country. Since 1994, newspapers such as the French-language *Le Monde* and *Liberation* have been subjected to distribution bans on numerous occasions for their unfavorable coverage of Tunisia. In 1997, CPJ documented distribution bans of at least 37 issues of *Le Monde*. The London-based daily *Al-Quds al-Arabi*, meanwhile, estimates that the paper was banned an average of five to seven times a month for what it believed was the paper's coverage of topics such as the activities of Islamist groups in Algeria and Egypt.

The World Association of Newspapers on June 4 decided to expel the Tunisian Association of Newspaper Editors—formerly one of the most independent press associations in the Arab world in the 1970s and 1980s—for its failure to speak out against government violations of press freedom.

Two journalists remain in prison: Hamadi Jebali and Abdellah Zouari of the now-defunct weekly *Al-Fajr*, which was closed by authorities in February 1991 after repeated harassment by authorities. Jebali, the newspaper's editor, was arrested in January 1991 and sentenced to one year in prison under the country's press law for a news article published in *Al-Fajr* condemning the government's use of military courts against civilians. During Jebali's imprisonment, a second case was raised against him, Zouari, and 279 other people accused of being members of the Islamist Al-Nahda movement. On August 28, 1992, a military court sentenced Jebali and Zouari to 16 years and 11 years in prison, respectively, for their alleged membership in an illegal organization and "attempting to change the nature of the state." According to international human rights organizations, their trial fell far short of international fair-trial standards, and in the cases of Jebali and Zouari, the state failed to present credible evidence, relying instead on the journalists' association with *Al-Fajr*.

In separate letters sent to Tunisian President Zine Abdine Ben Ali and U.S. Secretary of State Madeleine K. Albright on August 27, the eve of the bicentennial of U.S.-Tunisian diplomatic relations, CPJ called for joint government efforts to end the Tunisian government's ongoing harassment of the press.

Turkey

Despite positive steps taken since the new government took office in July, press freedom in Turkey remains severely constrained by repressive statutes which criminalize leftist and pro-Kurdish political commentary and effectively ban independent reporting from or about the southeast. There were at least 29 journalists in jail in Turkey at year end, still more than in any other country. This represents a dramatic improvement from 1996, when CPJ reported 78 journalists in jail at the end of the year (see "The Case of Turkey: Verifying Reports of Imprisoned Journalists," p. 49). The release of 37 jailed journalists and the virtual halt to new prosecutions—CPJ was able to confirm one new case of imprisonment this year, as compared to 30 or more yearly between 1994 and 1996—was one of the most positive press freedom developments of the year.

Under the Islamist-oriented government of Necmettin Erbakan and his predecessor and coalition partner, Tansu Çiller, the prosecution of journalists had escalated to unprecedented levels. Repression of the news media was marked by the imprisonment of a record number of journalists, the brazen refusal of indicted policemen to appear for their murder trial in the death of reporter Metin Goktepe, and the temporary shutdowns ordered by the State Security Court of such newspapers as the now-defunct, pro-Kurdish *Demokrasi*.

The political transition in the summer presented a new opportunity for CPJ to press its long-standing concerns about imprisonment of Turkish reporters and editors. On June 18, Erbakan resigned under fierce pressure from the military, and Mesut Yilmaz of the staunchly secular, centrist Motherland Party was asked by the president to form a new government. On July 13—just one day after Yilmaz's new minority coalition survived a parliamentary vote of confidence—a CPJ-led coalition of international press freedom organizations and Turkish journalist groups began a series of discussions with the president, prime minister, other senior cabinet officers, and influential minority party leaders. The CPJ delegation was headed by vice chairman Terry Anderson and included board members Peter Arnett of CNN and Josh Friedman of *Newsday*, executive director William A. Orme, Jr., and Middle East program coordinator Joel Campagna. Joined by the executive directors of Reporters sans Frontières and the International Press Institute, and the chairmen of the Press Council of Turkey and the Turkish Union of Newspaper Owners, the CPJ delegation urged the Yilmaz government to place press freedom at the top of its agenda and to take immediate action to secure the release of imprisoned journalists—including 1996 International Press Freedom Award recipient Ocak Isik Yurtçu. In private meetings with the CPJ group and in public statements afterwards to the Turkish press, Yilmaz and his cabinet ministers pledged to take immediate steps to release Yurtçu and several other jailed journalists, and to introduce legislation before year end revising or eliminating provisions of the Anti-Terror Law and Penal Code under which journalists have been prosecuted in the past.

On August 14, the government fulfilled its first pledge to the CPJ delegation, pushing through parliament a limited amnesty bill that resulted in the release of seven imprisoned newspaper editors. Among those freed was Yurtçu, who had received front-page and prime-time local media coverage when Anderson presented him with his CPJ press freedom award in Saray Prison in July. Yet Yilmaz's fragile coalition was unable or unwilling to introduce its promised reform of the Anti-Terror Law and Penal Code. Police and prosecutors continued to harass reporters for leftist and pro-Kurdish newspapers. In September, authorities banned distribution of the pro-Kurdish and leftist dailies *Ükede Gündem* and *Emek* in the Southeastern cities of Diyarbakir, Tunceli, Hakkari, Siirt, Sirnak, and Van. The military-dominated National Security Council (NSC) excoriated private Islamist television and radio stations and urged the government to "take legal action against media organizations operating in violation of the constitution's basic and indispensable principles." In November, CPJ asked Prime Minister Yilmaz to request the release from Aydin Prison of Hasan Özgün, the former Diyarbakir bureau chief for *Özgür Gündem*, who is said by his attorney to be suffering from internal bleeding and heart tremors and had reportedly been denied medical treatment by prison authorities. At year end, Özgün remained in prison, serving a 12-year term.

January 2
Bulent Balta, *Özgür Gündem* IMPRISONED

Balta, a former editor of the now-defunct pro-Kurdish daily *Özgür Gündem*, was sentenced to 30 months in prison by a State Security Court for violating statutes of Turkey's Anti-Terror Law. The conviction stemmed from articles in *Özgür Gündem* during Balta's tenure criticizing aspects of the Turkish military's conflict with Kurdish separatists in the southeast region of the country. Balta had served only 12 days as the newspaper's editor in 1993 before he was arrested and charged.

On August 18, Balta was released from Pinarhisar Prison after the Turkish parliament passed a limited amnesty for jailed editors. Additional charges that were pending against him were also suspended.

February 4
Ahmet Erkanli, *Tavir* IMPRISONED

Authorities imprisoned Erkanli, a cartoonist for

the leftist magazine *Tavir*, after the Court of Cassation upheld a previous conviction under Article 159 of the Penal Code, criminalizing defamation of the Turkish armed forces. He was sentenced to 10 months in prison. Erkanli's conviction stemmed from a cartoon he published in *Tavir* in 1994 which parodied the 1991 "Yesilyurt Incident," in which Turkish soldiers allegedly forced prisoners to eat excrement. Erkanli, who is handicapped, applied for and was granted a humanitarian pardon by President Suleyman Demirel in June. He was subsequently released from Metris Prison.

February 17
Radikal CENSORED

The February 17 edition of the daily *Radikal* was seized by order of a Turkish court in Istanbul. The court said the newspaper slandered Mustafa Kemal Ataturk, the founder of the modern Turkish Republic. *Radikal* had reprinted an article from the French newspaper *Le Figaro*, which referred to Ataturk as an authoritarian ruler. It is against Turkish law to slander Ataturk.

March 2
Stephen Kinzer, *The New York Times*
IMPRISONED

Kinzer, *The New York Times*' correspondent in Turkey, was detained at a military checkpoint near the town of Kozluk and taken to the town of Batman, where he was held for 19 hours before being released. Kinzer was interrogated for seven hours and accused of spying for the outlawed Kurdistan Workers' Party (PKK).

During the detention and interrogation, he was denied requests to contact the U.S. Embassy or his newspaper.

May 2
Flash TV ATTACKED, CENSORED

A group of about 50 armed assailants entered the Istanbul office of the independent Flash TV and opened fire, shooting randomly. The men fled the scene after the attack, which lasted five minutes. No one was injured during the incident, but the office was substantially damaged. The attackers, who shouted threats at station employees, appeared to have been motivated by a live telephone interview with fugitive organized-crime figure Alaattin Cakici. In the interview, aired on Flash TV the previous day, Cakici implicated the husband of Foreign Minister Tansu Çiller in financial improprieties and said he had contacts with the criminal underworld.

After the attack, Turkish police sealed Flash TV's headquarters in Bursa, forcing the station off the air. They cited the station's alleged improper satellite licensing as the reason for their action. The station eventually was allowed to resume broadcasting.

May 3
Demokrasi LEGAL ACTION, CENSORED

An Istanbul State Security Court ordered the pro-Kurdish daily *Demokrasi* to close for one month, after ruling that the paper had "incited hatred" in an article it published on August 9, 1996. The article, titled "After the Resistance," reported on a 1996 hunger strike by leftist inmates and also talked about what it referred to as a government campaign to assimilate Kurds in Turkey. Ali Zeren, editor of *Demokrasi*, also received a 20-month prison sentence for having published the article.

May 6
Izzet Baran, *Ozgür Halk* IMPRISONED

Baran, a correspondent for the pro-Kurdish monthly magazine *Ozgür Halk*, was arrested and charged with violating Article 312 of the Penal Code (inciting racial hatred) for carrying an *Ozgür Halk* banner in a May Day parade in the town of Mersin, where he is based. He was released on October 2, pending trial.

May 12
Hürriyet ATTACKED

An assailant armed with a knife and a toy gun forced his way into the Istanbul office of the daily *Hürriyet*. The man, Huseyin Vuran, seized an automatic weapon from a guard and said he was looking for the newspaper's publisher, Aydin Dogan. Vuran opened fire on a custodian, injuring him in the legs, before turning himself in to police. Vuran, who was described as an Islamist sympathizer, was reported to have been motivated by *Hürriyet*'s harsh editorial line against the Islamist-led government of Prime Minister Necmettin Erbakan.

May 20
ATV ATTACKED
Sabah ATTACKED

Three unidentified gunmen opened fire on the building housing the Istanbul offices of ATV and the daily newspaper *Sabah* from a nearby highway. The gunfire shattered windows on the building's fifth floor, but no one was injured. The assailants fled the scene of the attack.

June 2
Abulkader Konuksever,
ATV IMPRISONED, LEGAL ACTION

Konuksever, a cameraman in Diyarbakir for the mainstream television station ATV, was detained by authorities after two separate interviews he and a team from ATV conducted with two former members of the Kurdistan Workers' Party (PKK). The former PKK members had allegedly carried out clandestine activities for the government. He was subsequently charged under Article 169 of the Penal Code (aiding an outlawed organization). Following Konuksever's arrest, ATV closed its bureau in Diyarbakir, in the southeast region of Turkey. He was released on October 6, pending trial.

June 4
Mahmut Ovur, ATV ATTACKED

Ovur, a journalist and director of a legal affairs program broadcast on the privately owned television channel ATV, was shot near his home in Istanbul. Ovur was attacked from behind and hit five times, in his left hand and right thigh. He was treated at a nearby hospital.

Ovur, who reports regularly on Turkey's criminal underworld, had been investigating alleged government contacts with organized crime figures. Prior to the attack, he had received numerous threatening telephone calls as a result of his reporting.

June 4
Ahmet Sümbül, *Demokrasi* IMPRISONED, LEGAL ACTION

Sümbül, a Diyarbakir correspondent for the pro-Kurdish daily *Demokrasi*, was detained and charged under Article 169 of the Penal Code (aiding an outlawed organization) after conducting an interview with two former members of the Kurdistan Workers' Party (PKK), who had alleged that they had carried out terrorist activities for the state. He was released on October 6, pending trial.

July 29
Hayri Ozugur, ATV ATTACKED
Durak Dogan, Kanal D ATTACKED
Abdullah Koltuk, CTV ATTACKED
Fevzi Gonulay, Ilhas News Agency (IHA) ATTACKED
Cemalettin Alan, IHA ATTACKED
Ismail Yesilyurt, Anatolian News Agency (ANA) ATTACKED
Mustafa Abadan, ANA ATTACKED
Selahattin Sonmez, *Turkish Daily News* ATTACKED

Ozugur, a cameraman for ATV; Dogan, a cameraman for Kanal D; Koltuk, a cameraman for

CTV, Gonulay, a reporter for IHA; Alan, a reporter for IHA; Yesilyurt and Abadan, ANA reporters; and Sonmez, a photographer for the *Turkish Daily News*, were beaten by police with batons while covering a demonstration in Ankara attended by Islamist and other activists. The attacking police officers were encouraged to assault the journalists by the crowd of demonstrators.

In a letter to Turkey's Prime Minister Mesut Yilmaz, CPJ urged an immediate investigation of the incident and that the responsible officers be held accountable for their actions.

July 31
Zeynel Bagir, *Demokrasi* IMPRISONED, LEGAL ACTION

Bagir, Diyarbakir bureau chief for the pro-Kurdish daily *Demokrasi*, was detained by Turkish authorities after interviewing two former members of the Kurdistan Workers' Party (PKK) who had alleged that they had carried out clandestine activities for the government. He was charged under Article 169 of the Penal Code (aiding an outlawed organization) and released on October 6, awaiting trial.

November 4
Mehmetcan Toprak, Radyo Karacadag IMPRISONED, HARASSED
Vedat Bakir, Radyo Karacadag IMPRISONED, HARASSED

Anti-terror police detained Toprak and Bakir, the director and manager respectively of Radyo Karacadag, after they reported on a police action at a bookstore in the town of Sanliurfa, in southeastern Turkey. Police also raided the radio station's office and the homes of both men, confiscating numerous audio cassettes and publications. Toprak and Bakir were released the following day.

Yemen

In comparison to its neighbors on the Arabian peninsula, the Yemeni press has enjoyed a considerable degree of press freedom. The 1990 unification of north and south Yemen ushered in democratic reforms that sparked a proliferation of private newspapers. In the years following the country's 1994 civil war, however, the state has reversed some of this progress.

The state's exploitation of the press law and penal code to prosecute journalists who write critically of the government or public officials threatens the independent press. One particularly shocking case in 1997 was the libel conviction of Abdul Jabbar Saad and Abdullah Saad from the weekly *Al-Shoura*, who were sentenced to 80 lashes and banned for a year from practicing journalism for "defaming" a leading politician of the opposition Islah party. Officials also displayed their displeasure with independent reporting by suspending newspapers that were outspoken in their criticism of the state.

Political Security agents kept up their harassment of the press, intimidating and detaining reporters, or confiscating issues of newspapers.

April 6
Al-Ahram al-Arabi CENSORED

Yemeni authorities banned distribution of the April 5 issue of the Cairo-based, Arabic language weekly *Al-Ahram al-Arabi*. The apparent reason for the move was an article that discussed the activities of Saudi dissident and Islamist militant Osama Bin Laden. The article reported that Muslim militants maintained a strong armed presence in areas along the Saudi-Yemeni border.

May 27

Abdul Jabbar Saad, *al-Shoura* LEGAL ACTION, CENSORED

Abdullah Saad, *al-Shoura* LEGAL ACTION, CENSORED

Reporter Jabbar Saad and editor Abdullah Saad, both of the opposition newspaper *al-Shoura*, were convicted of libel. They were sentenced to 80 lashes each and banned from practicing journalism for one year. The newspaper was also suspended for six months.

The journalists were convicted of writing a series of articles critical of Sheikh Abdul Majid Zendani, a leading politician in the al-Islah party.

July 30

Alawi Ben Sumait, *Al-Ayyam* IMPRISONED

Saleh Jareery, *Al-Ayyam* IMPRISONED

Ben Sumait and Jareery, reporters for the biweekly *Al-Ayyam*, were detained by Yemeni Political Security forces in the towns of Seyeun and Mukallah, respectively, amid a security round-up of political opposition figures in Hadrahmut province. The operation followed several weeks of protest by political opposition groups and others against a government proposal to partition Hadrahmut into different administrative entities. The journalists' detention appeared related to news articles they wrote for *Al-Ayyam* in which they criticized the government plan. They were later released on an unspecified date.

September 6

Al-Haqiqah CENSORED

The Ministry of Information ordered the 3-month closure of the weekly *Al-Haqiqah* after the newspaper published an interview with exiled opposition figure Abdel Rahman Jaafri in its September 4 edition.

October 11

Ma'in CENSORED

The Ministry of Information confiscated all issues of the September 30-October 15 edition of the official fortnightly *Ma'in* and banned its publication indefinitely. The action appeared to have been taken in retaliation for an editorial written by chief editor Abdel Fattah Al-Hakimi titled "From the Revolution of the Poor to the Poor Revolution!" (Min Thawra al-Faqr ila Faqr al-Thawra!), which strongly criticized state policies and prevailing socio-economic conditions in Yemen. Al-Hakimi and his staff were also dismissed from their jobs.

November 20

Al-Ayyam CENSORED

Police and Political Security agents seized approximately 4,000 copies of the November 19 issue of the biweekly newspaper *Al-Ayyam* before it was distributed in the towns of Al-Mukallah, Seyun, and Ashahr. The action appears to have stemmed from the biweekly newspaper's publication of two front-page stories about recent government arrests of oppositionists in Hadrahmaut Province.

December 13

Nabil al-Amoudi, *Al-Ayyam* IMPRISONED

Al-Amoudi, a reporter for the biweekly newspaper *Al-Ayyam* in Abyan Province who is also a lawyer, was detained by agents from Yemen's Political Security (PS) in the town of Zinjibar, after being summoned to PS headquarters the previous evening. He was held for eight days before his release on December 21.

During his detention, security agents attempted to pressure al-Amoudi into signing a statement saying that he would give the Press and Publications Department copies of his stories before publication. He refused to sign the statement.

Prior to his detention, al-Amoudi had received threats from PS agents in October, warning him against his continued work for *Al-Ayyam*.

Jordan Reins in the Press
by Joel Campagna

Since Jordan began a process of political reform in the late 1980s—one which included the lifting of martial law and the legalization of political parties—the kingdom has burnished its international image as a nascent democracy. But the government's moves in the last three years to narrow the political space have had serious consequences for the country's democratic institutions, especially compromising press freedom. In 1997, the state stepped up its restrictions on Jordan's independent press, and by the beginning of 1998, press freedom in Jordan hung in the balance.

The High Court of Justice ruled in January that last May's highly restrictive amendments to the Press and Publications Law (PPL), sharply curtailing the work of the country's outspoken independent weekly newspapers, were unconstitutional. But the reprieve is temporary, since the court ruling faulted the means of ratification—royal decree, without public or parliamentary debate—and not the substance of the amendments. The next battle for Jordan's free press is thus destined to be fought in parliament, since the government is likely to try the constitutional route to enacting amendments similar to the ones that triggered a firestorm of domestic and international criticism last spring.

On May 17, six months before Jordan's parliamentary elections, the cabinet of Prime Minister Abdel Salam Majalli promulgated temporary amendments to the 1993 press law that severely restricted the independent weeklies, which had flourished since the lifting of martial law in 1992. This surprise unilateral move by the executive branch while parliament was out of session prompted vocal and furious opposition in Jordan. The amendments followed nearly four years of legal harassment of the weeklies, which have been the primary outlet for independent news and opinion about the increasingly unpopular October 1994 Israel-Jordan peace treaty, the country's economic performance under IMF-led structural adjustment reform, government corruption, and human rights abuses. The targeting of the independent weeklies is part of a broader pattern of increasing state restrictions on free expression, assembly, and association. "The king wants everything to be under his control. The weekly press weakened him," said a publisher who requested anonymity.

CPJ has documented a pattern of harassment and criminal prosecution of independent Jordanian journalists since privately owned newspapers began to appear in the early 1990s. In October, I traveled to Jordan and spent a week meeting with and interviewing newspaper editors and reporters—many of whose cases CPJ had taken up over the last few years—who provided detailed accounts of the state's techniques for muzzling the press. In addition, I met with government officials, including Minister of State for Information Affairs Samir Mutawe and Bilal al-Tal, director of the Ministry of Information's Press and Publications Department, to express the committee's concern about the deterioration of press freedom in Jordan. And during a two-day seminar on press freedom in Jordan organized by two local nongovernmental organizations, the New Jordan Research Center and the Arab Media Institute, and the London-based ARTICLE 19 (International Centre Against Censorship), I sampled the full range of views about the climate for the press, hearing from Jordanian journalists, local and international human rights activists, and senior government officials.

The May press amendments came at a time when the convergence of political and economic pressures made the state particularly sensitive to scrutiny. According to Jordanian political scientist Radwan Abdullah, "The policies of the regime are mostly faltering, domestically and in foreign policy, and [the king] finds them increasingly difficult to defend. So he's growing more insecure, more defensive and less tolerant of attacks by the opposition." Public frustration has been intertwined with— some would say fueled by—worsening economic conditions for most Jordanians. According to a 1997 report by the United States Agency for International Development (USAID), unemployment and inflation increased between 1995 and 1996 and there was a 13-percent drop in the standard of living. USAID noted that "since the Gulf War, the condition of the poor and the income gap between the middle class and the poor has widened. Many

Jordanians unfortunately blame this reality on the economic reform process which exacerbates underlying skepticism regarding the peace process, the benefits of which are considered unrealized by the vast majority of Jordanians." A Jordanian political observer who asked not to be named said: "This government speaks about democracy and free expression, but after the peace with Israel, the situation changed drastically. Plus, the election of Netanyahu intensified the popular resentment in Jordan—the settlements, the punishment of Palestinians. Such events affect Jordan directly."

The amendments imposed sweeping restrictions on the press, giving the state broad powers to suspend, fine, and permanently close newspapers found to be in violation of the many vaguely worded provisions. "We have brought the martial law mentality into law," said Leith Shubeilat, a former member of parliament and a leading government critic. The amendments also ushered in a new era of self-censorship among journalists and editors. "Before the new law, we would never talk about the king but we would criticize the government for its concessions to Israel," said a representative of a now-suspended weekly newspaper. "Now, we can't say anything." Even the partially government-owned dailies have been affected by the new law. A journalist from the daily *Al-Dustur* said that the newspaper had withheld some 20 articles and columns that he had written about "the retreat of democracy in Jordan."

As the November parliamentary elections approached, tensions rose between the government and opposition parties. In July, eight secular opposition groups and the country's largest political opposition party, the Islamic Action Front (the political arm of the Muslim Brotherhood) announced that they would boycott the elections. One of the demands of the boycotters was revocation of the press law amendments. Former member of parliament Fares Nabulsi observed in late October: "I think that the government wanted this law because [it] didn't want any opposition. Sure there were unfavorable things in the press, but this should not make you close down newspapers just before the elections."

Despite the suspension of martial law in April 1992 and the passage of the PPL in May 1993, which allowed for the private ownership of newspapers, Jordanian journalists remained burdened by restrictions. Although the PPL canceled the state's previously unlimited powers to censor, suspend, or permanently close newspapers, it permitted authorities wide berth to discourage and punish independent journalism. Since the law's inception, the Ministry of Information has employed its vaguely worded bans to haul journalists to court for coverage of sensitive topics such as government corruption, criticism of the peace treaty with Israel, and negative reporting about friendly Arab states. Another favored tool has been the penal code, whose ambiguously worded provisions allow lengthy prison sentences and stiff fines for journalists convicted of such offenses as "inciting sedition," defamation, innuendo, or publishing false news. "Let's call the Press and Publications Law the first line of defense," said Leith Shubeilat. "If [a journalist] gets by that, then [the authorities] can use the penal code ... The journalists are terrified of this."

Between July 1993 and July 1996, the state prosecuted newspapers under the press law and penal code 63 times—all but five of them against weekly newspapers. *Al-Bilad*, one of the papers that had its license revoked, currently has 26 cases pending against it, the majority dating back to 1993. Another paper, the popular weekly *Shihan*, which continues to publish, had 29 pending cases in September 1996.

"The weekly press played a large role in providing information about government corruption," noted a journalist from *Shihan*. "And Jordan's relationship with Israel opened the door for the weekly press to seize the issue from the dailies." Indeed, in the period leading up to and following the peace treaty between Israel and Jordan, the weeklies took the lead in reporting and advocating opposition to the accord and normalization of relations with Israel.

In response, the Ministry of Information kept the pressure on the weeklies throughout 1994. On August 2 of that year, Nidal Mansour, then-editor in chief of *Al-Bilad*, was detained for what authorities described as "publishing an article on the activities of parties fighting against normalization with Israel." Mansour was detained a second time later in the month for publishing what prosecutors said were statements by political parties opposed to peace. In September, Fahd Rimawi and Hilmi Asmar, editors in chief of the weeklies *Al-Majd* and *Al-Sabeel* respectively, were summoned by prosecutors for questioning about their newspapers' editorial policy of opposition to peace with Israel. In all, a dozen cases were brought against the weeklies during 1994 for coverage of opposition to the Israel-Jordan peace treaty.

In reaction, eight opposition political parties issued a letter to Prime Minister Abdel Salam Majalli on September 25, 1994, condemning the government's moves to stifle the dissemination of independent views. "Any criticism is considered slander against the government and any word is interpreted as harmful to national unity because this interpretation justifies legal action," the statement read. "The government position aims at preventing views opposed to normalization of ties with Israel from reaching the people." Expressing its view of the state's attempts to monopolize news and commentary about the Israel-Jordan peace process, the Islamist weekly *Al-Sabil* noted: "The policy being pursued by the official and semi-official mass media organs is clearly forging the will of the Jordanians. Not all Jordanians support the government's policy and its panting after Rabin and Peres, not all Jordanians are happy over upcoming meetings with Rabin and Peres, not all Jordanians believe in the government's justifications for its rush."

Criticism of the peace treaty was not the only source of irritation, however. The Ministry of Information invoked the PPL and penal code against journalists who wrote critically of friendly Arab regimes. In one prominent case in 1995, authorities charged *Al-Majd* editor in chief Fahd Rimawi with defamation under the penal code for publishing an opinion piece titled "Glubb Pasha Should Leave," which called for the removal of Bahrain's British-born security chief, Ian Henderson. Another suit was triggered by an article about capital punishment in Saudi Arabia. "[One] of the phony accusations that [has] been made [is] that the press [is] slandering other countries and Jordan's image abroad," said Taher Adwan, editor in chief of the independent, privately owned daily *Al-Arab al-Youm*, launched in May 1997. "This is actually factual reporting, but the government says that it is harming the country's international relations."

The desire to restore damaged relations with the Gulf states in the wake of the 1991 Gulf War played a role in the government's sensitivity to the pro-Iraqi tilt of the weekly press. In January 1994, Prime Minister Majalli criticized the press for harming improved relations with Saudi Arabia and Kuwait as a result of its pro-Iraq positions: "Unfortunately, and I say it clearly to the Jordanian media, the Jordanian media play a part in not getting this relation back...Every time we almost get it back, a couple of articles go in some of these media and it becomes strained again."

The weekly press sustained its critical stance, and the king reacted by threatening reprisal. The king was infuriated by caustic commentary that followed the assasination of Israeli Prime Minister Yitzhak Rabin in November 1995 and his attendance at Rabin's funeral. One article in *Al-Sabil*, titled "One Less Murderer," (a reference to a statement made by Shimon Peres, then Israel's foreign minister, after the assassination of Islamic Jihad leader Fathi Shikaki in Malta), provoked the king to lash out at the press upon his return to Jordan. "Do not destroy in the name of democracy," Hussein admonished, adding that those who threaten national unity will be "my foe forever." Shortly thereafter, he asked that parliament consider a tougher law to keep the press in line. In June 1996, the king again referred to a new law: "I believe the law will be sent to the House of Representatives soon.... Then, God willing, the media will be in the hands of responsible people who can perform their role in serving the homeland and the nation and in reflecting the true picture of this country." Although a parliamentary committee discussed possible amendments to the PPL, no action was taken. Journalists and other observers predicted then that it was just a matter of time before the government would impose tighter restrictions on the press.

In 1996, a marked increase in prosecutions and government warnings against "irresponsible" journalism set the stage for a clampdown in September. The weekly press increasingly came under fire for its often-sensational, tabloid-style news coverage and failure to check facts and sources. Headline stories such as "Four-Year-Old Child is Married to a Fairy and Practices Sexual Intercourse with Her" and "Parties Start After Midnight and Homosexuals are Known" were sometimes splashed across the front pages of newspapers, causing outrage in parliament, particularly from Islamist deputies and the Jordan Press Association. Articles such as these made easy targets in the government's attacks against the weekly press. "The government took advantage of the morals issue. They said: 'This is our excuse,'" said a former government official who requested anonymity. "It had some support on that."

In the wake of internationally publicized riots and unrest in the southern town of Kerak in August 1996, following the government's decision to lift state subsidies on bread, several journalists were arrested for their coverage of the disturbances. Among them were four journalists from *Al-Bilad* who were charged under the penal code with "inciting strife" and "publishing false information." They face up to three years in prison if convicted of the charges, which are still pending. Following the arrests, one editor said: "They are trying to teach journalists not to touch sensitive issues."

In the days leading up to the abrupt implementation of the press amendments, two news stories reportedly enraged the king. One charged that he had given money to the families of the Israeli school girls who were murdered by a Jordanian soldier, Ahmed Dakamseh, in March, and another alleged that the king's daughter had studied in Israel. Shortly after their publication, the king said in a speech on May 14: "This is enough. We can no longer take it."

On May 17, while the parliament was out of session, the cabinet promulgated the 14 amendments to the press law, introducing broad and ambiguous content bans; greater powers to suspend or close publications; exorbitant fines; and sharply increased capital requirements for both daily and weekly publications. The amendments were "temporary," subject to approval or amendment by the new parliament, but the measures had an immediate impact on the press.

The first casualty was the weekly *Abed Rabbo*, which often satirized public officials and had run into legal difficulties under the 1993 law. It voluntarily closed down in June, fearing financial penalties. "The new law is elastic, and it can be applied to almost any article we publish," said Yusuf Gheisan, the paper's editor. Gheisan was referring to the sharp increases in fines mandated under the amendments, ranging from JD 15,000 (US$21,135) to JD 25,000 (US$35,225) for violations of the content bans.

On September 2, *Al-Bilad* became the second casualty when the Court of First Instance ruled that the paper had unlawfully published information about the security forces when it ran a news story about the arrest of the husband of a woman who had carried out an armed attack against Israeli soldiers. Although the article had been based on a Reuters story, the paper was fined 15,000JD (US$21,135). Four other cases are pending, and the newspaper faces up to 200,000JD (US$281,800) in fines. The weekly *Al-Hadath* was also charged for publishing a summary of the Reuters article.

But it was Article 24 of the amendments that had the greatest impact on the weekly press. It requires daily newspapers to increase their capital base from 50,000JD (US$70,450) to 600,000JD (US$845,400), and weeklies from 15,000JD (US$21,135) to 300,000JD (US$422,700). Government officials attempted to justify the exorbitant capital requirements as a mechanism for ensuring that newspapers meet their financial obligations. "All that we have done is to raise the level of capital that media organizations must have so that they can meet their obligations, at least toward their workers who are complaining about their wages [not] being paid," Prime Minister Majalli said in an interview with the London-based weekly *Al-Wasat*. But most observers agree that the new capital requirements were specifically designed to target the financially shaky weekly newspapers. "If we don't manage to raise our capital, then we don't have any other option but to close and give up," said Fahd Rimawi, editor in chief of *Al-Majd*, after the amendments were implemented, adding that these sums "can hardly be met."

Indeed, few weeklies were able to meet the requirement. Thirteen were eventually suspended by order of the Ministry of Information between September 23 and 24, for failure to comply with the registered capital minimum, leaving only four independent weeklies publishing. In November, 12 of the 13 papers had their publishing licenses revoked—only the weekly *Al-Majd* was able to raise the required capital mandated by the law and resume publishing.

The secrecy surrounding the May amendments provoked widespread condemnation from the daily and weekly press, as well as Jordan's independent professional associations—a major locus of organized political opposition in Jordan. Attempts by opposition deputies to convene an extraordinary session of parliament to debate the new measures failed.

In May and June, the heads of the professional associations threatened to resign in protest, only to back down later under pressure. Meanwhile, successive attempts by the 450-member Jordan Press Association to convene a session to oppose the amendments failed to meet the required quorum. The opposition fizzled. "It's fear," said Leith Shubeilat. "They're scared to death." Veiled government threats against the professional associations may have also contributed to the retreat.

King Hussein continued to criticize the press after the passage of the amendments. In a June 8 speech in Irbid, he said: "One reads columnists' articles cursing America one day, President Clinton on another, Turkey the next day, Netanyahu on a third [sic] day and so on, in addition to cursing the state, the government, the performance of the government...all without any objective reasoning and without defining the problems or exerting positive efforts to address these problems."

The pressure worked. "We used to publish the press releases of the leftist opposition parties but after the amendments, we stopped," one publisher explained. "We refrained from publishing certain cartoons and some information related to the army. Nothing was published about the police. I stopped writing about Jordanian affairs and began to write columns about [political developments in] other countries. If there were good relations between King Hussein and [Egyptian President Hosni] Mubarak, I would write something good about Mubarak."

In addition to the explicit content bans mandated under the law, authorities have also used indirect means to pressure the independent newspapers. One target of these intimidation tactics was the newly formed daily *Al-Arab al-Youm*, which has made a name for itself through its often-provocative news coverage of sensitive political issues. After the newspaper provided detailed coverage of the Israeli Mossad's failed attempt in September to assassinate Hamas political leader Khaled Meshaal in Amman, editorial staffers were summoned by intelligence officers in an apparent attempt to curb their investigative zeal. Editor in chief Taher Adwan described the government officials' strong-arm tactics. "It started with telephone calls," he said. "[Deputy Prime Minister] Jawed Anani called and asked that we retract the information we published about the arrest of armed groups," a reference to an article published in June about individuals arrested for smuggling arms into Jordan. Adwan said that he had received a telephone call from Minister of Information Samir Mutawe, who demanded that the paper publish a front-page story about the Ministry's criticism of the press, or face prosecution for having published the article. "One week later, we were referred to court...At the time the Minister threatened me, he said he would take me to court if I didn't publish news on the front page [attacking the press]." Government ministries then temporarily withdrew their advertising, in one case following a story about falsified voter cards in the lead-up to the elections. Also, in late October, the Ministry of Tourism distributed a circular to government agencies advising they stop advertising in *Al-Arab al-Youm* after it published an article about corruption at the ministry.

Adwan insists that his newspaper's coverage will not be compromised by government pressure. However, *Al-Arab al-Youm* journalists said that that the paper has refrained from crossing certain boundaries. "This week the editor in chief refused to run three columns," columnist Yousef Gheishan said on November 2. He added that two of his columns defended an opposition candidate whose son had been arrested for allegedly selling drugs, hinting that the arrest had been a set up designed to discredit the candidate. Gheisan estimates that 30 to 40 of his columns have been rejected by *Al-Arab al-Youm* because of politically sensitive content since he began writing it in June 1994. Leith Shubeilat, who writes a weekly column for *Al-Arab al-Youm*, maintained that editorial self-censorship was a fact of life now for the Jordanian press. He said that editors had rejected three of his columns because of positions he took on politically sensitive topics, and he offered copies of several articles which he said his editors had toned down or cut to omit material that might anger the government. An open letter that Shubeilat addressed to the director of Jordan's General Intelligence Department, calling for the release of Ali Sneid, a young writer who was arrested in September, was rejected by every newspaper in Jordan. At the time, Sneid was on trial in the State Security Court for violating the dignity of King Hussein, a penal code offense that carries a maximum prison term of three years.

Atef Joulani, editor in chief of the Islamist weekly *Al-Sabil*, described telephone calls that he received from Bilal al-Tal of the Ministry of Information's Press and Publications Department, warning that his paper "should be careful." He also received calls from other government officials: "Two months ago, we published an article about how a minister had appointed one of his nephews in the ministry. We published it without any mention of his name or the ministry," Joulani said. "The minister called me after the article was published and said that 'I am the person who you mean in the article.' We then published his response."

Along with the assault on the weeklies, the state has stepped up the frequency of distribution bans on foreign newspapers for what authorities have deemed their undesirable coverage of Jordanian affairs. Censorship of foreign publications—the responsibility of the Ministry of Information's Press and Publications Department—was ostensibly ended in February by the government of then-Prime Minister Abdel Karim Kabariti, which chose instead to refer "violators" of the law to the courts. But the Majalli government has reversed this policy. In the months leading up to the elections, numerous foreign newspapers—including the London-based daily *Al-Hayat*—were barred from distribution in the country. In October alone, 15 issues of the London-based daily *Al-Quds al-Arabi* were seized in 18 days. Journalists from the paper suspect that the crackdown stemmed from its detailed follow-up coverage of the failed assassination attempt against Khaled Meshaal.

Some journalists and political observers in Jordan remain convinced that the government intended to use the amendments to sideline the weekly press in advance of the elections. "[The government] want[s] to show international opinion [makers] that Jordan will have free and fair elections," one journalist said in late October. "There are already problems with the elections and the falsification of voter cards. The weeklies would have publicized these issues." A journalist from the daily *Al-Dustur* added: "The government didn't want the weeklies to support the opposition."

The election was certainly an important proximate factor in the clampdown on the press. But, given the pattern of harassment of the weekly press in the 1990s, the enactment of the amendments marked the culmination of the state's growing intolerance of the segment of the press which voiced criticism of state domestic and foreign policy. The pre-election period was the critical time to take decisive action.

Whether Jordan's parliament will put its stamp of approval on a similar press law in 1998 remains uncertain. In light of the events of the past year, journalists are prepared for the worst. As Taher Adwan of *Al-Arab al-Youm* put it: "These people pretend that they are the protectors of the free press, but they are really its executioners."

A version of this article appeared in the spring 1998 issue of Middle East Report [*vol. 28, no.1*].

The author would like to thank the Jordanian journalists who made this piece possible. Special thanks to Nidal Mansour.

Facts About the Organization and Its Activities

The Committee to Protect Journalists is a nonpartisan, nonprofit organization founded in 1981 to monitor abuses against the press and promote press freedom around the world.

How did CPJ get started?
A group of U.S. foreign correspondents created CPJ in response to the often brutal treatment of their foreign colleagues by authoritarian governments and other enemies of independent journalism.

Who runs CPJ?
CPJ has a full-time staff of 15 and five part-time research and editorial staffers at its New York headquarters, including an area specialist for each major world region. The committee's activities are directed by a 31-member board of prominent U.S. journalists.

How is CPJ funded?
CPJ depends on private donations from journalists, news organizations and independent foundations. CPJ accepts no government funding.

The press is powerful; why does it need protection?
The press in the United States does have great power and enjoys legal protection. But that is not the case in most countries. Scores of journalists are imprisoned every year because of what they have reported. Hundreds more are routinely subjected to physical attack, illegal detention, spurious legal action and threats against themselves or their families. And, on average, at least one journalist is killed every week somewhere in the world. Even in the United States, journalists have been murdered—in New York; California; Florida; Virginia; Washington, D.C.; Colorado; and Arizona.

How does CPJ protect journalists?
By publicly revealing abuses against the press and by acting on behalf of imprisoned and threatened journalists, CPJ effectively warns journalists and news organizations where attacks on press freedom are likely to occur. CPJ organizes vigorous protest at all levels—ranging from local governments to the United Nations—and, when necessary, works behind the scenes through other diplomatic channels to effect change. CPJ also publishes articles and news releases, special reports, a quarterly newsletter and the most comprehensive annual report on attacks against the press around the world.

Where does CPJ get its information?
Through its own reporting. CPJ has full-time program coordinators monitoring the press in the Americas, Asia, the Middle East, Africa, and Europe. They track developments through their own independent research, fact-finding missions and firsthand contacts in the field, including reports from other journalists. CPJ shares information on breaking cases with other press freedom organizations worldwide through the International Freedom of Expression Exchange (IFEX), a global E-mail network.

When would a journalist call upon CPJ?

• In an emergency. Using local contacts, CPJ can intervene whenever foreign correspondents are in trouble. CPJ is also prepared to immediately notify news organizations, government officials, and human rights organizations of press freedom violations.

• When traveling on assignment. CPJ maintains a database of local journalist contacts around the world. CPJ also publishes practical "safety guides" that offer advice to journalists covering dangerous assignments.

• When covering the news. Attacks against the press are news, and they often serve as the first signal of a crackdown on all freedoms. CPJ is uniquely situated to provide journalists with information and insight into press conditions around the world.

• When becoming a member. A basic membership costs only US$35, and each donation helps assure that CPJ will be there to defend you or a colleague if the need arises. Members receive CPJ's quarterly newsletter, *Dangerous Assignments*, and a discount on other publications.

CPJ Publications

To order the publications listed below, please call (212) 465-9344 x350. Members receive a 50-percent discount on the cost of publications. We accept Visa, MasterCard, American Express, checks, or money orders. Please make checks and money orders payable to CPJ in U.S. currency drawn on a U.S. bank or U.S. resident branch. Several of the publications can also be found on-line at CPJ's website (http://www.cpj.org).

Attacks on the Press   **$30**
A comprehensive annual survey of attacks against journalists and news organizations around the world.

Dangerous Assignments Quarterly $35/year
CPJ's newsletter reports on international press conditions and attacks on the press. Free to members.

Freedom Under the Dragon: Can Hong Kong's Press Still Breathe Fire?   **$10**
China resumed control over Hong Kong in July 1997. But even before the handover, Hong Kong's vibrant press began to prepare for the handover. Asia program coordinator A. Lin Neumann and a variety of Hong Kong watchers explore press freedom in Hong Kong 100 days after the handover.

The Anatolian Archipelago: CPJ's Campaign to Free Turkey's Imprisoned Journalists   **$10**
After an intensive media campaign to raise international awareness of Turkey's woeful press freedom record, CPJ sent a mission to Turkey to meet with the new prime minister and push for reforms. This report chronicles CPJ's campaign, the meetings in Turkey, and the aftermath of the mission: Six freed editors and promises of far-reaching reforms. Includes CPJ's updated records on Turkey's record number of imprisoned journalists.

Paradoxes in the Caucasus: A Report on Freedom of the Media in Azerbaijan and Armenia   **$10**
Veteran journalist Nicholas Daniloff explores the maze of contradictions faced by independent journalists in Armenia and Azerbaijan—two Caucasian republics which must shed the legacy of Soviet-era attitudes and institutions to reach their goal of democratization.

Clampdown in Addis: Ethiopia's Journalists at Risk   **$10**
Based on a fact-finding mission to Ethiopia, this comprehensive report by Africa program coordinator Kakuna Kerina documents how the Ethiopian government uses provisions of a restrictive press law to limit the news the independent press may report and to silence opposing viewpoints. Introduction by Josh Friedman. October 1996

Briefing on Press Freedom in Bosnia and Herzegovina Before the September 14 Elections   **$10**
A comprehensive review of press freedom violations in Bosnia and Herzegovina in the run-up to the September 14 national elections. The report also cites all clauses in the 1995 Dayton peace accords that specifically seek to protect the freedom of the press. September 1996

Briefing on Press Freedom in Russia Before the Presidential Elections   **$10**
This report details the numerous murders, attacks, and other difficulties Russian journalists have endured under President Boris Yeltsin's rule; highlights potential threats to a free press; and offers background on the economic hardships of the Russian media that foster a continued dependence on the government. June 1996

On a Razor's Edge: Local Journalists Targeted by Warring Parties in Kashmir $10
Based on a fact-finding mission to Kashmir, this report documents how local journalists are attacked by Indian armed forces and militant separatists for their reporting on the battle for control of the Indian-held state. July 1995

Double Jeopardy: Homophobic Attacks on the Press, 1990-1995 $10
A sampling of 21 cases from 14 countries, this report demonstrates that in nations as politically and culturally disparate as Canada, Russia, and Zimbabwe, censorship is imposed selectively against gay journalists and news outlets covering gay issues. October 1995

Silenced: The Unsolved Murders of Immigrant Journalists in the United States, (1976-1993) $10
This study of journalists killed in the United States reveals that when foreign-born journalists are murdered, their cases are rarely solved. December 1994

Journalists' Survivial Guide: The Former Yugoslavia $10
This essential booklet provides advice from journalists for journalists on everything from where to get flak jackets, insurance, and rental cars to tips on avoiding sniper fire in Sarajevo. It includes a list of phone numbers for U.N. and other relief agencies in the area, as well as organizations to call when making travel plans or in case of emergency. November 1994

Don't Force Us to Lie: The Struggle of Chinese Journalists in the Reform Era $20
A detailed study of the determined efforts of Chinese journalists to speak and write freely throughout the 1980s and early 1990s, this book is one of the most comprehensive accounts available of how journalism works in the world's most populous country. With a foreword by Dan Rather and contributions by China scholar Anne Thurston. January 1993

In the Censor's Shadow Journalism in Suharto's Indonesia $10
A comprehensive account of media repression in Indonesia, this report includes eyewitness accounts by two American reporters of the army massacre in Dili, East Timor. November 1991

The Soviet Media's Year of Decision $10
Pulitzer Prize-winning journalist Hedrick Smith analyzes the press in Gorbachev's Soviet Union and events leading up to the attempted coup of August 1991. This report includes a comprehensive guide to media organizations, primarily in Russia. September 1991

How to Report an Attack on the Press

CPJ needs accurate, detailed information in order to document abuses of press freedom and help journalists in trouble. CPJ corroborates the information and takes appropriate action on behalf of the journalists and news organizations involved.

What to report:

Journalists who are:
- Missing
- Killed
- Arrested or kidnapped
- Wounded
- Assaulted
- Threatened
- Harassed
- Wrongfully expelled
- Wrongfully sued for libel or defamation
- Denied credentials
- Censored

News organizations:
- Attacked, raided, or illegally searched
- Closed by force
- Wrongfully sued for libel or defamation
- Censored
- Materials confiscated or damaged
- Editions confiscated or transmissions jammed

Information Needed:

CPJ needs accurate, detailed information about:
- Journalists and news organizations involved
- Date and circumstances of incident
- Background information

Anyone with information about an attack on the press should call CPJ.
Call collect if necessary: (212) 465-1004

Or send us a fax at (212) 465-9568

Contact information for regional programs:
Africa:
(212) 465-9344, x103
E-mail: africa@cpj.org
Americas:
(212) 465-9344, x104
E-mail: americas@cpj.org
Asia:
(212) 465-9344, x109
E-mail: asia@cpj.org
Central Europe and the republics of the former Soviet Union:
(212) 465-9344, x106
E-mail: europe@cpj.org
Middle East and North Africa:
(212) 465-9344, x105
E-mail: mideast@cpj.org

What happens next:

Depending on the case, CPJ will:
- Confirm the report.
- Pressure authorities to respond.
- Notify human rights groups and press organizations around the world, including IFEX, Article 19, Amnesty International, Reporters Sans Frontières, PEN, International Federation of Journalists, and Human Rights Watch.
- Increase public awareness through the press.
- Publish advisories to warn other journalists about potential dangers.
- Send a fact-finding mission to investigate.

Ways to Participate in CPJ

Become a Member (see membership form, p. 433)
CPJ welcomes the participation of **individual members** interested in supporting press freedom and staying informed about press conditions around the world. Gift memberships are also available. All memberships include a subscription to CPJ's quarterly newsletter, *Dangerous Assignments*. Levels of $100 and higher also include a complimentary copy of *Attacks on the Press*.

CPJ works on behalf of journalists everywhere. If you represent a **news organization**, your membership commitment will send a powerful message that journalists throughout the globe are looking out for the rights of their colleagues. Demonstrate your organization's commitment to the profession and to your colleagues' safety by joining CPJ. For corporations, the free flow of information is vitally important to business in the global marketplace. Private-sector institutions in the legal, financial services, and communications industries have become increasingly involved in supporting the freedom of the press to report on political and economic conditions. Show your company's support for CPJ's critical analyses and actions by becoming a **corporate member**.

Support our Membership and Fundraising Campaigns

Encourage your colleagues to become members of CPJ by distributing our membership materials at your office. Contact your public/corporate affairs office and find out if your company will match your contribution to CPJ.

In-kind donations and services can also make a significant difference to CPJ. Consider donating a broad range of products and services, including research; technology; advertising; publicity; printing; graphic design; photography; video; computer equipment; and even office space.

Match CPJ's Challenge Grant (see Knight Challenge Grant form, p. 436)

CPJ has been awarded a three-year, $300,000 challenge grant from the John S. and James L. Knight Foundation, to help establish the Emergency Response Fund. The Knight Foundation will match every new contribution and every increase above your last contribution on a dollar-for-dollar basis. Already in its second year, the Emergency Response Fund has made it possible for CPJ to respond swiftly and effectively to press freedom crises in Asia, Central Europe, the Middle East, and Latin America. By supporting the Knight Challenge Grant, you will be significantly advancing the cause of global press freedom.

Support the Eighth Annual International Press Freedom Awards Dinner, Fall 1998, New York City

The International Press Freedom Awards Dinner honors the efforts of journalists who risk their lives to report the news. The annual gala is a major media industry gathering of journalists, publishers, and communications professionals, as well as leaders of the entertainment, finance, and legal communities. A highlight of New York's fall benefit season, the gala historically has raised more than half of CPJ's operating funds. Show your support for freedom of the press by attending, or by contributing direct gifts to CPJ in honor of the press freedom awardees. **Corporations** can demonstrate their commitment to CPJ's work by becoming **corporate sponsors** of the gala program and of the awardees' tour of major U.S. cities.

Buy CPJ's Publications (Members receive a 50-percent discount)
For **journalists** and **media executives**, CPJ's safety manuals and press freedom reports are invaluable tools. Buy them for your newsroom and help us defray the costs of this important service. The **general public** also can follow emerging developments through CPJ's reports on press conditions around the world. They are essential reading for anyone interested in freedom of expression or human rights. **International businesses** can benefit as well from CPJ's publications, which shed light on political and economic developments.

Provide Information on Cases and Support CPJ's Efforts on Behalf of Endangered Journalists
CPJ should be contacted at once whenever a colleague or news organization is threatened, harassed, or attacked. **Journalists**, **media executives** and **concerned individuals** should provide CPJ with accurate and reliable information immediately. Letters, petitions, and communiqués from journalists in support of colleagues under attack or in prison do make a difference. Stay on top of late-breaking developments by visiting CPJ's website at http://www.cpj.org.

Becoming a Member of CPJ

I wish to join as an individual member:

[ ] Participant $35
[ ] Contributor $100
[ ] Supporter..............................$500
[ ] Benefactor..........................$1,000 and above
[ ] Student...................................$15
    (must submit identification)

My company is subscribing to a corporate membership:

[ ] Activist $1,000
[ ] Champion $2,500
[ ] Advocate $5,000
[ ] Catalyst $10,000
[ ] Corporate Supporter.......$15,000
[ ] Corporate Leader.............$20,000

Contingent on the level of support, CPJ offers a range of services to our corporate members. Among these are an annual by-invitation-only forum with key CPJ board members; availability of select news reports; special consultation with CPJ staff about specific areas; as well as advertising opportunities in the CPJ newsletter *Dangerous Assignments*.

Member Name Mr./Miss/Mrs./Ms. (as you wish to be listed for acknowledgement)

Corporation

(Please indicate preferred mailing address)   [ ] Home [ ] Business

Title

Company

Street

City   State   Zip

Home Phone   Business Phone

Fax   E-Mail

PAYMENT INFORMATION

My corporation will match my gift to CPJ: [ ] Yes [ ] No (Enclosed is the relevant matching gift form.)

Enclosed please find my tax-deductible contribution of $_____, or charge my gift of $_____.

[ ] Visa   [ ] MasterCard   [ ] American Express   [ ] Check Enclosed

Card Number   Expiration Date

Name On Card   Signature

Please write checks or money orders to Committee to Protect Journalists (funds must be drawn on a U.S. bank or U.S. resident branch), or indicate charge information, and send to:

Director of Development • CPJ • 330 Seventh Avenue, 12th Floor, New York, NY 10001, USA
(212) 465-9344 ext. 113 • Fax: (212) 465-9568 • E-Mail: lharrop@cpj.org

Contributions in Support of the Challenge Grant from the John S. and James L. Knight Foundation

The Committee to Protect Journalists is extremely proud to recognize the following major contributors whose generous gifts have been instrumental in helping us meet the three-year matching challenge grant from the John S. and James L. Knight Foundation:

Leader
$50,000 and above
The Times Mirror Foundation

Philanthropist
$25,000 and above
Tom Brokaw
The New York Times Company Foundation

Guardian
$10,000 and above
James S. Copley Foundation
Gene Roberts

Grantor
$5,000 and above
Kati Marton
James C. and Toni K. Goodale
Mr. and Mrs. James E. Burke
Henry Grunwald
Drue Heinz
Ted and Grace Anne Koppel
Dan and Silvia Lufkin
National Broadcasting Company, Inc.
PaineWebber
Peter G. Peterson
Mr. and Mrs. W.J. Ruane
Howard Stringer
Universal Studios, Inc.
Ted Waitt
John C. Whitehead

Provider
$1,000 and above
Franz and Marcia Allina
Isobel and Ron Konecky
The Phillips-Green Foundation, Inc.
Walter Haskell Pincus and Ann Terry Pincus
Joyce Purnick and Max Frankel
The Steven H. and Alida Brill Scheuer Foundation
The Ruth and Frank Stanton Fund
Star Tribune/Cowles Media Company
Thomas Winship

(To contribute to this matching campaign, please fill out and return the form on the next page.)

Challenge Grant from the John S. and James L. Knight Foundation

All donors supporting CPJ's Challenge Grant at these levels will be given permanent recognition on a plaque at CPJ headquarters, and will also be listed in the annual report, *Attacks on the Press*, as well as in other CPJ literature

[ ] Sponsor ....$100,000 and above
[ ] Leader ....$50,000 and above
[ ] Philanthropist ....$25,000 and above
[ ] Guarantor ....$20,000 and above
[ ] Guardian ....$10,000 and above
[ ] Grantor ....$5,000 and above
[ ] Provider ....$1,000 and above

Donor Name Mr./Miss/Mrs./Ms. or Institution/Organization
(as you wish to be listed for acknowledgement)

(Please indicate preferred mailing address)　　　　　[ ] Home　[ ] Business

Title

Company

Street

City　　　　　　　　　　State　　　　　　　　Zip

Home Phone　　　　　　　Business Phone

Fax　　　　　　　　　　　E-Mail

PAYMENT INFORMATION

My corporation will match my gift to CPJ: [ ] Yes [ ] No (Enclosed is the relevant matching gift form.)

Enclosed please find my tax-deductible contribution of $_____, or charge my gift of $_____.

[ ] Visa　　　　[ ] MasterCard　　　　[ ] American Express　　　　[ ] Check Enclosed

Card Number　　　　　　　　　　　　　　　　　Expiration Date

Name On Card　　　　　　　　　　　　　　　　Signature

Please write checks or money orders to Committee to Protect Journalists, (funds must be drawn on a U.S. bank or U.S. resident branch), or indicate charge information, and send to:

Director of Development • CPJ • 330 Seventh Avenue, 12th Floor, New York, NY 10001, USA
(212) 465-9344 ext. 113 • Fax: (212) 465-9568 • E-Mail: lharrop@cpj.org

Contributors

The Committee to Protect Journalists is extremely grateful to the following foundations, corporations, and individuals for their invaluable support of our annual fund during 1997:

Executive Leadership—$100,000 and above
The Ford Foundation
The Freedom Forum
John S. and James L. Knight Foundation
Robert R. McCormick Tribune Foundation

Leadership—$50,000 to $99,999
Open Society Institute
The Walt Disney Company

Underwriters—$25,000 to $49,999
Allen & Company Incorporated
Bloomberg News
Phil Donahue and Marlo Thomas
Katharine Graham
The John D. and Catherine T. MacArthur Foundation
The McGraw-Hill Companies
The Menemsha Fund
Merrill Lynch & Co., Inc.
NTV Russian Television
National Broadcasting Company, Inc.
The New York Times
Dan Rather
Reuters America Holdings
The Star-Ledger
Time Warner Inc.

Patrons—$10,000 to $24,999
ABC, Inc./ABC News
The Abernathy/MacGregor Group, Inc.
BankAmerica Corp.
Bankers Trust Company
Tom Brokaw
CBS Foundation
CBS News
Cahill Gordon & Reindel
The Coca-Cola Company
Condé Nast Publications, Inc.
Credit Suisse First Boston
Joan and Joseph F. Cullman 3rd

Dow Jones & Company
Ford Motor Company
Nicholas C. Forstmann
Fox News
James C. and Toni K. Goodale
Harper's Magazine
The Hearst Corporation
Johnson & Johnson
Kati Marton
The New Yorker
Philip Morris International, Inc.
Times Mirror Newspapers
Viacom Inc.
The Washington Post Company
Worldwide Television News Corporation
Yazhou Zhoukan

Donors—$5,000 to $9,999
Franz and Marcia Allina
American Lawyer Media
Amway Corporation
Baker & Hostetler
Bear, Stearns & Co. Inc.
Bell Atlantic Foundation
Brill Media Ventures, L.P.
CNN
Debevoise & Plimpton
Dow Jones Foundation
Hachette Filipacchi Magazines
Hilton Hotels Corporation
Lifetime Television
Kenneth & Evelyn Lipper Foundation
Lockheed Martin
McClatchy Newspapers, Inc.
Tim Metz and Geraldine Fabrikant
Microsoft Corporation
Montgomery Securities
National Amusements
New York Magazine
Newsday
Newsweek

Nike, Inc.
Offitbank
Prudential Insurance Company of America/Prudential Securities Inc.
Random House
Rockwell
Sony Corporation of America
Thomson Newspapers
Mr. and Mrs. A. Robert Towbin
Turner Broadcasting System, Inc.
U.S. News & World Report
Katrina vanden Heuvel
WABC-TV
Barbara Walters
Weil, Gotshal & Manges LLP

Benefactors—$1,000 to $4,999
Altman/Kazickas Foundation
Ken Auletta and Amanda Urban
A. H. Belo Corporation Foundation
Robert and Helen Bernstein
The Boston Globe
Thomas R. Bettag
Blum-Kovler Foundation
James E. Burke
José Carreño
Helen K. Copley
Cox Newspapers, Inc.
Walter Cronkite
Daedalus Foundation
Robert P. DeVecchi
Edelman Public Relations Worldwide
Clay Felker and Gail Sheehy
Samuel N. Friedman
Global Village Fund
Alice Gottesman and Laurence Zuckerman
Mr. and Mrs. Henry Grunwald

HBO
H.J. Heinz Company
Peter Jennings
Mr. and Mrs. Gilbert Kaplan
Knight-Ridder, Inc.
Richard A. Leibner
LEXIS-NEXIS
Stuart H. Loory
Vincent and Anne Mai
David and Kerry Smith Marash
Cynthia G. McFadden
Judith and Harry Moses
Anne and Victor Navasky
Mr. Charles Osgood and Mrs. Jean Wood
Alan and Hannah Pakula
Jane Pauley and Garry Trudeau
Pearson plc
Peter G. Peterson
The Playboy Foundation
Public Concern Foundation
The Reebok Foundation
Cokie and Steven Roberts
Andrew Rooney
S. I. Newhouse Foundation
J. E. Smothers, Sr., Memorial Foundation
Joan and Rollin Sontag
Star Tribune/Cowles Media Company
Robert A.M. Stern Architects
Seymour and Audrey Topping
Peter and Francesca Tufo
Mr. and Mrs. Richard N. Winfield

We also extend our deepest gratitude to the many individuals and organizations who support the Committee to Protect Journalists with gifts below $1,000 and cannot be recognized in this list because of space limitations.

We thank the following for their in-kind services and contributions during the past year—critical resources that help make possible the work of CPJ.

ABC News
Agence France-Presse
Peter Arnett
Associated Press
CNN

Columbia Journalism Review
Walter Cronkite
IDT
NBC News
Reuters America Inc.

The Committee to Protect Journalists is proud to work in continuing partnership with LEXIS-NEXIS, whose in-kind donation of information technology services is vital to the implementation of our mission.

In memory of two esteemed journalists, the following funds were created during 1997:

J. Anthony Lukas Memorial Fund
Joan Bingham
Arthur Dubow Foundation
Frances Kiernan
Thomas Mallon
Jeanne L. Morton
Kristine K. Petersen
Ernest and Victoria Pryor Volkman
Robert Whiting
Galen Williams

William N. Oatis Memorial Fund
Jane and Alan Carey
Barbara Cornell
Jonathan W. Oatis
Pierre and Dorothea Signorat
Ian Simpson
Jake Simpson
Paul Simpson

Staff

EXECUTIVE DIRECTOR
William A. Orme, Jr.
(212) 465-9344, ext. 102
orme@cpj.org

**PROGRAM AND
EDITORIAL DIRECTOR**
Alice Chasan
(212) 465-9344, ext. 110
achasan@cpj.org

Jesse T. Stone
Associate Editor
(212) 465-9344, ext. 112
jstone@cpj.org

**DIRECTOR OF MEDIA
RELATIONS**
Judith Leynse
(212) 465-9344, ext. 105
jleynse@cpj.org

**DIRECTOR OF
DEVELOPMENT**
Lucy Mayer Harrop
(212) 465-9344, ext. 113
lharrop@cpj.org

Amy Bodow
*Development and Special Projects
Assistant*
(212) 465-9344, ext. 117
abodow@cpj.org

Nina Dubin
*Development and Special Projects
Assistant*
(212) 465-9344, ext. 142
ndubin@cpj.org

**REGIONAL PROGRAMS
Africa**
Kakuna Kerina
Program Coordinator
(212) 465-9344, ext. 103
africa@cpj.org

Selam Demeke
Research Assistant
(212) 465-9344, ext. 118
sdemeke@cpj.org

The Americas
Joel Simon
Program Coordinator
(212) 465-9344, ext. 108
americas@cpj.org

Marylene Smeets
Research Assistant
(212) 465-9344, ext. 107
msmeets@cpj.org

Asia
A. Lin Neumann
Program Coordinator
(212) 465-9344, ext. 140
asia@cpj.org

Shumona Goel
Research Assistant
(212) 465-9344, ext. 115
sgoel@cpj.org

**Central Europe and the
Republics of the Former
Soviet Union**
Chrystyna Lapychak
Program Coordinator
(212) 465-9344, ext. 101
europe@cpj.org

Irina Faion
Research Assistant
(212) 465-9344, ext. 119
ifaion@cpj.org

**Middle East and North
Africa**
Joel Campagna
Program Coordinator
(212) 465-9344, ext. 120
mideast@cpj.org

ADMINISTRATION
Lanny Mitchell
*Director of Finance and Admin-
istration*
(212) 465-9344, ext. 116
lmitchell@cpj.org

Angelo Machipisa
*Systems Administrator/
Webmaster*
(212) 465-9344, ext. 104
amach@cpj.org

Anitra Pavlico
Office Manager
(212) 465-9344, ext. 106
apavlico@cpj.org

Ellen Baxt
Receptionist
(212) 465-1004

Harry Wang
HTML Assistant
(212) 465-9344, ext. 104

Sarig Armenian
Intern

Save on *Attacks on the Press in 1997*

Libraries • Schools • Teachers • Orders of five or more copies
Save 50%—US$15.00 per copy *(cover price: US$30.00)*

Please send me _____ copies of *ATTACKS ON THE PRESS IN 1997* at _____ **US$15.00 each (discount)**

Name: _____

Title: _____

Institution/Affiliation
Street Address: _____

_____

City: _____ State: _____

Zip Code: _____

Telephone number:
(home) _____

(office) _____

E-mail: _____

Payment Information
Enclosed is a (check) (money order) in the amount of US$_____
or
Charge my credit card:

Type: _____

Card number: _____

Expiration date: _____

Please make checks or money orders payable to:
Committee to Protect Journalists (funds must be drawn on a U.S. bank or U.S. resident branch).

Mail this order to:
Committee to Protect Journalists
330 7th Avenue, 12th Floor, New York, NY 10001 USA

Index of Countries